THE OXFORD HISTORY OF

WESTERN MUSIC

THE OXFORD HISTORY OF
WESTERN MUSIC

THE OXFORD HISTORY OF

WESTERN

MUSIC

Richard Taruskin

Volume 2

THE SEVENTEENTH AND EIGHTEENTH
CENTURIES

OXFORD
UNIVERSITY PRESS
2005

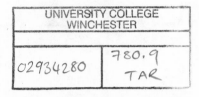

OXFORD
UNIVERSITY PRESS

Oxford   New York

Auckland   Bangkok   Buenos Aires   Cape Town   Chennai
Dar es Salaam   Delhi   Hong Kong   Istanbul   Karachi   Kolkata
Kuala Lumpur   Madrid   Melbourne   Mexico City   Mumbai   Nairobi
São Paulo   Shanghai   Taipei   Tokyo   Toronto

Copyright © 2005 by Oxford University Press, Inc.

Published by Oxford University Press, Inc.
198 Madison Avenue, New York, New York 10016
http://www.oup.com/us

Oxford is a registered trademark of Oxford University Press

Library of Congress Cataloging-in-Publication Data
Taruskin, Richard.
The Oxford history of western music / by Richard Taruskin.
p. cm.
Includes bibliographical references and index.
ISBN 0-19-516979-4
1. Music — History and criticism. I. Title.
ML160.T18 2004
780′.9 — dc22
2004017897
ISBN Vol. 1 0-19-522270-9
ISBN Vol. 2 0-19-522271-7
ISBN Vol. 3 0-19-522272-5
ISBN Vol. 4 0-19-522273-3
ISBN Vol. 5 0-19-522274-1
ISBN Vol. 6 0-19-522275-X

1   3   5   7   9   8   6   4   2
Printed in the United States of America

Contents of Volume 2

The beautiful and the sublime • Classic or Romantic? • Beethoven and "Beethoven" • *Kampf und Sieg* • The *Eroica* • Crisis and reaction • The "Ninth" • Inwardness

Devotion and derision • Transgression • *Morti di Eroi* • Germination and growth • Letting go • The music century

THE OXFORD HISTORY OF

WESTERN MUSIC

Opera from Monteverdi to Monteverdi

PRINCELY AND PUBLIC THEATERS; MONTEVERDI'S CONTRIBUTIONS TO BOTH

COURT AND COMMERCE

Nino Pirrotta, an outstanding historian of Italian music, once proposed the title of this chapter as a joke, but it contains an important insight and provides an excellent frame for discussing some issues of major consequence.[1] Claudio Monteverdi (1567–1643), whom we met two chapters back as a great madrigalist, was also a major player in the "monodic revolution." Owing to the unusual length of his career and the places where he happened to live, moreover, he made distinguished contributions to the early repertoire of music for the stage during more than one phase of its development. His first "musical tale" dates from 1607, his last from shortly before his death, thirty-six years later. The first was performed before an invited assembly of nobles in Mantua and had a mythological theme. The last was performed before a paying public in Venice and had a theme from history. Stylistically as well as socially and thematically, the two works were worlds apart. To all intents and purposes, whether historical, theoretical, or practical, they belonged to different genres. It was the second that actually bore the designation *opera*, and that still looks like one.

The first was called *Orfeo*, and it was a *favola in musica* on the same music-myth previously musicalized by Peri and Caccini. The other, *L'incoronazione di Poppea* ("The crowning of Poppea," the emperor Nero's second wife), was designated a *dramma musicale* or *opera reggia* ("staged work"), *work* being the literal meaning of the word *opera*, which has stuck to the genre ever since. Both works still have a toehold on the fringes of today's repertory, although neither is without interruptions in its performance history.

FIG. 20-1 Claudio Monteverdi.

They are the earliest and for today's audiences the exemplary ("classic") representatives of the noble musical play and the public music drama, respectively. To put it a little more loosely and serviceably, they are the prime representatives of the early court and commercial operas. As Pirrotta implied, comparing them, the common author notwithstanding, will be a study in contrasts and a powerfully instructive one.

Because he was so widely recognized by his contemporaries as the most gifted and interesting composer in Italy, Monteverdi (though he had no hand in its inception) became willy-nilly the spokesman and the scapegoat of the new manner (or *seconda prattica*, as Monteverdi himself called it). It was captious criticism from detractors like Giovanni Maria Artusi (quoted in chapter 17) that made it necessary for Monteverdi to engage in defensive propaganda. But that redounded to our good fortune, because it enables us directly to compare his preaching with his practice, his professed intentions with his achievement.

FROM MANTUA TO VENICE

By the time he composed *Orfeo*, Monteverdi had been an active composer for a quarter of a century. His first publication, a book of three-voice motets, came out in 1582, when he was the fifteen-year-old pupil of Marc'Antonio Ingegneri, an important Counter-Reformation composer who had studied with Vincenzo Ruffo and who was the *maestro di cappella* at the cathedral of Cremona, Monteverdi's birthplace. By the late sixteenth century Cremona, a city in Lombardy southeast of Milan, was already famous as a manufacturing center for string instruments. The Amati family had established there the workshop where the design of the modern violin family began to be standardized in the earlier part of the century. Antonio Stradivari (1644–1737), who apprenticed with Niccolo Amati, and who is still thought of as the greatest of all violin makers, inherited the Cremonese art and brought it to its peak.

In view of his city's traditions, it is perhaps not surprising that Monteverdi's first official appointment should have been as a *suonatore di vivuola*, a string player, in the virtuoso chamber ensemble maintained by Vincenzo Gonzaga, the Duke of Mantua. (As far as we know, however, Monteverdi never composed a single piece of textless instrumental music.) He was engaged in 1590 and remained at the Mantuan court until a few months after Vincenzo's death in 1612, when he was summarily fired in a notable show of ingratitude by the new Duke Francesco, in whose honor *Orfeo* had been originally performed.

By then Monteverdi was a famous musician. He had been *maestro di cappella* at Mantua for eleven years. By the time of his accession to the post in 1601 he had already published four books of madrigals (one of them containing sacred madrigals) and had already been attacked by Artusi for harmonic liberties in madrigals that would eventually be published in his next book (1603). The controversy enhanced his reputation enormously, especially when he joined in himself, first (and sketchily) in the preface to his Fifth Book of Madrigals (1605). That book made him by common consent, and by virtue of the debates that surrounded his work, the leading composer of madrigals at the tail end of the genre's history.

Two years later — in 1607, the year of *Orfeo* — Monteverdi fully responded to his critics. The answer was included in a new book of what were actually rather innocuous little convivial compositions that he called *scherzi musicali* (literally "musical jests"): strophic, homophonic canzonetti and balletti (love songs and dance-songs) in three parts to racy "Anacreontic" (wine-women-song) verses by the poet Gabriello Chiabrera, full of catchy "French" rhythms (as Monteverdi called them) based on hemiolas, but without harmonic audacities or any adventurous word paintings to speak of. But it was Monteverdi's first publication to include a basso continuo, and the strophic songs had instrumental ritornelli between the stanzas. This demonstrative use of the concerted

EX. 20-1   Claudio Monteverdi, *Scherzi musicali: O rosetta*

EX. 20-1 (*continued*)

pu - ra don - zel - let - ta che spo - sa - ta an - cor non è.

pu - ra don - zel - let - ta che spo - sa - ta an - cor non è.

pu - ra don - zel - let - ta che spo - sa - ta an - cor non è.

1. Oh, little rose, what a rose
   Amid the bright green of your branches
   Shamefully you hide
   Like a pure young maiden
   Who is not yet married.

2. Se dal bel cespo natio
   Ti torrò non te ne caglia
   Ma con te tanto mi vaglia,
   Che ne lodi il pensier mio
   Se servigio ha sua mercè.

2. If from the bush that bore you
   I would pluck you, do not anger
   For it is worth so much to be with you,
   So much my thought would praise you
   If you have served your purpose.

3. Caro pregio il tuo colore
   Tra le man sia di colei,
   Che governa i pensier miei,
   Che mi mira il petto, e'l core
   Ma non mira la mia fè.

3. So valued be your color
   Between the hands of her
   who rules my thoughts,
   Who delights in my bosom and my heart
   But scorns my faithfulness.

style, albeit on a chamber scale, was in itself already a deposition in favor of the latest musical techniques and their implied esthetic (for a sample see Ex. 20-1). But the book also contained a formal statement of principles, one that ever since the seventeenth century has been among the most quoted documents in music history.

The full title of the 1607 publication was this: *Scherzi musicali a tre voci di Claudio Monteverde, raccolti da Giulio Cesare Monteverde suo fratello, con la dichiaratione di una lettera che si ritrova stampata nel quinto libro de suoi madrigali* ("Musical jests in three voices by Claudio Monteverdi, collected by his brother Julius Caesar Monteverdi, with a declaration based on a letter that is found printed in his Fifth Book of Madrigals)." Using his younger brother, also a composer, as a mouthpiece, Monteverdi wrote what amounted to a manifesto of the "second practice." The term became standard, as did his famous slogan — "Make the words the mistress of the music and not the servant" (*far che l'oratione sia padrona del armonia e non serva*), which managed to sum up in a single sound bite the whole rhetorical program of the radical humanists.

The discussion of the first and second practices in the Declaration is itself a masterpiece of rhetoric. The chief appeal of Artusi and other upholders of the polyphonic tradition had always been to the authority of established practice. The *ars perfecta* was supreme because it was the hard-won culmination of a long history, not the lazy whim of a few trendy egotists. At first the Declaration seems to honor that pedigree.

The first practice, defined as "that style which is chiefly concerned with the perfection of the harmony," is traced back to "the first [composers] to write down music for more than one voice, later followed and improved upon by Ockeghem, Josquin des Prez, Pierre de la Rue [court composer to the Holy Roman Emperor in the early sixteenth century], Jean Mouton, Crequillon, Clemens non Papa, Gombert, and others of those times." Finally granting flattering recognition to Artusi's own chief authorities, the Declaration concludes that the first practice "reached its ultimate perfection with Messer Adriano [Willaert] in composition itself, and with the extremely well-thought-out rules of the excellent Zarlino." Just what Artusi might have said.

But this recognition of the *ars perfecta*'s pedigree was only a rhetorical foil. In the very next breath Monteverdi claimed for himself a much older and more distinguished pedigree. "It is my brother's aim," wrote Giulio Cesare, "to follow the principles taught by Plato and practiced by the divine Cipriano [de Rore] and those who have followed him in modern times," namely Monteverdi's teacher Ingegneri, plus Marenzio, Giaches de Wert, Luzzasco Luzzaschi (a madrigalist who worked at Ferrara and accompanied a famous trio of virtuoso sopranos — the so-called *concerto delle donne* — at the harpsichord), Peri, Caccini, "and finally by yet more exalted spirits who understand even better what true art is." Plato, the Monteverdian argument implies, beats Ockeghem any day. Who, in the age of humanism, would dare disagree?

As early as 1610 Monteverdi, rather spectacularly mistreated by his patrons in Mantua, was casting about for a more satisfactory position. Several of his letters testify to his resentment of the high-handed way in which the Gonzagas dealt with their servant despite his standing in his profession. Like the anecdotes concerning Josquin, they testify to what we might call artistic self-consciousness and "temperament" of a sort that later came to be highly prized by artists and art lovers. But where the Josquin anecdotes are apocryphal, the Monteverdi letters are hard documents, the earliest we have of artistic "alienation." His hair-raisingly sarcastic reply to an invitation to return to Mantua in 1620 still makes impressive reading, and while it probably marked him as nothing more than a crank so far as the Gonzagas were concerned, it marks him for what we now might call a genius; it has in consequence become far and away the most famous letter by a composer before the eighteenth century.[2]

By the time he wrote it, Monteverdi had been living in Venice for seven years, serving as *maestro di cappella* at St. Mark's. He had attracted the interest of the Venetians with a large book of concerted psalm motets for Vespers, plus some continuo-accompanied madrigalistic "antiphons" and a couple of Masses, one of them, unexpectedly, in the *stile antico*; it has been mentioned in chapter 15 in connection with the Gombert motet that served as its "parody" model. This Vespers collection was actually written, it seems, in hopes of gaining employment in Rome; and yet its appeal to the home city of the grand concerted style seems almost predestined.

Monteverdi's tenure in Venice did not overlap with that of Giovanni Gabrieli, who had died in 1612; there is no evidence that the two greatest Venetian church composers ever met. Nor, contrary to the easy assumption, was Monteverdi hired to replace Gabrieli, who had served not as choirmaster but as organist. (Monteverdi replaced the previous choirmaster at St. Mark's, a minor figure named Giulio Cesare Martinengo, who died in July 1613.) The position suited him magnificently, in part because Venice was a republican city where the chief cathedral musician enjoyed a higher social prestige than he could ever have attained in a court situation. He stayed on the job for three decades, until his death; after about 1630, however, he occupied the post only nominally, living chiefly on a pension in semiretirement. This, as we shall see, freed him for other kinds of work in his late years.

Once in Venice, Monteverdi composed only in the concerted style. He did not publish the service music he wrote in his actual job capacity until his retirement, but he continued to issue madrigals with some regularity, beginning with the Sixth Book in 1614, his last publication in which traditional polyphonic madrigals, left over from his late Mantuan period, appeared cheek by jowl with continuo compositions. They include what could probably be called Monteverdi's *a cappella* masterpiece (and probably his last non-continuo composition) — a spectacular cycle of six madrigals, *Lagrime d'amante al sepolcro dell'amata* ("A lover's tears at his beloved's grave"), composed in 1610 to a cycle of poems by Scipione Agnelli that poured subject matter in the recent, racy pastoral mode into an ancient, rigid mold: the old *sestina* form of Arnaut Daniel, the most virtuosic fixed form of the troubadours, as later adapted by Petrarch.

(The term *sestina*, derived from the word "six," denotes a cycle of six six-line stanzas in which the poet is limited to six rhyme words — that is, three rhymed pairs — that have to be deployed in each stanza in a different prescribed order; the six stanzas exhaust the possible permutations. Writing sensible, let alone moving verse under such constraints is a feat that few poets manage successfully; most sestinas, including Agnelli's in the opinion of some connoisseurs, fall into the category of valiant attempts.)

By the time he composed the *Lagrime d'amante*, even Monteverdi's polyphonic style had been touched by the monodic *stile recitativo*, as the opening of the first madrigal (*Incenerite spoglie*, "Ashen Remains") vividly suggests. Here, certainly, the words of the spiritually benumbed and torpid mourner at the tomb (clearly identified with the tenor) are the "mistress of the music" (Ex. 20-2), and the static harmony mimics Peri's motionless basses.

Monteverdi's Seventh Book of Madrigals, issued in 1619, actually bore the title *Concerto*. One of its most characteristic items, however, the famous "Lettera amorosa" (love letter), is a monody, the most extended one that Monteverdi ever conceived outside of an actual theatrical situation, or for a single soliloquizing voice. And yet it is theatrical all the same, as Monteverdi recognized by designating the piece as being *in genere rappresentativo*, "in the representational style." The style had its technical requirements, notably the static bass, and these are met entirely, so that the whole work becomes an unprecedented 12-minute unstaged *scena*: music for staging in the theater of the mind (Ex. 20-3).

Monteverdi's Eighth Book (1638), his last and most lavish in its instrumentation, was called *Madrigali guerrieri, et amorosi* ("Madrigals of love and war,") and also included a few little works (*opuscoli*) specially designated as being *in genere rappresentativo*. The earliest item in the book and, in its inextricable mixture of the martial and the erotic, possibly its conceptual kernel, was a setting Monteverdi had made in 1624 of a sizeable chunk from *Gerusalemme liberata* ("Jerusalem delivered," 1581), the celebrated epic poem of the crusades by Torquato Tasso, whom Monteverdi might have known during his early years in Mantua.

EX. 20-2   Claudio Monteverdi, *Sestina* (Madrigals, Book VI), no. 1 (*Incenerite spoglie*), mm. 1–9

The poem, like any epic, is a narrative, but Monteverdi solved the problem of turning it into a dramatic representation by selecting one of its best-known episodes, called the "Combattimento di Tancredi e Clorinda," in which the hero Tancred engages in ferocious hand-to-hand combat with a soldier whom he finally kills, but who in dying reveals herself to be his former lover Clorinda. It is a scene with dialogue, suitable for dramatic treatment, plus a narrator (or the *testo*, the "text-reciter," as Monteverdi calls him) who gets most of the lines, and whose graphic description of the gory fight is acted out by the protagonists in mime.

To give adequate expression to this exceptionally violent text, Monteverdi invented a new style of writing, which he called the "agitated style" (*stile concitato*), and which consisted of repeated notes articulated with virtuosic rapidity. In his preface, Monteverdi

EX. 20-3   Claudio Monteverdi, *Concerto* (Madrigals, Book VII), *Lettera amorosa (Se i languidi miei sguardi)*, mm. 1–22

O my idol, if my languishing glances, my interrupted sighs, my faltering words, have not been able to make you believe in the sincerity of my passion, then read these notes, believe this paper, this paper on which I have poured out my heart.

related his *stile concitato* to the Pyrrhic foot of Greek dramatic poetry, which "according to all the best philosophers . . . was used for agitated warlike dances."[3] (This correspondence was no doubt arrived at after the fact, but like a good humanist Monteverdi reports the "discovery" as if it had been some sort of disinterested scholarly research.) Most of the *concitato* effects were assigned to the basso continuo and to the concertato string instruments; it was the origin of the string *tremolo* that has been a dependable resource ever since for imitating agitation both physical (as in stormy weather) and emotional, and linking them. In the *Combattimento*, the concitato rhythms move imperceptibly from strictly mimetic imitations (the hoofbeats of Tancred's horse, the clashing of swords, the exchange of physical blows) to more metaphorical representations of conflict. At the very climax of battle, the *testo* gets to match speed with the instrumentalists to electrifying effect (Ex. 20-4).

EX. 20-4   Claudio Monteverdi, *Combattimento*, fifth stanza, *L'onta irrita lo sdegno a la vendetta*

In another "theatrical opuscule" from the Eighth Book, a setting of Rinuccini's famous canzonetta *Lamento della ninfa*, "The nymph's lament" (Ex. 20-5), Monteverdi again turned a narrative into a dramatic *scena* by framing the complaint of a rejected lover, sung as a solo aria over a ground bass, with narration by a trio of male singers (satyrs?), as if eavesdropping on her grief. The ostinato bass line is no longer one of the standard aria or dance tenors of the sixteenth century, but a four-note segment (tetrachord) of the minor scale, descending slowly by degrees from tonic to dominant—a figure that Monteverdi, through his affecting use of it, helped establish as an "emblem of lament" (so dubbed by Ellen Rosand, a historian of the Venetian musical theater) that would remain standard for the rest of the century and a good deal beyond.[4]

This was a new sort of dramatic or representational convention: a musical idea that is independent of any image in the poem, that does not portray the nymph's behavior iconically or hook up with any observable model in nature; a musical idea associated with a literary one, in short, not through *mimesis* or direct imitation but by mere agreement among composers and listeners. This, of course, is the way most words acquire their meaning. The new technique could be called lexical (as opposed to mimetic) signification, and it became increasingly the standard way of representing emotion in the musical theater. The most fascinating aspect of Monteverdi's use of it is the way he plays off its regularity by making the phrasing of the voice part unprecedentedly irregular and asymmetrical for an aria, and the similar way in which he uses its strong and regular harmonic structure to anchor a wealth of strong, "ungrammatical" and otherwise possibly incomprehensible dissonances between voice and bass.

Monteverdi issued most of his Venetian church music in 1641 in a huge retrospective collection titled *Selva morale et spirituale* ("A Righteous and Spiritual Forest [i.e., large accumulation])." Most of its contents resemble the contents of the 1610 Vespers collection: continuo madrigals on sacred or liturgical texts, and grand *concerti* in the Gabrieli mode. One of the latter, a Mass *Gloria*, sometimes known as the "Gloria concertata," is a spectacular "theatricalization" of the liturgy, as originally sanctioned by the Counter Reformation. It is utterly unlike any liturgical setting we have so far encountered, and the very opening is the chief symptom of that difference. Monteverdi's setting is possibly the first Mass *Gloria* in which the actual words "Gloria in excelsis Deo" are set to original music by the composer rather than being left for the celebrant to intone as a memorized chant formula. And the reason for this considerable liberty—one that, if not expressly forbidden, would not likely have occurred to any composer as desirable before the seventeenth century—lay in an old madrigalist's inveterate eye for musically suggestive antitheses, and an old theatrical hand's ability to render them vivid. What could be more irresistible than to contrast bright "glorious" melismas and the high angelic voices of sopranos caroling "on high" (*in excelsis*) with low-lying "terrestrial" sonorities and the slow-moving rhythms of peace, its tranquil enjoyment affirmed with mellow chromatic inflections?

So Monteverdi's Venetian music, while chiefly written for church and chamber, was increasingly couched in theatrical terms: church-as-theater as determined by the Counter Reformation ideal, and chamber theater in the form of *opuscoli in genere rappresentativo.* What life in Venice did not give him much opportunity to create was actual theatrical music, and that was because Venice, being a republic, had no noble court and consequently no venue for the performance of *favole in musica.* What actual theatrical music Monteverdi composed during his tenure at St. Mark's was written on commission from north Italian court cities (including Mantua, his old stamping

EX. 20-5   Claudio Monteverdi, Madrigals, Book VIII, *Non havea febo (Lamento della ninfa),* mm 1–12

"Love, where is the fidelity that the traitor swore?
Love," she said: looking at the sky, she stayed her feet.

ground), where there continued to be a demand for *intermedii*, for *favole* and *balli*, or court ballets. Monteverdi wrote (or is thought to have written) at least seven theatrical works between 1616 and 1630, but for the most part their music has been lost.

POETICS AND ESTHESICS

The situation in Venice changed drastically when the Teatro San Cassiano opened its doors during the carnival season of 1637. This was the Western world's first public music theater—the world's first opera house, it is at last appropriate to say—and it seems in retrospect inevitable that it should have been Venice, Europe's great meeting place and commercial center, that brought it forth. "There and then," as Rosand has written, "opera as we know it assumed its definitive identity—as a mixed theatrical spectacle available to a socially diversified, and paying audience: a public art."[5] This was a greater novelty, perhaps, than we can easily appreciate today, after centuries of public music-making for paying audiences. But it made a decisive difference to the nature of the art purveyed, and learning to appreciate this great change will teach us a great deal about the nature of art in its relationship to its audience. In a word, it will teach us about the politics of art and (for our present purposes even more pressing) about the politics of art history, which like the music theater itself is a *genere rappresentativo*, an artful representation of reality.

In classical times, and again since the "Renaissance," most history has actually been biography, the story of great men and great deeds. Since the nineteenth century, which

was not only the "Romantic era" but also the era of Napoleon and Beethoven, and of a triumphant middle class of "self-made men," the great men celebrated by historians have typically been great neither because of high birth or hereditary power, nor because of their election by God, but rather by virtue of their individual talents and their ability to realize their destinies, especially in the face of obstacles. (This, we can easily see, is an exact description of both the Napoleonic myth and the myth of Beethoven.) Like Josquin des Prez (see chapter 14), Monteverdi has been Beethovenized by historians. For a long time, the standard account of his life

FIG. 20-2   Carnival festivities on the Piazza San Marco, Venice.

and works was a book by the German musicologist Leo Schrade called *Monteverdi, Creator of Modern Music.*[6]

An art historiography that is centered on great creative individuals will be a historiography centered on what is called *poetics.* This word has an etymology similar to the words "poetry" or "poetic", but has an altogether different meaning and a very useful one that should be kept free of the more commonly used words that resemble it. All of these words stem from the Greek verb *poiein,* "to make." The word "poetics" remains close to this original meaning and refers to the creative process, the actual making of the artwork.

The near-exclusive focus on poetics — on making — that is typical in post-Romantic historiography can lead to what is sometimes called the "poietic fallacy." (The peculiar spelling "poietic," derived from the Greek root word, is used here simply to lessen the possibility of confusion with the more ordinary meaning of "poetic.") The poietic fallacy is the assumption that all it takes to account for the nature of an artwork is the maker's intention, or — in a more refined version — the inherent (or immanent) characteristics of the object that the maker has made.

There has been considerable (quite diversely motivated) resistance to this model of art historiography in the twentieth century, and some revision of it. This book has been reflecting that resistance and revision to some extent. In the last few chapters, the ones devoted to the supplanting of the *ars perfecta,* as much or possibly more attention has been paid to larger social, economic, and religious forces as to the personal intentions of composers and theorists. (It could go without saying, but perhaps it had better be said anyway, that complete disregard of such intentions would be just as partial and just as distorted a viewpoint as its opposite: composers are influenced by all sorts of "larger forces," as are we all, but subjectively — and directly — they are most of all influenced by music.)

And yet when it came to the neoclassical impulse that gave birth to dramatic music, as discussed in the previous chapter, this book has so far followed the "poietic" model, putting things mainly in terms of artists' and theorists' expressive aspirations and achievements. But like any other form of art (at least those that have been successful), dramatic music, of course, had an "esthesic" side as well (from the Greek *aisthesis,* "perception"), reflecting the viewpoint and the expectations of the audience. ("Esthesics," like "poetics," has a more common cognate — "esthetics," the philosophy of beauty — with which it should not be confused.) In fact the esthesics of dramatic music is perhaps more of a determining factor (or at least more obviously a determining factor) in its development than in any other branch of musical art, and it is very closely bound up with politics. Before we can understand "opera from Monteverdi to Monteverdi" — that is, the differences between Monteverdi's *Orfeo* of 1607 and his *Incoronazione di Poppea* of 1643 — that bond has to be explored.

OPERA AND ITS POLITICS

At least one aspect of the "esthesics" of early dramatic music was given its due in the last chapter, namely its descent in part from the Florentine *intermedii.* All the earliest *favole in*

FIG. 20-3 Francesco Gonzaga (1466–1519), depicted on a Mantuan coin.

musica were fashioned to adorn the same kind of north Italian court festivities, flattering the assemblages of "renowned heroes, blood royal of kings" who were privileged to hear them, potentates "of whom Fame tells glorious deeds, though falling short of truth," as La Musica herself puts it in the prologue to Monteverdi's *Orfeo*—first performed during the carnival season of 1607 to fête Francesco Gonzaga, the hereditary prince of Mantua, where the composer was employed. The words were written by the prince's secretary, Alessandro Striggio (the son of a famous Mantuan madrigalist of the same name), and the whole occasion had a panegyric (prince-praising) subtext.

Thus the revived musical drama—the invention, after all, of a coterie of Florentine nobles—reflected (and was meant to reflect) the recovered grandeur and glory of antiquity on the princes who were its patrons. Like most music that has left remains for historians to discuss, it was the product and the expression of an elite culture, the topmost echelons of contemporary society. To put it that way is uncontroversial. But what if it were said that the early musical plays were the product and the expression of a tyrannical class—a product and an expression, moreover, that were only made possible by the despotic exploitation of other classes? That would direct perhaps unwelcome attention at the social costs of artistic greatness. Such awareness follows inescapably from an emphasis on the "esthesic," however; and that is perhaps one additional reason why the "poietic" side has claimed so vast a preponderance of scholarly investigation.

One scholar who did not flinch from the social consequences of the untrammeled pursuit of artistic excellence was Manfred Bukofzer, in a still unsurpassed essay, "The Sociology of Baroque Music," first published in 1947. Bukofzer characterized the early musical plays, of which Monteverdi's *Orfeo* was the crowning stroke, as the capital artistic expression of the twin triumphs of political absolutism and economic mercantilism, an expression that brought to its pinnacle the traditional exploitations of the arts "as a means of representing power." It was precisely this exploitation that, in Bukofzer's view, brought about the stylistic metamorphosis that we have been tracing for the last few chapters and that, following the terminology of his time, he called the metamorphosis from "Renaissance" to "Baroque." His description is vivid, and disquieting:

> Display of splendor was one of the main social functions of music for the Counter Reformation and the baroque courts, made possible only through money; and the more money spent, the more powerful was the representation. Consistent with the mercantile ideas of wealth, sumptuousness in the arts became actually an end in itself. . . . However, viewed from the social angle the shining lights of the flowering arts cast the blackest of shadows. Hand in hand with the brilliant development of

court and church music went the Inquisition and the ruthless exploitation of the lower classes by means of oppressive taxes.[7]

With the spread of musical plays from the opulent courts of Italy to the petty courts of northern Europe — chiefly Germany, where the first musical play was *Dafne*, a setting of Rinuccini's libretto for the earliest of all *favole in musica* as translated by Martin Opitz, court poet of the Holy Roman Empire, with music by Heinrich Schütz, a former pupil of Gabrieli, performed to celebrate a princely wedding at the court of Torgau in 13 April 1627 — the costs became ever more exorbitant and the bankrolling methods ever more drastic. "The Duke of Brunswick, for one, relied not only on the most ingenious forms of direct and indirect taxation but resorted even to the slave trade," Bukofzer reports. "He financed his operatic amusements by selling his subjects as soldiers [in the Thirty Years' War] so that his flourishing opera depended literally on the blood of the lower classes."[8] The court spectacles thus bought and paid for apotheosized political power in at least three ways. The first and most spectacular — and the most obvious — was the fusion of all the arts in the common enterprise of princely aggrandizement, familiar to us since the time of the earliest Medici wedding-shows in the early sixteenth century. The monster assemblages of singers and instrumentalists (the former neoclassically deployed in dancing choruses like those of the Greek drama, the latter massed in the first true orchestras) were matched, and even exceeded, by the luxuriously elaborate stage sets and theatrical machinery. Second, the plots, involving mythological or ancient historical heroes caught up in stereotyped conflicts of love and honor, were transparent allegories of the sponsoring rulers, who were addressed directly, as we know, in the obligatory prologues that linked the story of the opera to the events of their reign.

Third, most subtly but possibly most revealing, severe limits were set on the virtuosity of the vocal soloists lest, by indecorously representing their own power, they upstaged the personages portrayed, or worse, the personages allegorically magnified. The ban on virtuosity reflected the old aristocratic prejudice, inherited from Aristotle, that found its most influential neoclassical expression in Castiglione's *Book of the Courtier*, in which noble amateurs are enjoined to affect *sprezzatura* ("a certain noble negligence," or nonchalance) in their singing lest they compromise their standing as "free men" by an infusion of servile professionalism. We have already seen that Giulio Caccini revived the concept of *sprezzatura* in the preface to his *Nuove musiche*, and in so doing gave some precious insight into the manner and purpose of the moderate, intimate, elegantly applied throat-music called *gorgia*, which we have already had occasion to compare with crooning.

Withheld from the earlier discussion, but now relevant, was Caccini's cranky comparison of the subtle *gorgia* he employed with the unwritten (extemporized or memorized) *passaggii*—real virtuoso fireworks—with which more popular singers peppered their performances. *Passaggii*, Caccini sneered, "were not invented because they were necessary to the right way of singing, but rather, I think, for a certain titillation they afford the ears of those who do not know what it is to sing with feeling; for were this understood, then passages would no doubt be abhorred, since nothing can be more contrary to producing a good effect." The matter is couched outwardly in terms of fastidious taste, but the social snobbery lurking within is not hard to discern. Virtuosity is "common." Those who indulge it or encourage it with their applause are to be despised as vulgar, "low class." (To find Caccini's heirs in this antipopulist bias, chances are one need only read one's local music critic or record reviewer.)

Not surprisingly, virtuosity found a natural home in the commercial music theater. It is only one of the reasons for regarding the Venetian Teatro San Cassiano and the year 1637, not the Florentine Palazzo Pitti or the year 1600, as the true time and place of the birth of opera as we know it now. Where the court spectacles, even *Orfeo*, now seem like fossils — ceremonially exhumed and exhibited to sober praise from time to time (and dependably extolled in textbooks) but undeniably dead — the early commercial opera bequeathed to us the conventions by which opera has lived, in glory and in infamy, into our own time. From now on, the word *opera* as used in this book will mean the commercial opera. Anything else will be called by a different name, whether or not its creators chose to do so.

As Ellen Rosand has written, modern operagoers can still recognize in seventeenth-century Venetian works "the roots of favorite scenes: Cherubino's song, Tatiana's letter, Lucia's mad scene, Ulrica's invocation, even Tristan and Iseult's love duet."[9] With these references to characters and scenes from operas by Mozart, Chaikovsky, Donizetti, Verdi, and Wagner, all pillars of the modern repertoire, and surely not by accident, Rosand has named four potent female roles, one fairly neutered masculine partner, and a delectable cross-dresser. Ever since opera opened its doors to a paying public — a public that had to be lured — it has been a prima-donna circus with a lively transsexual sideshow, associated from the very beginning with the carnival season and its roaring tourist trade. Uncanny, nature-defying vocalism easily compensated for the courtly accoutrements — the sumptuous sets, the intricate choruses and ballets, the rich orchestras — that the early commercial opera theaters could not afford. Never mind the noble union of all the arts: what the great Russian basso Fyodor Chaliapin called "educated screaming" is the only bait that public opera has ever really needed, and its attraction has never waned.

SEX OBJECTS, SEXED AND UNSEXED

The greatest screamers of all, and the most completely "educated" (that is, cultivated), were the male prima donnas known as *castrati*, opera's first international stars, whose astounding sonority and preternaturally florid singing style confirmed opera in an abiding aura of the eerie. Although castrati originated not in the theater but in the churches of sixteenth-century Italy, where females could not perform but a full range of singers was desired, and where (as the historian John Roselli has put it) "choirboys were no sooner trained than lost,"[10] the burgeoning commercial opera stage with its exhibitionism and its heroics gave these unearthly singers their true arena. In an age that valued finely honed symbolic artifice, these magnificent singing objects — artists made, not born — were "naturally" the gods, the generals, the athletes, and the lovers. Seventeenth- and eighteenth-century "serious opera" is unthinkable (and unrevivable) without them.

Here too there are social costs to consider; for if it was to be musically effective, castration had to take place, so to speak, in the nick of time. That meant that the necessary surgery had to be performed on boys before they reached the age of consent. For this reason the operation was always officially illegal, even though the practice catered in large part to the most official social strata. When Charles Burney, the English music historian, went in search of information on the practice, he was given a royal runaround: "I was told at Milan that it was at Venice; at Venice, that it was at Bologna; but at Bologna the fact was denied, and I was referred to Florence; from Florence to Rome, and from Rome I was sent to Naples."

Greedy parents were often responsible; a prospective castrato was supposed to be brought to a conservatory to be tested "as to the probability of voice," as Burney put it.

But, he continued,

> it is my opinion that the cruel operation is but too frequently performed without trial, or at least without sufficient proof of an improvable voice; otherwise such numbers could never be found in every great town throughout Italy, without any voice at all, or at least without one sufficient to compensate such a loss.[11]

And as other travelers reported, no churchyard in Italy was without a contingent of unemployed or failed castrati, begging for their subsistence. The eunuchs of Italy were not all heroes.

By the end of the seventeenth century the serious — the noble and the heroic — was only one of the available operatic modes. The commercial opera was from the first a bastard genre, in which crowd-pleasing comic characters and burlesque scenes or interludes compromised lofty classical or historical themes in violation of traditional (that is, Aristotelian) dramatic rules, before being segregated by snobbish dramatic purists (in the eighteenth century) into discrete categories of "serious" (*opera seria*) and "comic" (*opera buffa*). And this was the other great difference — an even more significant difference — between court music spectacles and commercial opera: the latter, at first under cover of comedy, introduced oppositional, anti-aristocratic politics into the genre. The commercial (later the comic) opera, originally instituted as a carnival entertainment, became a very hotbed of what the Russian critic Mikhail Bakhtin called "carnivalism": authority stood on its head.

It was already a license to display operatic divas (women singers, literally "god-desses"), veritable warbling courtesans, to the public gaze, and a notorious Jesuit critic, Giovan Domenico Ottonelli, lost little time in rising to the bait. In a treatise of 1652 called *Delle cristiana moderazione del theatro*, he denounced the theaters of the *"mercenarii musici"* (money-grubbing musicians) as voluptuous and corrupting in contrast to the edifying spectacles mounted *"ne' palazzi de' principi grandi"* (at the palaces of great princes).[12] But the most significant licenses were as much political as moral and marked the public opera indelibly. Public opera became a world where satyrs romped and Eros reigned, where servant girls outwitted and chastised their masters, where philandering counts were humiliated, and where — later and more earnestly — rabbles were roused and revolutions were abetted. No one had to be sold into slavery to support it; and yet, for the most cogent of reasons, opera became the most stringently watchdogged and censored of all forms of art until the twentieth century, when that distinction passed to motion pictures.

Examples of opera's disruptive and destabilizing vectors can be drawn from any phase in its history, beginning with the earliest, and the promised comparison of Monteverdi's two most famous theatrical pieces, sole survivors in the repertory of the court and market genres of seventeenth-century Italy, will make an ideal vantage point for observing them since they epitomized the two artistic and political poles.

THE QUINTESSENTIAL PRINCELY SPECTACLE

Orfeo was officially mounted not by the Mantuan court itself but by an Academy — the Accademia degli Invaghiti ("Academy of those captivated [by the arts]") as it was called — but that was just a front to make the production look like a gift, since the academicians (whose ranks included both the librettist Striggio and the princely honoree) were all courtiers. Its orchestra surpassed that of any *intermedio* in its range of colors, although no more than a fraction of the full assembly of instruments plays at any one time, so that relatively few musicians were required as long as their ranks included "doublers" who could take different nonoverlapping parts.

The published score (Venice, 1609) calls for a ceaselessly churning *fundamento* or continuo contingent of five keyboard instruments (two harpsichords, two flue organs, one reed organ or regal), seven plucked instruments (three *chitarroni*, two mandolinlike citterns, and two harps), and three bass viols. The string ensemble, which mainly played ritornellos between the stanzas of the strophic numbers, consisted of a basic band of twelve *ripieni* or ensemble members and two soloists on "French violins" (evidently meaning small dancing-master "pocket fiddles" or *pochettes*). Finally there was an assortment of wind and brass, some of them reserved for the infernal scenes: two end-blown whistle flutes or recorders, two cornetti, three *trombe sordini* ("mute trumpets," probably with slides), five trombones, and a *clarino*, meaning a trumpet played in its highest register.

The brass colors were to be flaunted first in a *toccata* (= tucket in English, *Tusch* in German) — a quasi-military fanfare that, according to the published score, was to be played three times from various places around the hall to silence the audience and invest the proceedings with appropriate pomp. (Contemporary accounts of the premire suggest that a tucket — perhaps this very one — was played before all Mantuan court spectacles; the one in *Orfeo* — as so often in the case of apparent innovations — was just the first to get written down.) Bukofzer's point about the interest in ostentatious displays of power that the Counter Reformation church shared with the "baroque courts" is nicely confirmed by Monteverdi's reuse of the *Orfeo* toccata three years later in a very uncustomary way to back up the choral *falsobordone* (choral recitation) for the Invitatory (opening Psalm verse) in his Vespers of 1610 which, we recall, was originally intended for Rome, the Counter Reformation command center. The concluding doxology is sampled in Ex. 20-6.

EX. 20-6   Claudio Monteverdi, *Vespro della beata virgine* (1610), *Deus in adiutorium meum intende* (doxology), mm. 14–18

EX. 20-6 *(continued)*

As in the case of Rinuccini's libretto for *Euridice*, Striggio's for *Orfeo* revises its mythological subject to avoid a tragic conclusion. In the myth, after losing Eurydice a second time, Orpheus turns against all women, for which reason a rioting chorus of jealous Bacchantes tears him to pieces. In the *Orfeo* libretto Orpheus's father Apollo, the divine musician, translates Orpheus into the heavenly constellation that bears his name, substituting serene apotheosis for bloody cataclysm. There is also a somewhat didactically pointed clash between virtuosity and true eloquence in Orpheus's great act III aria *Possente spirto*, his plea to the ferryman Charon to transport him across the river Styx to the Underworld. The aria consists of five strophes over a ground bass. The first four are decorated with flowery *passaggii* that exploited the famous skills of Francesco Rasi, a pupil of Caccini, who sang the title role. His florid stanzas are sung in alternation with fancy instrumental solos for the "French violins" mentioned earlier, for harp (standing in for the Orphic lyre), and for cornetto. When all of this artifice leaves Charon unmoved, Orpheus, in desperation, drops all pretense of crafty rhetoric and makes his final appeal in unadorned *recitativo* to a bare figured bass, the very emblem of sincerity. (Charon, while too oafish to respond, nevertheless falls asleep at this, possibly charmed by Apollo, and Orpheus steals his boat; it is the single touch of comic relief.) Above all, and perhaps strangely to us who know what opera has become, there is virtually no love music in this tender *favola*, for all that it concerns the parting and reuniting of lovers. Orpheus sings on and on about his love for Eurydice, but he does not express it directly through music—that is, to her. Indeed, as it took a feminist critic, Susan McClary, finally to point out, Eurydice, with only a couple of very plain-sung lines in act I and a couple more in act IV, is hardly a character at all in what is at bottom a very decorous, an inveterately "noble," and an insistently masculine spectacle in its focus on natural male vocal ranges and on the ideal of self-possession.[13] This focus is made explicit in the scene where Orpheus loses Eurydice for the second time and a chorus of spirits sing the moral (intended not only for Orpheus but for the young prince Francesco in whose honor the *favola* was performed): only he who can subdue his passions with reason is worthy of reward. Indeed, the original performance observed the interdiction on female singers in serious places like the *palazzi de' principi grandi*, casting the solo feminine roles—from La Musica to the Messenger to Eurydice herself—for castrati or, in some cases, possibly, for boys.

What, then, can account for this oddly restricted work's enduring hold on audiences, even nonnoble ones, even to this day? Of all the individual acts, the second might best suggest the answer in the way Monteverdi's music mirrors the implicit point of the whole *favola*, which is in essence a music-myth, a demonstration of music's power to move the affections. For in the second act Monteverdi and his librettist contrived a determined clash between "phenomenal" and "noumenal" music, as defined in the previous chapter. It concentrates the radical humanist message into a more powerful dose than any other contemporary composer imagined.

The act begins with a celebration of the wedding of Orpheus and Eurydice. Orpheus, surrounded by his friends the shepherds, celebrates his love. They do it as a kind of concert consisting, after an invocation by the title character, of no fewer than four strophic arias, veritable *scherzi musicali* with lavishly scored instrumental ritornelli, in all likelihood danced as well as sung. The first three are sung respectively by a shepherd, by two shepherds, and by the full chorus. Then comes Orfeo's big number, the aria *Vi ricorda o bosch'ombrosi*, in which he gives catchy vent to his joy, using the elegant hemiola meter Monteverdi designated in his *Scherzi* of 1607 as "French" (=elegant, as in "French pastry"). Repeated references in the verses to Orpheus's lyre leave no doubt that he is playing along to accompany the singing, and that the songs and dances are literally that — actual songs and dances performed "phenomenally" on stage.

After Orpheus has finished, one of the shepherds bids him strike up another song with his golden plectrum; but before Orpheus can comply, the baleful "Messenger" (actually the nymph Sylvia) bursts in with the horrible news of Eurydice's death and silences the stage music for good and all (Ex. 20-7). But the phenomenal music is silenced only so that the noumenal music, the real music of lyric eloquence, can work its wonders on the audience. From here until Orpheus and the Messenger depart the scene (he to fetch Eurydice back, she to hide in shame at having broken such bitter news) no instrument is heard but those of the *fundamento*, whose music goes symbolically "unheard" on stage.

EX. 20-7   Claudio Monteverdi, *Orfeo*, Act II, messenger breaks in on song and dance

EX. 20-7 (*continued*)

The central business of the act is the exchange between Orpheus and the nymph Sylvia (fulfilling the same function as the nymph Daphne in Rinuccini's *Euridice* libretto), which is clearly modeled on, but just as clearly far surpasses, the analogous scene in Peri's and Caccini's *favole* (Ex. 20-8). Monteverdi actually pays Peri the homage of imitation in his deployment of jarring tonalities; but where Peri had contrasted the harmonies of E major and G minor in large sections corresponding to the main divisions of Orpheus's soliloquy, Monteverdi uses the contrast at very close range to underscore the poignancy of the dialogue psychologically.

EX. 20-8   Claudio Monteverdi, *Orfeo*, Orfeo gets the horrifying news from the messenger

EX. 20-8 (*continued*)

The harmonic disparity between Orpheus's lines and Sylvia's symbolizes his resistance to the untimely news she has brought him. He breaks in on her narrative with G minor — *Ohimè, che odo?* ("Oh no, what am I hearing?") — as soon as she has mentioned the name of Eurydice (on an E-major harmony), as if to deflect her from the bitter message she is about to deliver, but she comes right back with E major and resolves the chord cadentially to A on the word *morta*, "dead." When Orpheus responds with another *Ohimè*, this time he takes up the same harmony where she left it and confirms it with D, the next harmony along the circle of fifths: the message has sunk in, and he must accept it.

Once again, as in *Euridice*, the same horrific events are recounted rather than portrayed: not only out of delicacy, but because the composer's interest is in portraying not events but emotions, those of the Messenger herself and those of Orpheus. When Orpheus finds his voice again after temporarily becoming (as one of the shepherds puts it) "a speechless rock," Monteverdi again shows his reliance upon Peri as a model, but once again only to surpass his predecessor. Monteverdi's central soliloquy, like Peri's, builds from stony shock to resolution, but does so with a fullness of gradation that mirrors much more faithfully — and recognizably! — the process of emotional transmutation (Ex. 20-9). The secret lies in the bass, which begins with Periesque stasis but gradually begins to move both more rhythmically and with a more directed harmonic progression, approaching some middle ground between *recitativo* and full-blown song. (Later this middle-ground activity would be called *arioso*.) Orpheus having spoken and left, the chorus strikes up a formal dirge by turning the messenger's opening lines ("Ah, grievous mischance. . .") into a ritornello, the messenger's notes forming the bass, against which a pair of shepherds sing lamenting strophes that recall the previous rejoicing with bitter irony (Ex. 20-10). Whether to regard the dirge as phenomenal or noumenal music is a nice question; but in any event it is formalized and ritualized emotion that is here being expressed, rather than the spontaneous outpouring that provides the act with its center of dramatic gravity. In this most affecting act of *Orfeo*, then, the dramatic strategy has been to frame dramatic recitative with decorative aria. The commercial opera would eventually reverse this perspective.

EX. 20-9   Claudio Monteverdi, *Orfeo*, Orfeo's recitative ("Tu se' morta")

THE CARNIVAL SHOW

In one of the most impressive feats of self-rejuvenation in the history of music, the septuagenarian Monteverdi, bestirred by the institution of public opera theaters, or else offered terms he could not refuse, came out of retirement and composed a final trio of operas for the Teatro SS. Giovanni e Paolo, one of several competitors that quickly sprang up to challenge San Cassiano, the original opera house. The first was *Il Ritorno d'Ulisse in patria* (*Ulysses' Return to His Homeland*), after Homer's *Odyssey*. The second, now lost, concerned another mythological subject, the wedding of Aeneas. The last was *L'incoronazione di Poppea*, not a mythological but a historical fantasy based on Tacitus and other Roman historians. The librettist was Giovanni Francesco Busenello, a famous poet who was active in the Accademia degli Incogniti (the Academy of the Disguised), a

EX. 20-10   Claudio Monteverdi, *Orfeo*, Chorus ("Ahi caso acerbo")

society of libertines and skeptics who dominated the early Venetian commercial theater and did their best to subvert the values of court theatricals for the greater enjoyment of the paying public.

Busenello's libretto celebrates neither the reward of virtue nor (as in *Orfeo*) the chastisement of vice. It is a celebration of vice triumphant and virtue mocked. The librettist's own *argomento* or synopsis, published in 1656 in his collected works, puts the story very concisely:

> Nero, enamored of Poppaea, who was the wife of Otho, sent the latter, under the pretext of embassy, to Lusitania [Portugal], so that he could take his pleasure with her — this according to Cornelius Tacitus. But here we represent these actions differently. Otho, desperate at seeing himself deprived of Poppaea, gives himself over to frenzy and exclamations. Octavia, wife of Nero, orders Otho to kill Poppaea. Otho promises to do it; but lacking the spirit to deprive his adored Poppaea of life, he dresses in the clothes of Drusilla, who was in love with him. Thus disguised, he enters the garden of Poppaea. Love [i.e., the god Eros] disturbs and prevents that death. Nero repudiates·Octavia, in spite of the counsel of [the philosopher] Seneca, and takes Poppaea to wife. Seneca is sentenced to death, and Octavia is expelled from Rome.[14]

Monteverdi's setting of this most unedifying — and in places virtually obscene — entertainment has the skimpiest of orchestras (just a little ritornello band notated in three or four staves for unspecified instruments, most likely strings), but it is cast throughout for flamboyant voice types that could never have existed in the court *favole*: two superbly developed prima-donna roles (the more virtuosic of them the fork-tongued, string-pulling title character, the more poignantly monodic one the wronged and rejected wife), two *male* parts for shrill castrato singers (the higher of them the feminized, manipulated Emperor Nero, the other the stoical wronged husband), and a quartet of low-born comic characters — one of them, a ghastly crone (Poppaea's former wet nurse Arnalta) often played by a male falsettist in drag — who spoof, intentionally or not, the passions and gestures of their betters.

As often in Shakespeare, Monteverdi's shorter-lived contemporary, the comic scenes are paired with the most serious ones. Thus, the scene in which Seneca carries out Nero's sentence of death by committing suicide surrounded by his loving disciples is immediately followed by one in which Octavia's page is shown chasing her lady-in-waiting, coyly singing the while that he is "feeling a certain something" (*Sento un certo non so che*) between his legs. And the opera's most tragic moment, Octavia's farewell to Rome as she boards the ship that is to take her into exile (Ex. 20-11), is followed immediately by the most farcical — Arnalta's gloating at her mistress's impending elevation, and her own (Ex. 20-12). Elsewhere the page, the opera's "lowest" character, directly mocks Seneca, its most exalted one (Ex. 20-13).

The relationship between Nero and Poppaea is represented frankly as lustful, and that lust is given graphic musical representation. In an early lovers' dialogue, Poppaea flaunts her lips, her breasts, and her arms at Nero, and the composer, taking on the role of stage director, seems to prescribe not only her lines and their delivery but her lewd gestures as well. Nero, in response, makes explicit reference to their sexual encounters,

EX. 20-11 Claudio Monteverdi, *L'incoronazione di Poppea*, Act III, scene 6 (Octavia), mm. 1–18

Octavia: Farewell, Rome, farewell, my homeland, farewell.
Innocent, I am going to leave you,
I am going to suffer bitter grief.
I am sailing in despair across the deaf sea.

EX. 20-12 Claudio Monteverdi, *L'incoronazione di Poppea*, Act III, scene 7 (Arnalta), mm. 1–28

EX. 20-12 (continued)

Arnalta: Today Poppea will be empress of Rome.
I, her nurse, will climb the steps of status.
No, I will not slum it with the vulgar.
Those who were on familiar terms with me
will now embellish a new harmony,
"Your ladyship!"

EX. 20-13   Claudio Monteverdi, *L'incoronazione di Poppea*, Act I, scene 6, mm. 113–41

EX. 20-13   (*continued*)

Page: I cannot do my duty, no, no, no,
while he bewitches others with golden words.
They are mere inventions of his brain.
He touts them as mysteries, but they're just songs.

even to "that inflamed spirit which, in kissing, I spilled in thee" (Ex. 20-14). And in the opera's famous culminating number, the duet *Pur ti miro*, an arching, bristlingly sensual lust duet (for two sopranos, impossible to savor today at full outlandish strength even when the part of Nero is not transposed to the range of a "natural" man but sung by a woman), the music, in its writhing, coiling movements, the increased agitation of the middle section, and the dissonant friction between the singers' parts (or between them both and the bass: see especially the setting of the words *più non peno, più non moro* in Ex. 20-15), leaves no doubt that the lovers are enacting their passion before us, whether or not the stage director dares show them in the act.

This duet, of which the final, opera-ending section is given in Ex. 20-15, symbolizes and formally celebrates in the guise of a *ciaccona*, a slow dance over a mesmerizing ground

EX. 20-14   Claudio Monteverdi, *L'incoronazione di Poppea*, Act I, scene 10, mm. 1–38

EX. 20-14 *(continued)*

Poppea: How sweetly, my lord, how smoothly did you enjoy last night the kisses of this mouth?
Nero: The sweeter they were the more they bit me.
Poppea: The apples of this bosom?
Nero: Your breasts deserve a sweeter name.
Poppea: The sweet embraces of these arms?

EX. 20-15 Claudio Monteverdi, *L'incoronazione di Poppea*, final scene, no. 24 (ciaccona: *Pur ti miro*), end

EX. 20-15 (*continued*)

o _ mia vi - ta, o_mio te - so - ro. _____

o _____ mia _____ vi - ta, o mia te - so - ro. _____

I gaze on you, I enjoy you.
I hug you, I entwine you.
No more pain, no more death.
O my life, O my treasure.
I am yours. I am yours,
my joy, say you love me too.
You are truly my idol.
Yes, my love, yes my heart, my life, yes.

bass (again a descending tetrachord at the beginning and the end, but in the lubricious major rather than the lamenting minor), a craving that has subverted all moral and political codes. (Its form, with a contrasting middle section and a reprise of the opening "from the top" [*da capo*], would become increasingly popular with opera composers and eventually replace the strophic aria.) Where *Orfeo*, the court pageant, celebrated established order and authority and the cool moderation that its hero tragically violates, *Poppea*, the carnival show, brings it all down: passion wins out over reason, woman over man, guile over truth, impulse over wisdom, license over law, artifice (in persuasion, in the singing of it, in the voice itself) over nature.

Scholars now agree that *Pur ti miro*, once thought to be the aged Monteverdi's sublime swan song, was not written by him at all, but by a younger composer (maybe Francesco Cavalli, Monteverdi's pupil; maybe Benedetto Ferrari; maybe Francesco Sacrati, now regarded as the prime suspect) for a revival in the early 1650s. Only that version, presumably one of many that circulated in the theaters at the time, has survived. And so it is now the standard text, but it had no such status in its own day. That is another difference between the court spectacles and the earliest real operas. The court operas, performed once only, were then printed up as souvenirs of the festivities for which they were composed in fully edited, idealized texts that resembled books. These scores could become the basis of later productions (and did so in the case of *Orfeo*), but that was not their primary purpose.

Commercial operas, by contrast, were not published at all until comparatively recent times. Like today's commercial (e.g., "Broadway") musical shows, they existed during their runs and revivals in a ceaseless maelstrom of negotiation and revision, existing in a multitude of versions — for this theater, for that theater, "for the road," for this star or that — and never attained the status of finished texts. It distorts them considerably even to contemplate them from the purely "poietic" standpoint that has become the rule for "classical music." They were esthesic objects par excellence, not texts but performances, embodying much that was unwritten and unwritable, directed outward at their audience, not at history, the museum, posterity, the classroom, or any other place where poietics is of primary interest.

Once again we observe that the fully textual (or textualized) condition we associate with "classical music" and its permanent canon of masterpieces came into being much later than many types of music that eventually entered its orbit, sometimes with distorting or invidious result. And yet the commercial opera never did altogether supplant the courtly, since they occupied differing social spheres and have only lately met, uneasily, on the modern operatic stage.

Ever since 1637, then, the world of opera has been a divided world, its two political strains — the edifying and the profitable, the authoritarian and the anarchic, the affirmational and the oppositional — unpeacefully coexisting, the tension between them conditioning everything about the genre: its forms, its styles, its meanings (or its attempts to circumvent meaning), its performance practices, its followings, its critical traditions. The same political tension lies behind every one of the press skirmishes, reforms, and "querelles" that dot operatic history (and that we shall be tracing in due course), and it informs the intermission disputes of today. Nothing else attests so well to opera's cultural significance, and nothing else so well explains the durability of this oldest of living musical traditions in the West.

Fat Times and Lean

ORGAN MUSIC FROM FRESCOBALDI TO SCHEIDT; SCHÜTZ'S
CAREER; ORATORIO AND CANTATA

SOME ORGANISTS

Whoever wrote it, and however it may have related to Monteverdi's original design, the ending of *L'incoronazione di Poppea* was a harbinger. The seventeenth century was the great age of the ground bass. Infinitely extensible formal plans (if "plan" is indeed the word for something that is infinitely extensible) enabled musical compositions to achieve an amplitude comparable to the extravagantly majestic Counter Reformation church architecture that provided the spaces in which they were heard (and to which the word "baroque" was first applied).

These forms, as we have had more than one occasion to observe, grew directly out of an oral or "improvisatory" practice that continued to flourish alongside its written specimens. The written examples, especially those meant for solo virtuosos to perform, represented the cream of the oral practice—particularly effective improvisations retained (as "keepers") in memory for repeated performance and refinement and eventual commitment to paper, print, and posterity.

That certainly seems to be the case with Girolamo Frescobaldi (1583–1643), the organist at St. Peter's basilica in Rome from 1608 to his death, whose mature works were among the most distinctive embodiments of practices arising in the wake of the Counter Reformation. He was at once the most flamboyantly impressive keyboard composer of his time and the most characteristic, because it was characteristic of early seventeenth-century music to be flamboyantly impressive. The theatricalized quality that virtually all professional music making strove to project was as avidly cultivated by instrumentalists as by vocalists and those who wrote their material. The stock of the instrumental medium rose in consequence to the point where a major composer could

FIG. 21-1 Girolamo Frescobaldi, by Claude Mellan (1598–1688).

FIG. 21-2   Interior of St. Peter's basilica, Rome, painted in 1730 by Giovanni Paolo Pannini (1692–1765).

be concerned primarily with music for instruments. Before the seventeenth century that had never happened.

Many of Frescobaldi's compositions circulated during his lifetime only in manuscript, but the composer did personally oversee the publication of sixteen volumes between 1608 and 1637. Of the sixteen, only four volumes contained vocal compositions: one of motets, one of madrigals, and two of continuo arias written during a brief sojourn in Florence. The remaining twelve were devoted to instrumental works. Eight of them were issued *in partitura*, that is, laid out in score with strict voice leading, in most cases with parts provided so that they could be performed by ensembles as well as at the keyboard. The remaining four were *libri d'intavolatura*, idiomatic keyboard compositions laid out like modern keyboard music on a pair of staves corresponding to the player's two hands, with free voice leading and other effects that precluded ensemble performance.

When he played them himself, the composer certainly adapted his ricercari, fantasias, and canzonas to the idiomatic style of his "intabulations." Nevertheless, the *libri d'intavolatura* contained Frescobaldi's most novel, most theatrical, and most elaborately "open-ended" compositions, and in that sense they reflected his most vividly over-the-top (i.e., "baroque") side. Such compositions came in two main types — *partite* (that is, variations) over a ground bass, and formally capricious, unpredictable *toccate*. We will sample both at their most flamboyant.

A visiting French viol player named André Maugars left a revealing description of the mature Frescobaldi at work (or at play) in 1639, "displaying a thousand kinds of inventions on his harpsichord [*spinettina*] while the organ stuck to the main tune," adding that "although his printed works give sufficient evidence of his skill, still, to get a true idea of his deep knowledge, one must hear him improvise toccatas full of admirable refinements and inventions."[1] Maugars well knew whereof he spoke. As an internationally famous musician from whom no written music survives, he if anyone knew that the musical daily business of seventeenth-century instrumentalists continued to be transacted *ex tempore*. On the same trip to Rome, Maugars enjoyed his own success before Pope Urban VIII, Frescobaldi's patron, improvising in the organ loft during Mass on a theme presented as a challenge by the organist, who then repeated it as an accompaniment "while I varied it with so much imagination and with so many different rhythms and tempi that they were quite astonished." Frescobaldi's famous *Cento partite sopra passacagli* ("A Hundred Variations on Passacalles"), the concentrated residue of years of similar improvising, is nothing if not astonishing, with its frequent surprising forays into contrasting rhythms and tempi and its startling harmonic effects. It comes from the last of his keyboard publications, called *Toccate d'intavolatura di cembalo et organo, partite di diverse arie, e correnti, balletti, ciaccone, passacagli*, published in Rome in 1637. The title lists four other keyboard genres besides toccatas and partitas:

— The *corrente* was a dance in triple meter (*courante* in French) that could occur either with a quick step notated in $\frac{3}{4}$ or $\frac{3}{8}$ or in a more stately variant notated in $\frac{3}{2}$ with many hemiolas.

— The *balletto*, as Frescobaldi used the term, was a dignified dance of German origin (hence *allemande* in French), usually in a broad duple meter. Balletti and correnti were often cast in melodically related pairs, like the pavanes and galliards of old.

— The *ciaccona* was a fast and furious dance in syncopated triple meter, which in the sixteenth century had been imported into Spanish and Italian courtly circles from the New World. (The first literary use of the word *chacona*, the Swiss music historian Lorenzo Bianconi has disclosed, came from a Spanish satire on Peruvian customs published in 1598.[2]) Its first appearance in a musical print was in an Italian guitar book of 1606, where it was given as a formula for singing poetry in the manner of an old-fashioned "aria."[3] As a dance, the ciaccona was built over repetitive chord progressions similar in practice to the traditional Italian dance tenors, and was considered so inveterately lascivious that it was banished — as an actual dance — from the Spanish stage. An air of forbidden fruit surrounded it thereafter, which is why it was the inevitable choice of Sacrati (or whoever it was who renovated *L'incoronazione di Poppea*) for the lubricious final duet. The Italian poet Giambattista Marino (1569–1625), whose highly mannered, flamboyant verses Monteverdi often set, aimed some mock curses at this "immodest, obscene dance, with its thousand twisted movements" in his epic *Adonis*: "Perish the foul inventor who first amongst us introduced this barbaric custom,... this impious profane game, which the *novo ispano* [i.e., the denizen of "New Spain," meaning the Americas] calls *ciaccona*!"[4] These lines were written in 1623. Nine years later, Monteverdi published his setting of Ottavio Rinuccini's imitation of Petrarch's famous sonnet *Zefiro torna* ("The breeze returns") in the form of a "ciacona" (Ex. 21-1), and from then on it was a major Italian medium for love poetry, for stage music, and for instrumental virtuosity.

— *Passacagli* is Italian for *passacalles*, a related Spanish genre consisting of variations on cadential patterns that apparently grew out of the habits of guitarists who accompanied courtly singers, and who introduced and bestrewed the songs with casual ritornellos — the kind of thing accompanists in today's nonliterate ("pop") genres call "vamping." Like today's popular guitarists and keyboardists, who often take off on their vamping figures for impressive flights of fancy, so the players of *passacagli* often elaborated them into long instrumental interludes, eventually into independent instrumental showpieces.

The repetitive cadential phrases of the ciaccona and the passacagli were a natural for adaptation to traditional ground-bass techniques, and that is how they entered the domain of written music. The first literate instrumental adaptations of the two related genres were by Frescobaldi. His second *libro d'intavolatura*, published in 1627, contained

EX. 21-1   Claudio Monteverdi, *Zefiro torna*, beginning

both a set of *Partite sopra ciaccona* (roughly "variations on the chacona") and one of *Partite sopra passacagli* ("variations on passacalles"). Eventually the name of the latter variations genre was standardized in Italian as *passacaglia*, and the ciaccona, owing (as we shall see) to its many adaptations on the French stage, has become falsely but firmly identified with France and is now most widely known as the *chaconne*.

Frescobaldi's enormous *Cento partite* ("hundred variations") of 1637, though nominally another passacaglia set, actually mixes several of the genres just described. A total of 78 actual *passacagli* or varied two- or four-bar cadence figures alternate first with a *corrente* and then with some forty *ciaccona* progressions, producing a total far in excess of one hundred, from which the player was invited to choose ad libitum. As the composer wrote in the preface, "the passacaglias can be played separately, in accordance with what is most pleasing, by adjusting the tempo of one part to that of the other, and the same goes for the ciacconas."[5]

It is even possible that the word *cento* in the title was chosen for its resonance with the earlier Latin usage, chiefly used in connection with chant, which denotes not literally "one hundred" but rather a patchwork or mixture of formulas. The title, then, would mean something like "A mixed bag of variations on passacaglias [and other things]" or "Passacaglias mixed with other ground-bass formulas." In any case, Frescobaldi's fanciful mixture of sameness and contrast gave instrumental music access to a whole new temporal plane, and a newly dramatized character. This was music with real "content," not just an accessory to vocal performances or a liturgical time-filler.

Yet tonally speaking, and in keeping with its character as compendium rather than a work of fixed content, Frescobaldi's mixed bag is extremely, even disconcertingly, loose. The first set of passacagli, as well as the corrente that they surround, are in D minor. A sudden cadence to what we call the "relative major" on F, duly labeled "altro tono" ("the other mode"), leads to the first section labeled ciaccona, also in F. From there on the tonal behavior of the composition is altogether unpredictable, as is the final cadence on E. This lack of "tonal unity" has led some writers to suggest that the work is no "composition" at all, but just an assortment of goods. Other writers have even suggested that the components were printed in the wrong order as the result of "some sort of mishap at the printer's office," to cite one scholar's particularly rash proposal.[6] The composer's presence on the scene, and his presumable role as proofreader, makes this somewhat implausible. While granting that the performer had many options besides the printed order ("in accordance with what is most pleasing," as the composer allowed), the printed order must surely be counted as one of the available options. The only conclusion the evidence supports is that the "tonal unity" we look for now in an extended composition was not (yet) considered a necessary criterion of coherence for works of this type. Ex. 21-2 shows the final section, in E. Note the cadences in every other bar. Their regularity is in fact a guide to tempo; from their placement we can tell, for example, that the note values following the triple meter signature should be read at *doppio movimiento* or double speed.

THE TOCCATA

The earliest recorded use of the word "toccata" in a musical source occurs in a lute collection of 1536, where it refers to the kind of brief improvisatory prelude formerly called *preambulum* or *ricercar* or even *tastar de corde* ("checking to see if the strings are in tune"). The new term was evidently coined to substitute for "ricercar" when the latter term had become firmly associated with "strict" imitative compositions in motet style. Over the next hundred years the term saw a variety of uses; we have already

EX. 21-2 Girolamo Frescobaldi, *Cento partite sopra passacagli*, conclusion

seen it applied by Monteverdi to the curtain-raising flourish before his *Orfeo*, a kind of theatrical preambulum. Later on, pieces called "toccata" achieved greater dimensions and independent status, but they always remained "free" and open in form, deriving their continuity from discontinuity, to put it paradoxically. That is, they relied on contrast — in texture, meter, tempo, tonality — between short striking sections, rather than the continuous development of motives, to sustain interest. "Striking" meant virtuosic as well; toccatas, like the preluding improvisations of old, were often festive display pieces that turned the very act of playing (or "touching" — *toccare* — the keys) into a form of theater.

Frescobaldi inherited the toccata from Claudio Merulo (1533–1604), whose two books of toccatas, published in Rome shortly before Frescobaldi took up his duties at St. Peter's, had established what would become the genre's basic modus operandi as an alternation of "free" chordal and "strict" imitative sections. With his horror of regularity, Frescobaldi turned Merulo's placid interchanges into another sort of "mixed bag," in this case a dazzling bag of tricks. In the very lengthy and detailed preface to his first book of toccatas, the epochal *Primo libro d'intavolatura* ("First book of intabulations," 1615), reprinted in every subsequent book, Frescobaldi explicitly gave the performer the last say as to the form his toccatas took, just as he himself must have done when performing them. "In the toccatas," he wrote, "I have taken care not only that they be abundantly provided with different passages and affections but also that each one of the said passages can be played separately; the performer is thus under no obligation to finish them all but can end wherever he thinks best."[7]

This option would seem to apply particularly to the famous *Toccata nona* or ninth toccata from Frescobaldi's second book (1637), which set a new and widely emulated standard for fireworks (Ex. 21-3). It begins with a bit of cursory lip service to imitation between the hands, but motivic consistency is not maintained past the second bar; and although the piece ends where it began, in F, the tonal vagaries along the way are seemingly as wayward as possible. It is that sense of wandering through a harmonic labyrinth, as well as the mounting rhythmic figuration and the frequent superimposition of conflicting divisions of the beat ("threes against twos"), that must

EX. 21-3   Girolamo Frescobaldi, Toccata IX (*Toccata nona*), mm. 11–22

EX. 21-3   (*continued*)

have prompted the curious note of mingled self-congratulation and lampoonery that Frescobaldi appends in conclusion: *Non senza fatiga si giunge al fine* ("You won't make it to the end without tiring"). The many apparent changes of time signature along the way are really proportion signs: $^{12}_{8}$, for example, literally means 12 sixteenth notes in the time of eight, later cancelled by its seemingly inscrutable reciprocal, $^{8}_{12}$. It is the sort of thing indicated in more modern notation by the use of triplet signs and the like (Ex. 21-3).

In the hands of Frescobaldi's pupils like Michelangelo Rossi (1602–56), the toccata could become truly bizarre, seemingly in the spirit of the late polyphonic madrigal. In Rossi's *Toccata settima*, the seventh toccata in his first *libro d'intavolatura* (published in Rome without a date, most likely around 1640) the weird harmonic successions of Gesualdo's madrigals or Sigismondo's monodies are elevated to the level of broad sectional contrasts (Ex. 21-4). Music like this is clearly contrived to

EX. 21-4   Michelangelo Rossi, Toccata VII (*Toccata settima*), mm. 9–16

knock listeners for a loop, the way an outlandish twist of plot might do the spectators in a drama.

In Frescobaldi, stupefying chromatic effects are most often found in a special subgenre called *toccate di durezze e ligature* ("toccatas with dissonances and suspensions") that inhabits a very different expressive world from the histrionic self-assertion of the showpiece toccatas. Such pieces are found among the other toccatas in Frescobaldi's *libri d'intavolatura* (and they are found in the work of some earlier organists as well), but they may be seen in their natural habitat, so to speak, in his largest collection, *Fiori musicali* ("Musical flowers," 1635), which contains music designed for specific liturgical use, arranged in three "organ Masses."

This wonderfully suggestive volume enables us to imagine the way in which organists, still for the most part working *ex tempore*, actually accompanied the church service in the years following the Counter Reformation. Each Frescobaldi organ Mass begins with a short flourish of a toccata (*Toccata avanti la Messa*) that functions as an *intonazione*, a fancy way to give the choir its pitch. The next (and longest) section is a complete and very old-fashioned cantus firmus setting of the Kyrie, the organist's equivalent of the choir's *stile antico*. Ex. 21-5 shows the beginning of the Kyrie setting from the second organ Mass in *Fiori musicali*, the *Messa della Madonna* ("Mass of the Virgin Mary"), based on the Gregorian Kyrie IX ("Cum jubilo"), which we have known since chapter 3.

EX. 21-5   Girolamo Frescobaldi, *Messa della Madonna* (in *Fiori musicali*), opening section of Kyrie, mm. 13–23

Then follow a lively *Canzon dopo la Pistola*, a "canzona [for playing] after the Epistle [and before the Gospel]," to preface or stand in for the Gradual; a strictly imitative *Recercar dopo il Credo*, a "ricercar [for playing] after the Credo," to introduce the Offertory and accompany the collection (sometimes itself preceded by a short toccata, giving the effect of what was later known as a prelude and fugue); and to conclude, a *Canzone post il Comune*, a "canzona [for playing] after [the singing of] the communion [chant]," also sometimes introduced by a little toccata, to accompany the distribution of the wine and wafer.

The *toccata di durezze e ligature*, sometimes called the *toccata chromatica*, is played *per le levatione*, "for the Elevation," the moment when the priest performs the transubstantiating miracle that turns the wine and wafer into the blood and body of Christ, as his ordination empowers him to do. It is the most mysterious moment of the Mass, a moment of sublime contemplation, and it is that mood of self-abasement before a truth that passes human understanding that the elevation toccata, in its unearthly harmony, is designed to capture, or induce.

The Elevation toccata from Frescobaldi's *Messa della Domenica*, the Mass for Sundays throughout the year, is both his most chromatic composition and the one most poignantly riddled with suspensions. Its obsessive contemplation of an "irrational" idea, in which an apparent leading tone turns tail and descends dissonantly through semitones (an effect later classified by German theorists, among other "unnatural progressions," as the *passus duriusculus*, "the hard way down"), makes the toccata an epitome of the Counter Reformation ideal, long since associated with St. Theresa, that envisaged "religious experience" as deeply felt emotion on the very threshold of pain.

SWEELINCK—HIS PATRIMONY AND HIS PROGENY

Surely the most spectacular workout ever given the *passus duriusculus* was in a *Fantasia chromatica* by the Dutch organist Jan Pieterszoon Sweelinck (1562–1621), Frescobaldi's older contemporary, who succeeded his father as chief organist at Amsterdam's Oude Kerk (Old Church) while still in his teens, and held it until his death. Unlike Frescobaldi, Sweelinck was not a church organist in the full sense of the word. The Dutch Reformed Church, Calvinist in outlook, forbade the use of "figural" (polyphonic or instrumental) music during services. Rather, Sweelinck was employed to perform what amounted to daily organ recitals—an hour of uninterrupted music making—to follow the morning and evening services. Like Frescobaldi, and like every other keyboard virtuoso of the day, Sweelinck was best known for his improvisations, and the works he noted down and allowed to circulate (in manuscript only) represented the skimmed cream of this daily exercise.

For publication Sweelinck composed a great deal of vocal music, most of it secular and none of it meant for actual service use. It was intended for the international music trade and was therefore composed to texts in international languages: French (chansons and metrical psalms), Latin (motets), and Italian (madrigals). Although some of his publications were equipped with basso seguente parts to make them commercially viable, none of Sweelinck's music is actually "concerted." His vocal music is all fully polyphonic in the sixteenth-century style; never does the instrumental bass play an independent role, nor did Sweelinck publish so much as a single solo song or monody. That makes him the youngest continental composer never to write in the concerted or monodic styles of vocal music, and he therefore looms in retrospect as the last of the legendary "Netherlanders" of the polyphonic Golden Age.

But his dual preoccupation with old-fashioned vocal music and extremely up-to-date keyboard compositions puts Sweelinck in a position comparable to no other Netherlander, but rather like that of William Byrd, his older English contemporary (see chapter 16). The similarity was not fortuitous. While he never met Byrd, Sweelinck was well acquainted with several other English composers who had settled in the southerly (Catholic) part of the Netherlands that is now Belgium. Peter Philips (1560–1628) came to Brussels in 1589 in the entourage of a recusant nobleman, Lord Thomas Paget, who had fled England to avoid religious persecution. After Paget's death the next year, Philips relocated in Antwerp. He was joined in 1612 by John Bull (1562–1628), who also claimed to be a religious refugee but is now thought to have been evading some sort of "morals" charge (possibly adultery or pederasty). Philips and Bull were the conduits through which the very advanced art of the Elizabethan keyboard composers established, through Sweelinck, a continental base. Sweelinck composed variations on a pavan (a slow keyboard dance) by Philips, and after his death Bull based a fantasia on a theme by Sweelinck.

Once he had absorbed the English styles and genres, moreover, Sweelinck's work began circulating in England along with native wares. A fantasia by Sweelinck is found in the so-called Fitzwilliam Virginal Book, a mammoth collection of English keyboard music and the chief source for much of Philips and Bull. Its present name comes from its present location, the Fitzwilliam Museum in Cambridge, but it may actually have been assembled at the Fleet Prison in London, where its compiler, Francis Tregian, was confined for recusancy from 1614 until his death three years later. "Virginal" was the name of the English version of the harpsichord: a small box, often in the shape of a pentagon, that contained only a single set of strings. Several virginals of various sizes were often piled atop one another to gain a fuller range of pitch and color. The origin of the name is obscure, but it was popularly associated with the girls who were most often taught to play it as a social grace, and it became the inevitable pretext for a lot of coarse punning.

The Sweelinck fantasia—one of many, especially by English composers, that used the Guidonian hexachord (ut–re–mi–fa–sol–la) as cantus firmus—was entered in the Fitzwilliam manuscript in 1612. Equally a tour de force of keyboard virtuosity and of counterpoint, it contains twenty officially numbered statements of the familiar scale segment, both ascending and descending, in various transpositions, diminutions, and syncopated forms, and against many countersubjects and accompaniment figures. And it harbors many hidden variations as well, including strettos. More organ-specific yet are Sweelinck's four fantasias "op de manier van een echo" (in the manner of an echo),

FIG. 21-3   Pentagonal virginal (Italian, 1585) at the Russell Collection, University of Edinburgh.

or echo-fantasias, in which the middle section of the piece consists of little phrases marked *forte* and repeated *piano*, calling the multiple keyboards or manuals of the organ into play. The effect is transferable to a multiple-manual harpsichord as well, and Sweelinck's fantasias are often played on that instrument. But on the organ, with its spatially separated ranks of pipes, such passages come out as literally antiphonal, reflecting the Venetian polychoral style.

The Chromatic Fantasia (Ex. 21-6), on the *passus duriusculus* tetrachord, pitches the titular chromatic descent on D, A, and E, so that all twelve notes of the chromatic scale are eventually employed in stages over the course of the composition. The piece is thus a magnificent reconciliation of the venerable academic counterpoint of the sixteenth century with the burgeoning affective or pathetic style of the seventeenth. It is also a summit of virtuosity, displaying the cantus firmus at four rhythmic levels (from whole notes to eighth notes in the transcription) and reaching a peak of rhythmic excitement with sextolets (sixteenth notes grouped in sixes like double-time triplets) and thirty-second notes, very much in the style of English keyboard figuration.

EX. 21-6   Jan Pieterszoon Sweelinck, *Fantasia chromatica*, mm. 1–16

English sextolets can be seen in their natural habitat in Giles Farnaby's *Daphne*, from the Fitzwilliam Virginal Book (Ex. 21-7). This is a set of variations (or divisions, to use the contemporary word) on a bawdy popular song that retold the myth, popularized by Ovid, of Apollo's (or Phoebus's) lascivious pursuit of the nymph Daphne and her rescue by the earth-goddess Gaea, who transformed her into a laurel tree. These variation sets were the virginalist composer's most characteristic genre. Their main precedent were sets of *diferencias* — Spanish for divisions — on popular songs that were published by Iberian lutenists and organists beginning with Luis de Narváez in 1538; the most famous such set is the one by the blind organist Juan de Cabezón on the folk tune *Guárdame las vacas* — "Watch over my cattle" — printed in 1578, twelve years after his death. Farnaby (1563–1640), a "joiner" or carpenter by trade, was eventually a builder of virginals as well as a performer on them and composer for them. His extant work is preserved almost complete in the Fitzwilliam Virginal Book and is hardly found elsewhere.

EX. 21-7   Giles Farnaby, *Daphne*, mm. 1–13

Whether through Farnaby's work or Byrd's, or through personal contact with Philips and Bull, this type of variation writing passed to Sweelinck, who wrote the best-known examples of it, of which some are still played by organ recitalists today. The set on the French love song "Est-ce Mars?" uses a tune known far and wide in many guises. (Farnaby wrote a version under the silly name "The New Sa-Hoo" — i.e., "Say Who?") The words as Sweelinck knew them mean, "Could this be Mars, the great battle-god, whom I espy? To judge by his arms alone, so I'd think. But at the same time it's clear from his glances that it's more likely Cupid here, not Mars." Sweelinck is just as droll and whimsical as Farnaby and reaches the obligatory rhythmic peak with sextolets; but unlike his English counterpart he is concerned to show off his contrapuntal technique as well as his eccentric fancies, with a suggestion of stretto as early as the second variation and a brief canon in the last. Oddly enough, and with only a couple of exceptions, the only sacred melodies to which Sweelinck devoted variation sets were Lutheran chorales. This unexpected preoccupation on the part of a non-German, non-Lutheran organist seems to have come about as a by-product of Sweelinck's extensive teaching activity. He was much sought after by pupils, to whom he devoted a great deal of time, and his best ones were German. For a time the three principal organ posts in Hamburg, the largest North German city, were all held by former pupils of "Master Jan Pieterszoon of Amsterdam," which led Johann Mattheson, an eighteenth-century composer and music historian, to dub Sweelinck the "hamburgischen Organistenmacher" (the Hamburg-organist-maker).[8]

With his prize pupil, Samuel Scheidt (1587–1654), who came from the Saxon town of Halle in eastern Germany and apprenticed himself to Sweelinck in Amsterdam around 1608 or 1609, Sweelinck engaged in some friendly rivalry, recalling the emulation-games of the early Netherlanders. Scheidt's monumental organ collection *Tabulatura nova*, issued in three volumes in 1624, contains examples of every genre that Sweelinck had practiced, including those, like the echo-fantasia, that Sweelinck had pioneered. The first volume even has a set of variations on a "cantio gallica" (French song) that turns out to be *Est-ce Mars?*. It was no doubt a tribute or a memorial to Sweelinck, but the pupil's set is twice as long and twice as elaborate as the teacher's. Also unlike Sweelinck's, Scheidt's set begins with a bald statement of the "theme" before proceeding to the ten *variationes* (singular *variatio*), a term that in fact first appears in print (with its modern meaning, anyway) in the *Tabulatura nova*.

FIG. 21-4   Samuel Scheidt, woodcut from *Tabulatura nova* (Hamburg: Michael Hering, 1624), the earliest German keyboard publication (its title notwithstanding) printed in open mensural score rather than tablature. The sheet of music contains a four-part canon in contrary motion on the final words of the Te Deum prayer: *In te, Domine, speravi; non confundar in aeternim* ("In thee, O Lord, have I trusted; let me not ever be confounded").

Yet since Scheidt worked for the Lutheran church, which unlike the Calvinist or "Reformed" church integrated organ-playing into its actual liturgy, the *Tabulatura Nova* contains many works in genres that Sweelinck did not compose in, and that Scheidt presumably picked up from the work of German predecessors, particularly those from the Catholic southern regions of Germany, like Hans Leo Hassler (1564–1612), who came from Nuremberg and studied with Andrea Gabrieli in Venice, or Christian Erbach (1568–1635), the Augsburg cathedral organist. The most important of these liturgical genres were the chant-based "versets," or organ settings of alternate lines of text in Kyries, Glorias, hymns, and Magnificats. These were interpolated — *alternatim-fashion*, as it was called — into choral or congregational performances. It was yet another instance of an "oral," extemporized genre (one that in Germany went back at least as far as the fifteenth century) that had only lately begun the process of transformation — or ossification — into a literate one. A great many of these snippets, organized into "organ Masses" and "organ Vespers," can be found in Book III of *Tabulatura nova*. As the largest collection of German liturgical organ music of the seventeenth century, Scheidt's volumes could be thought of as the Protestant counterpart to Frescobaldi's *Fiori musicali*, which came out about a decade later.

LUTHERAN ADAPTATIONS: THE CHORALE PARTITA

Most of Sweelinck's chorale compositions are found in a huge manuscript of organ scores, now at the Deutsche Staatsbibliothek (German National Library) in Berlin, dating most likely from the early 1630s. It is otherwise devoted to chorale variations by a dozen or so of his German pupils, some in the form of collaborative sets, with individual variations contributed by both master and disciples.

In all these works, both Sweelinck's own and those of the pupils, the basic technique is the same. The variations correspond to the verses of the chorale. In each of them the traditional melody is treated strictly — that is, with little or no embellishment — as a cantus firmus in a single voice. Where the secular variations keep the tune consistently in the uppermost voice, the chorale variations not only allow the lower voices to be tune-bearers in the old cantus-firmus manner but also allow the hymn tune to migrate through the texture as verse succeeds verse. The accompanying voices vary freely in number from a single one (producing a two-part or "bicinium" texture) on upwards. Sometimes they incorporate aspects of the chorale tune, thus integrating it into the polyphony; sometimes they contrast with it as countersubjects.

This, too, was a technique that Sweelinck had picked up from the English and passed along to his pupils. It corresponds exactly to the hymn-setting technique of John Bull, which derived in turn from that of Bull's teacher, John Blitheman (ca. 1525–91), a Gentleman of the Chapel Royal from 1558 to his death. Tracing it gives us a particularly crisp example of the way in which traditions of personal emulation can serve as the means through which the larger, less personal phenomenon of stylistic dissemination takes place. A technique that English organists had developed for accompanying and supplementing choral hymnody was transferred in stages to a new geographical terrain and a new, music-hungry church, which had an even greater need for organ music to supplement a choral hymnody that had spread from the elite choir to full congregational participation. Sweelinck was the middleman who brokered the transaction.

The end result was the Lutheran chorale partita, as practiced first by Scheidt, most spectacularly by J. S. Bach, and by Lutheran organist-composers to this day. Scheidt's partita on the "cantio sacra" *Christ lag in Todesbanden* (Ex. 21-8; cf. Ex. 18-2) comes from the second volume of *Tabulatura nova*, printed exactly one hundred years after the earliest polyphonic settings of the chorale appeared (see Ex. 18-4). In five verses, Scheidt's set begins with two connected settings of the chorale in the highest part: the first is an integrated motetlike setting with some old-fashioned *Vorimitation* (imitative foreshadowing of the cantus firmus) in the accompanying voices, of a kind that Luther himself would surely have recognized; the second is more à la Sweelinck, with successive lines of the chorale set in relief against a series of ever more rhythmically active countersubjects, each treated in imitation (Exx. 21-8a-b).

The third verse, the centerpiece, is a "free" variation: an intricate bicinium in which the individual phrases of the chorale are independently developed in dialogue between the player's hands, sometimes broken up into motives, sometimes superseded altogether by episodes (Ex. 21-8c). The fourth and fifth variation return to a stricter cantus-firmus style. In the fourth, after a brief foreshadowing in the bass, the cantus firmus, placed in the middle voice (the "tenor"), is pitted against two exceptionally florid outer voices

EX. 21-8A   Samuel Scheidt, *Christ lag in Todesbanden*, first versus, mm. 1–7

EX. 21-8B   Samuel Scheidt, *Christ lag in Todesbanden*, second versus, mm. 1–5

that sometimes develop countersubjects in imitation, sometimes contrast with one another as well as with the subject, creating toward the end an "obbligato" texture with a fast-flowing line above the tenor, a slower "walking bass" beneath it (Ex. 21-8d).

The fifth and last variation is presented and harmonized in a very unusual fashion that could be considered either tonally wayward (to adopt the viewpoint and expectations of an observer contemporary with Scheidt) or tonally "progressive" (to adopt the viewpoint and expectations of an observer contemporary with us). It is a fascinating case to consider, for the difference between the two historical and aesthetic vantage points is rarely so clear-cut or easily identified. Do we get more aesthetic gratification from the standpoint that sees the piece as intriguingly capricious or "deviant," or from the one that sees it groping, so to speak, toward a more modern (familiar? higher? more integrated?) conception of tonality? Can we somehow view it from both standpoints at once?

Here is how the piece works. The bass carries the complete cantus firmus (though the "cantus" and "tenor" also get to quote phrases from it), but its various constituent

EX. 21-8C   Samuel Scheidt, *Christ lag in Todesbanden*, third versus, mm. 1–19

EX. 21-8D   Samuel Scheidt, *Christ lag in Todesbanden*, fourth versus, mm. 39–44

phrases are independently transposed. The music thus seems to oscillate between implied mode finals on D, on A (the upper fifth), and on G (the lower fifth), staking out the tonal areas we now think of as "tonic," "dominant," and "subdominant." Particularly "modern" in its tonal effect is the last phrase in the bass, ending on A (the dominant) so as to prepare the grandiose final cadence (Ex. 21-8e).

EX. 21-8E   Samuel Scheidt, *Christ lag in Todesbanden*, fifth versus, mm. 65–end

THE CHORALE CONCERTO

The Lutheran chorale partita had its vocal counterpart as well, in which sacred genres that had developed elsewhere were adapted to specifically Lutheran use. The result was the so-called chorale concerto, a mixed vocal-instrumental genre that in its more modest specimens seemed a direct outgrowth of Viadana's pioneering *Cento concerti ecclesiastici* of 1602 (pirated by a German publisher seven years later) and that in its more opulent ones could vie with the most extravagant outpourings of the Venetians. Its two main exponents, besides Scheidt, were Michael Praetorius (1571–1621), organist to the Duke of Brunswick (Braunschweig), and Johann Hermann Schein (1586–1630), the cantor of St. Thomas's School in Leipzig, where J. S. Bach would occupy the same position a hundred years later.

Schein (like Sweelinck before him and Bach after him) was a contracted civil servant who reported to a town council, not a court or church employee who served at the pleasure of a patron. He published a great deal of secular music as well as sacred, including the *Banchetto musicale* (Leipzig, 1617), an early book of dances-for-listening organized into standardized sequences or *suites* (though Schein does not use the word). Played by ensembles of viols and violins, they probably served originally as dinner music (*Tafelmusik*, literally "table music") at the noble

FIG. 21-5   Johann Hermann Schein, woodcut portrait at the Musical Instrument Museum, University of Leipzig.

houses where he served briefly before being elected "Thomaskantor." Each suite in the collection consists of an old-style pair — a slow duple-metered padouana or pavan followed by a quick triple-metered gagliarda — and a new-style pair consisting of the same genres (courente and allemande, as Schein called them) that we saw in Frescobaldi. Each suite ended with a quick-time sendoff in the form of a fast triple-metered variation on the allemande called the *tripla*. What so distinguished Schein's suites was his application to them of the keyboard variation technique pioneered by the virginalists and Sweelinck. The components of each suite, as Schein put it, were integrated both in mode and in "invention," meaning that they were fashioned out of a common fund of melodic ideas so that they became in effect not only a suite but a set of variations as well.

Schein made three settings of *Christ lag in Todesbanden*. Two of them were *Cantionalsätze*, simple chorale harmonizations to accompany congregational singing. The third comes from Schein's first continuo publication, *Opella nova* ("A new collection of works," 1618), which consisted, according to its title page, of *geistliche Concerten auff italiänische Invention componirt*: "sacred concertos composed on the Italian plan." It is scored for two sopranos (boys) and a tenor over a very active basso continuo. For instructions in realizing his continuo parts, Schein actually referred the user of his book to the preface of Viadana's *Cento concerti*.

It looks at first as though the two boys are going to sing a paraphrase of the chorale melody, but it turns out that it is only *Vorimitation*, preparing the way for the tenor, the true bearer of the cantus firmus. In the second part of the concerto, corresponding in the original melody to the "B" of the AAB chorale form, the boy sopranos and the tenor are pitted against one another in true concertato style (Ex.21-9). The boys sing fanciful diminutions on the chorale phrases, full of imitations and hockets, that sound like countersubjects against the tenor's rather stolid enunciations of the same phrases, unadorned. Take away the boys, replace them with violins or cornetts, and the piece would still be a viable chorale concerto. (In fact it might easily have been performed that way on occasion.)

EX. 21-9 Johann Hermann Schein, *Christ lag in Todesbanden* from *Opella nova* (1618), mm. 20–25

The incredibly industrious Michael Praetorius, who is said to have died pen in hand on his fiftieth birthday, produced in his relatively brief career well over a thousand compositions, most of which were issued in 25 printed collections published between 1605 and the year of his death. Except for eight chorale settings for organ and a very successful and influential book of ensemble dance music (*Terpsichore*, pub. 1612) — and also apart from five treatises, including the *Syntagma musicum*, a giant musical encyclopedia that came out in three volumes between 1614 and 1618 — Praetorius's works consist almost entirely of psalm motets (nine volumes called *Musae sioniae*, issued between 1605 and 1611) and chorale concerti. His most grandiose compositions were reached in what turned out to be his culminating publication, a three-volume monster issued between 1619 and 1621 and named, significantly, after the ancient Muse of oratory and sacred poetry: *Polyhymnia caduceatrix et panegyrica* (Polyhymnia, bringer of peace and singer of praise).

The concerti in this collection, some scored for as many as twenty-one mixed vocal and instrumental parts, were written (possibly on commission) after Praetorius had visited the court of Dresden, where the musical establishment was the envy of all Germany. The concerto on *Christ lag in Todesbanden*, from the second volume, is composed in such a way that it can be performed in various concerted combinations: by two boys with basso continuo, by two boys and two basses with basso continuo, or by two boys and a three- or four-part instrumental ensemble plus basso continuo, for a maximum of seven sounding parts.

In addition, when the two boys perform without competition from other concerted parts they are given the option of singing highly embellished lines — or rather, the composer supplied for them the sort of vocal diminutions more experienced singers habitually extemporized when performing concerted music. Ex. 21-10 shows how Praetorius decorated the chorale's famous opening line. It is the rare instance like this one, where the composer went to the trouble of furnishing in advance what was normally left to the promptings of the moment, that give us our scarce and precious clues to what the written music whose physical remains we now possess really may have sounded like in life — that is, in performance.

EX. 21-10   Michael Praetorius, *Christ lag in Todesbanden* from *Polyhymnia caduceatrix et panegyrica*, vol. II (Cantus I)

RUIN

All this Italianate splendor was not fated to last. The second quarter of the seventeenth century was a horrendous period for the German-speaking lands, marked by an unremitting series of territorial, dynastic, and religious conflicts collectively known as the Thirty Years War. What had started in 1618 as an abortive revolt of the Protestant nobility in Bohemia against the dominion of the Holy Roman (Austrian) Empire spread all over Germany as the Scandinavian kings to the north of Germany opportunistically took up the offensive against the Austrians to the south. By the mid-thirties the German Protestant territories were one huge blood-soaked battlefield.

A peace was declared in 1635 that gave the Empire the advantage. This antagonized France, the other great centralized European power. France joined forces with Sweden and the final stage of what had in effect become a general European war began. The German princes were forgotten as the French and the Austrians, with their various allies, contended everywhere: in the Netherlands, in Spain, in Italy, and in the north, where the Scandinavian powers were now divided. Peace negotiations were begun even before 1640, but hostilities continued sporadically until 1648. The result was a vastly weakened Austrian Empire, a vastly strengthened France, and a completely ruined Germany.

Powerful repercussions of this virtual world war were felt immediately in the arts. The military successes that made France the richest and most prosperous land in Europe laid the foundations for what the French still call their *grand siècle*, their Great Century. The musical results of that flowering will be the subject of the next chapter. The impoverishing effects of the war on the arts of the German-speaking countries, on the other hand, can scarcely be imagined.

A CREATIVE MICROCOSM

The "high" or courtly arts managed to hang on through their vicissitudes, though not without crucial adaptive change. In music, that process of adaptation may be viewed with exceptional clarity thanks to the presence on the German scene of a composer of irrepressible genius, whose long career, mirroring in an intense creative microcosm the general fate and progress of his art, furnishes us with an ideal prism. His name was Henrich (or more commonly, Heinrich) Schütz. Despite the conditions in which he was forced to work, he became the first internationally celebrated German master.

Born in 1585 to a family of innkeepers in the Saxon (east German) town of Köstritz near Gera, a musical instrument center, Schütz early displayed his gifts. His singing voice was noticed by a music-loving nobleman, the Landgrave Moritz of Hessen, who happened to stay at his father's inn in 1598, when the boy was just entering adolescence. Over the objections of his parents, the Landgrave had the lad brought to his residence in Kassel for instruction and training "in all the good arts and commendable virtues." After his voice changed, Schütz ostensibly gave up music for university studies in law, also underwritten by Landgrave Moritz, who had become a surrogate father to him.

But then one day in 1609, when his protégé was twenty-four, the Landgrave came to visit him at school with a proposition: "Since at that time a very famous if elderly musician and composer was still alive in Italy," as Schütz recounted his patron's words in old age, "I was not to miss the opportunity of hearing him and gaining some knowledge from him."[9] Since the proposal was backed up with a generous cash stipend, the young man "willingly accepted the recommendation with submissive gratitude,... against my parents' wishes."

The musician in question was Giovanni Gabrieli. Schütz spent three years in Venice under his tutelage, right up until the master's death, by which time the young Saxon had become his prize pupil. "On his deathbed," Schütz recalled, "he had arranged out of special affection that I should receive one of the rings he left behind as a remembrance of him." This gift not only signaled the passing of the Venetian musical heritage to a new generation, but also symbolized its becoming, through Schütz, an international standard.

The year before, Schütz had composed a book of Italian madrigals that Gabrieli thought worthy of publication. It was issued in Venice in 1611 with an attribution to *Henrico Sagittario allemanno* — "Henry Archer (i.e. Schütz) the German" — but its

FIG. 21-6 Heinrich Schütz, portrait by Christoph Spetner (ca. 1650) at the University of Leipzig.

contents are completely indistinguishable in style from the native product. Schütz wanted nothing else. He went back to Germany in 1613 with the intention of fulfilling his promise to his patron by adapting the glorious Venetian style to the needs of the Lutheran church, just as Praetorius and others were also doing, but with the added benefit of authenticity arising out of training at the source.

For the rest of his life Schütz saw himself primarily as the bringer of Italianate "light to Germany" (as his tombstone reads), and saw the composition of grand concerted motets and magnificent court spectacles as his true vocation. Given that ambition, his career was dogged by cruel frustration. His actual contributions, not only to the musical life of his time but to the historical legacy of German music, tallied little with his intentions. But his musical imagination was so great, and his powers of adaptation so keen, that what he did accomplish was arguably a greater fulfillment of his gifts than what he set out to achieve.

On returning to Germany with his sterling credentials, Schütz went back to work, as expected, for Landgrave Moritz of Hessen. The very next year, however, the Elector of Saxony, a personage far superior in rank to the Landgrave, called Schütz to his legendarily appointed court at Dresden, the very court that Praetorius was adorning so splendidly with his *Polyhymnia* motets, and Moritz had to release him. Schütz

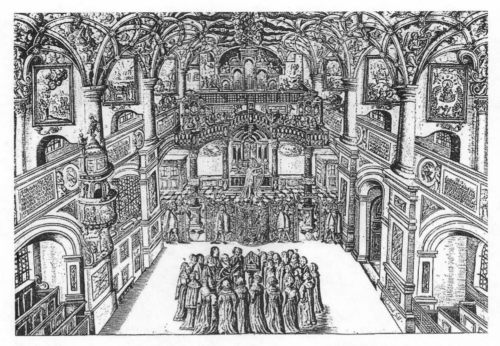

FIG. 21-7   Schütz directing his choir at the Dresden court chapel. Copperplate engraving from the title page of his pupil Christoph Bernhard's *Geistreichen Gesangbuch* ("Artful songbook") of 1676.

arrived in 1615 and spent his entire subsequent career at Dresden (from 1621 as court Kapellmeister), serving faithfully through thick and thin for almost sixty years.

At first the times were "thick," indeed downright opulent. Schütz's first German publication, issued at Dresden in 1619, was *Psalmen Davids* ("The psalms of David") a book of twenty-six sumptuous concerted motets for up to four antiphonal choruses with continuo ("organ, lute, chitarrone, etc.," according to the title page) and parts for strings and brass *ad libitum*. There are also archival records of gala court performances of secular compositions by the young Kapellmeister. They included "The Miraculous Transport of Mount Parnassus" (*Wunderlich Translocation des . . . Berges Parnassi*), a mythological ballet performed for the visiting Holy Roman Emperor Matthias, and a polychoral birthday ode for the Elector on the subject of Apollo and the Muses. The most tantalizing such reference is to an opera, the first ever composed to a German text, on the time-honored subject of Apollo and Daphne, for the marriage of his first patron's son to his second patron's daughter. The libretto was in fact an adaptation by a court poet of Rinuccini's libretto for Peri's *Dafne* of 1597, the first musical tale of all. Except for the early book of madrigals, though, Schütz's secular output, comprising as well an Orpheus opera and a whole series of court ballets, has perished with only the most negligible exceptions. The five hundred or so works by which he is known to us are virtually all sacred.

And from his Latin-texted *Cantiones sacrae* of 1625 to his German-texted *Geistliche Chor-Music* of 1648, Schütz's output reflects to varying degrees the austerity of wartime conditions, when court establishments were decimated by conscription and budgets for the fine arts were ruthlessly slashed. Schütz was forced to renounce the polychoral style in favor of simpler choral textures and even sparser forces. In 1628, he issued a new collection of settings from the Psalter, again called *Psalmen Davids*. But where the first collection, counting on the Dresden court chapel forces at their most lavish, had assumed the grand manner, the new one consisted of simple part-songs with continuo, based on metrical psalm paraphrases by Cornelius Becker, a Leipzig churchman, which (as the "Becker Psalter") were then popular.

Faced with increasingly difficult conditions in Dresden, Schütz petitioned for leave so that he could visit Venice again and wait out the war. He departed in August 1628 and stayed for about a year. He seems to have become acquainted this time with Monteverdi, now the *maestro di cappella* at St. Mark's, and to have experimented on the scene with the new declamatory styles that Monteverdi had pioneered. While in Italy he published a book of fifteen sacred concerti to Latin texts, which he called *Sacrae symphoniae* in tribute to his late teacher Gabrieli. These are comparatively modest works, scored for one or two solo voices (in one case for three) with obbligato instrumental parts. Only one of them is antiphonal in the literal sense of employing spatially separated ensembles, but all of them remain Venetian in spirit by extracting a maximum of color and interplay out of their reduced forces.

O quam tu pulchra es ("O how comely art thou"), one of the best known items from the *Symphoniae sacrae* of 1629, is set to a text from the Song of Songs that had already served countless composers going back as far as Dunstable (see chapter 11). The reason for its popularity, and also the reason why this particular concerto of Schütz has served so long as a favorite introduction to his work, surely lies in the spectacularly erotic text, replete with a catalogue of the beloved's anatomy, that furnished Schütz, as it had furnished Dunstable, with both a wonderful opportunity to display the attractions of a new "luxuriant" style, and a pretext for pushing the style to new heights of allure.

LUXURIANCE

The term "luxuriant style" (*stylus luxurians*), meaning a style brimming abundantly with exuberant detail in contrast to the "plain style" (*stylus gravis*) of old, was coined by Christoph Bernhard (1628–92), Schütz's pupil and eventual successor as the Dresden Kapellmeister, in a famous treatise on composition that circulated widely in manuscript in the later seventeenth century and was widely presumed to transmit Schütz's teachings. What mainly abounded in the luxuriant style was dissonance, which makes the *stylus luxurians* the rough equivalent of what Monteverdi called the *seconda prattica*.

Like Monteverdi, Bernhard stipulated that freely handled dissonances arose out of (and were justified by) the imagery and emotional content of a text.[10] They were an aspect of rhetoric: ornamental figures, so to speak, of musical speech. That is why Bernhard called them *figurae* (*Figuren* in German), and why his theory of composition, which treats the novel dissonances of the luxuriant style as ornaments on the surface of the plain style, is known as the *Figurenlehre* (the doctrine of figures). Bernhard's *Figurenlehre*, which may derive from Schütz's own take on Monteverdi, was the first of many theories of composition, mainly put forth by German writers, that conceptualized and analyzed music in terms of an ornamental surface projected over a structural background.

But the *stylus luxurians* was anything but a passive response to the contents of a text. On the contrary, and as *O quam tu pulchra es* shows especially well, the composer actively shaped the text to his musical purposes even as he shaped the music to conform to the text's specifications. It was a process of mutual enhancement and intensification — indeed, of mutual impregnation — that bore an offspring more powerfully expressive than either words or music alone could be.

Reading Schütz's setting of the concerto's opening words in terms of Bernhard's opposition of plain background and luxuriant surface (Ex. 21-11a), we might characterize it as descending through the notes of the tonic triad (A–F–D in D minor) with lower neighbors ("overshooting" — *quaesitio notae*, literally "searching for the note" — in Bernhard's parlance) decorating the F and the D in the manner of what we would now call an *appoggiatura* (see Bernhard's illustration of the practice in Ex. 21-11b). The neighbor to the root of the triad is raised a half step to function as a leading tone, resulting in a diminished fourth — in Bernhard's parlance a "hard leap" (*saltus duriusculus*) — from F to C♯. This chromaticized interval coincides by finely calculated design with the main "operator" in the text, the word *pulchra*, or "beautiful".[11]

The lilting triple-metered refrain thus created is heard again and again over the course of the concerto. After addressing a series of endearments to the bride that intensify through sequences to a drawn-out hemiola cadence, the baritone soloist returns to the opening phrase, this time joined by the tenor in imitation. When the pair of vocal soloists have repeated the baritone's invocation to the bride, the opening phrase jumps up into the range of the instrumental soloists, the violins, who fashion

EX. 21-11A   First line of Heinrich Schütz's *O quam tu pulchra es* rhetorically parsed

EX. 21-11B   Christoph Bernhard, example of *Quaesitio notae*

EX. 21-11B *(continued)*

Naturally it stands thus:

from it a *sinfonia* or wordless interlude — wordless, but still texted in a way, since the opening melody has been so strongly associated with the opening words. Finally, the vocal soloists join the violins for a final invocation in four parts over the basso continuo to finish off the first section of the concerto.

From this point on the text of the concerto consists of the famous inventory of the bride's body, in which every part named is made the object of a vivid simile — a verbal figure. Since the music performs a similar "figurative" function, Schütz radically abridged the text, leaving most of the actual work of description to the music. This gives him time to bring back the opening phrase in both words and music as a *ritornello* to follow each item in the enumeration. Its dancelike triple meter contrasts every time with the freer declamatory rhythms of the simile verses.

The first simile is the most straightforward; the beloved's eyes are compared with the eyes of a dove. The music is comparably straightforward, consisting of recitative in what for Schütz was a new style. The next, comparing her hair (presumably as it is blown by the wind) with a flock of (frisking) goats, is matched by trills and wide leaps in the music. The cadence on *greges caprarum* (mm. 66–67) is similar to that on *oculi columbarum* (mm. 56–57), but is intensified harmonically very much à la Monteverdi: by interpolating the subdominant (G) in the bass, the melody note (F) is turned into a dissonant suspension that does not resolve directly, but only through an intervening ascent to a more strongly dissonant ninth (A), from which a (goatlike?) leap is made to the note that would have resolved the original suspension by step (Ex. 21-12a). In such a passage it is especially easy to see the "structural" voice leading that underlies the frisky "ornamental" figures on the surface.

After a return to recitative for the simile comparing the bride's teeth to the whiteness of shorn sheep, there is a steady increase in musical floridity with every extravagant textual figure. From here on the tenor and baritone are in constant, quasi-competitive duet, their intertwining lines suggesting the scarlet ribbon to which the beloved's lips are compared, the winding staircases that encircle the tower to which her long neck is likened (Ex. 21-12b), and the cavorting of the twin fawns that symbolize (the jiggling of) her two breasts (Ex. 21-12c). The last being an especially potent sexual symbol, it is played out at length, with the violins at last taking part in the simile.

EX. 21-12A   Heinrich Schütz, *O quam tu pulchra es* (*Symphoniae sacrae I*), mm. 56–58, mm. 66–68

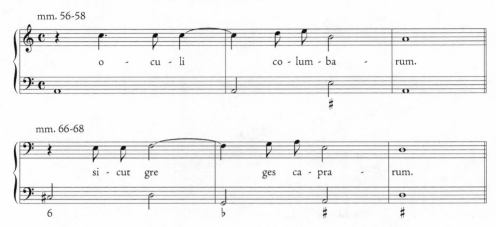

EX. 21-12B   Heinrich Schütz, *O quam tu pulchra es* (*Symphoniae sacrae I*), mm. 91–95

EX. 21-12C   Heinrich Schütz, *O quam tu pulchra es* (*Symphoniae sacrae I*), mm. 100–111

EX. 21-12C (*continued*)

It is followed by what is quite obviously a musical representation of a sensual climax, the violins' mounting arpeggios introducing a passage in which the singers vocalize on similar arpeggio figures, their text shrunk back to mere moaning iterations of the opening O, and with the violins now sounding the aching *saltus duriusculus* (the diminished fourth) not as a neighbor but as a harmonic interval, producing arpeggios of augmented triads. The baritone, it seems hardly necessary to add, reaches his highest note on his final O. The final cadence is packed with extra cathartic force by adding arbitrarily to its dissonance: the tenor's C, on the "purple" word *pulchra*, is not only a dissonance approached by leap but also a false relation with respect to the C♯ immediately preceding it in the baritone and basso continuo parts (Ex. 21-12d). (The apparent ending on the dominant is resolved by the next concerto in the collection, *Veni de Libano*, set to a continuation of the same passage from the Song of Songs.)

The most remarkable aspect of *O quam tu pulchra es* is the refrain. There was nothing new, of course, about the idea of the refrain as such. It was one of the most ancient of all musical and poetical devices, with a literally prehistoric origin. The way Schütz employs it here, however, it acts in a double role — or rather, it combines two roles in a singularly pregnant way. It is of course a musical (or "structural") unifier, quite a necessary function in a composition that otherwise sets so many contrasting textual images to contrasting musical ideas. It is at the same time the bearer of the central affective message both of the text and of the music, its constantly reiterated and intensifying diminished fourth saturating the whole with the "lineaments of desire," to borrow a neat phrase from the English Romantic poet William Blake. The refrain, being both the concerto's structural integrator and its expressive one, erases any possible line between the expressive and the structural. From now on, musical ideas would tend increasingly to function on this dual plane; ultimately that is what one means by a musical "theme."

EX. 21-12D   Heinrich Schütz, *O quam tu pulchra es* (*Symphoniae sacrae I*), mm. 112–end

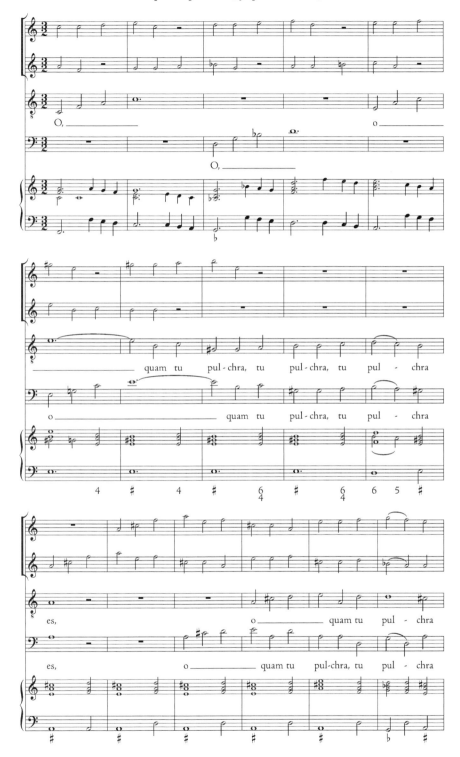

EX. 21-12D *(continued)*

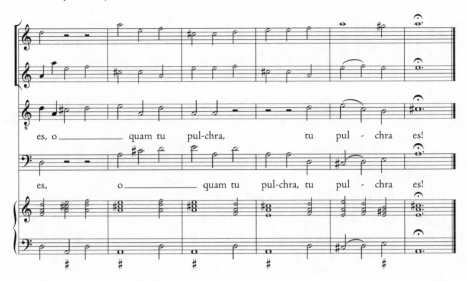

es, o _____ quam tu pul-chra, tu pul - chra es!

es, o _____ quam tu pul-chra, tu pul - chra es!

SHRIVELED DOWN TO THE EXPRESSIVE NUB

Schütz returned from his second Italian sojourn to find conditions in Germany greatly worsened. The war economy interfered more directly with musical opportunities than ever, and in the autumn of 1631 Saxony became an active belligerent in alliance with Sweden. Most of Schütz's singers were drafted into the army; by 1633, the Dresden musical establishment, once the envy of Germany, was to all intents and purposes disabled, "like a patient *in extremis*," as Schütz put it in a letter to his patron, and so it remained until the mid 1640s. The Gabrielian side of Schütz's Venetian heritage was deprived of an outlet. "I am of less than no use," the unhappy composer complained in another letter from the time. The only gainful employment he had during this dismal period came from courts to the north and west that continued to function, particularly that of King Christian IV of Denmark in Copenhagen, which Schütz was permitted to visit from 1634 to 1635 and again from 1642 to 1644, and that of Hildesheim, where he spent some months from 1640 to 1641.

During these bleak years Schütz's "Monteverdian" side came into its own, as if by default. In 1636 and in 1639 he published collections of what he called *Kleine geistliche Concerte* or "Little Sacred Concertos," vastly scaled-down compositions for from one to five solo voices with organ continuo, completely without the use of concertante instruments (with one exception, a dialogue setting of the Ave Maria in the second book). These ascetic compositions were characterized not only by drastically curtailed forces but by a mournfully penitential, subjective mood as well. The ones for single solo voices and continuo, performable by only two musicians, were perhaps the most characteristic of the lot, amounting to what Italian musicians would have called sacred monodies in recitative style, or (as Schütz called it) the *stylus oratorius*.

The opening concerto in the first book, *Eile mich, Gott, zu erretten* ("Hasten, O God, to deliver me!"), a complete setting of the tiny Psalm 70, sets the tone (Ex. 21–13). In this earliest German recitative (labeled *in stylo oratorio* — "in the style of an oratorio" — in the original print), the flamboyance of Schütz's earlier style is replaced by terse declamation. There is not a single melisma. Emphasis comes not from a proliferation of notes but from repetition of key words and phrases, usually without any corresponding repetition of music. A certain amount of word-painting remains — the melody "turns back" on itself on the word *zurückekehren* in mm. 6–7; the words *hoch gelobt* ("highly praised") are repeated in mm. 14–15 on the way to a high note — but it is very restrained. Instead of seeking out madrigalian imagery, Schütz now seems bent on distilling a more generalized, concentrated emotion in the spirit of Monteverdi's *seconda prattica*, achieving it through dissonant leaps (see especially the taunts in mm. 11–12) and syncopated rhythms.

Perhaps the most poignant reminder of the straitened circumstances in which Schütz was now forced to work is the puny little *symphonia* between the stanzas of the psalm (just after Ex. 21-13 breaks off), a single optional (*si placet*) measure scored for just the bare figured bass. The absence of any tune save what the organist may extemporize searingly dramatizes the absence of the court instrumentalists whose corpses were piling up on the Saxon battlefields.

EX. 21-13   Heinrich Schütz, *Eile mich, Gott, zu erretten (Kleine geistliche Concerte I)*, mm. 1–16

In Schütz's new-found techniques of poignant text-expression, we may observe the beginnings of a tendency that would reach a remarkable climax in the Lutheran music of the coming century: the deliberate cultivation of ugliness in the name of God's truth, an authentic musical asceticism. It is often thought to be a specifically German aesthetic, and as evidence of a special Germanic or Protestant profundity of response to scripture (as distinct from Italianate pomp and sensuality). And yet the musical means by which it was accomplished, as Schütz's career so beautifully demonstrates, were nevertheless rooted in Catholic Italy. Schütz was only the father of modern German music to the extent that he served as conduit for those Italianate means.

Rebuilding of the impoverished German courts and their cultural establishments could only begin after the signing of the Peace of Westphalia on 24 October 1648, which effectively terminated the Holy Roman Empire as an effective political institution (although it would not be formally dissolved until 1806). The German Protestant states, of which Saxony was one, were recognized as sovereign entities, leaving only France as a united and centralized major power on the continent of Europe. Schütz's patron, the Elector Johann Georg, emerged from the war as one of the two most powerful Protestant princes of Germany. (The other was the Elector of the state of Brandenburg, which later became the kingdom of Prussia.)

Schütz's last publications reflected these improved fortunes. In 1647 he issued a second book of *Symphoniae sacrae*, scored like the first for modest vocal/instrumental forces, but with texts in German. The next year saw the publication of his *Geistliche Chor-Music*, beautifully crafted polyphonic motets specifically intended for performance by the full chorus rather than *favoriti* or soloists. Finally, in 1650, aged sixty-five, he issued what is now thought of as his testamentary work, the third book of *Symphoniae sacrae*, scored for forces of a size he had not had at his disposal since the time of the *Psalmen Davids*. The music, though, was still characterized by the terseness and pungency of expression he had cultivated during the lean years. Schütz's Gabrielian and Monteverdian sides had met at last in a unique "German" synthesis.

One of the crowning masterworks in this final collection is *Saul, Saul, was verfolgst du mich*, scored for six vocal soloists, two choruses, and an instrumental contingent consisting of two violins and *violone* (string bass), all accompanied by a *bassus ad organum* (continuo). The text consists of two lines from the Acts of the Apostles (chapter 26, verse 14), containing the words spoken by Christ to the Jewish priest Saul on the road toward Damascus. As Saul, according to the Biblical account, later reports to Agrippa I, the grandson of King Herod:

> I myself once thought it my duty to work actively against the name of Jesus of Nazareth; and I did so in Jerusalem. . ... In all the synagogues I tried by repeated punishment to make them renounce their faith; indeed my fury rose to such a pitch that I extended my persecution to foreign cities.
> On one such occasion I was travelling to Damascus with authority and commission from the chief priests; and as I was on my way, Your Majesty, in the middle of the day I saw a light from the sky, more brilliant than the sun, shining all around me and my travelling-companions. We all fell to the ground, and then I heard a voice saying to me in the Jewish language, *"Saul, Saul, why do you persecute*

me? It is hard for you, this kicking against the goad." I said, "Tell me, Lord, who you are"; and the Lord replied, "I am Jesus, whom you are persecuting. But now, rise to your feet and stand upright. I have appeared to you for a purpose: to appoint you my servant and witness, to testify both to what you have seen and to what you shall yet see of me" (translation from *The New English Bible*).

Thus did Saul become the Apostle Paul. The italicized words are the ones that form the text of Schütz's concerto. It is no straightforward setting, but one designed to fill in a great deal of the surrounding narration of Paul's miraculous conversion by means of dramatic symbolism. The words echo and reecho endlessly in the prostrate persecutor's mind, which we who hear them seem to inhabit. The echo idea is portrayed in the music not only by repetition but also by the use of explicitly indicated dynamics, something pioneered in Venice by Schütz's first teacher.

The musical phrase on which most of the concerto is built is sounded immediately by a pair of basses, then taken up by the alto and tenor, then by the sopranos, and finally by the pair of violins as transition into the explosive tutti. (Divine words were often set for multiple voices, so as to depersonalize them and prevent a single singer from "playing God.") The syncopated repetitions of the name Saul are strategically planted so that, when the whole ensemble takes them up, they can be augmented into hockets resounding back and forth between the choirs, adding to the impression of an enveloping space and achieving in sound something like the effect of the surrounding light described by the Apostle. The words *was verfolgst du mich* ("Why dost thou persecute me?") are often set in gratingly dissonant counterpoint: a suspension resolution in the lower voice coincides with an anticipation in the higher voice, producing a brusque succession of parallel seconds (later known, albeit unjustly, as a "Corelli clash" owing to its routinized use in Italian string music).

The second sentence of text is reserved for the soloists (*favoriti*), whose lines break out into melismas on the word *löcken* (*lecken* in modern German), here translated as "kick." Against this the two choirs and instruments continually reiterate the call, "Saul, Saul," as a refrain or ritornello. In the final section of the concerto, the soloists declaim the text rapidly in a manner recalling Monteverdi's *stile concitato*. Meanwhile, the tenor soloist calls repeatedly on Saul, his voice continually rising in pitch from C to D to E, the two choirs interpreting these pitches as dominants and reinforcing each successive elevation with a cadence, their entries marking "modulations" from F to G to A, the last preparing the final return to the initial tone center, D (Ex. 21-14).

The ending, rather than the climax that might have been expected, takes the form of reverberations over a fastidiously marked decrescendo to *pianissimo*, the forces scaled down from tutti to favoriti plus instruments, and finally to just the alto and tenor soloists over the continuo, the fadeout corresponding to the Apostle's "blackout," his loss of consciousness on the road to Damascus. Through the music we have heard Christ's words through Saul's ears and shared his shattering religious experience. Schütz has in effect imported the musical legacy of the Counter Reformation into the land of the Reformation, reappropriating for Protestant use the musical techniques that had been originally forged as a weapon against the spread of Protestantism.

EX. 21-14 Heinrich Schütz, *Saul, Saul, was verfolgst du mich* (*Symphoniae sacrae III*), mm. 67–74

EX. 21-14 *(continued)*

EX. 21-14 *(continued)*

Schütz's largest surviving works are oratorios, or as he called them, *Historien*—Biblical "narratives," in which actual narration, sung by an "Evangelist" or Gospel reciter, alternates with dialogue. Oratorios were most traditionally assigned to Easter week, when the Gospel narratives of Christ's suffering (Passion) and Resurrection were recited at length. Sure enough, of Schütz's six *Historien*, five were Easter pieces: a Resurrection oratorio composed early in his career, in 1623; a setting of Christ's Seven Last Words from the Cross, evidently from the 1650s; and three late settings of the Passion according to the Apostles Matthew, Luke, and John, respectively. These last, in keeping with Dresden liturgical requirements for Good Friday, are austerely old-fashioned *a cappella* works in which the chorus sings the words of the crowd (*turbae*), and the solo parts (the Evangelist, Jesus, and every other character whose words are directly quoted) are written in a kind of imitation plainchant for unaccompanied solo voices.

The remaining oratorio, called *Historia der freuden- und gnadenreichen Geburth Gottes und Marien Sohnes, Jesu Christi, unsers einigen Mitlers, Erlösers und Seeligmachers* ("The Story of the Joyous and Gracious Birth of Jesus Christ, Son of God and Mary, Our Sole Intermediary, Redeemer and Savior"), performed in Dresden in 1660, is by contrast a thoroughly Italianized, effervescent outpouring of Christmas cheer in which the Evangelist's part (printed by itself in 1664) is in the style of a continuo-accompanied monody. The words given to the other soloists (Herod, the angel, the Magi) and chorus in ever-changing combinations are set as eight little interpolated songs (*Intermedia*), accompanied by a colorful assortment of instruments: recorders, violins, cornetti, trombones, and "violettas," the last probably meaning small viols; and there are introductory and concluding choruses—the former announcing the subject, the latter giving thanks—in which voices resound antiphonally against echoing instrumental choirs in a manner recalling the Venetian extravaganzas of the composer's youth.

CARISSIMI: ORATORIO AND CANTATA

The chief Italian composer of oratorios in the time of Schütz was Giacomo Carissimi (1605–74), a Roman priest who served as organist and choirmaster at the Jesuit German College (Collegio Germanico) from 1629 until his death. His fourteen surviving works in the genre probably represent only a fraction of the biblical narratives he composed, beginning in the 1640s, for Friday afternoon performances during Lent at the college and at other Roman institutions, notably the Oratorio del Santissimo Crocifisso (Oratory of the Most Holy Crucifix), which lent its name to the genre. His many foreign pupils at the College included Christoph Bernhard, who had already trained with Schütz, and the French composer Marc-Antoine Charpentier, who brought the practice of setting dramatic narratives from the Latin bible back with him to his native country.

Jephte, Carissimi's most famous biblical narrative, was composed no later than 1649 (the date on one of its manuscripts). The story, from the Book of Judges (chapter 11), is a celebrated tale of tragic expiation. The Israelite commander Jephte vows that if God grants him victory over the Ammonites, he will sacrifice the first being who greets him on his return home. That turns out to be his beloved daughter, a virgin, who is

FIG. 21-8   Jephte recognizes his daughter. Painting by Giovanni Francesco Romanelli (1610–1662).

duly slaughtered after spending two months on the mountaintop with her companions, lamenting her fate.

The last part of Carissimi's setting, consisting of two laments, the daughter's and (in the final chorus) the community's, is introduced by a portion of narrative text sung by the *historicus*, as Carissimi calls the narrator's part. (In Carissimi's setting, the function of *historicus* is a rotating one, distributed among various solo voices and, as here, even the chorus.) The daughter's lament, a monody in three large strophes, makes especially affective use of the "Phrygian" lowered second degree at cadences, producing what would later be called the Neapolitan (or "Neapolitan-sixth") harmony. These cadences are then milked further by the use of echo effects that suggest the reverberations of the daughter's keening off the rocky face of the surrounding mountains and cliffs. Like Schütz (in *Saul, Saul*), Carissimi uses the music not only to express or intensify feeling, but to set the scene. The double and even triple suspensions (on *lamentamini*, "lament ye!") in the concluding six-part chorus are a remarkable application of "madrigalism" to what is in most other ways a typically Roman exercise in old-style (*stile antico*) polyphony. Its emotional power was celebrated and widely emulated. The chorus was quoted and analyzed by Athanasius Kircher in his music encyclopedia *Musurgia universalis* (Rome, 1650), and "borrowed" almost a hundred years later by Handel (who also wrote a *Jephtha*) for a chorus in the oratorio *Samson*.

Carissimi's other major service appointment was as *maestro di cappella del concerto di camera* (director of chamber concerts) for Queen Christina of Sweden (1626–89), patroness of the philosopher René Descartes, who lived in Rome following her notorious abdication in 1654 and subsequent conversion to Catholicism. For her, and for many another noble salon, Carissimi turned out well over one hundred settings of Italian love poetry in a new style known generically as *cantata* (a "sung" or vocal piece as opposed to *sonata*, a "played" or instrumental one).

Carissimi wrote so many cantatas that he is sometimes credited with inventing the genre. The cantata, however, was well established as a genre in Rome by the time Carissimi began contributing to it. The first composer known to have used the term was Alessandro Grandi (1586–1630), a member of Monteverdi's choir at St. Mark's in Venice, in a book published around 1620.

Like the monody, the cantata was a solo successor to the madrigal. It eventually came to denote a relatively ambitious setting that mixed several forms — strophic or ground-bass arias, little dancelike songs called *ariette*, recitatives, etc.— in a quasi-dramatic sequence. The more or less regular alternation of narrative and lyric items — recitatives that set the scene and arias that poured out feeling—first became standardized in the Roman cantata. It soon characterized all dramatic genres, especially opera. Most of the conventional aria types that later provided Italian opera with its stock in trade were first tried out in the cantata as well. The genre could thus be viewed as a kind of musico-dramatic laboratory.

From Rome, the cantata radiated out to more northerly Italian cities, chiefly Bologna and Venice (the latter still the great publishing center). Ex. 21-15 samples an especially rich cantata, *Lagrime mie* ("My tears"), by the Venetian singer and composer Barbara Strozzi (1619–77), a pupil of Francesco Cavalli, the foremost Venetian opera composer at midcentury, and the adopted daughter and *protégée* of Giulio Strozzi, a famous academician and poet-librettist whose words were set by almost every Venetian composer from Monteverdi on down. The fact that Barbara Strozzi published eight books of madrigals, cantatas, and arias, and did so at a time when prejudice against the creative abilities of women ran high, bears impressive witness to her excellence as a composer in the eyes of her contemporaries. *Lagrime mie* comes from her seventh book, titled *Diporti di Euterpe* ("Euterpe's Recreations") after the muse of lyric poetry and music, published

FIG. 21-9 Barbara Strozzi. Portrait with bass viol by Bernardo Strozzi (ca. 1640).

in 1659, when the composer was forty years old and done with her career as singer and aristocratic hostess.

The text, following convention, is composed from the male perspective. A lover laments the loss of his beloved, locked away in her father's castle. The vocal range is soprano, however, and might as well have been taken by a female singer such as Strozzi herself as by a castrato. The setting of the opening line (Ex. 21-15a), which will return later as a refrain, is identified by the harsh (and unconventionally resolved) dissonances, and by the somewhat decorated scalar descent in the bass from tonic to dominant, as a *lamento*. Expressive dissonance in the manner of the *seconda prattica* arrives as a palpable

EX. 21-15A   Barbara Strozzi, Cantata: *Lagrime mie*, mm. 1–13

Tears of mine, why do you hold back, why don't you wash away the pain

EX. 21-15B   Barbara Strozzi, Cantata: *Lagrime mie*, mm. 49–55

And you, eyes of mine, are not weeping! What are you waiting for?

twinge when the bass leaps from A♯ to D♯ under the voice's sustained E on — what else? — the word *dolore*, giving concrete auditory representation to the lover's pain.

The second stanza is divided quasi-operatically into narrative and lyric segments. The culminating, albeit fleeting aria (*E voi lumi dolenti*) is cast in the stately triple meter we have already encountered in *Pur ti miro*, the concluding duet in *L'incoronazione di Poppea* (Ex. 20-15). It was the lyric aria meter *par excellence*, partly because of the way it lent itself to expressive suspensions of the kind that Strozzi provides at this point in such abundance (Ex. 21-15b). In each measure, the first beat contains the dissonance, the second beat the resolution, and the third the preparation for the next suspension. The resolutions take place through slurred anticipations calculated to sound like sobs, a resemblance that was probably emphasized by the singer's voice production. ("Sobbing" remains a specialty of Italian tenors.) The final stanza is the most obvious harbinger

EX. 21-15C   Barbara Strozzi, Cantata: *Lagrime mie*, mm. 88 – 108

But I am well aware that in order to torture me even more, Fate even denies me death.
It is true then, oh God, that destiny desires only my tears.

of the recitative/aria pairing that would soon become standard operating procedure (Ex. 21-15c). The first couplet is set in a free, unpredictable style that follows the rhythm of speech in good *seconda prattica* fashion. The second couplet returns to the flowing triple meter; its first line unfolds over the emblematic bass tetrachord, and the last line (not included in the example) provides a lyric capstone, ascending to the highest note in the cantata's range and signaling the end by means of a full harmonic closure.

WOMEN IN MUSIC: A HISTORIANS' DILEMMA

Because the history of European and Euro-American art music is the story of a literate tradition — that is, to a very great extent the story of musical texts and their making — women are seriously but inevitably underrepresented in it. Even this book, despite its strenuously "foregrounded" efforts not to forget the oral side of musical traditions or neglect the effects of performance, will necessarily fail to reflect the full extent of women's contribution, since no matter what we may assume or conjecture, the historical sources on which the narrative is necessarily based consist overwhelmingly of musical texts.

It is a question that must be dealt with in the open, since the right of women to participate in public and cultural life as the social and economic equals of men has never been a more important or hotly debated a political issue than it became in late twentieth-century America. It is therefore incumbent on the historian — the teller of the tale — to explain the reasons for the glaring absence of female participants in the story that is told, lest it be assumed (as it has been, often) that the reasons lie in the nature of women, or the nature of music, rather than in the nature of the story.

A well-known example of how easy it is to fall prey to such assumptions is the answer Aaron Copland (1900–90), a famous American composer, gave some time ago to what was once a much-asked question: "Why have there been no great women composers?"[11] Copland opined that there may be "a mysterious element in the nature of musical creativity that runs counter to the nature of the feminine mind." His answer, while seemingly dogmatic and misogynistic, was not made in any such spirit and was not singled out at the time for criticism by readers or reviewers of the book in which it appeared. In fact, it comes from a tribute to an important woman musician, Nadia Boulanger (1887–1979), Copland's early composition teacher, who had once aspired to a composing career of her own. It was an answer typical of its time and reflected a viewpoint that was widely shared by men and women alike.

That, of course, did not make it correct. After decades of cogent feminist critiques of age-old cultural assumptions, it is very easy to spot the fallacies that inform it. Copland was asked a question that reflected a situation that everyone acknowledged, but one that he could not effectively explain. It was, in short, a mystery. And so the explanation had to be a "mysterious element" that women lacked. The mystery was "solved" simply by calling it a mystery. That is what is known in logic as a tautology — a mere repetition of a premise in other words, or (in this case) an arbitrary definition.

How can we do better? First by acknowledging that the "problem" of women's creativity in the arts, and in music particularly, is one that we do not see directly but through a screen of social and esthetic issues. These involve the value placed on the composer (and, more specifically, on the "great composer") in our modern musical culture, which follows, as already suggested, from the high value placed by modern musical culture on written texts. Once this is realized, economic and political factors such as *access* and *dissemination* suddenly stand revealed.

Before the twentieth century (indeed, the *late* twentieth century), it was only under exceptional circumstances that women enjoyed access to media of textual preservation and dissemination. It was because she was an abbess, the head of an exclusively female religious institution, that Hildegard of Bingen (discussed in chapter 3) had the means at her disposal to record her inspired religious poetry and the extraordinary melodies to which she sang them. Before they were committed to writing (probably not by Hildegard herself but by a scribe to whom she as a socially privileged person could dictate them), Hildegard's poems and songs were worked out in memory. In this activity she was hardly alone. Countless other nuns, as well as countless forgotten monks, surely made up liturgical songs. But only those with the power to command the necessary material and human resources got to preserve their works and make them available, so to speak, to the modern historian. The same is true of Beatriz di Dia, the *trobairitz* whose work was discussed in chapter 4. As a noblewoman, she had privileged access to the means of inscribing and disseminating her work.

It was this power of access, rather than powers of verbal or musical inspiration, that was disproportionately commanded by men, because men commanded the overwhelmingly greater part of the political and (especially) the ecclesiastical power structures in European society. To gain access to the means of inscription and dissemination, a creatively gifted male musician sought institutional connections as an employee of court or church. Such positions were rarely open to women. For a creatively gifted woman to gain such access, she would have had to be the employer, not the employee. And that is why, until the nineteenth century, practically all women composers came, like Hildegard, from the higher echelons of the monastic hierarchy or from the hereditary aristocracy.

More than one reviewer of the exhaustive *Norton/Grove Dictionary of Women Composers* (New York and London, 1994) — an unprecedented biographical compilation covering almost nine hundred musically creative women who managed to contribute materially to the literate tradition — expressed astonishment at the number of titled names the book contained, from Schütz's contemporary Sophie Elisabeth (1613–76), Duchess of Brunswick, to Amalia Catharina (1640–97), Countess of Erbach, to Wilhelmina (1709–58), Princess of Prussia, to Maria Barbara (1711–58), Queen of Spain, and so on.

Yet the astonishment is misplaced, and the fact easily misinterpreted. Noblewomen proportionately outnumber noblemen in the ranks of aristocratic dilettantes precisely because the rank of noble dilettante was virtually the only rank to which a woman composer could aspire. So there is no real mystery about male dominance in music, and no lack of data to account for it. The illusion of gendered disparity in musical endowment (Copland's "mysterious element") turns out to be the result of gendered disparity of access to the means of inscription and dissemination, something for which historical evidence could hardly be more abundant.

The late sixteenth and seventeenth centuries (the "early modern" period) began to witness exceptions to this pattern, as we have observed in the case of Barbara Strozzi. New careers opened up to women as performers with the advent of professionalized court singing, particularly at the music-loving court of Ferrara in northern Italy, which maintained a famous *concerto delle donne*, a "consort" of virtuoso women singers for whom several important (male) composers wrote flamboyantly ornate madrigals near the end of the sixteenth century. With the advent of public opera in Italy beginning in the 1630s, women performers reached new heights of accomplishment and renown.

And yet their musical accomplishments did not bring women performers enhanced social status; rather the opposite. Women who sang or danced in public still bore a stigma in Christian Europe, where such activities were traditionally associated with prostitutes (or courtesans, as they were known in more elevated social circles). Thus a recent study by the music historian Anthony Newcomb of the *concerto delle donne* and other professional court singers of the time bears the title "Courtesans, Muses or Musicians?" and confirms the fact that, unless married to a nobleman, a professional woman singer was thought of as "a remarkable renegade to be looked at, applauded, but not included in polite society."[12] Even Barbara Strozzi, in the words of her biographer Ellen Rosand, "may, indeed, have been a courtesan, highly skilled in the art of love as well as music."[13]

Strozzi was nevertheless able to function as a professional composer — a creator — as well as a performer, and this was an "early modern" novelty. Many of the women performers at Ferrara and other north Italian courts were known to have composed a significant part of their own repertoires, but with only a single notable exception — Maddalena Casulana, who issued three books of madrigals in Venice between 1568 and 1583 — they did not publish their work and are lost as composers to history. Strozzi, by contrast, was considered an important composer in her day, as was her older contemporary Francesca Caccini (1587 – ca. 1641), who published a book of monodies in 1618 and had an opera performed at the Medici court in Florence in 1625. (This opera, *La liberazione di Ruggiero dall'isola d'Alcina* — "Ruggiero's deliverance from the island of Alcina" — may have had the unforeseen and unrelated distinction of being the first Italian opera to be performed outside of Italy when it was given in Warsaw in 1628.)

Just to name these two composers, however, is to explain their exceptional status and to realize that they are only exceptions that (as the saying goes) "prove the rule." Both of them were daughters (in one case natural, the other adopted) of famous fathers who commanded great prestige in musical circles. It was on their fathers' coattails that the daughters could find an outlet for their talents where other talents, perhaps equally great, could find no outlet. Strozzi, in an effort to mitigate the audacity of her career objectives, paid tribute to the prejudice against women composers even as she overcame it, writing in the preface to her first publication that "as a woman, I publish [it] all too anxiously," and in her second, dedicated to the Emperor of Austria, that "the lowly mine of a woman's poor imagination cannot produce metal to forge those richest golden crowns worthy of august rulers."

Caccini left the service of the Medici on the death of her husband in 1626. Recent research by Suzanne Cusick has shown that she married again a year later, to a wealthy nobleman and musical dilettante, and that she continued to compose music for entertainments at her new home — but anonymously, as befit her new social rank.[14] Thus, ironically, access to a private fortune through marriage — a marriage probably contracted precisely because of her musical talents — actually took away from Caccini the outlet she had formerly possessed, by virtue of her father's fame, to the public profession of music and the dissemination of her works.

Indeed, she now outranked her father socially. After her second husband's death, she returned to the Medici court, but as a lady-in-waiting rather than as a designated musician. (She did, however, sing in chapel services and also taught music in a convent school — a "gynocentric" environment, as Cusick calls it, and an oral one that is for both reasons hidden from the purview of conventional historiography.) In a final touch of irony, she refused permission to have her daughter sing in a dramatic spectacle such as she had participated in during her own previous stint in service, lest it damage the girl's prospects for a good marriage. Francesca Caccini recognized, in short, that her own lucky combination of musical and social success had been freakish, and not likely to be repeated in the next generation.

So, to pose once more the question Copland so glibly answered and answer it anew: There have been no "great women composers" because of a virtual catch-22. Without social rank, feminine access to the means of dissemination was impossible for one reason, but with it access could become impossible for another reason. Besides, the problem as we pose it today is compounded by a subtle nuance in the wording of the question. As we will see in greater detail when we investigate the musical results of the romantic movement, the concept of artistic greatness (a far more recent concept than one might assume) is itself a gendered one. Even earlier, the concept of artistic creation was linked with the notion of the biblical Creator, traditionally a patriarchal rather than a matriarchal figure. So the question itself, like many questions that purportedly seek simple "natural" answers, is not innocent of cultural bias.

So what do we do? One way of restoring women to the history of music, informally known as "mainstreaming," is to give the works of women composers disproportionate representation so as to offer a constant reminder that (*pace* Copland) men have no monopoly on compositional talent. The choice of Strozzi's cantata as a specimen for analysis in this book, rather than one by the more famous and prolific Carissimi (or Luigi Rossi, another Roman specialist in the genre), is an example of mainstreaming. Its immediate purpose, however, was more to provide an opening for the present discussion than to even the score between men and women in the history of composition. There is simply no way of evening that score; and while mainstreaming may constructively counteract the unfounded assumption that women are lacking in innate capacity to compose, it, too, distorts the historical record. Nor does concealing the fact of any group's historical exclusion serve to advance its current prospects for equality.

Another way of restoring women to music history is to change the nature of the story, giving less emphasis to composition and more to performance, patronage, and other areas in which the contributions of women have been more commensurate with those of men. The present account, with its constant reminders that the literate repertory is not the sole subject of music history and its constant attention to the social contexts in which music has been made, shows the influence of this trend. And yet to the extent that it remains the aim and obligation of a text like this not only to narrate the story of past musical activities and deeds but also to provide an introduction to the material products — the textual remains — of those activities, the literate repertory must, despite all caveats, retain its privilege and remain the primary focus of the story.

Whatever the quantity of women's contributions to that repertory and whatever the extent of its representation in a book like this, another question remains to be asked about it. Is its quality, or essence, distinct in any observable way from that of men? Is there something peculiar about the musical expression of women (and, it follows, of men) that is the direct result of the composer's gender? Do men or women, as composers, possess a particular group identity, the way they do as participants in the act of sexual reproduction? And if so, is that identity truly a biological given and a determinant of their behavior, as it is in reproduction, or is it the result of habit and socialization (that is, behavior one learns from other people)?

These questions — which can be applied not only to matters of gender but to a broad range of differences among human groups including race, nationality, religion, erotic preference, and as many others as we can describe — have become increasingly common in recent years, and increasingly fraught, as different human groups (especially minority groups) have demanded, and been accorded, increasing respect in many modern societies. Answers to them have been extremely various, and they have been subject to heated, often acrimonious debate as befits the important political and economic issues that are at stake behind them, even when asked in the relatively serene context of the arts and their history.

An inclination toward affirmative answers to questions about the reality of group identity as a determinant of individual behavior is generally called the *essentialist* position, while the tendency to answer such questions in the negative marks one as a *social constructionist* or *constructivist*. These extreme positions are rarely espoused in pure form except by political activists. And even political activists sometimes recognize that the political implications of these positions are seldom unambiguous. Asserting an essentialist notion of women's writing, as certain literary critics have done (especially in France, so that "women's writing" is often called *écriture feminine* even by English or American writers), has been a useful tactic in calling attention to the existence of such literature and gaining a readership for it. And yet women writers have often resisted the notion, thinking it a predefinition of their work, hence more a limitation on them than a liberation. There has been a certain amount of musicological criticism along such lines (an example is Cusick's work on Francesca Caccini, whom she has termed a "proto-feminist").

But there is little consensus on the matter, and it will be noticed that the present discussion of Strozzi's style as evinced by her cantata has sought a neutral or agnostic (some might call it an evasive) stance. On the one hand, it is evident that Strozzi follows practically all of the same expressive conventions previously observed in the work of men like Monteverdi and Schütz. On the other, her work does possess distinguishing characteristics that, some might argue, involuntarily reflect her group identity. Questions of essentialism *vs.* constructionism, in any event, cannot be approached on the basis of a single example, and a broader empirical survey lies beyond the scope of a book like this. As in all such controversies, the burden of proof lies with those who assert the critical relevance of the issue.

Courts Resplendent, Overthrown, Restored

Tragédie Lyrique from Lully to Rameau; English Music in the Seventeenth Century

SENSE AND SENSUOUSNESS

The story is told of King Louis XIV of France that once a courtier fond of the brilliance and grandeur of Italian music brought before the king a young violinist who had studied under the finest Italian masters for several years, and bade him play the most dazzling piece he knew. When he was finished, the king sent for one of his own violinists and asked the man for a simple air from *Cadmus et Hermiorie*, an opera by his own court composer, Jean-Baptiste Lully. The violinist was mediocre, the air was plain, nor was *Cadmus* by any means one of Lully's most impressive works.

But when the air was finished, the king turned to the courtier and said, "All I can say, sir, is that that is my taste."[1]

Invoking taste, the thing that is proverbially beyond dispute, is always a fine way of putting an end to an argument, especially when invoked by one to whom nobody may talk back. But while a king's taste may not be disputed, it may still be worth investigating. Nor can we say we really understand a story unless we know who is telling it, and why.

This particular story comes from a pamphlet, *Comparaison de la musique italienne et de la musique française* ("A comparison of French and Italian music"), issued in 1704 by one French aristocrat, Jean Laurent Lecerf de la Viéville, Lord of Freneuse, in answer to a likenamed pamphlet, *Paralèle des Italiens et des Français* ("Differentiating the Italians from the French"), issued in 1702 by

J. Bapt. Lully Surintendant de la Musique du Roy

FIG. 22-1 Jean-Baptiste Lully, Superintendent of the King's Music. Engraving by Henri Bonnart (1652–1711).

another French aristocrat, Abbé François Raguenet. It was the opening salvo of a press war that would last in France throughout the eighteenth century — that is, until the revolution of 1789 rendered all the old aristocratic controversies *passé*.

The reason why it enters into our story a little ahead of schedule, and why it was so very typical of France, is that the musician it defended had been dead for almost twenty years at the time of writing, and *Cadmus*, his second opera, had had its first performance more than thirty years before. Nowhere else in Europe had operas become classics, nor had any other composer of operas been exalted into a symbol not only of royal taste but of royal authority as well. Authority is what French music was all about, and Lully's operas above all. They were the courtiest court operas that ever were.

Lurking behind the story, as behind every discussion of opera in France, was a political debate. It was touched off by Raguenet's admiring description of castrato singing, probably the most vivid earwitness account ever penned of singers the likes of which we will never hear. Sometimes, wrote Raguenet (in the words of an anonymous eighteenth-century translator):

> you hear a ritornello so charming that you think nothing in music can exceed it till on a sudden you perceive it was designed only to accompany a more charming air sung by one of these castrati, who, with a voice the most clear and at the same time equally soft, pierces the symphony of instruments and tops them with an agreeableness which they that hear it may conceive but will never be able to describe.
>
> These pipes of theirs resemble that of the nightingale; their long-winded throats draw you in a manner out of your depth and make you lose your breath. They'll execute passages of I know not how many bars together, they'll have echoes on the same passages and swellings of a prodigious length, and then, with a chuckle in the throat, exactly like that of a nightingale, they'll conclude with cadences of an equal length, and all this in the same breath.
>
> Add to this that these soft — these charming voices acquire new charms by being in the mouth of a lover; what can be more affecting than the expressions of their sufferings in such tender passionate notes; in this the Italian lovers have a very great advantage over ours, whose hoarse masculine voices ill agree with the fine soft things they are to say to their mistresses. Besides, the Italian voices being equally strong as they are soft, we hear all they sing very distinctly, whereas half of it is lost upon our theatre unless we sit close to the stage or have the spirit of divination.[2]

And yet, Raguenet emphasizes, these desexed singers were not only the best male lovers, they were the best females as well:

> Castrati can act what part they please, either a man or a woman as the cast of the piece requires, for they are so used to perform women's parts that no actress in the world can do it better than they. Their voice is as soft as a woman's and withal it's much stronger; they are of a larger size than women, generally speaking, and appear consequently more majestic. Nay, they usually look handsomer on the stage than women themselves.[3]

To us, living in an age when sexual identity has become a "hot button," Raguenet's comfortable enjoyment of masculine cross-dressing is perhaps the most striking aspect of his description. It is a facet of a general comfort with artifice, and a willingness to accept all manner of make-believe, that contrasts strongly with more modern theatrical esthetics. But at the time the most provocative aspect of Raguenet's discourse — and the one regarded as most potentially degenerate — was his ready receptivity to the purely sensuous pleasure of singing and his willingness to accept it as opera's chief, most characteristic, and therefore most legitimate, delight. This went not only against the grain of Lecerf de la Viéville's argument, which ends with strenuous exhortations to "yield to reason" and heed the admonitions that "reason pronounces for us" (that is, for us French) — it went against the whole history of operatic reception in France, and England too.

Opera had a difficult time getting started in France. Indeed, it had to succeed as politics before it had any chance of succeeding as art. Like their English counterparts, who also possessed a glorious tradition of spoken theater (as the Italians did not), the aristocrats of seventeenth-century France saw only a child's babble in what the Italians called *dramma per musica* (drama "through" or "by means of" music). To their minds, the art of music and the art of drama simply would not mix. "Would you know what an Opera is?" wrote Saint-Evremond, an exiled French courtier and a famous wit, to the Duke of Buckingham.[4] "I'll tell you that it is an odd medley of poetry and music, wherein the poet and musician, equally confined one by the other, take a world of pains to compose a wretched performance." Music in the theater, for the thinking French as for the thinking English, was at best an elegant bauble, more likely a nuisance. High tragedians made a point of spurning it. Pierre Corneille, the greatest playwright of mid-century France, would admit music only into what was known as a *pièce à machines* — a play that already adulterated its dramatic seriousness for the sake of spectacle in the form of flying machines on which gods descended or winged chariots took off. And even then, he wrote in 1650 in the preface to his drama *Andromède*, "I have been very careful to have nothing sung that is essential to the understanding of the play, since words that are sung are usually understood poorly by the audience."[5] But then artists and critics who value intellectual understanding have always resisted opera. From the beginning dramatic music has been reason's foe, as indeed it was expressly designed to be.

THE POLITICS OF PATRONAGE

The irrational, though, can have its rational uses, and nobody knew that better than Jules Mazarin, the seventeenth century's most artful politician. It was Cardinal Mazarin (né Giulio Mazzarini), the Italian-born de facto regent of France, who took the first steps, in the earliest years of the boy-king Louis XIV's reign, to establish opera in his adopted country. He recruited the services of Luigi Rossi (ca. 1597–1653), the leading composer of Rome, to write an opera expressly for the French court. Fittingly, indeed all but inevitably, this first officially sponsored French opera, performed at the Palais Royal on 2 March 1647, was another *Orfeo*, another demonstrative setting of the myth of music's primeval power to move the soul.

Forty years after Monteverdi's treatment of the same tale, the new work showed the influence of opera's commercial popularization, so that it resembled Monteverdi's *Poppea* more than it did his *Orfeo*. Where Monteverdi's *Orfeo* had only the briefest of duets for Orpheus and Eurydice (to celebrate their happiness, not express their love), Rossi's gave the nuptial pair (both sopranos) no fewer than three extended love scenes. Orpheus, a natural tenor in Monteverdi's setting, is a soprano castrato in Rossi's, so that these scenes closely resemble the ones for Nero and Poppea in Monteverdi's last opera. Also in the spirit of *Poppea* rather than Monteverdi's *Orfeo*, Rossi's *Orfeo* has a pair of comic characters (one of them a satyr) who mock the lofty passions of the main characters.

But like Monteverdi's *Orfeo*, and like all the early aristocratic musical tales, Rossi's *Orfeo* was fitted out with sumptuous scenery, with dancing choruses, with lavish orchestral scoring and with machines (the most splendid one reserved for Apollo, who descends in a fiery chariot that illuminates a fantastic garden set). Above all, it had the requisite sycophantic prologue that showered praises on the young King Louis from the mouths of gods and allegorical beings.

By masterminding this display, Cardinal Mazarin secured for himself a prestige that rivaled that of his own mentor, the Roman cardinal Antonio Barberini, Rossi's patron. The Italian spectacles, full of everything *merveilleux*, bedizened the French court more gloriously than any rationalistic drama could do, for "the purpose of such spectacles," wrote the moralist Jean de la Bruyère (1645–96), a court favorite and a converted operatic skeptic, "is to hold the mind, the eye and the ear equally in thrall."[6]

And there was something else as well. Rossi, in his turn, recruited for his performances a troupe of Roman singers and instrumentalists, a little colony of Italians in the French capital who were personally loyal to Mazarin, and who, in the time-honored fashion of traveling virtuosi, could serve him as secret agents and spies in his diplomatic maneuvers with the papal court. All of this was a lesson to Mazarin's apprentice, the young king, who thus received instruction, as a French historian has put it (using the French word for lavish arts patronage), in "the political importance of *le mécénat*."[7] The foundations were laid for what the French still call their *grand siècle*, their great century, and opera was destined to be its grandest manifestation.

Yet it was a very special sort of opera that would reign in France, one tailored to accommodate national prejudices, court traditions, and royal prerogatives. The French autocracy was the largest ethnically integrated political entity in Europe. Its royal court was the exemplary aristocratic establishment of the day, and its musical displays would classically embody the politics of dynastic affirmation. Like every other aspect of French administrative culture, the French court opera was wholly centralized. Its primary purpose was to furnish "propaganda for the state and for the divine right of the king," as the music historian Neal Zaslaw has written, and only secondarily to provide "entertainment for the nobility and bourgeoisie."[8] No operatic spectacle could be shown in public anywhere in France that had not been prescreened, and approved, at court.

At the same time, however, French opera aimed far higher than the "musical tale" of the Italians, which was essentially a modest pastoral play. The French form aspired to the status of a full-fledged *tragédie en musique* (later called *tragédie lyrique*), which meant that the values of the spoken drama, France's greatest cultural treasure, were as far as possible to be preserved in the new medium despite the presence of music.

To reconcile the claims of court pageantry with those of dramatic gravity was no mean trick. Only a very special genius could bring it off. At the time of Luigi Rossi's momentous sojourn in France, another far less distinguished Italian musician — just an apprentice, really — was already living there: Giovanni Battista Lulli, a Florentine boy who had been brought over in 1646, aged thirteen, to serve as *garçon de chambre* to Mme. de Montpensier, a Parisian lady who wanted to practice her Italian. She also supported his training in courtly dancing and violin playing. When his patroness, a "Frondist" (that is, a supporter of a failed parliamentary revolt against Louis and Mazarin), was exiled in 1652, Lulli secured release from her employ and found work as a servant to Louis XIV's cousin, Anne-Marie-Louise d'Orleans (known as the "Grande Mademoiselle"), and as a dancer and mime at the royal court, where he danced alongside, and made friends with, the teenaged king. Upon the death of his violin teacher the next year, Lulli assumed the man's position as court composer of ballroom music.

His rise to supreme power was steady and unstoppable, for Lulli was a veritable musical Mazarin, an Italian-born French political manipulator of genius. Shortly after the founding in 1669 of the Académie Royale de Musique, Louis XIV's opera establishment, Jean-Baptiste Lully, who like Mazarin had been naturalized and Gallicized his name, managed to finagle the rights to manage it from its originally designated patent holder. From then on he was a musical Sun King, the absolute autocrat of French music, which he re-created in his own image.

He had a crown-supported monopoly over his domain, from which he could exclude any rival who threatened his preeminence. He squeezed out his older, native-born contemporary Robert Cambert (ca. 1628–77), who, despairing of ever producing his masterpiece, *Ariane* (1659), withdrew embittered to London where in 1674 he did finally see a much-modified version of it performed in Drury Lane to a partially translated libretto. Likewise Marc-Antoine Charpentier (1643–1704), a younger competitor who, though trained in Italy and employed by the king's cousin and later by the *dauphin* (the future Louis XV), had to wait until the age of fifty before he could get a *tragédie en musique* (*Medée*, 1693) produced at court, several years after Lully's long-awaited death in 1687. (The old monopolist had died with his boots on, so to speak, following a celebrated mishap with a time-beating cane that resulted in gangrene.) By then Lully had produced thirteen *tragédies lyriques*, averaging one every fifteen months. The pattern that he set with them became the standard to which any composer aspiring to a court performance had to conform. Two generations of French musicians thus willy-nilly became Lully's dynastic heirs. His works would dominate the repertory for half a century after his death, in response not to market forces or to public demand but by royal decree, giving Lully a vicarious reign comparable in length of years to his patron's and extending through most of the reign of Louis XV as well. His style did not merely define an art form, it defined a national identity. *La musique*, he might well have said, *c'est moi*.

DRAMA AS COURT RITUAL

The ultimate theatrical representation of power, the Lullian *tragédie lyrique* was from first to last a sumptuously outfitted — but, in another sense, quite thinly clad — metaphor for the grandeur and the authority of the court that it adorned. The monumental mythological or heroic-historical plots, some chosen by the king himself, celebrated the implacable universal order and the supremacy of divine or divinely appointed rulers.

Themes of sacrifice and self-sacrifice predominated. Lully's *Alceste* (1674), his second *tragedie lyrique* and one of his most successful, was based on the myth of Alcestis (as embodied in Euripides' tragedy of the same name), about a queen who gives up her life so that her husband's life-threatening malady may be cured. The adaptation was by Philippe Quinault (1635–88), a court poet and member of the Académie Française, who became Lully's principal librettist. (The same Euripides tragedy would serve about ninety years later as plotline for a similarly lofty, French-style libretto by Ranieri de' Calzabigi, a Vienna court poet, austerely set to music by the great opera reformer Christoph Willibald von Gluck to honor the Empress Maria Theresa for her devotion to her consort, who had died the year before.)

Idomenée (1712), a *tragédie en musique* by André Campra, a member of the post-Lully generation, concerns Idomeneus, the king of Crete during the Trojan Wars, who makes a hasty vow to Neptune to sacrifice the first living thing he espies on returning home in return for deliverance from a shipwreck, and is forced to sacrifice his own son at the cost of his throne and his sanity. (Its libretto, based on a fourth-century commentary to Virgil's *Aeneid*, was later translated, revised, and expanded for Mozart's *Idomeneo*, performed for the court of Munich in 1781.) Later, the almost identical biblical story of Jephtha (already the subject of an oratorio by Carissimi described in chapter 21), who makes a similar vow and suffers a similar fate, was turned into a *tragédie en musique* by

FIG. 22-2   Illuminated evening performance of *Alceste*, a *tragédie en musique* by Lully and Quinault, at the Marble Court of Versailles, 1674. Engraving by Jean Le Pautre (1618–1682).

Michel Pignolet de Montéclair (*Jephté*, 1732). By then, tastes had changed sufficiently to permit a happy ending: Jephtha's daughter is spared in Montéclair's opera by divine intervention. Lully's greatest successor, Jean-Philippe Rameau, honored Louis XV with *Castor et Pollux* (1737), concerning the mythological twins, immortalized in the constellation Gemini, who were each tested and found willing to sacrifice his life for the sake of the other.

A metaphor of grandeur and authority from first to last, beginning with the march-like *ouverture* or "opener" whose stilted dotted rhythms (enclosing a faster jiglike fugue) became for eighteenth-century composers — and even later ones — a universal code for pomp. The "French overture" was actually Cambert's invention, in his pastorale *Pomone* (1671), performed a year

FIG. 22-3   Jean-Philippe Rameau, portrait by Jacques Aved (1702–1766).

before Lully managed to secure the royal patent and ruin his rival, meanwhile taking over all his stylistic innovations and expanding them into their "classic" form. Ex. 22-1 shows the beginnings of the two main sections of the *ouverture* to Lully's opera *Atys* of 1676.

What the *ouverture* served to introduce was an obligatory panegyric prologue of a full act's duration, vastly outstripping its Italian courtly prototype. Here mythological beings were summoned to extol the French king's magnificent person and his deeds of war and peace with choral pageantry and with suites of dances modeled on the actual *ballet de cour*, an elaborate ritual, in which the king himself took part, that symolized the

EX. 22-1A   Jean-Baptiste Lully, Overture to *Atys* (1676), opening section

EX. 22-1A   (*continued*)

EX. 22-1B   Jean-Baptiste Lully, Overture to *Atys* (1676), beginning of middle section

divinely instituted social hierarchy. (A description of "the King's Grand Ball" by Pierre
Rameau, Louis XV's dancing master, may be found in Weiss and Taruskin, *Music in
the Western World*, No. 53.) At times the mythological characters could be joshed a
little, as in Rameau's *Castor et Pollux*, where Louis XV's successful mediation of the

War of Polish Succession is symbolized textually by an amorous concord of Venus and Mars, the gods of love and war, and musically by a delightfully incongruous love duet of flute and trumpet that only Rameau, a master of the grotesque, could have brought off (Ex. 22-2); or as in Montéclair's *Jephté*, where Roman deities scurry out of the way of the Holy Scripture. Such levity was tolerable in a prologue, for it only enhanced the exaltation of the king above his mythological admirers.

EX. 22-2 Jean-Philippe Rameau, *Castor et Pollux*, Prologue

EX. 22-2 (*continued*)

Throughout the spectacle that followed, dancing—ceremonial movement accompanied by *les vingt-quatre violons du Roi* ("the twenty-four royal fiddlers"), the grandest and most disciplined orchestra in Europe—would furnish a lavish symbolic counterpoint to the words. Sometimes the dance enlarged directly on the dramatic action, sometimes it contrasted with it, as when Jupiter, in the second act of *Castor et Pollux*, orders up a lengthy *divertissement* or dance-diversion just to show his errant son what pleasures he will have to give up if he goes through with his planned self-sacrifice.

Everything reached culmination in a monumental *chaconne* or *passacaille*, a stately choral dance over one of the ground basses described in chapter 21. It often went on for hundreds of measures, enlisting all the dramatis personae for the purpose of announcing an explicit moral. "C'est la valeur qui fait les Dieux/Et la beauté fait les Déesses" ("Valor makes gods and beauty goddesses") is the one proclaimed in *Castor et Pollux*; and the metaphorical signifance of the final dance is spelled out with special clarity in that opera. "C'est la fête de l'univers!" ("Let the whole universe rejoice!"), Jupiter declares, and his words are taken up as a refrain by the ensemble, representing all the planets and the stars in the sky in an orgy of royal panegyric.

The champion Lully *passacaille* comes from the fifth act of *Armide* (1686), his last *tragédie en musique*, composed to a libretto adapted by Quinault at Louis XIV's behest from a celebrated episode in Tasso's 1581 epic *Gerusalemme liberata* concerning the love of Armida, a Saracen sorceress, for Rinaldo, a crusader, culminating in her conversion and her renunciation of pagan vengefulness in favor of Christian humility and conciliation. (The story became the subject of close to one hundred operas and ballets, from Monteverdi in the early seventeenth century to Dvořák in the early twentieth.) The work was kept in repertory until 1766, eighty years after its première—a record run, not to be matched till Mozart, whose late operas never left the standard repertory.

The *passacaille* (Ex. 22-3), which if performed complete (that is, with all repeats observed) lasts upwards of twelve minutes, comprises a divertissement performed by a troupe of allegorical Pleasures and *amants fortunés* (happy lovers) to entertain Renaud (Rinaldo) while Armide seeks advice from the Underworld on what to do about her lovesickness. The fact that it is based largely on the traditional descending minor tetrachord (occasionally garnished chromatically into the *passus duriusculus*) is a tip-off to the audience that things will not end as happily as they did in Tasso's original, but with a denouement better suited to the requirements of the French court and its mores. And sure enough,

FIG. 22-4   Destruction of the magic palace at the conclusion of Lully's *Armide* (1686). Stage design for the original production by Jean Berain.

when Armide returns Renaud surprises her with the declaration that he will sacrifice love to duty and leave her; Armide, enraged, humiliated, and despairing, orders the destruction of her magic palace (and Renaud within it) then departs on a flying chariot. Thus Renaud, the true hero of the tale (and the royal patron's surrogate) ends up sacrificing not only love but life itself on the altar of social obligation.

EX. 22-3   Jean-Baptiste Lully, *Armide*, Passacaille, beginning

EX. 22-3 (*continued*)

The contemporary allegorical relevance of the plot, proclaimed at the first in the prologue and affirmed at the last by the *passacaille*, was what really counted in a *tragédie lyrique*. To drive it home the players wore "modern dress," adapted from contemporary court regalia, just as the dances they performed were the sarabandes, the gavottes, and the passepieds of their own ballroom, albeit performed at a supreme level of execution. Thus the theatrical pageant was no mere reminiscence of a social dance, it *was* a social dance enacted by professional proxies. The whole drama was conceived as a sublimated court ritual. Royal and noble spectators did not seek transcendence of contemporary reality but rather its cosmic confirmation. They did not value the kind of verisimilitude that makes the imaginary seem real. They wanted just the opposite: to see the real — that is, themselves — projected into the domain of fable and archetype.

Along with this feast of symbolic movement and rich sonority went an unparalleled, completely un-Italianate prejudice against virtuoso singing, which was abjured not only for the usual negative reasons — uppity singers symbolizing a polity in disarray — but for more positive reasons having to do with the theatrical traditions of France. Here verisimilitude of a very particular sort—fidelity to articulate language, which is the first thing to go in florid, legato, "operatic" singing—suddenly loomed very large. The lead performers in French court opera remained nominally *acteurs*, and the voice of the castrato went unheard in the land—even when, in Lully's *Atys* (1676), after Ovid, the plot actually hinged on castration.

ATYS, THE KING'S OPERA

But of course the brave castrato voice referred to anything but itself. The one thing its brassy timbre never symbolized was actual eunuchhood. And so the last character a castrato might have effectively represented was Atys, or Attis, the hero of the ultimate courtly sacrifice-spectacle, known in its time as "the king's opera" and cited not only as an operatic but as a literary classic by Voltaire, seventy-five years after its first production.[9] Attis was a god of pre-Hellenic (Phrygian) religion, later taken over as a minor deity by the Greeks. Like Adonis, he was a beautiful youth over whom goddesses fought jealous battles. Cybele, the earth or mother goddess, fell in love with the unwitting and insouciant Attis, and so that none other shall ever know his love, caused him to castrate himself in a sudden frenzy. Like Adonis, he was worshiped by the Greeks as a god of vegetation who controlled the yearly round of wintry death and vernal resurrection.

In Quinault's libretto, Cybele's rival for the love of Attis is the nymph Sangaride, to whom Attis has actually declared his affections. At the end of the opera, Cybele causes Attis to kill Sangaride in his frenzy, and then to stab himself fatally. Before he can die, Cybele transforms him into a pine tree whose life is renewed yearly, so that she will be able to love it forever. According to a gossipy courtier who authored several highly revealing letters about the preparations for the *Atys* première and about the staging, this ending was contrived expressly so as to avoid having to show an act of castration on stage. The very avoidance, however, testified to everyone's awareness of the real nature of the hero's sacrifice and lent an added resonance to the contemporary subtext, no doubt well known to Lully and Quinault: "Word has it," one of the letters divulges, "that the King recognizes himself in this Atys, apathetic to love, that Cybele strongly resembles the Queen, and Sangaride Mme. de Maintenon, who enraged the King when she wanted to marry the Duke of B****."[10]

In other words, the opera gave symbolic representation to a love triangle that was even then being played out in the king's own household; for "Mme. de Maintenon" (that is, Françoise d'Aubigné, marquise de Maintenon), the widow of a court poet and an influential royal adviser, became the second wife of Louis XIV in 1684. No wonder *Atys* became known as "the king's opera." It was, even beyond the obligatory prologue, an opera about the king. And in its famed artistic "chastity"—(almost) no comic interludes, (almost) no subplots, in short (almost) no popular "Venetian" trappings of any kind—*Atys* reflected on the artistic plane the same tendency toward serenity and exalted moderation that Mme. de Maintenon advocated in court life.

The third act of *Atys*, at once the most succinct of the opera's five acts and the most varied, is a perfect model of courtly opera at the peak of its prestige. It begins with a short soliloquy for the title character, cast as an *haute-contre*, the highest French male voice range, a soft tenor shading into falsetto and the very antithesis of the plangent castrato (Ex. 22-4a). Atys laments the loss of Sangaride to her betrothed, King Celenus of Phrygia. This little number epitomizes Lully's deliberate avoidance of big Italianate vocal display in the interests of dramatic realism; as the anonymous letter writer describes it, "all in half-tints: no big effects for the singers, no grand arias, but small courtly airs and recitatives over the bare continuo, and their alternation is what will give shape to the action."

EX. 22-4A   Jean-Baptiste Lully, *Atys*, Act III, Atys's opening *air* (sarabande)

Of what use are Fortune's favors when Love makes us miserable?

Atys's solo is just such a "courtly air" (*air de cour*). The text consists of a single quatrain, of which the first pair of lines (*couplet*) is used as a refrain to round it off into a miniature ABA (*da capo*) form. This little rounded entity is further enclosed between a pair of identical *ritournelles*, in which the first measure already discloses the characteristic meter and rhythm of the sarabande. Thus even the vocal solos reflect the underlying basis of the French court opera in the court ballet, and beyond that, in ballroom dance itself. The setting of the text is entirely syllabic and responsive to the contours, stresses, and lengths of the spoken language, reflecting the other underlying basis of the court opera, namely high-style theatrical declamation.

These values were hard-won. They ran counter to "musicianly" instincts, and Lully's famous skills as autocratic disciplinarian, with unprecedented authority stemming directly from his patron the king, were necessary ones to the success of his undertaking—as the anonymous letter writer confirms in a delightfully written, somewhat cynical passage that conjures up a vivid sense of something new in music: haughty, easily offended authorial pride.

> Lully is ranting at everybody. Everyone wants to shine in *Atys*, and there is no way to shine in this work of Lully's. Everything is fashioned, calculated, measured so that the action of the drama progresses without ever slackening. This singer takes it upon himself to add ornaments, slowing down the beat; and in order to remain on stage longer and arouse a little more applause, drags out an air that Lully intended to be simple, short and natural. That dancer begs for a futile repetition; the violins want to play when Lully asks for flutes . . . ,. Everybody seeks his own reflection in *Atys*. Lully has to defend his work.[11]

After Atys's solo, the nymph Doris and her brother Idas enter to urge Atys to act on his passion and spurn his official duty as Celenus's protégé and chief sacrificer to Cybele, thus crystallizing the moral dilemma on which the drama turns. Like most scenes of dialogue, it is carried by a rhythmically irregular recitative that alternates between measures containing four big beats and measures containing three. But when the two confidants come to their principal argument ("In love's realm duty is helpless"), they come together in another minuscule *air* in minuet tempo, into which (and out of which) they slip almost imperceptibly: that is the deft "alternation that shapes the action," in the words of the anonymous letter writer. And when they win Atys over, he joins them in a tiny trio in the style of an allemande with dotted rhythms recalling the imperious strains of the overture (Ex. 22-4b).

EX. 22-4B   Jean-Baptiste Lully, *Atys*, Act III, *Air à trois* (allemande)

EX. 22-4B   (*continued*)

-mour et le re-con-nois-san - ce, L'A - mour tou-jours em - por-te la ba - lan-ce.

-mour et le re-con-nois-san - ce, L'A - mour tou-jours em - por-te la ba - lan-ce.

-mour et le re-con-nois-san - ce, L'A - mour tou-jours em - por-te la ba - lan-ce.

In vain, a heart, uncertain of its choice, puts Love and gratitude
a thousand times upon the scales. Love always tips the scales.

FIG. 22-5   Costume design by Jean Berain for
the *Sommeil* ("sleep scene") in Lully's *Atys* (1676).

Left alone once again to reflect on his amorous prospects, Atys launches what appears to be another sarabande, heralded by another orchestral ritournelle. (Its give-away rhythm is the accented and length-ened note on the second beat of the mea-sure.) But he is quickly distracted by the counterclaim of duty and lapses into a recitative, from which he lapses further into sleep. This is an enchanted slum-ber that Cybele has engineered in order to apprise him of her love without hav-ing to confess it (degrading for a god-dess). The scene thus conjured up is the most famous scene in the opera—the subtly erotic *Sommeil*, literally the "sleep scene" or "dream symphony," so widely copied by later composers and librettists that it became a standard feature of the *tragédie lyrique*.

It begins with a Prelude (Ex. 22-4c) in which soft, sweet-toned whistle-flutes (what the French simply called *flûtes*, or recorders in English) are spotlighted in a somewhat concerto-like dialogue with the string band. The rocking rhythms, slurred two-by-two and surely performed with the characteristic French lilt (the so-called *notes inégales*), literally cradle the entranced title character and serve as the prologue to a charmed vision of Sleep himself (haute-contre), who sings a hypnotic refrain in alternation with his sons Morpheus (another haute-contre), Phobétor (bass), and Phantase or "Dream" (tenor).

EX. 22-4C Jean-Baptiste Lully, *Atys*, Act III, *Sommeil*

Morpheus's short recitative, in which he informs Atys that he has the honor (or in view of the outcome, the curse) of being loved by the exalted Cybele, introduces a typical process of alternating recitatives and accompanied airs with refrains, the chief refrain being the quatrain sung by the three sons of Sleep that continually reminds Atys that Cybele's love exacts duty and constancy in return. Exhortations give way to a ballet of sweet dreams (*des songes agréables*), in which the minuet danced by the corps de ballet forms a refrain to alternate with that of the sons.

The ballet of the sweet dreams is suddenly disrupted by one of nightmares (*songes funestes* or "evil dreams"), who enter, heralded by a bass who warns against offending a divine love, to the strains of an allemande in pompous overture style, its regal rhythms reflecting the high station of the goddess at whose behest the nightmares have appeared. The chorus of evil dreams that follows (Ex. 22-4d) is in one of Lully's specialty styles: the rapid-fire "patter chorus," which reached its peak the next year with the chorus of "Trembleurs" — People from the Frozen Climates whose bodies quake and whose teeth chatter with the cold — in Lully and Quinault's pastoral *Isis*. Having sung, the evil dreams launch into a lusty *courante*, full not only of the usual hemiolas but of rattling military tattoos as well. The nightmare sequence is dispelled by the awakening of the startled Atys and the arrival of Cybele herself, who comforts him, distressed though she is to learn, through an exchange of minuscule airs, that Atys properly reveres her but does not return her passion. Sangaride enters for a long scene in recitative that encloses the drama's (would-be) turning point, when Cybele (alas, only temporarily) promises to aid her rival out of unselfish love for Atys. Her crucial decision is rendered as a maxim: "The gods protect the freedom of the heart," set as a tiny march or allemande for the goddess, immediately repeated by the mortal pair.

EX. 22-4D Jean-Baptiste Lully, *Atys, Choeur des Songes Funestes*

EX. 22-4D *(continued)*

Love insulted turns to fury and won't forgive the most charming appeal.

Sangaride and Atys exit to seek the aid of Sangaride's father, the river Sangarus. (His scene, in act IV, is the opera's one comic divertissement.) Cybele's confidant, the priestess Melissa, now enters to console the unhappy goddess, whose complaint that "the ungrateful Atys loves me not" is set against the all-but inevitable *passus duriusculus*, the chromatically descending tetrachord, in the continuo (Ex. 22-4e). She sings in recitative style throughout, while Melissa's attempts to console her take the form of *petits airs* (little songs without repeats), the first of them a gavotte (Ex. 22-4f), identifiable by its characteristic two-quarter upbeat in quick "cut time" (two half notes to the bar).

EX. 22-4E Jean-Baptiste Lully, *Atys*, Act III, Cybele's complaint

How doth Atys mix indifference with respect! The ungrateful wretch
loves me not; Love demands love, any substitute is an offence.

Finally, Melissa leaves Cybele alone on stage and the goddess delivers herself of an impassioned yet dignified lament, the most extended solo turn in the opera. Impassioned though it is, however, it is far from what one would expect from a contemporary Italian opera at such a point. Rather, it harks back directly to such masterworks of the

EX. 22-4F   Jean-Baptiste Lully, *Atys*, Act III, Melissa's *petit air* (gavotte)

It is not so great a crime to express oneself poorly; A heart
that has never loved knows little about how love is expressed.

early, courtly Italian style as Monteverdi's famous lament for Ariadne—Lully surely
knew it—in the otherwise lost opera *Arianna* of 1608, named for her (Ex. 22-4g).
Introduced and concluded by a ritournelle in an elegiac sarabande style, Cybele's lament
(Ex. 22-4h), like Ariadne's, is a recitative built around a three-fold textual and musical
refrain: "Hope, so cherished, so sweet, Ah, . . . ah, why dost thou deceive me?" Between
the two consecutive "Ahs," Lully inserts a quarter rest, called a *soupir* ("sigh") in French,
on the downbeat. (A teaser: Was the rest called a sigh because it was used like this,
or did Lully use it like this because it was called a sigh? The history of the term is not
well enough established to answer the question, but it raises the prospect that even the
most obviously "onomatopoietic" or "iconic" musical imitations are actually mediated
through language concepts and are, in effect, puns.)

EX. 22-4G   Claudio Monteverdi, *Lamento d'Arianna*, refrain

EX. 22-4H   Jean-Baptiste Lully, *Atys*, Act III, Cybele's lament (sarabande)

Hope, so dear and sweet, Ah! Why dost thou deceive me?
From supreme heights thou hast brought me down;
A thousand hearts adore me, I neglect them all;
I ask for only one; he will hardly give himself up to me.
I feel nothing but distress and jealous suspicions
Is this the lovely fate I was to have expected?
Hope, so dear and sweet, Ah! Why dost thou deceive me?

As we see from the third act of *Atys*, French singing actors were rarely if ever called upon to contend with the full orchestra. Their scenes and confrontations were played against the bare figured bass in a stately, richly nuanced recitative whose supple rhythms in mixed meters caught the lofty cadence of French theatrical declamation. Lully, for whom French was a second language, was said to have modeled this style directly on the closely observed delivery—the contours, the tempos, the rhythms and the inflections—of La Champmeslé (Marie Desmares, 1642–98), the leading tragedienne of the spoken drama, who created most of the leading roles in the works of the great dramatist Jean Racine. Racine personally coached her, and thus indirectly coached Lully, whose *tragédies en musique* were exactly contemporaneous with Racine's great tragedies for the legitimate stage. Cybele's concluding lament in act III of *Atys* was an obvious instance of this musicalized tragic declamation.

Roulades and cadenzas would only have marred this lofty style, but Lully's singers employed, as if in compensation, a rich repertoire of "graces" or *agrémens*: tiny conventional embellishments—shakes, slides, swells—that worked in harness with the bass harmony to punctuate the lines and to enhance their rhetorical projection. And there were all kinds of subtly graded transitions in and out of the *petits airs*, the tiny, simply structured couplets and quatrains set to dance rhythms, which animated the prosody while placing minimum barriers in the way of understanding.

This, then, was the perfect opera for snooty opera haters like Saint-Evremond: an eyeful of spectacle, one ear full of opulent instrumental timbre, the other ear full of high rhetorical declamation. Vocal melody was far from the first ingredient or the most potent one, and the singers were held forcibly in check. Vocal virtuosity was admitted only in a decorative capacity on a par with orchestral color and stage machinery, never as a metaphor for emotion run amok. For passions out of control, the title character's harrowing final mad scene in Campra's *Idomenée* marked the absolute limit (Ex. 22-5). The tragic agitation is conveyed by brusque orchestral roulades, not vocal ones, and by the use of extreme tonalities, whose timbres were darkened by lessened string resonance, and whose unfamiliar playing patterns and vocal placements caused the performers to strain.

EX. 22-5   André Campra, *Idomenée*, from the final mad scene

EX. 22-5 (continued)

*Here Idomenée tries to kill himself with his sword.

By contrast, virtuoso singing could only emanate from the lips of anonymous *coryphées*: soloists from the general corps, representing members of the crowd, shades, athletes, even planets—whatever the dramatic or allegorical circumstances required. The singing planet in Ex. 22-6—a brilliant *ariette* to greet a new heavenly constellation—is from Rameau's *Castor et Pollux*, part of the *fête de l'univers* decreed by Jupiter. It embodies a kind of singing otherwise uncalled for in the opera—one that, while eminently theatrical, is essentially foreign to the dramatic purposes of the *tragédie lyrique* and therefore only suitable for an undramatic ornamental moment in a divertissement.

The resplendent general impression to which this coldly dazzling ariette contributed took precedence over the personality of any particular participant. The concert of myriad forces in perfect harness under the aegis of a mastermind was the real message, whatever the story. While even the prejudiced Saint-Evremond had to admit that "no man can perform better than Lully upon an ill-conceived subject," he turned it into a barb: "I don't question but that in operas at the Palace-Royal, Lully is 100 times more thought of than

EX. 22-6 Jean-Philippe Rameau, *Castor et Pollux*, Act V, ariette, *Brillez, brillez astres nouveaux*

EX. 22-6 (*continued*)

Theseus or Cadmus," his mythological heroes. But that was all right, since the king was even more thought of than Lully.

Rameau's planetary *ariette* shows the influence of a later Italian style than Lully could have known. (We will give it fuller consideration when we turn to the operas of Alessandro Scarlatti and George Frederick Handel.) In a sense it belongs to another age; but although Rameau is obviously later than Lully, and novel enough to have inspired resistance, he is not essentially dif-

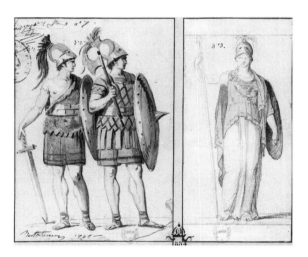

FIG. 22-6 Costume designs for Rameau's *Castor et Pollux* (1737).

ferent; and that is important to keep in mind. The eighteenth-century philosopher Denis Diderot had it right when he called Lully *Monsieur Ut–mi–ut–sol* (C–E–C–G)—roughly, "Mr. Music"—but called Rameau *Monsieur Utremifasollasiututut* (CDEFGABCCC)![12] For the Rameau style was the Lully style advanced—in no way challenged, but intensified: richer in harmony, more sumptuous in sonority, more laden in texture, more heroic in rhythm and rhetoric, more impressively masterminded than ever.

When André Campra said of the fifty-year-old Rameau's first opera that it contained enough music for ten operas, he did not mean it as a compliment. That same opera, *Hyppolite et Aricie* (1733), was the very first musical work to which the adjective "baroque" was attached, and as we know, that was no compliment either. Rameau's prodigality of invention and complexity of style were taken by some as a hubris, a representation of personal power and therefore a *lèse-majesté* (an affront to the sovereign), offensive not only to the memory of the great founder, whose works were in effect the first true "classics" in the history of music, sacramentally perpetuated in repertory, but also to what the founder's style had memorialized.

Indeed, if (as we have done) one compares Lully's dulcet *Atys* of 1676 with Rameau's pungent, even violent *Castor et Pollux* of 1737, one can experience a bit of a shock—until one reckons that the span of time separating these two works is greater than the span that separates Palestrina's *Missa Papae Marcelli* from Monteverdi's *Combattimento di Tancredi e Clorinda* (or, more recently, Bach's Mass in B Minor from Beethoven's "Eroica" Symphony, or Verdi's *Il Trovatore* from Stravinsky's *Rite of Spring*). Then the shock of the new gives way to amazement at the hold of tradition, a hold that testifies first of all to the potency of administrative centralism and absolute political authority.

The real challenge, to look ahead briefly, came about fifteen years later, with the so-called *Guerre des Bouffons*, the "War of the Buffoons," an endless press debate that followed the first performances of Italian commercial opera in Paris, when the French court opera received, according to the great philosopher Jean-Jacques Rousseau, "a blow from which it never recovered."[13] Rousseau was a dilettante composer in addition to being a philosopher, and he had an interest in seeing the grand machinery of the official French style, with which he could never hope to cope, replaced with the sketchy "natural" spontaneity of the Italians. He even rode the coattails of the Italians in Paris to some popular success with his own little rustic one-acter called *Le Devin du village* ("The village soothsayer").

But of course Rousseau was much more than a musician, and his intense interest in the War of the Buffoons suggests that much more than music was at stake. Historians now agree that what seems a ludicrously inflated press scuffle about opera was in fact a coded episode, and an important one, in the ongoing battle between political absolutism and Enlightenment that raged throughout the eighteenth century. As always, the Italian commercial opera—epitomized this time by a farce (we'll take a close look at it later) in which a plucky maidservant cows and dominates her master, subverting the social hierarchy it was the business of the French opera to affirm—exemplified and stimulated the politics of opposition.

ART AND POLITICS: SOME CAVEATS

The political conflict embodied or symbolized in the War of the Buffoons has a great deal of resonance for contemporary politics, or so one might be inclined to think, and for American politics in particular. The basic philosophical contradiction eventually transcended philosophy and passed into political action, culminating in revolutions not only in France, the original site of operatic contention, but in the American colonies as well. The anti-aristocratic, egalitarian ideals expressed in America's foundational documents, the Constitution and (especially) the Declaration of Independence, arose precisely out of the political ferment adumbrated by the War of the Buffoons. The *tragédies en musique* of the *grand siècle* speak eloquently for a social order unalterably opposed to every principle Americans are supposed to hold dear.

And yet we are not likely to be any more troubled by the political content or implication of these works — at least while listening to them — than we are likely to be troubled on hearing "popish ditties" like the Missa Papae Marcelli if we are Protestants (as long as we do not hear them in church). Nor are we apt to be troubled by our equanimity when (as now) it is pointed out. But why should that be so? Why does our appreciation of such works now tend to be almost completely nonpolitical, when their political content was so much a part of their original meaning and value?

Answers to these questions are not simple; indeed, they are questions with which we will have to struggle repeatedly from this point on, just as composers and listeners have struggled with them ever since the notion — the ever-expanding notion — of modern participatory politics (or democracy, as we call it now) was born. Suffice it to say at this point that the answers will have to do both with the artworks with which we engage and with ourselves. Since the nineteenth century the concept both of "the work of art" and of its social import have changed radically.

Once the idea of autonomous art, existing in some sense for its own sake, was born, the tendency has been to apply it to all art that we value. We tend therefore not to expect works of "classical music" to engage with political or social issues, even if they did so at an earlier phase of their history. We are often content to enjoy it and not ask questions. And yet opera — a genre that contains much more than music, and that so often engages explicitly with political and social issues to this day — remains a somewhat ambiguous category. It is hard to regard it wholly as art for art's sake.

So if we are not troubled by the art of the *ancien régime* and its absolutist politics — politics that would have consigned the vast majority of those who now enjoy that art to what we would certainly now regard as a miserable existence — it must also be because we no longer regard the figure of Louis XIV or his policies as politically active agents. The War of the Buffoons is over, we are apt to think, and Louis lost. He and his despotic policies are "history"; they do not threaten us. His victims (as we would now define them) are all dead, along with those who mourn them, and we take no umbrage at an art that glorifies his power.

When dealing with more recent despotisms — Nazi Germany, for example, or Soviet Russia, whose victims are still remembered keenly and with anguish — some remain disinclined to regard the art that glorified them as entirely innocent or politically denatured. Studying history, moreover, makes it harder to ignore the fact that it was the political absolutism they celebrated that gave the practitioners of French court music (and Lully above all) the right to institute in their own artistic sphere their own tyrannical exercise of power. Absolute authority — especially as vested in choral and, later, orchestral conductors — has remained part of the ethos of musical performance in the West long after it disappeared from the political scene. Only recently, in fact, has it been moderated by the advent of labor unions representing musicians.

Moreover, whereas modern Protestants, living in societies that have long protected their rights, or where they make up the majority population, may not regard the messages of Counter Reformation art as threatening, it may be a different matter with today's minority populations. There is a great deal of Christian art, even very old Christian art, that makes modern Jews uncomfortable; there is a great deal of Western art that deals troublingly with "oriental" peoples; and there is much music, now regarded as "classical," set to texts deriding the rights of women, the elderly, the handicapped, and so on.

We will encounter many examples as we continue our story into the modern age. It is important, at least in a book like this, to take the opportunity historical discussion grants us to air these matters dispassionately. As we are nearing the beginning of the age of modern politics, it seems the right time to raise the issue and make a couple of cautionary observations. One is that it may not be wise simply to assume that an artwork's status as "classical" is enough to render it politically and socially innocuous. Another is that the impulse to dismiss such considerations as mere sanctimony or "political correctness" may be similarly imprudent.

In today's society, it may not be superfluous to observe, the charge of "political correctness" is almost invariably made by members of privileged groups against the claims and concerns of the less privileged. It is a way of warding off threats to privilege. "Classical music," like all "high art," has always been, and remains, primarily a possession of social and cultural elites. (That, after all, is what makes it "high.") This is so even in a society like ours, where social mobility is greater than in most societies, and where entry into elites can come about for reasons (like education, for example) that may be unrelated to birth or wealth. To maintain that "classical music" is by nature (or by definition) apolitical is therefore a complacent position to assume, and a rather parlous one. Complacency in support of a not universally supported status quo can serve, in today's world, to marginalize and even discredit both the practice and the appreciation of art. With these matters explicitly raised and fresh in mind, we may return to our historical narrative with heightened awareness, perhaps, of their ubiquitous implicit presence.

Our next topic, the fate of music (and particularly of opera) in England during the seventeenth century, will underscore with special intensity the relationship between high art and the fortunes of social and political elites. It will also help delineate the difference between the elite attitudes of yesterday and those of today. The hereditary elites of old regarded art as something "there for them" — something that was at their disposal, that awaited their pleasure. The cultural and intellectual elites of today often seem to regard art with a respect formerly reserved for the holy and the mighty. High art has been placed on a pedestal, and we, so to speak, are there for it. And in this attitude of submission to art we have perhaps identified another rationale for our curious habit of purging the notion of art of its social and political component: we now think of art as bigger than its patrons.

These notions are recent, they are virtually restricted to "the West," and they are decidedly odd when placed in a historical or a global context. But they are the ones most of us have grown up with, and so they can seem "natural" to us. To see them historically means seeing them as strange. Observing a radically different scale of values at work can help us achieve detachment from the familiar and better evaluate our acceptance of it.

JACOBEAN ENGLAND

Whether courtly or commercial, opera (or, for that matter, any full-blown music in the theater) simply did not take hold in England for most of the seventeenth century. "Spoken drama with musical decorations" was about as far as the English were prepared to go. Shakespeare's plays made provision for a bit of incidental music, not only in occasional popular-song texts — for instance "It was a lover and his lass, with a hey and a ho and a hey nonny no" from *Twelfth Night*, of which Thomas Morley made a still-famous setting — but also in the stage directions, which call for trumpets, "hautboys" (high woodwinds, or what would later become oboes), and so on, playing "alarums" (signals for attention), or "sennets and tuckets" (flourishes and "toccatas," as Monteverdi called them). And a stronger case of the same prejudice that prevented the French from tolerating a virtuoso aria from the mouth of a major character prevented the English from tolerating any music at all from such a mouth. Dramatic "verisimilitude" — sheer believability — would not stretch that far in England. Music, when used at all in the theater, was consigned to the gaudy periphery.

MASQUE AND CONSORT

During the early Stuart reigns — called the "Jacobean" period after James I (reigned 1603–25), the Scottish king whose ascent to the throne of England created what is now officially known as the "United Kingdom" — music found its chief theatrical outlet in dance entertainments called masques, which lay somewhere between a costume ball and the prologue to an early Italian or (especially) French court opera. The name of the genre recalls its early link with mummery — masked ceremonial and carnival dancing. By the time of James I such entertainments were organized around mythological or allegorical plots in praise of the ruler or some aristocratic patron. (One early Jacobean masque took as its theme "The Virtues of Tobacco," recently imported to England from the New World colonies and thought to have medicinal properties.) The participants were noble amateurs, who often selected dance partners from the audience for a central episode (or "entry," from the French *entrée*) called "revels," that amounted to a suite of plotless social dances.

The chief Jacobean masque-maker was the playwright Ben Jonson (1572–1637), whom James I chose as "Master of the Revels" before elevating him in 1617 to become the first British poet laureate. The few individual songs and dances that survive from Jonson's masques were mainly the work of James's stable of court composers, including Robert Johnson (ca. 1583–1633), Thomas Campion (1567–1620), Alfonso Ferrabosco II (ca. 1575–1628), and John Cooper (alias Coprario, d. 1626). The closest the Jacobean masque ever came to opera was Jonson's *Lovers made Men* of 1617, in which the music, by Nicholas Lanier (1588–1666), was "sung after the Italian manner, *stilo recitativo*," according to the published libretto. The music does not survive, however, and so it is impossible to say how continuous it really was.

It is also difficult to say how much masque music survives in the many Jacobean manuscripts that contain dances for lute or for "consorts" (or as we would say, ensembles) of viols. The great profusion of Jacobean instrumental music, especially consort music, compared with the relative paucity of vocal or theatrical music, seems a reliable guide to the musical tastes of the period no matter how low a survival rate we assume. Jacobean England may well have been the earliest European society to value instrumental music more highly than vocal. The preference was as much a social as an esthetic indicator.

Jacobean consort music was, in effect, the earliest instrumental chamber music. It had its forerunners, chiefly in northern Italy—the instrumental chanson reworkings published by Petrucci, the ensemble ricercars and canzonas of sixteenth-century Venice, and so on. But the English repertory was not only larger and more varied than these; it also came much closer to our modern idea of what chamber music is. Although "chamber music" performance in our own time has by now been thoroughly professionalized and takes place as much or more on the concert stage than it does in homes, the idea of chamber music originally implied private conviviality. In chamber music, audience and performers are ideally one.

Thus it was in its origins a wholly secular art and largely a domestic one, without significant or necessary social ties to the contemporary court or church (although, as we shall see, there were some residual musical ties to the latter). It was an art addressed to amateurs and connoisseurs, implying privacy and leisure, and ultimately affluence. But its uniqueness lay in the fact that it was an art not primarily of noblemen or courtiers but one of "gentlemen"—aristocrats of commerce and education rather than by way of birthright. Only England had a class of this kind—"self-made men" (though not yet a "bourgeoisie" since they resided for the most part on country estates)—sufficiently numerous and developed to support a distinct musical subculture.

One of the best descriptions of this musical subculture was written by Roger North (1651–1734), a latter-day member or descendent of the class that nurtured it. He belonged to a very distinguished family, a few of whose members held baronies, estates that carried with them minor titles of nobility. The untitled members of the clan distinguished themselves in learning, in trade, and in civil service. Roger North spent his early years in law and politics, holding the offices of solicitor general to the Duke of York and attorney general to the queen consort of King James II. His elder brothers had even more distinguished careers. One, Sir Dudley North (1641–91), amassed a huge personal fortune in trade with the Ottoman Empire and, not altogether surprisingly, became an important early advocate of laissez-faire economics ("free trade").

Roger North was rather early excluded from politics as a result of the "Glorious Revolution" of 1688 that dislodged the Stuart dynasty from the throne, and he spent the rest of his life as a country squire and scholar with a special interest in music. In this he followed in the footsteps of his grandfather, Dudley, the third Lord North, an exemplary Jacobean gentleman who

> took a fancy to a wood he had about a mile from his house, called Bansteads, situated in a dirty soil, and of ill access. But he cut glades, and made arbors in it. Here he would convoke his musical family, and songs were made and set for celebrating the joys there, which were performed, and provisions carried up for more important regale of the company. The consorts were usually all viols to the organ or harpsichord . . . . When the hands were well supplied, then a whole chest went to work, that is six viols, music being formed for it; which would seem a strange sort of music now . . . [14]

Indeed, it was even by the time Sir Roger wrote a somewhat strange sort of music, and one that has long attracted the special interest of musical sociologists.[15] It was a socially and politically "progressive" repertory in that it was cultivated by very early members of an entrepreneurial class that, over the next couple of centuries, would challenge the power of the aristocracy all over Europe and that appears to us now as the truest harbinger of the capitalist or "free market" societies of the modern world. At the same time, it was stylistically about the most conservative repertory to be found anywhere in the world. That very combination — economic libertarianism and cultural conservatism — characterizes "business" attitudes to this day.

The two main genres of Jacobean consort music were both inherited directly from the Elizabethan, and even pre-Elizabethan, past. The fantasy or fancy as it was colloquially known (or "fantazia," to give the more formal designation found in the musical sources) was, in North's unimprovable phrase, an "interwoven hum-drum" made up of successive points of imitation — known as *fantazies*, as we know, since the fifteenth century — occasionally relieved by chordal writing. In other words, it was a textless motet.

Thomas Morley, writing at the end of the sixteenth century, called it "the chiefest kind of music which is made without a ditty," that is, without words, and emphasized the freedom that this gave the composer, who "taketh a point at his pleasure and wresteth and turneth it as he list, making either much or little of it according as shall seem best in his own conceit," so that "in this may more art be shown than in any other music because the composer is tied to nothing, but that he may add, diminish, and alter at his pleasure." Morley's description, with its enthusiastic emphasis on freedom of enterprise, is consistent with the social status of the genre, even in Morley's day a gentleman's occupation par excellence, and also consistent with Morley's own status as England's foremost musical entrepreneur.

The genre's extreme stylistic conservatism — conservatism in the most literal, etymological sense of "keeping old things" — can be dramatically illustrated by focusing on one of its most popular subgenres, a special type of fancy called the "In Nomine." The odd name, which means "in the name of," is derived from the text of the Mass Sanctus ("Benedictus qui venit *in nomine* Domini".) Indeed, the instrumental genre goes back to a particularly grand and venerable English cantus-firmus Mass, John Taverner's six-voice *Missa Gloria tibi Trinitas*, based on a pre-Reformation (Sarum) Vespers antiphon for

Trinity Sunday, "Glory to thee, O Trinity." Taverner probably composed the Mass around 1528. The chant-derived cantus firmus from the *In nomine* section of Taverner's Sanctus, scored for a reduced complement of four solo voices (already given in Ex. 15-8), became the ever-present cantus firmus for the whole repertory of instrumental *In Nomines*, a repertory numbering in the hundreds and practiced for almost a century and a half after Taverner's death in 1545.

How did such an improbable tradition get started? Although Taverner's original *In nomine* was copied out for instruments and is found in many manuscripts containing fancies, the instrumental *In Nomine* repertory as such evidently goes back to Christopher Tye (ca. 1505–73), an Elizabethan composer best known for his Anglican hymns and anthems, who wrote no fewer than twenty-one *In Nomine* fancies (mostly in five parts) over Taverner's cantus firmus as a sort of sideline or hobby. As usual with a big series of similar pieces, the composer eventually began to show off his craft by indulging in various sorts of gimmicks.

One of his *In Nomines*, for example, called "Crye," has a subject consisting of a series of rapid repeated notes that mimic a street vendor's cry. (Weaving plebeian "Cries of London" or "Country Cries" into the otherwise abstract texture of viol fancies was another standard subgenre that amused the gentlemen patrons of the medium.) Another, called "Howld Fast" (i.e., "hang on") casts the Taverner cantus firmus in dotted semibreves that crosscut the implied meter of the other parts. Yet another, called "Trust," is cast in what we would now call a $\frac{5}{4}$ meter (Ex. 22-7).

E X. 22-7A   Christopher Tye, *In Nomines*, "Crye" (opening)

EX. 22-7B   Christopher Tye, *In Nomines*, "Howld Fast" (opening)

EX. 22-7C   Christopher Tye, *In Nomines*, "Trust" (opening)

As in the case of the "L'Homme Armé" Masses of the previous century (described in chapter 12), Tye's prolific output of *In Nomines*, both technically impressive and whimsical, seems to have stimulated the emulatory impulse that led to the creation of the genre. The great upsurge of interest in consort music during the Jacobean years led to a flood tide in which every composer of fancies participated. The aged William Byrd composed seven *In Nomines*, a total exceeded only by Tye himself. After Byrd, the next most prolific *In Nomine* composer was Alfonso Ferrabosco II, the English-born son of Byrd's early Italian motet mentor, who composed six, of which three were scored for the full "chest" of six viols, thought not only by North but by all contemporary writers to be the ideal consort medium: "your best provision (and most complete)," in the words of Thomas Mace, seventeenth-century England's most encyclopedic theorist, who specified that a "good chest of viols" were "six in number, 2 Basses, 2 Tenors, 2 Trebles, all truly proportionably suited."[16] As time went on and the tradition developed, the style of writing became increasingly idiomatic and "instrumental," further belying the genre's vocal, ecclesiastical origins.

The *In Nomine* by Ferrabosco excerpted in Ex. 22-8, which dates from around 1625, is scored for just such a full complement of viols (Fig. 22-7). The old cantus firmus (cf. Ex. 15-8) is given, rather unusually, to one of the treble viols, and was probably played by a novice on the instrument. (The inevitable presence of a part playable by a child has been counted one of the reasons for the *In Nomine*'s popularity, given the family surroundings in which English consorts were apt to be played.) Meanwhile, the other parts converse motet-fashion, approaching, toward the end, the kind of "perpetuall intermiscuous syncopations and halvings of notes" that North cited as one of the chief pleasures of the genre.

The bass viols, in particular, are given some elaborate "divisions" to play during the last point of imitation; these reflect the solo repertoire that was also growing up at the time, which mainly consisted of bass viols doing what contemporary musicians called

EX. 22-8   Alfonso Ferrabosco II, *In Nomine a 6*

EX. 22-8 (continued)

FIG. 22-7 A chest of viols (the ensemble near the right), shown in an anonymous painting (ca. 1596) of the wedding masque for Sir Henry Unton, Queen Elizabeth's special envoy to the French court.

"breaking a base": performing ever more elaborate variations over a ground. Like most virtuoso repertories, that of the "division viol" was as much an improvisatory practice as a literate one. (Its greatest exponent was a gentleman virtuoso named Christopher Simpson, who published a treatise on the subject, called *The Divisionviolist, or the Art of Playing Extempore upon a Ground*, in 1659). The consort fancy, however, depended entirely on writing for its dissemination and performance. It represents positively the last outpost of what on the continent had already been consigned once and for all to the "first practice" or *stile antico*: a final wordless flowering of the motet, and even, in the case of the *In Nomine*, of traditional cantus-firmus composition.

AYRES AND SUITES: HARMONICALLY DETERMINED FORM

The other main genre of consort music was the "ayre," a general term no longer meaning a song, but rather any sort of dance-style composition. (Its etymology was chiefly by way of the "lute ayre," which in the hands of Dowland, as we saw in chapter 17, usually took the form of a pavane or galliard with two or three repeated strains.) The later composers of consort music tended to write their pieces in "setts" that began with one or two numbers in the more elaborate fancy form and concluded more lightly with an ayre or two. The ayre by William Lawes, whose ending is shown in Ex. 22-9, is the final item in what the key signature of two flats already identifies as an unusually serious set: on the way to it there are two lengthy fantasies and an "Inominy," all in what we would call the key of C minor. (In the seventeenth century minor keys with flats generally carried "Dorian" signatures, that is, with one less flat than their modern counterparts; flatting of the sixth degree was usually done at sight, by applying already ancient rules of chromatic adjustment.)

This ayre, which is really an *alman* or allemande ("German dance"; cf. Frescobaldi's *balletto*) in a dignified duple meter, is cast in a form that will remain with us for centuries to come. Its two dance strains make cadences respectively on the dominant (replete with borrowed leading tone) and tonic, producing an effect of harmonic (or "tonal") complementation. This "there and back" or "to and fro" effect was immediately found to be an exceedingly stable and satisfying plan for structuring a composition. Indeed, the very concept of autonomous musical "structure" was in large part enabled by the seemingly inherent coherence of this complementary (or "binary") harmonic relationship. The binary form, originally associated, as here, with dance-derived compositions, would undergo a glorious evolution that quickly transcended the utilitarian genre in which it originated and provided the basis for what has long been known as "absolute music."

That evolution, of course, lay largely in the future when Lawes composed his "setts," but his use of the binary form already entailed a good deal of "transcendence of the utilitarian." The genre of chamber music is itself an embodiment of transcendence, since its constituent genres — the motet-derived fantasy, the Mass-derived *In Nomine*, the dance-derived ayre — have all been thoroughly divested of their original functions and have become the bearers of abstract or "absolute" tonal patterns for performing or for listening (or, ideally, for both at once) as a form of social recreation.

Yet "abstract" or "absolute" by no means precluded a high level of purposeful expressivity. Flat keys, as we have observed, already connoted pathos, and Lawes followed through with pungent suspension dissonances in the first strain and chromatic inflections in the second (including a really acrid augmented triad in the third measure of Ex. 22-9). These "madrigalisms" without a motivating text show the tardy but inexorable infiltration of what the Italians called *seconda prattica* effects into the consort repertory.

EX. 22-9   William Lawes, Ayre in six parts

Lawes (1602–45), whose career reached its peak under Charles I, King James's son and successor, cultivated a highly pathetic style in all his works, as a few of his expressively contorted fantazia themes will vividly attest, their wide leaps and striking arpeggiations seeming to parallel the "mannerist" elongations and foreshortenings of an El Greco torso (Ex. 22-10). Lawes's remarkably "purple" manner made the already idiosyncratic mixture of old and new in the English consort idiom seem all the more noteworthy and bizarre. Some accounts of Lawes' spectacular "manneristic" tendencies attribute them to sheer composerly appetites and creative genius; others have sought the origins of the style in broader historical and political conditions. But there is no reason to regard these alternatives as incompatible. Like everyone else, musicians respond to varying degrees, and with varying degrees of consciousness, to historical and political conditions; but — perhaps needless to say — musicians also respond, and respond with the keenest consciousness, to music.

EX. 22-10A   William Lawes, fantazia themes, Suite in G Minor

EX. 22-10B   William Lawes, Suite in C Minor in five parts

EX. 22-10C   William Lawes, Suite in C Major (two variants)

EX. 22-10D   William Lawes, Suite in C Minor in six parts

DISTRACTED TIMES

The broader historical and political conditions to which musicians of the mid-seventeenth century perforce responded are reflected deliberately and directly in "A Sad Pavan for These Distracted Times" by Thomas Tomkins, originally for keyboard but transcribed for strings as well (Ex. 22-11). Tomkins (1572–1656), formerly organist of the Chapel Royal, was one of the oldest English musicians still alive and semi-active during the times in question.

EX. 22-11 Thomas Tomkins, "A Sad Pavan for These Distracted Times"

The phrase "these distracted times" was a standard contemporary euphemism for the greatest political upheaval in British history: the Civil War of 1642–48 that culminated in the trial of King Charles I for treason and his beheading on 30 January 1649, after which a republican form of government, called the Commonwealth, was instituted under the nominal rule of Parliament, but in actuality under the personal dictatorship of Oliver Cromwell, the leader of the Puritan party, who in 1653 took the title of Lord Protector. Tomkin's Sad Pavan bears the date 16 February 1649, roughly a fortnight after the regicide, and its tone bears witness to his loyalty and his sorrow at his former patron's fate.

Although it is often called the Puritan Revolt, the English Civil War is no longer thought of as a primarily religious conflict. Historians now view it as a collision between the country gentry and urban merchants (the very classes whose support had made possible the growth of English chamber music) on the one hand, and the crown and nobility on the other, whose restrictive trade policies were inhibiting the economic growth of the self-made classes. The most lasting result of the Civil War was the victory of the "common law" over the so-called divine right of the king and the eventual establishment (after the Glorious Revolution of 1688) of the world's first constitutional monarchy.

Despite the popularity of their chamber music among the classes who broke with the crown, the loyalties of composers, as of all artists and entertainers, were overwhelmingly on the royalist side, for that is where artists and entertainers dependent on patronage had always perceived their self-interest to lie, and that must account in part for the elegiac tone that is so conspicuous in the instrumental music of the Caroline years, the years of King Charles's ill-fated reign. In the exaggerated but colorful words of the mid-nineteenth-century historian Thomas Macaulay, "the Puritan austerity drove to the King's faction all who made pleasure their business, who affected gallantry, splendour of dress or taste in the lighter arts, and all who live by amusing the leisure of others, . . . for these artists well knew that they might thrive under a superb and luxurious despotism, but must starve under the rigid rule of the precisians [religious ascetics]."[17]

Indeed, one of the casualties of these tumultuous events was William Lawes himself, who fought and died in the 1645 Siege of Chester, one of the King's signal defeats. As the very partisan poet Thomas Jordan put it in a eulogy for the fallen musician,

> When pestilential Purity did raise
> Rebellion 'gainst the best of Princes, And
> Pious Confusion had untun'd the Land
> When by the Fury of the Good old cause
> Will Lawes was slain by such whose Wills were
> Laws.[18]

Puritan hostility to the arts, and to music in particular, is often exaggerated. Unlike the early Anglicans they did not instigate search-and-destroy missions against musical artifacts. But of course the absence of a royal court, both under the republican

Commonwealth and under the military dictatorship (Cromwell's Protectorate) that succeeded it in the 1650s, meant that patronage for musicians reached an all-time low. As Calvinists, the Puritans did not tolerate an elaborate professional church music, and so the musical establishments of the Church of England reached a low musical point as well, and the most exalted of British musical traditions suffered disruption and virtual extinction. The Puritans were indeed hostile to the theater, and from 1649 to 1660 closed it down in England; but as we have seen, musical theater had failed to establish itself in England for reasons unrelated to the fall of the royal court or the rise of the Puritan party to power.

RESTORATION

The fortunes of music in England, and of theatrical music in particular, took a decisive turn with the Stuart Restoration, the reestablishment of the British monarchy less than a dozen years after its abolition. Charles II, the 30-year-old son of the deposed king, was summoned back from France, where he had been exiled (with interludes in Germany and the Netherlands) since 1646, and crowned in 1660. A shrewd diplomat and skillful politician, Charles II reigned relatively peacefully until 1685, the last three years actually as an absolute monarch without a parliament, but—in marked contrast with this father—a very popular despot. One of the sources of his popularity was the cosmopolitan, libertine character of his court, a most welcome contrast with the times that had gone before. It was a court where (in the waggish words of Keith Walker, a literary historian), "anything went, where actresses were regularly rogered, where whores were ennobled to duchesses, where the arts flourished, where if greed wasn't yet good, hypocrisy certainly was."[19]

In its very cynicism, this sentence neatly encapsulates the contemporary attitude toward the arts and their place in the Restoration scheme of things. No matter how heroic or serious their content, they were viewed and cultivated as an aspect of luxurious living on a par with other sensual and gustatory delights. That hedonism, tinged as it was with licentiousness, may seem to us attractive enough; but in the context of seventeenth-century England it meant a resurgence of aristocratic tastes, values, mores, and privileges. We have another choice example of the beneficial effect of absolutist politics—an ugly politics, most would agree today—on the growth of the fine arts; and again the question starts nagging, whether the élite arts that we treasure can truly flourish in a political climate that we would approve.

Having spent his late adolescence and early adulthood in France, Charles naturally modeled his idea of kingship not on his tragically aborted father but on his near contemporary (and distant cousin) Louis XIV, for whom song, dance, and theater were both a political symbol and a personal passion. Where the first Charles "had insisted on the divine rights of a king, and the sanctity of his office," and paid for his insistence with his very life, Charles II, the little sun-king, "lent his coronation robes to the players in the recently re-established playhouse," as Walker reminds us, and counted many of them among his friends and intimates. He famously fathered two sons by the actress Nell Gwynn, the leading lady of the London stage and the most celebrated of his many

FIG. 22-8 Eleanor (Nell) Gwynn, seventeenth-century English comic actress, as Cupid. She was the mistress of Charles II.

mistresses. Leaving behind no legitimate offspring, he was succeeded by his brother, James II, a confessed Catholic whose short and troubled reign was cut short by the Glorious Revolution that finally put an end to absolutist politics in England.

This was the atmosphere that conditioned the "Restoration period," the brilliant rebirth of English art and literature — and music, too, but on a new footing. The theater that Charles II reestablished and revived was, to an extent previously unimaginable in England, a musical (or better, a musicalized) theater. While opera as such remained with a few equivocal exceptions beyond the pale, virtually all plays featured specially composed musical scores (what is now called "incidental music"), often the work of teams or committees of composers. They consisted typically of a French-style overture, dances and jigs (the latter being not a specific dance but a song-and-dance medley), songs (chiefly for minor or allegorical characters), and instrumental curtain-music ("act tunes") for the end of each act. No more sad pavans would be composed in England — in fact no more pavans or galliards of any kind. The Restoration at last brought English music up-to-date vis-à-vis the continent.

In addition, most Restoration plays included masques of a much more elaborate type than their Elizabethan or Jacobean predecessors. Restoration masques were extended song-and-dance interludes — sometimes with spoken dialogue, sometimes with recitatives, often only tenuously related or even unrelated to the main plot but (unlike the Renaissance *intermedii*) with well-defined dramatic plots of their own. At their most elaborate they could amount to virtual one-act operas or opera-ballets. An especially resonant example of the type was the masque interpolated into the fourth act of *The Empress of Morocco*, a heroic drama by Elkanah Settle, the Lord Poet of London, first performed at the royally patronized Duke's Theater in Lincoln's Inn (later called the Dorset Garden) in 1673. It took the form of a miniature Venetian-style opera on the time-honored subject of Orpheus and Eurydice.

Its composer was Matthew Locke (ca. 1622–77), who seems already to have been in Charles's employ during his Netherlands exile, and who became the leading stage musician of the early Restoration period. Equally adept at dance compositions in the French manner and recitatives in the Italian, Locke was the virtual inventor of a peculiarly English mixed genre called the "dramatick opera" (or "semi-opera," as it is now usually called) in collaboration with the playwright Thomas Shadwell and Thomas Betterton, the manager of Dorset Garden, who had seen Lully's works in Paris and wanted to create something comparable for the suddenly ready English market.

Semi-operas, in effect, were *comedies-ballets* or *tragédies lyriques* adapted to the tastes, and above all to the longstanding prejudices, of the English theatergoing public. To the decorative songs and dances and instrumental tunes of the masque, now present in greater profusion than ever, was added the spectacular stage machinery for which the French court opera was particularly renowned. The major compromise was the insistence that major characters never sing, following the old pre-Lullian prejudice (quoted earlier in this chapter from Pierre Corneille) that sung words are poorly understood, and that therefore a sung drama could not really be a drama but only a concert in costume. The result was a peculiar split between protagonists who never sang and incidental characters who only sang, making the new genre quite literally a semi-sung play.

Some of the most celebrated semi-operas were adaptations of Shakespeare — or, rather, readaptations of the lightweight Shakespeare adaptations, often by poet laureate John Dryden, that were standard on the Restoration stage. The first major success was *The Tempest* (1674), in which Ariel was the main singing character. The music was supplied by a committee of five, headed by Locke. Perhaps the greatest and most ambitious "dramatick opera" — certainly the most lavish and expensive according to Curtis Price, the leading historian of the early English musical stage — was *The Fairy Queen*, based on an anonymous adaptation (probably Betterton's) of *A Midsummer Night's Dream*.[20] It was produced at Dorset Garden in 1692, with music by a former pupil of Locke named Henry Purcell.

PURCELL

Chiefly employed as an organist (first at Westminster Abbey and later at the Chapel Royal), Purcell (1659–95) was as close to an all-round musical genius, within the practices of his day and the institutions he served, as England has ever produced. He excelled in every genre, from Anthems and Services and royal odes and "welcome songs" — these being the genres he was officially employed to produce — to instrumental chamber music and harpsichord pieces. For the London stage he produced songs and instrumental pieces for more than forty plays between 1680, his twenty-first year, and 1695, the year of his untimely and much-mourned death.

An idea of his brash and pungent style, and that of Restoration theater music generally, is startlingly conveyed by his Overture in D minor (Ex. 22-12), a work that must

FIG. 22-9   Henry Purcell by John Closterman (1695). This painting, now in the National Portrait Gallery, London, served as a prototype for the frontispiece engraving in *Orpheus Britannicus* (1698), a posthumous collection of Purcell's songs.

have started life as a dramatic curtain-raiser but that is now found only as a free-standing composition for four stringed instrument parts and continuo. The play, one tends (perhaps naively) to think, must have been a tragedy, for the dissonance level is remarkably high. In the first measure, for example, both violin parts skip down from a seventh that is itself approached by skip; in the fourth and fifth measures, every beat carries brusque suspensions between the outer parts (seventh–ninth–seventh–ninth) that are resolved only on the fourth sixteenth, which in the French style is performed extra short; in the sixth measure a seventh between the outer voices is resolved through a chromatic "escape tone"; and so on. The part writing is so forcefully directed, however, that long-range harmonic goals are never lost sight of; instead, the dissonances, especially when they occur in sequential passages, impel the harmony on its way with special vigor.

Chromatic writing not only enhances the sense of pathos but also the remarkable thrust with which Purcell propels the part writing toward the main cadences. The ending of the first section of the overture is expedited (Ex. 22-12a) by an amazing chromatic ascent that leads (albeit with a couple of breaks) through an eleventh (an octave plus a fourth); as it nears its climax it is joined by a chromatic descent in the bass from tonic down to dominant (the familiar *passus duriusculus*), which is decorated with neighbor notes whose resolutions contradict the direction of the overall line and lend an extra sense of effort to the "difficult pass." The middle section seems to hark back to the motetlike fantazia (of which Purcell had written several outstanding specimens in his prentice days) in its use of two successive points of imitation instead of the single-subject fugato favored by Lully and his successors. The final section reverts not only to the original tempo but also to the original tone of high pathos. Every instrument gets to subside through a moaning diminished fifth (as indicated by brackets), and the outer parts are given veritable sequences of chromatic plunges (Ex. 22-12b). Purcell's pompous theatrical style is a far cry from the immediate expressivity of Lawes or Tomkins, however. Stage music strikes showy attitudes of sentiment rather than, as in the earlier chamber style, speaking intimately or "subjectively" and stirring sympathy.

The Fairy Queen was Purcell's third "dramatick opera," commissioned from him by Betterton's theater after Purcell had become without dispute the star composer of the London stage. In addition to the overture and entr'actes (suites of act tunes), the score

EX. 22-12A   Henry Purcell, Overture in D Minor, beginning

EX. 22-12A (continued)

EX. 22-12B Henry Purcell, Overture in D Minor, end

consists entirely of interpolated masques, one per act. As first performed in 1692, these began in act II with a Masque of Sleep (compare the French *sommeil* as in Ex. 22-4c) to follow title character Titania's request for a lullabye entertainment. Purcell might have set Shakespeare's own "Fairies Song" ("Ye spotted Snakes...."), but instead he was given by his librettist a far more elaborate scene in which two fairy choruses are followed by sleep-inducing songs by the spirits of Night, Mystery, and Secrecy, and a final air with chorus to depict the actual onset of sleep.

Secrecy's song, "One charming night," with ritornello for obbligato recorders (*flûtes douces*), is set for a male alto voice, modeled perhaps on the French *haute-contre* but sung in the "head voice" or "falsetto" range throughout (Ex. 22-13). This peculiarly English voice category, called "countertenor" in England since the seventeenth century, has been universalized in the twentieth century by the "early music" revival, following the precedent set by the widely imitated English falsettist Alfred Deller (1912–79), who made a remarkable recording of Secrecy's song.

In act III the masque consists of an entertainment called up by Titania to entertain ass-headed Bottom, with whom she is temporarily enamored. In act IV a Masque of Four Seasons is ordered by Oberon, the Fairy King, to celebrate his reconciliation with his spouse, and in act V the Masque, ordered by Juno herself to entertain the two pairs of human lovers, provides a brilliant finale to the whole spectacle. (It sports a florid

EX. 22-13 Henry Purcell, *The Fairy Queen*, Act II masque, Secrecy's song

trumpet aria, "Hark! the ech'ing air," that dazzlingly imitates the very latest Italian fashions.) It is characteristic of the semi-opera that, although he might well have done so (or so it seems to us), Purcell did not set a single line of Shakespeare's to music. The score was meant not as a medium for the original play but rather, as Curtis Price aptly puts it, as "an extended meditation on the spell it casts."

The act I masque, composed for the revised and expanded revival of *The Fairy Queen* in 1693, is a comic interlude completely unrelated to Shakespeare's plot. It consists of a rather cruel slapstick entertainment, ordered up by Titania, in which the band of fairies torments a defenseless drunken poet. With its quick repartee and its broadly "realistic" portrayal of the poor victim, the Masque of the Drunken Poet is the closest episode in Purcell's London stage works to full-fledged opera as the Italians knew it.

DIDO AND AENEAS AND THE QUESTION OF "ENGLISH OPERA"

He came closer still in *Dido and Aeneas*, his single stage work that, while still technically a masque, was meant to be sung straight through from beginning to end. The plot was adapted by the poet Nahum Tate from the fourth book of the *Aeneid*, the Roman poet Virgil's epic poem that tells of the hero Aeneas's return from the Trojan War. On the way he stops at Carthage, in North Africa, where the Queen, Dido, having given him hospitality, conceives a passionate love for him. But the gods send Mercury to bid the hero continue on his journey (in Virgil, that is; in the libretto it is a false Mercury sent by scheming witches) and Aeneas departs, leaving Dido bereft. She dies (that is, kills herself) out of grief and shame.

The one documented performance of this little opera took place in 1689 at a London girls' school ("Mr. Josias Priest's Boarding-School at Chelsey," as the libretto's title page says); but as historians now mostly agree, that performance was probably not the first. Tate, the librettist, was a prominent figure who was chosen poet laureate by William and Mary a few years later. It seems unlikely that he and Purcell would have collaborated on a major work for so lowly a venue; but then again, *Dido and Aeneas*, as a through-composed if miniature tragic opera, was not a work that would have been welcomed on the Restoration stage. For its time and place it was an anomaly, probably meant for court performance (around 1687, for James II), and—as scholars now contend—embodying a now obscure political allegory favorable to the ill-fated king.[21]

Even so, it was not entirely without precedent. If by "English opera" one means a continuous musical setting of a dramatic text in English in more than a single act, then *Dido and Aeneas* was probably the fourth of its kind. The earliest surviving one is *Venus and Adonis* (1683) by John Blow (ca. 1649–1708), another of Purcell's teachers, who served as the Westminster Abbey organist both before and after his famous pupil's tenure. It consists of a kind of sing-song melodic recitative modeled on those of Locke, alternating with danced choruses à la Lully.

Charles II could not have liked it very much, because he snubbed its composer a couple of years later in conspicuous and painful fashion. After weathering a political crisis and an attempted assassination in 1681, Charles decided to commission a grandiose operatic allegory of his restoration and reign to celebrate the deliverance of the house of Stuart. Poet laureate Dryden concocted a libretto called *Albion and Albanius*, in which the two title characters (both of whose names were derived from archaic names of England) stood transparently for Charles and his brother, the later James II. The action depicts the defeat of the three nefarious opponents of Christian monarchy, namely Democracy, Zelota ("Zeal," meaning Puritanism), and Asebia (Atheism).

When it came to commissioning the music, though, all native-born composers were passed over in favor of Luis Grabu, a Spaniard then living in Paris, who years earlier had already aroused the envy of English musicians when Charles II appointed him to a brief term as Master of the King's Musick. In the event, Grabu's operatic panegyric to the king was ill-fated. On 6 February 1685, days before its scheduled première, Charles II suddenly died, and its rescheduled run in June was cut short after six performances by another political crisis (the Duke of Monmouth's Rebellion). Nevertheless, despite its musical sterility, the *Albion and Albanius* episode is historically significant for the way the resentment it stimulated led to the first expressions of musical nationalism, as we understand the word today.

The chief cause for nationalistic disparagement was always Grabu's asserted inability to set English words correctly. The specialness of English prosody has been a critical watchword ever since, and Purcell has always been looked upon as its greatest master. The difficulty of setting English is said to consist in the language's unusual accentuation patterns, in which stressed syllables and long syllables do not necessarily coincide, the way they do in Italian. (And indeed, Grabu's recitatives, in mixed meters adapted directly from Lully, would have been better suited to a language that, like French but unlike English, does not have a heavy tonic stress.) But Purcell's musical prosody in recitatives was not his original discovery; it derived from that of his teachers, Blow and Locke.

The very first recitative in *Dido and Aeneas* — Dido's exchanges with her handmaiden Belinda and a second woman about Aeneas's virtue, and her fear of unrequited love — is an ideal introduction to this idiosyncratic English declamation (Ex. 22-14). In most ways the setting follows the conventions of Italian recitative as we have observed them as far back as Peri and Monteverdi at the dawn of opera. There are a few residual madrigalisms: rapid melismas on "storms" and "fierce," a melisma in regal dotted rhythms on "valour," and the like. There is also a great deal of conventionally affective harmony, such as the chromatic inflection on "woe." Where the setting is syllabic, however, it follows the rhythms of English speech very strictly, as we may still confirm by testing our modern

EX. 22-14   Henry Purcell, *Dido and Aeneas*, recitative and dance song

EX. 22-14 (continued)

soft_____ in peace, and yet how fierce,_____ how fierce_ in_

Belinda

arms! A tale so strong____ and full of

woe__ Might melt_____ the_ rocks, as well as__ you.

English pronunciation against Purcell's notation. Another English feature, taken over from Lawes and Locke, is the characteristic progression in the bass line from long notes into "walking" quarters and eighths (the kind of thing that we now call "arioso").

The most conspicuously "English" prosodic effect is the frequent use of short–long rhythms ("Lombards" or "Scotch snaps") on accented beats to reflect the distinctive English short stress. In the very first measure, the rhythm of "so much" is fastidiously distinguished in this way from the rhythms that precede and follow it. Other short–long pairs occur on "did he" in m. 3 and "full of" in m. 10. And in the typically masquelike (hence typically English) dancing-air-plus-chorus that follows the recitative ("Fear no danger to ensue"), the short–long rhythm, alternating with its opposite, is turned into a characteristic metric pattern.

For the most part, however, the "Englishness" of *Dido and Aeneas* consists of an original synthesis of French and Italian ingredients that is more attributable to Purcell's individuality (and to his exceptional familiarity with, and receptivity to, foreign trends) than to his nationality as such. In his case, an apparently insular style was really cosmopolitanism in disguise. It is easy enough to catalogue the imported ingredients. Group activities—choruses, dances, orchestral numbers—are governed by French conventions, as often observed, and solo behavior by Italian.

And yet the French and Italian strains were not wholly discrete in the seventeenth century. Both made conspicuous use of ground basses, for example; and ground-bass numbers, for which Purcell had an uncanny gift, are one of the special glories of *Dido and Aeneas*. The ending of act I puts a French spin on the device, that of act III, the opera's final scene, puts an Italian one; both, however, are at the same time inimitably Purcellian.

Act I ends with a celebration by the chorus of the title couple's as-yet-undeclared love. After singing, they do a "Triumphing Dance" in the form of a chaconne, the customary celebratory dance of the French lyric stage. Like most of the numbers in *Dido and Aeneas*, it is a miniaturized adaptation of its model, but it has lots of tonal and rhythmic variety. The twelve statements of the four-measure bass are organized into two little ternary forms around modulations to the dominant ($3 + 1 + 3$; $1 + 1 + 3$). In between come two surprising bars, not shown in the example, that have no bass at all and throw the measure count delightfully off symmetry.

The second scene of act III, the opera's dénouement, consists of a dramatic recitative in which Aeneas takes leave of the forlorn and lovesick Queen, a sadly sympathetic comment from the chorus, and Dido's suicide aria (Ex. 22-15), to which a final chorus of lamentation is appended. Dido's diminutive aria is usually called her lament, because it is written in the style of a Venetian *lamento*, a form we have traced from its Monteverdian origins (see Ex. 20-5, the "Lamento della Ninfa"). By the end of the seventeenth century it had become a virtual cliché. Purcell is true to the established convention in his choice of a descending tetrachord as ground bass, and he is also conventional in the chromatic interpolations that turn the tetrachord into the standard *passus duriusculus*.

EX. 22-15   Henry Purcell, *Dido and Aeneas*, Act III, sc. 2, Dido's lament

EX. 22-15 (continued)

EX. 22-15 (*continued*)

for - get my — fate.

Altogether unconventional and characteristic, however, is the interpolation of an additional cadential measure into the stereotyped ground, increasing its length from a routine four to a haunting five bars, against which the vocal line, with its despondent refrain ("Remember me!"), is deployed with marked asymmetry. That, plus Purcell's distinctively dissonant, suspension-saturated harmony, enhanced by additional chromatic descents during the final ritornello and by many deceptive cadences, make the little aria an unforgettably poignant embodiment of heartache.

THE MAKING OF A CLASSIC

Unforgettable, yet long forgotten. Within a few years of Purcell's death, *Dido and Aeneas* was in typical "Restoration" fashion ruthlessly cannibalized as a masque within a performance of Shakespeare's *Measure for Measure*, and then laid aside. It was not the time or place for "classics." The opera was rediscovered during the nineteenth century — a great age for classics! — and published for the first time in 1841. The first modern staged revival took place in 1895, the bicentennial of Purcell's death; like the first documented performance, it was a student production. Yet George Bernard Shaw, not yet a famous dramatist but London's leading music critic, traveled out of his way to cover it, and informed his readers that the two-hundred-year-old "first English opera" was "not a bit the worse for wear."[22] Since then, usually as part of a double bill, it has been a staple of the Anglo-American musical stage. The advent of recordings and, later, the vogue for "early music" or period performance-style, has further enhanced its popularity.

So it was that this very late, atypical, and geographically peripheral seventeenth-century opera, from a country where opera was practically unknown, managed to become the twentieth-century "classic" of the genre; and that is how Dido's immensely moving yet stylistically rather offbeat lament has become the main representative of the ubiquitous seventeenth-century ground bass in modern repertory. The main agent of this lucky though improbable transformation was burgeoning English nationalism. In the late nineteenth century, English composers were trying hard to establish a distinctive national identity after a long period of aping continental fashions. English musicians and music writers of all kinds, Shaw very conspicuous among them, were trying to recover from the written remains of English music what cultural historians call "a usable past" — a legacy that could serve as a model for constructing a distinctive national identity in the present.

Purcell fit the bill. The unusualness of his idiom (his "freshness," as Shaw put it), and in particular "his unapproached art of setting English speech to music," provided English composers with their model, and one of the least typical of his works became the very archetype of Englishness in music.

Class and Classicism

OPERA SERIA AND ITS MAKERS

NAPLES

Returning now to Italy after a chapter spent in France and England, it is worth a reminder that (with the exception of Portugal) France and England were the only countries in seventeenth-century Europe whose borders then were pretty much what they are today. They were also, and not by coincidence, the only nations in Europe that were ethnically and linguistically more or less coextensive with their territory. The other European nations were either empires — multiethnic, polyglot dynastic states — or small hereditary or republican enclaves whose political boundaries had little to do with language or ethnicity. The much-weakened "Holy Roman" (Austrian) Empire, Charlemagne's tattered legacy, was the main representative of "supra-ethnicity." Its main rival, and avid foe, was the Ottoman (Turkish) Empire that in the fifteenth and sixteenth centuries expanded aggressively into southeastern Europe from Asia Minor and as late as 1683 threatened the walls of Vienna, the Austrian capital. The main areas of fragmented "subethnic" political division were Germany and Italy.

Northern Italy was dominated by the republic of Venice, which in the mid-seventeenth century reached its height of power, controlling much of the eastern Adriatic coast (territory belonging now to Slovenia and Croatia) and extending its rule as far as Crete in the eastern Mediterranean. The other main north Italian city states were Florence and Genoa, both of which had expanded territorially far beyond their municipal borders, with Genoa controlling the Mediterranean island of Corsica. Extending like a stripe through the middle of the Italian peninsula was the Papal State (or Papal Estates), the temporal domain of the Roman Catholic church. The south of Italy was occupied by the Kingdoms of Naples and Sicily, both of which belonged to the Spanish crown in the seventeenth century and were ruled by provincial viceroys, one in the city of Naples, the other in Palermo, the Sicilian capital, each backed up by an army of occupation.

This period of subjugation, which lasted from the beginning of the sixteenth century to the beginning of the eighteenth, was an economic disaster for southern Italy, the repercussions of which continue to this day. The city of Naples swelled with an influx of dispossessed peasants, making it by the end of the seventeenth century, with close to 200,000 inhabitants, perhaps the largest but also the most squalid metropolis in Europe. Historians of Neapolitan culture call the sixteenth and seventeenth centuries the city's "iron age."

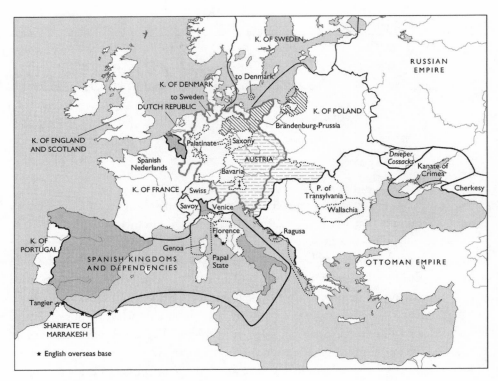

FIG. 23-1   Europe, ca. 1680.

Musically, however, and in seeming paradox, the same conditions created a golden age. In direct consequence of the urban poverty that viceroyal rule had engendered, a number of orphanages and foundling homes had to be set up in the city. These houses where homeless boys were harbored were called "conservatories" (*conservatorio* in the singular, meaning "place of safekeeping" in sixteenth-century Italian). They were self-maintaining organizations. Money spent in providing for the inmates was recouped by putting them to work. And one of the obvious ways in which you could employ an orphan was to make him a choirboy. So the training of choirboys became a major preoccupation of the Naples conservatories, training that was eventually expanded to include secular and instrumental music, as the need arose.

That need was greatly stimulated by the importation of opera—"Venice-style music," as it was at first called by the Neapolitans—beginning around 1650 at the instigation of Count d'Oñate, the mid-century Spanish viceroy. (The first opera production in the city, it is said, was *Il Nerone*, an adaptation, by a traveling company, of Monteverdi's *Poppea*.) The first Neapolitan opera house, the renovated Teatro di San Bartolomeo (St. Bartholomew's), opened in 1654. Though a public theater, it enjoyed the direct patronage of the viceroyal court. By the 1680s, the court and chapel musical establishments, staffed chiefly by musicians educated at the conservatories, had in large part been siphoned off to San Bartolomeo, which became one of the best-endowed opera houses in Europe. Around the same time, too, its repertoire began shifting over from a transplanted Venetian to a local Neapolitan one that soon became itself a major international force.

FIG. 23-2 Interior of the Teatro San Bartolomeo, Naples (eighteenth-century engraving at the Bibliothèque et Musée de l'Opéra, Paris).

SCARLATTI

The guiding genius behind the Neapolitan ascendency was a Palermo-born composer named Alessandro Scarlatti (1660–1725), who dominated the Neapolitan musical scene from 1683 to 1702, and again (after Naples had passed from Spanish to Austrian rule) from 1709 to 1721. His career was international, or at least pan-Italian; he had important stints of service in Rome, in Florence, and elsewhere. But the bulk of his voluminous output of operas (114 by his own count) and cantatas (more than 800 by modern scholarly count) was written for Naples, where in 1696 the theater was expanded and newly outfitted just for him by the viceroy, the Duke of Medinaceli, who was a great *melomaniaco* (as the Italians called an opera fan). The inheritor and transformer of the Venetian tradition, Scarlatti could be looked upon as the culminating figure of opera's first century. By reshaping and standardizing the legacy he inherited, he laid the foundation for the next century of operatic development, especially as regards what came to be known as "serious" opera (*opera seria*).

Scarlatti served his apprenticeship in Rome, where he was a favorite of the aging

FIG. 23-3 Anonymous portrait of Alessandro Scarlatti at the Civico Museo Bibliografico Musicale, Bologna.

Queen Christina. When the Spanish ambassador to the papal court was named viceroy of Naples, he brought Scarlatti along with him as *maestro di cappella*. The twenty-three-year-old maestro's duties were staggering. He was under contract to compose, as well as rehearse and perform, an average of four operas a year. He had to provide the music for the viceroy's chapel, including a yearly oratorio for Lent and an annual Te Deum or two for occasions of state. And he furnished on commission untold cantatas and miniature operas known as serenatas for various noble salons. No wonder, then, that he tended to standardize his *modus operandi*. In the words of Donald Jay Grout, his biographer, the hard-pressed maestro was "forced to make as many minutes as possible of music at the cost of as few minutes as possible for getting the notes written down."[1] His methods of standardization were widely emulated by his contemporaries and immediate successors, who were just as overworked as he was.

Since much of Scarlatti's work remains unpublished, or available only in scholarly editions, and since a whole opera or even a single act would tax our available space, the best way of observing Scarlatti's standard operating procedure is within the more modest confines of a cantata, the form to which he was the last (and by far the most) prolific contributor. *Andate, oh miei sospiri* ("Go, O my sighs") was written in 1712, during Scarlatti's second stint as chief composer in Naples. It was, for Scarlatti, an especially labored-over composition, since he wrote it in friendly competition with his younger contemporary Francesco Gasparini, a leading Venetian composer of the day. Each composer had to compose two settings of the same text, as different from one another as possible.

The one we are sampling here was Scarlatti's second setting, composed, as he put it on the title page, *"in idea inumana, ma in regolato cromatico; non è per ogni professore"* ("in a devilish style, but within the rules of chromatic writing; not for your average tootler"). The harmonic extravagances to which he refers — and which begin at the very beginning (Ex. 23-1a) with two successive tritones on the repeated opening word, a flattened second degree (the so-called "Neapolitan" harmony) almost immediately following, and many diminished-seventh chords throughout (a particular Scarlatti mannerism) — are not really all that unusual. Rather, they place the work within the old tradition of the "mannered" madrigal that (as we have seen) stood parent to the cantata. They are quite comparable to the expressive harmonic effects in Barbara Strozzi's cantata, composed half a century earlier, which was discussed in chapter 21. The most "mannered" moment comes in a later recitative at the parenthetical line *"(ma s'infinge / quel suo barbara cor)"*, which means "(while her cruel heart pretends otherwise)." The sudden, radical harmonic excursion (Ex. 23-1b) is indeed a perfect analogue to a parenthetical thought, especially one that is not only parenthetical but also antithetical to the main sense of the words.

Such bizarre rhetorical effects were nothing new, as comparison with Strozzi's work will quickly show. Completely new, however, and completely unlike Strozzi's cantata, is the thoroughgoing formal regularity of Scarlatti's setting. It is cast in four discrete sections that form two recitative–aria pairs. The poetry is made for this division. The recitative sections are cast in *versi sciolti* ("free verses") in which eleven-syllable lines alternate irregularly with sevens. These lend themselves to the flexible declamation of

EX. 23-1A   Alessandro Scarlatti, Cantata: *Andate, oh miei sospiri*, opening recitative.

EX. 23-1B   Alessandro Scarlatti, Cantata: *Andate, oh miei sospiri*, third recitative, harmonic "aside".

EX. 23-1B *(continued)*

segue Aria

recitative. The arias are cast in shorter lines with a regular meter and (especially in the case of the second one) a simpler rhyme scheme.

Not only is the setting fixed and formal in its alternation of recitative and aria, but the arias themselves are also uniform in structure. The texts are cast in two sections, each consisting of a single sentence. These sentences are given discrete musical settings. The first, by far the longer thanks to a continuo introduction and many repetitions of words and phrases, cadences on the tonic. The second is not only shorter, it is tonally distinguished from the first as well, beginning and cadencing on a different scale degree (in effect, in a different key).

Obviously the aria cannot end with this tonally subsidiary second section. The words *da capo*, written at its conclusion, confirm this point. They mean "from the top," and direct the performers to repeat the first section, in its entirety or up to the word *fine* ("end"), so that the whole has a tonally stable, recapitulatory form that could be designated ABA. This tripartite form, known informally as the "da capo aria," remained the absolutely standard aria form for the rest of the eighteenth century. Its advantage for the composer was obvious: he had to write only two parts out of three, amounting to perhaps three-fifths of the total duration. The rest was taken care of by the unwritten repeat. Its advantage for the performer consisted in the opportunities the unwritten repeat offered for spontaneous embellishment. The da capo aria was (or became) the virtuoso display aria par excellence, ensuring the kind of spectacular performance on which public opera has always thrived.

The origins of the form are a bit obscure. Scarlatti, though his name is now firmly associated with it, certainly did not invent it. It appears to be an abridgement of an earlier strophic form, as befits the use of the word "aria," which (as we may recall) originally designated a poem declaimed stanza by stanza to a musical formula. Indeed, in Scarlatti's earliest operas each aria had two strophic stanzas separated by refrains. Shrink such an aria down to a single stanza framed by the refrain, enlarge and embellish the simple structure thus achieved, and the "da capo aria" is the result.

The second aria in *Andate, oh miei sospiri* belongs to a type that was particularly characteristic of Scarlatti and of Neapolitan music in general. Identifiable by compound meter ($\frac{6}{8}$ or, more commonly, $\frac{12}{8}$), leisurely or languid tempo, lilting rhythms (with much use of the figure ♩. ♪ ♩ ♪) and (usually) by an eighth-note pickup, such an aria was called a *siciliana* and is often assumed, although without any real evidence, to stem from a jiglike Sicilian folk or popular dance. Very often, too, *siciliana* arias exhibit at their cadences the "Neapolitan sixth" harmony that emerges when the already-observed flatted second degree in the tune coincides with the fourth degree in the bass. This distinctive harmonic mannerism, which quickly caught on in other repertoires, reinforces the impression that the *siciliana* may have originated in some local musical dialect. Ex. 23-2 shows the main

EX. 23-2A   Alessandro Scarlatti, Cantata: *Andate, oh miei sospiri*, second aria (in *siciliana* style), setting of opening line.

EX. 23-2B   Alessandro Scarlatti, Cantata: *Andate, oh miei sospiri*, second aria (in *siciliana* style), section break.

EX. 23-2C   Alessandro Scarlatti, Cantata: *Andate, oh miei sospiri*, second aria (in *siciliana* style), end of middle section.

tune, as sung by the soloist on entering (after a little introduction for the accompanists); the join between the A and B sections; and the end of the B section, marked *da capo*. (The "Neapolitan sixth" occurs in the penultimate bar, on the word *sparga*.)

The main difference between cantata arias and their operatic counterparts is in scoring. Cantatas are chamber music; the basic ensemble of voice plus basso continuo—sustaining bass, usually string, and chordal "realizer," usually keyboard—generally suffices for them. In the opera house a small "Venetian style" string band (like the one encountered in Monteverdi's *Poppea*) was employed to accompany the voice part or set it off with ritornellos, as in the siciliana aria in Ex. 23-3, from Scarlatti's opera *L'Eraclea* (Heraclia) first performed at the Naples opera house in 1700. Note the "Neapolitan" throb in m. 5 that emphasizes—what else?—the words "I love you"!

Like the da capo aria itself, the siciliana was something Alessandro Scarlatti used so abundantly that his name became identified with it, but again he was not (as sometimes stated) its inventor. Yet a third important operatic convention not invented by Scarlatti but standardized and popularized by (and hence often attributed to) him was a new type of *sinfonia* (that is, overture) consisting of a brilliant opening in fanfare style, a central slow episode (often with "affective" harmonies involving suspensions or chromatics), and a concluding dance.

This last section, as was by then standard for dance movements, was cast in two repeated strains, the first cadencing on the dominant or some remoter degree, and the second on the tonic. Like the da capo aria, then, the "binary" dance movement embodied a "closed" tonal motion—away from the tonic and back. The resulting effect of harmonic contrast and closure, and its standard employment as the chief articulator of musical form, was perhaps the most powerful new idea that can be associated with late seventeenth-century Italian music, and certainly the most influential one. In all sorts of ways, it conditioned the development of European art music for centuries to come. Alessandro Scarlatti's stature in music history derives from his important role, by virtue of his prolific output and its high visibility, in establishing these new harmonic and formal norms.

EX. 23-3   Alessandro Scarlatti, *L'Eraclea*, "Ricordati ch'io t'amo," mm. 1–6.

Remember that I love you and
serve you and am silent.

Scarlatti employed the new overture form as early as 1681, in *Tutto il mal non vien per nuocere* ("Not Every Misfortune Is Harmful"), his third opera and first big hit, which played in six Italian cities in as many years. Perhaps not coincidentally, this was a comic opera, where a high-spirited curtain-raiser would have seemed especially fitting. But by the turn of the century such overtures were standard in operas of every plot type. Given in Ex. 23-4 is a sort of summary of the "Sinfonia avanti L'Opera" from *La caduta de' decemviri* ("The Fall of the Decemvirs"), a serious opera first given at San Bartolomeo in 1697, with a plot (like that of Monteverdi's *Poppea*) adapted from Roman history. The final dancelike section, given complete as Ex. 23-4c, is cast in Scarlatti's ubiquitous $\frac{12}{8}$ meter.

EX. 23-4A   Alessandro Scarlatti, *La caduta de' decemviri*, Sinfonia, mm. 1–7.

EX. 23-4B   Alessandro Scarlatti, *La caduta de' decemviri*, Sinfonia, mm. 29–36.

EX. 23-4C   Alessandro Scarlatti, *La caduta de' decemviri*, Sinfonia, m. 55–end.

EX. 23-4C *(continued)*

NEOCLASSICISM

In 1706, while living in Rome between his two stints as *maestro di cappella* in Naples, Scarlatti was honored by election, along with the keyboard virtuoso and composer Bernardo Pasquini and the great violinist Arcangelo Corelli, to a very prestigious association of musical and literary connoisseurs known as the Arcadian Academy. It had been founded in 1690, the year following the death of Queen Christina, Scarlatti's former patron, by former habitués of her salon. At its head was Pietro Cardinal

Ottoboni, grandnephew of the reigning pope, Alexander VIII. For more than fifty years Cardinal Ottoboni was far and away the most lavish patron of opera in Rome. He was also an amateur librettist, whose texts, whatever their shortcomings, were eagerly set by composers in hopes of an extravagant production and an outstanding performance supervised by Pasquini and Corelli. Two of Scarlatti's operas and several of his oratorios were set to Ottoboni librettos, including *La Statira*, the cardinal's maiden operatic effort.

The Arcadians preached, and to a considerable extent practiced, very lofty esthetic ideals. Following Aristotle, as they would have claimed, but also responding to the criticism of French dramatists who (as we saw in chapter 22) heaped scorn on theatrical music, they wanted to restore opera to its original "classical" purity. This meant cleansing it of the old Venetian comic and bawdy scenes with their conniving servants and aging wet nurses, which had catered to the tastes of paying audiences, and returning opera to the chaste pastoral or heroic historical spheres from which it had sunk. Like most operatic reformers (and as a venerable wag once put it, the history of opera is the history of its reforms), the Arcadians sought to recover the politics of affirmation that had attended the original invention of opera at the noble north Italian courts a hundred years before.

Thus librettos became vehicles for noble sentiment — noble in both the literal and the figurative sense of the word. Real tragedy, which according to Aristotle required a flawed hero and a terrifying dénouement, was deemed unsuitable for moral instruction in an enlightened age: therein lay one crucial difference between the actual classical drama and the "neoclassical" drama of the European courts. A happy ending (*lieto fine* in Italian) was mandatory in an opera libretto even if it contradicted historical fact; for as Marita McClymonds, a leading historian of "reform" opera, has observed, "poets were expected to portray what, according to an orderly moral system, should have happened rather than what actually did happen."[2] That, as far as opera was concerned, was what was meant by "verisimilitude." In practical terms, this requirement entailed a schematic, idealized cast of character types that, in Grout's words, represented "not a picture of the actual world in which people then lived, but rather a diagram of it."[3] This abstract diagrammatic representation of the social world implied, for its fullest delineation, the depiction of three social levels — rulers, confidants, and servants — each represented by a loving couple (or a would-be loving couple). The dramatic intrigue, always played out in three acts, involved the interplay among this set of characters, augmented by one or two others (villains, jealous or rejected lovers, false friends), until the inevitable happy ending, "where," as Grout writes, "all the couples are finally sorted out and launched on a life which presumably will continue happily ever after." Most important, he continues, "this consummation is usually brought about not by luck, still less by any intelligent planning by the persons chiefly concerned, but rather by the last-minute intervention of the ruler, in an exemplary act of renunciation inspired by pity and greatness of soul."

The ruler, in short, functioned in an ideal opera libretto the way a benevolently intervening deity — the proverbial *deus ex machina* or "god from out of a machine" — descended, like Apollo in Monteverdi's *Orfeo*, in ancient plays or the earliest courtly operas. Here is another important distinction between the "classical" and the "neoclassical." Intervention in the newly idealized opera could not be supernatural; it had to be human, but the human intervener, like the ruler in an absolutist state, was taken as the earthly representative of the divine. The neoclassical drama thus celebrated the "divine right of kings."

These Arcadian reforms were anticipated and paralleled in Venice, the former hotbed of "impure" opera, by Apostolo Zeno (1668–1750), a famous poet and scholar who had founded his own Academy for the restoration of taste and tradition, and whose librettos were set many times over by many composers. Like most operatic reformers, Zeno had high aristocratic patronage (in his case the "Holy Roman" Emperor, no less), and wrote librettos on commission from the Viennese court (where he was eventually in residence) which further idealized the role of the beneficent monarch. One of these, *Scipione nelle Spagne*, was set by Scarlatti and no fewer than eight other composers between 1710 and 1768: such libretto-longevity was not at all unusual in the eighteenth century.

Along with the purification and elevation of subject matter went the standardization of form and regularization of verse. In librettos like *Griselda* (on which Scarlatti, one of fourteen who set it, composed his last opera in 1721, twenty years after its creation), Zeno began to cast all the scenes in the same basic shape — recitative followed by a single da capo aria, after which the singer exits amid applause — and made every aria the bearer of a single vivid and consistent emotional message, cast in a simple and distinctive meter to facilitate its setting by the composer. It became a point both of technique and of esthetics to employ as great a variety of aria meters as possible. Thus Zeno and the Arcadians sought at the level of the libretto, the highest level of operatic "structure," to match Scarlatti's achievement in standardizing forms and procedures.

METASTASIO

Ultimate "classical" perfection was reached by the Roman poet Pietro Antonio Trapassi (1698–1782), a godson of Cardinal Ottoboni himself, who was virtually raised in the bosom of the Arcadian Academy and who eventually replaced Zeno as Austrian court poet in 1730. His pen name, Metastasio, has become the very emblem of the genre he perfected. It was a sort of pseudo-Greek translation of his family name: *trapasso* means transit or conveyance from one place to another (and by extension, death, or "passing on"); Metastasio substitutes Greek roots for Latinate ones (compare the medical term *metastasis*, meaning the spread or transference of a disease or a fluid from one part of the body to another). The "translation" signaled the poet's neoclassical leanings and his avowed aim, as usual, of re-resurrecting the ancient Greek drama, and all its effects, through opera.

Between 1720 and 1771 Metastasio wrote some sixty librettos, of which about half (twenty-seven) belonged to the genre of *opera seria* — "serious opera" — the term now used for what Metastasio, following tradition, had called *dramma per musica* ("drama through music"). Over the next century or more, Metastasio's texts were set more than eight hundred times by more than three hundred composers. During that long span of time, and at the hands of several generations of musicians, the music that clothed these texts underwent considerable stylistic change. (At the most basic level, the settings of the arias became steadily longer and more elaborate, and therefore fewer.) But the librettos remained relatively constant. That is what it means to be (regarded as) a classic. No other librettist ever achieved such a stature or so dominated the opera of his time.

The stylistic changes in the music will naturally be the subject of future discussions in this book. And of course Metastasio's librettos did undergo a certain amount of adaptation (or *refacimento* — "remaking" — to use the Italian word) as they circulated over time and from place to place. They had increasingly to be cut as the musical entities got longer. But their longevity, and their consistency, are nonetheless remarkable and have a great deal to teach us about the musical and social ideals of their age. It was an age of relative political and social stability, a stability that the very longevity and consistency of Metastasio's libretti can seem to symbolize. In advance of all musical discussion, then, the style and structure of the Metastasian libretto deserve consideration, since they embody a critical set of concepts with many important consequences.

The Metastasian libretto was a supreme balancing act, reconciling the theoretical ideals of the Arcadian reformers with the practical demands of the stage. Not only the audience but the performers had to be considered, for the star singers in an opera performance were in effect another hierarchical society, and a very demanding one. To meet and balance all demands, the older reform libretto was adjusted to feature six main roles, deployed in two pairs and a "remainder."

At the top was the first couple: the *primo uomo* or first man, almost always played by a castrato, and the *prima donna* or first lady, played by a soprano where women were allowed on the public stage, and by another castrato where they were not. The indifference to the actual sex of performers, which is evident in the casting not only of *opera seria* but also the contemporary spoken theater, is something that fascinates many historians in our present era of gender politics. In the case of *Artaserse*, a famous Metastasio libretto that will furnish our main example, the first performance of its first musical setting took place in Rome, where women could not sing on stage, and featured two male castratos in the main lovers' roles. Most subsequent performances cast the roles according to sex, although the male was always a eunuch, never a "natural" man. But in at least one production, a gala sung at Naples in 1738 on the birthday and wedding-eve of the King of the Two Sicilies, both "first" roles were sung by women. As the figurative meaning of "prima donna," which still survives in colloquial English, emphatically suggests, these favored singers, whatever their actual sex, had many prerogatives and insisted on them. Between the two of them, the first couple had to sing half the arias in the show, amounting to as many as half a dozen arias apiece. And only they could sing a duet.

The second couple, also noble, claimed three or four arias apiece. Afterwards came the "remainder": confidants, villains, servants, whatever. They could be given no more than two arias, and these arias had to be positioned less conspicuously than those of the higher-ranking roles. One of these characters, for example, had to sing the first aria in act II, because in many theaters that was when refreshments were served to the audience and nobody was listening. (The first aria in act II actually came to be known as the *aria di sorbetto* or "sherbet aria," and the hapless singer to whom it was assigned could expect to be drowned out by the clinking of spoons.)

In addition, the arias each character sang had to belong to different standard types that showed off different aspects of their vocal prowess. These included the *aria di bravura* or virtuoso aria full of difficult coloratura passages; the *aria d'affetto* or tender aria full of long-held, swelling notes; the *aria cantabile* or lyrical aria, in which the singer's ability to sustain long phrases was displayed, and so on. Not only were these types to be distributed within the roles; they also had to be distributed in their succession, so that there never be two arias of the same type side by side. Thus the librettist had to be able to anticipate the demands of singer and of composer alike, and also meet strict standards of plot propriety and literary style. It was specialist work, and in its profusion of rigorous conventions it was a "classical" art indeed. No wonder the works of Metastasio, who could manage all these staggering prerequisites within a style that apparently exemplified classical "simplicity" and "naturalness," were kept up in active use as long as they were.

Metastasio rationalized the artificiality of the neoclassical dramatic art he practiced and reconciled it with the principles of the classic drama he claimed to emulate by comparing the arias, which functioned as reflective monologues at the conclusion of every scene, not with soliloquies but with the chorus — the eternal commentator — in the classical Greek drama. In this way the aria differs in quality and function even from the recitative soliloquy that might precede it. The essential difference is that the recitatives exist within the stage world; they are addressed to the *dramatis personae*, the characters on stage, even if the singer and the addressee are one and the same (as in a true soliloquy, an "internal dialogue").

The arias, like the Greek choruses, are addressed outward to the audience; they are emotional weather reports, so to speak, delivered in a sort of stopped time, or "time out." As traditionally staged, the arias were actually sung stage front, facing the spectators, accompanied by appropriate stylized poses or attitudes. A "character," in such a drama, was only the sum of the prescribed attitudes he or she was called upon to strike.

The artificiality of this scheme is proverbial and often mocked. And yet no matter how much opera may have changed after Metastasio, no matter how vehemently later operatic composers, librettists, or theorists may (in the name of one form of "realism" or another) have rejected his stylizations, this most fundamental stylization forever remained: the distinction between "recitative time" (public time, clock time, time for action) and "aria time" (internal time, psychological time, time for reflection). The formalization of this distinction was the great stroke of genius that gave opera not only more room for music but also a special dramatic dimension that modern spoken drama (despite many fruitless experiments with "asides") could never match.

Metastasio began his career in Naples, Scarlatti's old haunt, with *Didone abbandonata* ("Dido abandoned"), based on the same story as Purcell's famous little opera of 1689. Even though it was an early work and therefore somewhat atypical (lacking a *lieto fine*, for one thing), *Didone abbandonata* was one of Metastasio's most popular librettos. It was set more than sixty times by composers great and obscure over a period of precisely a century, from 1724 to 1824.

Comparing Metastasio's libretto with Virgil's original story as summarized in chapter 22, and with Purcell's setting as discussed there, will illuminate the special nature of *opera seria*. Like virtually all *opere serie* it is in three long acts. Where Nahum Tate, Purcell's librettist, had three main characters—Dido, Aeneas, and Belinda (Dido's confidante)—Metastasio's has the standard six. Dido (soprano) and Aeneas (alto castrato) make up the first couple. The second couple consists of Araspes (bass) and Dido's sister Selene (soprano), who at first is also in love with Aeneas: the remainder consists of the villains Iarbas (tenor), a Moorish king who is fruitlessly wooing Dido, and Osmidas (tenor), Dido's faithless confidant, who is plotting against her with the help of the jealous Iarbas.

In the first act, Aeneas informs Dido of his decision to leave Carthage; Iarbas, unaware of this, tries to kill Aeneas with the help of Araspes, his henchman. In the second act, Araspes declares his love to Selene who rejects him; Aeneas magnanimously intercedes with Dido on behalf of Iarbas, who has already been set free by Osmidas; Dido at first pretends to accept Iarbas's offer of marriage to test Aeneas's love; having been reassured, she rejects Iarbas. In the third act, Iarbas challenges Aeneas to a duel, whereupon the Moors and Trojans all begin fighting with one another; again Aeneas shows his magnanimity by defeating Iarbas but sparing his life; Selene declares her love to Aeneas but cannot deter him from leaving. Araspes comes with news that the Moors have set fire to Carthage, but even at this Dido does not give in to Iarbas's entreaties. Learning of Osmidas's betrayal and her sister's secret love, she sings a rage aria (modeled by Metastasio on the ending of Quinault's libretto for Lully's *Armide*, performed at Louis XIV's court some forty years before; see chapter 22), following which she throws herself into the fire and is killed.

A cluttered action, a confusion of lovers, a welter of superfluous characters (there is also "Arbaces," Iarbas in disguise), but ample opportunity to display the high virtues of fidelity, steadfastness of purpose, and noble generosity (all at grave personal cost) and express the high emotions of love in many variations. In writing it, the young Metastasio was guided by the singers who were to portray the leading couple: Maria Anna Benti, called La Romanina, Italy's reigning diva (at whose house the poet was staying), and her partner, the castrato Nicolo Grimaldi, called Nicolini. They gave the librettist, in seriousness, the indispensable advice he needed about role requirements and aria types, the notorious but inviolable rigmarole later parodied by so many satirists of the opera seria like Carlo Goldoni (see Weiss and Taruskin, *Music in the Western World*, No. 62). His early mastery of these absolute injunctions enabled Metastasio to cope, for the rest of his career and with seeming effortlessness, with all the competing demands of the librettist's craft.

The libretto Metastasio himself regarded as his masterpiece, at once typical and ideal, was *Attilio Regolo*, which more than any other highlighted the theme of noble self-sacrifice. The title character, Marcus Attilius Regulus (d. ca. 250 BCE), was, like so many *opera seria* heroes, an exemplary historical personage: "a Roman hero of consummate virtue," as Metastasio himself put it, "not only in principle but in practice," because he is "a rigid and scrupulous observer, not only of justice and probity, but also of the laws and customs which time and the great authority of his ancestors have rendered sacred to his country."[4] A Roman consul and general, Regulus invaded Africa and defeated the Carthaginians in 256 BCE but was defeated and captured by them the next year. Having promised to return whatever the outcome, he was sent by the Carthaginians to Rome in 250 to negotiate peace and exchange prisoners. Having failed in his mission, but remaining true to his promise, Regulus returned to Carthage and was tortured to death.

The distribution of the six roles emphasizes filial as opposed to erotic love. The main couple is Regulus (alto castrato) and his daughter Attilia (soprano), leaving the latter's husband (the impassioned Licinius, another castrato) to the "remainder." The second couple consists of Hamilcar, the Carthaginian ambassador, and Barce, a Carthaginian noblewoman who has been kept as a slave by Publius, Regulus's son, who also loves her. (In another act of noble magnanimity, Publius gives her back her freedom to return to Carthage with Hamilcar.) The remainder consists of Licinius, Publius (who must argue in the Senate against the proposed peace even though its rejection means his father's certain death); and Manlius, Regulus's successor as consul, who at first is ruled by envy of his predecessor, but is finally persuaded by Regulus's sterling example to act nobly on behalf of state and civic interests.

The libretto's ideology of civic fortitude and heroic sacrifice to the social order is most explicitly set forth by negative example, through the mouth of the uncomprehending Barce, the Carthaginian slave, who is portrayed with undisguised racial contempt. The librettist describes her as "a pleasing, beautiful and lively African," whose "temperament, like that of her nation, is amorous," not noble.[5] She cannot fathom the magnanimity of the Romans, Metastasio's idealized European patrons. "What strange ideas does the love of praise excite in Rome!" she declares (in the words of Metastasio's eighteenth-century translator, John Hoole), and continues:

> With envy Manlius views his rival's chains, while Regulus abhors the public pity that would save his life. The daughter glories in her father's sufferings, and Publius — this surpasses all belief! — Publius, my beauty's slave, for honor's sake, resigns the mistress whom his soul adores.[6]

That is the recitative preceding Barce's last exit aria, which begins, "But thanks be to Heaven, I don't have a Roman soul!"

Metastasio prepared this grand quintessence of everything that is meant by the word "august" for a gala performance in Vienna to honor Emperor Charles VI on his saint's name day in 1740. Charles's sudden death two weeks before the planned celebration prevented its performance. Instead of letting the work out for another occasion, Metastasio continued to work on it intermittently over the next nine years, during which time it was on several occasions performed at court under the Empress Maria Theresa as a spoken play despite its operatic structure that turned every character into an endlessly soliloquizing Hamlet. Metastasio always maintained that his librettos were suitable for spoken performance and that he would rather hear them that way than poorly set.

Metastasio finally let *Attilio Regolo* out for setting in 1749 at the request of King Frederick Augustus II of Saxony, who wanted to have it performed at his court in Dresden. The proposed composer, Johann Adolf Hasse (1699–1783), was a musician the librettist could trust. He had already composed 43 *opere serie*, fifteen of them to Metastasio libretti (one of them for Vienna, where it had triumphed in the poet's presence). Even so, Metastasio sent Hasse a long letter, now a classic text of music history, in which he detailed his wishes as to how his text should be set.

FIG. 23-4   Johann Adolf Hasse, copperplate engraving by C. F. Riedel after a painting by Pietro Antonio Rotari (1707–1762).

In particular, he bade the composer set certain key passages — mainly the title character's occasional soliloquies of impassioned self-doubt — in accompanied recitative (*recitativo obligato* in eighteenth-century Italian), a style reserved for very special effects, in which the whole orchestra, not just the continuo, accompanied the singer. And he counseled so, as he put it to Hasse, "for (you know this as well as I) the same words and sentiments may be uttered, according to the diversity of situation, in such a manner as to express either joy, sorrow, anger, or pity."[7] And music may underscore such nuances and ironies with peerless subtlety and truthfulness "by the judicious and alternate use of *pianos* and *fortes*, by *rinforzandos* [sudden loudening], by *staccatos*, slurs, accelerating and retarding the measure, *arpeggios*, shakes [trills], *sostenutos* [that is, *fermatas* or holds], and above all, by new modulation [of the harmony]." With the insight of the trained musician that he was, Metastasio presumed to instruct the composer how to let the music not merely transcribe or represent, still less duplicate, but actually *supplement* (at times by contradicting) the meanings of the words to which it is set. Hasse, it may be presumed, did not really need this lesson. It is something all successful opera composers know, for it is the very idea of the *dramma per musica* — not just "a play for music," as normally translated, but a play *through* music.

Metastasio's letter was dated 20 October 1749. The première of Hasse's lengthy opera took place on 12 January 1750, a mere 84 days later. That speediness was enough, from the point of view of its producers and consumers, to justify all the many easily derided conventions of the *opera seria*.

METASTASIO'S MUSICIANS

Partly because it was a fairly late work and partly because of its extraordinary literary demands, *Attilio Regolo* was not frequently set to music. Besides Hasse's setting there were only three others, the last in 1780. By contrast, Metastasio's most popular libretto, the most frequently reused operatic libretto of all time, was *Artaserse* (Artaxerxes). It was set first in 1730 by Leonardo Vinci, Scarlatti's successor as *maestro di cappella* in Naples, for performance in Rome. Vinci's setting became a frequently revived classic in its own right and helped establish the text as a must for budding composers. (Two very famous later composers of opera, Christoph Willibald Ritter von Gluck and Johann Christian Bach, made their debuts with settings of *Artaserse*, in 1741 and 1760 respectively.)

In all, over ninety settings of this libretto are known, the last being *The Regicide*, set in translation by a composer named Lucas for performance in London at the incredibly late date of 1840, some 110 years after the first setting was heard. On the way, just about every important composer of *opera seria* set it, including Giuseppe Scarlatti, a nephew or grandnephew (accounts differ) of Alessandro, who set it for Lucca in 1747; Baldassare Galuppi, who set it for Vienna, and Niccolò Jommelli, who set it for Rome, both in 1749 (each of them made at least one later setting as well); Giuseppe Sarti, who set it for the Royal Theater of Copenhagen in 1760; Thomas Arne, who set it for London in 1762; Niccolò Piccinni, who set it for Rome in 1762; Giovanni Paisiello, who set it for Modena in 1771; Josef Mysliveček, who set it for Naples in 1774; Domenico Cimarosa, who set it for Turin in 1784; and Nicolas Isouard, who set it for Livorno in 1794.

Hasse, Metastasio's favorite, set *Artaserse* three times: for Venice in 1730, close on the heels of Vinci; for Dresden in 1740; and for Naples in 1760. In 1734, following a common practice, a *refacimento* of Hasse's first setting was presented in London in the form of a *pasticcio* or hodgepodge (literally a pie), in which a lot of the original music was replaced with popular arias by other composers, including Nicola Porpora, a Neapolitan composer who was then enjoying a great vogue in the English capital, and Ricardo Broschi, another visiting Neapolitan, who wrote for it (under circumstances shortly to be described) one of the most celebrated arias of the century.

What has so far gone without saying, but had better be said now, is that with the sole exception of Arne's (for reasons that will emerge in a later chapter), and of course Lucas's anachronistic *Regicide* of 1840, every one of these settings was performed in Italian, wherever it was staged (whether in Denmark or in Russia, where a setting by Francesco Araja was given for the St. Petersburg court as early as 1738), whatever the composer's nationality (whether Czech like Mysliveček or Maltese French like Isouard), and whether or not the audience understood the language in which it was sung. And that is because wherever *opera seria* was sung, the singers were mainly Italian virtuosi, whose careers (like those of most Italian composers) were international.

The international status — indeed, the "world" hegemony — of Italian music (and not only opera) from the late seventeenth to the early nineteenth centuries is still reflected in the Western "classical" musicians' vocabulary, which to this day is an international patois based largely on the terminology the Italians brought with them wherever they went. (This is already demonstrated by the translation given above of Metastasio's letter to Hasse, which was published in 1796 by Sir Charles Burney, the English music historian; even in the adapted version given here, alterations are mainly substitutions of more familiar Italian words, like *fermata*, for the less common ones Burney employed.)

THE FORTUNES OF *ARTASERSE*

Because there is so much material to choose from, the ubiquitous *Artaserse*, in its various early settings, makes an ideal introduction to the music of the *opera seria*. Metastasio's own plot synopsis or *argomento* was published in all of the opera's printed *libretti* — the "little books" that were sold to the audience so that they could follow the text if they wished, including the lines of recitative that had been cut by the composer. The story, attributed to the third-century Roman historian Justin (Marcus Junianus Justinus), reads as follows:

> Artabanus, chief officer to Xerxes, King of Persia, seeing the power of the king diminish daily because of his losses to the Greeks, hopes to sacrifice to his own ambition the whole royal family, along with the abovementioned Xerxes, and ascend the Persian throne. Therefore, taking advantage of the ease of access to which his intimate friendship with his master entitled him, he gained entry to Xerxes' palace at night and killed him. Then, to dispose of the royal princes, Xerxes' sons, he sets them one against the other, causing Artaxerxes, one of the abovementioned sons, to kill his own brother Darius, believing him to be a parricide upon Artabanus's insinuation. The only thing the traitor fails to accomplish according to plan is the death of Artaxerxes. Through various accidents (which supply the episodes that adorn the present drama), in the end his treason is exposed and the safety of Artaxerxes is assured, which exposure and assurance are the main action of the drama.[8]

And yet it is a question what is the main action and what are the episodes, since the greater part of the libretto's actual events, and four of its six characters, were "freely" invented by Metastasio so as to meet the specific demands of opera. Artabanus and Artaxerxes are transferred from the historical account to the operatic plot, but neither of them belong to the "first couple." That pair, to whom the lion's share of arias are assigned, consists of Arbaces, Artabanus's son and Artaxerxes' bosom friend, and Mandane, Artaxerxes' sister, who is Arbaces's beloved. To round out the second couple and achieve a pleasing symmetry, Artaxerxes is also given a beloved: Semira, daughter of Artabanus and sister of Arbaces. Thus the sister of each main male character is the other's lover. And so as to have an "inferior" character as part of the remainder, Artabanus is given an evil confidant: Megabises, a corrupt army general.

Such an extreme symmetry of design cries out for a "structuralist" interpretation that will bring its motivating premises to light. Martha Feldman, a historian of the genre, has embodied the relationships in *Artaserse* in an ingenious diagram representing what she calls its "archetypal geometry."[9] It is laid out in the form of two "patriarchal triangles," with the rival fathers Xerxes (an unseen presence) and Artabanus at their heads (Fig. 23-5). Stripped to its most basic level, the story of the opera reduces to the fundamental narrative of all *opere serie*: "a moral tale of impure elements tamed and eradicated from the idealized body politic."

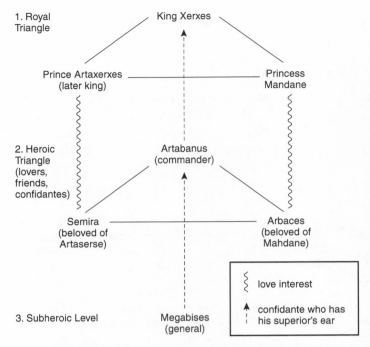

1. Royal Triangle

King Xerxes

Prince Artaxerxes (later king) —————— Princess Mandane

2. Heroic Triangle (lovers, friends, confidantes)

Artabanus (commander)

Semira (beloved of Artaserse) —————— Arbaces (beloved of Mahdane)

3. Subheroic Level

Megabises (general)

〰 love interest

↑ confidante who has his superior's ear

FIG. 23-5 "Geometry" of the dramatis personae in Metastasio's libretto *Artaserse* (after Martha Feldman).

The invention of Arbaces gives Artabanus a new motive for killing Xerxes, who has tried to prevent the marriage of his daughter to Artabanus's son, a social inferior. That is what makes Arbaces the central character in the drama, for it is he who symbolizes the basic conflict between love and duty.

In the first act, Artabanus exchanges swords with Arbaces so as to hide the murder weapon. But later, to exculpate himself, he reveals the bloody sword in Arbaces's possession to Artaxerxes and accuses the bewildered Arbaces of the murder. Artaxerxes, mourning his father and brother and loath to execute his friend and prospective brother-in-law, is bereft and confused. In the second act, Artabanus proposes to Arbaces a plan not only to escape but to usurp the throne; but Arbaces, the paragon of honor, refuses to cooperate, leaving his father at once enraged at his disobedience and awed by his probity. Semira pleads with Artaxerxes to show mercy for her brother, but Mandane, more loyal to her class and family ties than to her lover, calls for vengeance against the man she believes to have killed her father. Artaxerxes, still trusting Artabanus, bids him resolve the matter. Artabanus, to everyone's horror, condemns his son to death but is still secretly planning to dispossess Artaxerxes and put Arbaces on the throne.

In the third act, Artaxerxes, despite Arbaces's apparent treason, releases his friend from imprisonment on the condition that he exile himself forever. Artabanus then comes to his son's cell to rescue him, but finding it empty assumes that Arbaces has been executed. Mandane laments his death; but Arbaces, overhearing her, reveals himself alive and proclaims his love, vowing to die rather than leave her, showing his steadfastness.

Meanwhile Artabanus, still up to no good, poisons the wine in Artaxerxes' coronation cup. The coronation is interrupted, just as Artaxerxes is about to drink, by reports of a rebellion that has been fomented by Megabises on behalf of Artabanus. Arbaces, at first suspected of leading it, reveals himself as its suppressor and is reconciled with Artaxerxes. As a token of renewed friendship, Artaxerxes offers Arbaces the first sip from the coronation cup. Artabanus, who loves his son despite all his evil designs, intervenes and confesses. He is at first condemned, but Arbaces offers his life in place of his father's, thus proving once again his true nobility of spirit and making himself worthy of Mandane's hand. Artaxerxes, in an act of kingly magnanimity, commutes Artabanus's sentence to exile and the two loving couples are betrothed amid coronation festivities. The last number in the opera is a "chorus" (that is, an ensemble of all the principals minus the banished Artabanus) praising the clemency shown his enemies by Artaxerxes, the "Giusto Re" ("just king").

The opera contains thirty arias in all. Arbaces, the *primo uomo*, gets six (two per act); Mandane, the *prima donna*, gets five. In addition, the first couple, in accordance with their prerogative, sing the one duet in the opera, which occurs in the act III declaration scene, giving Arbaces a total of seven numbers and Mandane six. Artaxerxes, Artabanus, and Semira have five apiece. Last, and least, Megabises makes do with three (one per act), which is actually rather generous for an inferior role. As the main character, Arbaces gets to sing not only the most arias but also the most elaborate ones.

Particularly impressive is his *aria di bravura* in act III, sc. 1, which Arbaces sings upon leaving his cell and setting off for points unknown. It is a "simile aria," in which the singer's situation or emotion is pinpointed by means of a poetic image, here *L'onda dal mar divisa* — a wave severed from the sea. Vinci's setting (Ex. 23-5), from the original Rome production of 1730, is typical of his style, and that of the early *opera seria* generally. It also typifies the music that the great castratos sang. (The part was originally intended for Giovanni Carestini, already a famous soprano at the age of twenty-six, of whom Hasse would say, "he who has not heard Carestini is not acquainted with the most perfect style of singing."[10])

It was a style Vinci had in fact pioneered, making him historically a figure of considerable importance, even if his music is forgotten today, along (for the most part) with the *opera seria* itself. *Artaserse* was the short-lived Vinci's last opera (out of thirty-one, all composed between the ages of twenty-five and thirty-four!), and his

E X. 23-5A   Leonardo Vinci, "L'onda dal mare divisa" (*Artaserse*, Act III, scene 1), mm. 1–24.

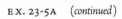

EX. 23-5A   (continued)

EX. 23-5B   Leonardo Vinci, "L'onda dal mare divisa" (*Artaserse*, Act III, scene 1), mm. 39–55.

EX. 23-5C   Leonardo Vinci, "L'onda dal mare divisa" (*Artaserse*, Act III, scene 1), mm. 136–56.

sixth setting of a Metastasio libretto. By the time he wrote it, the da capo aria format had undergone considerable transformation since Scarlatti's death, only a decade or so before.

The lengthy orchestral ritornello (Ex. 23-5a) consists of three distinct, indeed contrasting, parts: an initial statement of the main theme that will be taken up by the singer, a middle section "spun out" in sequences of triplets, and a final cadential phrase. The ritornello alternates with the voice three times during the aria's first section: $R^1V^1R^2V^2R^3$. Each vocal passage consists of a complete setting of the first sentence of the text, so that the entire text is repeated, giving the "A" section of the aria its greater amplitude. The repetitions are tonally contrasted: the first begins in the tonic

FIG. 23-6   Leonardo Vinci, caricature by Pier Leone Ghezzi (1674–1755).

and cadences in the dominant; the second, following the complementary trajectory, begins in the dominant and cadences in the tonic. The middle and final ritornellos are partial ones, consisting of a bit of the triplet material plus the cadence phrase. The "triplet material," as becomes evident when the singer takes it up in impressively "wavy" melismas (Ex. 23-5b), represents the motion of the metaphorical sea.

The aria's middle section (Ex. 23-5c) also embodies a tonal contrast, beginning in the relative minor and ending with a cadence on the subdominant. Thus the piece is laid out according to a clearly demarcated sectional plan, articulated by cadences and tonal "movement," that organizes a relatively long span of time. But if the format of the aria has become ampler and more complicated since the time of Scarlatti, the texture has been simplified. Dr. Burney, a great admirer of Vinci, gave him credit (perhaps a little too much credit) for virtually reinventing opera along lines similar to those that attended its original invention among the Florentines a century before.

"Without degrading his art," Burney exulted, Vinci "rendered it the friend, though not the slave to poetry, by simplifying and polishing melody, and calling the attention of the audience chiefly to the voice-part, by disentangling it from fugue, complication, and laboured contrivance."[11] And yet one of Vinci's contemporaries, Pier Francesco Tosi, a castrato and a famous singing teacher, complained in his *Observations on the Florid Song*, published in Bologna in 1723, that "poor Counterpoint has been condemn'd, in this corrupted Age, to beg for a piece of Bread in the Churches"[12] (where the *stile antico* still hung on).

The place to look, when judging texture, is the bass line, and Vinci's static bass gives credence both to Burney's delight, and to Tosi's complaint, that counterpoint had been banished from the theater. Vinci's bass is no longer in a contrapuntal relationship to the melody but rather its well-subordinated harmonic accompanist. Its cadential rests very often coincide with those of the melody, so that the phrases are very clearly set off and balanced one against another. For long passages, indeed, the bass is confined to reiterations of single pitches that change regularly on the bar line. It is most static, in fact, precisely when the voice part is the most florid, leaving no doubt about who is carrying the musical ball. Like everything else in the setting, the homophonic — indeed, newly "homophonized" — texture casts a spotlight on the virtuoso singer.

Also noteworthy is a new style of orchestration, in which two horns join the orchestral strings, never to play *obbligati* (that is, independent melodic lines) but only to double the string parts or provide harmonic support. The sound thus gained is handsome, but the use of natural brass instruments sets new and narrow limits on the harmony, virtually confining it to what we now call the "primary" chords — tonic, dominant, subdominant. These limits were not only acceptable but actually desirable within the new style; they were an additional simplification and clarification of design.

The use of horns or trumpets as supporting members of the band can be found in earlier Italian music — in the work of Scarlatti, for one, and in even older composers. Scarlatti used to be given credit for it along with so much else to which he is no longer thought entitled, not only because the work of his older contemporaries was even less well known today than his but also because innovations, historians tended to feel, had to have protagonists. More likely the practice originated in the unwritten repertories that provided the stylistic background to the new Italian idioms we are now discovering. Its incorporation into "art" music coincided with the "liberation of melody" so touted by Burney, among others, and the undisputed sovereignty of the singers who sang them.

Just how much the singers controlled the show in *opera seria* we cannot tell by looking at just one setting of a given libretto. We have to compare settings. So let's have a look at the analogous number — Arbaces's exit aria in act III, sc. 1 — in Hasse's *Artaserse*, composed in the same year as Vinci's for performance in Venice. And to our surprise, we find that it is a wholly different aria — different not only in music but in text as well. Metastasio's original simile aria has been bumped, as it were, in favor of another (by a poet unknown) consisting of an accompanied recitative ("Ch'io parta?"/"Should I go?"; Ex. 23-6a) and a much more florid, virtuosic aria in which the voice enters (Ex. 23-6b) with a long held note on the first syllable of the word "Parto" ("I go"), and then begins again with the main theme as foreshadowed by the ritornello: "Parto qual pastorello prima che rompa il fiume" ("I go like a shepherd lad before the flood"). Ex. 23-6c shows the beginning of the first main vocal passage, to give an idea of the extreme virtuosity required of the singer.

The reason for the substitution lies in the casting. The role of Arbaces was sung in Venice by the greatest of the eighteenth century castrati and very likely the greatest opera singer who ever lived: Carlo Broschi (1705–82), known as Farinelli, after the Farina family, a noble Neapolitan clan who were his earliest patrons. Although he was undisputed champion among the singers of his time and lived a long life, Farinelli had a short public career, beginning in Naples in 1720 and ending in London in 1737. Afterwards he joined the household of King Philip V of Spain, whom he served not only as court singer but as a trusted and powerful counselor as well. The development of Farinelli's career was mirrored in the music his talent inspired. He left behind a veritable wake of florid arias, indeed the fanciest, most embellished vocal music in the entire European operatic tradition.

The substitute aria interpolated into Hasse's version of *Artaserse* was very likely a "portfolio aria," composed by Hasse just for Farinelli to use as a signature piece.

EX. 23-6A   Johann Adolf Hasse, *Artaserse* (1730), recitativo obligato ("Ch'io parta?") mm. 1–9.

All the great castrati had such arias that they brought with them wherever they sang. When Hasse revised his setting of *Artaserse* thirty years later for performance in Naples, Farinelli was no longer active — and sure enough, the 1760 score reverts to Metastasio's original aria text, "L'onda dal mar divisa", set this time with only modest coloraturas and without any *recitativo obligato*.

The ultimate Farinellian signature tune was the famous shipwreck simile aria, "Son qual nave ch'agitata" ("I am like a storm-tossed boat at sea"), first heard in the London pasticcio version of *Artaserse* in 1734. Although published that same year in

EX. 23-6B   Johann Adolf Hasse, *Artaserse* (1730), aria ("Parto qual pastorello prima che rompa il fiume"), mm. 37–45.

a volume called "The Favourite Songs in the Opera call'd Artaxerxes by Sig. Hasse," this particular vehicle was actually the work of the singer's brother Ricardo Broschi (1698–1756), a minor Neapolitan composer who has ridden his sibling's coattails into the history books. (Except for the recitatives, the whole role of Arbaces was done over for this production, mainly by Farinelli's former teacher, Porpora, then one of the reigning composers for the London stage.)

Ex. 23-7 gives the first solo entrance of an abridged and simplified version of this virtually incredible display aria, published in 1734, with the orchestral accompaniment (the by-then standard strings and horns) reduced to a single violin line. The full

EX. 23-6C   Johann Adolf Hasse, *Artaserse* (1730), aria ("Parto qual pastorello prima che rompa il fiume"), mm. 49–57.

EX. 23-7   Riccardo Broschi, "Son qual nave ch'agitata"

Son qual na — — — — ve   Son qual na - ve ch' a-gi-ta - ta

seque

da più sco - gli in mezzo all' on - de   si   con-fon - de   si   con-fon - de

6   5   6
                            5   #

e spa-ven-ta — — — — — — —

2

- ta   va sol-can-do in   al - to mar

#6   7
                          #3

EX. 23-7 (*continued*)

score, with many more virtuoso turns, is found in a manuscript that the Spanish king (Farinelli's patron) sent Maria Theresa (Metastasio's patron) as a gift in 1753, containing the repertory with which the retired singer now entertained the Spanish court in private.[13]

OPERA SERIA IN (AND AS) PRACTICE

The first sung phrase in Ex. 23-7 is followed by a fermata in the printed score. Such fermatas in virtuoso arias signal not a pause but a "cadenza" (short for *cadenza fiorita*, "ornamented cadence"), an unwritten solo that can come (as here) after the textual "motto," but that more often precedes — and delays — an important cadence. Cadenzas are display vehicles abounding in what their singers called *passaggii*, from which we get our English term "passage" or "passagework," replacing the earlier English "divisions." In theory cadenzas were improvised by the singer on the spot, but in practice they were often worked out in advance and memorized.

There are three fermatas signaling cadenzas during the second vocal solo alone in the version of Farinelli's shipwreck aria in the Maria Theresa manuscript, and we have the word of many earwitnesses that singers considered all of the main cadences in an aria fair game for embellishment. As often happens, it was chiefly those who disapproved of the practice, or of what they took to be its abuse, who took the trouble to write about it. P. F. Tosi, himself a singer (but writing as a preceptor of singers), complained in 1723 that the ends of all three sections in da capo arias were becoming overgrown with cadenzas: during the first cadenza, "the orchestra waits"; during the second "the dose is increased, and the orchestra grows tired."[14] But during the last

FIG. 23-7   Jacopo Amigoni, portrait of Farinelli (center), surrounded by (left to right) Metastasio, Teresa Castellini, the artist, and the artist's page, holding his palette.

cadenza, chaffs Tosi, "the throat is set going like a weather-cock in a whirlwind, and the orchestra yawns." There was a touch of envy here, perhaps, for we do not find much indication of audiences complaining. Nor did Metastasio himself, who might have been expected to think the practice of interpolating cadenzas, and also of adding coloraturas by the bushel to the da capo repeat, an assault upon his handiwork. Quite the contrary: as we see in a group portrait (Fig. 23-7) by the Madrid painter Jacopo Amigoni (now hanging in the National Gallery of Victoria in Melbourne, Australia), Metastasio and Farinelli were the best of friends. They met in 1720, when the singer, then a teenager, made his Neapolitan debut on the very occasion at which the poet's verses for music were first sung in public, and remained on terms of intimacy until the end of their lives more than sixty years later. (The figures in the portrait, from left to right, are Metastasio, Farinelli's pupil the soprano Teresa Castellini, Farinelli, the artist, and his page.) The great librettist recognized the great singer as a major influence — a far greater one than any composer — on the development of the *opera seria* and its supremely ornate, aristocratic musical style. The two of them, Metastasio and Farinelli, were likewise universally regarded during the eighteenth century as being far more important to the art of opera than any composer, and so a historian must regard them as well.

"PERFORMANCE PRACTICE"

It is no easy task nowadays, even for a historian, to demote the composer from the top of the musical hierarchy or to acknowledge the fluidity of *opera seria* texts at the hands of the singers, not to mention the crucial importance of unwritten music to the genre. In an essay of 1957 devoted (with *opera seria* uppermost in mind) to the variable aspects of performance practice and the relatively weak integrity of musical texts during this period, Donald Jay Grout argued strongly, and against longstanding prejudice, that "the problem with regard to most old music is not to determine a single, fixed, invariable practice."[15] And yet in the very next sentence, he made an assertion with which no one involved with opera during the seventeenth or the eighteenth century would have agreed. The real problem, as he put it, was "rather to determine the limits within which the several aspects of performance might have fluctuated without leading to results that the composers would have found unacceptable."

We do not know what these limits were, we will never know them, and they do not matter, because during the period in question nobody ever consulted the composers about such things. The highest arbiter of taste and practice was the ruler or patron; next in order of clout came the audience; next the singer; next the librettist. The composer was there to serve them all. Now we ordinarily think just the opposite: that librettist and performer are there to serve the composer, and that even the audience must strive to adapt itself to the demands that composers make.

As we shall see, these familiar ideas were all tenets of Romanticism, and, in an even stronger form, of modernism. They are the philosophical foundations, in other words, of nineteenth- and twentieth-century art. They arose precisely in reaction to the decline of noble patronage, and they are utterly anachronistic to the esthetics of *opera seria*.

The fundamental values of the *opera seria*, as reflected in the ranking of librettists and singers above composers, are so remote from today's "classical" musical values that the culture that produced such a thing can seem entirely alien and paradoxical today. Apparent contradictions abound. One is the clash between the high-minded reformist mission that demanded the removal of comic scenes from librettos (thus enabling the very concept of "serious opera") and the spectacular antics of performers — often crowd-pleasing to the point of clownishness.

The liberties singers were *expected* to take with the written music, and *had* to take or lose all respect, would be thought a virtually inconceivable desecration today. But that was the very least of it: the great Neapolitan castrato Gaetano Majorano, known as Caffarelli (1710–83), another pupil of Porpora who was generally ranked second only to Farinelli, was actually arrested and imprisoned, according to the police report, for "disturbing the other performers, acting in a manner bordering on lasciviousness (on stage) with one of the female singer, conversing with the spectators in the boxes from the stage, ironically echoing whichever member of the company was singing an aria, and finally refusing to sing in the *ripieno* [the concluding "chorus" of principals] with the others."[16] He was released, however, by royal command and reinstated in the company, for he was the public's darling. They loved his monkeyshines.

Now what sort of public would tolerate such behavior, let alone delight in it? Nowadays only a circus audience, perhaps; surely not any sort of "serious" theatrical public. We, who expect (and are expected!) to sit still and pay attention when attending any theatrical performance, can only regard the behavior of the *opera seria* audience as something virtually other-planetary. That audience, a mixture of aristocracy and urban middle class (what we would now call "professionals" — doctors, lawyers, clergy, civil servants, and military officers), was famed throughout Europe for its sublime inattention. They "sat (or roamed) in a continuously well-lit auditorium," as one commentator remarked, having come to the theater "to see itself as much as to see the show." As Feldman reports (citing research by Kathleen Hansell), at San Bartolomeo in Naples, a particularly aristocratic house, "noise levels astonished diarists from abroad, nobility arrived with servants who cooked whole meals, talked, played [at cards], and relieved themselves in the antechambers that stood in back of each lavish box."[17] Even if we avoid judging such manners by contemporary standards of decorum, we are easily left bewildered. Never mind questions of mere etiquette. How is all of this evident anarchy on stage and in the hall to be reconciled with the nature of the dramas themselves, which (as we have observed in some detail) exalt a perfectly ordained, God-given, and rigidly hierarchical social order?

The explanation for all these apparent contradictions lies partly in the social mixture alluded to above. The *opera seria* had a dual inheritance. Its subject matter descended from the courtly opera of old and shared its politics of submission and affirmation. The theaters were maintained in most cases by royalty, and the performances *as occasions* were embedded, as historians are at pains to point out, in the forms and hierarchies of absolutism. The theatrical schedule itself reflected this: performances, particularly galas, were held on royal birthdays and name days, as well as church holidays. The librettos were metaphorical embodiments of these occasions. This, so to speak, was Metastasio's heritage.

Farinelli's heritage, on the other hand, was that of the commercial opera theater, even if, at its height, the art of the castrato was by virtue of its sheer price primarily an aristocratic property and even, in its floridity and flamboyance, a virtual symbol of noble aggrandizement. (The word *virtuoso*, which became an international word exactly at this time as applied to singers, comes from the Italian word *virtù*, "virtue"; in modern Italian *virtuosità* still means "virtuousness.") The art of such a singer only began with the written notes. Many theatrical virtuosi did not read music well, if at all, and learned their arias by rote as a basis for personalized embellishment. Recitatives were often improvised outright, based on the harmonies the singers could overhear from the pit, and the words that they overheard from the prompter's box. In a more literal sense than we would ever guess today, only the libretti (or more narrowly yet, only the words of the recitatives) were fully fixed and "literate" in *opera seria*.

There is no comparable genre in classical music today. The modern counterpart of the *opera seria* castrato is the improvising jazz ("scat") or pop singer. And the relationship such singers have with their audience is again sooner comparable to that between the *opera seria* audience and the castrato than that between any sort of contemporary "classical" musician and the modern concert or opera audience. However inattentive during recitatives or "sherbet arias," the audience sprang to attention when the *primo uomo* held forth, egging him on with applause and spontaneous shouts of encouragement at each vocal feat. The singers, striking their attitudes front and center, had to work to capture their hearers' attention. They had, quite literally, to seduce the noble boxholders, drawing them out from the backs of their boxes, because listening to the music was only one of the things the audience was there to do.

For nobles and urban professionals tended in those days to live their social lives outside of their houses, especially in the evenings. A box at the opera, rented for the season, was a virtual living space, and occupying it was a social ritual in which the musical performance was not the only component, or even necessarily the most important one, especially as the season consisted of only a few works, each of which had a run of twenty or thirty performances. The audience, in perpetual attendance, "could hardly have been expected to take a close interest in the action after the first few performances," as McClymonds notes.[18] "And since the literate part of it knew Metastasio's dramas virtually by heart," she continues, "they could dip in and out at will, interrupting the flow of social intercourse to attend to the most affecting scenes or the favorite arias of the leading singers."

In any case, as Feldman shrewdly observes, listening and reacting to the performance "was rarely prescribed."[19] The only occasions when you did have to behave and pay attention were those evenings when the king himself, the latent subject of the opera, was present, enacting his role of surrogate father (or "sire"). What could better attest to the nature of "patriarchy," the social system that the *opera seria* preeminently reflected? At other times, listening to the opera was only one option that could be "selected from a heavy menu of social choices."

The modern counterpart, again, is not any sort of classical musical performance, or indeed any musical performance. Rather, it is the living room TV, which in many homes today hums in the background all evening and is only occasionally watched. It works as the symbol and embodiment of at-homeness, and so did the *opera seria*. For all their obstreperous behavior, indeed *through* their obstreperous behavior, the *opera seria* audience demonstrated their at-homeness with the genre and with the patriarchal social structure that it validated. It is about the crispest example the history of European music can furnish of an art invested with, and affirming, a social and political system — a system with which no one educated according to the principles of the Enlightenment (which is to say, just about anyone reading this book) could possibly sympathize today.

So once again the questions nag: How do we relate to the artistic products that bolstered an ugly patriarchal, absolutist politics in their time? Can they be detached from it? Can we vote for the art and reject the politics? It is the job of a book like this one to raise these questions, not answer them. In any case, though, it would be a feat of understatement to note that the social use to which opera is put has changed, and changed radically, since the days of Scarlatti or Metastasio. It would make little sense to expect its content or its manner of execution to have remained the same — or to think that the *opera seria* could be revived today, in today's opera houses, for today's audiences. (To begin with what you'd have to begin with, the return of the castrato voice would be about as likely or as feasible as the return of public hangings.) Sometimes, though, it is just those aspects of bygone art that are most bygone from which we can learn the most about ourselves and our present world, and the place of art within it. That is enough to justify the long and lingering, if not exactly loving, look we have just taken at what is perhaps the most irrevocably bygone genre in the history of European art music.

The Italian Concerto Style and the Rise of Tonality-driven Form

CORELLI, VIVALDI, AND THEIR GERMAN IMITATORS

STANDARDIZED GENRES AND TONAL PRACTICES

As far as we know, Arcangelo Corelli (1653–1713) never set a word of text to music. A virtuoso violinist, he was the first European composer who enjoyed international recognition as a "great" exclusively on the strength of his finely wrought instrumental ensemble works. They circulated widely in print both during his lifetime and for almost a century after his death, providing countless other musicians with models for imitation. In his chosen domain of chamber and orchestral music for strings, he was the original "classic," playing a major role in standardizing genres and practices, and setting instrumental music on an epoch-making path of ascendency. His sonatas and concertos may no longer be played much except by violin students, and yet their historical significance is tremendous, affecting European music of every sort.

Corelli's career, based (after apprenticeship in Bologna) almost exclusively in Rome, outwardly paralleled Alessandro Scarlatti's: service to Queen Christina and Cardinal Ottoboni, membership in the Arcadian Society, and so on. His main activities were leading orchestras, sometimes numbering one hundred musicians or more, in the richly endowed churches and cathedrals of the city, and appearing as soloist at "academies" (*accademie*), aristocratic house concerts.

For sacred venues Corelli perfected an existing Roman genre known as *sonata da chiesa* (church sonata). Such pieces could be variously scored: for solo violin and continuo, for two violins and continuo (hence "trio sonata," albeit normally played by four instrumentalists), or amplified by a backup band known as the *concerto grosso* ("large ensemble"), which eventually lent its name to the genre itself. Thus when Corelli's collected orchestral music was finally published in 1714 (a year after the composer's death) by the Amsterdam printer Estienne Roger, the title page used the term *concerto grosso* in both senses at once: *Concerti grossi con duoi violini e violoncello di concertino obligato e duoi altri violini, viola e basso di concerto grosso ad arbitrio, che si potranno radoppiare, opera sesta.* Reissued the next year by the London house of John Walsh and John Hare, the title page was Englished thus: "*Concerti grossi*, being XII great concertos, or sonatas, for two violins and a violoncello: or for two violins more, a tenor, and a

FIG. 24-1   Arcangelo Corelli, portrait by Hugh Howard, adapted as the frontispiece engraving for a late edition of Corelli's trio sonatas, op. 1 (Amsterdam: Estienne Roger and Michel Charles Le Cène, ca. 1715).

thorough-bass: which may be doubled at pleasure, being the sixth and last work of Arcangelo Corelli." Church sonatas or concerti grossi were often played during Mass to accompany liturgical actions: typical placements were between the scripture readings (in place of the Gradual), at the collection (in place of the Offertory) or at Communion. At Vespers they could be played before Psalms in place of antiphons. A standardized outgrowth of the earlier canzona, the church sonata usually had four main sections in contrasting tempos ("movements"), cast in two slow – fast pairs resembling preludes and fugues such as organists were used to improvising. The more elaborate of these fugal movements was the one in the first pair; it was still occasionally labeled "canzona."

For aristocratic salons, Corelli adopted another standard violinist's genre, called *sonata* (or *concerto*) *da camera* (chamber sonata or concerto). This was essentially a dance suite, which Corelli adapted to the prevailing four-movement format (a "preludio" and three dances or connecting movements). Between 1681 and 1694 Corelli published forty-eight trio sonatas in four collections of twelve, alternating church sonatas (opp. 1 and 3) and chamber sonatas (opp. 2 and 4).

The eleventh church sonata from opus 3 (1689) and the second chamber sonata from opus 4 (1694) make an effective pair for comparison both with one another and with the works of other composers. They are both in the key of G minor, and illustrate between them virtually the full range of Corellian forms and styles. They also show the overlap in practice between the church and chamber genres. Their last movements, especially, might be interchanged (see Ex. 24-1a-b, which show their respective first halves). Although one is marked *corrente* (a fast triple-metered dance) and the other, untitled, is implicitly a fugal movement, they are virtually identical in form (binary), texture (imitative), and character (lively culmination). But where the second movement of the sonata da camera, the *allemanda*, is also a binary dance movement, the second movement of the sonata da chiesa (the "canzona" movement) is "abstract" and "through-composed" as befits its forebear. Stylistically, that "canzona" movement (presto) from op. 3, no. 11 (Ex. 24-3) may be the most revealing movement of all. A

EX. 24-1A Arcangelo Corelli, *Sonata da chiesa*, Op. 3, no. 11, final Allegro, mm. 1–12

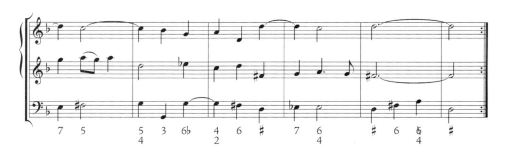

EX. 24-1B Arcangelo Corelli, *Sonata da camera*, Op. 4, no. 2, final Corrente, mm. 1–25

EX. 24-1B *(continued)*

brief comparison with a work (Ex. 24-2) by one of Corelli's Austrian contemporaries, Johann Joseph Fux (1660–1741), will indicate what was so novel about the work of the Italian composer, and so potent.

Fux, we may recall from chapter 16, was a conservative and academic musician. His best-known work was no musical composition but a textbook, *Gradus ad Parnassum*, which remained for more than a century the standard compendium of the *stile antico*, the mock-Palestrina style that counterpoint students still learn to imitate in school, using methods that are still derived from Fux's famous analysis of strict counterpoint into five rhythmic "species." The stately sonata for two viols and continuo in canonic style (published in 1701), of which the opening is given in Ex. 24-2, illustrates not the *stile antico* itself, but rather the kind of modern contrapuntal virtuosity that immersion in the *stile antico* was meant to instill.

Like Corelli's, Fux's is a church sonata, meant to replace the Mass Gradual on a festive occasion. Its measured, allemande-like tread lends it a noble "affect" or mood. The leisurely three-measure interval of imitation sets the standard "sentence-length" for the piece. The opening tune breaks that standard sentence into three asymmetrical, cunningly apportioned phrases, each longer than the last. The long last phrase is accompanied by a rhythmic diminution in the bass, creating a mild "drive to the cadence."

By comparison, Corelli's movement (Ex. 24-3) seems virtually jet-propelled, and not only by its faster tempo. Everything about the composition is pressured and intense. The opening three-note motif is identical to that of Fux's canon. But what a contrast in the way it is handled! What was only a beginning or a headmotive for Fux is the whole thematic substance for Corelli, as if Corelli had decapitated Fux's theme and tossed its "head" like a ball between the two violins.

EX. 24-2 Johann Joseph Fux, Canonic Sonata in G minor, I, 1–8

Meanwhile, the bass accompanies their agile game of catch with a so-called "running" pattern that moves steadily at a rate twice that of the beat value. The hocket effect between the violins is intensified after the first cadence (m. 7), their tossed motivic ball now consisting of only two notes in an iambic pattern (that is, starting with an upbeat), while the bass continues its frenetic run, made even more athletic by the use of large skips — octaves, ninths, even tenths. At the movement's midpoint (m. 21) the original motive is tossed again, this time beginning a fourth lower than the opening — i.e., on the fifth degree of the scale. Thus the movement over all has the satisfying harmonic aspect of a binary form: a run out from I to V, and a run back from V to I.

WHAT, EXACTLY, IS "TONALITY"?

And yet this description has so far omitted the most potent factor in the movement's extraordinary momentum. That factor is the harmony — the "tonal" harmony, as we now call it. The standardizing of harmonic functions, something going on in all music at the time but particularly foregrounded and made an "issue" in the Italian string

EX. 24-3 Arcangelo Corelli, *Sonata da chiesa*, Op. 3, no. 11, second movement (Presto)

EX. 24-3 (continued)

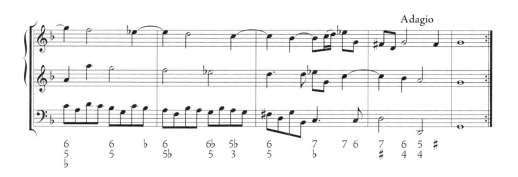

music of which Corelli was the foremost exponent, was his most transforming and enduring legacy.

The opening exchange between the violins describes a preliminary alternation of tonic (I) and dominant (V), that establishes on the smallest level the motion "out" and "back" that will give coherence to the whole. It necessitates a small adjustment in the intervallic structure of the "head motive." When describing the motion "out" from tonic to dominant, the motive consists of a rising fourth and a falling semitone; but when describing the motion "back" from dominant to tonic, the second interval is altered to a falling third. This kind of adjustment between the motive and its imitation is now called "tonal answer," because it arises in response to the exigencies of the tonal functions that are driving the music so forcefully.

When the movement "back" from dominant to tonic has been completed, the bass continues to move in the same harmonic direction, passing "Go" (as one says when playing Monopoly) and moving by half-measures through the tonic to the fourth degree or subdominant (C), the seventh degree (F), and the third or mediant (B♭), for a total of four moves along an exhaustive cycle that we now call the "circle of fifths." It was precisely in Corelli's time, the late seventeenth century, that the circle of fifths was being "theorized" as the main propeller of harmonic motion, and it was Corelli more than any other one composer who put that new idea into telling practice.

As a sort of harmonic curiosity, the circle of fifths and its modulatory properties had been recognized as early as the mid-sixteenth century. There is, for example, a curious motet by a German humanist musician named Matthias Greiter called *Passibus ambiguis* ("By sneaky steps"). Published in 1553, its text concerns the vagaries of Fortune, and its cantus firmus consists entirely of the six-note incipit of a famous old song called *Fortuna desperata* ("Desperate Fortune"), somewhat shakily attributed to the fifteenth-century Burgundian court composer Busnoys. The little snatch, consisting of the syllables *fa – fa – sol – la – sol – fa*, is repeated over and over, and is transposed up a perfect fourth (or down a perfect fifth) seven times, so that its tonic pitch proceeds in a perpetual "flatward" progression from F to F♭, thus: F – B♭ – E♭ – A♭ – D♭ – G♭ – C♭ – F♭. (Meanwhile, the other parts have to scramble for their notes by applying the rules of *musica ficta* in unheard-of profusion.) It is an amusing allegory for a serious idea. The circle of fifths symbolizes the fabled "wheel of Fortune," and by ending on a note that looks like F but sounds like E (and even looks like E on a keyboard or a fretted fingerboard), the composer has transformed the "happiest" final (Lydian *fa*) into the "saddest" one (Phrygian *mi*), illustrating the precariousness of luck and the transience of earthly joys (Fig. 24-2).

What was merely a curiosity to sixteenth-century musicians was bread and butter to their seventeenth-century successors. The circle of fifths was represented for the first time in a theoretical treatise composed in

Passibus am.   volubilis errat.

FIG. 24-2 Tenor (based on *Fortuna desperata*) from Matthias Greiter's *Passibus ambiguis*, in Gregorius Faber, *Musices practicae erotematum libri II* (Basel, 1553).

Polish by a Ukrainian cleric and singing teacher named Nikolai Diletsky (or Dilezki), who lived at the time in the city of Vilnius (see Fig. 24-3). (It was first printed in 1679, in Moscow of all places, in Russian translation.)

This earliest complete circle is a circle like Greiter's extended to its limit. That is, it is made up of twelve perfect fifths and shows all possible transpositions of a major scale (that is, all the possible keys) but does not define the harmonic relations implicit in a single key. On the contrary, a circle like Greiter's or Diletsky's leads ineluctably away from any stable point of tonal reference.

FIG. 24-3 Early diagram of the circle of fifths, from Nikolai Diletsky, *Ideya grammatiki musikiyskoy* (Moscow, 1679).

The decisive practical move was to limit the circle of fifths to the diatonic degrees of a single scale by allowing one of the fifths to be a diminished rather than a perfect fifth. When adjusted in this way the circle is all at once transformed from a modulatory device — that is, a device for leading from one key to others progressively more distant — into a closed system of harmonic functions that interrelate the degrees of a single scale. When thus confined, the circle of fifths became an ideal way of circumscribing the key defined by that scale by treating every one of its degrees as what we now call a harmonic root.

The progression by fifths thus became the definer of "tonality" as we now know it: a model for relating all the degrees of a scale not only melodically but also harmonically to the tonic, and measuring the harmonic "distance" both among the degrees within a single scale and between scales (Ex. 24-4). When the diatonic circle of fifths became the basis of harmonic practice, the major–minor tonal system (or "key system") can be said to have achieved its full elaboration.

EX. 24-4   Diatonic circles of fifths on C major and G minor

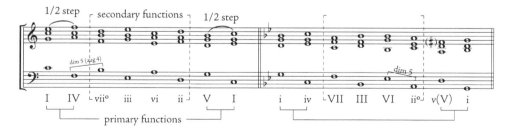

The fully elaborated system's birthplace was the Italian music of the 1680s. The earliest example known to the author of the use of a full diatonic circle of fifths to circumscribe and thus establish a diatonic tonality occurs in a tiny aria from the third

act of *L'Aldimiro*, Alessandro Scarlatti's third opera, first performed in the theater of the Royal Palace at Naples in November 1683. It functions here as a ground bass (the more elaborate *da capo* structure not yet having become the standard; see Ex. 24-5). Like all ground basses, this one surely had a "preliterate" prehistory in improvisation. And

EX. 24-5   Alessandro Scarlatti, *L'Aldimiro* (1683), "S'empia man" (Act III, scene 12)

ARSINDA: *If the evil band of an angry archer*
Wishes to deliver a mortal blow,
I will be sure, that the arrow
Will first open a path through my bowels.

EX. 24-5   (continued)

like all ground basses it is a static element, a bead for stringing, rather than a dynamic shaper of form.

The Presto from Corelli's op. 3, no. 11 (Ex. 24-3), published in Rome in 1689 but probably composed some years earlier, no longer shows the circle of fifths off as a "device" but simply harnesses it, a fully integrated element of technique, to drive a dynamically unfolding form-generating process. That much is typical of the north-Italian instrumental ensemble music of the time, which for that reason stands as one of the great watershed repertories in the history of European music. It is certainly no accident, moreover, that "tonality" as a fully elaborated system emerged first in the context of instrumental music. Instrumental music stood in far greater need of a potent tonal unifier like the circle of fifths than did vocal music, which can as easily take its shape from its text as from any internal process.

So for our purposes we can let Corelli stand as protagonist of this all-important development — one that put instrumental music on a path of ascendency that would ultimately challenge the preeminent status of vocal genres. For in no other composer of the time is the circle of fifths quite so conspicuously and copiously deployed. In the Presto of op. 3, no. 11, Corelli resorts to it over and over again. The instance already noted at the outset is the first segment of the circle of fifths to appear; but it is by no means the most extensive one, for it only takes the circle half way, to III (what we now call the "relative major"). For a complete circle, fully circumscribing the key of the piece (and then some!), see mm. 11–15.

Not only does Corelli use the circle here in its complete form, he also manages to enhance its propulsive force in two distinct ways: first, by doubling the rate of chord change (what is now often called the "harmonic rhythm") in the second half of the progression; and second, by adding sevenths to most of the constituent chords, especially in the latter (faster, more emphatic) portion. These sevenths, being dissonances, create the need for resolution, thus turning each progression of the circle into a simultaneous reliever and restimulator of harmonic tension. In this intensified form, the circle of fifths becomes more than just a conveyor belt, so to speak; it becomes, at least potentially, a channeler of harmonic tension and a regulator of harmonic pressure — phenomena that can be easily associated or analogized with emotional tensions and pressures, hence harnessed for expressive purposes (see Ex. 24-6).

EX. 24-6A   Circle of fifths in Corelli, Op. 3, no.11, II (Presto)

EX. 24-6B   Circle of fifths in G minor with interlocking sevenths

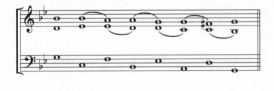

$$\text{i} \quad \text{IV}_7 \quad \text{VII}_7 \quad \text{III}_7 \quad \text{VI}_7 \quad \text{ii}^\circ_7 \quad \text{V}_7 \quad \text{i}$$

Note, finally, that when this inexorable cycle gets underway, Corelli (like Scarlatti before him) reinforces it with melodic sequences — another way of demonstrating the inexorability of the progression.

Another kind of standard sequence, not simply melodic but contrapuntal, is the suspension chain. It, too, is easily adapted to the circle of fifths, as Corelli demonstrates in mm. 34–36, the passage that sets up the final cadence: the suspensions between the two violins are accompanied by another supercomplete progression, VI–ii–v–I–iv–VII–III–VI–ii–V-i (Ex. 24-7a). Compare also the suspensions over the "walking bass" at the beginning of the Preludio from the sonata da camera, op. 4, no. 2 (Ex. 24-7b).

EX. 24-7A   Arcangelo Corelli, Op. 3, no. 11, II (Presto), mm. 34–36, analyzed to show *basse fondamentale*

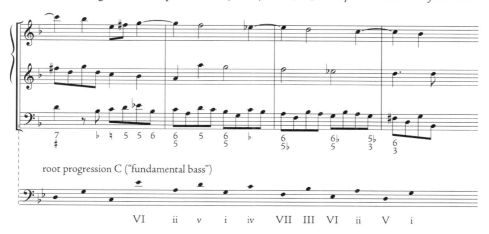

EX. 24-7B   Arcangelo Corelli, Op. 4, no. 2, I, mm. 1–5, analyzed to show *basse fondamentale*

These two techniques in tandem — melodic sequences or suspensions underpinned with dynamic circle-of-fifths harmonies — would become the standard by which all tonal progressions would henceforth be measured. They became, in effect, the basis of what is often called the "Era of Common Practice"; and the "sequence-and-cadence" model (shown at its most primitive in Scarlatti's ground bass) became the chief generator of form in "tonal" or "common-practice" music.

For a final illustration from Corelli's own work we can take a look at one of his most famous compositions, the "Pastorale ad libitum" from the Concerto Grosso, op. 6, no. 8, a *concerto da chiesa* "made for Christmas Night" (*fatto per la notte di natale*) and

usually called the "Christmas Concerto" in English. It was probably composed in the
1680s but first published in 1714.

This Pastorale movement is an appendage to the concluding fast movement in
the concerto, a dancelike number in binary form. (While untitled, as was the rule in
a concerto da chiesa, the movement is clearly a gavotte, and would surely have been

EX. 24-8A   Arcangelo Corelli, *Pastorale ad libitum* from the "Christmas Concerto", Op. 6, no. 8

EX. 24-8A   (continued)

EX. 24-8B   Arcangelo Corelli, *Pastorale ad libitum*, mm. 8–11, analyzed to show *basse fondamentale*

so labeled in a concerto da camera.) The Pastorale is marked "ad libitum" (optional) so that the concerto might be performed without it on other occasions, for it is the Pastorale alone that has obligatory or "programmatic" associations with the holiday theme. The Largo tempo and the $^{12}_{8}$ meter will bring the Scarlattian "siciliana" to mind with all its rustic associations, and the plangent bagpipe drones with which the backup band (*concerto grosso*) accompanies the soloists (*concertino*) in the opening ritornello (Ex. 24-8a), and on its later reappearances, leave no doubt that we are standing among the shepherds, and that the music is painting a manger scene.

That ritornello consists of nothing but three sequential repetitions of a three-bar "rocking" motif (Mary cradling the infant Jesus?) and a two-bar cadence. The little episode for the *concertino* in mm. 8–11 contains the first circle of fifths. As happens so often, the harmonic circle is unfolded through a suspension chain; in this case, somewhat unusually, the syncopated voice that creates the suspensions is the bass. Its dissonances and resolutions identify an essential root progression by fifths that is broken up and somewhat disguised in the voices above (Ex. 24-8b). The first theorist to employ the technique of "root extractions" used in this analysis and the preceding one was Jean-Phillippe Rameau, in his *Traité de l'Harmonie* or "Treatise on Harmony" of 1722; as usual, a theorist of the next generation has found a way of systematically rationalizing and representing a manner of writing—or rather of thinking musically—that had already become well established in practice.

THE SPREAD OF "TONAL FORM"

Having characterized the sequence-and-cadence model as a norm that would usher in an era of "common practice," we need to justify that remark by demonstrating its chronological and geographical spread. The chronological demonstration will emerge naturally enough in the course of the following chapters, but just to show how pervasive the model became within the sphere of Italian instrumental music, and how quickly it spread, we can sneak a peek at a concerto by a member of the generation immediately following Corelli's.

Alessandro Marcello (1669–1747) was a Venetian nobleman who practiced music as a *dilettante*—a "delighter" in the art—rather than one who pursued it for a living. His work was on a fully professional level, however, and achieved wide circulation in print. (His younger brother Benedetto, even more famous and accomplished as a composer, was also more prominent as a Venetian citizen, occupying high positions in government and diplomacy.) Marcello, like Corelli before him, was a member of the Arcadian Academy, and maintained a famous salon, a weekly gathering of artist-dilettantes where he had his music performed for his own and his company's enjoyment. It was for such a gathering that he composed his *Concerto a cinque* ("concerto scored for five parts") in D minor, which was published in Amsterdam in 1717 or 1718 and attracted the attention of J. S. Bach, who made it famous in an embellished transcription for harpsichord.

Although published only three or four years later than Corelli's *Concerti Grossi*, op. 6, Marcello's concerto belongs to a different type—one that much more closely resembles the type of concerto we know from the modern concert repertoire. Where Corelli's concerti were in essence amplified trio sonatas (and while such concerti continued to be written by many composers, particularly George Frederick Handel and his English imitators, long into the eighteenth century), Marcello's is modeled on the format of the contemporary *opera seria* aria, such as we encountered in the previous chapter. It is scored for a single solo instrument (replacing Corelli's "concertino"), in this case the oboe, accompanied by an orchestra (or *ripieno*, "full band") of string instruments that chiefly supplies ritornellos.

Concertos of this type usually dispensed with the opening "Preludio" of the Corellian model and consisted of three movements: fast ritornello movements at the ends, with a slow *"cantabile"* (lyrical accompanied solo) in between. This new genre of "solo concerto" seems to have originated in Bologna, at the Cathedral of San Petronio. Its earliest exponent was the violinist Giuseppe Torelli (1658–1709), a contemporary and rival of Corelli's, who led the Cathedral orchestra. Its "classic" exponent was Antonio Vivaldi (1678–1741), the outstanding Venetian composer of the early eighteenth century, to whom we will of course return.

Doubtless Marcello picked up the three-movement concerto form from fellow-Venetian Vivaldi. The first movement of his oboe concerto is in a straightforward ritornello form akin to the opening section of a da capo aria. The last movement crossbreeds the ritornello framework with the binary dance form familiar to us from the Corelli "da camera" style. (Marcello, recall, wrote not for the church service but for his own aristocratic salon.)

FIG. 24-4 Antonio Vivaldi, caricature by Pier Loene Ghezzi (the only authenticated life drawing of the composer).

Of particular interest is the structure of the main ritornello theme (Ex. 24-9a). It begins with a four-measure "head motive" over a bass that is clearly derived from the old "descending tetrachord" of chaconne and passacaglia fame. It ends, accordingly, on a half cadence. Ground basses remained popular in the Italian string repertory. The last sonata da camera in Corelli's opus 2, published in 1685, consisted of a single showy *ciaccona* over a descending tetrachord, and the most famous solo sonata in Corelli's opus 5, published in 1700, was a magnificent set of variations over the eight-bar *folia* ground, one of the old "tenors" first sighted as far back as Ex. 15-12. Corelli's "La Folia" has remained a virtuoso warhorse — usually in modernized and "violinistically enhanced" transcriptions — to the present day.

All resemblance to the ground bass, however, ends with the fifth measure of Marcello's ritornello. Instead of another four-bar phrase over the same bass, we now get a nine-bar monster consisting of four sequential repetitions of an angular scale-plus-arpeggio idea that unfolds over a single exact and complete circumnavigation of the circle of fifths, finally hooking up with a cadence formula that adds the "extra" ninth measure to its length. The ensuing oboe solo, a variation on the ritornello, reproduces and embellishes its harmonic structure: a four-bar approach to a half cadence followed by a full circle of fifths accompanying a series of melodic sequences (reduced this time to four measures by doubling the harmonic rhythm) and a concluding set of ascending sequences that reaches a cadence on III, the relative major.

A set of rising, unlike the falling type that arises more or less straightforwardly out of the circle of fifths, requires a different sort of harmonic support. The implied root movement is made explicit in the next oboe solo (mm. 36–52), a fascinating interplay of melodic and harmonic contours (Ex. 24-9b). It begins with the usual four-bar "head," followed by a sequential elaboration. The sequences in this case begin (mm. 36–41) by rising. The harmonies change bar by bar in a root progression that ascends by fourths and falls by thirds: F (III)–B♭ (VI)–G (IV)–C (VII)–A (V)–D (I). Immediately on reaching the original tonic, the circle of fifths kicks in and the sequences come tumbling down in double time (mm. 41–46), as if to remind us that rising is always more laborious than falling.

But notice that the rising progression is presented in such a way that if the "functional bass" notes were sampled at the bar lines beginning at m. 36, they would create a rising chromatic line that exactly reversed the old *passus duriusculus*, the chromatically descending groundbass tetrachord of old: (A)–B♭–B–C–C♯–D. In effect we have a series of interpolated leading tones (again familiar from longstanding

EX. 24-9A Alessandro Marcello, Oboe Concerto in D minor, III, beginning

practice, in this case the downright ancient principles of *musica ficta*); and if we now interpret those leading tones within the nascent system of harmonic functions (i.e., as the thirds of dominant triads), we have a new principle — the "applied dominant" — that will emerge over the years as the primary means of harmonic and formal expansion within the tonal practice that is just now reaching full elaboration.

We are witnessing a truly momentous juncture in the history of harmony: the birth of harmonically controlled and elaborated form. In the Italian instrumental music of a rough quarter-century enclosing the year 1700, we may witness in their earliest, "avant-garde" phase the tonal relations we have long been taught to take for granted. And yet from the very beginning this avant-garde style of harmony was easily and eagerly assimilated, both by composers and by listeners. For composers it made the planning and control of ever larger formal structures virtually effortless. To listeners it vouchsafed an unprecedentedly exciting and involving sense of high-powered, *directed* momentum, and promised under certain conditions a practically visceral emotional payoff. The tonal system at once gave composers access to a much more explicit and internal musical "logic" than they had ever known before, and also gave them the means for administering an altogether new kind of pleasurable shock to their audiences.

These new powers and thrills made the new style virtually irresistible and assured its rapid spread. Our geographical witness to that spread can be Henry Purcell. Up to now we have viewed Purcell chiefly through a French-tinted lens, as befits a composer for the Restoration stage. He was equally receptive to the new winds blowing from

EX. 24-9B   Alessandro Marcello, Concerto in D minor, III, mm. 22–25 and mm. 32–52, analyzed to show *basse fondamentale*

Italy, however, and equally reflective of them, provided one looks for the reflection in the right place. That place, of course, would be string ensemble music, an area in which Purcell's art underwent an astoundingly quick and thorough transformation at very nearly the beginning of his career. Rarely can one trace so sudden a change of style, or be so sure about its cause.

Purcell was heir to the rich and insularly English tradition of gentlemanly ensemble music for viols that we visited briefly in chapter 22. His first important body of compositions, in fact, was a set of consort "fantazias" that he wrote in the summer of 1680, the year he turned twenty-one. They well exemplify the somewhat archaic imitative polyphony the English held on to so long into the seventeenth century — the "interwoven hum-drum" Roger North affectionately described in his memoirs of rural music-making.

Ex. 24-10, the opening "point" in one of Purcell's fantasies of 1680, will give us one last look at this style, particularly poignant in its peculiarly English harmonic intensity, replete with false relations of an especially dissonant kind (sevenths "resolving" to diminished octaves!) on practically every cadence. The timing of the entries on the principle motif (first heard in the "tenor"), their progress through the texture, and, most of all, their transpositions seem to be waywardness itself. It is hard to imagine the composer of this piece and the composer of Corelli's sonatas and concertos as contemporaries, or to believe that Corelli's first book of trio sonatas was published less than a year after Purcell's fantasies were composed.

EX. 24-10   Henry Purcell, "Fantazia 7" a 4, mm. 1–26

EX. 24-10 (continued)

And yet hard on the heels of those fantasias, in 1683, Purcell published his own book of "Sonnatas of III Parts: Two Viollins And Basse: To the Organ or Harpsecord" that advertise his full capitulation to what old Roger North, who detested it, called the "brisk battuta" of the Italians.[1] *Battuta* is Italian for "beat," and so it was evidently the fast tempi and the heavy regularity of its rhythm (or maybe just the professional virtuosity that it required) that seems to have affronted traditional English taste in the new Continental fashion. But Purcell, although only six years younger than North, had no such scruple about appropriating for himself and his countrymen "the power of the Italian Notes, or [the] elegancy of their Compositions," as he put it in the preface to his collection.

The composer whose work Purcell chiefly aped in his trio sonatas was probably not Corelli (although Corelli's first book of church sonatas would have been available to him) but rather one Lelio Colista (1629–80), an older Roman contemporary of Corelli's, best known as a lutenist or "Theorbo man" (to quote an English traveler who heard him perform in church in 1661). His sonatas were never published and consequently fairly little known or admired—except, by chance, in England, where they circulated widely in manuscript. The third sonata from Purcell's set is modeled closely on the church sonatas of Colista, and therefore (somewhat curiously, but characteristically for the island kingdom) preserves the new Italian style at a slightly earlier stage of development than Corelli had already achieved.

THE FUGAL STYLE

There is another element, besides its harmonically driven form, that defines the new Italianate style. The use of the old-fashioned term "Canzona" for the second movement in Purcell's sonata (Ex. 24-11) is adopted directly from Colista, as are the movement's form and texture, somewhat more thoroughgoingly and conservatively contrapuntal than the Corellian norm. It is a very competently crafted *fugue*, worked out with the perhaps excessive regularity and rigor one might expect to find in a self-conscious (and still youthful) imitator. But since it is the first fully developed fugue (or to be painstakingly accurate, the first fully developed specimen of what would later be called a fugue) to be encountered in this book, it is worth studying in some detail. In the description that follows, the standard modern terminology for the fugue's components and events will be employed (and set off in italics), even though—like the word "fugue" itself—they are not strictly contemporaneous with the piece at hand.

A fugue is like a single extended and colossally elaborated point of imitation from the older motet or canzona. There is a single main motive or theme, called the *subject*, on which the whole piece is based. In the opening section of such a piece, called the *exposition*, the subject is introduced in every voice. In the present example, this has been accomplished by the time the downbeat of the seventh measure is reached. First the subject is heard alone (though doubled by the organ continuo) in the first violin. Then the second violin plays the subject "at the fifth" (meaning a fifth up or, as here, a fourth down); when played at this transposition, it is called the *answer*. The counterpoint with which the first violin accompanies the answer (here, a chain of

EX. 24-11 Henry Purcell, *Sonnatas of III Parts*, no. 3 in D minor, mm. 25–62

EX. 24-II (*continued*)

EX. 24-11   (*continued*)

syncopations/suspensions) is called the *countersubject* (CS). Next to enter is the cello, playing the subject in its original form, though down an octave; hence the entering voices continually describe a quasi-cadential "there and back" alternation of tonic and dominant to lend the newly important sense of tonal unity to the exposition. When the third voice to enter plays the subject, the second voice shifts over to the CS (suitably transposed), and the first voice plays a second CS that harmonizes with both the other melodies. These fixed components of the texture are given analytical labels in Ex. 24-11: S (for subject, or when transposed to the "fifth," the answer), **CS1** for the syncopated CS, and **CS2** for the second one.

By now, with all the voices in play, the exposition has performed its function and could end. But this fugue, as already noted, is very demonstratively, even compulsively worked out, and the composer is determined to display his complex of three voices in every possible permutation (for which reason this kind of extremely regular and thoroughgoing fugue is sometimes called a "permutation fugue"). Up to now the subject has always been found in the lowest sounding voice. And so in the seventh measure, still inexorably alternating subjects with answers, Purcell brings it back in the highest voice while keeping the two countersubjects as before.

The texture is now inverted, with subject above countersubjects rather than below. Thus, Purcell announces, this fugue is of the especially rigorous variety known as *double fugue* because it is written in "double" — that is, invertible — counterpoint. (As any student who has taken counterpoint knows, in order for counterpoint to be invertible it must conform to especially stringent rules of dissonance treatment.) This "double exposition" does not end until the subject (or answer) has circulated through the texture three times and been in every possible juxtaposition with the other voices. It is in fact a triple exposition.

The exposition ends in m. 19 and is followed by what is called an *episode*, which simply means a stretch of music during which the subject is withheld. Even the episode is contrapuntally complex in this very determined fugue: a three-beat phrase in anapests (short – short – long) that on its repetitions cuts across the four-beat bar and is capriciously alternated with its inversion. Also playful (and welcome, in compensation for the dogged regularity of the exposition) is the episode's asymmetrical five-bar length.

The subject reappears in m. 24, still whimsically accompanied by the episode figure, now extended and continuous. When the answer comes in at m. 26 (top voice) Purcell pulls one last contrapuntal stunt: the other voices now pile in with overlapping entries on the subject and answer, so that every part is eventually playing some part of it at the same time. This foreshortening device is called the *stretto* (Italian for "straitened" — tightened or made stricter) and is a common way of bringing fugues to a close. (Strettos have to be worked out in advance while the subject is being cooked up; not every subject will produce one.) Another conventional touch is the concluding passage (or *coda*, "tail") over a sustained dominant in the bass: the latter is known as a *pedal*, or "pedal point," because the device originated in organ music, where the player produces it by literally planting a foot on the rank of tone-producing pedals with which large built-in church organs are equipped. It is during the pedal point, which projects the cadential harmonic function so forcefully, that Purcell again goes playful, this time with chromatically inflected lines that give a tiny, perhaps nostalgic, whiff of the expressive harmony so endemic to the older English style exemplified in his own fantazia of a few years earlier (cf. Ex. 24-10).

It is interesting to compare the "canzona" in Purcell's sonata with the other fugal movement, the fourth (Allegro), which bursts in upon the sarabande-like third movement without pause (Ex. 24-12). Its subject descends from the fifth (dominant) degree of the scale to the first, which calls for a "tonal answer" that in effect transposes the subject (once past the first note) up a degree, so that the V-I descent will be balanced by a complementary descent from I to V (covering a fourth, not a fifth). This movement, too, has a first countersubject in syncopations, producing suspensions. But whereas the suspensions in the second movement resolved the old-fashioned "intervallic" way (sevenths resolving to sixths over a stationary bass), the suspensions in the last movement are channeled — as in the newer, Corellian style — through the bounding circle of fifths. The sense of harmonic purpose, of activity at once more intense and more directed than ever before, was as great a stylistic breakthrough for Purcell as it was for every other composer who took it up.

And yet to us, at the other end of its history, it can sound, paradoxically enough, like a step backward. "Those weaned on Purcell's great Fantasias of 1680," a recent commentator has observed, "with their superlative juxtaposing of archaic longings and innovative yearnings, might all too easily dismiss the composer's sonatas as formulaic and fashion-bound."[2] But the familiar "tonal" formulas and patterns were what struck late seventeenth-century ears as innovative, just as the harmonic vagaries that can sound so delightfully unexpected and personal to us — even "other-worldly," to quote the same critic — struck contemporary ears as familiar, hence entitled to what familiarity breeds.

Purcell was highly conscious that he was "advancing" the music of his homeland by bringing it into contact with the latest emanations from the continent. He underscored the point by retaining "a few terms of Art" from his Italian sources, namely the vocabulary of tempo and expression marks that are familiar to all musicians in the European literate tradition to this day.[3] It was Purcell who in his preface to the 1683 Sonnatas first defined words like Adagio, Grave, Largo, Allegro, Vivace, and Piano for English-speaking players.

EX. 24-12   Henry Purcell, *Sonnatas of III Parts*, no. 3 in D minor, m. 98–110

HANDEL AND "DEFAMILIARIZATION"

Not that a great and practiced musical imagination could not work refreshing and fanciful changes on the new styles, and keep them fresh. Purcell in 1683 represented the first English adoption of the Corellian (or slightly pre-Corellian) style. It was the style itself that was then new. Merely using it, even at its most basic level, was an innovative act. In a later chapter we will take a long look at the work of George Frideric Handel, a naturalized Englishman who belonged to the generation of Corelli's or Purcell's sons and daughters, and who was one of the great representatives of the "High Baroque" style (as it is now so often called) that flourished, particularly in northern Europe, in the first half of the eighteenth century. It will be worthwhile at this point to have a preliminary look at Handel, who knew and played with the venerable Corelli during his apprentice years in Rome, to see what he did with the Corelli style in his set of "Twelve Grand Concertos," opus 6, published in London in 1740 (more than a quarter of a century after Corelli's death), one of the very latest major collections of Concerti Grossi.

The seventh concerto grosso from the set is dated 12 October 1739 on its autograph manuscript. By Handel's day, and especially in England, the old distinction between church and chamber styles had become meaningless. The Anglican church service did not make room for sonatas or concerti *da chiesa*; instrumental chamber music was by definition secular entertainment. Handel's concerto has five movements, of which the first two, a kind of prelude and fugue, are a clear echo of the church style. Just as clearly, the last movement, a dance in binary form, echoes the chamber style.

The third and fourth movements, paired slow–fast like the first two, are played without repeats but go through an elaborate harmonic "round trip" such as one finds in binary movements. The Andante, with periodic returns of a rhythmically catchy opening melody in different keys (yet without any interplay of solo and tutti) seems to be a hybrid, combining the characteristic features of the ritornello style, typical of arias or concertos, with those of the dance, typical of suites. The whimsical, diverting quality of the whole concerto is most obviously suggested by the adoption of an English national dance, the hornpipe (also known, fittingly enough, as the "delight" or "whim") for the concluding movement (Ex. 24-13). As danced in the eighteenth century, the hornpipe was a "longways country dance," meaning (paradoxically) an urban, genteel couples dance in which the dancers assembled in long files. The rather complicated steps were adapted from an older solo dance often done competitively by sailors; the rhythms, as in Handel's adaptation, were often syncopated. Handel was surprising his English listeners and players with a delightful stylization of a dance they all knew "in situ," extended delightfully (and somewhat ridiculously) to monumental length. Ex. 24-13 shows just the first half, allowing the first violin part and the bass to stand in for the four-part texture.

The same whimsicality, the same aim to amuse, can be seen in the second, fugal movement of Handel's concerto. Using a style that by then had long since become a standard procedure to which nobody paid much attention *qua* style, Handel subtly "defamiliarizes" it in order to produce the same kind of diverting piquancy Purcell could achieve simply by using the style when it was as yet unfamiliar. Consider first

EX. 24-13   G. F. Handel, Concerto grosso in B-flat major, Op. 6, no. 7

the one-note subject itself, a famous joke. The impression of mindless jabber, "put on" like a comic mask, is actually the means by which Handel exercises a subtle control over the texture of the fugue and keeps it lucid. The progressive rhythmic diminution from half notes to eighths that must run its course before the subject is allowed to quit its initial pitch, and the continuation of the eighth-note pulse into the sequential patterns of the countersubject insure that the subject's rhythmic "head" in half notes will stand out against the eighth-note ground rhythm on its every entrance, wherever in the texture it may occur, and gives the composer an unusual freedom in placing or "voicing" surprising subject entries.

Another area of potential surprise is the timing of subject entries. We see an example of this within the first exposition (Ex. 24-14) in the little three-bar episode (on material derived from the countersubject) that breaks the implicit pattern defined by the second subject entry in mm. 9–11 and delays the third. Thereafter, the whole fugue consists of a game of hide-and-seek: when and where will the subject next turn up? The game is rendered all the more obviously (and amusingly) a game by the way episodes are made to "mark time" with static or obsessive repetitions (at times virtually denuded of counterpoint) of the four-eighths motif first heard in the second violin at the beginning of the countersubject (m. 5).

EX. 24-14   G. F. Handel, Concerto grosso in B-flat major, Op. 6, no. 7, Allegro, mm. 1–22

EX. 24-14 (continued)

So in the hands of its ablest practitioners, a style that derives its identity and its strength from the regularity of its patterns is subjected to calculated disruptions that honor the patterns (as the saying goes) "in the breach," and that turn "form" into a constant play of anticipations and (dis)confirmations. This process of setting up and either bearing out or letting down the listener's expectations has quite recently been termed the "implication/realization" model of musical form, and has been the focus of much investigation by psychologists, who regard it as a relatively pristine embodiment of the learning (or "cognitive") processes by which humans adapt to their environment.[4]

In the instrumental music of the early eighteenth century, the listener's interest is engaged by these abstract processes of "conditioned response" as if in compensation for the absence of a text as cognitive focus. They brought about a virtual revolution in listening, in which the listener's conscious mind was much more actively engaged than previously in these processes of forecast and delayed fulfillment, and in which the form may even be said to arise out of the play of these cognitive processes. When it was new, such abstract yet intensely engaging instrumental music seemed to some listeners to be very aggressive both in what it demanded from them in the way of active perceptual engagement, and in its effects on them in the way of intense passive experience.

One particularly uncomprehending listener, an aged French academician named Bernard le Bovier le Fontenelle (1657–1757), who was used to the idea of music not as abstract intellectual process but as "imitation" of feeling, reacted to a bit of Italianate string music with the exasperated question, "Sonate, que me veux-tu?" which means "Sonata, what do you want from me?"[5] He was not as uncomprehending as he thought. His indignation was aroused by his correct perception that the sonata wanted his active mental engagement. Music became a more strenuous experience but also a more powerful (and at the same time a more "autonomous") one. And yet, as we have seen, the process of attending to such an autonomous musical structure can be endlessly diverting. Handel's fugue, though far more sophisticated than Purcell's, is also lighter — prankish rather than dogged.

BACH AND "DRAMATIZED" TONALITY

We can witness the new instrumental style at its most sublime, and experience its newfound power to deliver both intellectual gratification and a powerful emotional payoff, by stealing an advance look at the work of Handel's exact contemporary, Johann Sebastian Bach. Bach's impressive organ Toccata in F major — probably composed between 1708 and 1717 while Bach held the post of organist at the court chapel of Weimar (a town in Eastern Germany, then known as Saxony) — is in some ways an old-fashioned work, but in others it is downright prescient. A virtuoso showpiece for the organist, Bach's Toccata belonged to an ancient tradition, one that we have traced back to the Gabrielis and Sweelinck at the end of the sixteenth century, and which lay behind the development of the Corellian "church sonata" as well. Toccatas, etymologically, were "touch pieces." They foregrounded the playing process itself. And what could be more characteristic of the organ's particular playing process than the activity of the player's feet? It was in the fancy footwork that organ playing differed from the playing of any other instrument of the time, and Bach spotlights that footwork in various highly contrasting ways.

The opening section of the piece (Ex. 24-15a) is accompanied through most of its duration by what may well be the longest "pedal point" ever written, one that

EX. 24-15A   J. S. Bach, Toccata in F, BWV 540, mm. 1–82

EX. 24-15A (continued)

EX. 24-15A   (continued)

dramatically advertises the derivation of what is often thought of as an abstract harmonic device from the practical technique of organ playing. The organist plunks his foot down on the F pedal and thereby opens up a flue pipe through which air will rush as long as the pedal is depressed. The low F thus produced can last indefinitely; Bach lets it sound for the two minutes or so that it takes to execute the canon that runs up above between the two keyboards (or manuals). The organ is the only instrument capable of sustaining a note of such a length without any break. The implied harmonies that it supports — notably the dominant — are often dissonant with respect to it, but Bach concentrates for the duration of the pedal on the tonic (I) and subdominant (IV) harmonies (both of which contain the F) and on the tonic-plus-E♭, which functions as an "applied dominant" of B♭ ("V of IV").

Bach lets the canon in the manuals peter out in mm. 53–54 without any real cadence, whereupon the pedals take over with one of the most extended solos for the feet that Bach or any organ virtuoso ever composed. It lasts 26 measures, roughly half the length of the preceding canon-over-pedal, and consists entirely of sequential elaborations of the canon's opening pair of measures, itself already a sequential elaboration of a "headmotif" with a characteristic contour consisting of a "lower neighbor" and its resolution, followed by a consonant leap down, a larger consonant leap up, and a return to the original note. The blow-by-blow description is cumbersome indeed, but the contour itself is instantly apprehensible. (Indeed, the sense of triple meter in the piece depends on our apprehending it, since the rhythm is just an undifferentiated stream of sixteenth notes, and the organ cannot produce accentual stresses; thus the only thing that can serve to define the measure as a rhythmic unit here is the recurrent pitch contour and its sequential repetitions.)

A 26-measure section or "period" comprising nothing except sequential repetitions of a single pitch contour is a quintessential display of the technique of melodic elaboration and form-building known as *Fortspinnung* ("spinning out"). This handy term was actually coined (by the Austrian music historian Wilhelm Fischer) in 1915, but it very neatly defines the techniques of melodic elaboration that arose with the concerto style as a sort of by-product of the circle of fifths and the other standard patterns of chord succession that we have already observed, the melody arising (for the first time in the history of musical style) out of an essentially harmonic process.

In Bach's long passage of pedal Fortspinnung, the circle of fifths acts as a long-range modulatory guide, within which many smaller cadences and sequences take their place. The long-range workings of the circle of fifths can best be gauged by noting accidentals as they occur. The first accidental to appear (in m. 61) is E♭, which has the effect, here as previously, of invoking the scale of B♭ major (IV), which in turn identifies A as leading tone ("vii of IV"). When E-natural occurs (in m. 66) as an accidental that explicitly cancels the E♭, it asserts its function as leading tone to the original tonic (I). The next accidental to appear (m. 70) is B-natural, the leading tone of C (V), and the next one after that (m. 78) is F♯, the leading tone of G (ii, but retaining the B-natural so as to turn ii into "V of V," and with the E♭ reinstated to suggest — colorfully but falsely, as it turns out — a cadence on C minor).

The whole passage may be summed up harmonically in terms of a slowly unfolding circle of ascending fifths: B♭ (IV)–F (I)–C (V)–G (ii/V of V), all preparing the bald cadence formula on C (V) in mm. 81–82. That the first explicit cadence in the piece takes place so late is a testimony to the efficacy of the Fortspinnung technique in organizing vast temporal spans. And the same vast span is now replayed on C (V), replete with 54-measure canon-over-pedal and mammoth pedal solo, now expanded to 32 measures in length.

Again a cadence on C (V) is elaborately prepared and the same cadential formula is invoked. But this time the cadential preparation is detached from the resolution and repeated no fewer than seven times (Ex. 24-15b), dramatically delaying the arrival of the keenly anticipated stable harmony (the "structural downbeat," as it is often called). When the C major triad in root position is finally sounded, it can no longer be merely taken for granted as the inevitable outcome of a standard harmonic process. The process of delay has "defamiliarized" it and made it the object of the listener's keenly experienced desire.

Bach's Toccata is one of the earliest pieces to so dramatize the working out of its form-building tonal functions, adding an element of emotional tension that is inextricably enmeshed in its formal structure. The listener's active engagement in the formal process is likewise dramatized. The listener's subjective reaction to the ongoing tonal drama is programmed into the composition. Subjectivity, one may say, has been given an objective correlate. It even makes a certain kind of figurative sense to ascribe the desire for resolution to the notes themselves, objectifying and (as it were) acting out the listener's involvement.

So far we have had a decisive tonal movement from I (the opening pedal) to V (the long-delayed and intensified arrival at m. 176, shown in Ex. 24-15b). We may now expect the usual leisurely return, by way of intermediate cadences on secondary degrees. And that is what we shall get — but not without dramatic withholdings and ever more poignant delays. The measures that immediately follow Ex. 24-15b unfold a sequential progression along the by-now-familiar descending circle of fifths: C (V) – F (I) – B♭ (IV) – E (vii°) – A (iii). The chord on A is expressed as a major triad, connoting an applied dominant to D (vi), just where one might expect the "medial cadence" on the way back to the tonic.

EX. 24-15B   J. S. Bach, Toccata in F, BWV 540, mm. 169 – 76

That expectation will indeed be confirmed, but only after a really hair-raising strategy of delay shown in Ex. 24-15c has run its course. At the short range the A major chord ("V of vi") is allowed to reach its goal (m. 191), but the D minor chord is immediately given a major third, a seventh, and even a dissonant ninth, turning it in its turn into an applied dominant ("V of ii") along the same circle of fifths. The G minor chord (ii) is also manipulated and compromised as a goal, first by harmonizing the G as part of a diminished seventh chord (m. 195), then as part of a "Neapolitan sixth" such as we observed in the last chapter in connection with Alessandro Scarlatti (m. 196). The Neapolitan sixth always acts as a cadential preparation to the dominant, and so the A returns (m. 197) with its previously assigned function ("V of vi") intact. Again (mm. 197 – 203) we get the elaborately stretched-out preparation we heard previously in mm. 169 – 76. But this time, the already much-delayed resolution is thwarted (m. 204) by what was probably the most spectacular "deceptive cadence" anyone had composed as of the second decade of the eighteenth century.

EX. 24-15C   J. S. Bach, Toccata in F, BWV 540, 188–219

A deceptive cadence (as it is called in today's analytical language) is not just any avoided or interrupted cadence. In a deceptive cadence the cadential expectation is partially fulfilled, partially frustrated, producing an especially pungent effect. Most often it is the leading tone that is resolved, the fifth-progression that is evaded; the most common way of achieving this is to substitute a submediant chord for the tonic (Ex. 24-15d).

EX. 24-15D Ordinary deceptive cadences in D major and D minor

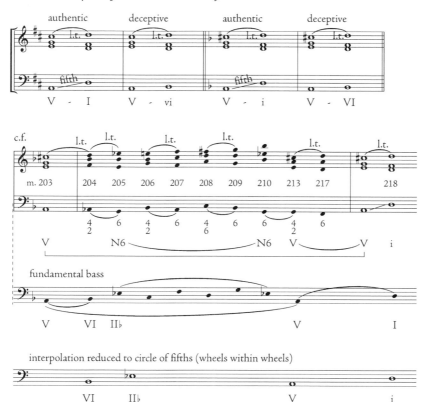

Bach does something similar, but much spikier. The leading tone, C♯, is resolved to D, the expected tonic, in m. 208; but the bass A proceeds, not along the circle of fifths to another D, but rather descends a half step to A♭, clashing at the tritone with the soprano D. And the tritone is harmonized with one of the most gratingly dissonant chords available in the harmonic language of Bach's time: a dominant seventh in the "third inversion" (also known as $\frac{4}{2}$ position), in which the bass note is the seventh of the chord, dissonant with respect to all the rest.

The $\frac{4}{2}$ chord is a chord in drastic need of resolution, and Bach resolves it in timely fashion. That local resolution, however, takes him far afield of his long-range harmonic goal. It is to the Neapolitan sixth chord. Bach first "normalizes" the Neapolitan harmony by treating it as part of a standard sequential progression (mm. 204–209) similar to the one noted in Marcello's oboe concerto, but made stronger by putting all the applied dominants in $\frac{4}{2}$ position. In m. 210 the Neapolitan is regained, reiterated, and (after yet another set of feints) finally directed "home" to the long-awaited D in mm. 217–19. The process of delay, from the initial adumbration of the cadence to its ultimate completion, has unfolded over an unprecedented span of 32 intensely involving measures, a passage full of finely calculated yet overwhelmingly powerful harmonic jolts and thrills.

The Toccata's progress from this point to completion can be briefly summarized. In the section that follows Ex. 24-15c, the familiar cadential formula is used to navigate through a complete circle of fifths and beyond, to a cadence on A minor (iii). Over the next 62 measures, an almost identical harmonic process (dramatically extended by the use of the deceptive cadence) is used to establish G minor (ii). From there to the end it is just a matter of holding off the inevitable V–I that will complete the main cadential circle of fifths, and with it the piece. Once achieved, the dominant pedal is held for twenty-three measures while the hands on the manuals go through a frenzy of sequential writing that descends, ascends, descends again, and ascends again in ever-increasing waves. The pedal gives way to a series of cadential formulas that only reach the home key after yet another eruption, like the one in Ex. 24-15c, of the bizarre deceptive cadence to the "V$_2^4$ of the Neapolitan," a chord of crushing disruptive force that makes the final attainment of the tonic seem an inspiring, virtually herculean achievement.

The Toccata in F is thus a tour de force not only of manual (and pedal) virtuosity but of compositional virtuosity as well. Bach deserves enormous credit for sensing so early the huge emotional and dramatic potentialities of the new harmonic processes, and for exploiting them so effectively — at first, presumably, in thrillingly experimental keyboard improvisations of which the "composed" Toccata is the distilled residue. By harnessing harmonic tension to govern and regulate the unfolding of the Toccata's form, he managed to invest that unfolding-to-completion with an unprecedented psychological import. Thanks to this newly psychologized deployment of harmonic functions — in which harmonic goals are at once identified and postponed, and in which harmonic motion is at once directed and delayed — "abstract" musical structures could achieve both vaster dimensions and a vastly more compelling emotional force than any previously envisioned. Harmonic tension could from now on be used at once to construct "objective" form and "subjective" desire, and to identify the one with the other.

VIVALDI'S FIVE HUNDRED

The main protagonist and establisher of the three-movement soloistic concerto, as already mentioned, was Antonio Vivaldi, a Venetian priest who from 1703 to 1740 supervised the music program at the Pio Ospedale della Pietà, one of the city's four orphanages. The word *ospedale* (cf. hospital), originally meant the same thing as *conservatorio* (whence "conservatory"); both were institutions that maintained and educated indigent children (orphans, foundlings, bastards) at public expense, and both emphasized vocational training in music. The Pietà housed only girls, and thanks to Vivaldi's extraordinary talent and energy, its program was outstandingly successful. The Sunday vespers concerts performed by its massed bands and choirs of budding maidens under Vivaldi's direction were regarded as something of a phenomenon and became one of the city's major tourist attractions.

Travelers' reports are split between those that emphasized the young performers' allure, and those that emphasized the fiery demeanor of *il prete rosso*, "the red-haired priest" who presided, when present, with his violin at the ready. "There is nothing so charming," wrote Charles de Brosses, a French navigator, "as to see a young and pretty nun in her white robe, with a sprig of pomegranate blossoms over her ear, leading the orchestra and beating time with all the grace and precision imaginable."[6] By contrast, Johann Friedrich Armand von Uffenbach, a German music patron who caught Vivaldi in action at the opera house, wrote that "his playing really frightened me."[7]

Vivaldi's official duties at the Pietà were the spur that caused him to produce concertos in such fantastic abundance. The most popular Venetian composer of opera and oratorio in his day, he was superbly prolific in those genres as well, and internationally famous. But it is with his five hundred surviving concertos (out of who can only guess how many composed?) that his name is irrevocably linked. About 350, almost three quarters, feature a single solo instrument, and of these about 230 (almost half the total) are for the violin, which was not only Vivaldi's own instrument but the one taught to the largest number of girls at the Ospedale. Runner-up, with thirty-seven concertos, is (perhaps unexpectedly) the bassoon. There are also numerous concertos for flute, for oboe, for cello, and occasionally for rarer instruments, including some (like the mandolin and the "flautino" or flageolet) that were most often used in folk or street music — that is, by nonliterate musicians.

Some three hundred Vivaldi concertos are found today in unique manuscript copies, many of them autographs, housed since the 1920s in the National Library of Turin in northern Italy. They were deposited there by the musicologist Alberto Gentili, who tracked them down and purchased them for the library with funds provided by a local banker named Roberto Foà and a textile manufacturer named Filippo Giordano. These manuscripts had belonged to Count Giacomo Durazzo (1717–94), the Imperial (Austrian) ambassador to Venice, who later served as the "intendant" or impresario-in-charge of the Vienna opera. It is thought that he purchased the collection — either in Venice or in Vienna, where Vivaldi happened to die in 1741 while visiting on operatic business — intact from the composer's estate, and that they represented the actual performing repertoire of the Pietà at the time of his death.

These are the concertos, in other words, that were expressly composed for the outstanding girl musicians — the *figlie privilegiati*, as they were called — whom Vivaldi trained and led. Published in the aftermath of World War II as a national treasure in a huge series of editions prepared by a leading Italian composer of the day, Gian Francesco Malipiero, these previously unknown Vivaldi concertos were a major spur to the so-called "postwar Baroque boom" that awakened active performing and recording interest in many forgotten repertories of "early music." They thus have significance in the history of the twentieth century's musical life as well as the eighteenth's.

A concerto in C major for bassoon from the Foà deposit can serve as well as any (and better than most) in the somewhat imaginary capacity of "typical" Vivaldi concerto. It once carried the misleadingly low number 46 in the catalogue of Vivaldi's works by Marc Pincherle, whose listing, once standard, was based on keys (starting with C); more recently it has carried equally misleading high number 477 in the catalogue of Peter Ryom, whose listings, based on instrumentation, are now supplanting Pincherle's. In any case it well exemplifies the basic principles of concerto-writing that were à la mode in the early eighteenth century, largely because of Vivaldi's commanding example.

Johann Joachim Quantz, a flutist and composer who in 1752 published (in the modest guise of a flute tutor) the most compendious encyclopedia of mid-eighteenth-century musical practice, called this type of concerto "a *serious* concerto with a large accompanying body" (the italics were his).[8] What made it so was the nature of the ritornello, "majestic and carefully elaborated in all the parts," in Quantz's words, and containing a variety of melodic ideas. In its full form this complex ritornello functions as a frame, launching the movement and bringing it to an end, as in the main ("A") section of a da capo aria. Elsewhere, as Quantz describes (or for any composers reading, prescribes), "its best ideas are dismembered and intermingled during or between the solo passages."

The twelve-measure ritornello that introduces our bassoon concerto (Ex. 24-16) consists of four distinct melodic ideas. The first (mm. 1–4) is "spun out" of a turn figure and a rising third. The second (mm. 4–7) is a spaciously textured derivation from our old acquaintance the *passus duriusculus*, the chromatic descent from tonic to dominant degrees, presented not as a bass but as a treble line in the first violins, played against a bass consisting of ostinato repetitions of the opening turn figure. (Mentally connect the first and last notes in every group of four eighths in the first violin part and the chromatically descending line will emerge to the eye as clearly as it does in performance to the ear; the octave Gs in between double the viola's "pedal." This kind of "compound" melodic line, containing two registrally separated "voices" in one, was common in Italian string music and in later music, including a lot of Bach's, that imitated it.) The third

EX. 24-16   Antonio Vivaldi, Concerto for Bassoon in C major, F VIII/13, mm. 1–12

EX. 24-16 (continued)

characteristic phrase in the ritornello (mm. 8–10) is marked by a radically contrasting texture, called *all'unisono* because it consists of unharmonized octaves. The fourth and last (mm. 10–12) is a cadential motive that (like the second phrase) makes a playful feint toward the parallel minor.

If we label these component phrases for reference with the letters from A to D, we can easily compare the partial (or "dismembered") internal repetitions of the ritornello with the full statement at opposite ends of the movement. In the first of them, the opening phrase (A) is balanced against a consequent phrase that telescopes truncated versions of B and D into a single four-bar span. The next internal ritornello consists of phrase A paired with phrase C, the one omitted in the previous statement. The next time, A is followed by fuller statements of B and D. The last internal ritornello is brief; it consists of nothing more than the second half of phrase B (in the major mode rather than the minor).

Each of these ritornellos is built on a different scale degree. Only the outer (full-blown) statements are based on the tonic; their harmonic stability reflects their important role in articulating the form of the piece. In between we get statements on V, vi, iii (the remotest point, articulated by the lengthiest internal ritornello), and (briefly) V again, providing a smooth "retransition" to the home key. The whole trajectory comprises a strongly directed tonal sequence embodying a characteristic "binary" or "round trip" motion: the initial swing to the dominant is prolonged through a deceptive cadence and a "regression" along the circle of fifths (that is, a move farther away from the tonic) before the dominant is picked up again and directed home: I–V–[vi–iii]—V–I.

Thus the sequence of ritornellos defines and unifies the structure of the concerto movement both melodically and tonally. In between come the solos, alternating not only with the ritornellos but with the "ripieni" or backup players who play them. In one sense—the public or "external" sense—the virtuosic solo turns are what the concerto is all about. It is the soloist one pays to hear, after all. In another sense—the structural or "internal" sense—the solos have a much less important role, merely providing modulatory transitions from one "tonicized" scale degree on which ritornellos are played to the next. They are the exact functional equivalent of the "episodes" between the expositions in a fugue.

In contrast to the ripieni, who are confined to repetitions (whether full or partial) of the ritornello, the soloist never repeats. Each episode (summarized in Ex. 24-17a-e) presents a new hurdle, progressively more challenging in its figuration: arpeggios, fast slurred scales, wide-leaping triplets, etc. Thus the typical concerto movement is a fascinating interplay of the fixed and the fluid: one body of players is confined to a single idea, while the other (here a group of one, plus continuo) is seemingly unconstrained in its spontaneous unfolding. One group only repeats, the other never repeats. One "role" is dramatically subordinate but structurally dominant, the other is dramatically dominant but structurally subordinate. Their effect together is one of complementation, of disparate parts fitting harmoniously into a satisfying, functionally differentiated whole, all of it grounded by the constant auxiliary presence of the basso continuo, everyone's companion and aide.

All of this suggests a social paradigm or metaphor. Indeed, the concerto form has always been viewed, in one way or another, as a kind of microcosm, a model of social interaction and coordinated (or competitive) activity. That is one of the things that has always invested its seemingly abstract patterns with "meaning" and fascination for listeners. And that fascination, along with the fascination of tonal relations with their

EX. 24-17A   Antonio Vivaldi, Concerto for Bassoon in C major, F VIII/13, mm. 12–14

EX. 24-17B   Antonio Vivaldi, Concerto for Bassoon in C major, F VIII/13, mm. 30–25

EX. 24-17C   Antonio Vivaldi, Concerto for Bassoon in C major, F VIII/13, mm. 44–48

EX. 24-17D   Antonio Vivaldi, Concerto for Bassoon in C major, F VIII/13, mm. 162–165

EX. 24-17E Antonio Vivaldi, Concerto for Bassoon in C major, F VIII/13, mm. 74–78

strong metaphorically "forward" drive to completion, is what allowed "large" forms of instrumental music to emerge and to assume a place of central importance in European musical culture.

The remainder of the concerto amplifies the sense of kinship with the *opera seria*. The broad (*largo*) second movement, scored for soloist and continuo alone, is a study in "florid" song (*coloratura*) over a static bass—a veritable *aria d'affetto* (or, more precisely, an *arietta*, in view of its binary form). The final movement, another ritornello-style composition, brings the ripieno back. Less "serious" than the first movement, it sports a ritornello theme with only two distinct parts and a pervasive *all'unisono* texture. As might be expected, the two halves of the theme are complementary or, more precisely, reciprocal. Tonally, they reproduce the functions of the binary form: the first phrase makes a half cadence on the dominant, the second a full cadence on the tonic. Melodically, too, the phrases are complementary. Both feature rushing scales, first ascending then descending. Taken as a three-part whole, the concerto reproduces in its texture the effect of a typical da capo aria: outer sections with ritornellos frame a contrasting middle section in which the soloist is accompanied by the continuo instruments only.

For an idea of Vivaldi not at his most typical but at his most bizarre or "frightening," consider one of his most unabashedly extravagant compositions, the Concerto in B minor for four violins. Its only rival in excess might be the concertos "per l'orchestra di Dresda," which Vivaldi wrote on order to show off the famous orchestra maintained by the Elector of Saxony Friedrich August II, whose titles included that of King of Poland, and who kept up a "royal" court in Dresden; this concerto had a colossal concertino consisting of six instruments: an especially showy violin part for the Elector's "concertmaster" Johann Georg Pisendel, Vivaldi's former pupil, along with two oboes, two recorders, and bassoon.

The concerto for four violins is written in what was then a very unusual, indeed hardly used key that was reserved for very special expressive—or (in this case) impressive—effects. In all of Vivaldi's vast instrumental output the key of B minor turns up only twelve times. One piece that uses it is a sombre "Sinfonia al Santo

Sepolcro" ("Sinfonia to be played before the holy tomb"). The four-violin concerto likewise exploits what was thought of as the harsh or crazed quality of the key for expressive effect. Originally played (one may assume) at the Ospedale by the master and three of his most headstrong *figlie* to an enthusiastic reception, the work is a veritable juggernaut. The four soloists are forever intruding with calculated unruliness on the ripieni and on one other, co-opting portions of the ritornellos, vying obsessively for the last word, forcing the music out of its harmonic sanctuaries, so to speak, and into the flux.

Very significantly, the ritornellos are highly truncated affairs, split between sequential patterning that allows harmonic "movement," and highly repetitive ostinato patterning (especially in the outermost ritornelli) that builds tension by inhibiting harmonic movement. The soloists jack up the tension further by dividing the ripienists' eighth notes into relentless chains of sixteenths that are maintained as a virtual rhythmic constant. The combination of this insistent rhythmic commotion with a harmonic plan that alternates between harmonically pent up, static repetition (as in Ex. 24-18a) and periodic harmonic discharge (as in Ex. 24-18b) produces an almost unbearably exciting impression of fluctuating tension and release. Compare a movement of this concerto with Gabrieli's sonata for three violins (Ex. 18-18), a comparably extravagant conception for its time, and one sees how the solidification of tonal routines and the forms accommodating them have given composers access to a kind of musical galvanism, resulting in a newfound ability to shock, startle, and manipulate the responses of the audience.

Which of course makes one wonder about the kind of expression audiences might have given their responses at the time. One of the most striking things we found when looking in the last chapter into the mores of the *opera seria* was the spontaneity and the uninhibitedness of the audience response, so unlike the behavior of "classical" audiences today. We might also reflect on the fact that interactive instrumental music — the "concertato" principle, if you will — is still practiced today as a contemporary art in various forms of "nonclassical" music. Audiences still tend to react to these musics, whether improvised (as in jazz) or memorized and reproduced (as in "heavy metal" and other forms of instrumental rock), with an unrestrained, demonstrative enthusiasm that recalls the behavior of eighteenth-century opera audiences. It is probable, therefore, that Vivaldi's concertos were greeted by their intended audience with the kind of intense reflex response one can find now only at pop performances. The sense of occasion thus created would go a long way toward explaining the extraordinary demand these pieces excited in their time. The immediacy of audience response quickens awareness of what is being responded to. If every solo brings (or fails to bring) applause, players are stimulated to take risks in hopes of keeping the noisy feedback coming.

To gain the full flavor of a Vivaldi concerto, then, it is probably not enough to listen to even the most aggressive performance. One must imagine an equally aggressive audience — a house full of shouting, clapping, stamping listeners, and the effect their demonstrations of approval may have had on the performers. (One doesn't have to work hard to imagine such a thing; any rock video will provide a living example.) The decorous audience behavior first demanded by composers and performers of instrumental music in the nineteenth century (for reasons we will take pains to discover) can cast a real pall on music written earlier, to say nothing of those who play it.

"CONCERTI MADRIGALESCHI"

During his lifetime, the Concerto for Four Violins was one of Vivaldi's best known works, thanks to its publication in his earliest concerto collection, *L'estro armonico* (roughly, "Music Mania"), op. 3, issued in Amsterdam in 1711. This book, actually printed (like most ensemble publications of the time) as a set of partbooks without score, traveled far and wide, spreading Vivaldi's fame and making his music a model to many a farflung imitator (including J. S. Bach, who made a boisterous arrangement of

EX. 24-18A   Antonio Vivaldi, Concerto for Four Violins Op. 3, no. 10, I, mm. 37–39

the Concerto for Four Violins for four harpsichords). It was followed by several other partbook collections bearing fanciful promotional titles: *La stravaganza, La cetra* ("The lyre"), and the biggest seller of all, *Il cimento dell'armonia e dell'inventione* (something like "The trial of musical skill and contrivance"), op. 8, a book of twelve concerti that came out in 1725 and made a sensation thanks to the first four items it contained.

These four concerti, originally written for a foreign patron of Vivaldi's, the Bohemian count Wenzel von Morzin, were arranged in a set called *Le quattro stagioni,* "The Four Seasons." Accompanied by explanatory sonnets that spelled out their imagery, they were inventively detailed evocations or "imitations" of nature as manifested (respectively) in spring, summer, autumn, and winter — and (perhaps more significantly) of the sensory and emotional responses the seasons inspired. The delight

EX. 24-18B   Antonio Vivaldi, Concerto for Four Violins Op. 3, no. 10, I, mm. 68–72

EX. 24-18B   (continued)

audiences took from the very beginning in the composer's powers of musical description is reflected in the popularity the *Seasons* already enjoyed in the eighteenth century, a popularity that crossed all national boundaries. Today, thanks to countless recordings, the set is practically synonymous with the composer's name.

In France, where descriptive music had an especially strong tradition, and where one of the earliest important public concert series (the *Concert spirituel*) got under way exactly in the year of the *Seasons'* publication, these concerti, particularly Spring (*La primavera*), became the very cornerstone of the emerging "standard repertory." In Italy, too, the *Seasons* put all the rest of Vivaldi in the shade. In 1761, only a couple of decades after the composer's death, the playwright and librettist Carlo Goldoni found it necessary to remind his readers that the famous violinist who composed *Le quattro stagioni* had also written operas.

La primavera quickly became the most popular one of the lot, and so it has remained. It was arranged for solo flute without accompaniment by none other than Jean-Jacques Rousseau, and even as a motet (for the Concert spirituel) by the French composer Michel Corrette, who simply superimposed choral parts declaiming the words of the psalm *Laudate Dominum* ("Praise ye the Lord") over Vivaldi's instrumental parts.

As a look at the first movement of *La primavera* will show, the concerto form, with its constant and fluid components, proved easy to adapt to illustrative or narrative purposes. (From here on we can use the literary critic's word *mimesis*—Greek for "imitation"—to encompass the gamut of illustrative or narrative functions.) Here are the first and second quatrains of the accompanying sonnet, corresponding to the movement in question:

A   *Giunt'è le primavera e festosetti*
B   *La salutan gli augei con lieto   canto,*
C   *E i fonti allo spirar de' Zeffiretti*
    Con dolce mormorio scorrono   intanto.
D   *Vengon coprendo l'aer di nero   amanto*
    E lampi, e tuoni ad annuntiarla   eletti
E   *Indi, tacendo questi, gli augelletti*
    Tornan di nuovo al lor canoro   incanto.

[Spring has come, and merrily the birds salute it with their happy song. And the streams, at the breath of little Zephyrs, run along murmuring sweetly.

Then, covering the air with a black cloak, come thunder and lightning, as if chosen to proclaim her; and when these have subsided, the little birds return once more to their melodious incantation.]

The letters running down the left margin are original. They mark the exact spots in the score to which the words refer—or rather, the exact spots where the music is designed to mime the words in question. There is no question, then, as to the composer's exact intentions. The imitations are obvious and hardly need pointing out; and yet it will be worth our while to consider the precise relationship at various points between the musical and verbal imagery.

Letter **A** corresponds to the ritornello (Ex. 24-19a), which (as befits its mimetic character) is rather unusual. Instead of the usual thematic complex there is a simple bouncy tune in binary form—an imitation folk song, as it were, whose implied words, as if sung by some implied rustics who will actually appear and dance in the last movement, are suggested by the sonnet's first line. The nature of the mimesis here is "affective," as one might find in the ritornello of a "happy" aria. Its periodic returns continually reinforce the overall mood of rejoicing at spring's arrival.

The remaining images, **B** through **E**, correspond exactly to the four episodes that come between the ritornelli. Letter **B**, the singing of the birds (Ex. 24-19b), is rendered in the most straightforward way that music, the "art of combining sounds," has at its disposal: *onomatopoeia*, direct "sound-alike" imitation. Birdsong had indeed long been a violinistic stock-in-trade, to the point where fastidious fiddlers like Francesco

Geminiani, a pupil of Corelli who worked in England and wrote a famous treatise on violin playing, were fed up with it. In a celebrated bilious aside, Geminiani complained that "imitating the Cock, Cuckoo, Owl, and other Birds . . . rather belongs to the Professors of Legerdemain and Posture-masters [i.e., magicians and charlatans] than to the Art of Musick."[9] He wrote this in 1751, twenty-six years after Vivaldi's *Seasons* had begun circulating in print and sounding forth from concert stages in France and England, and the composer of *La primavera* was surely one of the prime offenders.

EX. 24-19A   Antonio Vivaldi, *La primavera* (Op. 8, no. 1), I, mm. 1–3

EX. 24-19B   Antonio Vivaldi, *La primavera* (Op. 8, no. 1), I, mm. 15–18

Letter **C**, the episode of the brook and breezes (Ex. 24-19c), takes us back almost a century and a half, to Monteverdi's famous madrigal *A un giro sol* (Ex. 17-18), where the same textual images found the same mimetic response. Not that Vivaldi necessarily knew Monteverdi's work. (Such antiquarian knowledge would have been unusual in those days.) Even in Monteverdi's time the rendering of water by the use of wavelike motion — an instance of *metonymy*, the representation of an object through one of its attributes — was a stock device, the kind of thing we now call "madrigalism." And madrigalism would not be a bad term to use to characterize Vivaldi's mimetic devices as well, despite the transfer to the instrumental medium.

EX. 24-19C   Antonio Vivaldi, *La primavera* (Op. 8, no. 1), I, mm. 37 – 41

Using it would signal the easily overlooked, somewhat paradoxical fact that to incorporate mimesis into an instrumental concerto was actually to fall back on an old practice, one that the new Italian instrumental genres were widely perceived as threatening. (Recall old Fontanelle and his lugubrious plea, "Sonate, que me veux-tu?") Vivaldi was aware of this. He himself once used the term *concerto madrigalesco* to denote a piece in somewhat archaic style that used the kind of purply expressive chromatic harmonies the old madrigalists had formerly used to "paint" emotively laden words.

If we adapt the term to cover other kinds of word-painting as well, then *Le quattro stagioni* are also *concerti madrigaleschi*, and so are quite a number of other famous Vivaldi concerti, including *La tempesta del mar*, the item that immediately follows the Seasons in Vivaldi's opus 8, which "paints" a storm at sea, or again the eighth concerto in the book, called *La caccia*, which incorporates hunting signals (and which has antecedents going all the way back to the fourteenth century—see Ex. 10-2b).

What all this shows once again, and it is something never to forget, is that new styles and genres do not actually replace or supplant the old in the real world, only in history books. In the real world the new takes its place alongside the old and, during the period of their coexistence, the two are always fair game for hybridization.

To return to our catalogue: letter **D**, the sudden storm (Ex. 24-19d), juxtaposes low *tremolandi* for the ripieni, mimicking thunder, with high scales that depict lightning.

EX. 24-19D   Antonio Vivaldi, *La primavera* (Op. 8, no. 1), I, mm. 45–46

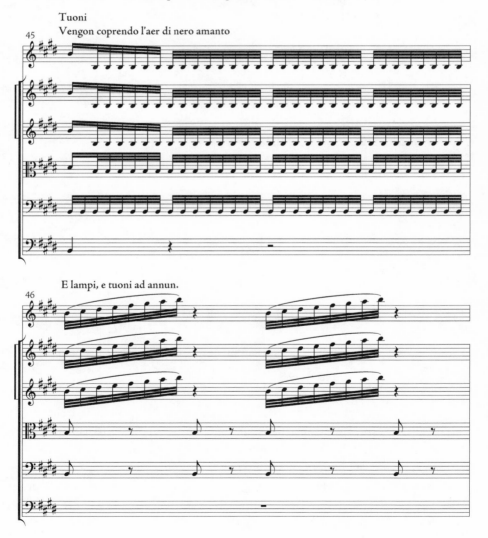

EX. 24-19E   Antonio Vivaldi, *La primavera* (Op. 8, no. 1), I, mm. 60–65

Canto d'uccelli
Indi, tacendo questi, gli Augelletti

Tornan di nuovo al lor canoro incanto

Thunder, like birdsong, is onomatopoeia—a natural for music. But how can music imitate lightning, which is a visual, not an aural phenomenon? Again by means of metonymy: the adjectives one might use to describe the violin scales—bright, quick, even "flashy"—apply to lightning as well; the shared attributes are what link the images. Following the storm, the ritornello takes on its minor-mode coloration, as if an affective reflection on the spoiling of the day.

Letter E, the birds' return (Ex. 24-19e), is the masterstroke: the way the solo violins steal in diffidently on chromatic scale fragments (yes, the *passus duriusculus*), as if checking out the weather before resuming their song, adds a "psychological" dimension to the onomatopoetical. This is no longer the work of a professor of legerdemain or a posture-master but the work of an expert musical dramatist. And that is the other obvious resonance that lies behind Vivaldi's mimetic practices: the opera house, where winds and storms, birds, rustic song, and all the rest were regularly evoked and compared—in the ritornelli of "simile arias"—with dramatic situations and the emotions to which they gave rise.

Class of 1685 (I)

Careers of J. S. Bach and G. F. Handel Compared; Bach's Instrumental Music

CONTEXTS AND CANONS

The year 1685 is luminous in the history of European music, because it witnessed the birth of three of the composers whose works long formed the bedrock of the standard performing repertoire, or "canon," as it crystallized (retrospectively) in the nineteenth century. In fact, the three composers in question — Johann Sebastian Bach (1685–1750), George Frideric Handel (1685–1759), and Domenico Scarlatti (1685–1757) — were for a long while the three earliest composers in active repertory, and so the number 1685 took on the aspect of a barrier, separating the music of common listening experience from a semiprehistoric repertoire called "early music" (or "pre-Bach music" as it was once actually termed), of concern only to specialists.

The contents, indeed the very existence, of this book show that this barrier has softened considerably, perhaps (some might argue) to the point of nonexistence. Concert life has been enriched by many performing artists and ensembles who confine themselves to music earlier than that of the class of 1685. Excellent recordings of such music abound. It is widely studied, analyzed, and critiqued. It has become familiar to a degree that would have been unthinkable even half a century ago. And yet artists who perform this music still specialize in it, and one aspect of the popularization of "pre-Bach" music has been an effort to reclaim the class of 1685 as specialist repertoire, which paradoxically means separating it from the "standard performing canon as crystallized in the nineteenth century" and placing it in the "pre-Bach" category.

Now we are apt to find Bach, Handel, and Scarlatti performed on the resurrected instruments of their time, not the standard instruments of today, by performers who have made a specialized study of the conventions that governed the performance practices of the early eighteenth century, and who are keen to emphasize the differences between those conventions and those to which "modern" listeners have become accustomed. The newfound familiarity of "early music" has led paradoxically to an effort to "defamiliarize" (or even "re-defamiliarize") it. This is something that happened in the twentieth century, and so the reasons for it will be best studied as part of the history of twentieth-century music.

The formation (or "canonization") of the old performing repertory was something that happened in the nineteenth century, and so, it follows, the reasons for *it* will be something to study as part of the history of nineteenth-century music. (The revival of Bach, whose music had temporarily fallen out of use except as teaching material, is an important and revealing part of that story.) And yet there were good reasons — "objective" reasons, one could argue — why the music of the class of 1685 became the foundation stone of the standard repertory once it was formed, and why even today their music (plus a few later rediscoveries like Vivaldi's *Four Seasons*) remains the earliest music that nonspecialist performers and "mainstream" performing organizations like choral societies and symphony orchestras routinely include in their active repertoires.

Theirs is also the earliest music that today's concertgoers and record listeners are normally expected to "understand" without special instruction, partly because general music pedagogy is still largely based on their work. No child learns to play the violin without encountering Vivaldi, or the piano without encountering Bach and (if one gets serious) Scarlatti. As soon as one is old enough to participate in community singing, moreover, one is sure to meet Handel.

The main reasons for this were broached in the previous chapter. These composers were the earliest to inherit from the Italian string players of the seventeenth century, and then magnificently enlarge upon, a fully developed "tonal" idiom. From the same Italian virtuosi they also inherited a standardized and highly developed instrumental medium — the "ripieno" string band or orchestra, to which wind and percussion instruments could be added as the occasion demanded. The new harmonic idiom and the new instrumental media acted symbiotically to foster the growth of standard instrumental and vocal-instrumental forms of unprecedented amplitude and complexity, and these were the forms on which the later standard repertory rested.

It follows, then, that the works of the class of 1685 that loom largest in the standard repertory will be those that coincide with, or that can be adapted to, standard performing media and esthetic purposes. Those of their works that are apt to be familiar today will therefore represent only a portion of their outputs, and not necessarily those portions considered most important or most characteristic by the composers themselves or by their contemporaries. *Opera seria*, the reigning genre of their day, has long dropped out of the repertoire. Therefore much of the music that both Handel and Scarlatti regarded as the most important music of their careers has perished from active use, while a lot of music that they regarded as quite secondary (Scarlatti's keyboard music, Handel's suites for orchestra) is standard fare today. Bach, who never even wrote an opera, was an altogether atypical and marginal figure in his day. Seeing him, as we do, as being a pillar of the standard performing repertory means seeing him in a way that his contemporaries would never have understood.

Thus to see Bach, Handel, and Scarlatti as standard repertory composers is to see them in a historical context that is not theirs. It will be our job to view them in their own historical context as well as in ours. The most fascinating historical questions about their work will be precisely those that concern the relationship between the two contexts. The most surprising aspect of the comparison will be the realization that Bach and Handel, whom we regard from our contemporary vantage point as a beginning, were regarded more as enders in their own day: outstanding late practitioners of styles and genres that were rapidly growing moribund in their time.

It was their very "conservativism," paradoxically enough, that later made them "canonical." The styles that supplanted theirs were destined to be ephemeral. Meanwhile, Handel's conservative idiom chanced to appeal to conservative members of his contemporary audience — and as we shall see, these members constituted the particular social group that inaugurated the very idea of "standard" or "timeless" repertory. It was logical that Handel's music should have been the earliest beneficiary of that concept.

With Bach the situation was more complicated. He came back into circulation, and achieved a posthumous status he never enjoyed in life, because the conservative aspects of his style — in particular, his very dense contrapuntal textures and his technique of "spinning out" melodic phrases of extraordinary length — made his music seem weighty and profound at a time when the qualities of weightiness and profundity were returning to fashion (and, as we shall see, served political and nationalistic purposes as well).

A mythology grew up around Bach, according to which his music had a unique quality that lifted it above and beyond the historical flux and made it a timeless standard: the greatest music ever written and (ideologically far more significant) the greatest music that would or could ever be written. That myth of perfection begot in its turn a myth of music history itself. It was given an elegant and memorable expression by the great German musicologist Manfred Bukofzer (1910–55). "Bach lived at a time when the declining curve of polyphony and the ascending curve of harmony intersected, where vertical and horizontal forces were in exact equilibrium," Bukofzer wrote, adding that "this interpenetration of opposed forces has been realized only once in the history of music and Bach is the protagonist of this unique and propitious moment."[1]

There was indeed a unique moment of which Bach was the protagonist. It took place, however, not during Bach's lifetime but in the nineteenth century, when the concept of impersonally declining and ascending historical "curves" was born. It was a concept born precisely out of the need to justify Bach's elevation to the legendary status he had come to enjoy as the protagonist of an unrepeatable, mythical golden age and the fountainhead of the Germanic musical "mainstream." The "equilibrium" and "interpenetration" of which Bukofzer wrote, and to which he assigned such a high value, were qualities and values created not by Bach but by those who had elevated him. The *history* of any art, to emphasize it once again, is the concern — and the creation — of its receivers, not its producers.

CAREERS AND LIFESTYLES

Bach and Handel were born within a month of one another, only a few miles apart, in adjoining eastern German provinces (then independent princely or electoral states). Handel, whose baptismal name was Georg Friederich Händel, was born on 23 February, in Halle, one of the chief cities in the so-called March of Brandenburg (a "march" being a territory ruled by a Margrave). Bach came into the world on 21 March a little to the south and west, in the town of Eisenach in Thuringia, a province of Saxony. Because of their nearly coinciding origins and their commanding historical stature, Bach and Handel are often thought of as a pair. In most ways, however, their lives and careers were a study in contrasts.

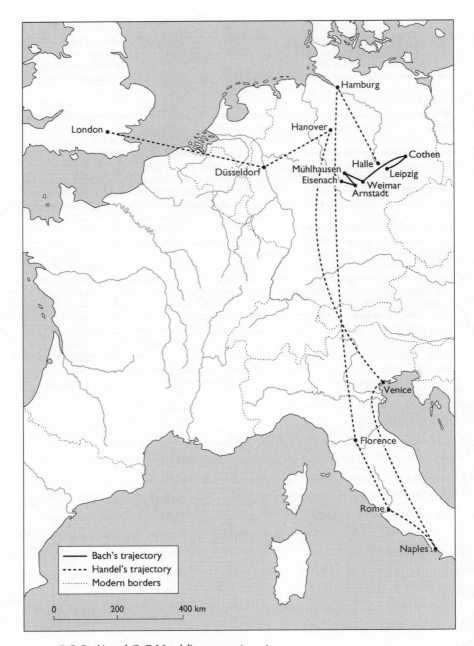

FIG. 25-I   J. S. Bach's and G. F. Handel's career trajectories.

Handel spent only the first eighteen years of his life in his native city, where he studied
with the local church organist, Friedrich Wilhelm Zachow, and attended the university.
In 1703 he moved to Hamburg, the largest free city in northern Germany, which had
a thriving opera house maintained by the municipal government and supported by
the local merchants. There he played harpsichord (continuo) in the orchestra and
composed two operas for the company. Having found his métier in the musical theater,

Handel naturally gravitated to Italy, the operatic capital of the world. He spent his true formative years—from 1706 to 1710—in Florence and Rome, where he worked for noble and ecclesiastical patrons and met and played with Alessandro Scarlatti, Corelli, and other luminaries of the day, and where he was known affectionately as *il Sassone*, "the Saxon," meaning really "the Saxon turned Italian" in the musical sense. In 1710 he became the music director at the court of George Louis, the Elector of Hanover, one of the richest German rulers. There, Handel had to assimilate the French style that all the German nobles affected in every aspect of court life, including court music.

The great turning point in Handel's life came in 1714, when his employer, without giving up the Electoral throne in Hanover, was elected King George I of England. (Queen Anne had died without a living heir and George Louis, as the great-grandson of King James I, was the closest Protestant blood claimant to the English throne.) George I never learned to speak English and was personally unpopular in England. He continued to spend much or most of his time in Hanover, leaving the running of the English government largely to his ministers of state, chief among them Robert Walpole, the powerful Prime Minister.

Handel had actually made his English debut as an opera composer before George's accession to the throne. With the King a virtual absentee ruler, his court composer was left remarkably free of official duties, and gained the right to act as a free agent, an independent operatic entrepreneur on the lively London stage. Over the rough quarter century between 1711 and 1738, Handel presented thirty-six operas at the King's Theatre in the London Haymarket (with a few, toward the end, at Covent Garden, which is still called the Royal Opera House), averaging four operas every three years. Acting at once as composer, conductor, producer, and, eventually, his own impresario, he made a legendary fortune, the first such fortune earned by musical enterprise alone in the history of the art. (Palestrina also died a very rich man, but his fortune came from his wife's first husband's fur business.)

Beginning in the 1730s, operatic tastes in London began to catch up with the continent. A rival company, the Opera of the Nobility, managed to engage the latest Italian composers and (far more important) the services of the castrato singer Farinelli (see chapter 23), around whom a virtual cult had formed. After a few seasons of cutthroat competition, both Handel and his competitors were near bankruptcy, and Handel was forced out of the opera business. With his practically incredible business sense he divined a huge potential market in English oratorios: Biblical operas presented without staging, along lines already familiar to us from the Lenten work of the Roman composers such as Carissimi.

Handel's adaptation of this old-fashioned genre was really something quite new: full-length works in the vernacular rather than Latin, without a narrator's part, but with many thrilling choruses, sometimes participating in the action, sometimes reflecting on it ("Greek chorus" style) to represent as a collective entity the pious yet feisty nation of Israel, with which the musical public in England—a public of "self-made men," aristocrats of wealth and opportunity, not birth, exulting in England's mercantile supremacy—strongly identified.

FIG. 25-2   J. S. Bach (?) at age thirty. Oil portrait by Johann Ernst Rentsch (ca. 1715), at the Municipal Museum of Erfurt.

Though ostensibly religious in their subject matter, the subtext of Handel's English oratorios — twenty-three in all, produced between 1732 and 1752 — was stoutly nationalistic. It was the first important body of musical works motivated by nationalism — a nationalism in which the composer, a naturalized British subject who had benefited greatly from his adopted country's economic prosperity and the opportunities it offered, enthusiastically shared — just as England, since the "revolutions" of the mid- and late seventeenth century, was the first country larger than a city state to identify itself as a nation in the modern sense of the word: a collectivity of citizens.

Handel's was thus the exemplary cosmopolitan career of the early eighteenth century, a career epitomized by his operatic

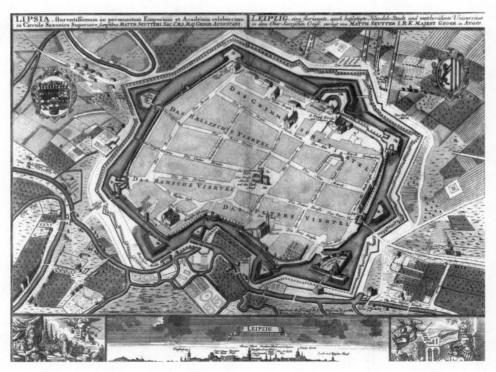

FIG. 25-3   A bird's-eye view of Leipzig in 1712. St. Thomas Church, where Bach would find employment eleven years later, stands by the south wall at right. The churches of St. Paul and St. Nicolai, where he also supervised musical performances, are at the other end of town.

"middle period," in which a German-born composer made a fortune by purveying Italian-texted operas to an English-speaking audience. Handel's style was neither German nor Italian nor English, but a hybrid that blended all existing national genres and idioms, definitely including the French as well. France was the one country where Handel, though an occasional visitor, never lived or worked; but its music, an international court music, informed not only the specifically courtly music that he wrote for his kingly patron but the overtures to his oratorios as well, which paid tribute to the "Heavenly King." Handel was the quintessential musical polyglot and the consummate musical entrepreneur. He commanded "world" (that is, pan-European) prestige. He has been a role model to "free market" composers ever since.

FIG. 25-4 St. Thomas Square, Leipzig, in an engraving by Johann Gottfried Krügner made in 1723, the year of Bach's arrival. The church is at right; the school, where Bach lived and worked, is at left.

Johann Sebastian Bach never once left Germany. Indeed, except for his student years at Lüneburg, a town near Hamburg to the north and west, his entire career could be circumscribed by a small circle that encompassed a few east German locales, most of them quite provincial: Eisenach, his Thuringian birthplace; Arnstadt, where he served between 1703 and 1707 as organist at the municipal Church of St. Boniface; Mühlhausen, where he served at the municipal Church of St. Blasius for a single year; Weimar, where he served the ducal court as organist and concert director from 1708 to 1717; Cöthen, a town near Halle, Handel's birthplace, where he served as Kapellmeister or music director to another ducal court from 1717 to 1723; and finally Leipzig, the largest Saxon city (but not the capital), where he served as cantor or music director at the municipal school attached to the St. Thomas Church from 1723 until his death.

FIG. 25-5 Interior of St. Thomas Church, with a view of the organ loft.

One of the larger German commercial cities even in Bach's day, Leipzig was nevertheless only a fraction of London's size and far from a cosmopolitan center. Still, it was a big enough town to have sought a bigger name than Bach as its municipal cantor. He was chosen only after two more famous musicians, Georg Philipp Telemann (1681–1767) and Christoph Graupner (1683–1760), had declined the town's offer in favor of more lucrative posts (in Hamburg and Darmstadt, respectively). One of the Leipzig municipal councillors grumbled that since the best men could not be had, they would have to make do with a mediocrity. Bach, for his part, felt he had been forced to take a step down the social ladder by going from a Kapellmeister's position at Cöthen to a cantorate at Leipzig. Until age put him out of the running, he repeatedly sought better employment elsewhere, including the electoral court at Dresden, the Saxon capital. Leipzig was the best he could do, however, and Bach was the best that Leipzig could do. Neither was very happy with the other.

Bach's, then, was the quintessential "provincial" career—humble, unglamorous, workaday. He remained for life in the musical environment to which he had been born, and which Handel quitted at his earliest opportunity. Handel had an unprecedented, self-made, entrepreneurial career that brought him glory and a very modern kind of personal fulfillment. Bach's, by contrast, was entirely predefined: it was the most traditional of careers for a musician of his habitat and class. For a musician of exceptional talent it was downright confining.

ROOTS (DOMESTIC)

It was as "predefined" as that because J. S. Bach happened to come from an enormous clan or dynasty of Lutheran church musicians dating back to the sixteenth century. So long and firmly associated was the family with the profession they plied that in parts of eastern Germany the word "Bach" (which normally means "brook" in German) was slang for musician. The *New Grove Dictionary of Music and Musicians* lists no fewer than eighty-five musical Bachs, from Veit Bach (ca. 1555–1619), a baker from Pressburg (now Bratislava in Slovakia) who enjoyed a local reputation for proficiency on the cittern (a plectrum-plucked stringed instrument related to the lute and the mandolin), down ten generations to Johann Philipp Bach (1752–1846), court organist to the Duke of Meiningen.

Fourteen members of the family were distinguished enough as composers to earn biographical articles in the dictionary. They include two of Johann Sebastian Bach's uncles (Johann Christoph and Johann Michael), three of his cousins (Johann Bernhard, Johann Nicolaus, and Johann Ludwig), four of his sons (Wilhelm Friedemann, Carl Philipp Emanuel, Johann Christoph Friedrich, and Johann Christian), and his grandson Wilhelm Friedrich Ernst (1759–1845, son of Johann Christoph Friedrich), who died childless and extinguished his grandfather's line.

The outward shape of Johann Sebastian Bach's career did not differ from those of his ancestors and contemporaries, and was far less distinguished than those of his most successful sons, Carl Philipp Emanuel and especially Johann Christian, whom we have already met briefly as a globe-trotting composer of *opera seria*. Most of the elder

Bachs were trained as church organists and cantors. That training included a great deal of traditional theory and composition, and as church musicians the elder Bachs were expected to turn out vocal settings in quantity to satisfy the weekly needs of the congregations they served.

The greatest composers of this type in the generations immediately preceding Bach — or at least the ones Bach sought out personally and took as role models — were three: Georg Böhm (1661–1733), whom Bach got to know during his student years at Lüneburg and whose fugues he particularly emulated; the Dutch-born Johann Adam Reincken (1643–1722), a patriarchal figure who had studied with a pupil of Sweelinck, and who died in his eightieth year; and, above all, Dietrich (or Diderik) Buxtehude (1637–1707), a Dane who served for nearly forty years as organist of the Marienkirche in the port city of Lübeck, one of the most important musical posts in Lutheran Germany.

Within that cultural sphere Buxtehude's fame was supreme, and he received numerous visits and dedications from aspiring musicians, including both Handel (who came up from Hamburg in 1703) and Bach (who took a leave from Arnstadt to make a pilgrimage on foot to Buxtehude in the fall and winter of 1705–1706). According to a story related by one of his pupils in a famous obituary, the aged Reincken, having heard Bach improvise on a chorale as part of a job audition, proclaimed the younger man the torchbearer of the old north-German tradition: "I thought this art was dead," the patriarch is said to have exclaimed, "but I see that in you it lives!" The story may well be apocryphal, but it contains an important truth: Bach did found his style on the most traditional aspects of north German (Lutheran) musical culture — a culture that was by most contemporary standards an almost antiquated one — and brought it to a late and (in the eyes of some of his contemporaries) virtually anachronistic peak of development. The keyboard works he composed early in his career while serving as organist at Arnstadt and Weimar show this retrospective side of Bach most dramatically.

One such apprentice piece, a harpsichord sonata in A minor, was based on a *sonata da camera* by Reincken himself, originally published in 1687 when Bach was two. Reincken had scored the piece for a trio sonata ensemble of two violins and continuo, enriched by a viola da gamba part that sometimes doubled the basso continuo line, sometimes embellished it, and sometimes departed from it to add a fourth real part to the texture. This kind of saturated texture was very much a German predilection and harks back to the full polyphony of the *stile antico*. Another Germanic trait was the sheer length of Reincken's fugal subjects, a length achieved by the use of

FIG. 25-6 Johann Adam Reincken, engraving after a portrait by Gottfried Kneller.

very long measures ($\frac{12}{8}$ meter being the most note-heavy meter in general use) and through devices of *Fortspinnung* or "spinning out" such as we have already associated in the previous chapter with Bach.

In Ex. 25-1, the first section of Reincken's last movement, a gigue in typical fugal style, is juxtaposed with Bach's reworking. It is a true emulation: not just an imitation, not just an homage, but an effort to surpass. One way in which Bach sought to accomplish this was by a sheer increase in size — in two dimensions. Reincken's nineteen measures are swollen to thirty, and his three-voiced exposition is augmented by a fourth fugal entry in Bach's version. At a time when many composers — especially composers of opera — were pruning and simplifying their styles in the interests of directness of expression, Bach remained faithful to an older esthetic tradition, seeking instead a maximum of formal extension and textural complexity. Throughout his life he was famed for the density of his music — sometimes praised for it, sometimes mocked.

At the same time, Bach managed, by varying the texture and pacing the harmony, to give his fugal exposition a much shapelier, more sharply focused design than Reincken's, despite the increase in length and (so to speak) in girth. At the beginning, Bach allows the initial exchange of subject and answer to take place without accompaniment, dispensing with Reincken's bass line as if getting rid of clutter. Then he gives greater point to the cadence at the end of the subject (m. 3) by spinning the sequence down as far as the leading tone, where Reincken had marked the end by repeating the approach to the tonic pitch.

This sharpening of tonal focus could be thought of as a modernizing touch: a response to the newly focused tonal style that was emanating from Italy, and that had quickly established itself, for musicians of Bach's generation, as a norm. Indeed, Bach greatly intensifies the harmony both in color and in "functionality," accompanying Reincken's long sequences of three-note descents with explicit circle-of-fifths harmonizations that sometimes (as in the full-textured "fourth entrance" in mm. 11–13) go into a sort of chromatic overdrive thanks to the use of secondary or "applied" dominants. For the rest, Bach expands the length of the exposition by devising an "episode" motive consisting of a decorated suspension chain (first heard in m. 7 between the two subject/answer pairs) that is finally brought rather dramatically into contrapuntal alignment with the subject on its last appearance.

Both Reincken's and Bach's versions are followed a couple of measures into the second section before Ex. 25-1 breaks off, to show the way in which both composers, following an old tradition, invert the subject to complement its initial statement. Here, too, Bach managed to outdo Reincken by building the inverted exposition from the bottom up instead of repeating the original top-down order of entries, thus achieving inversion, as it were, on two compositional levels at once.

Devices like these, and competition in their ingenious application, were standard operating procedure for church organists, who learned to do such things extemporaneously. More than anything else, they hark back to the learned artifices and contrivances of the *stile antico*. Bach delighted in these erudite maneuvers that he learned in his prentice years, employed them in every genre, and in his last years brought them to a peak of virtuosity that has been regarded ever since as unsurpassable. His son Carl Philipp Emanuel recalled that when listening to an organist improvise, or even when hearing a composed fugue for the first time, his father would always try to predict all the devices that could be applied to the subject, taking special pleasure in being surprised by one that he had failed to predict, and, contrariwise, reproaching the player or composer if his expectations went unmet.

EX. 25-1A   J. A. Reincken, *Hortus musicus*, Sonata no. 1, Gigue, mm. 1–21

EX. 25-IA (*continued*)

EX. 25-1B J. S. Bach, the same, arranged as a keyboard sonata, mm. 1–34

Gigue

EX. 25-IB (continued)

EX. 25-1B   (continued)

From Buxtehude, Bach inherited the toccata form sampled in the previous chapter. The Toccata in F included there as Ex. 24-15 may have originally been paired with a fugue (in F minor), according to a process that Buxtehude had pioneered, whereby the "strict" and "free" sections of a toccata—that is, the rigorously imitative or "bound" vs. the improvisatory passages—became increasingly separate from one another and increasingly regular in their alternation, with the improvisatory passages serving as introductions to the increasingly lengthy fugal ones.

By the early eighteenth century these sectionalized toccatas had developed into pairs of discrete pieces, the free one prefacing (or serving as "prelude" to) the strict. Such a pair, although still called "Toccata" or "Toccata and fugue" when the "free" part was especially lengthy or virtuosic (as in Ex. 24-15), or "Fantasia and fugue" when the free part had strongly imitative or motif-developing tendencies, was by Bach's time most often simply designated "Prelude and fugue."

Bach was the latest and greatest exponent of the prelude-and-fugue form, to which he contributed more than two dozen examples for organ, along with works in even more traditional genres, like his famous organ Passacaglia in C minor. Most of these are early works, the bulk of them composed at Weimar, where he was employed primarily as an organ virtuoso. One of Bach's most famous and mature compositions, however, was a monumental cycle of forty-eight paired preludes and fugues called *Das wohltemperirte Clavier*, in two books, the first composed in Cöthen in 1722, the second in Leipzig between 1738 and 1742.

Das wohltemperirte Clavier means "The Well-Tempered Keyboard." Its subtitle reads "Praeludia und Fugen durch alle Tone und Semitonia," or "Preludes and Fugues through all the Tones and Semitones." This meant that each of the books making up Bach's famous "Forty-Eight" consisted of a prelude-and-fugue pair in all the keys of the newly elaborated complete tonal system, alternating major and minor and ascending by semitones from C major, the "purest" of the keys since it has an accidental-free signature, to B minor (thus: C, c, C♯, c♯, D, d, and so on). Only a keyboard tuned in something approaching "equal temperament," with pure octaves divided into twelve equal semitones, can play equally well-in-tune throughout such a complete traversal of keys.

Equally well-in-tune actually means equally out-of-tune. Except for the octave, intervals composed of equal semitones do not correspond to those produced by natural resonance, known (after the well-known legend of their discovery) as "Pythagorean" intervals. The whole history of tuning has been one of compromise between natural resonance and practical utility. Since musical practice almost always demanded the ability to move from key to key—that is, to transpose scales so that their tonics and other harmonic functions are "keyed" to different pitches—and since the musical practice of the late seventeenth and eighteenth centuries suddenly demanded the ability to do this with increasing freedom and variety within single pieces, it was precisely then that the idea of equalizing the semitones decisively overcame the long-standing resistance of fastidious musicians who objected to the total loss of undeniably beautiful "pure" fourths, fifths, and thirds.

Bach's own preferred tuning was probably not yet quite equal. His practice may have accorded with that of Andreas Werckmeister (1645–1706), the author (in 1691) of the earliest treatise on equal temperament, who nevertheless declared himself willing "to have the diatonic thirds left somewhat purer than the other, less often used ones." Bach and his contemporaries may in fact have relished the dramatizing effect of greater harmonic "impurity" in remote tonalities. And yet Bach's twofold exhaustive cycle of preludes and fugues in all the keys celebrated what he clearly regarded as an ongoing triumph of practical technology, enabling a greatly enriched tonal practice that Bach, as we already know from the Toccata in F, was very quick to exploit.

For this, too, Bach had an immediate model. Twenty years before he wrote the first volume of the "WTC," in 1702, a south German organist and Kapellmeister named Johann Caspar Ferdinand Fischer published a collection of preludes and fugues under the title *Ariadne musica*, after the mythological princess who led the hero Theseus out of the Cretan labyrinth. The labyrinth, or maze, had long been a metaphor for wide-ranging tonal modulations, and Fischer's nineteen prelude-and-fugue pairs are cast in as many keys. (The fact that five "remote" keys are missing from his traversal probably means Fischer presupposed one of several tunings in use at the time that, while basically "well-tempered," were farther from equal than the one used by Bach.) As early as the sixteenth century, modulatory sets of this kind, placing tonics on all the semitones, had been written as curiosities for the lute, whose frets even then were set in something like equal temperament. But Fischer was undoubtedly Bach's model, for Bach paid him tribute by quoting a few of his fugue subjects, for example the one in E major (no. 8 in Fischer, no. 9 in Bach).

EX. 25-2A   J. C. F. Fischer, *Ariadne musica*, subject of the E-major Fugue

EX. 25-2B   J. S. Bach, *Das wohltemperirte Clavier*, Book II, subject of the E-major Fugue

And yet just as in the case of Reincken, Bach far surpassed his model even as he kept faith with it. Not only did Bach complete the full representation of keys; he also greatly expanded the scope and the contrapuntal density of his model. And perhaps most significantly of all, he invested the music with his uniquely intense and emphatic brand of tonal harmony.

To take the full measure of the WTC in a brief description is impossible; yet something of its range of technique and its intensity of style may be gleaned by juxtaposing the very beginning and the very end of the first book: the C-major prelude and the exposition of the B-minor fugue (Ex. 25-3).

These are both famous pieces, albeit for very different reasons. The C-major prelude is a piece that every pianist encounters as a child. It is in a classic "preludizing" style that goes back to the lutenists of the sixteenth century. That style had been kept alive through the seventeenth century by the French court harpsichordists (or *clavecinistes*) who took over from their lutenist colleagues like the great Parisian virtuoso Denis Gaultier (1603–72) both the practice of composing suites of dances for their instrument, and also many "lutenistic" mannerisms such as the strumming or arpeggiated style Bach's prelude continues to exemplify.

EX. 25-3A   J. S. Bach, *Das wohltemperirte Clavier*, Book I, Prelude no. 1 (C major)

The French called it the *style brisé* or "broken [chord] style"; early written examples, like those of the *claveciniste* Louis Couperin (ca. 1626–61), preserve many aspects of what was originally an impromptu performance practice akin to the old lute ricercar, in which the player prefaced the main piece with a bit of preparatory strumming to capture the listeners' attention and to establish the key. Couperin's "unmeasured" preludes, like

EX. 25-3A   (*continued*)

EX. 25-3B   J. S. Bach, *Das wohltemperirte Clavier*, Book I, Fugue no. 24 (B minor), mm. 1–19

the one in Ex. 25-4, are especially akin to improvised lute-strumming. Their notation actually leaves the grouping and pacing of the arpeggios to the player's discretion.

Thus, descending from a literally improvisatory practice, Ex. 25-3a is cast in a purely harmonic, "tuneless" idiom. (It was so tuneless as to strike later musicians as beautiful but incomplete. The French opera composer Charles Gounod [1818–93] actually wrote a melody, to the words of the antiphon *Ave Maria*, to accompany—or rather, to be accompanied by—Bach's prelude. It is a familiar church recital piece to this day.) Even without a tune, though, Bach's prelude has a very clearly articulated form—as well it

EX. 25-4 Louis Couperin, unmeasured prelude

Prélude
sol mineur

EX. 25-4   (continued)

might, since as we saw in the last chapter, it is harmony that chiefly articulates the form of "tonal" music even when melody is present.

The first four measures establish the key by preparing and resolving a cadence on the tonic. Measures 5–11 prepare and resolve a cadence on the dominant: and note that even though all the chords are "broken," the implied contrapuntal "voice leading" is very scrupulously respected. Dissonances, chiefly passing tones and suspensions, are always resolved in the same "voice." Thus the suspended bass note C in m. 6 resolves to B in the next measure; the suspended B in m. 8 resolves to A in m. 9; the suspended G in the middle of the texture in m. 9 (its "voice" identifiable as the one represented by the fourth note in the arpeggio—let's call it the alto) resolves to F♯ in m. 10; while the suspended C in the soprano in that same measure resolves to B in m. 11. (Ex. 25-5 shows this progression in block chords, so that the voice leading can be traced directly.)

EX. 25-5   J. S. Bach, Prelude no. 1, mm. 5–11, analyzed for voice leading

Measures 12–19 lead the harmony back to the tonic, characteristically employing a few chromaticized harmonies as a feint, to boost the harmonic tension prior to its final resolution. That resolution turns out not to be final, however: the tonic chord sprouts a dissonant seventh, turning it into a dominant of the subdominant; and the subdominant F in the bass, having passed (mm. 21–24) through a fairly wrenching chromatic double neighbor (F♯/A♭), settles on G, which is held as a dominant pedal for a remarkable eight measures (remarkable, that is, in a piece only 35 measures long) before making its resolution—a resolution accompanied by more harmonic feinting so that full repose is only achieved after four more measures. This apparently simple and old-fashioned composition conceals a wealth of craftsmanship, and in particular, it displays great virtuosity in the new art of manipulating tonal harmony.

That new art is really put through its paces in the B-minor fugue (Ex. 25-3b), famous for its chromatic saturation and its attendant sense of pathos—a pathos achieved by harmony alone, without any use of words. The three-measure subject is celebrated in its own right for containing within its short span every degree of the chromatic or semitonal scale, a sort of maximally intensified *passus duriusculus*, which at the same time symbolically consummates the progress of the whole cycle "through all the tones and semitones." What gives the subject, and the whole fugue, its remarkably poignant affect is not just the high level of chromaticism, but also the way in which that chromaticism is coordinated with what, even on their first "unharmonized" appearance, are obviously dissonant leaps—known technically as *appoggiaturas* ("leaning notes"). The two leaps of a diminished seventh in the second measure are the most obviously dissonant: the jarring interval is clearly meant to be heard as an embellishment "leaning on" the major sixth that is achieved when the first note in the slurred pair resolves by half step: C-natural to B, D to C♯. But in fact, as the ensuing counterpoint reveals, *every* first note of a slurred pair is (or can be treated as) a dissonant appoggiatura.

A thorough analysis of mm. 9–15, encompassing the entries of the third (bass) and fourth (soprano) voices, will reveal an astonishing level of dissonance on the strong beats, where the appoggiaturas fall. The bass G in m. 9 is harmonized with a tritone; the B on the next beat clashes with the C♯ above; the E on the downbeat makes the same clash against the F♯ above; the C that follows is harmonized with a tritone; the F♯ that comes next, with a fourth and a second; and the D on the fourth beat of m. 10 creates a seventh against the suspended C♯. Most of these dissonances are created not by suspensions but by direct leaps—the strongest kind of dissonance one can have in tonal music. Turning now to the soprano entrance in m. 13, we find a tritone and a diminished seventh against the D on the third beat; a leapt-to seventh on the fourth; a simultaneous clash of tritone, seventh, and fourth on the ensuing downbeat; a tritone against the sustained B on the second beat; another leapt-to seventh on the third beat, and so it goes.

It will come as no surprise to learn that these slurred descending pairs with dissonant beginnings were known as *Seufzer*—"sighs" or "groans"—and that they had originated as a kind of madrigalism. The transfer of vivid illustrative effects, even onomatopoeias, into "abstract" musical forms shows that those forms, at least as handled by Bach, were not abstract at all, but fraught with a maximum of emotional baggage. What is most remarkable is the way Bach consistently contrives to let the illustrative idea that bears the "affective" significance serve simultaneously as the motive from which the musical stuff is spun out.

Structure and signification, "form" and "content," are thus indissolubly wedded, made virtually synonymous. That was the expressive ideal at the very root of the "radical humanism" that gave rise to what Monteverdi (unbeknown to Bach) had called the *seconda prattica* a hundred years before. Monteverdi could only envisage its realization in the context of vocal music (where "the text will be the master of the music"). He never dreamed that such an art could flourish in textless instrumental music. That was what Bach, building on a century of musical changes, would achieve within an outwardly old-fashioned, even backward-looking career.

Clearly, Bach's art had a Janus face. Formally and texturally it looked back to what were even then archaic practices. In terms of harmony and tonally articulated form, however, it was at the cutting edge. That cutting edge still pierces the consciousness of listeners today and calls forth an intense response, while the music of every other Lutheran cantor of the time has perished from the actual repertory.

The other traditional genre that Bach inherited directly from his Lutheran organist forebears, and from Buxtehude most immediately, was the chorale setting. This was a protean genre. It could assume many forms, anywhere from a colossal set of improvised or composed variations (the type with which Bach enraptured Reincken and called forth his blessing) to a minuscule *Choralvorspiel* or "chorale prelude," a single-verse setting with which the organist might cue the congregation to sing, or provide an accompaniment to silent meditation. The chorale melody in such a piece might be treated strictly as a cantus firmus, or else melodically embellished, or else played off against a ritornello or a ground bass, or else elaborated "motet-style" into points of fugal imitation based on its constituent phrases.

Toward the end of his Weimar period, ever the encyclopedist and the synthesizer, Bach set about collecting his chorale preludes into a liturgical cycle that would cover the whole year's services. He had only inscribed forty-six items out of a projected 164 in this manuscript, called the *Orgelbüchlein* ("Little organ book"), when he was called away to Cöthen. But in their variety, the ones entered fully justify Bach's claim on the manuscript's title page, that in his little book "a beginner at the organ is given instruction in developing a chorale in many diverse ways." We can compare Buxtehude and Bach directly, and in a manner that will confirm our previous comparisons, by putting side by side their chorale preludes — Bach's from the *Orgelbüchlein* — on *Durch Adams Fall ist ganz verderbt* ("Through Adam's fall we are condemned," Ex. 25-6).

Although the first line makes reference to what for Christians was the greatest catastrophe in human history, the real subject of the chorale's text is God's mercy by which man may be redeemed from Adam's original sin through faith in Jesus Christ.

EX. 25-6A Dietrich Buxtehude, *Durch Adams Fall*, mm. 1–23

EX. 25-6A   (continued)

EX. 25-6B   J. S. Bach, *Durch Adams Fall* (*Orgelbüchlein*, no. 38)

EX. 25-6B *(continued)*

Nevertheless, it is the first line that sets the tone for the setting, since the first verse is the one directly introduced by the prelude. Both Buxtehude's prelude and Bach's, therefore, are tinged with grief. The chorale melody, treated plain by Bach, with some embellishment by Buxtehude, is surrounded by affective counterpoints.

In Buxtehude's case the affect is created by chromatically ascending and descending lines that enter after a curious suppression of the bass. In Bach's setting, the most striking aspect is surely the pedal part. This in itself is no surprise: spotlighting the pedal part was one of Bach's special predilections, as we already know from the Toccata in F (Ex. 24-15), and fancy footwork was one of his specialties as an organ virtuoso. On the title page of the *Orgelbüchlein*, which he intended to publish on completion, Bach included a little sales pitch, promising that the purchaser will "acquire facility in the study of the pedal, since in the chorales contained herein, the pedal is treated as wholly *obbligato*," that is, as an independent voice.

What is a powerful surprise, and further evidence of Bach's unique imaginative boldness, is the specific form the obbligato pedal part takes in this chorale setting: almost nothing but dissonant drops of a seventh — Adam's fall made audible! And not just the fall, but also the attendant pain and suffering are depicted (and in a way evoked), since so many of those sevenths are diminished. A rank madrigalism, the fall, is given emotional force through sheer harmonic audacity and is then made the primary unifying motive of the composition. Again the union of illustration and construction, symbolic image and feeling, "form" and "content," is complete. And if, as seems likely, Buxtehude meant the three falling fifths that accompany the first phrase of the chorale in the bass to symbolize the fall, we have another case of Bach's propensity to emulate — to adopt a model and then surpass it to an outlandish degree, amounting to a virtual difference in kind.

ROOTS (IMPORTED)

The same attitude Bach displayed in intensifying and transforming the traditional techniques of his trade characterized his relationship to all the styles of his time. Despite the seemingly cloistered insularity of his career, he nevertheless mastered, and by his lights transcended, the full range of contemporary musical idioms. In part this was simply a matter of being German. At a time when French and Italian musicians were mutually suspicious and much concerned with resisting each other's influence, German musicians tended to define themselves as universal synthesists, able (in the words of

Johann Joachim Quantz, a colleague of C. P. E. Bach's at the Prussian court) "to select with due discrimination from the musical tastes of various peoples what is best in each," thereby producing "a mixed taste which, without overstepping the bounds of modesty, may very well be called the German taste."[2] Bach became its ultimate, most universal, exponent.

But he had many predecessors. We know how eagerly Heinrich Schütz, born a hundred years before Bach, had imported the Italian styles of his day to Germany. A younger contemporary of Schütz, the sometime Viennese court organist Johann Jacob Froberger (1616–67), a native of Stuttgart in southern Germany, traveled the length and breadth of Europe, soaking up influences everywhere. After a period (approximately 1637 to 1640) spent studying with Frescobaldi in Rome, Froberger visited Brussels (then in the Spanish Netherlands), Paris, England, and Saxony. He died in the service of a French-speaking German court in the Rhineland, the westernmost part of Germany.

The first whole book of pieces by Froberger to be (posthumously) published was eminently Frescobaldian: *Diverse curiose partite, di toccate, canzone, ricercate etc.* ("Assorted off-beat toccatas, canzonas, ricercars and so on"). Four years later, there followed a book containing *Dix suittes de clavessin* ("Ten suites for harpsichord"), in a style that comported perfectly with the language of the title page. This book of suites would be by far Froberger's most influential publication. By century's end, the French style had become a veritable German fetish, the object of intense envy and adaptation. Envy played an important role because it was envy of the opulent French court on the part of the many petty German princelings that led to the wholesale adoption of French manners by the German aristocracy. French actually became the court language of Germany, and French dancing became an obligatory social grace at the many mini-Versailleses that dotted the German landscape.

With dancing, of course, came music. Demand for French (or French-style) ballroom music, and for instruction in composing and playing it, became so great that by the end of the seventeenth century a number of German musicians, sensing a ready market, had set themselves up in business as professional Gallicizers. One of these was Georg Muffat (1653–1704), an organist at the episcopal court at Passau, who had played violin as a youth under Lully in Paris. In 1695 he published a set of dance suites in the Lullian mold, together with a treatise on how to play them in the correct Lullian "ballet style." His rules, especially those concerning unwritten conventions of rhythm and bowing, have been a goldmine to today's "historical" performers, who need to overcome a temporal distance from the music comparable to the geographical distance Muffat's original readers confronted.

Another Gallicizer was J. C. F. Fischer, with whose *Ariadne* we are already acquainted. His Opus 1 was a book of dance suites for orchestra called *Le journal de printems* ("Spring's Diary," 1695), in which he prefaced the dances, originally composed for the ballroom of the Margrave Ludwig of Baden, with Lully-style overtures. Although the components were all French, this type of orchestral "overture suite" was in fact a German invention, pioneered by Johann Sigismund Kusser (or "Cousser," *à la française*) a sort of Froberger of the violin who studied in Paris with Lully and then plied his trade all over Europe, ending up in Dublin, where he died in 1727. Orchestral suites of this kind, actually called *ouvertures* after their opening items, remained a German specialty. Telemann, cited by the *Guinness Book of World Records* as the most prolific composer of all time, composed around 150 of them.

Fischer's op. 2, titled *Musicalisches Blumen-Büschlein* ("A little musical flower bush," 1696), was a book of harpsichord suites on the Froberger model. Between the two of them, Froberger's publication and Fischer's managed to establish a standard suite format that provided the model for all their German or German-born successors. Froberger's contribution was the truly fundamental one: it was he who adopted a specific sequence of four dances as essential nucleus in all his suites, setting a precedent that governed the composition of keyboard suites from then on. Fischer prefaced his suites with preludes, some patterned on the *style brisé*, others on the toccata. This, too, became an important precedent, albeit not quite as universally observed by later composers. (Bach, for example, composed suites both with and without preludes, but always included Froberger's core dances.)

It is worth emphasizing that Froberger's core dances had, by the time he adapted them, pretty much gone out of actual ballroom use. They had been sublimated into elevated courtly listening-music by the master instrumentalists of France, which meant slowing them down and cramming them full of interesting musical detail that would have been lost on dancers. The typical French instrumental manuscript or publication of the day, whether for lute, for harpsichord, or for viol, generally consisted of several vast compendia of idealized dance pieces in a given key, each basic type being multiply represented. The French composers, in other words, did not write actual ready-made suites, but provided the materials from which players could select a sequence (that is, a *suite*) for performance. It was Froberger and his German progeny who began, as it were, "preselecting" the components, thus casting their suites as actual multimovement compositions like sonatas.

The four favored dances, chosen for their contrasting tempos and meters (and, consequently, their contrasting moods), were these:

1. *Allemande*. This dance had a checkered history. As its name suggests, it originated in Germany, but by the time German composers borrowed it back from the French it had changed utterly. In its original form — previously encountered in Corelli (Ex. 24-1b) — it was a quick dance in duple meter. The first keyboard examples are by the English virginalists, who called it the *alman*, and Frescobaldi, who called it the *bal tedesco* or *balletto*. It was Gaultier and his *claveciniste* contemporary Jacques Champion de Chambonnières (1602–72) who slowed it down into a stately instrumental solo in a broad four beats per bar and a richly detailed texture. It was this elegantly dignified *allemande*, never before heard in Germany, that Froberger borrowed back and ensconced permanently in the opening slot of his standard suite.

2. *Courante*. In its older form, more often called (in Italian) *corrente*, this was a lively mock-courtship dance, notated in $\frac{3}{4}$ or even $\frac{3}{8}$ meter. (Examples can be found in any Corelli *sonata da camera*.) The idealized French type borrowed

by Froberger was just the opposite: the gravest of all triple-time suite pieces, notated in $\frac{3}{2}$ with many lilting hemiola effects in which $\frac{6}{4}$ patterns cut across the $\frac{3}{2}$ pulse.

3. *Sarabande.* Of all the suite dances, this one underwent the most radical change in the process of sublimation. It originated in the New World and was brought back to Europe, as the *zarabanda*, from Mexico. In its original form it was a breakneck, sexy affair, accompanied by castanets. Like the passacaglia or chaconne, it consisted originally of a chordal ostinato and is first found notated in Spanish guitar tablatures. Banned from the Spanish ballroom by decree for its alleged obscenity, it was idealized in a deliberately denatured form, becoming (like the chaconne) a majestic triple-metered dance for the ballet stage, often compared to a slow minuet. As borrowed by Froberger, it usually had an accented second beat, rhythmically expressed by a lengthened (doubled or dotted) note value.

4. *Gigue.* Imported to Europe from England and Ireland, the jig was (typically) danced faster in Italy (as the *giga*), in more leisurely fashion by the more self-conscious bluebloods of the French court and their German mimics. In its idealized form, the gigue usually began with a point of imitation, which (as we have already observed in Reincken and Bach) was often inverted in the second strain.

A "binary" or double-strain structure (AABB), supported by a there-and-back harmonic plan, was a universal feature of suite dances, particularly as adopted by Germans. (In France there was an alternative: the so-called *pièce en rondeau*, in which multiple strains alternated with a refrain.) In the hands of Bach and his contemporaries, the binary dance became another important site for developing the kind of tonally articulated form that conditioned new habits of listening and formed the bedrock of the standard performing repertory.

BACH'S SUITES

As we know, Bach never went to France. Instead, France came to him through the musical publications that circulated widely in the Gallicized musical environment that was Germany. Bach made his most thorough assimilation of the French style when he was professionally required to do so. That was in 1717, when he left Weimar for the position of Kapellmeister in Cöthen. This was an entirely secular position, the only such position Bach ever occupied and an unusual one for any "Bach." His new employer, Prince Leopold of Anhalt-Cöthen, was a passionate musical amateur, who esteemed Bach highly and related to him practically on terms of friendship. (He even stood godfather to one of Bach's children.) Leopold not only consumed music avidly but played it himself (on violin, bass viol or viola da gamba, and harpsichord) and had even studied composition for a while in Rome with Johann David Heinichen (1683–1729), a notable German musician of the day. He maintained a court orchestra of eighteen instrumentalists, including some very distinguished ones. And he was a Calvinist, which meant he had no use for elaborate composed church music or fancy organ playing. So

FIG. 25-7 Title page of Anna Magdalena Bach's music book (*Clavier-Büchlein*), 1722.

Bach had no call to compose or play in church and could devote all his time to satisfying his patron's demands for musical entertainments.

Thus for six years Bach wrote mainly instrumental music. The first book of the WTC dates from the Cöthen period, as we know, but that was done on the side. The kind of entertainments demanded of Bach as part of his official duties would have taken the form of sonatas, concertos, and above all, suites. Bach turned out several dozen of the latter, ranging from orchestral *ouvertures* through various sets for keyboard, to suites for unaccompanied violin and even cello, the latter unprecedented as far as we know. He even wrote a couple of suites for the practically obsolete lute, the historical progenitor of the idealized suite-for-listening, which still had a few devotees in Germany.

Most of Bach's keyboard suites are grouped in three sets, each containing six of them. The earliest is a set of six large suites with elaborate preludes and highly embellished sarabandes, probably composed in Weimar around 1715. They were published posthumously as "English Suites," and have been called that ever since, although no one really knows why. The set published (also posthumously) as "French Suites" are close to the Froberger model. The four dances standardized by Froberger provide the core, with a smaller group of faster and lighter "modern" dances interpolated between the sarabande and the gigue. Of the six French Suites, five are found in one of the music books of Anna Magdalena Bach, the composer's second wife. They were probably composed for the private enjoyment of Bach's family and the instruction of his children.

The final group of six, though written at Cöthen, were assembled, engraved, and published by Bach himself at Leipzig in 1731, as the first volume of an omnibus keyboard collection unassumingly titled *Clavier-Übung* ("Keyboard practice"). Bach borrowed the name from his predecessor as Leipzig cantor, Johann Kuhnau, who published a set of keyboard suites under that title in 1689. Bach also followed Kuhnau in calling the suites contained therein by the old-fashioned (and somewhat misleading) title "partitas." When we last encountered it (chapter 21), the word "partita" referred to a set of variations, in Lutheran countries often based on chorale melodies. Bach's fame has firmly implanted his unusual usage in the common vocabulary of music. When musicians use the word "partita" now, it almost always means a dance suite.

A CLOSE-UP

The nucleus of Bach's fifth French Suite, in G major, consists of the Frobergerian core of allemande, courante, sarabande, and gigue, augmented by a trio of slighter dances (a gavotte, a bourée, and a loure) interpolated before the gigue. Bach himself used the term *Galanterien* (from the French *galanteries*) on the title page of the *Clavier-Übung* to classify these interpolated dances and distinguish them from the core, describing his suites (or partitas) as consisting of "Präludien, Allemanden, Couranten, Sarabanden, Giguen, Menuetten, und anderen Galanterien." Note that the obligatory or core dances are listed (after the preludes) in order, while the variable category of "minuets and other *galanteries*" is mentioned casually, out of order, as if an afterthought. This contrast in manner is very telling.

Even though the word *galanterie* can be translated as a "trifle," it denotes a very important esthetic category. It is derived from what the French called the *style galant*, which stemmed in turn from the old French verb *galer*, which meant "to amuse" in a tasteful, courtly sort of way, with refined wit, elegant manners, and easy grace. It was a quality of art — and life — far removed from the stern world of the traditional Lutheran church, and Bach never fully reconciled the difference between the sources that fed his creative stream.

EX. 25-7A   J. S. Bach, French Suite no. 5 in G major, Allemande

EX. 25-7A   (*continued*)

To put Bach's allemande (Ex. 25-7a) alongside one written sixty or seventy years earlier by Froberger (Ex. 25-7b) is to marvel at the sheer persistence of the French courtly style in Germany. The old *style brisé*, in which the harpsichord aped the elegant strumming of a lute, informs both pieces equally, although Froberger learned it directly from the lutenists (one of his best known pieces being a *tombeau*, or "tombstone," an especially grave allemande or pavane composed *in memoriam*, for the Parisian lutenist Blancrocher, a friend), while Bach would have learned it from Froberger, from Kuhnau, and from their followers.

EX. 25-7B   Johann Jakob Froberger, Suite in E minor, Allemande

The difference between the pieces is the usual difference between Bach and his predecessors or contemporaries. Although not much longer than Froberger's (twenty-four measures as against twenty), Bach's makes a far more distinctive and developed impression thanks to two characteristic features, one melodic and the other harmonic. The opening motive of Bach's allemande, a three-beat ascent of a third (with pickups and a distinguishing trill), is treated *thematically*—that is, as a form-definer—in a way that was unknown to Froberger.

While Froberger had at his disposal characteristic ways of articulating the melodic shape of his composition—for example, the three-note pickup that begins each half—Bach uses the opening motive to lend the two halves of his allemande a sense of thematic parallelism, echoing on the melodic plane the overall symmetry of design that is chiefly articulated by the harmony. Coordination of the harmonic and melodic spheres is additionally confirmed by the use of the opening motive, replete with defining trill, to point the cadences in m. 4 (which establishes the tonic) and in m. 5 (which launches the movement to the dominant). For an even more dramatic illustration of how conscious and deliberate Bach's motivic writing could be, compare a passage from one of his concertos (for two harpsichords in C major, probably composed later in Leipzig), in which the same opening figure from the allemande is dramatically proclaimed as a "headmotive" that introduces the main ritornello and is also developed antiphonally as an episode (Ex. 25-7c and d).

As to harmony, both allemandes follow the same there-and-back pendular motion between tonic and dominant that defines the "binary" form of a dance, but Bach's ranges wider and is at the same time more sharply focused. Each half of Froberger's dance follows a single motion between harmonic centers with no major stops along the way. Each half of Bach's, by contrast, is divided into two distinct phrases, keenly marked by cadences. The first phrase, mm. 1–4, begins and ends with the tonic, thus reinforcing it by closure. The balancing phrase, mm. 5–12, establishes the dominant as cadential goal. (Actually, the dominant is reached at m. 8, so that the phrase has two equal components, one that "moves" and the other that "re-arrives" after some interesting chromatic digressions.)

EX. 25-7C   J. S. Bach, Concerto in C for Two Harpsichords, BWV 1061, I, mm. 1–4

mm. 1 - 4

EX. 25-7D   J. S. Bach, Concerto in C for Two Harpsichords, BWV 1061, I, mm. 28–32

mm. 28 - 32

The second half of Bach's allemande is divided more equally than the first. Its first phrase, mm. 13–18, moves from the dominant not straight back to the tonic but to a "secondary function" (that is, a chord with opposite quality from the tonic), in this case E minor, the submediant. The concluding phrase finally zeroes back on the tonic, harking back to the "interesting chromatic digressions" from the first half to signal its impending arrival.

That shape will henceforth serve as paradigm for a fully "tonal" binary form. The new elements include the care with which the tonic is established (almost the way a ritornello might establish it in a concerto movement), and the compensating feint in the direction of some "far out point" (henceforth FOP) in the second half of the piece to redirect the harmonic motion home with renewed force. Once again Bach is out in front of his contemporaries in harnessing the power of tonality to steer the course of a composition through a sort of journey, and to take the measure of its distance, at all points, from "home."

The other movements in the French Suite all confirm this basic pattern of harmonic motion, in which the simple "binary" there-and-back is amplified and extended by means of an initial closure on the tonic to emphasize departure, and an excursion to a FOP on the way back, thus: Here-there-FOP-back. In the Italian-style courante or corrente (Ex. 25-8a), the cadential points are distributed with perfect regularity, as follows: m. 8 (I), m. 16 (V), m. 24 (vi), m. 32 (I). Compare the tonally much more elusive French-style courante from the third French Suite in B minor (Ex. 25-8b), in which the cadence points are quite unpredictably and asymmetrically distributed among its 28 spacious measures: m. 5 (i), m. 12 (V), m. 19 (iv), m. 28 (i).

Note, too, how every pre-cadential measure in Ex. 25-8b (i.e., mm. 4, 11, 18, and 27) foreshadows the cadence by speeding up the harmonic rhythm (that is, the rate of harmony-change) and by regrouping the measure's six quarter notes by pairs rather than by threes, producing a so-called "hemiola" pattern of three beats in the normal time of two. (The pre-cadential bars are not the only ones that are felt in "$\frac{3}{2}$" rather than "$\frac{6}{4}$": the surest signal for hemiola grouping is the presence of a dotted quarter note, usually trilled, on the fifth beat.) By comparison with the stately old-style French courante (the

EX. 25-8A   J. S. Bach, French Suite no. 5 in G major, Courante

EX. 25-8B   J. S. Bach, French Suite no. 3 in B minor, Courante

EX. 25-8B (*continued*)

only kind Froberger knew), the Italianate type—by virtue of its rhythmic evenness, its regular cadences, and its uncomplicated, predominantly two-voiced texture—is practically a *galanterie*.

In the sarabande (Ex. 25-9), the cadence points again evenly divide the first half. In contrast, the second half is elaborately subdivided into sections cadencing on two FOPs (ii in m. 20 and vi in m. 24), and the trip back to the tonic is subarticulated with stops on the subdominant (m. 28) and the dominant (m. 36) before finally touching

EX. 25-9 J. S. Bach, French Suite no. 5 in G major, Sarabande

EX. 25-9   *(continued)*

down at the end (m. 40). The result is a colorfully lengthened, but also strengthened, harmonic structure.

While of course slighter, the *galanteries* (Ex. 25-10a-c) observe similar tonal proportions. The *gavotte* (Ex. 25-10a), a buoyant dance with beats on the half note and a characteristic two-quarter pickup, has cadences on mm. 4 (I), 8 (V), 16 (vi), and 24 (I). Notice that the tendency to expand the second half, already apparent in the sarabande, is maintained here as well by doubling the phrase lengths, though without the addition of any supplementary cadence points. The *bourrée* (Ex. 25-10b), a rambunctious stylized peasant dance in two quick beats per bar, has its cadences more irregularly placed: mm. 4 (I), 10 (V), 18 (vi), 30 (I). That irregularity is part of its *galant* or witty charm: each phrase is longer than the last, and the listener is kept guessing how much longer.

The *loure* (Ex. 25-10c), one of the rarer dances, might be described as a heavy *(lourd)* or rustic gigue in doubled note values. (In the sixteenth century the word *loure* was

EX. 25-10A   J. S. Bach, French Suite no. 5 in G major, Gavotte

EX. 25-10B   J. S. Bach, French Suite no. 5 in G major, Bourée

EX. 25-10B (continued)

EX. 25-10C   J. S. Bach, French Suite no. 5 in G major, Loure

EX. 25-10C (continued)

used for a certain kind of bagpipe, but whether that is the source of the dance's name is unclear.) Its meter and note values resemble those of the "true" French courante (as in Ex. 25-8b), but its rhythms—particularly the pattern ♩ ♪ ♩, already familiar from the Scarlattian siciliano—are gigue-like. Altogether unlike those of the courante in Ex. 25-8b, the cadences of Bach's loure are distributed with perfect regularity (mm. 4, 8, 12, 16). The supertonic (ii), somewhat unusually, is used in place of the submediant (vi) as FOP.

Finally, the gigue (Ex. 25-11): with its 56-bar length (distributed 24 + 32) and its fugal expositions in three real parts, it is the most elaborate dance of all. Tracking cadences here is complicated by the behavior of the fugal writing, which has its own pendular rhythm. The first fugal exposition makes its final tonic cadence on the third beat of m. 9, and the dominant is reached by the third beat of m. 14, when the bass enters with the subject. Final confirmation of arrival on V comes, after a lengthy episode, in m. 24. The second half begins, just as Bach's gigue after Reincken (Ex. 25-1b) had begun, with an inversion. As befits a dance (if not a fugue), this inverted exposition ends, somewhat indefinitely, on a FOP (either vi in m. 37 or ii in m. 38). The bass then enters with the subject on the dominant of vi, to start steering the course through a slow circle of fifths toward home.

"AGRÉMENS" AND "DOUBLES"

To conclude this little study of the French Suite No. 5, two more comparisons are in order, one "internal," and the other "external." The internal distinction, of course, is that between the styles of the traditional "obligatory" dances and the galanteries. Putting the allemande next to the gavotte shows how radically they differ. The textural and harmonic richness of the allemande's style brisé contrasts with the virtual homophony of the gavotte; the subtle spun-out phrases of the one with the square-cut strains of the other; the placid, equable rhythms of the former with the highly contrasted, vivacious rhythms of the latter.

These musical ("technical") differences are symptomatic of a fundamental difference in taste, one that would eventually mark the eighteenth century as a kind of esthetic battleground. With Bach, the *galant*, while certainly within his range, is nevertheless the exceptional style — the sauce rather than the meat. With most of his contemporaries, the balance had rather decisively shifted to the opposite.

Here is where the external comparison comes in. Consider another gigue to set beside Bach's: the one that opens the fourteenth *ordre*, or "set," of harpsichord

EX. 25-11   J. S. Bach, French Suite no. 5 in G major, Gigue

EX. 25-11 (continued)

pieces (published in 1722) by Bach's greatest keyboard-playing contemporary, François Couperin (1668–1733), royal organist and chief *musicien de chambre* to Louis XIV (Ex. 25-12). Couperin's is a "set" rather than a suite because, following traditional French practice, the pieces in it, while related by key, are too numerous to be played or heard in one sitting and are not placed in performance order. One fashioned one's own suite from such a set *ad libitum*.

Couperin's gigue (Ex. 25-12a) is not identified as such by title. It is, rather, identifiable by its rocking $\frac{6}{8}$ meter. That is the normal gigue meter; Bach's $\frac{12}{16}$ is a diminution, betokening a faster tempo than usual. That tempo, since it is conventional, can be conveyed by the notation alone,

FIG. 25-8 François Couperin (ex collection André Meyer).

without any ancillary explanation. And indeed, none of the dances in Bach's suite carry any verbal indications as to their tempo. Such indications were not needed. The name of the dance, the meter, and the note values conveyed all the essential information.

But the situation with Couperin's gigue, one of his most famous pieces (and rightly so), is just the opposite. It is not called "gigue," but *Le Rossignol en amour*, "The Nightingale in Love"! It is not really a dance at all, but a "character piece" or (to use Couperin's own word) a sort of "portrait" in tones, cast in a conventional form inherited from dance music. The subject portrayed is ostensibly a bird, and the decorative surface of the music teems with embellishments that seem delightfully to imitate the bird's singing. But since (according to the title) the bird in question is incongruously experiencing a human emotion, the musical imitation is simultaneously to be "read" as a metaphor — a portrait not just of the bird but of the emotion, too, in all its tenderness, its languorousness, its "sweet sorrow."

Since the conventional tempo of a gigue contradicts tenderness or languor, Couperin had to countermand it with a very detailed verbal indication, directing the performer to play "slowly, and very flexibly, although basically in time." At the stipulated tempo there is room for a great wealth of embellishment, all indicated with little shorthand signs that Bach also used, and that are (mostly) still familiar to piano students today. The first sign in order of appearance, which Couperin called the *pincée* (a "pinched note") and which we now call a mordant, is a rapid alternation of the written note with its lower neighbor on the scale. The second, which Couperin called *tremblement* ("trembling") and we now call a short trill (or, sometimes, a shake), is a rapid and repeated alternation of the written note with its upper neighbor.

Such conventionalized, localized ornaments, called "graces" in English at the time, and *agrémens* in French, were learned "orally"—by listening to one's teacher and imitating, the way instrumental technique has always been (and will always be) imparted. There were tables of reference, of course, and many composers compiled

EX. 25-12A   François Couperin, *Le Rossignol en amour* (14th Ordre, no. 1), beginning

them. Couperin's (published as an insert to his first book of harpsichord pieces in 1713) is shown in Fig. 25-9. For an even more intense or less conventionalized expression, one resorted to specifically composed embellishments.

That is what Couperin does in his coda or *petite reprise*, where he notes that the speed of the written-out trill is to be "increased by imperceptible degrees" for an especially spontaneous (or especially ornithological) burst of feeling. And then he follows the whole piece with a "fancy version" or *double* (Ex. 25-12b), in which the surface becomes a real welter of notes, and where it becomes the supreme mark of skillful performance to keep the lineaments of the original melody in the fore-

FIG. 25-9 "Explication des Agremens, et des Signes," from Couperin's first book of *Pièces de clavecin* (Paris, 1713).

ground. (Perhaps that is why Couperin recommends in a footnote that the piece be played as a flute solo, for the flutist can use flexible dynamic shading and a true legato, while a harpsichordist must "fake" both.) *Agrémens* are still used plentifully in a *double*, but they are supplemented with turns and runs that have no conventional shorthand notation. Bach's most notable *doubles* are those he wrote for the sarabandes in his "English" suites (although he called them, a little incorrectly, "agrémens").

Miniatures that display the kind of exquisitely embellished, decorative veneer Couperin knew so well how to apply are often called *rococo*, a kind of "portmanteau word" formed by folding together two French words: *rocaille* and *coquille*, the "rock-" or "grotto-work" and "shell-work" featured in expensively textured architectural surfaces of the period. Were the decorative surface stripped away from Couperin's *pièce*, the simplest of shapes would remain: cadences come every four bars (the last one delayed by two bars of "plaintive iterations"), describing a bare-bones tonal trajectory of I – V/V – I. Nor is the emotion expressed one of great vehemence or intensity. Rococo art expressed the same sort of aristocratic, "public" sentiments (including the sort of amorous or melancholy sentiments that can be aired in polite society) that we have already identified as *galant*. The strong pathos of Bach's B-minor fugue (Ex. 25-3b) would have been as out of place in such company as it would be in the music of Couperin.

There was a place for such emotion, of course, and for a style of embellishment that expressed it, in the Italian art associated with the opera; and although Bach wrote no

EX. 25-12B   François Couperin, *Le Rossignol en amour* (14th Ordre, no. 1), "Double de Rossignol"

operas, he was well acquainted with the music of his Italian contemporaries and much affected by it. By Bach's time a great deal of Italian instrumental music aspired to an "operatic" intensity of expression; recall some of the "frightening" work of Corelli and Vivaldi from the previous chapter. And there was a concomitant style of instrumental embellishment, allied to, and perhaps in part derived from, the *fioritura* of the castrati and the other virtuosi of the Italian opera stage.

Italianate ornamentation was "free," or so the story went. In fact it was governed by just as many rules or conventions as the French, but it was applied with a much broader brush — not to single "graced" notes, but to the intervals between notes, even to whole phrases. In effect it meant making up your own "double" on the spot. Such a deed required real composing skills — a ready "ear" for harmony and counterpoint at the least — and was therefore far more a creative act than French ornamentation. But of course the extent to which a fully embellished Italian instrumental solo was really a spontaneous invention, rather than a studied and memorized exercise, must have varied greatly from performer to performer, just as it did in the opera house.

Even more than the French, Italian ornamentation was a practice that had to be learned by listening and emulating. Such written guides as there are consist not of tables or rules but of models for imitation. The most widely distributed and influential publication of this type was an edition of Corelli's solo sonatas issued in 1716 (two years after the composer's death) by the Amsterdam printer Estienne Roger, in which all the slow movements were fitted out with an alternate line showing *"les agrémens des Adagio de cet ouvrage, composés par M. Corelli, comme il les joue"*: "the embellishments to the Adagios, composed by Mr. Corelli, just the way he plays them" (see Ex. 25-13).

The claim may be doubted. There was no guarantee in those piratical days that any composer had actually written what was published under his name, and it is downright implausible to think that Corelli needed to write such things out for himself. Nevertheless, even if these are not "Corelli's graces" (as an English publisher who had pirated them from Roger called them), they fairly represented the going style, as attested by many other publications, manuscripts, and compositions in the Italianate manner.

Among the most telling such corroborating documents is the slow movement — marked "Andante," but in style a true Adagio — from Bach's *Concerto nach italiänischem Gusto* ("Concerto after the Italian Taste"), probably written at Cöthen but published in the second volume of his *Clavier-Übung*, issued in Leipzig in 1735 (Ex. 25-14). This bracing composition, usually called the "Italian Concerto" in English, is a tour de force for composer and performer alike. The compositional feat is the transfer to a single keyboard instrument of the whole complex Italian concertato style, with its interplay of solo and tutti. A single keyboard instrument, that is, but not a single keyboard: large harpsichords, like pipe organs, had double keyboards that controlled different sets (or "ranks") of strings. By engaging a device called a coupler that made both keyboards respond to a single touch, Bach could achieve a solo/tutti contrast between keyboards. And so he did in the rollicking outer movements, cast in ritornello style.

In the slow middle movement, Bach reverted to the older ground bass format, over which he cast a lyrical ("*cantabile*") line for a metaphorical Corelli who pulls out all the stops in embellishing a hypothetical "original" tune (suggested in an alternate staff at the beginning of the music as given in Ex. 25-14). Note that Bach throws in a few "French" ornaments as well, especially on entering pitches and melodic high points. These do not so much represent a mixture of styles (though as a German, Bach would not have balked at such a mixture) as they do a means of achieving the equivalent of a dynamic accent, unavailable on the harpsichord. (Indeed, when transferring cantabile lines from the harpsichord to other instruments, as in *Le Rossignol en amour*, even Couperin suggests leaving out some of the signed graces, suggesting that French ornaments may actually have originated as a way of compensating for the physical limitations of the instrument.)

Bach's invigorating keyboard arrangement, so to speak, of an imaginary Italian violin concerto was preceded by many keyboard arrangements of actual concertos. While at Weimar, Bach arranged some nineteen Italian concertos (five for organ, the rest for harpsichord), including several that we looked at in the previous chapter, like Vivaldi's

E X. 25-13   Arcangelo Corelli, Sonata in D major, Op. 5, no. 1

EX. 25-13 (continued)

EX. 25-13 (*continued*)

for four violins and Marcello's for oboe. Making these arrangements is undoubtedly how Bach gained his mastery not only of the trappings of the Italian style but of the driving Italianate harmonic practices that he took so much further than his models, marking him as not just an imitator but a potent and very idiosyncratic emulator.

STYLISTIC HYBRIDS

By the time he reached creative maturity, Bach had thus assimilated and encompassed all the national idioms of his day. Indeed, like all Germans he made a specialty of commingling them; but his amalgamations were singular, even eccentric. They disclosed what even today can seem an unrivaled creative imagination, but one that was uniquely complicated, inexhaustibly crafty, even (while always technically assured and unfailingly alluring) at times incomprehensible and disturbing.

EX. 25-14   J. S. Bach, slow movement from the "Italian Concerto" with the Incipit of a hypothetical "original"

A relatively mild and sensuously ingratiating example of Bach's stylistic complexity is the opening movement of his third orchestral suite or *ouverture*. It was possibly composed at Cöthen, but Bach revised it in Leipzig for performance by the Collegium Musicum, a society of professional instrumentalists and students (founded by Telemann in 1702) that gave weekly afternoon concerts at a popular local "coffee garden." Bach became its director in 1729.

In its general outline, the movement follows the plan of a "French overture," such as we encountered in chapter 22 in the work of Lully and Rameau, although Bach's is far lengthier and more elaborate than any functional theatrical overture. The use of this format was standard operating procedure for German orchestral suites and the reason why they were called "ouvertures" to begin with. A regal march in binary form, full of pompous dotted rhythms, frames an energetic fugue. The march (Ex. 25-15a) sounds more regal than ever owing to the size and makeup of the orchestra, which in addition to the standard complement of strings includes a pair of oboes to reinforce the violin parts, and a blaring contingent of three trumpets — the first of them in the sky-high *clarino* register that only specialists could negotiate — plus timpani.

EX. 25-15A   J. S. Bach, Ouverture (Orchestral Suite) no. 3, I, beginning

The use of this brass and percussion unit is the first level of stylistic admixture here, for the virtuoso brass ensemble was a fixture of German municipal music-making. Such players, known as *Stadtpfeiferei* ("town pipers"), had been employed by free German towns as combined watchmen and signal corps as long as there had been free towns — that is, since the fourteenth century — and by the eighteenth century they formed a venerable guild or trades hierarchy of highly skilled musicians, to which admission was severely restricted. Their civic duties included performance at all official celebrations and ceremonial observances, and also regular morning and evening concerts (called *Turmmusik* or "tower music" because they were played from the tower of the *Rathaus*, the town council hall) that signaled the beginning and end of the public day.

Along with Nuremberg to the south, Leipzig was one of the greatest centers for municipal music. The most illustrious Stadtpfeifer in history, to judge by his contemporary reputation and his written legacy, was a Silesian named Johann Pezel (or Petzoldt, 1639 – 94), who worked in Leipzig from 1664 until 1681 (even at one point aspiring to the position of town cantor) and published five books containing tower and occasional music of all kinds. But if Pezel was the greatest of his line, surely the runner-up was the long-lived Gottfried Reiche (1667 – 1734), a renowned trumpeter whose period of service in Leipzig overlapped with Bach's. Although Reiche was nearing sixty by the time Bach came to Leipzig, he was a uniquely qualified clarino specialist, and Bach wrote many of his most brilliant first trumpet parts for him, including the one in the third orchestral suite.

Thus far we have a French courtly overture played by a band that included German town musicians. But stylistic mixture does not stop there. In the fugal middle section of the overture (Ex. 25-15b), the expositions are played by the full orchestra, the Stadtpfeifers capping them off with a blast at cadences. The episodes, how-

ever, are scored for a virtuoso solo violinist backed up with a string *ripieno* — an Italian concerto ensemble! And the fugue indeed behaves like a concerto if we regard the expositions, which after all always have the same thematic content, as ritornellos. So the panorama is complete: specifically French, Italian, and German elements have fused into a unique configuration that at the same time uncovers unsuspected affinities between forms and genres of diverse parentage and customary function.

Indeed, it can seem as though Bach's special talent — or special mission — was to uncover the hidden affinities that united the ostensibly diverse. Or to put it another way, by creating his unique and unsuspected joinings of what were normally separate entities,

FIG. 25-10 Gottfried Reiche, the Leipzig clarino trumpeter. Portrait by E. G. Haussmann, 1727.

EX. 25-15B   J. S. Bach, Ouverture (Orchestral Suite) no. 3, I, end of fugal exposition and beginning of episode

Bach knew how to make the familiar newly strange. As a self-conscious artistic tendency, such an aim is usually thought to be quintessentially "modern"; it sits oddly with Bach's reputation (in his own day as well as ours) as an old-fashioned composer. And yet his way of uniting within himself both the superannuated and the unheard-of was perhaps Bach's crowning "synthetic" achievement.

THE "BRANDENBURG" CONCERTOS

These ideas apply with particular conviction to Bach's most familiar body of instrumental music and can serve to "defamiliarize" it interestingly, perhaps illuminatingly. In 1721, while serving at Cöthen, Bach gathered up six instrumental concertos that he had composed over the last decade or so, wrote them out in a new "fair copy" or presentation manuscript, and sent them off with a suitably obsequious calligraphic dedication page, elegantly composed in French (the German court language), to Christian Ludwig, the Margrave of Brandenburg (Fig. 25-11), hoping for an appointment to the latter's court in Berlin. (Several of Bach's best known compositions, in fact, were written or assembled in connection with job- or title-hunting, often unsuccessful; they include his "B-minor Mass," about which more in the next chapter.)

The rest of the story is well known: the Margrave never acknowledged receipt of the manuscript and seems never to have had the concertos performed. Their fame dates from the acquisition of the calligraphic manuscript by the royal library in Berlin and their subsequent publication as a set. To the Margrave they must have seemed bizarre, and they were most likely quite unsuited to the resources of his court, for in their scoring they all differ radically from one another, and not one of them uses a standard orchestral complement. Their fame, plus the sheer fact that "The Brandenburg Concertos" have so long been standard repertory works, has hidden their strangeness behind a cloak of canonical familiarity. (So has the esthetic attitude that in the nineteenth century gave rise to the very idea of a standard repertory, which paradoxically regarded uniqueness as a "standard" feature of masterworks worthy of inclusion.) Perhaps the most absorbing exercise of the historical imagination, where Bach's music is concerned, is the recovery of that hidden strangeness.

Merely to list the ensembles the concertos call for is to make a start toward grasping their eccentricity. The first concerto, in F major, has for its *concertino* or solo group a weirdly assorted combination of two horns, three oboes, a bassoon, and a *violino piccolo* (a smaller, higher-pitched type of violin, then rare, now altogether obsolete). The movements are an equally weird

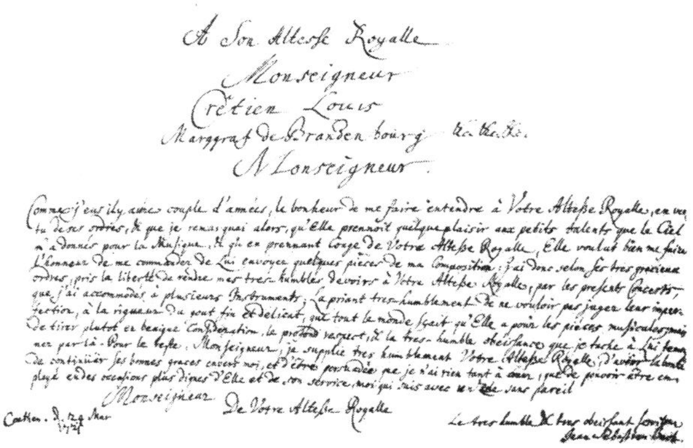
A Son Altesse Royalle
Monseigneur
Cretien Louis
Marggraf de Brandenbourg
Monseigneur

FIG. 25-11 Bach's calligraphic dedication of the Brandenburg Concertos.

assortment, mixing ritornello movements and courtly dances. The second concerto, also in F major, uses four soloists, their instruments starkly contrasting in their means of tone production and strength of voice: in order of appearance they are violin, oboe, recorder (end-blown whistle flute), and clarino trumpet. Balancing the recorder's whisper with the trumpet's blast must have been as daunting a prospect then as it is now. The third concerto, in G major, has no *concertino* at all; it is scored for a unique ripieno ensemble comprising nine string soloists: three violins, three violas, and three cellos, plus a continuo of bass and harpsichord. The fourth, also in G major, uses a violin and two unusual recorders pitched on G (designated *flûtes d'echo* in the score).

The last two concertos are the most bizarrely scored of all. The fifth, in D major, has for its *concertino* a violin, a transverse flute (the wooden ancestor of the modern metal flute), and — of all things! — a harpsichord in a fully written-out, soloistic (rather than continuo) capacity. This is apparently the earliest of all solo keyboard concertos. To us it seems the beginning of a long line, but no one could have foreseen that when Bach had the idea. The sixth concerto, in B-flat major, finally does away with the otherwise ubiquitous solo violin. Indeed, it banishes the violin from the orchestra altogether — something for which there seems to be no precedent in the prior (or for that matter, the subsequent) history of the concerto, which is so intimately bound up with the history of the violin.

Instead, the sixth concerto promotes two violas, normally the least conspicuous members of the ripieno, to soloist position, and dragoons a pair of viols (*viole da gamba*), not normally a part of the orchestra at all but soft-toned chamber music instruments, to fill the gap left in the middle of the texture by the "elevation" of the violas. Like the third concerto, the sixth minimizes the distinction between solo and ripieno; the concerto requires only seven instruments for performance — the two violas, the two gambas, and a continuo of cello, bass, and harpsichord.

Were these bizarrely fanciful and colorful scorings the product of sheer caprice, meant as "ear candy" and nothing more? Were they the product of immediate need or personal convenience? (Bach's patron at Cöthen played the gamba; Bach himself, of course, was a matchless keyboard virtuoso.) Or were they somehow meaningful, in a way that more normally scored or "abstract" instrumental music was not? These are questions to which answers can only be speculative. Such questions, to the historian, are in one sense the most frustrating kind, but in another sense the most fascinating.

To answer them, it is necessary to ask other questions. Was the standard concerto scoring, or the standard makeup of an orchestra, really "abstract" and nonsignificant? Or did it, too, mean something? If so, what did its alteration or negation mean? And even more basically, *to whom did it mean whatever it meant?*

Recent research on the history of the orchestra shows that, from the very beginning, the orchestra — the most complex of all musical ensembles — was often explicitly (and even more often, it would probably follow, tacitly) regarded as a social microcosm, a compact mirror of society. The orchestra, like society itself, was assumed to be an inherently hierarchical entity. This assumption was already implicitly invoked a few paragraphs back when the violas were casually described as the "least conspicuous members of the ripieno." Their inconspicuousness was the result of the kind of music they played: harmonic filler, for the most part, having neither any substantial tunes to contribute nor the harmonically defining function of the bass to fulfill. Musically, their role could fairly be described as being, while necessary, distinctly less important than those of their fellow players above (the violins) and below (the continuo instruments). Even today, the violas (and the "second violins") in an orchestra — the "inner parts" — are proverbially subordinate players, by implication social inferiors. Our everyday language bears this out whenever we speak of "playing second fiddle" to someone else.

And if "second fiddle" implies inferiority, then "first fiddle" tacitly implies a superior condition. In Bach's day, before there were baton conductors, the first violinist was in fact the orchestra leader. (Even today, when the leadership role has long since passed to the silent dictator with the stick, the first violinist is still called the "concertmaster.") So when Bach banishes the violins from the ensemble, as he does in the sixth concerto, and puts the violas in their place, it is hard to avoid the impression that a social norm — that of hierarchy — has been upended.

Or consider the fifth concerto, which begins (Ex. 25-16a) with a fiery tutti played by every instrument in the ensemble except the flute. For one actually watching the performance as well as listening to it — a point that may require some underscoring in an age when our primary relationship to musical sound may be to its recorded and therefore disembodied variety — the clear implication is that the flute is to be the protagonist, and that the rest of the instruments belong to the ripieno. So the fact that the violin and the obbligato harpsichord continue to play after the first tutti cadence is already a surprise.

At first it is not entirely clear that the harpsichord part in the solo episodes is a full social equal to the flute and the violin; continuo players often improvised elaborate right-hand parts in chamber music, and Bach himself was known to be especially adept at doing so. The triplets in measure 10, unprecedented in the opening tutti but later much developed by the other soloists, can be read in retrospect as the first clue that the harpsichord is to be no mere accompanist. The triplets, like the slurred pairs of eighth notes in the second solo episode (already identified in the B-minor fugue from the WTC as "sighs"), are unmistakable emblems of what Bach would have called the *affettuoso* (tender) style. (They were conspicuous in the castrato music sampled in chapter 23.) In their contrast with the agitated repeated sixteenth notes of the ritornello, recalling the dramatic *concitato* style that goes all the way back to Monteverdi, the triplets and slurs are a signal to us that the dulcet solos and the spirited tuttis are going to be somewhat at odds in this concerto, and that the "scenario" of the piece will involve their reconciliation — or else their failure to achieve reconciliation.

It is the harpsichord that impedes reconciliation. By the time the first "remote" modulation gets made (to B minor), the harpsichord has already made it clear that it will not be content with its usual service role. Indeed, it is determined to dominate the show. In m. 47 it actually abandons the bass line (leaving it contemptuously to the viola and ripieno violin) and launches into a toccata-like riff in thirty-second notes that lasts for only three measures (Ex. 25-16b), but that succeeds in knocking things for a loop — a condition symbolized first by the failure of an attempted tutti in the tonic to achieve its cadence, and then by the long dreamlike tutti that marks the movement's FOP in the very unusual mediant key of F♯ minor (iii).

EX. 25-16A   J. S. Bach, Brandenburg Concerto no. 5, I, opening

In this long section (mm. 71–101) a new theme, related neither to the ritornello nor to the original soloist's material, is traded off between the flute and violin soloists (Ex. 25-16c) while the harpsichord keeps up a relentless tramp of sixteenth notes. Eventually the other soloists' stamina gives out and the music becomes entirely

EX. 25-16A (continued)

harmonic, a slow march around the circle of fifths in which nothing sounds but arpeggios at various levels of speed. At m. 95 the motion is further arrested (Ex. 25-16d), with the long-held dissonances in the flute and violin, trilled pianissimo, seeming to go out of time as if everyone were falling asleep — everyone, that is, except the harpsichord and its continuo cohort, the cello.

EX. 25-16B   J. S. Bach, Brandenburg Concerto no. 5, I, mm. 47–51

EX. 25-16B (*continued*)

At m. 101 everyone snaps out of their trance with a ritornello on the dominant that seems to be pointing the way toward home. The flute and violin conspire to direct the harmony tonicward with a sequential episode, and succeed in bringing about a small cadence on I that the harpsichord seems to abet with an entrance that apes its very first solo. The flute and violin join in with reminiscences of *their* first solos, and when the ripieno chimes in to cap things off with a full repetition of the opening ritornello — the normal ending for a movement like this — the piece seems about to end on the expected note of fully achieved concord.

But it has all been a diabolical ruse, and the movement, which has already reached more or less average Vivaldian length, turns out to be only half over. On the third beat of m. 125 (Ex. 25-16e) the end so agreeably promised is aborted by a classic deceptive cadence, engineered by the bass, which (in a manner that recalls the Toccata in F, explored in the previous chapter) assaults the tonic D with a fiercely dissonant and chromatic C-natural that forces the music out of its tonal bed, so to speak, and forces it to keep going at least long enough to repair the abruption. A new purchase on the same ritornello is thwarted again, once more by the bass, which feints to the third of the chord rather than the root, producing an inversion that cannot support a close.

There will be no more attempts at closure for a long time, because the harpsichord, as if seizing its moment, launches once again into the toccata riff it had initiated some ninety or so measures earlier, and this time it proves to be truly irrepressible. The thirty-second notes keep up for fifteen measures, changing in figuration from scales to decorated slow arpeggios, to very wide and rapid arpeggios. With every new phase in the harpsichord's antics comes a corresponding loss of energy in the other instruments (now clearly their former accompanist's accompanists), until they simply drop out, leaving their obstreperous companion alone in play.

What follows is something no eighteenth-century listener could ever have anticipated. It had no precedents of any kind in ensemble music—and (outside of a few outlandish violin concertos by latterday Italian virtuosi like Pietro Locatelli and

EX. 25-16C   J. S. Bach, Brandenburg Concerto no. 5, I, mm. 71–74

EX. 25-16D   J. S. Bach, Brandenburg Concerto no. 5, I, mm. 95–99

Francesco Maria Veracini, who probably never heard of Bach) it would have no successors, either. The unimaginably lengthy passage for the *cembalo solo senza stromenti*, as Bach puts it ("the harpsichord alone without [the other] instruments"), is an absolutely unique event in the "High Baroque" concerto repertory.

It is often called a cadenza, on a vague analogy to the kind of pyrotechnics that opera singers like Farinelli would indulge in before the final ritornello in an *opera seria* aria. And perhaps Bach's listeners might eventually have made such a connection as the

EX. 25-16E   J. S. Bach, Brandenburg Concerto no. 5, I, mm. 151–59

EX. 25-16E (*continued*)

harpsichord's phantasmagoria wore on and the remaining instruments sat silent for an unheard-of length of time. But the actual style of the solo is more in keeping with what Bach's contemporaries would have called a *capriccio*—a willfully bizarre instrumental composition that made a show of departing from the usual norms of style. (Locatelli would actually call the extended—and optional—unaccompanied display passages in his violin concertos *capriccii*, and later collected them into a book of études in all the keys called *L'Arte del violino*; but even these were passages for the expected soloist, not a usurping would-be Farinelli from the continuo section!) Bach's capriccio begins like a virtuoso reworking of the original soloist's themes — the previously "dulcet" music now played with fiery abandon. Later there is a return to the relentless tread of sixteenth notes that had accompanied the F♯-minor episode described above. Finally, there is a mind-boggling explosion of toccata fireworks that lasts for over twenty measures before resuming the earlier thematic elaboration and bringing it at last to cadence. By the time it has run its course and allowed the tutti finally to repeat its opening ritornello one last time and bring the movement to a belated close, the harpsichord's cadenza/cappriccio/toccata has lasted sixty-five measures, close to one-third the length of the entire movement, and completely distorted its shape.

"OBBLIGATO" WRITING AND/OR ARRANGING

The remaining movements in the Fifth Brandenburg Concerto have nothing to compare with this disruption. By now the harpsichord has made its point, and its status as a full partner to the other soloists is something the listener will take for granted, so there is no need to insist on it. The middle movement, explicitly marked *affettuoso*, is actual chamber music, scored for the soloists alone. Although played by three instruments, it is really a quartet, since the left and right hands of the keyboard have differing roles. The left hand, as always, is the continuo part, sometimes joined in this function by the right hand (where figures are marked) to accompany the other soloists at the imitative beginnings of sections. Elsewhere, the right hand takes part on an equal footing with the flute and violin, sometimes participating in imitative textures along with them, at other times alternating with them in a kind of antiphony.

This kind of obbligato harpsichord writing in chamber music is something one finds a great deal in Bach and in other German composers, too, especially Telemann. It may have been the conceptual origin of the Fifth Brandenburg Concerto, in which an obbligato-style chamber ensemble is turned into a concertino. Usually, in ensembles of this kind, the obbligato harpsichord is paired with one other instrument to make a sort of trio sonata in which the right hand at the keyboard is a "soloist" and the left hand the "accompanist." Bach wrote three sonatas of this kind for flute and harpsichord, six for violin and harpsichord, and (at Cöthen, where his patron was an amateur of the instrument) three for viola da gamba and harpsichord.

The first gamba and harpsichord sonata actually began life as a trio sonata for two flutes and basso continuo before Bach transcribed it for the more compact medium. This suggests that any trio sonata might be performed with a harpsichordist taking two of the parts. (Bach surely did this sort of thing often at Cöthen and later with his Collegium Musicum at Leipzig.) In other words, the use of the obbligato harpsichord, at least when it does not involve highly idiomatic toccata-like passagework, could be looked at as a performance practice rather than a hard-and-fast compositional genre. The second gamba sonata does have a toccata-like passage in the last movement, suggesting that it was originally written for the obbligato medium, not merely adapted to it. The third gamba sonata, in G minor, is especially odd and interesting: a very extended affair with a first movement cast like a concerto in ritornello form. This, too, is a type of sonata for which there are precedents in Germany and only in Germany, where it was called a *Sonata auf Concertenart* ("Sonata in concerto style").

The point is that performance genres and media were much more fluid in Bach's day than they later became. For Bach, a piece did not necessarily have the kind of definitive form it later assumed with, say, Beethoven (and which, thanks largely to Beethoven, we now expect all pieces to have). A piece was always fair game for cannibalization in other pieces, for transplantation to other media, or seemingly arbitrary adaptation. The line between creating it and performing it was not as finely drawn as we might nowadays tend to assume. Thus it should not surprise us to learn that Bach arranged many violin concertos, including some otherwise lost ones by himself, to perform as harpsichord concertos with his Collegium Musicum, or that individual movements from the Brandenburg Concertos turn up in other works, even vocal ones.

The final movement of the Fifth Brandenburg Concerto is an excellent example of "fused" genres. It seems to have a hard time deciding whether it is a fugue, a gigue, or a concerto. But of course it is all of those things at once. We have already seen how often the two sections of a gigue begin with little fugal expositions. In the Fifth Brandenburg Concerto, the exposition is extended into quite an elaborate affair — in four parts, two of them assigned to the harpsichord — that lasts 28 measures before the ripieno joins in to second it with another extended exposition of 50 measures' length, the whole 78-bar complex in effect making up one huge ritornello.

WHAT DOES IT ALL MEAN?

Here, too, there is significant role reversal: in a way the soloists, who begin alone, and the ripieno, who follow, have exchanged functions. Once again a breach of traditional social hierarchies is suggested, albeit nothing on the scale of the colossal trespass or transgression committed by the harpsichord in the first movement, which one commentator has aptly compared to a hijacking.[3] What do all these reversals, mixtures, and transgressions signify?

For a long time they were thought to signify only the fertility of Bach's composerly imagination. And yet (without wishing to slight that imagination in any way) interpreting them so may not do their strangeness justice. Historians have lately begun to wonder whether, given the frequency with which the orchestra was compared with a social organism and described in terms of social or military hierarchy, Bach's musical transgressions might not resonate with ideas of social transgression.

Two such hypotheses have attracted scholarly attention (and provided the grounds, it should be obvious, for a great deal of scholarly debate). One, put forth by Susan McClary in an article that appeared during Bach's tricentennial year, 1985, straightforwardly compared the harpsichord's behavior with political subversion. By suggesting "the possibility of social overthrow, and the violence implied by such overthrow," McClary argued, Bach may have been weighing the pros and cons of "an ideology that wants to encourage freedom of expression while preserving social harmony."[4] Such a vision or fantasy did indeed preoccupy many social thinkers in the eighteenth century. Historians refer to the period during which this vision gained ground as the age of "Enlightenment," an age of secularism and anti-aristocratic thinking during which the ideals of an economically empowered middle class were cast as "universal" progressive ideals. In McClary's view, the harpsichord's behavior was a kind of symbolic "storming of the Bastille" some seventy years before the French Revolution turned Enlightened fantasy into political reality.[5] She suggested that the concerto as a whole symbolically enacted "the exhilaration as well as the risks of upward mobility, the simultaneous desire for and resistance of concession to social harmony."

Resistance to this hypothesis was swift and stout, fueled on the one hand by the absence of any corroborating evidence that Bach was interested in—or even knew about—the political theories of the Enlightenment, and on the other hand by an unwillingness to let the music alone provide the evidence. Yet once the idea had been broached that unusual musical behavior could be, and probably was, motivated by (or at least resonant with) ideas or circumstances that were abroad in the wider world, it became difficult to ignore the possibility without appearing to slight or disregard the unusualness of the music, and thereby diminish it.

An alternative proposal was offered by Michael Marissen, a Bach scholar who sympathized with McClary's general tendency to seek explanations for exceptional musical phenomena in the world of historical ideas, but who had misgivings about her ascription to Bach of social ideas that were so little shared among German Lutherans. Following Luther himself, Bach and his co-religionists entertained conservative social attitudes and placed great value on the stability of existing institutions—exactly what Bach's harpsichordist (indeed, Bach himself, as the imagined protagonist of the part) seemed bent on destroying.

And yet, as Marissen pointed out, Lutheran theologians, while supporting the necessity of social hierarchies on earth, have always reminded believers that there will be no social hierarchy in the world to come. Bach is known to have actively endorsed the notion that accepted musical hierarchies also represent "the God-ordained order of things in this world."[6] And therefore, Marissen suggests, if Bach appears to violate or transgress those musical hierarchies, the aim "is not to show that Bach advocated or foresaw revolutionary action against contemporary social hierarchies but rather to suggest that he may be telling or reminding his listeners of the significant Lutheran viewpoint that such figurations have only to do with the present world and therefore are without ultimate significance." If this view is accepted, then an apparent contradiction in McClary's argument would seem to have been resolved, while leaving the social commentary in place. And yet to accept this view of the Fifth Brandenburg Concerto may require of us an even greater tour de force of historical imagination, leading to an even greater sense of Bach's strangeness. McClary's reading of the concerto, even if it is anachronistic or foreign to Bach himself, nevertheless resonates strongly with the beliefs and values of many listeners today, especially in the United States of America, a country founded on the Enlightenment principles that occupy the foreground of McClary's discussion (a discussion that perhaps could only have been authored by a twentieth-century American).

Marissen's reading, while it attributes to Bach himself no foreign or anachronistic belief, is fundamentally foreign to the beliefs and values of Bach's likely listeners today and to the "use" that we are likely to make of the music. It asks us to believe that a set of instrumental concertos, composed in one secular environment (the domestic musical establishment of a German prince) and destined to be consumed in another (today's public concerts and recording industry), nevertheless expresses in its essence a fundamentally religious outlook on the world. By implication it requires us to be prepared to regard all of Bach's secular music as possibly containing a hidden religious advisory.

Of course (as Marissen reminds us), Bach wrote for a very different audience from the one that he willy-nilly addresses today, and a much smaller one. That audience might well have been primed to receive messages we no longer look for in music. And the enthusiastic embrace today's audience has given Bach's music is surely enough to show that appreciating its religious message is by no means a requirement for enjoying it. And yet there may be ways in which the idea that Bach was an essentially religious composer even in his secular instrumental works might nevertheless enhance modern understanding and enjoyment of his music, even by listeners who will never set foot in a Lutheran church or set much store by the religious message Bach's works might embody.

To test the notion, we will return in the next chapter to Handel, of all Bach's German contemporaries perhaps the most secular in inspiration and expression, and give his work a look of comparable closeness. That work will chiefly be vocal, since Handel's chief contribution was to vocal genres. But then so was Bach's, although the place of his instrumental music in the standard repertory has somewhat occluded and belied that important fact. And so after revisiting Handel, we will return once more to Bach and to the vocal music that reveals him as an explicitly, not merely an implicitly, religious composer.

Class of 1685 (II)

Handel's Operas and Oratorios; Bach's Cantatas and Passions; Domenico Scarlatti

HANDEL ON THE STRAND

The paradox is that Handel, the worldly spirit, is most characteristically represented in today's repertory by his vocal music on sacred subjects, while Bach, the quintessential religious spirit, is largely represented by secular instrumental works. And yet it may be less a paradox than a testimonial to the thoroughly secular, theatrical atmosphere in which all music is now patronized and consumed, and the essentially secular, theatrical spirit that informs even Handel's ostensibly sacred work—a spirit that modern audiences instinctively recognize and easily respond to. The modern audience, in short, recognizes and claims its own from both composers; and in this the modern audience behaves the way audiences have always behaved. Nor is it in any way surprising: Handel, not Bach, was present at the creation of "the modern audience." Indeed, he helped create it.

Not that Handel's secular instrumental output was by any means inconsiderable or obscure. We have already had a look at one of his two dozen concerti grossi, works that (simply because they were published) were far better known in their day than the Brandenburg Concertos or any other instrumental ensemble works of Bach (see Exx. 24-13 and 14). Handel also composed a number of solo organ concertos for himself to perform between the acts of his oratorios. In their origins they were thus theatrical works, but two books of them were published (one of them as a posthumous tribute) and became every organist's property.

In addition, more than three dozen solo and trio sonatas by Handel survive, of which many also circulated widely in print during his lifetime. Except for a single trio sonata and some instrumental canons in a miscellaneous collection called *The Musical*

FIG. 26-IA   Portrait by Christoph Platzer, ca. 1710, believed to be the twenty-five-year-old Handel, who was then completing his Italian apprenticeship.

FIG. 26-1B Full-length statue of Handel by Louis François Roubillac (1705–1762).

Offering, and a single church cantata published by a municipal council to commemorate a civic occasion, the only works of Bach that were published during his lifetime were the keyboard compositions that he published himself.

Handel's largest instrumental compositions, like Bach's, were orchestral suites. And as befits the history of the genre, Handel's orchestral suites were among the relatively few compositions of his that arose directly out of his employment by the Hanoverian kings of England. One was a kind of super-suite, an enormous medley of instrumental pieces of every description (but mostly dances) composed for performance on a barge that kept abreast of George I's pleasure boat during a royal outing on the River Thames on 17 July 1717, later published as "Handel's Celebrated Water Musick." A whole day's musical entertainment, it furnished enough pieces for three separate sequences (suites in F, D, and G) as arranged by the publisher.

Handel's other big orchestral suite was composed for an enormous wind band (twenty-four oboes, twelve bassoons, nine trumpets, nine horns, and timpani, to which strings parts were added on publication) and performed on 27 April 1749 as part of the festivities surrounding the Peace of Aix-la-Chapelle that ended the War of the Austrian Succession. This was a great diplomatic triumph for George II, who had personally led his troops in battle (the last time any British monarch has done so) and won important trade and colonial concessions from the other European powers, including a monopoly on the shipping of slaves from Africa to Spanish America. Handel's suite was published as "The Musick for the Royal Fireworks." In arrangements for modern symphony orchestra by the English conductor Sir Hamilton Harty, these suites of Handel's were for a while staples of the concert repertoire—especially in England, where they served as a reminder of imperial glory. They are the only Handelian instrumental compositions ever to have gained modern repertory status comparable to that enjoyed by the "Brandenburgs," and they lost it when England lost her empire. Handel's instrumental music was always a sideline, and so it remains for audiences today, even though modern audiences value instrumental music far more highly than did the audience of Handel's time and are much more likely to regard instrumental works as a composer's primary legacy.

For Handel was first and last a composer for the theater, the one domain where Bach never set foot. His main medium was the *opera seria*, the form surveyed in chapter 23. There we had a close look at the genre as such. Here we can concentrate on

Handel's particular style as a theatrical composer. For our present purpose it will suffice to boil his entire quarter-century's production for the King's Theatre on the London Strand down to a single consummate example. Such an example will of course have to be a virtuoso aria giving vent to an overpowering emotional seizure; for an *opera seria* role, as we know, was the sum of the attitudes struck in reaction to the complicated but conventionalized unfolding of a moralizing plot in a language that was often neither the composer's nor the audience's. The great opera composer was the one who could give the cut-and-dried, obligatory attitudes a freshly vivid embodiment, and who could convey it essentially without words.

Nothing could serve our purpose better than an aria from *Rodelinda*, one of Handel's most successful operas, first performed at the King's Theatre on 13 February 1725, right in the brilliant middle of Handel's operatic career, and revived many times thereafter. The libretto was an adaptation — by one of Handel's chief literary collaborators, Nicola Francesco Haym, an expatriate Italian Jew who also acted as theater manager, stage director, and continuo cellist — of an earlier opera libretto, produced in Florence, that was based on a play by the French tragedian Pierre Corneille that was based on an episode from a seventh-century chronicle of Lombard (north Italian) history.

The title character is the wife of Bertrarido, the heir to the throne of Lombardy, who has been displaced and forced into exile by a usurper, Grimoaldo, the Duke of Benevento, who has succeeded in his plan with the treasonable aid of Garibaldo, the Duke of Turin, a former ally of Bertrarido. The moral and emotional center of the plot

FIG. 26-2   Caricature of the alto castrato Senesino, the natural soprano Francesca Cuzzoni, and the alto castrato Gaetano Berenstadt in a performance of Handel's opera *Flavio* at the King's Theater, London, in 1723.

is the steadfastness of Rodelinda's love for Bertrarido and his for her, enabling both their reunion and Bertrarido's restoration to his rightful throne.

The aria on which we focus, Bertrarido's "Vivi, tiranno!" (Ex. 26-1), was actually added to the opera for its first revival, in December 1725, so as to give the noble Bertrarido a more heroic aspect and also to favor the famous alto castrato Senesino with a proper vehicle for displaying his transcendent vocal artistry. It is sung when Bertrarido, having killed Garibaldo off stage, returns to confront Grimoaldo. Instead of killing him outright, he hurls his sword to the ground at his rival's feet and sings, contemptuously:

A	*Vivi, tiranno,*	Live, o tyrant!
	io t'ho scampato;	I have spared thee;
	svenami, ingrato,	cut me open, ingrateful man,
	sfoga il furor!	pour out thy rage!

B	*Volli salvarti*	I chose to save you
	sol per mostrarti	only to show you
	ch'ho di mia sorte	that my fate has granted me
	più grande il cor!	the greater heart!

Like a good *seria* character, Grimoaldo capitulates to this demonstration of austere magnanimity and gives up his claim to the throne.

"Vivi, tiranno!" is a perfect — and perfectly thrilling — specimen of aria as "concerto for voice and orchestra." Its "A" section is structured exactly like a Vivaldi concerto, with a three-part ritornello that frames the whole, and returns piecemeal in between the vocal episodes (Ex. 26-1a). It symbolizes the aria's affect — stormy indignation, thundering wrath (both as felt by Bertrarido and as summoned forth from Grimoaldo) — with string tremolos that can be related either to the old *stile concitato* or to the onomatopoetical writing we encountered in the storm episode from Vivaldi's "Spring" concerto. As we know from chapter 23, such devices were standard procedure in the "simile arias" that formed the opera seria composer's stock-in-trade. The tremolo clearly retains its meaning in Handel's aria, even though there is no explicit simile (that is, no direct textual reference to the storm to which the characters' emotions are being musically compared).

As in the most schematic concerto movement, the vocal part in "Vivi, tiranno!" never quotes or appropriates the music of the ritornello and never carries material over from episode to episode. It is a continually evolving part cast in relief against the dogged constancy of the ritornello. Indeed the opposition of solo and tutti is dramatized beyond anything we have seen in an instrumental concerto. It is made exceptionally tense — even hostile — by having the instruments continually insinuate the ritornello within the episodes whenever the singer pauses for breath, only to be silenced peremptorily on the voice's return. This, too, is expressive of an unusually tense and hostile affect.

The most spectacular representation of rage, however, is reserved to the singer and takes the most appropriate form such a thing can take within a dramatic context.

EX. 26-1A   George Frideric Handel, "Vivi, tiranno!" from *Rodelinda*, Act III, scene 8, mm. 1–18

EX. 26-1B   George Frideric Handel, "Vivi, tiranno!" from *Rodelinda*, Act III, scene 8, mm. 68–81

The progressively fierce and florid coloratura in this aria is calculated to coincide on every occurrence with the word *furor* — "rage" itself. The singer literally "pours it out" as the text enjoins, setting Grimoaldo a compelling and exhausting example. The most furious moment of all comes when one of the singer's rage-symbolizing roulades is cast in counterpoint against the stormy tremolandos in the accompanying parts (Ex. 26-1b).

The aria, in short, is a triumph of dramatically structured music — or of musically structured drama, if that seems a better way of putting it. The "purely musical" or structural aspects of the piece and the representational or expressive ones are utterly enmeshed. There is no way of describing the one without invoking the other. An intricately worked out and monumentally unified, thus potentially self-sufficient, musical structure serves to enhance and elevate the playing-out of a climactic dramatic scene. And the structure, in its lapidary wholeness, with contrasting midsection and suitably embellished reiteration, enables the singer-actor to reach a pitch that is both literally and figuratively beyond the range of spoken delivery.

Comparing Handel's aria with the *opera seria* arias examined in chapter 23 — mostly by actual Italian composers writing for actual Italian audiences — points up the somewhat paradoxical relationship of this great outsider to the tradition on which he fed. It is Handel who, for many modern historians and the small modern audience that still relishes revivals of *opera seria*, displays the genre at its best, owing to the balancing and tangling of musical and dramatic values just described. Handel's work is indeed more craftsmanly and structurally complex than that of his actual Italian contemporaries, who were much concerned with streamlining and simplifying those very aspects of motivic structure and harmony that Handel continued to revel in.

His work, in short, was at once denser (and, to an audience foreign to the language of the play, perhaps more interesting) and stylistically more conservative. In his far more active counterpoint (just compare his bass line to Vinci's or Broschi's in chapter 23) he affirms his German organist's heritage after all, for all his Italian sojourning and acclimatizing. And by making his music more interesting in its own right than that of his Italian contemporaries, he gave performers correspondingly less room to maneuver and dominate the show.

In this way, for all that Handel seems to dominate modern memory of the *opera seria*, and despite his unquestioned dominance of the local London scene (at least for a while), he was never a truly typical *seria* composer, and as time went on, his work became outmoded. Unlike the actual Italian product, his operas never traveled well but remained a local and somewhat anomalous English phenomenon, admired by foreign visitors but nevertheless regarded as strange. A crisis was reached when Farinelli — the greatest of the castratos, with whose typical vehicles we are already familiar — refused to sing for Handel and in fact joined a rival company set up in ruinous opposition to him. The 1734 pastiche production of *Artaserse* sampled in chapter 23 was in fact a deliberate effort, on the part of the rival Opera of the Nobility, to depose Handel from his preeminence and, Grimoaldo-like, usurp his place in the affections of the London opera audience.

FIG. 26-3   A scene from Gay and Pepusch's *Beggar's Opera* as painted in 1729 by William Hogarth. The wife and the lover of Macheath the highwayman plead with their respective fathers to spare his life.

Handel's grip on the London public, or at least its most aristocratic faction, had already been challenged somewhat in the 1720s by a series of easy, tuneful operas by Giovanni Bononcini (1670–1747) imported to London together with their composer, a somewhat older man than Handel but one whose style was more idiomatically Italian and up-to-date. Another bad omen for Handel, the worst in fact, was the huge success in 1728 of *The Beggar's Opera*, a so-called "ballad opera" by John Gay, with a libretto in English, spoken dialogue in place of recitative, and a score consisting entirely of popular songs arranged by a German expatriate composer named Johann Pepusch (1667–1752).

This cynical slap in the face of "noble" entertainments like the *seria* had an unprecedented run of sixty-two performances during its first season (for a Handel opera a run of fifteen performances was considered a great success), and, altogether amazingly, was revived every season for the rest of the eighteenth century and beyond. (It has had hit revivals even in the twentieth century and spawned a huge number of spinoffs and adaptations, including some very famous ones that will figure in later chapters.) On every level from its plot (set among thieves and other London lowlifes) to its "moral" (namely, that morals are sheer hypocrisy) to its musical and dramatic allusions (full of swipes at operatic conventions and lofty "Handelian" style), *The Beggar's Opera* has been characterized as "frivolously nihilistic."[1] But it also played into a prejudice that was the very opposite of frivolous or nihilistic—namely, a peculiarly English version of the old prejudice (as old, we may recall, as Plato) against "delicious" music as a corrupting force that was inimical to the public welfare. The "soft and effeminate Musick which abounds in the *Italian* Opera," wrote the playwright John Dennis (1657–1734), a particularly vociferous London critic, "by soothing the Senses, and making a Man too much in love with himself, makes him too little fond of the Publick; so by emasculating and dissolving the Mind, it shakes the very Foundation of Fortitude, and so is destructive of both Branches of the publick Spirit."[2] In an *Essay upon Publick Spirit* published in 1711, a year before Handel's London debut, Dennis even argued that British wives should keep their men away from the opera lest they become "effeminate" (by which he meant homosexual). And he proceeded to attach this issue to one that mattered in Britain as it mattered at that time nowhere else on earth — the issue of patriotism, and its attendant religious bigotry:

> Is there not an implicit Contract between all the People of every Nation, to espouse one another's Interest against all Foreigners whatsoever? But would not any one swear, to observe the Conduct of [opera lovers], they were protected by *Italians* in their Liberty, their Property, and their Religion against *Britons?* For why else should they prefer *Italian* Sound to *British* Sense, *Italian* Nonsense to *British* Reason, the Blockheads of *Italy* to their own Countrymen, who have Wit; and the Luxury, and Effeminacy of the most profligate Portion of the Globe to *British* Virtue?

One need hardly add that all of these fears and intolerances intersected on the sexually ambiguous figure of the castrato, the very epitome of Italian license and excess, who added insult to injury by commanding princely fees far beyond the earning power of domestic singers. In the same year that Dennis's essay appeared, Joseph Addison, the eminent satirist, poked malicious fun at the castrati and their fans through an invented character, "Squire *Squeekum*, who by his Voice seems (if I may use the Expression) to be 'cut out' for an *Italian* Singer."[3]

The Beggar's Opera gave all of these resentful views a colossal boost. Its success was a presage that the *opera seria*, even Handel's, could no longer count on the English audience to take it seriously. And indeed, within a decade of its production, both Handel's own opera company and the Opera of the Nobility had gone bankrupt. Neither Handel nor the castrati were the losers, though. As Christopher Hogwood, a notable performer of Handel's music and a leader in the revival of an "authentic" period style of presenting it, has shrewdly observed, if *The Beggar's Opera* was a bad omen it was because it "killed not the Italian opera but the chances of serious English opera"[4] — something that would not emerge until the twentieth century, and then only briefly.

LOFTY ENTERTAINMENTS

Meanwhile, if Handel was to continue to have a public career in England, it would have to be on a new footing. It would take another kind of lofty entertainment to recapture his old audience. Here is where Handel's unique genius — as much a genius for the main chance as for music — asserted itself. Whenever opera had encountered obstacles on its Italian home turf — for example, those pesky ecclesiastical strictures against operating theaters during Lent — its creative energies had found an outlet in oratorio, especially in Rome, where Handel had served his apprenticeship. Handel had even composed a Roman oratorio himself (*La resurrezione*, 1708) and on a trip back to Germany in George I's retinue he composed a German oratorio on the same Easter subject: *Der für die Sünde der Welt gemartete und sterbende Jesus* ("Jesus, who suffered and died for the sins of the world"), usually called the *Brockes Passion* after the name of the librettist.

In fact, Handel had already composed some minor dramatic works on English texts, including *Acis and Galatea* (1718), a mythological masque, and another masque, *Haman and Mordecai* on an Old Testament subject, both commissioned by an English patron,

FIG. 26-4 Handel directing a rehearsal of an oratorio, possibly at the residence of the Prince of Wales.

the Duke of Chandos, for performance at his estate, called Cannons. Handel had also enjoyed great success with some English psalm settings he had written on commission from the same patron (now called the Chandos Anthems), in which he had drawn on indigenous choral genres for which Purcell had set the most important precedents: anthems and allegorical "odes" to celebrate the feast day of St. Cecilia (music's patron saint), royal birthdays, and the like.

A pastiche revival of *Haman and Mordecai*, expanded and refurbished (though not by Handel) and retitled *Esther*, was performed in 1732 in the explicit guise of "an oratorio or sacred drama" and attracted so much interest that Handel himself conducted a lucrative performance on the stage of the King's Theatre, where business that year was otherwise slow. The next year Handel wrote a couple of English oratorios himself (*Deborah*, *Athalia*). As operatic bankruptcy loomed, these experiences gave Handel an idea that the English public might welcome a new style of vernacular oratorio tailored to its tastes and prejudices. The result was *Saul* (1739), a musical theater piece of a wholly novel kind that differed in significant ways from all previous oratorio styles. As a genre born directly out of the vicissitudes of the British entertainment market, the Handelian oratorio was a unique product of its time and place.

How was it new? The traditional Italian oratorio was simply an *opera seria* on a biblical subject, by the early eighteenth century often performed with action, although this was not always allowed. In England, the acting out of a sacred drama was prohibited by episcopal decree, but *Saul* was still more or less an opera in the sense that its unstaged action proceeded through the same musical structures, its dramatic confrontations being carried out through the customary recitatives and arias, making it easy for the audience to supply in their imagination the implied stage movement (sometimes vivid and violent, as when Saul, enraged, twice throws his spear, although the actual singer of the role makes no move).

The listener's mind's eye was helped in other ways as well. The imaginary action was "opened out" into outdoor mass scenes unthinkable in opera, with opulent masque-like choruses representing the "people of Israel." Among the main advertised attractions, moreover, was an especially lavish orchestra replete with a trombone choir, with evocative carillons, and with virtuoso instrumental solos, as if to compensate for the diminished visual component. All the same, *Saul*—like *Esther* and *Deborah* before it, and *Samson, Belshazzar, Judas Maccabeus, Solomon,* and *Joshua* after it—remained centered in its plot on dramatized human relations, the traditional stuff of opera. It was in a sense the most traditionally operatic of all of Handel's oratorios, since the title character—the melancholy and choleric ruler of Israel, racked by jealousy and superstition—is complex, and the action implies a judgment of his deeds.

The other Old Testament oratorios listed above (excepting only *Belshazzar*) are all tales of civic heroism and national triumph. Esther, Deborah, Samson, Judah Maccabee, and Joshua were all saviors of their people, the Chosen People. All were heroes through whom the nation, over and over again, proved invincible. (And even *Belshazzar*, while not directly about Israel's heroism, depicts the destruction of Israel's adversary.) Here is where Handel truly showed his mettle in catering to his public, for the English audience—an insular people, an industrious and prosperous people, since the revolutions of the seventeenth century a self-determining people ruled by law, and (as we have seen) a latently chauvinistic people—identified strongly with the Old Testament Israelites and regarded the tales Handel set before them as gratifying allegories of themselves. "What a glorious Spectacle!" wrote one enraptured observer

> to see a crowded Audience of the first Quality of a Nation, headed by the Heir apparent of their Sovereign's Crown [the future George III], sitting enchanted at Sounds, that at the same time express'd in so sublime a manner the Praises of the Deity itself, and did such Honour to the Faculties of human Nature, in first *creating* those Sounds, if I may so speak; and in the next Place, being able to be so highly delighted with them. Did such a Taste prevail universally in a People, that People might expect on a like Occasion, if such Occasion should ever happen to them, the same *Deliverance* as those Praises celebrate; and Protestant, free, virtuous, united, Christian England, need little fear, at any time hereafter, the whole Force of slavish, bigotted, united, unchristian Popery, risen up against her, should such a Conjuncture ever hereafter happen.[5]

As the historian Ruth Smith has observed, the author of this letter "deploys the analogy of Britain with Israel to present the idea of a unified nation as natural, desirable, and, in the face of foreign aggression, essential," and praises Handel's music as an impetus that "can not only allude to, but actually create, national harmony and strength."[6] Handel's oratorios, in short, were the first great monuments in the history of European music to nationalism. That was the true source of their novelty, for nationalism was then a novel force in the world.

The letter just quoted, printed in the *London Daily Post* in April 1739, referred to the première performance of *Israel in Egypt*, the next oratorio Handel composed after *Saul*, which transformed the genre yet further away from opera and made it yet more novel and more specific to its time and place. For *Israel in Egypt* almost completely abandons the dramatic format—that is, the representation of human conflicts and confrontations through recitatives and arias—in favor of impersonal biblical narration, much of it carried out by the chorus (i.e., the Nation) directly, often split into two antiphonal choirs as in the Venetian choral concerti of old. It is thus the most monumental work of its kind, and in the specific sense implied by the writer of the letter, which relates to vastness and impressiveness, the most sublime.

This specifically Handelian conception of the oratorio as an essentially choral genre—an invisible pageant, it would be fair to say, rather than an invisible drama—completely transformed the very idea of such a piece. So thoroughly did Handel Handelize the oratorio for posterity that it comes now as a surprise to read contemporary descriptions of his work that emphasize its novelty, indeed its failure to conform to prior expectations. One contemporary listener wrote in some perplexity about Handel's next biblical oratorio after *Israel in Egypt*—namely *Messiah*, now the most famous oratorio in the world and the one to which all others are compared—that "although called an *Oratorio*, yet it is not dramatic but properly a Collection of *Hymns* or *Anthems* drawn from the sacred Scriptures."[7] That is precisely what the word "oratorio" has connoted since Handel's day. Now it is the dramatic oratorio that can seem unusual.

Israel in Egypt, the prototype of the "anthem oratorio," recounts the story of the Exodus, with a text compiled from scripture by Charles Jennens, a wealthy dilettante who paid Handel for the privilege of collaborating with him, and who had already written the libretto for *Saul*. This new "libretto" was no original creation but a sort of scriptural anthology that mixed narrative from the Book of Exodus with verses from the Book of Psalms. Its first ten vocal numbers (seven of them choruses) collectively narrate the story of the Ten Plagues of Egypt. In musico-dramatic technique they collectively embody a virtual textbook on the state of the "madrigalistic" art—the art of musical depiction—in the early eighteenth century, an art of which Handel, perhaps even outstripping Vivaldi, was past master.

Even the little recitative that introduces the first chorus contains a telling bit of word painting—the dissonant harmony and vocal leap of a tritone illustrating the "rigor" with which the Israelites were made to serve their Egyptian masters (Ex. 26-2a). The fact that these effects of melody and harmony do not exactly coincide with the word they illustrate does not lessen the pointedness of the illustration: the sudden asperities, incongruous with the rest of the music in the recitative, send the listener's imagination off in search of their justification, which can only be supplied by the appropriate word.

EX. 26-2A   George Frideric Handel, *Israel in Egypt*, no. 2, recitative, "Now there arose a new king"

The first of the plagues — the bloody river — is a choral fugue (Ex. 26-2b), in which we again encounter some time-honored devices: melodic dissonance in the subject (a diminished seventh) to portray loathing, and a *passus duriusculus* to combine that loathing with the river's flow as the fugue subject recedes from the foreground to prepare for the answer. The next plague (no. 5, "Their land brought forth frogs") is set not as a chorus but as an "air" — a truncated aria (very common in Handel's oratorios) in which the "da capo" is represented by its ritornello alone (Ex. 26-2c). Handel chose to make this number a solo item not only to provide some variety for the listener (and some respite for the choristers) but also because he evidently thought the illustrative idea — leapfrog! — would work better as an instrumental ritornello for two violins than in the voice.

The idea of purely instrumental "imitation of nature" was a Vivaldian idea, as we know from the *Four Seasons*, but no other composer had ever taken instrumental imitations to such lengths as Handel resorted to in *Israel in Egypt* — epoch-making lengths, in fact, since the art of "orchestration" as "tone-color composition," serving expressive or poetic purposes and requiring an extended instrumental "palette," achieved a new level in Handel's oratorios, and nowhere more spectacularly than in no. 6, "He spake the word" (Ex. 26-2d). The word here, of course, is the word of God, and so the burnished sound of the trombone choir, associated with regal and spectacular church music since the Gabrielis in Venice, was the inevitable choice to echo the choral

EX. 26-2B   George Frideric Handel, *Israel in Egypt*, no. 4, chorus, "They loathed to drink of the river," mm. 1–13

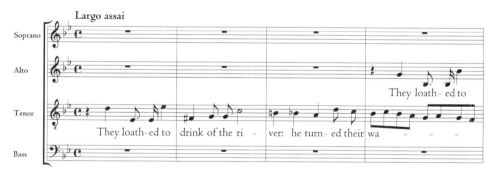

EX. 26-2B (continued)

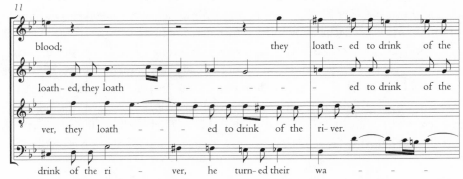

EX. 26-2C George Frideric Handel, *Israel in Egypt*, no. 5, aria, "Their land brought forth frogs," mm. I–II

announcement that God had spoken. Later, the two insects mentioned in the text (flies and locusts) are imitated by string instruments in two sizes. The massed violins are treated especially virtuosically. Demanding of ripienists all a soloist's skills is another mark of "gourmet" orchestration, marking not only the player but the composer as a virtuoso.

EX. 26-2D George Frideric Handel, *Israel in Egypt*, no. 6, chorus, "He spake the word," mm. 1–3

EX. 26-2D (continued)

The gathering storm leading to the representation of the "hailstones for rain" in no. 7 (Ex. 26-2e) calls a large assortment of new (woodwind and timpani) colors into play. Here Handel had a precedent in the French court opera, where orchestrally magnificent storm scenes had been a stock-in-trade since Marin Marais's *Alcyone* (1706), which spawned a legion of imitators (culminating with a volcanic eruption in Rameau's *Les Indes galantes* of 1735) and which, like many court operas, had been published in full score. No. 8, "He sent a thick darkness" (Ex. 26-2f), introduces a new, unheard-of color — high bassoons doubling low violins, but later descending to their normal range and trilling — as well as softly sustained but very dissonant chromatic harmonies to represent the covering gloom. The huge tutti chords slashing on the strong beats in no. 9 ("He smote all the first-born of Egypt") make almost palpable the grisliest calamity of all (Ex. 26-2g).

Yet no matter how lofty or how grisly the theme, Handel's representation of the plagues remains an entertainment — an entertainment that an exhaustive description like the one offered here threatens to impair. It has indeed been a tiresome exercise, and apologies are offered to those rightly exasperated by it, for tediously cataloguing the means by which such vivid effects are achieved has the same dampening effect as does the explanation of a joke.

But although the dampening may dull the joke, it may also serve a good purpose if it forces us to realize and confront, through our annoyance, what might be otherwise overlooked or forgotten — that these marvelous and musically epochal illustrations are indeed, for the most part, no more (and no less) than jokes. Like all "madrigalisms," they depend on mechanisms of humor: puns (plays on similarities of sound), wit (apt conjunctions of incongruous things), caricature (deliberate exaggerations that underscore a similarity). And, as Handel knew very well, audiences react to such effects, despite the awfulness of the theme, as they do to comedy. We giggle in appreciation when we "get" the representation of the leaping frogs and the buzzing flies, and we guffaw when the latter give way to the thundering locusts.

But what of the smiting of all those Egyptian boys? Do we laugh at that, too? We do — or, at least, so the music directs us — just as we have laughed at crop failures, bloody rivers, "blotches and blains." The withholding of empathy for the Egyptians is an essential part of the biblical account of the Exodus, and the scorn of the biblical Israelites and their religious descendants for the ancient oppressor is what enables the success of Handel's strategy. This separation of self and other plays also into the ideology of nationalism; a great deal of English national pride (or any nation's national pride) depends on a perception of separateness from other nations, and superiority to them. Of all of Handel's oratorios, it is perhaps easiest to see in *Israel in Egypt* how the manifest religious content coexists with, enables, and is ultimately subordinate to the nationalistic subtext. Hence the essential secularism of its impulse and its enduring appeal.

MESSIAH

This applies even to *Messiah* (1741), the one Handel oratorio that was performed within the composer's lifetime in consecrated buildings and could count, therefore, as

EX. 26-2E   George Frideric Handel, *Israel in Egypt*, no. 7, chorus, "He gave them hailstones," mm. 22–26

EX. 26-2E (*continued*)

EX. 26-2F   George Frideric Handel, *Israel in Egypt*, no. 8, chorus, "He sent a thick darkness," mm. 1–13

EX. 26-2G George Frideric Handel, *Israel in Egypt*, no. 9, chorus, "He smote all the first-born of Egypt," mm. 1–4

a religious observance. The work, or excerpts from it, is still regularly performed in churches, Anglican and otherwise, especially at Christmas time (although its original performances took place at the more traditional Eastertide). But it is much more often performed in concert halls by secular choral societies. That is appropriate, since, like the rest of Handel's oratorios, *Messiah*'s true affinities remain thoroughly theatrical.

What distinguished it from its fellows and gave rise to its occasional special treatment was its subject matter. Practically alone among Handel's English oratorios, it has a New Testament subject and a text, again compiled by Jennens, drawn largely from the Gospels. That subject, the life of Christ the Redeemer with emphasis first on the portents surrounding his birth, and then on his death and resurrection, brings the work into line with the most traditional ecclesiastical oratorios, and with the even older tradition of narrative Passion settings.

Messiah may have been commissioned by the Lord Lieutenant of Dublin to raise money for the city's charities. Handel wrote the music with his usual legendary speed — in twenty-four days, from 22 August to 14 September 1741 — and finished the orchestral score on 29 October, setting out for Dublin two days later. The first performance took place at the New Music Hall on Fishamble Street on 13 April 1742.

The première performance of *Messiah* is an especially important date in the history of European music because Handel's atypical New Testament oratorio is the very oldest work in the literature to have remained steadily in active repertory ever since its first performance. Unlike any other music so far mentioned or examined in this book, with the single equivocal exception of Gregorian chant — and even the chant lost its canonical status at the Second Vatican Council in 1963 — *Messiah* has never had to be rediscovered or "revived," except in the sense the word is used in the theater, whereby any performance by a cast other than the original one is termed a revival. The continuous performing tradition of European art (or literate) music — which we can now (and for this very reason) fairly call "classical music" — can therefore be said to begin with *Messiah*, the first "classic" in our contemporary repertoire, and Handel is therefore the earliest of all "perpetually-in-repertory" ("classical") composers.

Handel himself conducted yearly London "revivals" of *Messiah*, beginning the next year at the Theatre Royal, Covent Garden. The work became a perennial and indispensable favorite with the London public when Handel began giving charity performances of it in the chapel of the London Foundling Hospital, starting in 1750. These were the "consecrated" performances that led to the work's being regarded as an actual "sacred oratorio," although that was not the composer's original intention. By the time of Handel's death on 14 April 1759 (nine days after conducting his last Foundling Hospital *Messiah*), the British institution of choral festivals had been established, and these great national singing orgies (particularly the Three Choirs Festival, which has continued into our own day) have maintained *Messiah* as a unique national institution, vouchsafing the unprecedented continuity of its performance tradition (although the style of its performances has continued to evolve over the years, in accord with changing tastes — another sign of a "classic").

By the end of the eighteenth century *Messiah* was accepted and revered as true cathedral music. It is all the more illuminating, therefore, to emphasize and demonstrate its secular and

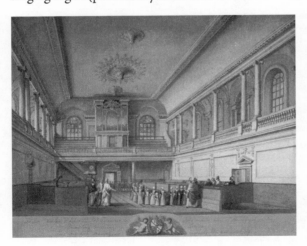

FIG. 26-5   Chapel at the Foundling Hospital, Dublin, where *Messiah* was first performed.

theatrical side. This aspect of the work can be vividly illustrated both from its fascinatingly enigmatic creative history and from its performance history.

"BORROWING"

In order to compose at the kind of speed required by the conditions under which they worked, seventeenth- and eighteenth-century composers frequently resorted to what have come to be called "parody" techniques — that is, to the reuse or recycling of older compositions in newer ones. Every church and theater composer indulged in the practice. There was really no choice. The only question involved the nature of the sources plundered and the specific means or methods employed. Was it only a process of "cannibalization" — eating one's own young (adapting one's own works) — or did it involve what would now be regarded as plagiarism? And if the latter, did the practice carry the ethical stigma now attached to plagiarism — or, for that matter, any stigma at all?

The question comes up with particular inevitability in connection with Handel, since he seems to have been the champion of all parodists, adapting both his own works and those of other composers in unprecedented numbers and with unprecedented exactness. Indeed, ever since the appearance in 1906 of a book (by one Sedley Taylor) entitled *The Indebtedness of Handel to Works by Other Composers*, the matter has been a cause for inescapable concern on the part of the composer's admirers, and a whole literature on the subject has sprouted up — two literatures, in fact: one in prosecution of the case, the other in Handel's defense.

The prosecutors have built an astonishing record. Several of Handel's works consist largely — in extreme cases, almost entirely — of systematic "borrowings," as they are euphemistically called. *Israel in Egypt* is among them. Of its twenty-eight choruses, eleven were based on pieces by other composers, some of them practically gobbled up whole. Three of the plagues choruses — including "He Spake the Word" and "He gave them hailstones," both singled out for their epoch-making orchestration — were based on a single cantata (or more precisely a *serenata*, music for an outdoor evening entertainment) by Alessandro Stradella (1639–82), a Roman composer whose music Handel encountered during his prentice years. Compare, for example, Ex. 26-3 with Ex. 26-2d.

Other famous cases detailed by Taylor include a setting of John Dryden's classic *Ode for St. Cecilia's Day*, performed in 1739, the same year as *Israel in Egypt*, based practically throughout on themes and passages appropriated from a then brand-new book of harpsichord suites (*Componimenti musicali*) by the Viennese organist Gottlieb Muffat. More recently it has been discovered that no fewer than seven major works composed between 1733 and 1738 draw extensively on the scores of three old operas by Alessandro Scarlatti that Handel had borrowed from Jennens. Perhaps Handel's most brazen appropriation involved the "Grand Concertos" (*concerti grossi*), op. 6, familiar to us from chapter 24. They were composed in September and October of 1739 and rely heavily for thematic ideas on harpsichord compositions by Domenico Scarlatti, a fellow member of the Class of 1685, which had been published in London the year before.

Noticing how many of Handel's "borrowings" involved works from the 1730s, and particularly the exceptionally busy years 1737–39, some historians have tried to connect his reliance on the music of other composers with a stroke suffered in the spring of 1737, brought on by overwork, that temporarily paralyzed Handel's right hand and kept him from his normal labors. Whether as evidence of generally deteriorated health or as a reason for especially hurried work following his enforced idleness, the stroke has been offered as an extenuating circumstance by some who have sought to defend Handel from the charge of plagiarism.

EX. 26-3   Alessandro Stradella, *Qual prodigio e ch'io miri*, plundered for *Israel in Egypt*

Stronger defenders have impugned the whole issue as anachronistic. To accuse Handel or any contemporary of his of plagiarism, they argue, is to invoke the Romantic notion of "original genius" at a time when "borrowing, particularly of individual ideas, was a common practice to which no one took exception" (as John H. Roberts, one of Handel's ablest "prosecutors," has stated the case for the defense).[8] Going even further, some of Handel's defenders have claimed his "borrowing" to have been in its way a good deed. "If he borrowed," wrote Donald Jay Grout (paraphrasing Handel's contemporary Johann Mattheson), "he more often than not repaid with interest, clothing the borrowed material with new beauty and preserving it for generations that otherwise would scarcely have known of its existence."[9]

The philosopher Peter Kivy, in a general discussion of musical representation, once cited a piquant example of such "improvement": a bit of neutral harpsichord figuration from one of Muffat's suites that Handel transformed into an especially witty "madrigalism" by summoning it to illustrate Dryden's description, in the *Ode for St. Cecilia's Day*, of the cosmic elements — earth, air, fire, and water — *leaping* to attention at Music's command (Ex. 26-4).[10] And surely no one comparing the choruses in Ex. 26-2 with their models in Stradella can fail to notice that everything that makes the *Israel in Egypt* choruses noteworthy in historical retrospect — the lofty trombone chords, the insect imitations, the storm music — came from Handel, not his victim.

Historical distance affects the case in other ways as well: Handel and his quarries being equally dead, it may no longer be of any particular ethical or even esthetic import to us whether Handel actually thought up the themes for which posterity has given him credit. (Nor could he, or any other composer of his day, have had an inkling of the eventual interest posterity would take in his reworkings.) Indeed, comparing Handel's dazzling reworkings with their often rather undistinguished originals can even cast some doubt on the importance of *inventio* (as Handel's contemporaries called facility in the sheer dreaming up of themes) in the scheme of musical values, and cause us to wonder whether that is where true "originality" resides.

And yet it does considerably affect our view of Handel and his times to know that recent scholarship, and particularly John Roberts's investigations, have pretty well demolished the foundations of the old "defense." Roberts has shown that what we call plagiarism was so regarded in Handel's day as well; that, while widespread, "it frequently drew sharp censure"[11]; and that Handel was often the target of rebuke. One of his critics, ironically enough, was Johann Mattheson, so often cited in Handel's defense,

EX. 26-4A   Gottlieb Muffat, *Componimenti musicali*, Suite no. 4

Muffat, *Componimenti Musicali*, Suite IV

who openly and angrily accused Handel of copping a melody from one of his operas. Another was Jennens, of all people, who wrote to a friend (in a letter of 1743 that came to light only in 1973) that he had just received a shipment of music from Italy, and that "Handel has borrow'd a dozen of the Pieces & I dare say I shall catch him stealing from them; as I have formerly, both from Scarlatti & Vinci."[12]

We know from chapter 23 that Leonardo Vinci, unlike Alessandro Scarlatti, was a contemporary and a rival of Handel's. Handel "borrowed" from Vinci as a way of making his style more up-to-date, which is to say more profitable. This begins to sound like a familiar plagiarist's motive for "borrowing," and Roberts has discovered a unique case where Handel both borrowed from a Vinci score (*Didone abbandonata*, first performed in 1726) and "pastiched" it as well — that is, arranged it for performance in London under its original composer's name. Sure enough, Handel rewrote the passages he had borrowed for his own recent operas so as to obscure his indebtedness to Vinci's.

EX. 26-4B   George Frideric Handel, *Ode for St. Cecilia's Day*

If the old defense — that borrowing carried no stigma — were correct, there would have been no reason for Handel to cover his tracks. And that may also explain why, of all the borrowings securely imputed to him, Handel altered the ones he made from Domenico Scarlatti the most. It may well have been because, of all the music he borrowed, Scarlatti's keyboard pieces were most likely to be recognized by the members of his own public.

In the case of *Messiah*, Handel's known borrowings were of the "cannibalistic" kind — the kind that even now entails little or no disrepute. Self-borrowings, which do not raise any question of ownership, can be called borrowing without euphemism. They are generally regarded, even in the strictest accounting, as a legitimate way for a busy professional to economize on time and labor. And yet they, too, can be revealing in what they tell us about Handel's (and his audience's) sense of what was fitting — in a word, about their taste.

Several of the most famous choruses in *Messiah* are of an airy, buoyant, affable type that contrasts most curiously with the "sublime" and monumental style of *Israel in Egypt*. Ornately melismatic, they require a kind of fast and florid, almost athletic singing that is quite unusual in choruses, and they sport an unusually light, transparent contrapuntal texture, in which the full four-voice choral complement is reserved for climaxes and conclusions only. Their virtuosity and their trim shapeliness of form are completely unlike anything one finds in the actual sacred choral music of the day — that is, music meant for performance in church, whether by Handel (who, never having an ecclesiastical patron, wrote very little) or by anyone else.

They are, however, utterly in the spirit of latter-day "madrigalian" genres — genres based on Italian love poetry — such as the chamber cantata pioneered by Carissimi and Alessandro Scarlatti (a genre in which Handel especially excelled during his Italian apprenticeship), and related breeds like the serenata or the *duetto per camera*.

The last-named (the "chamber duet" as it is sometimes called, rather stiltedly, in English) was simply a cantata for two voices. It became popular enough by A. Scarlatti's time to be regarded as a separate genre — replete with specialist composers, like Agostino Steffani (1654–1728) — partly because in matters of love, two, as they say, is company. Of all the postmadrigalian genres, the duetto was likeliest to be explicitly pagan and erotic. A typical text for such a piece might address or reproach Eros (Cupid) himself, the fickle god of amorous desire:

No, di voi non vo' fidarmi,	No, I do not wish to trust you,
cieco Amor, crudel Beltà!	blind Cupid, cruel Beauty!
Troppo siete menzognere,	You are too wily,
lusinghiere Deità!	O flattering deities!
Altra volta incatenarmi	Another time you did manage
già poteste il fido cor;	to net my trustful heart;
So per prova i vostri inganni:	so from having experienced your tricks
due tiranni siete ognor.	I know you both for tyrants.

These are the words of a duetto by Handel himself, and as a glance at Ex. 26-5a will show, he wove his paired vocal lines into garlands that wrap around one another to illustrate the "netting" to which the text refers (and behind that, of course, the physical writhing for which the textual words are a metaphor). Should it surprise or dismay us to discover that this erotic duet became the basis for not one but two choruses in *Messiah*? Handel reworked the opening section into "For unto us a Child is born" (no. 12, Ex. 26-5b) and the closing section (not shown) into "All we like sheep have gone astray" (no. 26).

EX. 26-5A   George Frideric Handel, duetto, *No, di voi non vo' fidarmi*

EX. 26-5A   (*continued*)

In fashioning the chorus shown in Ex. 26-5b, Handel tossed the duet material as a unit between the high male/female pair (sopranos and tenors) and the low one (altos and basses). Only once, briefly, near the end, does Handel amplify the duet writing into a quartet by doubling both lines at consonant intervals. Elsewhere the choral tutti consists of a chordal outburst ("Wonderful Counsellor!") that is newly composed for

EX. 26-5B *Messiah*, no. 12 ("For unto us a child is born"), mm. 1–14

EX. 26-5B (continued)

Messiah and caps every section of the chorus with a climax. In "All we like sheep," we have another case where one of Handel's happiest descriptive ideas (the wayward lines at "gone astray") turns out to have been not composed but merely adapted to the words it so aptly illustrates.

The use of such material as the basis for an oratorio on the life of Christ has tended to bemuse those for whom the sacred and the secular are mutually exclusive spheres. One way of excusing the apparent blasphemy has been to declare that the *duetti,* composed during the summer of 1741, were actually sketches for *Messiah,* composed that fall, and that therefore the text was merely a matter of convenience — "little more than a jingle, words of no significance whatever, serving merely as a crystallizing agent for music which was later to be adapted to a text that had not even yet been chosen," according to one squeamish specialist.[13] Another writer, the influential formalist critic Eduard Hanslick (whose ideas will merit further discussion in their proper nineteenth-century context), used the apparent incongruity to argue that the expressive content of music was unreal, and that any music could plausibly go with any text!

These circumlocutions are easily refuted, for the esthetic discomfort that gave rise to them was not Handel's. It is obvious, for one thing, that the main melody of "For unto us a Child is born" was modeled carefully on the Italian text, simply because the very first word of the English text is quite incorrectly set. (Say the first line to yourself and see if you place an accent on "for.") But then, the texts (and, consequently the music) of the duetti will seem incongruous, something to be explained away, only if we regard *Messiah* as being church music, which it was not. Despite its embodying the sacredest of themes, it was an entertainment, and its music was designed to amuse a public in search of diversion, however edifying. The musical qualities of the duets, being delightful in themselves, could retain their allure in the new context and adorn the new text — and even, thanks to Handel's "madrigalistic" genius, appear to illuminate its meaning.

The character of the entertainment *Messiah* provided — in particular, the absence of any contradiction between the oratorio's means and aims and those of the secular shows with which it originally competed — is also clarified by its performance history. The aria "But who may abide the day of His coming?" (no. 6) was originally assigned to the bass soloist, and like many oratorio arias, was cast in a direct and simple two-part form that harked back to the earlier style of Alessandro Scarlatti. The Scarlattian resonance is especially marked in this aria (Ex. 26-6a) because of its slowish (*larghetto*) gigue-like meter and its rocking *siciliana* rhythms, relieved only by some fairly perfunctory coloratura writing on the word "fire."

In 1750, Handel replaced the bass aria with a new one for alto that retained the original beginning, but regarded the two halves of the text as embodying a madrigalian antithesis, requiring a wholly contrasting setting for the part that compares God to "a refiner's fire." Here the music suddenly tears into a duple-metered section marked *Prestissimo*, the fastest tempo Handel ever specified, heralded by string tremolos and reaching a fever pitch of vocal virtuosity. A return to the *larghetto* seems to mark the piece as an operatic *da capo* aria, but a second *prestissimo*, even wilder than the first, turns it into something quite unique in both form and impact (Ex. 26-6b).

One way of explaining the replacement is to regard the first version as unsatisfactory and the alteration as an implicit critique, motivated by sheer artistic idealism. In this variant, Handel, on mature reflection, decided that the aria demanded the change of range and character, and then went looking for the proper singer to perform it. If that is what happened, it was a unique occurrence in the career of a theatrical professional who always had to know exactly for whom he was writing in order to maximize his, and his singers', potential effect.

In the case of "But who may abide," he knew, and we know, for whom the new aria was intended: the alto castrato Gaetano Guadagni (1729–92), one of the great singers of the eighteenth century, who was then near the beginning of his career, and who had

EX. 26-6A *Messiah*, no. 6 ("But who may abide"), 1741 version, mm. 1–18

EX. 26-6B *Messiah*, no. 6 ("But who may abide"), 1750 version, m. 139 – end

EX. 26-6B   (*continued*)

just come to England with a touring troupe of comic singers. Guadagni's virtuosity, his histrionic powers, and his ability to improvise dazzling cadenzas had taken London by storm. Handel rushed to capitalize on his drawing power, transferring to him all the alto arias in *Samson* (his latest oratorio) and the perennial *Messiah*, and specially composing for Guadagni, in the form of the revised "But who may abide," what his oratorios otherwise lacked: a true virtuoso showpiece for a castrato singer. "But who may abide" was the obvious candidate for this operation, since its "fire" motif gave

Handel the opportunity to revert to his old operatic self and compose a simile aria in the old "rage" or "vengeance" mode typified by "Vivi, tiranno!" (Ex. 26-1).

It has been the great showstopper in *Messiah* ever since. And it all at once erased the distinction between Italianate sissification and manly British dignity that the institution of the English oratorio was supposed to bolster. For here a symbol of "Italian-Continental degradation,"[14] as the cultural historian Richard Leppert puts it (or what Lord Chesterfield, in his famous "Letters to His Son," would call "that foul sink of illiberal vices and manners"[15]), was holding forth in the very midst of what had even by then become an official emblem of proud British piety.

Handel must have loved the moment. He was getting his own back in many ways. By hiring the latest divine *"ragazzo"* or Italian boy, he was getting his own back against Farinelli, who had so disastrously snubbed him. By scoring such a hit with his new *aria di bravura* he was vindicating the exotic entertainments he had been forced so long ago to give up. And by making the British public love the infusion of Italian manners into the quintessential British spectacle (for the original "Who May Abide" was never revived, although the British have often rather incongruously tried to give the florid alto version back to the cumbrous bass), he may have been taking a sweetly secret personal revenge on the stolid tastemakers who had forced him to deny his predilections in more ways than one — for as many scholars now agree, Handel, a lifelong bachelor, was probably what we would now call a closeted gay man.

But what chiefly mattered was the success. Again the old theatrical entrepreneur had seized the main chance. His protean nature, his uncanny ability continually to remake himself and his works in response to the conditions and the opportunities that confronted him — that was Handel's great distinguishing trait. It marks him as perhaps the first modern composer: the prototype of the consumer-conscious artist, a great freelancer in the age of patronage, who managed to succeed — where, two generations later, Mozart would still fail — in living off his pen, and living well.

BACK TO BACH: THE CANTATAS

Turning back now to Bach, and to his very different world, we are ready to assess the music he and his coreligionists unanimously regarded as his major contribution. That music is his vocal music, composed to a large extent in forms familiar to us from our acquaintance with Handel's operas and oratorios, but serving an entirely different audience and an entirely different purpose. With only the most negligible exceptions (birthday odes and the like) chiefly arising out of his Collegium Musicum activities or his nominal role as civic music director, Bach's vocal music is actual church music.

We have seen in the previous chapters how even in his eminently enjoyable instrumental secular music, and in his sometimes monumentally thrilling keyboard music, Bach managed to insinuate an attitude of religious contempt for the world, the polar antithesis to Handel's posture of joyous acceptance and enterprising accommodation. In his overtly religious vocal music we shall of course encounter that attitude in a far more explicit guise, even though it was often communicated through the outward forms of secular entertainment.

By the time of Bach's Leipzig tenure even the music of the Lutheran church had made an accommodation with the music of the popular theater, and this new style of theatricalized music became Bach's medium. Even though he never wrote an opera and maintained a lifelong disdain of what he called "the pretty little Dresden tunes" (Dresden being the nearest city with an opera theater, which Bach occasionally visited), Bach became a master of operatic forms and devices. But he managed—utterly, profoundly, hair-raisingly—to subvert them.

The forms of opera came to Lutheran music through the work of Bach's older contemporary Erdmann Neumeister (1671–1756), a German poet and theologian, who revolutionized the form and style of Lutheran sacred texts for music.

FIG. 26-6   Erdmann Neumeister, the German religious poet who adapted the forms of Italian opera to the requirements of Lutheran church services.

Traditionally, Lutheran church music, even at its most elaborate, had been based on chorales. By the 1680s a Lutheran "oratorio" style had been developed, in which chorales alternated with biblical verses and—the new ingredient—with little poems that reflected emotionally on the verses the way arias reflected on the action in an *opera seria*. This style was used especially for Passion music at Eastertime. Bach would write Passion cycles of this kind as well, more elaborate ones that reflected some of Neumeister's innovations. In his early years (up to his stint at Weimar), Bach also wrote shorter sacred works in the traditional style, closely based on chorales and biblical texts.

Around the turn of the century, Neumeister began publishing little oratorio texts in a new style, for which he borrowed the name of the Italian genre that had inspired him. Consisting entirely of vividly picturesque, "madrigalesque" verses, and explicitly divided into recitatives and arias, they were dubbed "cantatas" by their author, and they provided the prototype for hundreds of church compositions by Bach (who, however, continued to designate such pieces with mixed voices and instruments as "concertos," retaining the term in use since the time of Schütz and the latter's teacher, Gabrieli).

Neumeister's cantata texts were published in a series of comprehensive cycles covering the Sundays and feasts of the whole church calendar, and they were expressly meant for setting by Lutheran cantors like Bach, whose job it was to compose yearly cycles of concerted vocal works according to the same liturgical schedule. Bach wrote as many as five cantata cycles during the earlier part of his stay at Leipzig, of which almost three survive complete. This remainder is still an impressive corpus numbering around 200 cantatas (a figure that includes the surviving vocal concertos from Bach's earlier church postings). Only a handful of Bach's surviving cantatas were composed to actual Neumeister texts, but the vast majority of them adhere to Neumeister's format, mixing operalike recitatives and *da capo* arias with the chorale verses. Bach at Leipzig became, willy-nilly, a sort of opera composer.

But cantatas were reflective, not dramatic works. The singers of the arias were not characters but disembodied personas who "voiced" the idealized thoughts of the congregation in response to the occasion that had brought them together. Indeed, the Lutheran cantata could be viewed as a sort of musical sermon, and its placement in the service confirms this analogy.

The numbering system used for Bach's cantatas has nothing to do with their order of composition. It was merely the order in which the cantatas were published for the first time, by the German Bach Society (Bach-Gesellschaft), in an edition that was begun in 1850, the centennial of Bach's death. (The numbering was later taken over in a thematic catalogue called the *Bach-Werke-Verzeichnis*, published in the bicentennial year, 1950, and is now called the "BWV" listing.) Dating the Bach cantatas, as a matter of fact, has been one of the knottiest problems in musicology.

In dating a body of compositions like the Bach cantatas, one starts with those for which the date is fortuitously known thanks to the lucky survival of "external" evidence. One such is the Cantata BWV 61, on whose autograph title page Bach happened to jot down the year, 1714, which puts it near the middle of his Weimar period.

Cantata No. 61 also happens to be one of Bach's few settings of an actual text by Neumeister, and it was probably the earliest of them. For all these reasons, it can serve us here as an model of the new "cantata" style, to set beside an older "chorale concerto." It bears the title *Nun komm, der Heiden Heiland*—one of the most venerable Lutheran chorales (Ex. 26-7b), adapted by the Reformer himself (as noted in chapter 18) from the Gregorian Advent hymn *Veni, redemptor gentium* ("Come, Redeemer of the Heathen") (Ex. 26-7a). The cantata was composed for the first Sunday of Advent, the opening day of the liturgical calendar (in 1714 it fell on 2 December), and was therefore based on the opening text in one of Neumeister's cycles, perhaps indicating that Bach was planning to set Neumeister's whole book to music, as several of his contemporaries, including Telemann, did.

EX. 26-7A Gregorian hymn, *Veni redemptor gentium*

EX. 26-7B   Chorale: *Nun komm, der Heiden Heiland*

Nun komm, der Hei-den Hei— land, der Jung-frau-en kind er-kannt,

dess sich wun-dert al - le Welt, Gott solch' ge-burt ihm— be-stellt.

Now come, redeemer of the heathen, known as the Virgin's child;
Let all the world marvel, that God chose such a birth.

THE OLD STYLE

For its chorale-concerto counterpart, Cantata BWV 4, one of Bach's earliest surviving cantatas but also one of the best known, would make an appropriate choice. First performed at Mühlhausen—possibly on Easter Sunday (24 April) 1707 as part of Bach's application for the organist's post there—it consists of a set of variations on another venerable chorale, *Christ lag in Todesbanden* ("Christ lay enchained by death"), which Luther had adapted from the Gregorian Easter sequence *Victimae paschali laudes* (Ex. 18-2).

The text of Cantata no. 4 is exactly that of the chorale, its seven sections corresponding to the seven verses of the hymn, with a diminutive *sinfonia* introducing the first verse. That first verse setting is almost as long as the rest of the cantata put together. The *sinfonia* (Ex. 26-8a), which serves a kind of "preluding" function, is cleverly constructed out of materials from the chorale melody. The first line of the tune is quoted by the first violin in mm. 5–7; the second line, minus its cadential notes, is played by the second violin in mm. 8–10; the expected cadence is finally made by the first violins at the end. The first four measures are built on a neighbor-note motif derived from the melody's incipit (first in the continuo, then in the first violins). The obsessive repetitions, a seeming stutter before the first line of the tune is allowed to progress, effectively suggest constraint—"death's bondage."

The elaborate first chorus is an old-fashioned cantus-firmus composition in "motet style," in which the successive lines of the unadorned chorale tune in the soprano are pitted against points of imitation (some of them "*Vorimitationen*," pre-echoes of the next line) in the accompanying voices. Although adapted here to a more modern harmonic idiom, and further complicated by the intensely motivic instrumental figuration (often drawn from the neighbor-note incipit), the procedure dates back in its essentials to the sixteenth century, where we first discovered it. By 1707 such a piece would have been considered entirely *passé* (or at best an exercise in *stile antico*) in any repertory but the Lutheran. For the final *Hallelujah!*, Bach livens things up by doubling the tempo and shifting over to an integrated motet style in which the soprano part moves at the same healthy speed as the rest of the choir. Still, the whole piece, like the church whose worship it adorned, fairly proclaims its allegiance to old ways.

And so does verse 2 (Ex. 26-8b), in which a somewhat "figural" version of the chorale melody in the soprano is shadowed by a somewhat freer alto counterpart, while the two sung parts are set over a ground bass the likes of which we have not seen, so to speak, since the middle of the seventeenth century. The style of verse 3, with its neatly layered counterpoint, is like that of an organ chorale prelude: the tenor sings the cantus firmus in the "left hand," while the massed violins play something like a ritornello in the "right hand," and the frequently cadencing continuo supplies the "pedal." Verse 4 is perhaps the most old-fashioned setting of all. It is another cantus-firmus setting (tune in the alto) against motetlike imitations, with a very lengthy *Vorimitation* at the

EX. 26-8A   J. S. Bach, *Christ lag in Todesbanden*, BWV 4, Sinfonia

beginning that takes in two lines of the chorale. The continuo is of the *basso seguente* variety, following (in somewhat simplified form) the lowest sung voice whichever it may be, never asserting an independent melodic function of its own. This usage corresponds to the very earliest continuo parts, such as we may recall from Venetian music around 1600, as described in chapter 18. Like the earliest Venetian "ecclesiastical concertos," this verse could be sung *a cappella* without significant textural or harmonic loss. It is, in short, a bona fide example of *stile antico*.

EX. 26-8B   J. S. Bach, *Christ lag in Todesbanden*, BWV 4, Verse II, mm. 1–8

By contrast, verse 5 (Ex. 26-8c), with its initial reference to the ancient *passus duriusculus* (chromatic descent) in the bass, shows how the chorale may be recast as an operatic lament, for which purpose Bach adopts a somewhat (though only somewhat) more modern stance. For the first time Bach relinquishes the neutral "common time" signature and employs a triple meter that has ineluctable dance associations. With its antiphonal exchanges between the singer and the massed strings (in an archaic five parts), this setting sounds like a parody of a passacaglia-style Venetian opera aria, vintage 1640, or (more likely) of an earlier German ecclesiastical parody of such a piece, say by a disciple of Schütz.

When, toward the end (Ex. 26-8d), the textual imagery becomes really morbid (blood, death, murderer, etc.), Bach seems literally to torture the vocal part, forcing it unexpectedly to leap downward a twelfth, to a grotesquely sustained low E♯ on "death," and leap up almost two octaves to an equally unexpected, even lengthier high D on "murderer," while the violins suddenly break into a rash of unprecedented sixteenth notes. Comparing this tormented imagery with the jolly imagery we encountered in Handel's *Israel in Egypt* (albeit equally grisly and violent, at times, in its subject matter), we may perhaps begin to note a widening gulf between the two masters of the "High Baroque." It is an important point to ponder, and we will return to it.

In verse 6, Bach expands the scope of his imagery to incorporate, possibly for the first time in his music, the characteristic regal rhythms of the French overture as a

EX. 26-8c   J. S. Bach, *Christ lag in Todesbanden*, BWV 4, Verse V, mm. 1–12

way of reflecting the meaning of *So feiern wir* ("So mark we now the occasion"), which connotes an air of great solemnity and ceremony (Ex. 26-8e). Later, when the singers break into "rejoicing" triplets, the dotted continuo rhythms are probably meant to align with them. (There was no way of indicating an uneven rhythm within a triplet division in Bach's notational practice.)

The final verse (composed later for Leipzig, probably replacing a *da capo* repeat of the opening chorus) is set as a *Cantionalsatz*, or "hymnbook setting," the kind of simple "Bach chorale" harmonization one finds in books meant for congregational singing. (The term was actually coined in 1925 by the musicologist Friedrich Blume, but it filled an annoying terminological gap and has been widely adopted.) Bach ended many cantatas with such settings (enough so that his son Carl Philipp Emanuel could publish a famous posthumous collection of 371 of them), and it is possible that the congregation was invited to join in. We do not know this for a fact, but it does make sense in terms of Leipzig practice as Bach once listed it, where "alternate preluding and singing of chorales" by the congregation customarily followed the performance of the "composition."

EX. 26-8D J. S. Bach, *Christ lag in Todesbanden*, BWV 4, Verse V, 64–74

EX. 26-8E J. S. Bach, *Christ lag in Todesbanden*, BWV 4, Verse VI, mm. 1–5

THE NEW STYLE

The text of Cantata no. 61 has the more varied structure prescribed by Neumeister, with "madrigals" (recitative-plus-aria texts) and biblical verses intermixed with the chorale stanzas. Such a text is more literally homiletic, or sermonlike, than the chorale concerto. In the present case, for example, only the first verse of the actual chorale is used; the rest is commentary. That single verse (Ex. 26-9a) is given a remarkable setting: not just in "French overture style" but as an actual French overture — a stately march framing a jiglike fugue — scored, as Lully himself would have scored it, for a five-part string ensemble (two violins, two violas, cello plus bassoon continuo) supporting the usual four-part chorus (perhaps even, in Bach's own church performances, only one singer to a part). This unusual hybrid, the kind of thing we have learned to expect from Bach, resonates in multiple ways with the chorale's text and the cantata's occasion.

With respect to the text, the overture format gives Bach a way of emphasizing its most madrigalian aspect — the antithesis between the stately advent of Christ and the joyous amazement of mankind (marked *gai*, à la française) that greets him. By depicting Christ's coming with the rhythms that accompanied the French king's *entrée*, Bach effectively evokes Christ as King. Most notable of all is the absolute avoidance, in this first section, of choral counterpoint: a single line of the chorale is given a unison enunciation by each choral section in succession, and then they all get together for the second line in a "hymnbook" texture.

In this way the traditional, generic use of imitation in the fast middle section of the overture gains by way of contrast a symbolic dimension, evoking in its multiple

EX. 26-9A   J. S. Bach, *Nun komm, der Heiden Heiland*, BWV 61, Overture, mm. 1–7

EX. 26-9A *(continued)*

Nun komm, der Hei - den Hei - land,

entries a crowd of marveling witnesses. With respect to the cantata's function, it has been suggested that by actually—and, from the liturgical point of view, gratuitously—labeling his chorus "Ouverture," Bach meant to call attention to its placement at the very *opening* of the liturgical year. (Or else, conversely, the chorus's placement at the beginning of the first Advent cantata may have prompted Bach's choice of the *Ouverture* format.) Again, we are struck by the singlemindedness of Bach's expressive purpose. For the sake of the affective contrast between the stern beginning and the "gay" continuation, he is willing to "harden" and distort the chorale melody on its every appearance with a dissonant, indeed downright ugly, diminished fourth. Such a choice reveals an altogether different scale of values from those of the ostensible model, the brilliant French court ballet. In fact, Bach appears deliberately to contradict, even thwart that brilliance with his dissonant melodic intervals and clotted texture.

From the French court we now move to the Italian opera theater—or at least to the aristocratic Italian salon (where the original "cantatas" were sung)—for a tenor recitative and aria on a reflective text by Neumeister. But both the recitative and the aria differ enormously from any that we have encountered before. The recitative itself (Ex. 26-9b) ends with a little aria, where the bass begins to move (m. 10), and engages in imitations with the singer to point up the metaphorical "lightening" of the mood. This sort of lyricized recitative, called *mezz'aria* ("half-aria") in the Italian opera house, was a throwback to the fluid interplay of forms in the earliest operas and cantatas. By the

EX. 26-9B J. S. Bach, *Nun komm, der Heiden Heiland*, BWV 61, no. 2, recitativo

eighteenth century it was a German specialty (and one of the ways, incidentally, in which Handel often betrayed his German origins in his Italian operas for English audiences).

The aria (Ex. 26-9c), a sort of gloss on the word "Come" from the chorale, is a gracious invitation to Christ set as a lilting $\frac{9}{8}$ gigue. The ritornello, unlike the Vivaldian type with its three distinct ideas, is all "spun out" of a single five-note phrase. It is played by the whole orchestra, massed modestly in a single unison line, creating with the voice and the bass a typical (that is, typically Bachian) trio-sonata texture. The singer's entry would come as a surprise to connoisseurs of Italian opera, but not to connoisseurs of trio sonatas, for the voice enters with the same melody as the "ritornello" and spins out the same fund of motives. For this reason Bach can dispense with the lengthy instrumental ritornello on the *da capo*. Instead, he writes *dal segno* ("from the sign"), placing the sign at the singer's entry, which fulfills the "return" function perfectly well. This hybridization of operatic and instrumental styles is rarely if ever encountered in the opera house but standard operating procedure in Bach's cantatas.

EX. 26-9C   J. S. Bach, *Nun komm, der Heiden Heiland*, BWV 61, no. 3, aria, mm. 1–5, 17–21

The next recitative/aria pair is of a kind equally rare in Italian cantatas or operatic *scenes*: the recitative is sung by one singer and the aria by another. That is because Neumeister has cast the recitative (Ex. 26-9d) as Christ's answer to the invitation tendered in the previous aria. It is a biblical verse, sung by the bass, the only voice of sufficient gravity to impersonate the Lord. The singer emphasizes the word *klopfe* ("I knock") in two ways, first by a short melisma, and then by a quick repetition. And that is our signal as to the reason for the curious accompaniment *senza l'arco* ("without the bow," or *pizzicato* in more modern, standard parlance). The periodic plucked chords (with a top voice that is as stationary as Bach could make it) are Bach's way of rendering Christ's knocking at the church door.

EX. 26-9D   J. S. Bach, *Nun komm, der Heiden Heiland*, BWV 61, no. 4, recitativo, mm. 1–4

The soprano aria (Ex. 26-9e), sung by a disembodied soul-voice to its heart, is the Christian's answer to Christ's knock. Scored for voice and continuo only, it is an even more modest aria than the one before. Again the two parts share melodic material. Although only the motto phrase ("Open ye!") is obviously repeated when the voice enters, the whole vocal melody turns out on analysis to be a simplified version of the cello's ritornello, shorn of the gentle string-crossings. The fact that the singer's part is simpler than its accompaniment — especially when the high range of the part is taken into account — is already proof that although an operatic form has been appropriated, we are worlds away from the theater.

Indeed, soprano arias are likely to be the least adorned of all (and therefore especially suitable for "heartfelt" emotions, as here) because they were sung not by a gaudy castrato or a haughty prima donna but by a choirboy. (As in the Catholic church, so in the Lutheran, only male voices could be heard within its walls.) A Bach soprano aria, even one as simple as this one, was likely to strain the vocal and musicianly resources of the boy called upon to sing it. And yet when the text required it, Bach did not hesitate to write very difficult parts for the boys he trained.

EX. 26-9E J. S. Bach, *Nun komm, der Heiden Heiland*, BWV 61, no. 5, aria, mm. 1–16

MUSICAL SYMBOLISM, MUSICAL IDEALISM

Nor did he hesitate to write music of utter magnificence, despite the wan forces at his disposal. Undoubtedly his most splendid cantata was BWV 80, written at Leipzig for performance on the Feast of the Reformation, 31 October 1724. (Several of its parts were based on a much smaller cantata written at Weimar.) The *Reformationsfest*, as it is called in German, is the anniversary of the famous Ninety-five Theses, or articles of protest, which Luther posted on the door of the Castle Church at Wittenberg, 31 October 1517. It is thus the most important feast day specific to the German Protestant church and is always given a lavish celebration.

Bach's Cantata BWV 80 takes its name from *Ein' feste Burg* ("A mighty fortress"), Luther's most famous chorale, with a tradition of polyphonic settings going back to the early sixteenth century, sampled in chapter 18. It takes its musical shape from an alternation of choral movements based on chorale verses with recitatives and arias drawn from *Evangelisches Andachts-Opffer* ("Evangelical devotional offering," 1715), a book of devotional verse à la Neumeister by Salomo Franck, the Weimar court poet. At some later time, Bach's eldest son, Wilhelm Friedemann (1710–84), made the piece even more splendid by adding a *Stadtpfeifer* contingent (three trumpets and timpani) to the scoring, possibly for a special performance to celebrate (in 1730) the bicentenary of the "Augsburg Confession," the official creed of the Lutheran church, which Protestants regard as their declaration of independence from the authority of Rome. A tour of the chorale movements from this work in its final, collaborative realization will be a trip to the very summit of traditional Lutheran church polyphony in its latest and ripest phase.

To get the full effect of the tour, we will survey the four settings in reverse order, beginning with the concluding *Cantionalsatz* (no. 8), a setting of the final hymn verse, included here simply as a reminder of the tune (Ex. 26-10a). Passing back over a tenor recitative (no. 6) and an alto/tenor duet (no. 7), praising those who show a steadfastness comparable to Luther's and promising them a reward in the next world, we come to no. 5, a setting of the third chorale verse, which speaks of Christians standing firm in their faith, and through it repelling a host of devils and fiends.

EX. 26-10A   J. S. Bach, *Ein' feste Burg*, BWV 80, the four chorale movements, the concluding *Cantional-satz*

What a natural for a concerto-style setting! The steadfast Christians are represented by the chorus, singing the successive lines of the hymn in unison (or to be literal, in octaves), alternating with a richly raucous instrumental ensemble — trumpets, alto and tenor oboes, and strings — that portrays the grimacing surrounding host with a wild Vivaldian ritornello, which begins with a diminution of the chorale incipit (Ex. 26-10b), continues through a sequence, and ends with "thundering" rage-tremolandi in the strings and literally unplayable lip-trills for the clarino trumpet that produce the aural equivalent of a scowl or an obscene gesture (Ex. 26-10c). A close look at the score will turn up many extra diminutions of the chorale, thrown in wherever they can be made to fit by dint of a deceptive cadence.

Once again we skip over a recitative/aria pair on a text by Franck (nos. 3–4), except to note that (Franck being a literary disciple of Neumeister) it is a virtual replay of the second recitative-aria pair in Cantata no. 61: exhortations from the bass (concluding in an arioso) followed by an invitation, addressed by the chastened soprano to Jesus, to "Komm in mein Herzens Haus" ("Come dwell within my heart's abode"). The aria that comes before them (Ex. 26-10d), marked no. 2, is actually a fascinating hybrid: a duet that underscores the relationship between the reflective poetry and the emblematic chorale by combining text and gloss in a single contrapuntal texture.

The soprano sings the second chorale verse to a highly decorated or "figural" variant of the original melody, while the bass carols away to Franck's commentary on the same verse, set in an unusual (for bass) coloratura style that, by imitating the virtuoso manner of a soprano or even a castrato, seems to reflect the text's promise that all who accept Christ will triumph over the limitations of the flesh. (As we have already observed, and as we shall observe again, this preoccupation with human limitations was a particularly important principle for Bach. It found reflections of all kinds in his music, with the emphasis sometimes on their exposure, sometimes on their overcoming.) The heterogeneous result could be called a "cantus-firmus aria" or a "sung chorale prelude." It might be better, though, not to try to give such unique

EX. 26-10B J. S. Bach, *Ein' feste Burg*, BWV 80, the four chorale movements, no. 5, chorus, "Und wenn die Welt voll Teufel wär," beginning of ritornello

symbolic contrivances names; for they, too, are meant to display transcendence of normal (that is, humanly ordained) categories. At any rate, the unfolding of the cantus firmus takes precedence over the normal aria form, which, shorn of a contrasting section and *da capo*, resembles a concerto movement more than ever. Both vocal soloists are given instrumental correlates. The chorale-singing soprano is doubled by an oboe that contributes extra decorative contortions to the "figuration" of the traditional melody. Sometimes voice and instrument can even be heard ornamenting a melodic phrase in two different ways at once.

The bass, meanwhile, is paired with massed strings in unison (another typically Bachian effect we first saw in Cantata no. 61) to provide a "spun-out" ritornello at the beginning and the end and elsewhere to act as the bass's "obbligato" or accompanying counterpoint. The basic motive out of which this string ritornello is spun is enunciated in the very first measure: it is easily recognized as a stylized bugle call, a military tattoo that encapsulates the pervasive martial imagery of Luther's chorale poem, as it also did in operatic or madrigalian "rage" music going all the way back to Monteverdi.

Having traced the chorale now through three musical incarnations, at last we are ready to take on the cantata's opening number, a grandiose "chorale fantasia" of a kind peculiar to Bach's larger Leipzig cantatas. Even here, as everywhere in Bach's choral music, the method is basically archaic, albeit updated by the most sophisticated handling

EX. 26-10C   J. S. Bach, *Ein' feste Burg*, BWV 80, the four chorale movements, no. 5, end of ritornello of tonal harmony anyone anywhere had yet achieved. The form, in its essentials, is that of the motet—a form that goes back to pre-Reformation times and had been discarded everywhere save the Lutheran church, where alone it continued in living and evolving use. (When Catholic composers used the motet style, as we know, it was in the guise of an officially retrospective *stile antico* in which stylistic evolution was forbidden; eighteenth-century Catholics, when they wrote motets, adopted—or tried to adopt—the sixteenth century "Palestrina style": not a style whose history *went back to* Palestrina, but a style whose history *had stopped with* Palestrina.)

A motet, we may recall, takes shape as a series of discrete points of imitation (rather than a series of expositions of a single idea, like a fugue). In the opening fantasia of Cantata No. 80, the successive points of imitation (all accompanied by an independent and very active continuo and punctuated in Wilhelm Friedemann's arrangement by jocund ejaculations from the *Stadtpfeifer* band) are based on the successive lines of the chorale. The first of them sets the procedure that will be followed consistently

EX. 26-10D   J. S. Bach, *Ein' feste Burg*, BWV 80, the four chorale movements, no. 2, Aria con Choral, "Mit unser Macht," mm. 9–13

EX. 26-10E J. S. Bach, *Ein' feste Burg*, BWV 80, the four chorale movements, no. 1, Choral Fantasia, "Ein' feste Burg," mm. 23–30

EX. 26-IOE   (*continued*)

throughout. The chorale line is transformed by passing tones and a cadential flourish into a flowing "subject," which is then treated according to the rules of tonal counterpoint, in alternation with its "tonal answer," in which the first (tonic) and fifth (dominant) scale degrees are exchanged reciprocally. (Thus the tenors, entering with the subject,

EX. 26-10F   J. S. Bach, *Ein' feste Burg*, BWV 80, the four chorale movements, no. 1, harmonic "Far-Out Point"

descend a fourth from D to A; the altos, entering with the answer, descend a fifth from A to D, and so on.) This sounds like a normal enough fugal exposition, but in fact it would be hard to find another fugue that begins with the tenor and alto entries. All the fugues we have seen thus far have proceeded either from top to bottom or from bottom to top. Deviations from this pattern, being deviations, require reasons, and such reasons are most often to be sought in the "poetic" or symbolic realm. In this case, the reason for opening out from the middle of the choral texture to the extremes becomes clear after the vocal exposition of the first "point" is complete. Unexpectedly, it is capped by the instruments (Ex. 26-10e), playing the cantus-firmus melody, sans figuration, in a marvelous canon that is close-spaced in time but could hardly be wider-spaced in pitch register. Both instrumental lines are doubled at the octave in Wilhelm Friedemann's arrangement: the oboe by the clarino trumpet above (replacing Bach's original scoring for three oboes in unison), and the continuo both by the *violone* or double bass and by the 16-foot "trombone" (*Posaune*) pedal stop on the organ.

Bach hardly ever specified organ "registration," that is, the precise choice of "stops," the settings that determined exactly which ranks of pipes were to be activated by which keys and pedals. This, too, was a deviation from his normal practice and had a special "poetic" motivation. Thanks to these octave doublings, the capping statement of the "symbolum" — the emblem or article of faith — exceeds at both ends the range of the human voice, betokening transcendence. The special nature of this fugal exposition, then, has a multiple poetic purpose. The chorale is literally heard to spread out from the "midst" of the chorus — the human vehicles of the word — and pass into the all-encompassing universal reach of the divine.

This symbolism informs the exposition of the chorale's every line. What varies, once the basic format has been established through repetition (and recalling that the chorale is in the venerable AAB form), is the order of vocal entries. Bach's virtuosity in controlling this teeming contrapuntal microcosm is joyously displayed at a level that few composers, if any, could match. Study of the piece will bring many exhilarating discoveries, beginning with the way the fugal entries of the second line are dovetailed with those of the first, so that the chorale melody is actually set in counterpoint with itself.

Perhaps most noteworthy of all is the way Bach contrives a FOP — the harmonic far-out point, requisite for a fully articulated "tonal" form — between the penultimate line of the chorale and the final one. The penultimate line of the chorale melody ends on F♯. Bach interprets this note as an applied dominant ("V of vi") and follows it with a choral exposition (Ex. 26-10f) in which the last line of the text is sung to an adjusted version of the first phrase of the tune that goes through a circle of fifths — tenors cadencing on B (vi), basses on E (ii), sopranos on A (V), and altos on D (I), thence to the instruments who bring in the actual last phrase of the melody for a properly "achieved" conclusion in the tonic. In this way Bach supplies a "modern" harmonic structure that is unavailable in the original chorale melody (which of course was composed in "pre-tonal" times), without actually departing from or interrupting the progress of the tune.

The wonder is that, from all that we know of the conditions under which Bach worked, he never had at his disposal the musical forces that could do anything approaching justice to this mighty fortress of a chorus. Documents survive that inform us both as to the puny resources Bach had to work with, and those that he would have thought adequate if not ideal. The most telling document of this kind is a memorandum he submitted to the Leipzig Town Council on 23 August 1730, a couple of months before the celebrations at which Cantata no. 80 may have been performed in his son's "big band" arrangement.[16] The title already tells the story: "A Short but Most Necessary Draft for a Well-Appointed Church Music; Together with Certain Modest Reflections on the Decline of Same."

Bach's main concern was the choir, which consisted in large part of the boys he trained himself as head of the church music school. "Every musical choir should contain at least 3 sopranos, 3 altos, 3 tenors, and as many basses," he wrote, "so that even if one happens to fall ill (as very often happens, particularly at this time of year, as the prescriptions written by the school physician for the apothecary must show) at least a double chorus motet may be sung. (And note that it would be still better if the classes were such that one could have 4 singers on each part and thus could perform every chorus with 16 persons.)" Next Bach lists the minimum stable of instrumentalists who should be at the disposal of any self-respecting music director. It hardly seems a coincidence that (with the exception of the bassoons, which were probably assumed to be doublers of the continuo line) the ensemble he describes is exactly that called for in Cantata no. 80. Indeed, Bach immediately follows the list below with a supplementary list of instruments — flutes, recorders, etc. — that are also needed from time to time. But this is the minimum:

2 or even 3 for the	*Violino* 1
2 or 3 for the	*Violino* 2
2 for the	*Viola* 1
2 for the	*Viola* 2
2 for the	*Violoncello*
1 for the	*Violone*
2, or, if the piece requires, 3, for the	*Hautbois* (oboe)
1, or even 2, for the	*Bassoon*
3 for the	*Trumpets*
1 for the	*Kettledrums*

summa 18 persons at least, for the instrumental music

By Bach's own avowal, then, he considered thirty-four persons (plus himself and another keyboard player, who went without saying) to be the bare minimum required for a performance of a maximal piece like Cantata No. 80 — and that number would have been thought puny indeed at any aristocratic, let alone royal, court. (Just recall Handel's Music for the Royal Fireworks, with its band of fifty-five wind players.) Except for avowed attempts to re-create the conditions of Bach's time (as in the so-called "historically authentic" performances that have been popular since the 1970s), the number would be considered stingy for a professional performance today. Yet Bach declares himself content with it, *if only.*

For the same memorandum reveals that in reality Bach could only count on eight regular instrumentalists (relying on local students or his own choristers to pinch-hit when possible), and that of the choristers at the school, whose services were required not just at Bach's own church, St. Thomas's, but at all four Leipzig churches (and who also had to pinch-hit as instrumentalists, as noted), Bach considered only 17 to be "usable" for music of "artistry" and "*gusto*" (taste). It has been suggested (by Bach scholar and performer Joshua Rifkin) that Bach's church music was normally performed by no more than one singer or player to a part, if that (for, as Bach complains, most of the time some parts had to be omitted from the texture altogether due to absences).[17] One often daydreams about what the music heard today sounded like when first performed. It would seem that in the case of Bach, it might be better not to know.

WHAT MUSIC IS FOR

Or perhaps not. We might actually learn a good deal about music and its purposes if we could hear a Bach cantata at its first performance—but only if we are prepared for a lesson that challenges our most basic assumptions about the nature and purpose of music.

Those assumptions were given a classic articulation by Charles Burney (1726–1814), the great English music historian, who knew Handel in his youth and played occasionally in his orchestras. "Music is an innocent luxury, unnecessary, indeed, to our existence, but a great improvement and gratification of the sense of hearing," wrote Dr. Burney, who went on to define it more precisely as "the art of pleasing by the succession and combination of agreeable sounds."[18] These words, probably written in the early 1770s, were published in the front matter of Burney's *General History of Music*, which began appearing in 1776. They are still paraphrased in most English dictionaries, and few readers of this book will find them surprising. They will seem to most music lovers merely commonsensical.

But even "common sense" has a history, and Burney's definition of music reflects the intellectual history of the eighteenth century, when a complex of rationalistic (that is, antimystical, antimetaphysical) ideas now referred to as "The Enlightenment" rose to prominence and eventual dominance in Europe. They will receive a more extended discussion in a later chapter, when their musical manifestations (which we now call "Classicism") come into view. We have had a glimpse of them already in Handel, whose career was shaped by a taste comparable to the one Burney described, and who regarded all of his music, even the most exalted or profound, as a distinguished entertainment.

They have much less to do with Bach, and virtually nothing to do with Bach's church music, which embodied a pre-Enlightened—and when push came to shove, a violently anti-Enlightened—temper. Such music was a medium of truth, not beauty, and the truth it served—Luther's truth—was often bitter. Some of Bach's most striking works were written to persuade us—no, *reveal* to us—that the world is filth and horror, that humans are helpless, that life is pain, and that reason is a snare. Even in his most exuberant work, like Cantata no. 80, Bach's purpose in church was never just to please, and the sounds he combined there were often anything but agreeable.

When his music was pleasing, it was usually in order to indoctrinate or cajole. Just as often Bach aimed to torture the ear. When the world of man rather than that of God was his subject, he could write music that for sheer, deliberate ugliness has perhaps been approached (mainly by much later composers, after Bach's momentous nineteenth-century "rediscovery"), but never surpassed. The daring it took to write such passages is perhaps the best testimony to Bach's unique genius. They would have ruined Handel. But Bach's pious congregation would have understood his purpose in a way that we can do only by dint of great imaginative effort.

Take Ex. 26-11 to begin with. It is the ritornello to a bass aria, "Ächzen und erbärmlich Weinen/hilft der Sorgen Krankheit nicht" ("Groaning [literally, saying 'Ach'] and pitifully wailing or worrying won't relieve sickness") from Cantata BWV 13, *Meine Seufzer, meine Tränen* ("My sighs, my tears"). Despite its low BWV number, this is one of the later Leipzig cantatas, first performed 20 January (the second Sunday after Epiphany) 1726. With *Seufzer* in the title and *Ächzen* in the text, it is no wonder to see lots of slurred descending half steps—"sighs"—in all the parts. That was a conventional symbol that evoked the thing represented precisely the way a word does. Also to be expected were lots of dissonant appoggiaturas, a high degree of chromaticism, and (recalling Handel's "They loathed to drink of the river") chords of the diminished seventh.

But now consider the counterpoint in mm. 3–4: namely, the way in which the parallel "sighs" in the obbligato line and the basso continuo are harmonized. At the beginning of m. 3, the two voices move in parallel at the distance of nine semitones. This unusual way of specifying the interval is necessary here because, in terms of spelling and function, the intervals, though produced by parallel motion, are different. One voice progresses from one scale degree to another (E♭–D), while the other inflects a single degree (F♯–F). Thus the first harmonic interval formed between them is a diminished seventh, while the second is a major sixth. The harmonic progression, while unusual, can be rationalized as a "7–6 suspension" according to the traditional rules of counterpoint.

In the middle of m. 3, the intervals are still 7–6, even though the sixth is augmented and the constant parallel distance between the two voices is ten semitones, an interval always heard as a dissonance. This is a truly pungent progression that will take most listeners by unpleasant surprise, although on reflection it can be "justified" both in terms of counterpoint, and of course in terms of expression, since affliction and pain is the theme.

Only expression can justify what happens on the downbeat of m. 4, when the parallel doubling is again at the distance of ten semitones but both parts make degree progressions, so that both intervals are sevenths. By the rules—or, more pertinently, by customary *practice*—a progression of parallel sevenths is a solecism, a mistake. The writing is diseased. The effect on the naivest ear, all the more on a schooled one, is almost literally nauseous. This kind of direct analogy goes beyond Handel's ingratiating ways of representing horror. There is no way this passage could be described as pleasant or entertaining. That is not its purpose.

EX. 26-11   J. S. Bach, Cantata: *Meine Seufzer, meine Tränen,* BWV 13, bass aria, "Ächzen und erbärmlich Weinen" (ritornello and voice incipit), mm. 1–10

One can find such examples in abundance in Bach, many of them much stronger than this one. The text, of course, is the key to finding them. Cantata BWV 101, composed in Leipzig for performance on 13 August 1724, opens with a chorale fantasia that pits the melody of the Lutheran Lord's Prayer ("Vater unser im Himmelreich") as cantus firmus against a choral counterpoint that carries the text of a sixteenth-century hymn:

> Nimm von uns, Herr, du treuer Gott
> Die schwere Straf und große Not,
> Die wir mit Sünden ohne Zahl
> Verdienet haben allzumal.
> Behüt für Krieg und teurer Zeit,
> Für Seuchen, Feur und großem Leid.
>
> [Take from us, O Lord, thou faithful God
> The heavy punishment and great distress

That we with our numberless sins
Have only too well deserved.
Preserve us against war and famine,
Plague, fire and devastation.]

Ex. 26-12 is a "piano reduction" of Bach's setting of the second line, so that the scarcely credible dissonances with which he evoked punishment, distress, war, famine,

EX. 26-12   J. S. Bach, *Nimm von uns, Herr, du treuer Gott*, BWV 101, opening chorus

EX. 26-12   (*continued*)

EX. 26-12 (continued)

plague, fire, and devastation can be most compactly represented and easily observed. Almost all of them, semitonal clashes, false relations and all, arise out of a reckless deployment of "nonharmonic tones" that arise in turn out of expressive "sigh" motives or their inversions, equipped with pickups that render the first notes under the slurs maximally discordant both harmonically and melodically. This music will never bring a smile, the way Handel's famine, plague, fire, and devastation did in *Israel in Egypt*. And that is only partly because of the extremity of the musical means, which goes so far beyond the boundaries of what Handel or Burney or their audiences would have identified as good taste. It is also because the sufferers depicted are not "them" but "us."

Even more unsettling are the choruses and arias where Bach—following what Carl Friedrich Zelter, a choral conductor who played a major role in Bach's nineteenth-century rediscovery, called his "altogether contemptible German chuch texts"—gave vent to what not only Zelter but all "Enlightened" thinkers of his day despised as the "earnest polemic of the Reformation."[19] Indeed, many of Bach's texts express ideas that most listeners, not only in Zelter's day but in our own, would find abhorrent, for almost all modern ideas of social justice, reasoned discourse, and personal integrity are derived from the ideas of the Enlightenment.

There is no evidence that Bach believed in them. On the contrary: we have every reason to assume that he believed not in freedom, equality, and human institutions of justice as saving forces in the world, but in faith and God's grace—as we may learn from a harrowing tenor aria, "Schweig nur, taumelnde Vernunft!" ("Shut up, stumbling reason!") from Cantata BWV 178, composed in Leipzig in the summer of 1724. The text is a paraphrase of a verse from a sixteenth-century hymn. Past the first line the message of the text is one of comfort, but Bach is fixated on that fierce and derisive opening line—indeed, on just the opening word. Out of it he builds practically the whole first section of his *da capo* aria, crowding all the rest into a cursory and soon superseded middle section.

Over and over the tenor shrieks, "Schweig nur, schweig!" leaping now a sixth, now a seventh, now an octave (Ex. 26-13). Meanwhile, the accompanying orchestra, Reason's surrogate, reels and lurches violently. The effect is nothing short of terrifying—perhaps even more now than in Bach's own time, since we who remember the twentieth century have greater reason than Bach's contemporaries ever had to wince at the sound of a high-pitched German voice stridently shouting reason down.

EX. 26-13   J. S. Bach, Cantata: *Wo Gott der Herr nicht bei uns hält*, BWV 178, tenor aria, "Schweig nur, taumelnde Vernunft!", mm. 11–17

Even when Bach is not expressing actively anti-Enlightenment sentiments like these in his cantatas, his settings are pervaded with a general antihumanism such as we encountered (at least according to one interpretation) in the Brandenburg Concertos, with their implied religiously motivated contempt for human hierarchies and power relations. The contempt is much more overt in the cantatas and shows up precisely in Bach's seeming unconcern for practical performance considerations. A work like Cantata no. 80, plausibly beyond the capabilities of the performers to whom it was perforce assigned, could be looked upon as "idealistic" in this sense, deliberately contriving a splendor and suggesting a perfection beyond terrestrial accomplishment (though certainly not beyond imagining or aspiring to).

There is another side to this as well, when Bach seems deliberately to engineer a bad-sounding performance by putting the apparent demands of the music beyond the reach of his performers and their equipment. Ex. 26-14 contains two "middle sections" from cantata arias. The first (Ex. 26-14a), "Liebster Gott" ("Beloved God") from Cantata BWV 179, composed for Leipzig in 1723, is scored for a (boy) soprano and two *oboi da caccia* or "hunting oboes," ancestors of the modern English horn. The aria begins and ends in A minor, but the middle section weirdly modulates ever "flatward," so that it makes its final cadence in C minor.

Not only is the flatward modulation symbolic of *catabasis*, or "falling" in the theological sense (as a sharpward modulation symbolizes *anabasis* or elevation), the specific key chosen for the cadence also puts the instruments in a harmonic region where they are simply incapable of playing in tune, especially when playing, as Bach forces them to do, in their lowest, least tractable range.[20] The boy, too, is asked to descend to

EX. 26-14A   Cantata: *Siehe zu, daß deine Gottesfurcht*, BWV 179, soprano aria "Liebster Gott," mm. 62–81

EX. 26-14A (continued)

the very bottom of his range and even beyond, where he loses all tonal support. The whole performance will inevitably come out sounding loathsome and disgraceful. And these are the words (adapted from the prophet Habbakuk): "My sins sicken me like pus in my bones; help me, Jesus, Lamb of God, for I am sinking in deepest slime."

Nowadays, with instruments that have undergone more than a century of adaptation and with no strictures to prevent a secular performance by a well-trained mezzo-soprano, the technical demands of the aria could be easily met. But would the performance thereby become a better one? Or would an important part of the religious message of the piece — that humans are helpless and hopeless in their fallen state — be lost for the sake of mere sensory gratification?

The bass aria, "Beglückte Heerde, Jesu Schafe" ("O lucky herd of Jesus-sheep"), from the pastoral Cantata no. 104, *Du Hirte Israel, höre* ("Hear us, O shepherd of Israel") is on the face of it a sweet and gentle (if slightly macabre) lullaby, but it harbors within a veritable assault by the composer on the performer. The text of the middle section (Ex. 26-14b) reads, "Here you shall taste of Jesus's goodness and look forward, as your

EX. 26-14B   Cantata: *Du Hirte Israel, höre*, BWV 104, bass aria "Beglückte Heerde," middle section

EX. 26-14B (continued)

EX. 26-14B (*continued*)

Da Capo.

reward for faith, to the sweet sleep of death." The vocal line extends for eighteen measures in a stately $\frac{12}{8}$ meter without a single rest, and with notes lasting as much as nine beats. It will reduce any singer who assays it at an appropriate tempo to a gasping, panting state in which, were the aria to continue another two minutes, he would surely receive his reward.

This undermining of human agency is something that Bach engineers again and again. Unlike Handel's music, Bach's church music serves the purposes of the church — that is, ministering to the soul's salvation — and presents modern secular performers with a dilemma: either adapt the performance to the tastes of the modern secular audience (whether by modernizing the performing forces, for example, or by "secularizing" the tempos or the general demeanor) and risk losing the full force of the expressive message encoded in the music, or perform the music in an appropriate manner and risk perplexing, fatiguing, or even insulting the audience. That is why only a handful of Bach's cantatas can be said to have really joined the modern performance repertory, and a thoroughly unrepresentative handful at that.

Besides a couple of amusing secular items like the so-called "Coffee cantata" (about a young girl's passion for coffee — then a novelty — and the headaches it causes her father), composed for Bach's Collegium Musicum (which actually performed in a coffee shop), the "popular" cantatas include no. 51, *Jauchzet Gott in allen Landen* ("Rejoice in

God in every land"), a brilliant display piece for soprano and the only church cantata Bach ever composed for a women's voice (and one of the few pieces he actually called a cantata); and no. 140, *Wachet auf, ruft uns die Stimme* ("Wake up, the [watchman's] voice is calling"), in which Bach set a couple of love duets between Christ and the Christian soul in the style of "the pretty little Dresden tunes."

BACH'S "TESTAMENTS"

Bach's best-known religious pieces are the ones most comparable to Handel's oratorios and to even later, Catholic religious music. They include two Passion settings (out of five he is once reported to have composed), one based on the Gospel of Matthew and the other on the Gospel of John. And, a bit paradoxically, they include a grandiose concerted setting, for chorus in as many as eight parts and an exceptionally variegated orchestra, of the Latin Mass, a text for which there was no liturgical use at all in the Lutheran church. These were the works through which Bach was "rediscovered" and reclaimed for the performing repertoire in the nineteenth century.

The Mass was assembled out of settings that had accumulated over a period of more than two decades. About half of it is derived from known prototypes (cantata choruses, mainly), and most of the rest is presumed to consist of "parodies" of this kind as well, even though their prototypes are no longer extant. The work is therefore cast in a mixture of styles that reflects its miscellaneous origins. Some of the choruses, although never without an elaborate instrumental accompaniment, are written in a deliberately archaic style that comes closer than ever to the official Catholic *stile antico*. Some of the arias, by contrast, are cast in the kind of showy, courtly ("galant"), somewhat operatic idiom that Bach associated with Dresden.

The Catholic electoral court at Dresden, in fact, seems to have been the original destination of the Mass, or at least of the Kyrie and Gloria, which Bach sent in 1733 to the newly ascended Elector, Friedrich August II, who also reigned (as Augustus III) as the titular king of Poland. Friedrich August was already a notable patron of the arts, from whom Bach was now seeking a favor—not a job but a title (Hofkomponist) that would entitle him to better treatment and higher pay from the Leipzig town council. Bach eventually did receive the title but not until 1736, after sending another petition.

The music, meanwhile, languished unheard. Bach returned to it in the late 1740s, after he had effectively retired from his cantorate at Leipzig, and by adding to it a Sanctus he had partly composed as early as 1724 and assembling from parodies a Credo and an Agnus Dei, he turned it into a kind of testamentary piece—a summary of all types of ecclesiastical composition unified by the ancient Latin text of the Mass, but far too long and elaborate to have been intended for actual performance anywhere.

Performances began only when Bach had been assimilated to the secular concert repertory in the nineteenth century. (Hence the curiously secular name by which it is generally known: "Mass in B Minor," or "The B-Minor Mass," after the key of the opening Kyrie, although most of the music is actually in D major.) Thus it is a work that has existed, in a sense, only posthumously; and it is to later music only that it can be compared. The first of many "oratorio-style" Masses in the repertoire, it is the largest of them all, but it is in no real sense the progenitor of the line. That line originated in Austria and reached its peak some decades after Bach's death with the work of Haydn, Mozart, and Beethoven. But as we will learn in a later chapter, the antecedents to this Austrian genre were Italian, not German. Bach's Mass, although a famous work today and therefore an essential part of the history of music from our perspective, was from the perspective of its own time an isolated curio — or, given its size, perhaps a white elephant.

A description of the *Gloria*, part of the original offering to the Saxon elector, can be our entrée into this glorious anomaly. The text is broken up into nine separate segments, if one counts the two contrasting halves of the first chorus as two separate settings. Bach certainly did, because he is known to have adapted them from two separate preexisting pieces. The first, a quick gigue, marked *vivace* ("lively") and scored for an oversized orchestra of twenty or more (as per Bach's "Short but Most Necessary Draft"), features the trumpets and drums for a brilliant evocation of the title word (which, as we know, is merely intoned by the priest in an actual liturgical Mass). The second, a hushed evocation of "peace on earth," is suddenly in the slow "common time" of the *stile antico*. The trumpets and drums are silent for the most part, reintroduced only toward the end so that the piece can end grandly. Like Monteverdi's eight-part *Gloria* from the *Selva morale* (see chapter 20), Bach's "Gloria" chorus, with its vividly projected antithesis, is in effect a vaulting madrigal.

Thereafter, the Gloria proceeds as an alternation of choruses with arias for each of the five soloists in turn. The first aria ("Laudamus te"), for the second soprano, sets words of praise in an ingratiatingly ornate and courtly chamber style. The ritornello is a veritable violin concerto, and the vocal writing, with its trills and roulades, is as close to a castrato idiom as Bach ever came. This music was obviously meant for no choirboy, but for a Dresden court "canary." The chorus that follows ("Gratias agimus tibi") sets words of thanks in an austere, archaic idiom. Bach first used this music when setting the German equivalent of its text ("Wir danken dir, Gott") in a Leipzig cantata two years before.

Next comes another operatic showpiece ("Domine Deus"), a duet for the first soprano and the tenor, in which the consubstantiality of the Father and the Son is symbolized by the twinning of the two voices. Each sings in turn about the Father and the Son, but whenever the soprano is singing "Domine Deus" the tenor is singing "Domine Fili," and vice versa. Here the concertizing instrument in the ritornellos is the solo flute, playing for the most part in its most brilliant range, with typically "galant" affectations in the phrasing, such as slurred pairs (possibly also symbolic of consubstantiality) and long appoggiaturas.

The chorus that follows — "Qui tollis peccata mundi," "[O Thou] who takest away the sins of the world" — maintains the lightness of the preceding duet as it describes the gentle cleansing action of the Lamb of God. The music had previously served to introduce a Leipzig cantata, on the words "Schauet doch und sehet, ob irgend ein Schmerz sei" (Behold and see if there is any pain). In both of its contexts, then, the music represented the alleviation of distress.

The last part of the Gloria puts two arias back to back before a concluding chorus. The first aria ("Qui sedes") is an alto solo, with an obbligato for the *oboe d'amore* (halfway in size between modern oboe and English horn) that implies an *affettuoso* style of performance. The instrument closely matches the singer's range and twines all around the vocal part as the singer pleads operatically with the Son, sitting at the right hand of the Father, for mercy. The second aria ("Quoniam tu solus," "For only Thou"), a commanding item for the bass, features a rare obbligato for *corno da caccia* ("hunting horn," now called French horn) accompanied by not one but two bassoons, thus adding two more instruments to the already swollen instrumental roster. This aria may well have been adapted from a cantata in which the text used words like hunting, chasing, or pursuit as metaphors—words for which the horn itself could stand as a further metaphor. As adapted here to the Mass text, the singularity of the scoring may symbolize the singularity of Christ, as thrice detailed by the text.

The final chorus, "Cum sancto spiritu," invokes the glory of the Trinity with a return to the *vivace* tempo and the brassy scoring of the opening chorus. It is in three sections, the middle being a fast melismatic fugue somewhat reminiscent of the ones in *Messiah*, and adding an element of showy virtuosity to the choral writing that is as rare in Bach as it is frequent in the oratorios of Handel, his great expatriate contemporary.

There is nothing like this chorus in Bach's surviving Passion oratorios, which were written for church use on the afternoon of Good Friday, the most solemn day in the Christian year. The one based on the Book of John, written earlier, was first performed in Leipzig in 1724, during Bach's first year as Cantor there, and revived several times thereafter. Its text includes arias and a chorus drawn from the Passion poem by Brockes that Handel had set earlier. The St. Matthew Passion—conceived as a unity but on an enormous scale both as to duration and as to performing forces (two antiphonal choirs, each with its own supporting orchestra)—was composed in relative tranquillity after the maelstrom of cantata production had subsided, and was probably first performed in 1736.

In both Passions, following the post-Neumeister conventions of the genre, the text operates on

FIG. 26-7 Bach's autograph manuscript of the opening double chorus from the St. Matthew Passion.

three levels, which interact to produce a sort of biblical opera-with-commentary. The original Gospel text is set as semidramatic recitative. There is a narrator (called the Evangelist), but all direct discourse (lines spoken directly by the actors in the story) is assigned to other solo voices, and lines spoken collectively by the "people," following the "*turba*" (crowd) convention that goes back to the sixteenth century, were sung by the chorus, often in imitative textures that emphasized heterogeneity.

These recitatives are interrupted at strategic moments, just as they are in opera, by reflective arias — or "madrigals," as the Lutheran poets continued to call them — meant to be set in da capo form. As in the cantatas (where, however, there is no plot line), these arias are not sung by characters but by "voice-personas" who represent and give utterance to the poet's own meditations on the events of the biblical narration, and instruct the congregation on their Christian significance. In the St. Matthew Passion, all the arias, as well as the reflective choruses that open and close each part, are adapted from a single long Passion poem in *Erbauliche Gedancken* ("Edifying thoughts"), a cycle of texts for music by a friend of Bach's, a Leipzig lawyer and playwright named Christian Friedrich Henrici (1700–64), who wrote under the name Picander and provided the texts for many of Bach's Leipzig cantatas. The third textual element in Bach's Passions consisted of chorales in "Cantional" or hymnbook style that are frequently interpolated to provide an additional level of commentary (and, possibly, congregational participation).

The two Bach Passion settings are quite distinct in character. The shorter and faster-moving St. John Passion is as close to an opera as Bach ever wrote (if for the moment we ignore a few minor civic or coffeehouse comedies that Bach called *dramma per musica*). The *turba* scenes before Pontius Pilate, in particular, show the Roman viceroy, the crowd, and the Evangelist interacting with great dispatch. In the excerpt given in Ex. 26-15, Pontius Pilate offers Jesus back to the crowd, who reject him and call for his crucifixion. The sharp dactylic rhythms in the orchestra recall the cry of "Kreuzige!" ("Crucify!") from the previous chorus.

The St. Matthew Passion places more emphasis on contemplation than on action. Its emblematic sections are not the turba choruses but the monumental framing choruses on words by Picander. The one that opens the work, "Kommt, ihr Töchter, helft mir klagen" ("Come, O daughters, help me in my lamentation") is a conception of unparalleled breadth. By the use of antiphonal choruses (and orchestras) asking and exclaiming about the tragic scene at Golgotha, a panoramic scene is conjured up. The heavy bass tread and the slow harmonic rhythm in a broad $\frac{12}{8}$ meter at once sketches the movement of the procession of the cross and conveys the mournful affect of a traditional *lamento*.

And it all turns out to be a gigantic chorale prelude, when a third choir of boys (*soprano ripieno* as Bach puts it) chimes in with the so-called Passion Chorale (Ex. 26-16), set as a cantus firmus above the fray: *O Lamm Gottes unschüldig/am Stamm des Kreuzes geschlachtet* ("O spotless Lamb of God, slaughtered on the Cross's trunk"). The innocence of the victim is cast in relief against the enormity of the sacrifice by playing the G major of the chorale against the E minor of its environment. A whole panoply of tonal and

EX. 26-15 J. S. Bach, *St. John Passion, turba,* "Weg! Weg!," mm. 40–51

EX. 26-15   (continued)

EX. 26-15 *(continued)*

Pilate: "See ye your King, yea, behold Him."

Evangelist: They cried out ever:

Chorus: Away with Him, away with Him,
crucify Him.

harmonic effects of which Bach was then uniquely the master — modulations, deceptive cadences, and other feints — is enlisted to underscore this tragic contrast. Even without the external trappings of drama, Bach was able through his manipulation of tonal ("purely musical") procedures to express the essence of the dramatic conflict embodied in the Passion story as viewed from the Christian perspective.

Bach was well aware of the special place the St. Matthew Passion occupied within his vast output. He regarded it, too, as a testamentary work. He prepared a lavish calligraphic score of the work, replete with inks of different colors, to preserve it at a time when most music, including his, was composed for specific occasions, to be used and thereafter discarded. That fair copy passed into Carl Friedrich Zelter's possession and provided the vehicle for Bach's rediscovery and canonization as a musical Founding Father when the twenty-year-old Felix Mendelssohn, a pupil of Zelter who would have a distinguished career as composer in his own right, conducted a performance of the St. Matthew Passion at the Berlin Singakademie on 11 March 1829, a little over a century after its first performance in Leipzig.

THE BACH REVIVAL

This was an event of immense cultural significance. It placed Bach in a new context, one in which the very aspects of his style that had led to his temporary eclipse — its

EX. 26-16 J. S. Bach, *St. Matthew Passion*, opening chorus, mm. 34–36

complexity, its conservatism, its uncompromising religiosity, its very asperity, which caused it to be dismissed by some critics even during his lifetime as showing an "excess of art" and a "turgid and confused style"—could now be prized and held up as a model for emulation.[21] The conditions that brought about this change in Bach's status had a great deal to do with the burgeoning of Romanticism, to which we will return in a later chapter. There was another aspect to the reassessment of Bach, however, which needs our attention now.

The nineteenth-century Bach revival focused mainly on just a few works: the Passion oratorios, the B-minor Mass, the Well-Tempered Clavier, and a few later masterworks of an old-fashioned, abstract nature in which Bach gave full rein to his unrivaled contrapuntal virtuosity. This last group included the Goldberg Variations, a huge cycle of thirty keyboard pieces, including a series of intricate canons, all based on a single "aria" (ostinato) bass line. (The set is named—not by Bach but by posterity—after Johann Gottlieb Goldberg, one of Bach's pupils, who supposedly commissioned it on behalf of his patron, Count Kayserling, the Russian ambassador to the Saxon court, an insomniac who needed some engrossing music to divert him during sleepless nights.) For a really dazzling quick idea of Bach's contrapuntal wizardry we might look, not at the Goldberg Variations themselves, but at a little extra that he tossed off one day, and that remained undiscovered until the 1970s. In the flyleaf of his own personal copy of the printed edition of the work (the fourth volume of the *Clavier-Übung*, issued in 1747), Bach inscribed fourteen riddle canons, all based on the first eight notes of the Goldberg "aria" bass. Ex. 26-17 shows the bass line, the last canon ("Canon à 4, per Augmentationem et Diminutionem") as Bach wrote it, and a realization (by Christoph Wolff, who discovered and authenticated the canons). The first eight sixteenth-notes of the single notated line in Ex. 26-17b are an inversion of the Goldberg bass, transposed to the upper fifth and subjected to a threefold rhythmic diminution. The realization accompanies the notated part with its inversion at the upper fourth with note values doubled; with its literal transposition at the lower fourth with note values doubled again; and inverted at the lower fifth, with the note values doubled a third time, thus restoring the original bass.

It is probably fair to say that the sheer technical dexterity in the art of composition that Bach exhibits here has never been surpassed; it is all the more impressive in

EX. 26-17A   Goldberg bass

EX. 26-17B   Canon no. 14 as written by Bach

EX. 26-17C   Canon no. 14 as realized by Christoph Wolff

the context of little joke pieces like these, for only the truly learned can afford to wear their learning lightly. (Why exactly fourteen canons, by the way? Because the name Bach, if translated into numbers according to the positions of its constituent letters in the alphabet — a device called *gematriya* that goes back to Hebrew cabbalistic lore — comes out $2 + 1 + 3 + 8 = 14$. Bach's numerological virtuosity has only begun to be investigated. Some scholars suspect that it may rival his musical skills; others, favoring a more "Enlightened" view of Bach, remain skeptical.) A more formal exhibition of skill was the *Musikalisches Opfer* ("Musical offering"), a miscellany of canons, complicated ricercars (old-fashioned fugues), and a trio sonata, all based on a weirdly chromatic "royal theme" given Bach as a subject for improvisation by none other than Frederick the Great, the Prussian king, during a visit by Bach in May of 1747 to the Prussian court at Potsdam, where his son Carl Philipp Emanuel was employed. The ultimate "speculative" work, Bach's intended final testament, was *Die Kunst der Fuge* ("The art of fugue"), a collection of twenty-one *contrapuncti*, including canons, double fugues, triple fugues, fugues with answers by augmentation and diminution, inversion, and *cancrizans* ("crab motion," or retrograde), all based on a single D-minor subject.

Bach was working on this collection on the day he died, leaving unfinished the last *Fuga a 3 soggetti*, in which the musical anagram of his name was to be worked in as a chromatic countersubject (Ex. 26-18). The so-called B–A–C–H cipher has been a potent musical emblem ever since the Art of Fugue was published, in 1751, in an edition supervised by Carl Philipp Emanuel Bach, who refrained from finishing the last fugue (as he could easily have done), but let it trail off into a sketch, followed by a note explaining the reason.

It was no accident that the German musicians who created the Bach revival in the early nineteenth century fastened on just these pieces—the Passion oratorios and the encyclopedic, testamentary works. The Passions were the only vocal works by Bach that could find any sort of place in early nineteenth-century secular musical life. Their revival took place within the nineteenth-century German "concert oratorio" movement, something that had nothing to do with Bach or with the Lutheran tradition. Rather, it went back to Handel, or (more accurately) to the London Handelian tradition, both a prime fosterer and a beneficiary of British national sentiment.

As we will later observe in greater musical detail, the Handelian oratorio (the earliest type of oratorio meant expressly for concert performance) had been imported to the German-speaking lands by the Austrian composer Franz Joseph Haydn (1732–1809), who had encountered Handel's work on a visit to England, been bowled over by it, and emulated it in two oratorios of his own, "The Creation," first performed in 1798, and "The Seasons" (1801). Like most of Handel's oratorios, and like the German oratorios that followed them, Haydn's oratorios were performed in theaters and concert halls, not churches.

By the time Bach's Passions were revived, the main German venue for oratorio performances had become the music festival, first instituted in 1818. As the critic and historian Cecilia Hopkins Porter has shown, these festivals transformed the German musical establishment and created a new public—the first "mass public"—for music.[22] Their other main achievement was the creation of a sense of German national identity through music. It was Bach who provided a focal point for that, as Handel had done in England. (Of course, Handel—or rather, Händel—was "repatriated" and "reclaimed" by the Germans as well, and given back his umlaut, during this period.)

So burgeoning nationalism, perhaps the nineteenth century's signal contribution to European politics and culture, which had turned Handel into an institution in England a bit ahead of schedule thanks to British "national" precocity, caught up with Bach and turned him into a competing institution just when the familiar institutions of modern concert life were being established.

EX. 26-18A   The B-A-C-H cipher

EX. 26-18B   B-A-C-H cipher at end of *The Art of Fugue*

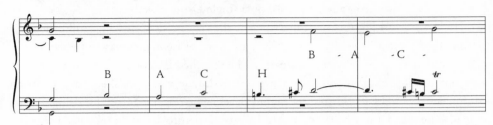

EX. 26-18B (*continued*)

EX. 26-18B (continued)

The specific nature of German nationalism also favored Bach's canonization. Where the British prided themselves on their commerce and industry, and on their liberal political institutions, the Germans, then lacking political unity, very backward industrially, and economically ruined by the Napoleonic wars, prided themselves on "art and learning," as the composer and critic Carl Kossmaly declared shortly after the Bach revival had got underway. Their nationalism was a nationalism of culture. "In the realm of ideas," Kossmaly averred, "in everything concerning intelligence and spiritual capacity, not only inner unity and national independence but also a decided superiority must be granted to the Germans."[23] In music, Bach was the proof. His profundity and complexity were all of a sudden national treasures; and the abstract musical speculations of his late years became harbingers of "absolute music," the highest of all the arts, where the Germans most vehemently asserted their supremacy.

This appropriation of Bach to the politics of German secular nationalism was already evident in the earliest biography of Bach, by Johann Nikolaus Forkel (1749–1818). This book, which appeared in 1802 (one year after Haydn's *Seasons*), was a landmark: it was not only the first biography of Bach, it was the first full-scale scholarly biography of any composer and one of the earliest books to be recognizably a work of musicology in the modern academic sense. It is dedicated to "patriotic admirers of true musical art." Its preface declares that "Bach's works are a priceless national patrimony; no other nation possesses anything to compare with it."[24] And this is its final paragraph:

> This man, the greatest orator-poet that ever addressed the world in the language of music, was a German! Let Germany be proud of him! Yes, proud of him, but worthy of him too![25]

So modern academic musicology, the tradition out of which (but also, in certain ways, against which) this book is written, originated, like the Bach revival and the musical canon of which Bach is now regarded as the cornerstone, as a by-product of German nationalism.

CURSED QUESTIONS

Does that matter? More generally, does it matter that Bach's music, little known in his time and forgotten soon after his death, has been called back to active cultural duty by a cultural program unrelated and perhaps alien to it? And does it matter that it is now admired for reasons that may have little to do with what motivated it?

Many lovers of the music will have no trouble answering these questions. Indeed, the Bach revival can seem a miraculous salvage operation, hardly in need of defense or excuse. But the "universalization" of music originally created within a narrowly specific cultural context does entail some difficulties, and cannot help raising some problems, especially if the original context was a religious one.

Look again at Ex. 26-15 and consider it from a different perspective. No mention was made the first time around of the fact that the *turba* in the St. John Passion, following the Book of John itself, is identified not as "*das Volk*" or "the people" (as it is in the Matthew Passion), but as "*die Juden*" or "the Jews." An accusation is being made, one that is no longer supported by responsible historical or theological scholarship, that the Jews rather than the Romans were responsible for Christ's death. That accusation, now often called the "blood libel," has had a bearing on a history of bloody persecutions, culminating in perhaps the most horrible page in the history of the twentieth century.

Obviously, Bach had no part of that. Nor was he, as far as anyone today can guess, personally anti-Semitic as the term is understood today, except insofar as he probably subscribed to Luther's doctrine that the Jews should submit to conversion on pain of punishment. In all likelihood he rarely, possibly never, met a Jew and thought little about them. The St. John Passion was intended for performance before a congregation of Christian believers for whom the Gospel text was . . . well, Gospel. The insult it contains to Jews was wholly incidental to its purpose.

But today it serves other purposes and is performed before other audiences. Bach is long dead, but the St. John Passion lives on. Jews not only hear it nowadays, they often participate in performances of it, and are sometimes shocked to learn what it is that they are singing. Are they wrong? Does Bach's music redeem the text? Would it impair Bach's work from the standpoint of its present social use if the text were emended to exclude the blood libel? And if people disagree about the answers to these difficult questions, on what basis can they be adjudicated?

It is no part of the purpose of this book to provide the answers to these questions. But it is integral to its purpose to raise them, for they crystallize important historical problems — problems of appropriation, universalization, recontextualization — that have arisen along with the practice of historiography itself, and that historiography not only poses but in large part creates. Precisely because these problems are part and parcel of historiography's essence and its legacy, historiography often remains blind to them, not regarding itself as a part of its own subject matter. But responsible historiography, most historians now concede, must contain an element of reflexivity — concern with itself as a historical entity and with its own potential cultural and social influence, alongside the entities it purports to study.

The problem of the anti-Semitic message in the St. John Passion, from which some people today may actually "learn" the "fact" that the Jews killed Christ, would never have become a problem had Bach never been revived. What was merely a latent message in Bach's time, stating an accepted truth to which no one would have paid much attention *per se*, has become a potentially explicit message in our time, and a potentially mischievous one. We have history — or rather the *sense* of history fostered by romantic nationalism — to thank for that. The peculiarly romantic sense of the timeless relevance of history, called "historicism," is what vouchsafed the work's survival. The problem comes in deciding just what it is in the treasured legacy of the past that should be regarded as timelessly relevant.

SCARLATTI, AT LAST

Bach lived his life in defiance of the Enlightenment and was revived in reaction to it. The remaining member of the class of 1685, Domenico Scarlatti, exemplified the esthetic of Enlightenment better, perhaps, than any other musician of his time.

The son of Alessandro Scarlatti, one of the giants of the opera seria, Domenico Scarlatti was at first groomed for a career in his father's footsteps, for which he showed a precocious aptitude. His first opera, *Ottavia ristituita al trono* ("Octavia restored to the throne"), was produced at Saint Bartholomew's in Naples, Alessandro's stamping ground, for the 1703 carnival season, when Domenico was all of seventeen years old. His last, the archetypical *Berenice, regina d'Egitto, ovvero Le gare di amore e di politica* ("Bernice, Queen of Egypt;" or, the "Contest of love and politics"), was produced for the Roman carnival fifteen years later, whereupon Scarlatti retired from the opera stage, at the age of thirty-two, with almost forty years of life still ahead of him.

The next year, 1719, he took a position as *maestro di cappella* at the cathedral of Lisbon, in Portugal, where he produced several oratorios and other sacred vocal works (some in a very chaste *stile antico*), and also supervised the musical education of the Infanta (crown princess) Maria Barbara, a gifted keyboard player. On her marriage to Fernando, the crown prince of Spain, in 1728, he followed Maria Barbara to Madrid, where he was known as Domingo Escarlatti, and served as courtier until his death in 1757, the last twenty years alongside the great castrato Farinelli, who (as we have seen) also retired to a sinecure at Madrid.

FIG. 26-8 Domenico Scarlatti, by Domingo Antonio de Velasco.

Scarlatti spent his years at Madrid as a pampered retainer, later a knight, and was free to compose whatever he wanted. What he wanted to compose was virtuoso harpsichord music for himself (and, presumably, his royal pupil) to perform. Unconstrained by any set requirements, yet prompted by a tremendous musical curiosity and imagination, he invented what amounted to a new style of composition, which he called "ingenious jesting with art."[26] The phrase is pregnant. It jibes presciently with Dr. Burney's comments on the nature and value of music, and reveals a wholehearted commitment to the ideal of delighting—rather than edifying, instructing, awing, or stirring—the listener. Nothing could be farther away from the monumental worlds of Bach and Handel.

Accordingly, Scarlatti became the great miniaturist of his age, spending the last thirty to forty years of his life turning out upwards of 550 short, freestanding compositions for the harpsichord (and, to an undeterminable extent, for other keyboard instruments to which they are adaptable, namely organ, clavichord, and early forms of the pianoforte). These pieces were individually called sonatas, but they were in only a single "movement" and were often published under different names (such as *essercizi*, "studies"), or even as *pièces* grouped in suites. None survives in the composer's autograph, and it is impossible to know, therefore, exactly what he called them or how he grouped them.

The reason for occasionally calling them *pièces* is clear enough: like those of Couperin and the other French *clavecinistes*, Scarlatti's pieces are uniformly in "binary" form—far more uniformly than Couperin's, which are often *rondeaux* (with recurrent refrains) or *passacailles* (variations over a ground). Scarlatti himself never gathered them into suites. Early copyists and editors liked to group them in pairs, similar in key but contrasting in tempo. This, too, is a practice that (while effective, and widely followed in performance) cannot with any certainty be associated with the composer.

Rather, Scarlatti evidently preferred to provide delight in single short doses—"by the shot," one could say. But unlike Couperin, who also deserves credit for pioneering the single characteristic piece (albeit published in "*ordres*" or suites), Scarlatti liked to make brash statements as well as tender ones. Like any jester, he had an exhibitionistic streak. He could never have said, with Couperin (in the preface to his first book of *pièces de clavecin*, 1713), that "I would rather be moved than astonished." Scarlatti's sonatas, though occasionally tender and lyrical, are, as a *corpus*, the most astonishing pieces of their time.

Their astonishing character draws on several sources. One is the outstanding instrumental virtuosity they require and display (particularly in the use of special effects like crossed hands and even *glissando*). Another is their harmonic extravagance, manifested both in terms of boldly handled dissonance and an often flamboyant, yet exquisitely graded use of modulatory chromaticism. Still another is the fantastic variety with which their single basic shape is treated.

Finally, there is a singular imprint of local color—a local color that to listeners in countries where the international music trade flourished seemed exotic (as it must have seemed to the foreign-born Scarlatti himself, hence his penchant for noticing and drawing on it). The Scarlatti sonatas are a very early instance of exotic local color being sought and valued for its "pure" musical allure, without any symbolically nationalistic overlay. (A century or more later, this allure was exploited nationalistically by Spanish musicians, notably the pianist-composer Enrique Granados, who pioneeringly programmed, edited, and emulated Scarlatti at a time when his work had largely lapsed into "historical" limbo.)

The most remarkable aspect of Scarlatti's sonatas, in fact, may be the absence in them (despite their frequent vivid "pictorialisms") of anything symbolic at all. At a time when music, like the other arts, was mainly valued for its mimetic properties, Scarlatti sought to convey what Thomas Twining, a friend of Dr. Burney, called "a simple original pleasure, . . . no more imitative than the smell of a rose, or the flavor of a pineapple."[27] In this, Scarlatti was true to the spirit, not of his father, but of the Italian string composers of his father's generation. His sonatas, unlike Couperin's character pieces, were works at which old French academicians like Fontanelle might have railed.

What made them the darlings of connoisseurs and epicures from the begin-ning—or at least from 1739, when a selection of them was published for the first time and immediately pirated far and wide (as well as plundered by Handel for his "Grand Concertos")—was what their British publisher Thomas Roseingrave, a famous harpsichordist in his own right, called "their Delicacy of Stile, and Masterly Composition."[28] The Scarlatti sonatas, from which the following examples have been drawn, were chosen to exemplify all these traits in turn—except sheer virtuosity, which is exemplified throughout. They are numbered here according to the catalogue of Ralph Kirkpatrick (1911–84), an eminent harpsichordist who in his biography of Scarlatti (1953) tried to put the sonatas in something resembling a chronological order. (The previously standard listing by Alessandro Longo had been an arbitrary one like the Bach-Gesellschaft ordering of Bach's cantatas.)

The Sonata in G, K. 105, has an overall shape that can be regarded as typical for Scarlatti: the usual swing from tonic to dominant in the first half, followed by a return in the second half by way of a FOP or "far-out point" (in this case, the cadence on B minor (iii) in mm. 118–19). As is also typical for Scarlatti, the endings of each binary half match up with their counterparts more closely than the beginnings, so that a drive to completion is achieved. What makes the sonata unforgettable, though, is not its general contours but the specific harmonic content, which is also "typically Scarlattian," but in an unusually, almost uniquely concentrated fashion. Beginning half-way through the first half, and even more pervasively in the second half, the harmony is rife with dissonant seconds, few of which can be considered "chord tones," and even fewer of which resolve in normally prescribed fashion to consonances. In mm. 39–41 (the beginning of Ex. 26-19) their actual function is best perceived. The harmony is clearly A major. The Ds in the left hand, however, show no tendency whatever to resolve to C♯; instead, they seem to cling to the E in a sort of decorative cluster.

In fact, this pungent decoration was widely employed by harpsichordists. Francesco Geminiani, an Italian violinist who worked in England, called particular attention to it in his *Treatise of Good Taste in the Art of Musick* (1749): "No performer should flatter himself that he is able to accompany well till he is master of this delicate and admirable secret which has been in use above a hundred years."[29] But before Scarlatti it was rarely written down (which was why it was a "secret"). A sort of simultaneous mordent, it was called *acciaccatura* (from *acciaccare*, to bruise or batter). Scarlatti was uniquely drawn to its use and, by notating it, put it "on the map."

The deliciously grotesque passage shown in Ex. 26-19, where the acciaccaturas are maintained throughout like a sort of pedal (or — more to the point — like a constantly strummed open string), discloses the reason for Scarlatti's seeming obsession with them. By combining the acciaccaturas with "Phrygian" neighbor notes (B♭ applied to A in the first half, E♭ applied to D in the second), Scarlatti unmistakably conjures up the sound of "Flamenco" guitars, the Andalusian gypsy style that has become pervasive in Spanish popular music, and that must have already been a conspicuous part of the sonic landscape in Scarlatti's day.

EX. 26-19   Domenico Scarlatti, Sonata in G, K. 105, mm. 39 – 54

The Sonata in E major, K. 264, is one of Scarlatti's most vagarious essays in modulation. The first half already contains chords whose roots lie the very maximum distance — namely, a tritone — away from the tonic on a complete (rather than diatonically adjusted) circle of fifths. The second half begins with a remarkable excursion (Ex. 26-20) in which the traditional FOP seems to be pushed much farther than ever before, requiring an enharmonic alteration of the key signature to avoid a huge proliferation of double (or even triple) sharps. The harmonic distance covered in Ex. 26-20, though covered very unconventionally (by a sequence of three successive ascending whole steps adding up to another tritone: B – C♯ [= D♭] – E♭ – F), turns out to be not all that great; the cadence point at the end of the example is C, merely the "minor vi" or "flat submediant" of E (that is, the submediant of the parallel minor), and though played around with at length, it is never exceeded. Far more significant, perhaps, is the fact that the strange modulation is carried by a melodic sequence drawn from the sonata's opening pair of measures, so that it could be regarded as a motivic development.

EX. 26-20   Domenico Scarlatti, Sonata in E major, K. 264, mm. 127–46

The "perhaps" is necessary, because a modulatory motivic development at the beginning of the second binary half, culminating in the FOP, was something that would later become a virtual *sine qua non* or mandate for "classical" sonata composers; but it happens only *ad libitum* ("when he pleases") with Scarlatti. For him it is only one of many ways of proceeding, and a rather exceptional one at that. Its "significance" is something that we judge, inevitably, with a hindsight the composer did not possess.

The same goes for the overall shape of the Sonata in F minor, K. 481, a plaintive *andante cantabile*, in which the beginning of the second half features another bold enharmonic modulation over a motive derived from the first half (compare Ex. 26-21a with Ex. 26-21b), again arriving at a bizarre FOP that is the exact reciprocal of the one in the previous sonata. Instead of the submediant of a major tonic's parallel minor, we have the submediant of a minor tonic's parallel major.

But there is something else to notice. In this sonata, the return of the original tonic happens to coincide with a return of the opening thematic material. This dramatic

EX. 26-21A   Domenico Scarlatti, Sonata in F minor, K. 481, mm. 9–12

EX. 26-21B   Domenico Scarlatti, Sonata in F minor, K. 481, mm. 36–44

"double return" (original key arriving together with the original theme) was something else that would become practically *de rigueur* by the last quarter of the eighteenth century, and a defining attribute of the "classical" sonata form. The double return is often thought typical of Scarlatti, because the most famous Scarlatti sonata of all — C major, K. 159, a favorite of piano teachers everywhere (Ex. 26-22) — happens to have one (compare the beginning with m. 43).

But the double return is actually a great rarity in Scarlatti's work. If we take an exclusively "horizontal" or synchronic view of his output (that is, comparing it only to what was going on in its own time), the double return will seem an insignificant caprice, even an eccentricity. If, on the other hand, we take a "vertical" or diachronic view (comparing it to what came before and after), it will appear momentously significant, even prophetic. Which view is the true view?

Obviously, it is a question of perspective. Both are true views, but neither is *the* true view. To Scarlatti's contemporaries, his sonatas, while much admired by connoisseurs, were admired as "original and happy freaks,"[30] to quote Dr. Burney — the offbeat products of an imaginative but isolated and pampered genius. (It was no doubt the self-indulgent quality of his work that gave rise to the rumor, contradicted at last by recently discovered portraits, that in his late years Scarlatti became too fat to reach the keyboard when seated.) As Ralph Kirkpatrick put it, a composer as fertile, as prolific, and as nonchalant as Scarlatti "would have been perfectly capable of discovering the classical sonata form and then throwing it away."[31] And yet to many other modern

EX. 26-22A   Domenico Scarlatti, Sonata in C, K. 159, mm. 1–6

EX. 26-22B   Domenico Scarlatti, Sonata in C, K. 159, mm. 38–47

historians and performers, Scarlatti's harmonic and formal experiments have made him seem no mere eccentric, but "an epoch-making composer,"[32] to quote Fernando Valenti (1926–90), an eminent harpsichordist who did a great deal to popularize Scarlatti's work. According to this view, Scarlatti was a more "advanced" composer than Bach or Handel, his fellows in the class of 1685. There are facts that may be cited to justify such a view. The most persuasive one, paradoxically enough, would be Scarlatti's retarded development.

Surely one of the latest bloomers among the major names in music history, Scarlatti only came into his own as a composer in 1738, with the publication of his first book, *Essercizi per gravicembalo*. By then the class of 1685 were all aged fifty-three, and Bach's and Handel's careers were largely behind them. Scarlatti was just beginning to be "Scarlatti," and thus his effective starting point coincided with Bach's and Handel's finish lines. As a composer, then, Scarlatti might better be regarded not as a contemporary of J. S. Bach but rather as an elder member of the generation of Bach's sons.

Such a view of Scarlatti, of course, reflects a general historical view that places the highest premium on teleological evolution, and on innovation, evolution's handmaiden. It is known as the "Darwinian" theory of history, after a fundamental misreading of the work of Charles Darwin, the biologist whose (entirely non-teleological) theory of evolution has dominated natural history since 1859, the year in which his masterwork, *The Origin of Species*, was published. By then, of course, the members of the class of 1685 had all been dead a hundred years or more. It is clearly anachronistic from the point of view of Scarlatti and his contemporaries. Does that make it an altogether irrelevant criterion of judgment?

Many historians and musicians in the twentieth century have not thought so. The Darwinian view of music history was given a memorable expression by Igor Stravinsky, a highly innovative modern composer, when commenting on an extravagantly Darwinian historical study by Edward Lowinsky called *Tonality and Atonality in Sixteenth-Century Music*. Lowinsky had contended that if a historian can show a trend or an accomplishment, no matter how small or how isolated, to have been "pregnant with the seed of future developments," then "it does not seem a matter of decisive importance whether it represents, say ten, fifteen, or twenty per cent" of the total musical output its time.[33] "Or, indeed, a smaller per cent still," Stravinsky enthusiastically chimed in, perhaps recalling the recent history of Russia, his native country, and the "Three Who Made a Revolution" (to cite the title of an influential study of Lenin, Stalin, and Trotsky by Bertram D. Wolfe).[34]

In back of an apparently scientific view, then, is a more general cultural assumption that significant history is the creation of small elites. When it is put in this way, the political implications (or foundations) of the view are more easily noticed. Exclusively diachronic views of historical phenomena, and the concomitant tendency to overrate innovation, have lost some ground as a result. But an exclusively synchronic view may tend to overrate eccentricity and obscure the reality of "trends and accomplishments." Again, it is more important for us right now to understand the question than it is to adjudicate it. Rather than attempt to decide the matter of Scarlatti's "true" significance or to harmonize the vividly conflicting perspectives on his achievement, we can regard him as an archetype of "peripheral" composers — composers who are geographically and temperamentally remote from the centers of institutional and commercial music making, but (perhaps seemingly, perhaps truly) "ahead of their time." Whether "seemingly" or "truly" depends on the manner in which the times make contact with the individual, and (inevitably) on the interests and biases of the historian.

The Comic Style

MID-EIGHTEENTH-CENTURY STYLISTIC CHANGE TRACED
TO ITS SOURCES IN THE 1720S; EMPFINDSAMKEIT, GALANTERIE;
"WAR OF THE BUFFOONS"

YOU CAN'T GET THERE FROM HERE

"Bach is the father, we are the kids" (*Bach ist der Vater, wir sind die Buben*),
Wolfgang Amadeus Mozart was once quoted, perhaps apocryphally, as
saying.[1] Only it was not J. S. Bach of whom he said it. "Old Sebastian," as
Mozart called him, was just a dimly remembered grandfather until the last decade of
Mozart's career, when (slightly in advance of the public revival described in the previous
chapter) Mozart first got to hear the works of J. S. Bach and G. F. Handel, then virtually
unperformed outside of the composers' home territory—northern Germany in the case
of Bach and Great Britain in the case of Handel. It was at the home of Baron Gottfried
van Swieten, a Dutch-born Viennese aristocrat who maintained a sort of antiquarian
salon, that Mozart made their acquaintance. The baron commissioned from Mozart
modernized scores of Handel's *Messiah* and other vocal works for performance at his
soirées. Although the works of Handel and Bach made a big impression on the van
Swieten circle, the very fact that they needed to be updated for performance in the
1780s shows how far their works had fallen out of the practical repertoire.

The Bach whom Mozart regarded as a musical parent was old Sebastian's second
son, Carl Philipp Emanuel (1714–88), who was indeed old enough to be Mozart's
father (or even his grandfather), and who along with his much younger half-brother
Johann Christian (1735–82) was indeed regarded by the musicians of the late eighteenth
century as a founding father. Their eminence has much receded, though, owing to
the historical circumstances that attended the rise of the modern "classical" repertory
and the writing of its history. That modern repertory (we still call it "standard")
began with the works of Mozart himself and his contemporaries, notably Franz Joseph
Haydn. When J. S. Bach was revived in the nineteenth century, he was appended to
an already-established "canon" of works and, along with Handel, was proclaimed its
founding father. The work of his sons, however, was not revived.

The false genealogy thus implied, in which the generation of Bach and Handel
was cast in a direct line that led straight to the generation of Haydn and Mozart, was
responsible for a host of false historical assumptions. Because of them, the interest and
attention of historians was diverted away from the music and the musical life of the mid-
eighteenth century, when the Bach sons, along with the later composers of *opera seria*

FIG. 27-1   Carl Philipp Emanuel Bach, J. S. Bach's second son, master of the *empfindsamer Stil* and author of the *Essay on the True Art of Keyboard Playing*.

(with whom we are already somewhat familiar from chapter 23) were at their height of activity and prestige. The result has been something of a historiographical black hole. The earliest attempts to plug it amounted to assertions and counterassertions that this or that repertory formed the "missing link" between the Bach–Handel and Haydn–Mozart poles. First came Hugo Riemann (1849–1919), a great German scholar who identified a once-famous but chimerical "Mannheim School" as "the so-long-sought predecessor of Haydn."[2] The Italian musicologist Fausto Torrefranca (1883–1955) found the missing link in Italian keyboard sonatas;[3] the Viennese Wilhelm Fischer (1886–1962) found it in the Viennese orchestral style; and so it went.[4]

Finally, in 1969, the American music historian Daniel Heartz blew the whistle on the game in an explosive four-page wake-up call of an article ("Approaching a History of 18th-Century Music"), and made the first comprehensive attempt at a new historiography in a magisterial eight-hundred-page book published twenty-six years later (*Haydn, Mozart and the Viennese School: 1740–1780*).[5] Heartz accounted for the notorious void by noting the fact—which many at the time found maddening to acknowledge—that the historiography of eighteenth-century music "has been done largely by, for, and about Germans."[6] But as he went right on to point out in a truly delicious passage, the Germanic historiography has affected everyone who conceives the history of eighteenth-century music in terms of the modern canon and its masters. The death of Bach in 1750, which seems so dramatically (and conveniently) to split the century into its early and late phases, Heartz observed,

> has a sentimental meaning for all music lovers today. It meant nothing at the time. For all that the Leipzig master participated upon the European musical scene of his day he might as well have died a generation earlier. He did not take the extra step that made [the opera seria composer Johann Adolf] Hasse the darling of Dresden and of Europe. . . and thank God for that! With Handel the case is different. Had he remained in the North we should probably honor him now no more than we do a hundred other Lutheran worthies. Italy coaxed him beyond his originally turgid and unvocal mannerisms. Had he remained to bask in Southern climes he might

have joined the Neapolitan thrust into the mainstream of 18th-century music. But he went instead to Augustan England. There, musical backwater though it was, he found himself in a land that led the world with regard to the freedom and dignity of the human spirit. To England, then, we owe thanks that Handel became one of the greatest of all masters. At the same time it should be borne in mind that Handel in London stood aside from the main evolution nearly as much as Bach.

We tend nowadays to recoil a bit from phrases like "mainstream" and "main evolution," seeing in them the likely pitfall of substituting one sort of blinkered or biased view for another. Evolutions are only "main" to the extent that their outcomes are valued. Heartz's "main evolution" is so described because of where it led—namely, to Haydn and Mozart. Meanwhile, the fact that Bach and Handel have returned to the canon in glory, and have exerted a potent influence on composers ever since their return, shows that the evolution from which they stood apart was not permanently or irrevocably "main." "Main-ness," in short is not something inherent in a phenomenon but something ascribed to it—inevitably in hindsight, and for a reason. But whether or not we wish to promote the slighted evolutionary line in this way, its reality must be accepted and coped with. Otherwise we have no history, if (to quote Heartz once more) history is an attempt "to seek the interconnection between events."

So in this chapter we will try to fill in the picture a bit, although the full story is still far from tellable. No period is in greater need of fundamental research than the period that extended from the 1730s to the 1760s: the period, in other words, in which the composers born in the first two decades of the century dominated the contemporary scene. That period, long commonly known as "Preclassic" (and thus relegated by its very name to a status of relative insignificance, a sort of trough between peaks), has been until recently the most systematically neglected span of years in the whole history of European "fine-art" music.

THE YOUNGER BACHS

One very dramatic way of pointing up the problem and suggesting solutions to it (even though it means staying for a while with the Germans) would be to begin with a close look at the work of Bach's sons, starting with the eldest, Wilhelm Friedemann (1710–84).

FIG. 27-2 Wilhelm Friedemann Bach, eldest son of J. S. Bach, who followed in his father's footsteps as a North German church organist.

We last heard of him as the arranger of his father's huge Reformation cantata for a gala performance on the anniversary of the Augsburg Confession. Thereafter, W. F. Bach (henceforth "WF") followed a career in his father's footsteps as Lutheran organist and cantor. Although far less successful than old Sebastian's in terms of steady employment, owing to what we would probably now diagnose as personality disorders, it was by no means an undistinguished career. WF's most prominent job, and the one he held longest, was as successor to Zachow, Handel's teacher, at the Liebfrauenkirche (Church of the Virgin Mary) in Halle, Handel's birthplace. And despite his career difficulties, WF inherited his father's reputation as the finest German church organist of his time.

It would be reasonable to expect his music basically to resemble old Sebastian's. Some of it, notably his church cantatas, did. And yet as the harpsichord sonata in F (Ex. 27-1) suggests, much more of it does not.

Although composed around 1745, that is to say within J. S. Bach's lifetime, the work occupies a different stylistic universe than anything the elder Bach composed. The very word "sonata" had come to mean something different to WF from what it meant to JS. For JS the word meant chamber music in the Italian style — basically trio sonatas, not keyboard works at all. For keyboard one wrote suites, not sonatas. The only exceptions were keyboard arrangements of chamber sonatas (like the one by Reincken we looked at in chapter 25), or else deliberate imitations of such works, like the set of six sonatas for organ composed in Leipzig around 1727, in which the two hands of the organist represent the two "melodic" parts of a trio sonata and the feet on the pedals played the very active and thematic bass. (The organ trios were thus pedal studies in effect; they were actually composed for WF to practice.) Even JS's sonatas for solo instrument and harpsichord were usually trio sonatas, thanks to obbligato writing for the keyboard. The most common formal approach in all of these works, especially in the outer (fast) movements, was to spin them out in fugal style.

JS never dreamt of writing keyboard sonatas like WF's (not just the one given here, but all of them), in which all three movements were in binary form and in which the texture is either two-part or else makes free use of harmonic figuration. But these large formal and textural differences, though significant, are really the least of it. The stylistic and rhetorical gulf is the mind-boggler, and it widens with each movement.

At first blush WF's first movement does not look all that "un-Bachlike." It actually begins with a canon. That canon, though, lasts all of two measures, and contains a repeated phrase that turns it into mere "voice exchange." Imitative counterpoint, though clearly something at WF's beck and call, is for him an occasional device, more a decorative touch than the essential modus operandi. But even that is not the most basic difference of approach between WF and his father. The most basic differences lie in the interpenetrating dimensions of melodic design and harmonic rhythm.

WF's melodic design, at the opposite pole from JS's powerfully spinning engine, is based on the dual principle of short-range contrast and balance. The first four measures tell the whole story. Both melodically and harmonically, they divide in the middle, two plus two. The first pair (our "canon") continually circles around the tonic, touching down on it at every second beat. The second pair of measures does the same with

EX. 27-1   W. F. Bach, Sonata in F (Falck catalogue no. 6), first movement

EX. 27-1 *(continued)*

EX. 27-1 (continued)

the dominant harmony and underscores the harmonic contrast with a motivic one. Melodically, the second pair has nothing to do with the first. But the contrast is forged into a sort of higher unity by the principle of balance when the tonic is restored in m. 5.

Melodic contrast then seems to run rampant. The fifth measure has a new motive (based on the opening rhythm in m. 1), and so does the sixth (no longer related to anything previous), *and so does the seventh*! These little melodic cells qualify as "motives" through independent repetition: in m. 5 directly in the right hand, in m. 6 by a twofold exchange between the hands, and in m. 7 by a single exchange; from this perspective, too, variety seems at first to know no bounds. Measure 8 continues with the same motive as m. 7, which once again creates a symmetrical divide (that is, a divide at the middle); measures 5–8 break down into (1 + 1) + 2.

Parenthetically, let us also note that these motives are cast in rhythms that carry definite associations to the "galant"—the "affable" (lightweight, courtly, "Frenchy") style that JS Bach tended to shy away from, even in the actual *galanteries* (the "modern" dances) from his suites. The fast triplets alternating freely with duple divisions are one specifically galant rhythm (exploited somewhat ironically by JS, we may recall, in the Fifth Brandenburg Concerto with its most ungallant juggernaut of a harpsichord solo). The "lombard" rhythms (quick short–long pairs) are even more distinctly galant, and even rarer in the work of Bach the father.

But all the surface variety and decorative dazzle in WF's writing is a feint that covers, and somewhat occludes, a very deliberate and structurally symmetrical tonal plan. Like any binary movement, this one will follow a there-and-back harmonic course, moving from tonic to dominant in the first half and from dominant to tonic, by way of a "far-out point" (FOP), in the second. What distinguishes one piece from another is not the foreordained basic plan they all share but rather the specific means of its implementation. Some pieces rush headlong from harmonic pole to pole. This one, to a degree we have never before encountered in instrumental music, takes time to smell the daisies (and, in the form of unpredictably varied motives, takes care to provide a lot of daisies to smell). That placidity is also part and parcel of what it meant to be galant. It's a bad courtier or diplomat who'll allow strong emotion to show.

A stroll around a garden, then—and a very meticulously laid out garden it is. Taking in the first half at a glance now, we count sixteen measures—and it's no accident. It means that the portion we have examined so far, exactly half of the total span, will be balanced by the rest, so that our observations about short-range harmonic and melodic symmetries will hold at the long range as well: $16 = (8 + 8) = (4 + 4 + 4 + 4)$, and so on down to pairs and units. The longest-range symmetry governing this half of the movement concerns harmonic balance. The establishment of the dominant as local tonic, or modulatory goal, takes place exactly on the downbeat of m. 9 and is repeatedly confirmed thereafter, thus dividing the whole span into 8 bars of tonic, 8 of dominant. Within the second 8 (that is, mm. 9–16), the motivic contrasts take place in a fashion that continues to emphasize symmetrical divisions on various levels simultaneously. Thus m. 9 introduces syncopes; m. 10 has exchanges of triplets between the hands; mm. 11–12 coalesce into one exchange of triplets and larger syncopes; mm. 13–14 feature a twofold exchange of motives; m. 15 has a single exchange, and m. 16 provides the cadence. Thus in summary we get $(1 + 1) + 2 + 2 + (1 + 1)$, which adds a kind of palindromic symmetry to the mix. The ideal, far from the "Baroque" aim of generating a great motivic and tonal momentum, seems to be to provide a maximum of ingratiating detail over a satisfyingly stable ground plan.

The second half starts off like a palindrome or mirror reflection of the first. Its first four measures (mm. 17–20) are a simple transposition to the dominant of the four-measure gambit that got the whole piece moving, and that we analyzed in some detail above. In m. 21, however, we hit a big jolt, expressed at once in every possible dimension—harmonic, textural, melodic. The harmony is a diminished-seventh chord, the most dissonant chord (as opposed to contrapuntal or "non-harmonic" dissonance) in the vocabulary of the time. The texture is disrupted by it: in fact this is the first actual chord we have heard in what up to now has been a strictly two-part texture, one that implied its harmonies rather than stating them outright. Melodically, too, there is disruption: obsessive (or constrained) syncopated repetition of single tones and dissonant leaps rather than smooth melodic flow. (And there is disruption in phrase length, too, as we shall see.)

In a way this is not unexpected, since it is time to move out to the FOP. But never yet have we seen the move so dramatized. The diminished-seventh at m. 21 is built over the leading tone of vi (d minor); and when resolution is made, the opening motive, familiar from both halves of the piece, returns, only to be brusquely shunted aside by a new diminished-seventh disruption on the third beat of m. 24. This is a far more serious disruption, because it is built over D♯, the leading tone to E, which is the seventh degree of the scale, and the only pitch in the scale of F major that cannot function as a local tonic because it takes a diminished triad. Therefore, when resolution is made to E major in m. 26, there can be no sense of stable arrival, even at a FOP, because the harmony still contains a chromatic tone and expresses no function within the original key.

Harmonic restlessness continues through an asymmetrical (because binarily indivisible) five measures—during which, with a single exception (find it!), every degree of the chromatic scale is sounded—before settling down on A minor (iii), the true FOP. At this point, stable thematic material is resumed for two measures—literally resumed at the very point at which it had been interrupted (compare mm. 31–32 with mm. 5–6)—only to be superseded by another five bars' restless modulation, aggravated this time by quickened syncopes, during which every degree of the chromatic scale is sounded without exception.

This last, extraordinarily chromatic, modulatory passage lets us off in m. 38 within hailing distance of the tonic—on IV, which proceeds to V, thence home. Again the return of stable harmonic functions is signaled, or accompanied, by the return of stable thematic material. The "retransitional" bar, the one that zeroes in on the tonic, brings back the "lombard" motives first heard in m. 7. When the tonic is reached in m. 39, however, the original melodic opening abruptly supersedes the lombards. This is the "double return"—original key and original theme simultaneously reachieved with mutually reinforcing or "synergistic" effect—that we first encountered, but only as an anomaly, in Domenico Scarlatti. Two bars later, in m. 41, the whole section originally cast in the dominant (mm. 7–16) returns transposed to the tonic and finishes the piece off with a sense of restored balance and fully achieved harmonic reciprocity.

In the music of W. F. Bach and his contemporaries, the double return and the large-scale melodic-recapitulation-cum-harmonic-reciprocation that it introduces are no longer anomalous features, as they had been with Scarlatti. They have become standard. Whereas Scarlatti's use of it created a little historiographical problem (what, precisely, was its relationship—or his—to the "main evolution"?), there is no question of its absolute centrality to the musical thinking of WF's generation and the ones that followed. Indeed, it would not be much of an exaggeration to dub the whole later eighteenth century the Age of the Double Return, so definitive did the gesture become.

The last movement of the present sonata, a rollicking Presto, offers immediate confirmation. Although it contrasts with the first movement in mood and texture, it follows the very same formal model and achieves the very same sense of roundedness and stability. Practically the whole of the first section of the piece is recapitulated in the second half. The first six measures are actually restated twice: at the very beginning of the second half, where they are transposed to the dominant, and towards the end, where they provide the double return. The middle movement (Ex. 27-2), a minuet (or a pair of minuets to be exact), is a simple *galanterie* such as J. S. Bach might have included in a suite. Simpler, in fact: JS would never have settled for such an uncomplicated texture, or for so much artless alternation of tonics and dominants, bar by bar, such as one finds here (especially at the beginning of the second minuet or "trio"). Yet we sense that WF is not "settling" for anything, but using the simplicity and "naturalness" of the unaffected dance as a foil for the very sophisticated constructions in the outer movements.

EX. 27-2 W. F. Bach, Sonata in F (Falck catalogue no. 6), second movement (Minuet and Trio)

By the use of this foil, the composer points up that very sophistication by reminding us that all the movements in his sonata are cast in what is basically the same form, and also showing us how much variety of surface detail and structural elaboration that basic form can accommodate. The outer movements, with their tremendous profusion of motives, their cunningly calculated harmonic jolts, and their dramatically articulated unfoldings, are teased-up versions of the old *galanterie*, set on either side of a basic version that provides a moment of repose.

But where did all these teasing-up devices come from? And where did WF learn them, if he did not learn them at home? Every distinctive feature of the son's style — its melodic profligacy, its reliance on the contrast and balance of short ideas, its frequent cadences, its self-dramatizing form, its synergistic harnessing of melodic and harmonic events, even its characteristic melodic and harmonic rhythms — were absolutely antithetical to his father's style, and to Handel's as well. To see this style surfacing all at once in Germany explains nothing; it merely makes the problem more acute. Its apparent suddenness is but the result of our skewed perspective on it — our skewed Germanocentric perspective, as Heartz might wish to warn us.

SENSIBILITY

Before trying to solve the problem, let's savor it for a while by making it "worse." We can expand the scope of our comparison by noting that the new "teasing" techniques not only created a stylistic contrast with the old but an esthetic and psychological one as well. A composition by J. S. Bach or one of his contemporaries was nothing if not musically unified. There is usually one main *inventio* or musical idea, whether (depending on the genre) we call it "subject," "ritornello," or by some other name, and its purpose is to project, through consistently worked out musical "figures" or motives, a single dominant affect or feeling-state, writ very large indeed.

The melodic surface of WF's sonata, as we have seen, presents not a unified but a highly nuanced, variegated, even fragmented, exterior. The many short-term contrasts, and their implicit importance, seem to undermine the very foundations of his father's style in both its musical and its expressive dimensions. In contrast to the inexorable consistency of JS's "spinning-out," the only predictable aspect of WF's melodic unfolding is its unpredictability. In place of a heroic affect, "objectively" displayed, there is consciousness of subjective caprice, of impressionability, of quick, spontaneous responsiveness or changeability of mood — in a word, of "sensibility," as eighteenth-century writers (most famously, Jane Austen) used the word.

The German equivalent of sensibility, in this sense, was *Empfindung*, meaning the thing itself, or *Empfindsamkeit*, meaning susceptibility to it. It was a new esthetic, which aimed not at objective depiction of a character's feelings, as in an opera, but at the expression and transmission of one's own; and, being based on introspection, it was "realistic" in the sense that it recognized the skittishness and fluidity of subjective feeling. "The rapidity with which the emotions change is common knowledge, for they are nothing but motion and restlessness," wrote the Berlin composer Friedrich Wilhelm (1718–95) in a famous treatise on music criticism.[7]

Yet while that rapidity was presumably as well known to the composers of theatrical and ecclesiastical music as it was to anyone else, it was not thought by them to be the most appropriate aspect of the emotions for musical imitation. Rather, they sought to isolate, magnify, and "objectify" the idealized moods of gods, heroes, or contemplative Christian souls at superhuman intensity, and use that objective magnification as the basis for creating monumental musical structures that would impress large audiences in theaters and churches. Composers of the *empfindsamer Stil*, composing on a much smaller scale for intimate domestic surroundings, sought to capture the way "real people" really felt. They sought to create an impression of self-portraiture in which the player (and purchaser) of their music would recognize a corresponding self-portrait.

The origins of artistic "sensibility" were literary. Its first great conscious exponent was the poet Friedrich Gottlieb Klopstock (1724–1803), who established the style with his odes (love poems) in the 1740s, and who lived in Hamburg beginning in 1770. The Hamburg connection is important to us because Klopstock's neighbor there was Carl Philipp Emanuel Bach (henceforth "CPE"), who in 1768 assumed the post of cantor at the so-called Johanneum (Church of St. John) after almost thirty years of service to the court of Frederick the Great, the King of Prussia, in Berlin and at the other royal residences. He and Klopstock were kindred spirits and quickly became friends. CPE set Klopstock's odes to music and carried on a lively and sympathetic correspondence with him about the relationship of music and poetry. He was in effect a musical Klopstock and the chief representative in his own medium of artistic *Empfindsamkeit*. The term is now firmly, if retrospectively, associated with him, and with his keyboard music in particular. He took to an extreme the kind of wordless "expressionism" we have already noted in the work of his elder brother.

He did it quite consciously and even wrote about it (though without using the actual E-word) in his famous treatise, *An Essay on the True Art of Playing Keyboard Instruments* (*Versuch über die wahre Art das Clavier zu spielen*), published in Berlin in two volumes (1753, 1762). (It was to this book that Mozart was supposedly paying tribute in the comment quoted at the beginning of this chapter.) CPE's *Essay* is of course full of technical information — about ornamentation, for example, and continuo realization — that is of great value to the historian of performance practice. But it also deals in less tangible matters, and that is what was new about it.

"Play from the soul," CPE exhorted his readers, "not like a trained bird!"[8] And then, lending his novel idea authority by casting it as a paraphrase of a famous maxim by the Roman poet Horace:

> Since a musician cannot move others unless he himself is moved, he must of necessity feel all of the affects that he hopes to arouse in his listeners. He communicates his own feelings to them and thus most effectively moves them to sympathy. In languishing, sad passages, the performer must languish and grow sad. . ... Similarly, in lively, joyous passages, the executant must again put himself into the appropriate mood. And so, constantly varying the passions he will barely quiet one before he rouses another.[9]

FIG. 27-3 Frederick the Great performing as flute soloist (probably in his own concerto) at a soirée in Sans Souci, his pleasure palace at Potsdam. His music master, Johann Joachim Quantz, watches from the left foreground. C. P. E. Bach is at the keyboard; leading the violins is Franticek Benda, a member of a large family of distinguished Bohemian musicians active in Germany, who spent fifty-three years in Frederick's service. Oil painting (1852) by Adolf Friedrich Erdmann von Menzel.

Although the author takes the point for granted, it is important for us to realize that he is describing not only a style of performance but a style of composition as well. The kind of mercurial changeability of mood he emphasizes, and the impetuous sincerity he demands of the player, would both be out of place in a work by his father or in a formalized aria by Handel. For practical examples of musical *Empfindsamkeit* we must turn to CPE's own works, like the Sonata in F (Ex. 27-3), chosen for the sake of its outward similarity to WF's sonata in the same key.

EX. 27-3A C. P. E. Bach, "Prussian" Sonata no. 1 in F (Wotquenne catalogue no. 48/1), first movement, mm. 1–4, 32–37

EX. 27-3B C. P. E. Bach, "Prussian" Sonata no. 1 in F (Wotquenne catalogue no. 48/1), second movement

This sonata is the first in a set of six, composed in Berlin between 1740 and 1742, as much as a decade before the death of J. S. Bach, and published with a dedication to Frederick the Great, for which reason they are called the "Prussian" sonatas. In style and texture the first movement is even simpler than WF's sonata and even more mercurial. The second half, for example, does not begin with a direct reference to the opening material but rather a fascinatingly oblique one. The first measure is a kind of free inversion of its counterpart; the left hand enters the way it did in the first half, but there is a new countermelody above it in the right, and so on (Ex. 27-3a). Thus when the double return comes, it is the first time the opening melody has been heard in anything like its original form since the beginning of the piece.

The magic movement, however, is the second (Andante). There is nothing like it in WF's sonata, and nothing remotely like it in the works of J. S. Bach. It is the kind of piece for which the term *empfindsamer Stil* was coined. The key is F minor, traditionally a key of tortured moods. But no key signature is used — not because the key is in any way unreal, but because the very wayward harmonic digressions from it would entail a lot of tedious cancellations of accidentals. Even before the digressions take place the harmonic writing is boldly "subjective" and capricious: in m. 2, for example, a sigh figure is immediately followed by a leap of a diminished octave.

After the half cadence in m. 3 the melody breaks off altogether in favor of something that at first seems a contradiction in terms: an explicitly labeled instrumental recitative! Even without the label, the texture and the nature of the melodic writing would have labeled it conclusively. The giveaways are the pairs of repeated eighth notes on the first three downbeats, representing the prosody of "feminine endings" (line-endings in which the last syllable is unaccented). A knowing performer would recognize the notational conventions of opera here and perform them like a singer, interpolating an accented passing tone (or "prosodic appoggiatura") in place of the first eighth, as indicated in the score.

The recourse here to a patently operatic style — and the style associated in opera with "speaking," at that — suggests that the *empfindsamer Stil* communicates, as it were, an unwritten or unspoken text. An operatic recitative (or *scena*, to cite the type of scene in which recitative alternates, as it does in CPE's sonata, with a rhythmically steady melody) is traditionally a "formless" style of music that follows the shape of its text — in this case its unwritten text. Without an actual text to set, the music comes, as CPE puts it in his treatise, directly "from the soul," and communicates, inchoately and pressingly, an *Empfindung* that transcends the limiting medium of words.

Thus instrumental recitative, the signature device of musical *Empfindsamkeit*, implies a direct address from the composer to the listener, who is taken into the composer's confidence, as it were, and confided in person to person. The impression created is that of an individual intimately addressing a peer — and CPE's favorite instrument for creating such an impression was the clavichord, an instrument capable of dynamic gradations unavailable on the harpsichord, but so soft that one has to be as near the performer in order to hear it as one would have to be in order to carry on a private conversation.

Also inchoate and pressing are the harmonies that support this wordless recitative — chromatic harmonies that deliberately depart from the model sequences of "normal" music and, if anything, recall the vagaries of the latest, most "decadent" madrigals. If a G natural is interpolated as a prosodic appoggiatura in m. 8, then the first recitative section (like WF's already rather *empfindsamer* modulations in the first movement of his sonata) contains every degree of the chromatic scale. While the wildest, most disruptive touch is surely the immediate progression of the V_2^4 chord of B♭ in m. 4 to the vii_3^{o4} of B in the next measure, surely the most sophisticated progression is the enharmonic succession in mm. 7–8, whereby G♯ is transformed to A♭, reversing its tendency and smoothly restoring the original key.

CPE would not have called this style of his madrigalian, of course; nor, as already observed, did he himself use the word *empfindsamer* to describe it. His term for this inchoate, pressing idiom, with its rhythmic indefiniteness and harmonic waywardness, was the "fantasia" style. It was a style more often improvised than actually composed, as he tells us in his *Essay*, giving us a helpful reminder that the written music on which we base our historiography was still — is always — just the tip of the iceberg. Indeed, the vogue for *Empfindsamkeit* lent improvisation a new prestige, CPE strongly implying that the ability to improvise is the sine qua non of true musical talent: "It is quite possible for a person to have studied composition with good success and to have turned his pen to fine ends without his having any gift for improvisation. But, on the other hand, a good future in composition can be assuredly predicted for anyone who can improvise, provided that he writes profusely and does not start too late."[10]

A fantasia, then, might be characterized as a transcribed improvisation. J. S. Bach, a master improviser, wrote down only a few, notably a famous "Chromatic fantasia and fugue" in D minor. For him a fantasia was the equivalent of a prelude — not a fully viable piece in its own right but an introduction to a strict composition. CPE wrote down many more, especially in his later years, and was inclined, in the spirit of *Empfindsamkeit*, to regard them as freestanding, complete compositions. His most famous fantasia is the one in C minor, which he published as a *Probestück*, or "lesson piece," to illustrate the *Essay* in 1753. Its beginning is shown in Ex. 27-4. Its many dynamic indications show it to have been conceived specifically in terms of the clavichord or the pianoforte, which was just then coming into widespread use.

The recitative style is again invoked at the outset, but a recitative sung by a supersinger with a multioctave range. There is a purely conventional signature denoting "common time," but there are no bars and hence no measures to count, signaling (according to CPE's instructions in the *Essay*) a restlessly fluctuating tempo. Approximately halfway through the piece, however, a time signature of $\frac{3}{4}$ will supersede the original signature, bars will be measured out so that the new tempo (Largo) is to be strictly maintained, and what amounts to an "arioso" will temporarily succeed the recitative. Here the power of dynamics to delineate quick emotional changes comes into its own; rapid-fire alternations of *fortissimo* and *piano*, with the *fortissimos* on the off-beats, amount to virtual palpitations. Once again, by casting the fantasia in a recognizable vocal form and employing an idiom that apes the nuances of passionate singing, an

EX. 27-4   C. P. E. Bach, Fantasia in C minor

imaginary text is suggested, of which the music is the intensified expression, faithfully and "truthfully" tracking every fugitive shade of meaning and feeling.

So clearly does "empfindsamer" instrumental music aspire to the condition of speech-song in its emotional immediacy, and so convincingly does this fantasia conjure up an imaginary or internal theater, that in 1767 the poet Heinrich Wilhelm von Gerstenberg (1727–1823), a close friend of Klopstock and an acquaintance of the composer, was moved to furnish the fantasia with not one but two vocal lines that mainly doubled what was singable in the right-hand figuration. The first is fitted to a German translation of Socrates's speech before committing forced suicide in Plato's dialogue *Phaedo*; the second carries a paraphrase in fevered doggerel of the celebrated suicide soliloquy ("To be or not to be. . .") from Shakespeare's *Hamlet*. These texts, the most searingly emotional outpourings Gerstenberg could find in all of literature, are overlaid to the beginning of the fantasia in Ex. 27-5. The Shakespearean travesty runs as follows:

Seyn oder Nichtseyn,	To be or not to be:
Das ist die grosse Frage.	That is the great question.
Tod! Schlaf!	Death! Sleep!
Schlaf! und Traum!	Sleep! and dream!
Schwarzer Traum!	Black dream!
Todestraum!	Death dream!
	(Trans. Eugene Helm)

Invoking Shakespeare was a particularly pointed commentary on the *empfindsamer Stil*. Gerstenberg was a leader in the so-called *Sturm und Drang* ("Storm and stress") movement, a loose literary association that sought to exalt spontaneous subjectivity and unrestrained "genius" over accepted rules and standards of art. Shakespeare (discovered by the Germans in the 1760s, in translations by the poet Christoph Martin Wieland) was their hero, worshiped and emulated for the way in which his plays "freely" mixed prose and poetry, tragedy and comedy, elevated and lowly characters and diction in a manner that—compared to the "neoclassical" style of the French theater or the Metastasian opera seria—seemed to subvert all restraints in the name of unmediated passionate expression.

A style that combined the declamatory freedom of recitative with the concentrated expressivity of the new instrumental music and the semantic specificity of words would synthesize, and hence surpass, all previous achievements in drama and music, thought Gerstenberg. He certainly implied as much when describing his Shakespearean adaptation of CPE's fantasia in a letter to a friend:

> I assume, first, that music without words expresses only general ideas, and that the addition of words brings out its full meaning. . .. On this basis I have underlaid a kind of text to some Bach keyboard pieces which were obviously never intended to involve a singing voice, but Klopstock and everybody have told me that these would be the most expressive pieces for singing that could be heard. Under the fantasy in the Essay, for example, I put Hamlet's monologue as he fantasizes on life and death. A kind of middle condition of his shuddering soul is conveyed.[11]

And Carl Friedrich Cramer, a professor of classics who edited a music magazine where he published Gerstenberg's experiment in 1787, described it to his readers in terms that capture the very essence of *Sturm und Drang*, and that may even remind us of the theorizing that had attended the birth of opera two centuries before:

> I believe that this eccentric essay belongs among the most important innovations that have ever been conceived by a connoisseur, and that to a *thinking* artist, one who does not always cringe in slavery to tradition, it may be a divining rod

EX. 27-5   C. P. E. Bach, Fantasia in C minor with Shakespeare text overlaid by Gerstenberg

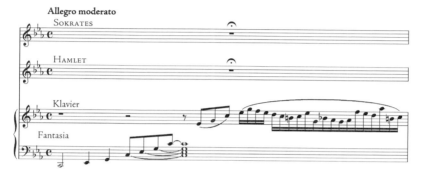

for discovering many deep veins of gold in the secret mines of music, in that it demonstrates in itself what can result from this dithyrambic union of instrumental and vocal music: an effect quite different from the customarily confined possibilities of self-willed forms and rhythms.[12]

But in an important and quite obvious sense both Gerstenberg and Cramer had missed the point. CPE Bach's intention, in creating his *empfindsamer Stil*, was not to express texts, however finely. For doing that, needless to say, there was plenty of precedent. Rather, his aim was to *transcend* texts—that is, to achieve a level of pure expressivity that language, bound as it was to semantic specifics, could never reach. This transcendently expressive music of which CPE was the fully self-conscious harbinger was later dubbed "absolute" music. It marked the first time that instrumental music was deemed to have decisively surpassed vocal music in spiritual content, and to be consequently more valuable as art.

And yet, to compound the paradox, the means by which the new instrumental music would transcend the vocal were nevertheless all borrowed from the vocal. To Gerstenberg himself, CPE once wrote that "the human voice remains preeminent"[13] as an expressive medium, and in his *Essay* he advises keyboard players to "miss no opportunity of hearing capable singers," for "from this one learns to think in terms of song."[14] Only thus can one translate one's ever fleeting, ever changing feelings into tones. And here at last we begin to get an inkling into the source of the tremendous metamorphosis in musical style and esthetics that took place over the course of the eighteenth century, ineluctably transforming the work of the Bach sons, along with everyone else's, and ineluctably opening up a gaping generation gap. The ferment was caused by opera. That was the "main evolution" to which Daniel Heartz drew attention.

But if the *empfindsamer Stil* was the most obviously and consciously "operatic" instrumental style of the period (taking "operatic" figuratively to mean intensely passionate and grandly eloquent), it was rather one-sidedly so. It placed emphasis on the formally unstable aspects of opera, particularly on recitative—musical "speech." (That is what can make it seem a throwback to the earliest days of opera, the days of the *seconda prattica* and the *stile rappresentativo*.) It was a kind of dramatic music that, as it happened, was practiced exclusively by composers who never wrote operas.

THE LONDON BACH

To see another side—a more direct and "purely musical" side—of opera's stylistic impact on instrumental music, we need to examine the work of a composer who wrote both operas and sonatas. And that means examining the work of one more son of JS Bach—the youngest one, Johann (or John) Christian (1735–82, henceforth "JC"), the half brother of WF and CPE, who by the end of his life was far and away the most famous of the eighteenth-century Bachs.

Unlike his elder brothers, and as we may remember from chapter 23, JC followed a career completely at variance with his father's. In some ways, in fact, it resembled Handel's—in its restlessness, in its worldliness, and even in its geographical trajectory.

His main teacher was his half brother CPE, with whom he went to live in Berlin after their father's death. In 1755, aged nineteen, he made the fateful trip to Italy. He took some additional instruction in Bologna from Giovanni Battista Martini (known as "Padre Martini"), a priest who was also a legendary music pedagogue; he found himself a patron in a Milanese count; and in 1760 he became an organist at Milan Cathedral, having first converted to Catholicism in order to qualify for the job. During the same year he wrote his first *opera seria*, *Artaserse*, to Metastasio's libretto (see chapter 23). From there he was summoned to Naples, the very nerve center of the *opera seria*, and in 1762 received an invitation to compose for the King's Theatre in London, Handel's old stamping ground.

FIG. 27-4   Portrait of J. C. Bach by Thomas Gainsborough.

Just as in Handel's day, music in London was to a larger extent than anywhere else a public, commercial affair. JC's career followed the ups and downs of the market. Squeezed out of the opera scene for a while by a jealous rival, he got himself appointed music master to Queen Charlotte, the German-born wife of King George III. Not only did this gain him a royal stipend, it also gave him a privilege to publish his works. The most lucrative prospects for printed music lay in keyboard and chamber music for domestic use ("such as ladies can execute with little trouble," to quote Dr. Burney, an admiring friend of the composer).[15]

In another entrepreneurial venture, JC joined forces with Carl Friedrich Abel, a composer and viola da gamba virtuoso whose father had been the gambist at the Cöthen court during J. S. Bach's tenure as music director there, and who was also by chance living in London. Together they founded the British capital's most successful concert series, the "Bach-Abel Concerts," which lasted until JC's death. At the same time he maintained his ties with the opera stage — ties as much personal as professional, since he married an Italian soprano, Cecilia Grassi, the prima donna at the King's Theatre. His fame brought operatic commissions from the continent — notably from the famously musical court at Mannheim, in the Rhineland, and even from Paris, where he set some ancient librettos that had previously served Lully.

All in all, John Christian Bach was the most versatile — and for a while, the most fashionable — composer of his generation, turning out music in every contemporary medium and for every possible outlet. Like Handel, he could boast of being a self-made man. But unlike Handel, he did not die a wealthy one. His last years were marked by several reverses in fortune and the declining popularity of his music. He died so deeply in debt that it took the queen's intervention to get him decently buried and enable his widow to return home to Italy.

FIG. 27-5   Portrait of Carl Friedrich Abel by Thomas Gainsborough.

John Christian Bach's first set of six keyboard sonatas was his opus 5 ("for the Piano Forte or Harpsichord" as the title page stipulates), printed in London in 1768. The second item in the set, sampled in Ex. 27-6, is in D major, a brilliant orchestral key in which strings and brass alike were at their most naturally resonant. The sonata catches a bit of that brilliance. It sounds like a transcribed orchestral piece—more specifically, like a transcribed operatic overture of a kind JC had composed by then in quantity. (It was literally child's play for the fifteen-year-old Mozart, already an experienced composer—and who had already met John Christian Bach in London during one of his early concert tours as an infant prodigy—to "restore" the sonata to full orchestral dress a few years later in the guise of a piano concerto.)

In style the sonata is in the purest "galant" idiom, witty and ingratiating. The balanced phrases and short-range contrasts that we have observed in the sonatas of JC's half brothers have become even more pronounced, to the point where they were regarded as J. C. Bach's personal signature. "Bach seems to have been the first composer who observed the law of *contrast* as a *principle*," wrote Dr. Burney in his *History*, exaggerating only slightly.[16] "Before his time, contrast there frequently was, in the works of others, but it seems to have been merely accidental," he went on (exaggerating a bit more, perhaps, in his enthusiasm), whereas Bach "seldom failed, after a rapid and noisy passage to introduce one that was slow and soothing."

And so it certainly is at the outset of JC's first movement (Ex. 27-6a): two bars of loud chordal fanfare followed immediately by two bars of soft continuous music, followed next by a balancing repetition of the whole four-bar complex. Contrast and balance operate in other dimensions as well: the loud bars describe an octave's descent, for example, while the soft ones describe an octave's ascent; the loud bars are confined to the tonic harmony, for another example, while the soft ones intermix tonic and dominant. Meanwhile the texture is the work of a composer who seems (despite his surname) never to have heard of counterpoint. It is, throughout and in many different (contrasting) ways, the kind of texture we nowadays call "homophonic," consisting of a well-defined melody against an equally well-defined accompaniment.

In overall form the sonata meets what by now must be our expectation: all three movements are binary structures. But the ways in which that same "there and back" structure is delineated differ very tellingly each time. The first movement, by far the

EX. 27-6A   J. C. Bach, Sonata in D, Op. 5, no. 2 (facsimile of original print), first page

EX. 27-6A   (*continued*)

EX. 27-6B   J. C. Bach, Sonata in D, Op. 5, no. 2, second page

EX. 27-6B   (continued)

longest, manages to cram a huge amount of finely contrasted and balanced material into its generous yet orderly unfolding. How that orderliness is achieved despite that abundance is the fascinating thing to observe. It is what made J. C. Bach the greatly influential figure that he was. Notwithstanding all appearances of profligacy, the movement is a study in economy and efficiency.

The arresting fanfare idea heard at the outset, for example, is heard only once again (not counting its "automatic" repetition as part of the unwritten sectional repeat) — namely, at the "double return." Despite its small share of the movement's running time, its strategic placement lends it an enormous structural importance, for it serves both to launch the movement's harmonic trajectory and to signal its completion. It thus plays the defining role in articulating a musical form that is equally the product of thematic and harmonic processes. The shape of the movement depends on our recognition of significant melodic and harmonic goals, and on our noticing their achievement. The "fanfare" theme is there to facilitate that recognition, and that makes it the movement's mainspring.

A similar functional efficiency characterizes all the other themes and melodic ideas in the movement. It is as if the older motivic (and "affective") prodigality we noticed and admired in the work of JC's brother WF — short-range contrast as its own reward — had been sorted and organized by JC into a higher and more energetic unity by assigning roles to each component. Thus the new idea — arpeggios in the left hand accompanied by tremolandos in the right — that follows at m. 9 introduces an unbroken span that lasts an asymmetrical ten bars until the next silent beat or caesura, and that seems to have as its assigned task the progressive introduction of new leading tones (first G♯, then D♯) along the circle of fifths so as to accomplish the "there" of the "there and back" on which all binary forms depend. It is the caesura (a term borrowed from poetry, where it means an empty foot) that serves to mark the arrival at the new tonic, A, in m. 19. Silence plays as important a role in articulating the form of a piece like this as the notes ever do.

We have seen this "modulatory" maneuver countless times by now, in arias, concertos, suites, and sonatas; but we have never before seen anyone make such a look-Ma-I'm-modulating production of it as here. From this point (m. 19) to the double bar, the music is stably in the key of A major. Stable tonality implies stable (that is, symmetrical) phrase structures, and so we are not surprised to find at this point a new, full-blown melody — the longest self-contained musical "section" in the piece so far — whose tuneful abundance is artfully organized into balanced "antecedent" and "consequent" phrases.

Its opening section, four bars ending with a caesura at m. 22, can be broken down into two sequential halves, the first ending with a piquant "lombard" rhythm, the second with a half cadence (i.e., a cadence on the dominant). Phrases ending on the dominant, requiring continuation, are "antecedents"; their balancing "consequents," as here, often begin like repetitions (compare the beginnings of m. 19 and m. 23), creating "parallel periods." The four balancing bars (mm. 23–26) also end with a half cadence, requiring yet another phrase to reach the (local) tonic.

This requirement is met — or (alternatively) this function is supplied; or (yet another way of putting it) this role is played — by a new eight-bar phrase (mm. 27 – 34), itself full of contrasts and balances, to balance the first. Its first four bars consist of two quick (one-measure) upward sweeps balanced by a slow (two-measure) undulating descent. The concluding four, which also break down into 1 + 1 + 2, finally bring back the A-major triad in root position, which alone can mark a "closure." From here on it's confirmation all the way: a pair of contrasting two-bar phrases, immediately repeated for a total of eight measures, that regularly reapproach the (local) tonic, reinforcing the sense of arrival and, finally, of closure (for which purpose a witty reference is made to the opening chordal idea).

To sum up the contents of Ex. 27-6a, the first half of the movement: it does what all such binary openings do, but does it in a newly dramatic and functionally differentiated way. Four main melodic/harmonic "areas" can be distinguished, which contrast and balance one another just as they are themselves made up of internal contrasts and balances:

1. The first eight measures, in which the tonic and dominant of the main key are introduced and alternated, provide the harmonic launching pad.

2. The next ten measures (asymmetrically divided 7 + 3) accomplish a "bridging" or "modulatory" function; the fact that their purpose is basically connective is equally apparent from their harmonic instability and from their melodic asymmetry. The two factors are always interdependent.

3. The next sixteen measures reestablish harmonic stability (in a new area) and melodic symmetry: the first eight are a parallel period that ends on a half cadence. They are balanced by eight bars ending on a full cadence.

4. The last eight measures, which contrast two-by-two and balance four-by-four, confirm arrival and effect closure. Now it is time to come "back" via the FOP. Again the familiar process unfolds through a remarkable diversity of material, but an equally remarkable functional organization.

The first thing heard after the double bar is a new melody (see Ex. 27-6b) over a characteristic arpeggiated accompaniment (three-note chords broken low-high-middle-high) that has been known ever since the eighteenth century as the "Alberti bass" after Domenico Alberti (d. 1746), an Italian composer who famously abused it. At first the new tune seems to be a stable melody in the dominant, but it makes its cadence after a telltale five measures, and its lack of symmetry is enhanced by the way the expected caesura is elided at its conclusion. Another obviously "modulatory" phrase of four bars impinges at that moment ("obviously" modulatory because it is modeled on the bridging material from the first half). It leads through a bass A♯ to an eight-bar melody consisting of a loud four-bar phrase and its echo that fully establishes a cadence on B minor (vi), the expected FOP.

And just as a four-bar bridge and a brief but full-blown symmetrical melody had led away from the dominant to the FOP, the same melodic complex leads from the FOP to the "double return." Note particularly how A, the dominant pitch, is sustained as a pedal through the whole eight-bar melody (mm. 65–73) that immediately precedes the return, creating a harmonic tension demanding especial relief. The double return palpably *impends*, creating the kind of suspense we associate with drama. Once again we may say that a familiar form is being newly "dramatized."

From the double return to the end of the movement, the music consists entirely of material introduced in the first half. Indeed, except for the shrinking of the bridge material (since it is no longer needed for modulatory purposes), the music is a veritable replay of the first half, with all the tunes stably confined to the tonic key, thus creating a sense of structural balance, of melodic invention governed by harmonic function, at the very longest possible range.

What we have just traced could be described, then, as a "maximized" binary form, in which harmonic departures and arrivals are dramatized and elaborated by drawing on a seemingly inexhaustible melodic well. The melodies draw on a common fund of figures and turns: note, for example, how the "new" material immediately after the double bar employs a skipping "lombard" heard previously (compare m. 20 with m. 43). But the dominant impression is one of maximum variety of material organized by the overriding harmonic motion into a maximum unity of concept.

The remaining movements of the sonata, like most sonata movements of the "Bach's sons" generation, are also cast in binary form—but not in the "maximized" version that gives the first movement (like most first movements, beginning with J. C. Bach) its special preeminent character. The second movement reverts to a procedure much closer to that of Bach the Father: the two halves closely mirror one another melodically as they trace the customary tonal progression, beginning and ending similarly though with reversed harmonic poles, and differing chiefly in the middle, where the second half makes its customary deflection toward the FOP—no actual cadence this time but just a chromatic color: an augmented-sixth harmony over ♭VI (E-flat).

The last movement, while also cast in a seemingly familiar traditional form—a pair of minuets (old-style *galanteries*), the second (marked "Minore") in the parallel minor—actually displays an interestingly novel feature. Like the first movement (and unlike any actual binary dance movement we have as yet encountered) both minuets sport "double returns" in their second halves. The functional association of theme with key has truly become a standard form-defining feature. Another feature that has (or will shortly) become standard is the substitution of III (the so-called relative major) as opposite harmonic pole for pieces in the minor mode, such as the second minuet.

SOCIABILITY MUSIC

Although it is notoriously easy to overdraw such matters, comparison of the sonata by C. P. E. Bach with that of his younger half brother shows up the two complementary sides of what might be called the "bourgeois" or "domestic" music of the mid-eighteenth century. Stylistically and formally they are similar enough, but "attitudinally" they contrast markedly. CPE's is solitary, introspective, "inner-directed" music; JC's is sociable, outgoing. The one explores personal, private, even unexpressed feelings; we easily imagine it performed for an audience of one (or even none but the player, seated

FIG. 27-6 "French concert" (actually a salon). Engraving by Duclos after a painting by St.-Aubin.

at the clavichord), late at night, in a mood of emotional self-absorption. It implies a surrounding hush. The other is party music, implying bright lights, company, a surrounding hubbub of conversation. That about sums up the difference between *Empfindung* and *galanterie*, and it is no accident that the one word is German and the other French.

It was the spirit of *galanterie* — conviviality, pleasant "causerie" (another French word in international use) — that gave rise to what we now call chamber music in its modern sense. The first pieces of this kind, in fact, grew directly out of the keyboard sonata, and it happened first in France. The earliest composers to attempt the transformation of keyboard sonatas into sociable ensembles were a couple of forgotten Parisian violinists: Jean-Joseph Cassanéa de Mondonville (1711–72) and Louis-Gabriel Guillemain (1705–70).

Their inclinations are well illustrated by the titles of Guillemain's sonata sets: *Premier amusement à la mode* (op. 8, 1740), for example, or *Six sonates en quators ou conversations galantes et amusantes* (op. 12, 1743). (In light of these titles, it is irresistible to mention that, in the words of the sonata-historian William S. Newman, Guillemain was "a neurotic, alcoholic misanthrope, who could not bring himself to perform in public, squandered his better-than-average earnings, and finally

FIG. 27-7 Jean-Joseph Cassanea de Mondonville, by Maurice Quentin de la Tour.

took his own life."[17] In this case, anyway, the style was not the man.) These were still old-fashioned continuo pieces, but as early as 1734 Mondonville—whose wife Anne Jeanne Boucon was a well-known harpsichordist who had studied with Rameau—took a decisive and much-imitated step in the name of *galanterie* that completely reversed the textural perspective. He published as his opus 3 a set of *Pièces de clavecin en sonates avec accompagnement de violon*, "harpsichord pieces grouped into sonatas, accompanied by a violin." What he offered merely as a piquant novelty quickly took root as a new musical genre. By the 1760s it had turned into a craze that finally marked curtains for the basso continuo style.

The "accompanied keyboard sonata" initiated by Mondonville was (in theory, at least) a fully composed, self-sufficient keyboard sonata to which an obbligato for the violin or flute could be added *ad libitum*. In theory this was something that could be done to any keyboard sonata, and there is evidence that accompanied sonatas existed for some time as a "performance practice" before the first expressly composed specimens saw the light. Indeed, we have already seen an instance—Couperin's "Le rossignol-en-amour" (Ex. 25-12)—where a composer explicitly suggested turning one of his keyboard pieces into an ensemble piece by giving its melody part to a flute.

In practice, from the very earliest composed specimens, the "accompanying" part added something indispensable to the texture, turning the piece into a true duo, to which a cello or viol could be added to double and lightly embellish the bass line, making a trio. Unlike Guillemain's continuo pieces, the result was a "conversation galante et amusante" for truly equal conversational partners, each with a melodic life of its own. As the excerpt in Ex. 27-7 from the minuet in Mondonville's fourth accompanied sonata shows, even at this early stage the texture is quite different from that of J. S. Bach's trio sonatas with obbligato harpsichord. There is no imitative polyphony, for one thing; the bass figuration shows Alberti-ish tendencies, for another; and for a third (possibly most crucial) thing, the texture is not so clearly laid out in contrapuntal "voices." The two hands of the harpsichord frequently combine in parallel motion to become a single "voice," and the violin (especially at such moments) is apt to dip beneath and take over the "bass."

Mondonville's earliest imitators were Rameau, his musical father-in-law (whose 1741 collection of *Pièces de clavecin en concert* for harpsichord solo and two obbligato parts contains a sarabande called "La Boucon," dedicated to Mondonville's wife), and Guillemain, who published a collection exactly modeled on Mondonville's, and identically titled, in 1745.

By the 1760s, accompanied keyboard sonatas were being written everywhere, and J. C. Bach and his London cohort Abel had become preeminent in the genre, of all musical forms and media the most quintessentially galant. In fact, JC published exactly twice as many accompanied keyboard sonatas (forty-eight) as unaccompanied ones, which gives an idea of the genre's quick ascendancy, a rise that testifies above all to its social utility. Even CPE was moved to try his hand at this profitable genre, but half-heartedly; according to a famous quip of JC's (like all such reported comments, possibly apocryphal), "my brother lives to compose and I compose to live."[18] It

EX. 27-7   Jean-Joseph Cassanéa de Mondonville, Accompanied Sonata in C, Op. 3, no. 4

would be hard to come up with a better encapsulation of *Empfindsamkeit* vis-à-vis *galanterie*!

For a last mid-century sonata let us turn to the fourth item in Abel's opus 2, a set of *Six Sonatas for the Harpsichord with Accompaniments for a Violin or German* [i.e., transverse or modern] *Flute and Violoncello*, published in London (with a dedication to the Earl of Buckinghamshire) in 1760. The style will be familiar from JC's sonata, but the piece is shorter, simpler, more schematic. There are only two movements, a moderately "expanded" or maximized binary followed by a minuet. This is commercial fare par excellence.

The principle of contrast is taken to such an extreme at the beginning of the first movement (Ex. 27-8a) as to amount practically to a spoof—"ingenious jesting with art," as Domenico Scarlatti, *galant avant la lettre* (galant before it had a name), might have said. The tonic is established with a deliberately over-pompous four-measure fanfare in orchestral style, thumped out with octaves in the bass. It is followed by a three-bar transition to a half cadence, after which the key, the texture, and even the scoring (thanks to the entrance of the obbligato) all change suddenly: a long, lyrical, legato melody in two distinct halves, cast in the key of the dominant and accompanied by a counterpoint-dissolving Alberti bass.

EX. 27-8A   Carl Friedrich Abel, Sonata in B-flat, Op. 2, no. 4, first movement, mm. 1–11

EX. 27-8B   Carl Friedrich Abel, Sonata in B-flat, Op. 2, no. 4 (facsimile of original print), end of second movement

The second half embarks on its journey from the dominant to the tonic with a reference to the opening fanfare—treating it, in other words, in the manner of a ritornello. Thus invoking or alluding to the concerto genre is another way of jesting ingeniously. This time the fanfare dissolves into a new melody whose job it is to lead (through some chromatic harmony and some asymmetrical phrase lengths) to the FOP, in this case D minor (iii), articulated by a reference to the second part of the lyrical theme introduced before the double bar.

The D minor cadence is followed unceremoniously by a brusque return to the tonic through the briefest of transitional motives in the bass. When the tonic arrives, of course, so does the opening fanfare (ritornello), and the movement proceeds to its conclusion through an only slightly abbreviated replay of the whole first half of the movement, the only differences being the omission of the no longer necessary transition to the dominant half cadence (mm. 5–7 in Ex. 27-8a) and the transposition of the long lyrical tune from its original pitching in the key of the dominant to the tonic. The second half of the piece could be described as containing virtually the whole first half, plus a bridging section devoted to harmonic caprice.

The minuet is about as ingratiating, unproblematic, and "popular" as the composer could have made it. The first half does not even leave the tonic; it consists of two parallel periods, the first ending on a half cadence, the second on a full—the sort of thing called "open" and "closed" as far back as the Middle Ages and still common in the eighteenth century in folk (i.e., "popular") tunes, of which Abel's minuet thus counts as a sort of sophisticated—or, in the etymological sense, "urbane"—imitation. Because the first half does not leave the tonic, the dominant can function in the second half as the FOP. There are no cadences at all on secondary functions, just an occasional whiff of chromaticism (including a lone diminished seventh) on the way to the last dominant cadence.

When the piece is effectively complete, the composer tacks on a 16-bar coda (Ex. 27-8b) over a satisfying tonic pedal, reasserting both tonal and rhythmic stability at maximum strength. The whole passage might as well have been written for the sake of this book, to provide a demonstration of phrase symmetry. The sixteen bars are really eight plus an exact repetition, and each eight breaks down to four plus four, in which the first four consists of a two-bar plagal cadence and its literal repetition, and the second four consists of the very same plagal cadence joined to an authentic one. More naively "natural" than this—as opposed to cunningly "artificial"—music could hardly get. (But of course to be this "natural" takes a lot of artifice.) It is in the second half of the minuet, by the way, that the harpsichord and the "accompanying" instrument get to engage in a bit of dialogue (the only imitative or even contrapuntal writing in the whole sonata), effectively precluding a performance of the piece as a straight keyboard sonata. It is genuine chamber music for actual chamber (that is, domestic) use, and its style and tone are wholly typical of the genre in its earliest stage.

"NATURE"

But whence this cult of the "natural"? And where, once and for all, did the style we have been tracking in this chapter originate? We still have not traced this very important river to its source, for all the hints and suggestions thrown out along the way. Far from solving the historical problem (the problem of the "black hole") with which we launched this chapter, all we have been doing is restating it over and over again, *da capo*, with variations and embellishments.

As the very existence of the "Alberti bass" already suggests, there was a slightly earlier but mainly concurrent repertoire of sonatas by Italian composers who deserted the violin family for the keyboard. Their work may indeed be compared with the music of the Bach sons and their friends, and has often been cited as its main model. Besides Alberti himself, whose name mainly lives on thanks to the term associated with it, the most famous member of this group was the Venetian opera composer Baldassare Galuppi (1706–85), a major international figure, who left in addition to his stage works almost one hundred keyboard sonatas of which only a fraction were published, mainly in two books of six issued by the London publisher John Walsh in the late 1750s.

In style, Galuppi's sonatas (and Alberti's, too) are eminently galant (see Ex. 27-9): their textures are homophonic, replete with arpeggiated basses and similar figurations;

they consist of two or three movements, almost uniformly in binary form; and the keyboardists proceed not by spinning out motives in great waves and sequences in the manner of the older violinists (or their best pupil, Bach the Father), but through short-breathed contrast and balance, and through lyrical, symmetrically laid-out and cadentially articulated melodies. Their evident model was not tireless bowing, but graceful singing. And what else would one expect from composers who worked mainly for the stage?

EX. 27-9A   Domenico Alberti, Sonata in C, Op. 1, no. 3 (London, 1748), mm. 1–4.

EX. 27-9B   Baldassare Galuppi, Sonata no. 2 (London, 1756), I, mm. 69–79

Once again we are returned to opera as source of it all; but now, having named Galuppi, we are in a position to make a more positive and specific identification of the operatic source. Beginning in the 1740s, Galuppi was the first major international protagonist of a new operatic genre, one that he and his main librettist Carlo Goldoni called *dramma giocoso* ("humorous drama"), but that took Europe by storm (and is now remembered) as *opera buffa*—from *buffo*, Italian for buffoon or clown. If the *opera seria*

was a form of nobly sublimated musical tragedy, *opera buffa* was musical comedy — the earliest form of full-fledged comic opera.

Here at last is where the body, as the saying goes, is buried. Here is the great stylistic transformer of European music, the spark that ignited what Daniel Heartz called the "main evolution" that somehow managed to take place behind the backs of Bach the Father and Handel. In the comic opera lies the common source for all the musical styles we have been tracking, even the nominally melancholy *empfindsamer Stil*. And as we shall see, by the late eighteenth century, *opera buffa* would decisively replace (or more precisely, displace) the *seria* as the most vital — and even serious! — form of musical theater.

But to appreciate the role of "humorous drama" as a hotbed of stylistic transformation or a plugger of historical holes, which after all is what we have set out to do in this chapter, we must look beyond it to its own antecedents. Then we shall have a proper starting point from which to tell at least the beginnings of a coherent story about the musical eighteenth century, and its relationship to the general social and intellectual currents of the time. One more flashback is necessary.

INTERMISSION PLAYS

During opera's first century, especially at the public theaters of Venice (and as we have known since chapter 20), it was considered good form to mix serious and comic scenes and characters, producing a kind of heterogeneous "Shakespearean" drama that afforded audiences the very utmost in varied entertainment. Then the reformers got to work. Seeking to restore the dignity of the earliest "neoclassical" (courtly) operas and justify the genre in light of classical poetic theory, librettists began to regard comic scenes as breaches of taste. Such scenes were banished, at first by the high-minded dilettantes who ran the learned academies, finally by the frosty Metastasio.

But what is kicked out the front door often climbs back in through the window. The public, especially in Venice, was unwilling to give up a favorite operatic treat — nor, more to the point, were they willing to forgo the pleasure of seeing and hearing their favorite *buffi*, many of whom had large followings. So a curious compromise was reached. The newly standardized *opera seria* remained free of any taint of comedy, but little comic plays with music were shown during the intermissions. These, naturally enough, were called intermezzos ("intermission plays"). They were usually in two little acts (called *parte*, "parts") to supply the intermissions required by a typical three-act *opera seria*, and almost always featured two squabbling characters, a soprano and a bass, these being the most typical ranges for *buffi*. Often enough they were at first loosely based on the comedies of Molière or his many imitators.

The first set of intermezzos for which a libretto survives was given in Venice in 1706 (it was called *Frappolone e Florinetta* after its bickering pair). Immediately specialist librettists and composers sprang up for the genre, and it assumed a very particular style. It is that style, which directly reflected the strange nature of the relationship between the intermezzos and their host operas, that played such a colossal — and entirely unforeseen — role in the evolution of eighteenth-century music. We have already seen some of the unforeseen products of that evolution. Their existence is the famous "problem" we have been addressing. Here, at last, are the beginnings of a solution to it, based on recent investigations and speculations by a number of scholars, particularly Piero Weiss and Wye J. Allanbrook, who have made progress at filling the black hole.[19]

The first big international hit scored by an intermezzo composer was *Il marito giocatore e la moglie bacchettona* ("The gambler husband and the domineering wife") by Giuseppe Maria Orlandini (1676–1760), a Florentine composer active in Bologna who was even older than Bach the Father, and who actually spent most of his life composing *opera seria* to lofty "Arcadian" libretti. The set contains three intermezzos, each depicting an episode in the rocky married life of the title characters: in the first, the wife, exasperated at the husband's behavior, resolves to divorce him; in the second the husband, disguised as the judge at the divorce court, promises to find in the wife's favor if she will sleep with him and, after she agrees, reveals himself and throws her out of the house; in the third, the wife comes back disguised as a mendicant pilgrim and soothes the husband into a reconciliation.

First performed in 1715 (as *Bajocco e Serpilla*, after the names of the title characters), Orlandini's intermezzos made the rounds of all the Italian theaters as actual intermission features, and, performed in sequence as a sort of three-act comic opera in their own right, conquered foreign capitals as well, reaching London (as *The Gamester*) in 1737, and Paris (as *Il giocatore*) as late as 1752. Everywhere it made a sensation. Perhaps the aria in which the distraught husband hurls imprecations at his wife will show why (Ex. 27-10).

In keeping with the strictest Aristotelian principles, according to which tragedy portrayed "people better than ourselves" and comedy "people worse than ourselves," this aria is "low" music with a perfect vengeance.[20] Everything about it is impoverished. The texture is reduced to unisons. The vocal line is reduced to barely articulate ejaculations of rage. The melody is reduced to asthmatic gasping and panting with insistently repeated cadences that prevent phrases from achieving any length at all. The structure is reduced to a patchwork or mosaic of these little sniffles, snorts, and wheezes. It might be thought a mere parody, and so the music of the early intermezzos is often described. And yet it came, *particularly to foreign audiences*, as a revelation.

One of the most precious testimonials to that revelation came from the pen of Denis Diderot, the famous French encyclopedist,

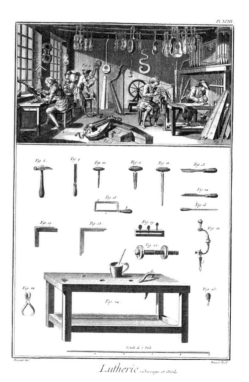

FIG. 27-8 "Instrument making" (*Lutherie*) from Diderot's *Encyclopédie*.

435

EX. 27-10 Bajocco's aria from Giuseppe Maria Orlandini's *Il giocatore*

in his satire *Rameau's Nephew*, written early in the 1760s, while the elder Rameau was still alive.

From the mouth of this fictional character (albeit based on a real person, a nephew of the great French composer who plied a modest trade as a music teacher and who had a considerable reputation in society as a "character"), Diderot voiced the widespread amazement of French artists and thinkers at the art of the *buffi*: "What realism! What expression!" he exclaims. And to those who might scoff — "Expression of what?!" — he spells it out with ardor bordering on anger, and with characteristically bizarre imagery:

> It is the animal cry of passion that should dictate the melodic line, and these moments should tumble out quickly one after the other, phrases must be short and the meaning self-contained, so that the musician can utilize the whole and each part, varying it by omitting a word or repeating it, adding a missing word, turning it this way and that like a polyp, but without destroying it.[21]

What the fictionalized nephew of Rameau is describing here is nothing other than the revolutionary new style of musical discourse we began investigating with the music of Bach's sons: short phrases that are musically and expressively self-contained so that they may be balanced and contrasted, so that they can express emotions the way they really present themselves in the real physical — or "animal" — world: the natural world.

The strange reference to the "polyp" is the most telling touch of all. In the eighteenth century the word referred not to a tumorous growth but to a class of marine animals that included the octopus and the squid — animals with soft, amorphous bodies and many feet. They were a symbol of changeability: an association, as Allanbrook has pointed out, that resonates with the more familiar word "protean," also nautical, which comes from Proteus, the Old Man of the Sea in Greek mythology, who could change himself into any shape he pleased.

It was its protean changeability — the very quality we have already isolated as the essential, inexplicable newness of mid-century instrumental music — that, coupled with its freshness and its elemental simplicity, gave the lowly comic music of the intermezzos its air of perfect naturalness and made it so influential. In an age that still regarded the nature and purpose of art as imitation of nature, this could be viewed as an improved art. Comparing Orlandini's imitation of rage with Handel's in *Vivi, tiranno!* (Ex. 26-1), we can be struck anew by its directness, compared with which Handel's elaborate melismas on the emblematic word *furore* can seem the height of stilted "baroque" contrivance.

The grand Handelian rhetoric stood revealed as the product of labored, unnatural artifice. Orlandini's simple syllabic setting with its frequent repeated notes and wide vocal leaps was "the animal cry of passion," intensified by an orchestral accompaniment that in its close tracking of the vocal part seemed to mirror not only the singing but even the gestures of the actor. The art of tragedy was the high rhetorical style. The low art of comedy was born of nature. It was "true." The music of change in the eighteenth century — Heartz's "main evolution" — was the music of comedy. What we have already traced has been its transfer into the wordless medium, which it transformed into another medium of nature and truth. The later eighteenth-century style was in effect the comic style.

THE "WAR OF THE BUFFOONS"

The great masterwork of the intermezzo genre — if such a contradiction in terms can be admitted — was *La serva padrona* ("The servant mistress") by the precocious Giovanni Battista Pergolesi (1710–36), a Neapolitan, who died of consumption at the age of 26 and who became, for that reason among others, a figure of enduring romantic fame. In his short life (with an active career lasting only five years) Pergolesi managed to compose ten works for the stage, of which four were *opere serie* (two to texts by Metastasio) and three were two-part intermezzos.

La serva padrona, written expressly to be played between the acts of one of Pergolesi's own *serie*, was first performed with it at the Teatro San Bartolomeo on 5 September 1733 in honor of the birthday of Elisabeth Christina, the consort of the Austrian Emperor Charles VI, then nominal ruler of Naples. The evening's main event, *Il prigioniero superbo* ("The proud prisoner"), was soon forgotten. The intermezzo, however, quickly became world famous, at first thanks to performances by traveling troupes of *buffi* who within ten years of its first performance took it all around Italy and as far away as Munich, Dresden, and even Hamburg in the north of Germany.

By the end of the 1740s it had been heard in Paris, and by the end of the '50s it had conquered London, St. Petersburg, and Madrid. And as we can tell from its printed librettos, it was (with a single main exception) still being performed then pretty much intact, the way it was originally written. That was extremely unusual for any opera in the eighteenth century, but particularly for a "low" piece. It means that the work was already regarded as a classic, a work exemplifying its type to perfection. And so it remains: *La serva padrona* is still occasionally performed and recorded as a two-act opera, the earliest comic opera in the standard repertory.

Its plot and cast of characters are of the usual kind. There are two sung roles, Serpina (soprano) and her master and guardian Uberto (bass), plus a mute role (Vespone, another servant) who gets to laugh once. The importance of conventions even to this supposedly "natural" genre is epitomized by the heroine's name.

FIG. 27-9A Caricature, ca. 1734, of Giovanni Battista Pergolesi, by Pier Leone Ghezzi. This is the only extant depiction of the composer from life.

Like Serpilla in *Il marito giocatore* it comes from *serpe* (snake), identifying Serpina as another "sharp-tongued" female, a stock figure ultimately derived from the old improvised *commedia dell'arte*, the traditional theater of masks and clowns. Her sharp tongue is the source of a great deal of the fast-paced patter that made the comic style so irresistible.

Both scenes contain little arias for each of the characters and a culminating duet. In the first, the master frets and stews over the maid's insolent behavior, finally ordering Vespone to go out and find him a wife. Serpina orders Uberto to marry her; he won't hear of it; she locks the doors to prevent Vespone from leaving, and the two of them erupt in sarcastic bickering. In the second, Serpina disguises Vespone as "Capitan Tempesta" ("Captain Storm"), her threatening bully of a fiancé,

FIG. 27-9B   Late eighteenth-century portrait of Pergolesi, done after his early death had made him a figure of romantic legend.

who is demanding from Uberto an impossible dowry. The only way out of a fight with the captain, she insinuates, is for him to agree to marry her himself. After a lot of coaxing and some agonized reflection, he gives in; Vespone removes his disguise; Uberto's been had, but he's happy. The newly engaged couple sing a duet of reconciliation.

Ex. 27-11 contains a sampling from the second half of the second intermezzo, beginning with Serpina's coaxing aria, "A Serpina penserete" ("Think of Serpina!"). She addresses Uberto to the strains of a melting *larghetto*; the repetitive bass, marking at least two cadences every measure, "truly" mimics the affection of cajolery. In between her approaches to Uberto, however, Serpina addresses us, the spectators, through ironic asides, set as perky little jigs of joy, in which she throws off her mask and revels in the effect she is having (Ex. 27-11a). This was a new dramatic situation for opera, and a new musical effect: contrast as irony—the very essence of comedy—replaces the "unity of affect" in which the *opera seria* had found its version of truth. Here we see the psychological, dramatic, and representational roots of the contrast-and-balance technique that became the universal stylistic medium of art music by century's end.

Uberto's little "tizzy aria," "Son imbrogliato io già" ("I'm really all snarled up"), is also full of irony. There is only one meter and tempo this time, but the whole joke of the piece lies in the contrast between his opening "fret motive" in eighth notes at a breakneck, practically unsingable tempo—a rapid-patter effect that became the very hallmark of the *basso buffo*—and his periodic attempts to take himself in hand, intoning in stately whole notes, "Uberto, pensa a te" (Uberto, think of yourself!), as if in ironic answer to Serpina. At those moments, the music slips into rather "distant" parallel-minor tonalities—another jokey contrast that became a standard operating procedure by century's end. A tantalizing question is whether there is any dramatic significance in the fact that the drolly repetitive cadential bass that underlies Uberto's fretting is the same as the one that underlaid Serpina's blandishments in the preceding aria. Or was it just a cliché of the style—one of the allurements that made it so popular and, for all its levity, so weighty in history?

The final lovers' duet, with its adorably silly imitations of Serpina's little heart-hammer and Uberto's thumping heart-drum, was originally composed for another opera of Pergolesi's—his last one, a full-length *commedia musicale* called *Il Flaminio*. Its passages in parallel thirds (that is, tenths) served as well as the original finale to symbolize the "harmonious" resolution of the little domestic farce, and by the 1750s it had already become customary to replace the original giguelike finale with this no less affectionate, but funnier, duet.

EX. 27-11A   Giovanni Pergolesi, *La serva padrona*, Act II, Serpina's aria, mm. 8–18

EX. 27-11B Giovanni Pergolesi, *La serva padrona*, Act II, Uberto's aria, mm. 12–15, 31–39

This slightly revised version of *La serva padrona* was the one brought to Paris, along with Orlandini's *Giocatore* and a dozen other intermezzos and newfangled comic operas, by a troupe of *buffi* under the direction of a canny impresario named Eustachio Bambini, for a run beginning in August 1752. The furor they touched off with their performances, and the debates to which it led, had extraordinary repercussions in the French capital, and in all of its cultural satellites both in France and abroad. The so-called *Querelle des Bouffons* ("press controversy about the *buffi*" or, more literally, "War of the Buffoons"), with its stellar cast of characters, presaged not only musical but also social and political change.

Press wars had always been a feature of France's lively intellectual life. There had been one only shortly before between the "Lullistes" and the "Ramistes," proponents of Lully's and of Rameau's operas. And there would be later ones too (including one to which we will have to pay attention, between the "Gluckistes" and the "Piccinnistes"). Always there were political and social subtexts, because under an absolute monarchy, where political, religious, and social issues could not be debated openly, they had to go

FIG. 27-10   Jean-Jacques Rousseau, by Maurice Quentin de la Tour.

underground, into highly suggestive and allusive art and literary criticism, among other things, for discussion. Such covert argumentation, often called "Aesopian discourse" because of the unstated but obvious "moral," has been a feature of modern intellectual life in totalitarian societies ever since. A great deal of music criticism—and of music, too—has carried hidden messages since the eighteenth century, which, precisely because they are necessarily hidden, are ever subject to conflicting interpretation.

Diderot's pamphlet, *Rameau's Nephew*, which has already been quoted, may be viewed as an aftershock of the *Querelle des Bouffons*. One of the most powerful salvos was fired off by Jean-Jacques Rousseau, in a scathing "Letter on French Music,"

published in November 1753, which elicited more than thirty rejoinders. Rousseau gave no quarter, ridiculing the *tragédies lyriques* performed by the royal musical establishment as stilted, labored, devoid of naturalness, ugly in harmony, and ungainly in prosody (text-setting). He went so far as to maintain that there was not and could not be such a thing as a truly French opera, for the phrase, he asserted, was a veritable contradiction in terms.

An enthusiastic if rudimentarily trained amateur composer, Rousseau had geared up for his attack with a one-act "intermède" of his own, *Le devin du village* ("The Village Soothsayer"), composed in obvious emulation of the Italian intermezzos and performed at Fontainebleau, a Paris suburb, on 18 October 1752, only a couple of months after Bambini's *buffi* had made their début. Although written to a French text (his own), and in a style that recalled French folksongs (*pastourelles*) more than anything Italian, this was nevertheless "comic" music, intended as an object lesson to his musical countrymen.

Its typical pastoral plot, concerning the triumph of "natural" rustic virtue over courtly sophistication, was a somewhat more didactic version of the usual intermezzo triumph of pluck over rank. But it was Rousseau's only successful opera (previous attempts to write *tragédies lyriques* having brought him nothing but ridicule). It played both in France and abroad until the end of the century and even a little beyond. Despite its implied politics, its catchy tunes even made it a court favorite for a while. After hearing it, Louis XV was observed by his palace staff tunelessly humming the opening number (Ex. 27-12) for the rest of the day.

But Rousseau was much more than a musician. His appeals to natural virtue and his denigrations of the traditional musical repertoire of the royal court were linked: both were veiled expressions of his philosophical and political hostility to the monarchical order. Diderot, too, expressed otherwise unprintable liberal ideas through his fictionalized "nephew of Rameau," who wished to cast his detestable uncle's work wholesale into oblivion while reveling in "the modern style" of the Italians.

For "modern style" here, we can read "modern philosophy" between the lines. For the likes of Rousseau and Diderot, the *Querelle des Bouffons* was a covert forum for disseminating the complex of ideas now collectively referred to as "Enlightened." Rousseau came close to making all of this explicit in his *Confessions*, where he gloated that Bambini's *buffi* "struck a blow from which French opera never recovered." It could be claimed with equal (imperfect but pithy) justice that the *Querelle des Bouffons*, a long generation before the French revolution, struck the beginnings of a blow from which not only the *tragédie lyrique* but the absolutist monarchy itself never fully recovered.

But were Diderot's and Rousseau's reasons for welcoming the comic style the same as the average composer's? The average keyboard player's? The average concertgoer's or music buyer's? To what degree did the spread of the "comic style" in music coincide

EX. 27-12 Jean-Jacques Rousseau, *Le devin du village*, no. 1, "J'ai perdu mon serviteur"

with, or even abet, the spread of Enlightened philosophy? Did the philosophy carry the music in tow? Or did the music carry the philosophy? These are questions that can hardly be answered with any precision. But the reality of the connection between the music and the philosophy, avidly acknowledged and as avidly resisted at the time, can hardly be denied.

Enlightenment and Reform

THE OPERAS OF PICCINNI, GLUCK, AND MOZART

NOVELS SUNG ON STAGE

Throughout the eighteenth century, opera and its endless "reforms" continued to encode the social history of the age. That is why opera criticism so often makes good and exciting reading, even when the composers and the operas of which it treats have been long forgotten. Both by design and by its nature, it can mean far more than it says.

And again both by design and by its nature, the burgeoning comic opera continued to bear the heaviest freight of what is now called "subtext" (that is, the stuff you read between the lines) even as it continued to be "the best school for today's composers," in the words of the German musician Johann Adam Hiller (1728–1804), who reacted to it both as composer and as critic.[1] "Symphonies, concertos, trios, sonatas — all, nowadays, borrow something of its style," Hiller wrote in 1768.

The composer whom Hiller had first in mind was his exact contemporary Niccolò Piccinni (1728–1800), who certainly qualifies today as "long forgotten." In his day, however, Piccinni was not only a prominent figure but a controversial one as well. He became the focal point of a "cause" and, in his rivalry with the somewhat older (and today much better-remembered) Christoph Willibald Gluck (1714–87), the object of a *querelle*, a Parisian press war. The issues his career raised for contemporary audiences, critics, and composers continued to reverberate long after the decades of his greatest fame. They were issues of social as well as musical import.

The best way of approaching Piccinni's "cause" and its social repercussions might be to note that his most famous opera, *La buona figliuola* ("The good little girl," or "Virtuous maiden"), was one of the earliest to be based on a modern novel, then a new literary genre with distinct social implications of its own. The opera's success was virtually unprecedented: between its Roman première (with an all-male cast) in 1760 and the end of the eighteenth century, *La buona figliuola* played every opera house in Europe, enjoying more than seventy productions in four languages.

Its plot came by way of Samuel Richardson's *Pamela; or, Virtue Rewarded* (1740), a novel in the form of letters that tells of a chaste maidservant who so resourcefully resists the crass advances of her employer's son that the young man finally falls seriously in love with her and marries her with his family's blessing. *Pamela* achieved phenomenal popularity with a new class of readers, the same "bourgeois" readership that made the novel the paramount literary genre for centuries to come, and who were especially susceptible to Richardson's idealistic moral: to wit, that natural virtues and emotions—pertinacity, honesty, love—can be practiced both high and low, and can level artificial barriers of rank.

This is only a variation, of course, on an ancient pastoral prototype with which we have been familiar, so to speak, since the twelfth century. (Recall the pastorelas of the medieval troubadours, in which virtuous maids fend off or are rescued from lascivious aristocrats). But it was indeed a novel variation, and a telling one, this sentimental version in which the bar of class is actually overcome and maid and aristocrat find happiness together. For aristocrats, then, the moral "love conquers all" could be a socially ominous one. The eighteenth-century English novel was, among other things, a celebration—and, potentially, a breeding ground—of social mobility. The *Pamela* motif has been a stock-in-trade of bourgeois fiction ever since, though by now more a cliché of "romance novels" and soap operas (like *Our Gal Sunday*, a radio staple from the 1930s to the 1950s: "the program that asks the question, Can a young girl from a small mining town in West Virginia find happiness as the wife of a wealthy and titled Englishman?") than of serious fiction.

Richardson's novel was soon translated into Italian, and attracted the attention of Carlo Goldoni, whom we met briefly in the previous chapter as the chief librettist of the early *opera buffa*. Actually, librettos were only a sideline for Goldoni, the leading Italian dramatist of the century. His main mission in life, as he saw it, was replacing the old improvised *commedia dell'arte* with literary comedies that had fully worked-out scripts and modern realistic situations, worthy of comparison with Molière and Congreve, the mainstays of the French and English stage. Goldoni saw in *Pamela* the makings of a hit, but as often happened, some funny things happened to the story on its way to the stage.

The trouble was that an Italian audience would not have found the plot sufficiently believable. Nor could such a thing be shown in the theater, which, being a site of public assembly, was in Italy (as elsewhere) far more strictly policed by censors than the literary press. The sticking point was the happy ending—or rather, what made it happy. The elevation of a poor commoner through marriage was not possible in Italy. According to Italian law, such a marriage would bring about not the ennobling of the commoner but the disgrace and impoverishment of the noble.

Hence Goldoni was forced to find another motivation or excuse for the happy marriage. He found it in the device of mistaken identity: Pamela's father turns out to be not a poor schoolteacher but an exiled count, and so she can marry her noble lover with impunity. As Goldoni put it in the preface to his adaptation,

> The reward of virtue is the aim of the English author; such a purpose would please me greatly, but I would not want the propriety of our Families to be altogether sacrificed to the merit of virtue. Pamela, though base-born and common, deserves to be wed by a Nobleman; but a Nobleman concedes too much to the virtue of Pamela if he marries her notwithstanding her humble birth. It is true that in London they do not scruple to make such marriages, and no law there forbids them; nevertheless it is true that nobody would want his son, brother, or relative to marry a low-born woman rather than one of his own rank, no matter how much more virtuous and noble the former.[2]

The emphasis was thus shifted away from the potential disruption of traditional social norms, but the satisfaction of natural love in a happy marriage was nevertheless retained, and the story could still capture the imaginations of idealistic lovers. Whereas we may think the device of mistaken identity a threadbare stratagem, in the context of eighteenth-century continental society and its rules, the device made the story more realistic and convincing, not less.

When Goldoni finally adapted his *Pamela* adaptation as an opera libretto, he had to make even more changes in order to satisfy the musical requirements of the opera stage. Now Pamela (rechristened La Cecchina) and her pursuer (Il Marchese della Conchiglia) are in love from the beginning, at first hopelessly. They are the main soprano/tenor pair, and sing duets. The Marchese's sister, Lucinda, also based on a Richardson character, is there to oppose the social mismatch. She is given a lover (Il Cavaliere Armidoro) who threatens her with rejection if her brother takes a common wife. There is a *basso buffo*, Mengotto, a gardener in love with Cecchina, and a sharp-tongued servant girl, Sandrina, in love with Mengotto. (She also gets a sidekick, Paoluccia, with whom she sings gossipy patter duets.)

The last of the newly invented characters is the swashbucking German mercenary soldier Tagliaferro, another *basso buffo* who gets wheezy laughs by mangling Italian in a manner we first observed some two hundred years ago in Ex. 17-11, Orlando di Lasso's "Song of the Lansquenet." It is he who clears up the matter of Cecchina's parentage in the last scene. All the tangled pairs are sorted out, and multiple happy weddings are forecast: Cecchina with the Marchese; Lucinda with the Cavaliere; Mengotto with Sandrina. The libretto ends with an invocation to Cupid from all hands: "Come unite each loving heart,/And may true lovers never part."

That would henceforth be the stock ending of the buffa, so that operas eventually divided into those in which people die (tragic) and those in which they marry (comic) — but both, increasingly, for love, not duty. That substitution was the great sentimental innovation and the great hallmark of "middle-class" (as opposed to aristocratic or "Family") values. It flew directly in the face of the *opera seria*, at first its chief competitor, which celebrated noble renunciation in dramas where people (or title characters, at any rate) neither died nor married. It marked the point at which the comic opera could begin to surmount the farce situations of the intermezzos and carry a serious or uplifting message of its own. That serious message was nothing less than a competing set of class aspirations — the aspirations of a self-made class whose power had begun to threaten that of hereditary privilege.

In Italian the new genre was eventually christened *semiseria*; in French, more revealingly, it was called *comédie larmoyante* ("tearful comedy"). In both, the happy end was reached by way of tears and therefore carried ethical weight. But instead of the weight of traditional social obligation, it was the weight of an implied injunction to be "authentic" — artlessly true to one's natural feelings. (And yet, as the opera historian William C. Holmes observes, the Marchese nevertheless "seems quite relieved when, in the dénouement, Cecchina is revealed as a German baroness."[3]) We know the device of mistaken identity the only way we can know it now—through a screen of cynical nineteenth-century satires (as in the operettas of Gilbert and Sullivan) that returned it to the realm of farce. Originally it was just as thrilling a concept as the intervention of a *deus ex machina* had been in an earlier age: it was the device through which the genre's approved values — true love and artless virtue — found their just reward.

For even though unwittingly a baroness by accident of birth, Cecchina is by nature and by her true character just *"una povera ragazza,"* a poor girl with a pure heart. The Italian phrase is the title of her main aria, the opera's most famous number (Ex. 28-1a), in which she exposes that heart for all to see — or rather hear (its very beating is famously represented by the second violins) — since the music, as in any opera, is the ultimate arbiter of truth. The social idealism that was the essence of the *comédie larmoyante* is made explicit by Piccinni's music and its canny contrast of styles. For Cecchina's aria, with its folklike innocence, is immediately contrasted with one that depicts the artful scheming of Lucinda (Ex. 28-1b), who as a "noble" character is given all the appurtenances of an *opera seria* role — in particular the virtuoso coloratura style of singing, replete with melismas on emblematic words (in this case *disperato*, "hopeless"). Of course in this ironic context it is just the "noble" aspects of Lucinda's music that cast her as ignoble, for she schemes to thwart the rightful consummation of true love. It is she, of course, who is thwarted in the end.

EX. 28-1A Niccolò Piccinni, *La buona figliuola*, "Una povera ragazza" (Act I, scene 12), mm. 5–9

EX. 28-IA   (*continued*)

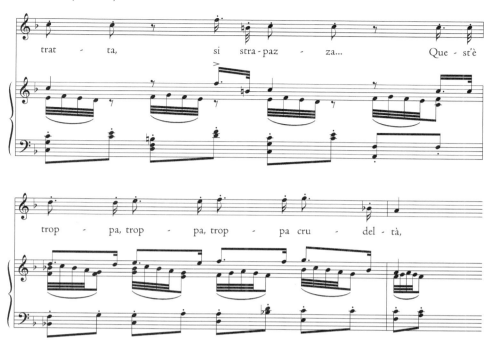

EX. 28-IB   Niccolò Piccinni, *La buona figliuola*, "Furie di donna irata" (Act I, scene 14), mm. 21–31

EX. 28-1B (*continued*)

So even if it typically ended with a perfunctory nod at aristocratic propriety, the *comédie larmoyante* was a genre in which the bourgeoisie, the optimistic "self-made" class, glorified itself and celebrated its dream of limitless opportunity. It was no accident, then, that the prototype was English. Indeed, the spread of *Pamela*, and of *Pamela*-inspired spinoffs, into continental artistic consciousness is an index by which to measure the spread of bourgeois ideals. Aristocratic audiences, needless to say, found the genre insufferable, and it quickly became just as popular a target for lampooning as the *opera seria* had been. Indeed, the adjective *larmoyante*, which in normal usage is just as disparaging in its implications as the English "lachrymose," was originally applied to the new genre by contemptuous aristocrats.

One aspect of comic opera, noticeable already in Pergolesi's *Serva padrona*, received a notable boost from Piccinni in *La buona figliuola*. The shape of a comic libretto depended on a plot that is first hopelessly tangled, then sorted out. The musical shape of the opera followed and epitomized this plan in a fashion that set the comic genre completely apart from the contemporary *seria*. Both the tangle (*imbroglio*) and the sorting were symbolized in complex ensemble finales in which all the characters participated. In an intermezzo like *La serva padrona* these were mere duets. In full-length *opera buffa*, they could be scenes of great length and intricacy, in which the changing dramatic situation was registered by numbers following on one another without any intervening recitative, all to be played at a whirlwind pace that challenged any composer's imaginative and technical resources. The first two acts of *La buona figliuola* end with quintets, the third and last with nothing less than an octet, representing the full cast of characters.

The second-act finale represents the height of imbroglio. Tagliaferro has just persuaded the ecstatic Marchese that Cecchina must be the lost baroness Mariandel on account of a distinctive blue birthmark on her breast. The Marchese rushes off to prepare their wedding forthwith, leaving Tagliaferro alone with the sleeping Cecchina. She calls tenderly in her sleep on her lost father. Tagliaferro, moved, responds in kind. Unfortunately this curious exchange is witnessed by Sandrina and Paoluccia. It is here that the finale begins.

At first it is dominated by the *buffi*, the characters most nearly recognizable from the earlier farce intermezzos like *La serva padrona* — namely Sandrina and Paoluccia, the sharp-tongued gossips, and Tagliaferro, the bumbling bass. They accuse him of trying to seduce Cecchina, and when the master returns (his entry underscored with a modulation to the subdominant), they denounce the hapless Tagliaferro. The Marchese, however, does not believe them, rejecting their malicious tale in a melting siciliano that expresses the purity of his love and faith. A quick change of tempo turns the siciliano into a madcap jig as the two girls argue back with the two men, finally reaching a peak of frenzied raving that is captured musically in a breathless *prestissimo* (Ex. 28-2) that returns to the opening patter tune of the finale, thus tying the whole imbroglio into a tidy musical package.

EX. 28-2   Niccolò Piccinni, *La buona figliuola*, Act II finale

EX. 28-2 (*continued*)

NOBLE SIMPLICITY

The *comédie larmoyante* was only one of many new departures in theater and theatrical music that burgeoned shortly after the middle of the eighteenth century. Another came to a head in an opera — ostensibly, an *opera seria* — that had its première performance in Vienna two years later than *La buona figliuola*, and is remembered today as the very model of "reform" opera, thanks to a deliberate propaganda campaign mounted on its behalf by the composer, the librettist, and their allies in the press. Although in many ways almost diametrically opposed to the style and the attitudes of Piccinni's masterpiece of sentimental comedy, it embodied a similar infusion of what was known as "sensibility." It too was in its way a quest for the "natural" and the "authentic."

The opera was called *Orfeo ed Euridice*, a knowing retelling of the legend that had midwifed the very birth of opera a century and a half before. The composer was Gluck, who was famous for declaring that when composing he tried hard to forget that he was a musician. What he meant by that, of course, was that he strove to avoid the sort of decorative musicality that called attention to itself — and away from the drama. The implicit target of Gluck's reform, like that of the comic opera in all its guises, was the Metastasian *opera seria* and all its dazzling artifices.

But where the *buffa*, as practiced by Piccinni, sought to replace those artifices with the "modern" truth of the sentimental novel, Gluck sought to replace them by returning to the most ancient, uncorrupted ways, as then understood. His was a self-consciously "neoclassical" art, stripped down and, compared with the *seria*, virtually denuded. In the preface to *Alceste* (1767), his second "reform" opera (based on a tragedy by Euripides), Gluck declared that in writing the music he had consciously aimed "to divest it entirely of all those abuses, introduced either by the mistaken vanity of singers or by the too great complaisance of composers, which have so long disfigured Italian opera and made the most splendid and most beautiful of spectacles the most ridiculous and wearisome," just as his librettist, Ranieri Calzabigi, had sought to eliminate "the florid descriptions, unnatural paragons and sententious, cold morality" of the unnamed but obviously targeted Metastasio.[4]

Thus in place of the elaborate hierarchy of paired roles that Metastasio had decreed, Gluck's *Orfeo* has only three char-

FIG. 28-1 Christoph Willibald Gluck, by Joseph Siffred Duplessis (1725–1802)

acters—the title pair plus Cupid, the hero's ally in his quest. The music they sing, despite the loftiness of the theme, is virtually devoid of the ritualized rhetoric of high passion—namely, the heroic coloratura that demanded the sort of virtuoso singing that had brought the *opera seria* its popular acclaim and its critical disrepute. That sort of musical "eloquence" was now deprecated as something depraved if not downright lubricious, and shed. Gluck's "reform" was in fact a process of elimination.

Gluck's ideals, and (even more) his rhetoric, derived from the ideals and rhetoric of what in his day was called "the true style" by its partisans. (Only later, in the nineteenth century, was it labeled "neoclassic" or "classical," and then only to deride it). The high value of art, in this view, lay in its divine power, sadly perverted when art was used for purposes of display and luxury. The legitimate connection between this attitude and notions of classicism or antiquity came about as a result of contemporary achievements in archaeology (most spectacularly the unearthing of Herculaneum and Pompeii between 1738 and 1748) and the theories to which they gave rise.

The main theorizer was the German archaeologist and art historian Johann Joachim Winckelmann (1717–68), Gluck's near-exact contemporary, whose most influential work in esthetics, *Thoughts on the Imitation of Greek Works*, appeared in 1755. The phrase he used to summarize the qualities in Greek art that he wanted to see imitated—"a noble simplicity and a calm grandeur" (*eine edle Einfalt und eine stille Grösse*)—became a watchword of the age, echoed and re-echoed in the writings of his contemporaries, including Gluck.

(There was a characteristic irony here, since many of the features of Greek art and architecture that Winckelmann most admired—its chaste "whiteness," for example—were the fortuitous products of time, not of the Greeks; we now know that the Athenian Parthenon, Winckelmann's very pinnacle of white plainness and truth, was actually painted in many colors back when it functioned as a temple rather than a "ruin." The "classicism" of the eighteenth century, a classicism of noble ruins, was in every way that very century's tendentious creation.)

Yet the heritage of the *opera seria* nevertheless survives in Gluck's *Orfeo*—most obviously in the language of the libretto, but also in the use of an alto castrato for the male title role, and in the high ethical tone that continues, newly purified and restored, to reign over the telling of the tale. Where Peri's or Monteverdi's Orpheus had looked back on Eurydice and lost her again out of sheer weakness (the inability to resist a spontaneous impulse), Gluck's hero does so out of stoic resolution and strength of character: in response to Eurydice's bewildered entreaties, Orpheus turns and looks to reassure her of his love, even though it means he must lose her. His act, in other words, has been turned into one of noble self-sacrifice: the classic *seria* culmination.

In other ways, the opera follows the conventions of the French *tragédie lyrique*, the majestic spectacle of the "ancient" and "divine" Lully, lately declared a classical model for imitation by French artists eager to relive the glorious achievements of the "grand siècle," the Great Age of Louis XIV. This unique mixture of what were normally considered inimical ingredients was typical of Gluck, the ultimate cosmopolitan. He had grown up in Austrian Bohemia. According to his pupil Antonio Salieri, his native language was Czech; "he expressed himself in German only with effort, and still more so in French and Italian . . . . Usually he mixed several languages together during a conversation."[5] And so he did in his music, too.

FIG. 28-2   Gluck's *Il Parnasso confuso* as performed at the Schönbrünn Palace, Vienna, in 1765.

His early career was practically that of a vagabond: from Prague to Vienna, from Vienna to Milan (where he worked with Giovanni Battista Sammartini, one of the lions of the operatic stage), from Milan to London (where his operas failed, but where he met Handel), thence as far north as Copenhagen and as far south as Naples. By 1752 he had resettled in Vienna, where he worked mostly as staff composer for a troupe of French actors and singers for whom he composed ballets and *opéras comiques*. That is where he absorbed the idioms of French musical theater.

The *tragédie lyrique*, the type of French musical theater Gluck chose to emulate in *Orfeo*, was, as we know, the courtliest of all court operas, and it might seem that Gluck's reform was aimed in the opposite direction from Piccinni's innovations. It was to be a reassertion of the aristocratic values that the latter-day *seria* had diluted with singerly excess, the values that the *opera buffa* owed its very existence to deriding. Here the main impetus came from Gluck's librettist, Calzabigi, an Italian-born poet then resident in Vienna, who had boldly set himself up as rival to the lordly court poet Metastasio. Calzabigi had actually trained in Paris, where he had learned to value the "Greek" dancing-chorus manner of the French opera-ballet over "*i passaggi, le cadenze, i ritornelli* and all the Gothick, barbarous and extravagant things that have been introduced into our music" by the pleasure-loving, singer-pleasing Italians, as he put it in a memoir of his collaboration with Gluck, published years later in a French newspaper.[6] (The English translation is by Dr. Burney.)

Thus the very first scene in the Gluck-Calzabigi *Orfeo* is a very formal choral elegy, sung by Orpheus's entourage of nymphs and shepherds, that corresponds roughly with the one at the end of the second act of Monteverdi's *Orfeo*. Eurydice is already dead. The horrifying news of her demise and Orpheus's reaction to it, so central to Monteverdi's confrontational drama, is dispensed with so far as the spectacle is concerned. This will be an opera of reflection — of moods savored and considered, not instantaneously experienced.

The aim of austerity — of striking powerfully and deep with the starkest simplicity of means — is epitomized by the role of Orpheus in this first scene. His whole part amounts to nothing more than three stony exclamations of Eurydice's name — twelve notes in all, using only four pitches (Ex. 28-3). It would be hard to conceive of anything more elemental, more drastically "reduced to essentials." Gluck once advised a singer to cry the name out in the tone of voice he'd use if his leg were being sawn off — Diderot's "animal cry of passion" in the most literal terms.

Orpheus then sends his mourning friends away in a grave recitative, whereupon they take their ceremonious leave of him through another round of gravely eloquent song and dance *à la française*. Orpheus's recitative is accompanied by the orchestral strings with all parts written out, not just a figured bass. "Accompanied" or "orchestrated recitative" (*recitativo accompagnato* or *stromentato*) had formerly been reserved for just the emotional highpoints of the earlier *seria*, to set these especially fraught moments off from the libretto's ordinary dialogue, for which ordinary or "simple" recitative — *recitativo semplice*, later known as *recitativo secco* or "dry" recitative — would have sufficed. In

EX. 28-3   Christoph Willibald Gluck, *Orfeo ed Euridice*, Act I, scene 1, chorus, recitative and pantomime

Gluck's opera, there was to be no "ordinary" dialogue, only dialogue fraught heavily with sentiment, hence no *recitativo semplice*, only *stromentato*.

As a result, *Orfeo ed Euridice* became the first opera that can be performed without the use of any continuo-realizing instruments. Considering that the basso continuo and the opera itself arose side by side as kindred responses to the same esthetic ferment (see chapters 19 and 20), there could hardly be any greater "reform" of the medium than this. Paradoxically, the elimination of the continuo had the same purpose as its invention: to adapt an existing (but constantly changing) medium to ever greater, and ever more naturalistic, expressive heights.

The same combination of high pathos and avoidance of conventional histrionics characterizes both of Orpheus's arias. The one in the third act, which takes place after Eurydice's second death, was very aptly described by Alfred Einstein, an admiring biographer of the composer, as "the most famous and most disputed number of the whole opera," possibly of all opera (Ex. 28-4).[7] Orpheus sings in grief—but in a noble, dignified grief that is in keeping with the nobility of his deed. That nobility and resignation constitute the aria's dominant affect, expressed through a "beautiful simplicity" (*bella simplicità*) of musical means, as Gluck put it (after Winckelmann, with Calzabigi's help) in the preface to *Alceste*. And that meant no Metastasian similes, no roulades, no noisy exits—for such things only exemplified pride.

The structure of the aria is French, not Italian: a *rondeau* with a periodic vocal refrain, not a *da capo* with an orchestral ritornello. The episodes between refrains are set in related keys—the dominant, the parallel minor—so that the return is always a refreshment. That and the shapely C-major melody of the refrain are what have given rise to the "dispute" to which Einstein referred—a dispute between those who have

EX. 28-4   Christoph Willibald Gluck, *Orfeo ed Euridice*, Act III, scene 1: "Che faro senza Euridice?", refrain, mm. 7–16

EX. 28-4 (*continued*)

rò,_____ do - ve an - drò,_____ che fa - rò sen - za il mio_____

ben, do - ve an - drò_____ sen - za il mio_____ ben?

J'ai perdu mon Eurydice,	I've lost my Eurydice,
Rien n'égale mon malheur,	Nothing can equal my sorrow;
Sort cruel, quelle rigueur,	O cruel fate, what hardship,
Je succombe à ma douleur.	I give myself up to despair.

found its "beautiful simplicity" simply too beautiful (and not expressive enough), and those who have seen in it the ultimate realization of music's power of transcendence.

The French composer Pascal Boyé, a friend of Diderot, used the aria as ammunition for a treatise entitled *L'expression musicale mise au rang des chimères* ("Musical expression exposed as an illusion"). Citing the aria by the opening words of the French version premièred in Paris in 1774 — "J'ai perdu mon Eurydice!" (I've lost my Eurydice!) — Boyé commented drily that the melody would have served as well or better had the text read "I've found my Eurydice!"[8] Nearly a century later, the critic Eduard Hanslick tried to generalize this remark of Boyé's and apply it to all music. "Take any dramatically effective melody," he suggested:

> Form a mental image of it, separated from any association with verbal texts. In an operatic melody, for instance one that had very effectively expressed anger, you will find no other intrinsic expression than that of a rapid, impulsive motion. The same melody might just as effectively render words expressing the exact opposite, namely, passionate love.[9]

And so on. Gluck would surely have found this notion bizarre, and might well have attributed it to the inability of "bourgeois" ears to appreciate a noble simplicity of utterance, awaiting completion (as Boyé recognized, but not Hanslick) by the expressivity of the singer's voice and manner. The singer for whom the aria was written, it so happens, is one whom we have already met—Gaetano Guadagni, for whom, a dozen years before, Handel had revised *Messiah* for showy "operatic" effect. Over that time Guadagni had transformed himself into a paragon of nobly simple and realistic acting under the influence of David Garrick, the great Shakespearean actor, with whom he had worked in London and whose then revolutionary methods of stage deportment he had learned to emulate. These, too, could be described with the phrase *bella simplicità*. A comparison of Handel's revised "But who may abide" (Ex. 26-6b) and Gluck's *Che farò senza Euridice?*, both written for Guadagni, makes a good index of simplicity's ascendancy. It was resisted by many among the aristocracy, however, who associated "natural" acting and stage deportment with comedy, and therefore with a loss of high "artfulness."

ANOTHER QUERELLE

Piccinni's rustic sentiment and Gluck's classical simplicity, though the one was directed at a bourgeois audience and the other at an aristocratic one, were really two sides of the same naturalistic coin. Both were equally, though differently, a sign of the intellectual, philosophical, and (ultimately) social changes that were taking place over the course of the eighteenth century. The famous rivalry that marked (or marred) their later careers might thus seem entirely gratuitous and therefore ironic from our historical vantage point. But although the two composers could have had no inkling of it in the 1760s, when they first became international celebrities, they were on a collision course.

Gluck naturally gravitated toward Paris, the half-forgotten point of origin for most of his innovatory departures. Having Gallicized the *opera seria*, he would now try his hand at the real thing—actual *tragédies lyriques*, some of them to librettos originally prepared as much as ninety years earlier for Lully. He arrived in the French capital in 1773 at the invitation of his former singing pupil in Vienna, none other than the princess Marie-Antoinette, the eighteen-year-old wife of the crown prince (*dauphin*) who the next year would be crowned Louis XVI ("Louis the last," as it turned out).

Under Marie-Antoinette's protection, Gluck at first enjoyed fantastic success. He even got old Rousseau to recant the brash claim he had made twenty years before, in the heat of buffoon-battle. After seeing *Iphigénie en Aulide*, Gluck's first *tragédie lyrique*, on a much-softened libretto after Euripides's bloody tragedy of sacrifice (adapted by Jean Racine), Rousseau confessed to Gluck that "you have realized what I held to be impossible to this very day"—namely, a viable opera on a French text.[10] The irony was that the same stylistic mixture that had spelled "Gallic" reform of Italian opera in Vienna was now read by the French as a revitalizing Italianization of their own heritage. Only a Bohemian—a complete outsider to both proud traditions—could have brought it off.

The best symbol of this hybridization of idioms was *Orphée et Eurydice*, a new version of Gluck's original "reform" opera, which amounted to a French readaptation of what had already been a Gallicized version of *opera seria*. Besides translating the libretto, this meant recasting the male title role so that an *haut-contre*, a French high tenor, could sing it instead of a castrato. Gluck also added some colorfully orchestrated instrumental interludes portraying the beauties of the Elysian fields, which are now performed no matter which version of the opera is employed.

In the summer of 1776, Gluck learned that the Neapolitan ambassador had summoned Piccinni to Paris for no other purpose than to be Gluck's rival, and had even "leaked" to him a copy of the very libretto Gluck was then working on (*Roland*, adapted from a *tragédie lyrique* formerly set by Lully, with a plot taken from French medieval history). Gluck, mortified, pulled out of the project, feeling with ample justification that he was being set up for a flop. "I feel certain," he wrote to one of his old librettists after burning what he'd written of the opera, "that a certain Politician of my acquaintance will offer dinner and supper to three-quarters of Paris in order to win fans for M. Piccinni. . .."[11] A couple of years later, though, it happened again, when Piccinni was induced to write an opera on the same story (albeit to a different libretto) as Gluck's last Parisian offering, a mythological tragedy loosely based on *Iphigenia in Tauris*, a famous play by Euripides whose story had already furnished the plot for quite a number of operas. The two settings were performed two years apart, Gluck's in 1779 and Piccinni's in 1781.

Their partisans (especially Jean François Marmontel, Piccinni's French librettist and sponsor) worked hard to cast the two composers as polar opposites — Gluck as the apostle of "dramatic" opera, Piccinni of "musical." Compared with the *Querelle des Bouffons*, however, the *querelle des Gluckistes et Piccinistes* was just a tempest in a teapot. The stakes, for one thing, were much lower. The main battle — the "noble simplification" and sentimentalization of an encrusted court art — was won before this later quarrel even started, and its protagonists, privately on friendly terms, were more nearly allies than rivals.

WHAT WAS ENLIGHTENMENT?

So perhaps it is from the operatic masterpieces of the age that we can best learn an important lesson: it is a considerable distortion of the way things were to describe the so-called Enlightenment exclusively as an "age of reason" — especially if we persist in assuming (as the romantics would later insist) that thinking and feeling, "mind" and "heart," are in some sense opposites. Gluck and Piccinni show us how far from true this commonly accepted dichotomy really is. The impulse that had led them and their artistic contemporaries to question traditional artifice and attempt the direct portrayal of "universal" human nature was equally the product of "free intellect" and *sympathy* — community in feeling. This last was based on introspection — "looking within." The community it presupposed and fostered was one that in principle embraced the whole of humanity regardless of race, gender, nationality, or class. The objective of "enlightened" artists became, in Wye J. Allanbrook's well-turned phrase, "to move an audience through representations of its own humanity."[12] And not only move, but also instruct and inspire goodness: free intellect and introspective sympathy went hand in hand — or in a mutually regulating tandem — as ministers to virtue.

The notion of free intellect — or "Common Sense," as the American revolutionary Thomas Paine put it in the title of his celebrated tract of 1776 — was the one that tended to attract attention by dint of its novelty and its political implications. "Man is born free; and everywhere he is in chains," wrote Rousseau at the beginning of his *Social Contract* (1762), perhaps the most radical political work of the eighteenth century, and the obvious source of Paine's main ideas. The chains to which he referred were not only the literal chains of enforced bondage, but also intellectual chains that people voluntarily (or so they may think) assume: religious superstition, submission to time-honored authority, acquiescence for the sake of social order or security in unjust or exploitative social hierarchies. The remedy was knowledge, which empowered an individual to act in accord with rational self-interest and with the "general will" (*sensus communis*) of similarly enlightened individuals.

Dissemination of knowledge — and with it, of freedom and individual empowerment — became the great mission of the times. The most concrete manifestation of that mission was the *Encyclopédie*, the mammoth encyclopedia edited by Diderot and Jean d'Alembert with help from a staff of self-styled *philosophes* or "lovers of knowledge" including Rousseau, who wrote the music articles among others. The first volume appeared in 1751, and the final supplements were issued in 1776. By the end, the project had been driven underground, chiefly by the Jesuits, who were enraged at its religious skepticism and persuaded the government of Louis XV to revoke the official "patent" or license to print. Even the clandestine volumes were subjected to unofficial censorship by the printer, who in fear of reprisal deleted the most politically inflammatory passages. These embattled circumstances only enhanced the prestige of the *Encyclopédie*, giving it a heroic aura as a new forbidden "Tree of Knowledge," and contributing to its enormous cultural and political influence.

That influence can be gauged by comparison with the famous essay *Was ist Aufklärung?* ("What Is Enlightenment?") by the German philosopher Immanuel Kant. It was published in 1784, four years after the *Encyclopédie* was completed. The answer to the question propounded by the title took the form of a popular Latin motto, originally from Horace: *Sapere aude!* ("Dare to know!").[13] "Enlightenment," Kant declared, "is mankind's exit from its self-incurred immaturity," defined as "the inability to make use of one's own understanding without the guidance of another."

"Enlightened" ideas quickly spread to England as well, where free public discussion of social and religious issues — both in the press and also orally, in meeting places like coffee houses — was especially far advanced. From England, of course, they spread to the American colonies, as already suggested by comparing Rousseau and Paine. Whether or not (as often claimed in equal measure by its proponents and detractors) the Enlightenment led directly to the French revolution of 1789, with its ensuing periods of mob rule, political terror, and civil instability, there can be no doubt that it provided the intellectual justification for the American revolution of 1776 — a revolution carried out on the whole by prosperous, enterprising men of property and education, acting in their own rational and economic self-interest. The Declaration of Independence, and the American Constitution that followed, can both be counted as documents of the Enlightenment. As mediated through two centuries of amendment and interpretation, moreover, the American Constitution, as a legal instrument that is still in force, represents the continuing influence of the Enlightenment in the politics and social philosophy of our own time.

It would be wrong, however, to think of the eighteenth-century Enlightenment within its own time as nothing but a vehicle of civic unrest or rebellion. The *philosophes* themselves believed in strong state power and saw the best realistic hope of freedom in the education of "enlightened despots" who would rule rationally, with enlightened sympathy for the interests of their subjects. A number of European sovereigns were indeed sympathetic to the aims of the Encyclopedists. Frederick II ("the Great") of Prussia—C. P. E. Bach's employer and a great patron of the arts and sciences, many of which (including flute-playing and even musical composition) he practiced himself—corresponded with Voltaire (François Marie Arouet, 1694–1778), the "godfather" of the Enlightenment, and entertained d'Alembert at Sans Souci ("Without-a-Care"), his pleasure palace in Potsdam. Catherine II ("the Great"), the German-born Empress of Russia and a protégée of Frederick's, corresponded enthusiastically with Diderot himself, whose much-publicized praise of Catherine and her liberality was largely responsible for her flattering sobriquet.

The liberality of an autocrat had its limits, though. Kant was a bit cynical about Frederick's: "Our ruler," he wrote, "says, '*Argue* as much as you want and about whatever you want, but *obey!*'"[14] And after the French revolution, which Frederick did not live to see, his protégée Catherine turned quite reactionary and imprisoned many Russian followers of her former correspondents.

The prototype of all the "enlightened despots" of eighteenth-century Europe was the Austrian monarch, Joseph II (reigned 1765–90). Beginning in 1780, when he came to full power on the death of his mother, the co-regent Maria Theresia, Joseph instituted liberal reforms on a scale that seemed to many observers positively revolutionary in their extent and speed. He wielded the powers of absolutism, just as the *philosophes* had envisaged, with informed sympathy for the populace of his lands. He annulled hereditary privileges, expropriated church properties and extended freedom of worship, and instituted a meritocracy within the empire's civil service. Above all, he abolished serfdom. (Catherine, by contrast, notoriously extended the latter institution into many formerly nonfeudalized territories of the Russian empire.) Yet few of Joseph's reforms outlived him, largely because his brother and successor, Leopold II, was impelled, like Catherine, into a reactionary stance by the revolutionary events in France, and Leopold's successor Francis II (reigned 1792–1835) created what amounted to the first modern police state. This anxious response to the French Revolution on the part of formerly "enlightened" autocrats is one of many reasons for regarding the political legacy of that great historical watershed as ambiguous at best.

MOZART

Joseph II was not a great patron of the arts. His sociopolitical reforms were his all-consuming interest, leaving little room for entertainment or intellectual pursuits. Music historians have tended to despise him a bit, because of his failure to give proper recognition or suitable employment to Wolfgang Amadeus Mozart (1756–91), the great musical genius of the age, whose music often perplexed him. (Joseph II is now best remembered by musicians not for his heroic reforms but rather for telling Mozart one day that there were "too many notes" in one of his scores.) But in fact Josephine Vienna, where Mozart made his home in the last decade of his life, and to whose musical commerce he made an outstanding contribution despite his failure to achieve a court sinecure, provides an ideal lens through which to view the work of one of European music's great iconic figures in a truly relevant — and "enlightening" — cultural context.

FIG. 28-3 Wolfgang Amadeus Mozart.

Posterity has turned Mozart, like Josquin des Prez before him (see chapter 14), into an "icon" — the "image of music," replete with an aura of holiness — for many reasons. One was his phenomenal precociousness; another was his heartbreaking premature demise. These as-if-correlated facts have long since converted his biography into legend. His earliest surviving composition, an "Andante pour le clavecin" in his sister Nannerl's notebook, was composed just after his fifth birthday (if his father, who inscribed the little harpsichord piece, can be believed). His last, as fate would have it, was a Requiem Mass, on which he was still working when he died, just 30 years, 10 months, and one week later. In that short span Mozart managed to compose such a quantity of music that it takes a book of a thousand pages — the *Chronological-Thematic Catalogue* by Ludwig Köchel, first published in 1862 and now in its seventh revised edition — just to list it adequately. And that quantity is of such a quality that the best of it (again like Josquin's legacy) has long served as a standard of musical perfection.

Mozart was born in Salzburg, an episcopal city-state near the Bavarian border, where his father, Leopold Mozart, served as deputy music director in the court of the Prince-Archbishop. By 1762, when the child prodigy was six years old, his father relinquished most of his duties and gave up his own composing career so that he could not only see properly to his son's musical education but also begin displaying his astonishing gifts to all the courts and musical centers of Europe. By the age of ten the boy Mozart was famous, having performed at courts throughout the German Catholic

FIG. 28-4 Mozart as a boy in Salzburg court uniform.

territories, the Netherlands, Paris, and finally London, where he stayed for more than a year, was fêted at the court of George III, became friendly with John Christian Bach, and submitted, at his father's behest, to a series of scientific tests by the physician and philosopher Daines Barrington, to prove that the boy truly was a prodigy and not a musically accomplished dwarf. Barrington's report, "Account of a Very Remarkable Musician," read at the Royal Society, a prestigious scientific association, marked an important stage in the formation of the Mozart legend, the "myth of the eternal child," as Maynard Solomon, the author of an impressive psychological biography of the composer, has called it.[15]

It is because of his uncanny gifts and his famously complicated relations with his father that Mozart has been the frequent subject of fiction, dramatization, "psychobiography," and sheer rumor (including the persistent legend of his death by poisoning at the hand of Gluck's pupil Salieri, a jealous rival). Before Solomon's sober psychological study there was a reckless one by the Swiss novelist Wolfgang Hildesheimer, not to mention Alexander Pushkin's verse drama "Mozart and Salieri" of 1830 and its subsequent Broadway adaptation by Peter Shaffer as *Amadeus*, later a popular movie. But Mozart's iconic status was also due to his singular skill at "moving an audience by representations of its own humanity." His success at evoking sympathy through such representations has kindled interest in his own human person to an extent to that point unprecedented, even by Josquin, in the history of European music, partly because the creation of bonds of "brotherhood" through art had never before been so central an artistic aim.

It is also for this reason that Mozart's music, in practically every genre that he cultivated, has been maintained in an unbroken performing tradition from his time to ours; he is the true foundation of the current "classical" repertoire, and has been that ever since there has been such a repertoire (that is, since the period immediately following his death). Except for Handel's oratorios, nothing earlier has lasted in this way. Franz Joseph Haydn, Mozart's great contemporary, whom we will meet officially in the next chapter, has survived only in part. (His operas, for example, have perished irrevocably from the active repertoire.) Bach, as we know, returned to active duty only after a time underground.

Mozart's operas have not only survived where Haydn's have perished. A half dozen of them (roughly a third of his output in the genre) now form the earliest stratum of the standard repertory. But for the Orfeos of Monteverdi and Gluck, they are the earliest operas now familiar to theatergoers. They sum up and synthesize all the varieties of musical theater current in the eighteenth century, as we have traced them to this point, and they have been a model to opera composers ever since.

Mozart composed his first dramatic work, a rather offbeat intermezzo composed to a libretto in Latin (!) for performance at the University of Salzburg, at the age of eleven, shortly after returning from London. It is a mere curiosity, like the composer himself at that age. Within a couple of years, however, Mozart was equipped to turn out works of fully professional calibre in all the theatrical genres then current. In 1769, the thirteen-year-old's first opera buffa, *La finta semplice* ("The pretended simpleton"), to a libretto by Carlo Goldoni, was performed at the Archbishop's Palace in Salzburg. (An earlier scheduled performance at Vienna was cancelled on suspicion that the opera was really by father Leopold.) Its style is most often compared with that of Piccinni. About eighteen months later, in December 1770, Mozart's first *opera seria*, called *Mitridate, re di Ponto* ("Mithridates, King of Pontus"), to a libretto based on a tragedy of self-sacrifice by Racine, was produced in Italy, opera's home turf, where the Mozarts, father and son, were touring. It was so successful that the same theater, that of the ducal court of Milan, commissioned two more *serie* from the boy genius over the next two seasons. Another early success was *Bastien und Bastienne*, a *singspiel* (a German comic opera with spoken dialogue) based loosely on the libretto of Rousseau's popular *Devin du village*, which was performed, possibly as early as the fall of 1768 when the composer was twelve, at the luxurious home of Franz Mesmer, the pioneer of "animal magnetism" or (as we would now call it) hypnotherapy.

These three—Italian opera both tragic and comic, and German vernacular comedy—were the genres that Mozart would cultivate for the rest of his career. What his early triumphs demonstrated above all was his absolute mastery of the conventions associated with all three: a mastery that enabled him eventually to achieve an unprecedented directness of communication that still moves audiences long after the conventions themselves have been outmoded. Mastery, rather than originality, was the objective all artists then strove to achieve. The originality we now perceive in Mozart was really a secondary function or by-product of a mastery so consummately internalized that it liberated his imagination to react with seeming spontaneity to the texts he set and achieve a singularly sympathetic "representation of humanity."

IDOMENEO

Mozart's first operatic masterpiece was *Idomeneo, re di Creta* ("Idomeneus, King of Crete"), an *opera seria* composed in 1780, first produced in Munich in 1781 and extensively revised five years later for performance in Vienna. By then, having quarreled over terms with the Archbishop of Salzburg and having requested and ungraciously received release from his position ("with a kick in the ass," he wrote to his horrified father), Mozart, with a wife and eventually a child to support, was living in the capital as a "free lance" musician, accepting commissions and giving "academies," or self-promoted concert appearances. Although he had craved the freedom to compose as he saw fit, the precariousness of his livelihood (exacerbated by gambling debts) and the attendant stress and overwork undoubtedly contributed to his early death, adding another leaf to the legend of his life—a legend that maintains, romantically but erroneously, that he died a pauper.

Idomeneo, a tragedy of child-sacrifice, was composed to a translation of a very old libretto, one that had served almost seventy years earlier as the basis of a *tragédie lyrique* (with music by André Campra) that was performed before Louis XIV during the last years of his reign (see Ex. 22-5). Mozart cast his opera, accordingly, in the severe style of Gluck's neoclassical "reform" dramas, two of which (on the myth of Iphigenia) had also treated the painful subject of a father sworn to sacrifice his child. By modeling his opera

FIG. 28-5   Act II of Mozart's *Idomeneo* as staged at the Metropolitan Opera House, New York.

on Gluck's, Mozart completed his assimilation of all the theatrical idioms to which he was heir.

At Mozart's request, his librettist, a Salzburg friend, added several choruses to the original libretto and also provided some exalted accompanied recitatives for a high priest and an oracle. As Daniel Heartz has shown, prototypes for all of these interpolations and more can be found in the French version of Gluck's *Alceste*, performed in Paris in 1776. This was the opera that carried, in the first edition of its score, the preface that set forth Gluck's famous principles of operatic reform. It had enormous prestige. Mozart's successful appropriation of Gluck's ideals and methods, in a manner that vividly illustrates the eighteenth century's outlook on artistic creativity, not only transcended his predecessor's achievement but at the same time went a long way toward transforming the reformer's innovations into conventions.

Both Mozart's indebtedness to Gluck and the astonishing boldness with which the twenty-four-year-old former prodigy exceeded his model can be judged from the High Priest's chilling recitative in the third act of *Idomeneo*, in which he exhorts the title character not to shrink from his obligation, incurred by a rash vow, to sacrifice his son Idamante to the god Neptune. It is modeled on the lengthy temple scene in the first act of *Alceste*, in which the high priest of Apollo issues a similar exhortation to the title character to prepare to sacrifice her life so that her husband, King Admetus of Thessaly, may recover from an illness and continue his propitious reign. Mozart in effect conflates several moments from Gluck's scene, of which the most prominent is an imperious unison arpeggio figure that modulates to the dark key of B♭ minor (Ex. 28-5).

EX. 28-5A Christoph Willibald Gluck, *Alceste*, Act I, scene 4, High Priest's exhortation, mm. 1–18

EX. 28-5A (continued)

Your prayers, O queen, and your gifts Apollo receives more favorably than is his custom. By a hundred clear signs I know that he is present. Behold, possessed by his sacred frenzy, I utter words that are more than human.

EX. 28-5B W. A. Mozart, *Idomeneo*, no. 23, mm. 2–23

EX. 28-5B (continued)

Mozart's intensification of the harmony, his transformation of the leading motive by obsessively repeating a nasty unison trill, and his antiphonal deployment of it over a restless modulation all contribute to a gruesome effect that some have interpreted as sarcastic, in keeping with the composer's presumed enlightened attitudes. The trills, according to Heartz, "tell us pretty plainly what Mozart thought of this particular high priest and how we are to respond to the 'holy' crime he exhorts."[16] Heartz relates this observation to a remark by Mozart's older contemporary, Baron Melchior von Grimm (1727–1807), one of the leaders of the German enlightenment who, as a result of his devotion to Voltaire, Rousseau, and Diderot, became a naturalized citizen of France. "What I want to see painted in the tragedy of Idomeneo," Grimm wrote, "is that dark spirit of uncertainty, of fluctuation, of sinister interpretations, of disquiet and of anguish, that torments the people and from which profits the priest."[17]

Whether Mozart's portrayal of the high priest actually intends or conveys such a judgment may be debated. What is certain, however, is that dramas like *Idomeneo* were becoming unfashionable in enlightened Vienna, where Mozart would shortly establish his permanent residence. Joseph II had an aversion to the *opera seria* (ostensibly because of its costliness). Although Mozart made an elaborate revision of *Idomeneo* in hopes of a performance in the capital, he succeeded only in having it done privately (possibly in concert form, as a sort of oratorio) at one of Vienna's noble residences during Lent in 1786 when the theaters were closed. Not until the end of Joseph's reign would Mozart have another opportunity to compose in the tragic style.

DIE ENTFÜHRUNG AUS DEM SERAIL

The 1780s, then, became Mozart's great decade of comic opera, a genre he utterly transformed. First to appear was a singspiel, composed in response to Joseph II's avid patronage of vernacular comedies, for which the Emperor had established a special German troupe at the Vienna Burgtheater (Court Theater), henceforth to be officially — though never colloquially — named the "Nationaltheater." It was there that Mozart's *Die Entführung aus dem Serail* ("The abduction from the Seraglio") was first performed, on 16 July 1782. (The production was to have been mounted in honor of the visiting Grand Duke Pavel Petrovich of Russia, who would later reign briefly as Tsar Paul I, but the visit was delayed.)

Although composed in the national language and performed in the national theater, the opera has an exotic rather than a national subject and locale. There had long been a great Viennese vogue for "Oriental" (or "Turkish") subject matter in the wake of the unsuccessful siege of the city by the Ottoman Turks in 1683. Making fun of the former enemy was a national sport, and Turkish military (or "Janissary") percussion instruments that had once struck fear in the hearts of European soldiers were now appropriated by European military bands — and eventually by opera orchestras. (The Janissaries, from the Turkish for "recruits," were originally Christian captives pressed into military service by the Ottoman Empire and forced to convert to Islam; the drafting of Christians waned during the seventeenth century, and the regiment gradually became the hereditary elite corps of the Turkish army.)

FIG. 28-6   The Vienna Burgtheater in 1783, engraving by Carl Schuetz (1745–1800).

The raucous jangling of the Janissary band (also imitated in a piano sonata by Mozart, concluding with a famous "Rondo alla Turca" that children often learn) is a special effect in the merry overture to *Die Entführung* (whose orchestra includes timpani, bass drum, cymbals, and triangle) and at various colorful points thereafter. The plot of the opera revolves around the efforts of Belmonte, a young Spanish grandee, to rescue Constanze, his beloved, who has been kidnapped by pirates, together with her English maidservant Blonde and Belmonte's servant Pedrillo, and sold into the harem of Pasha Selim—who turns out to be a runaway Christian himself and shows the lovers mercy. In the end the Christian lovers are reunited: Belmonte with Constanze (who, true to her name, had remained faithful to him despite temptation) and Pedrillo with Blonde (who had been wooed by the blustery and ridiculous Osmin, the keeper of the harem).

While at work in Vienna on *Die Entführung*, Mozart kept up a lively correspondence with his father, back home in Salzburg. One of his letters, dated 26 September 1781, has become famous for its very revealing descriptions of the arias he was writing for the various characters. About the frenzied last section of Osmin's rage aria in act I, where the "Janissary" instruments have a field day, he wrote:

> Just when the aria seems to be over, there comes the *allegro assai*, which is in a totally different measure and in a different key; this is bound to be very effective. For just as a man in a towering rage oversteps all bounds of order, moderation and propriety, and completely forgets himself, so must the music too forget itself. But

as passions, whether violent or not, must never be expressed in such a way as to excite disgust, and as *music, even in the most terrible situations, must never offend the ear, but must please the hearer, or in other words must never cease to be music,* I have gone from F (the key in which the aria is written), not into a remote key, but into a related one, not, however, into its nearest relative D minor, but into the more remote A minor.[18]

The oft-quoted words italicized above have been justly taken as a sort of emblem of "Enlightened" attitudes about art and its relationship to its audience. Bach, on one side of the Enlightenment, would have heartily disagreed; but so too would many composers on the other side of it, as we shall see, and even Mozart himself in at least one famous instance that we will encounter at the end of this chapter.

Mozart continues, in the same letter, with a description of the very next item in the singspiel, the brilliantly scored aria in which Belmonte expresses his anxieties about Constanze's fate (Ex. 28-6 a and b). This passage from the letter has also become a *locus classicus*—a place everyone cites—for its account of how finely Mozart calculated the orchestral effects to imitate the physical manifestations (or, as psychologists would say, the "iconicity") of Belmonte's feelings.

> Let me now turn to Belmonte's aria in A major, "O wie ängstlich, o wie feurig." Would you like to know how I have expressed it—and even indicated his throbbing heart? By the two violins playing octaves. This is the favorite aria of all those who have heard it, and it is mine also. You feel the trembling—the faltering—you see how his throbbing breast begins to swell; this I have expressed by a *crescendo.* You hear the whispering and the sighing—which I have indicated by the first violins with mutes and a flute playing in unison.[19]

EX. 28-6A   W. A. Mozart, *Die Entführung aus dem Serail,* Belmonte's aria, "O wie ängstlich," mm. 1–8

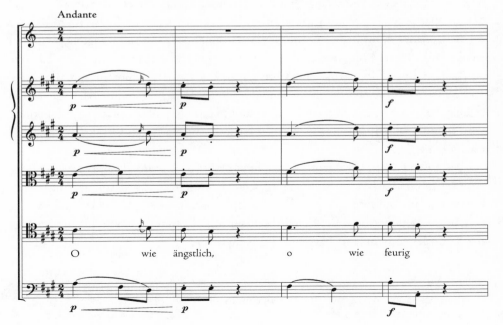

EX. 28-6A   (continued)

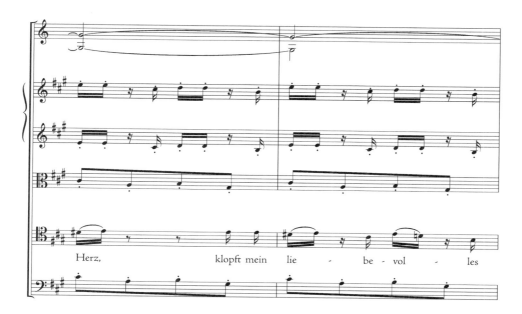

Mozart's list is far from exhaustive. He might also have mentioned the harmonic shifts toward the minor as Belmonte's thoughts darken, recalling the pain of separation. He might have mentioned the continuing heartbeat rhythm that underlies the "whispering and sighing" violins and flute, played by divided violas plucking four-part chords, *pizzicato* (Ex. 28-6b). (Such detailed writing for the lowly viola was practically unheard of at the time.) He might have mentioned the strangely lurching dynamic patterns and accents — an irregular pulse? — when Belmonte sings of trembling and wavering. The list could go on.

While not exactly a new technique—in cruder form we encountered it in the final duet from Pergolesi's *Serva padrona*—Mozart's mastery of iconic portraiture set a benchmark not only in subtle expressivity but in refinement of orchestration as well. These were new areas in which one could "move an audience through representations of its own humanity." Mozart's success was a dual one. In the first place it attracted, and continues to attract, an unprecedented "human interest" in the composer as a person. His portraits of his characters have been read, persistently though of course unverifiably, as self-portraits.

Nowhere is this more apparent than in the biographical interpretations often advanced to explain his composing, in swift succession, exemplary works in two such contrasting genres as opera seria (*Idomeneo*) and singspiel (*Die Entführung*). With another composer, adept powers of assimilation and mastery of convention might suffice to explain it. With Mozart, "mere" mastery of convention does not seem sufficient to account for such immediacy and versatility of expression. And so the grim *Idomeneo* is associated with Mozart's unhappy courtship of the German soprano Aloysia Weber, who spurned him in favor of the court actor and painter Joseph Lange, whom she married in 1780. And the blithesome *Entführung* is associated with Mozart's

EX. 28-6B   W. A. Mozart, *Die Entführung aus dem Serail*, Belmonte's aria, "O wie ängstlich," mm. 29–37

EX. 28-6B *(continued)*

marriage, a couple of weeks after its premiere in 1782, to Aloysia's younger sister, whose name happened to coincide with that of the leading feminine role in the opera, Constanze.

Are such explanations necessary? Perhaps not, but they are certainly understandable. Not only do Mozart's uncanny human portraits in sound seem to resonate with the reality of a concrete personality; they inspire empathy as well—and this was Mozart's other breakthrough. One is apt to respond to a work by him not only by thinking "it's about him," but also by thinking that, somehow, "it's about me." The bond of kinship thus established between the composer's subjectivity and the listener's—a human bond of empathy seemingly capable of transcending differences in age, rank, gender, nation, or any other barrier—is supremely in the optimistic spirit of the Enlightenment. When the feat is duplicated in the wordless realm of instrumental music, as we shall see in the next chapter, instrumental music is invested with a sense of importance—indeed, of virtual holiness—it had never known before. We can begin to see why Mozart could be worshiped, particularly by his nineteenth-century posterity, as a kind of musical god who worked a beneficent, miraculous influence in the world.

EX. 28-6B *(continued)*

THE "DA PONTE" OPERAS

After *Die Entführung*, Mozart did not complete another opera for four years. Part of the reason for the gap had to do with his burgeoning career in Vienna as a freelancer, which meant giving lots of concerts, which (as we will see) meant writing a lot of piano concertos. But it was also due to Joseph II's unexpected disbanding of the national singspiel company and its replacement by an Italian *opera buffa* troupe at court whose regular composers Giovanni Paisiello, Vincente Martìn y Soler, and Antonio Salieri — Italians all (Martìn being a naturalized Spaniard) — had a proprietary interest in freezing out a German rival, especially one as potentially formidable as Mozart.

Mozart's letters testify to his difficulty in gaining access to Lorenzo da Ponte (1749–1838, original name Emmanuele Conegliano), the newly appointed poet to the court theater. (There was a certain typically Joseph II symbolism in the fact that a specialist in *opera buffa* should have been chosen to replace the aged Metastasio, the paragon of the *seria*, who died in 1782 at the age of 84.) "These Italian gentlemen are very civil to your face," Mozart complained to his father in 1783. "But enough — we know them! If Da Ponte is in league with Salieri, I shall never get anything out of him."[20] It was these letters, and the intrigues that they exposed, that led to all the gossip about Salieri's nefarious role in causing Mozart's early death, and all the dubious literature that gossip later inspired.

Mozart's wish to compete directly with "these Italians" is revealed in another passage from the same letter to his father, in which he described the kind of two-act realistic comedy (but frankly farcical, not "*larmoyante*") at which he now aimed. This was precisely the kind of libretto that Da Ponte, a converted Venetian Jew, had adapted from the traditions he had learned at home and brought to perfection. In this he was continuing the *buffa* tradition of Carlo Goldoni, which sported lengthy but very speedy "action finales" at the conclusion of

FIG. 28-7 Lorenzo da Ponte, engraving by Michele Pekenino after a painting by Nathaniel Rogers (Mozarteum, Salzburg).

each act and a highly differentiated cast of characters. About this latter requirement Mozart is especially firm:

> The main thing is that the whole story should be really *comic*, and if possible should include two equally good female parts, one of them *seria*, the other *mezzo carattere*. The third female character, if there is one, can be entirely *buffa*, and so may all the male ones.[21]

This mixed genre insured great variety in the musical style: a *seria* role for a woman implied coloratura and extended forms; *buffa* implied rapid patter; "medium character" implied lyricism. Da Ponte's special gift was that of forging this virtual smorgasbord of idioms into a vivid dramatic shape.

Mozart (aided, according to one account, by the Emperor himself) finally managed to secure the poet's collaboration in the fall of 1785. The project was all but surefire: an adaptation of *La folle journée, ou le mariage de Figaro* ("The madcap day; or, Figaro's wedding"), one of the most popular comedies of the day. It was the second installment of a trilogy by the French playwright Pierre-Augustin Caron de Beaumarchais (1732–99), of which the first installment, *Le barbier de Séville* ("The barber of Seville"), had already been turned into a hugely successful *opera buffa* by Paisiello (1782; first staged in St. Petersburg, Russia). These plays by Beaumarchais were the very epitome of that old standby, the servant-outsmarts-master routine, familiar on every operatic stage since the very earliest intermezzi: *La serva padrona* was of course the first classic of this type. In the spirit of the late eighteenth century, the old joke became much more pointed and audacious than before—"outrageously cheeky," in Heartz's words.[22] And yet, with both master and servant now portrayed as rounded and ultimately likeable human beings rather than caricatures, the ostensible antagonists are ultimately united in "enlightened" sympathy.

Thus, contrary to an opinion that is still voiced (though more rarely than it used to be), Beaumarchais's Figaro plays were in no way "revolutionary." The playwright was himself an intimate of the French royal family. In his plays, the aristocratic social order is upheld in the end — as, indeed, in comedies (which have to achieve good "closure") it had to be. It could even be argued that the plays strengthened the existing social order by humanizing it. Hence Joseph II's enthusiasm for them, which went — far beyond tolerance — all the way to active promotion.

In the play Mozart and Da Ponte adapted for music as *Le nozze di Figaro*, the valet Figaro (formerly a barber), together with his bride Susanna (the *mezzo carattere* role), acting on behalf of the Countess Almaviva (the *seria* role), outwits and humiliates the Count, who had wished to deceive his wife with Susanna according to "the old *droit du seigneur*" (not really a traditional right but Beaumarchais's own contrivance), which supposedly guaranteed noblemen sexual access to any virgin in their household. All three — Figaro, Susanna, and the Countess — are vindicated at the Count's expense. But the Count, in his discomfiture and heartfelt apology (a moment made unforgettable by Mozart's music), is rendered human, and redeemed. On the way to that denouement there is a wealth of hilarious by-play with some memorable minor characters, including an adolescent page boy (played by a soprano *en travesti*, "in trousers") who desires the Countess, and an elderly pair of stock *buffo* types (a ludicrous doctor and his housekeeper) who turn out to be Figaro's parents.

Mozart and Da Ponte had such a success with this play that their names are now inseparably linked in the history of opera, like Lully-and-Quinault or Gluck-and-Calzabigi, to mention only teams who have figured previously in these chapters. The triumph led to two more collaborations. *Don Giovanni* followed almost immediately. It was a retelling of an old story, long a staple of popular legend and improvised theatrical farce, about the fabled Spanish seducer Don Juan, his exploits, and his downfall. Its first performance took place on 29 October 1787 in Prague, the capital of the Austrian province of Bohemia (now the Czech Republic), where *Le nozze di Figaro* had been especially well received; it played Vienna the next year. Its success was only gradual, but by the time he came to write his memoirs, Da Ponte (who died an American citizen in New York, where from 1807 he worked as a teacher of Italian literature, eventually at Columbia University) could boast that it was recognized as "the best opera in the world."[23]

Their third opera, produced at the Burgtheater on 26 January 1790 (a day before Mozart's thirty-fourth birthday), was the cynical but fascinating *Così fan tutte, ossia La scuola degli amanti* ("Women all act the same; or, The school for lovers"), which had only five performances before all the theaters in Austria had to close following the death of Joseph II. It would be Mozart's last *opera buffa*. The plot concerns a wager between a jaded "old philosopher" and two young officers. The old man bets that, having disguised themselves, each officer could woo and win the other's betrothed. Their easy success, much to their own and their lovers' consternation, has made the opera controversial throughout its history.

Many textual substitutions and alternative titles have seen duty in an attempt to soften the brazenly misogynistic message of the original. That message, preaching disillusion and distrust, is perhaps larger (and more dangerous) than its immediate context can contain. Its ostensible misogyny can be seen as part of a broad exposure of the "down side" of Enlightenment — a warning that reason is not a comforter and that perhaps it is best not to challenge every illusion. Some, basing their view on the assumption — the Romantic assumption, as we will learn to identify it — that the music of an opera is "truer" than the words, have professed to read a consoling message in Mozart's gorgeously lyrical score. Others have claimed that, on the contrary, Mozart and Da Ponte have by that very gorgeousness in effect exposed the falsity of artistic conceits and, it follows, unmasked beauty's amorality.

The tensions within it — at all levels, whether of plot, dramaturgy, musical content, or implication — between the seductions of beauty and cruel reality are so central and so deeply embedded as to make *Così fan tutte*, in its teasing ambiguity, perhaps the most "philosophical" of operas and in that sense the emblematic art work of the Enlightenment.

LATE WORKS

In his last pair of operas, both first performed in September 1791 less than three months before his death, Mozart reverted to the two genres in which he had excelled before his legendary collaboration with Da Ponte. *Die Zauberflöte* (*The Magic Flute*) is a singspiel to a text by the singing actor and impresario Emanuel Schikaneder, who commissioned it for his own Theater auf der Wieden, a popular playhouse in Vienna. Behind its at times folksy manner and its riotously colorful and mysterious goings-on, it too is a profoundly emblematic work of the Enlightenment, for it is a thinly veiled allegory of Freemasonry.

A secret fraternal organization of which both Mozart and Schikaneder were members (along with Voltaire, Haydn, and the poets Goethe and Schiller), the Order of Ancient Free and Accepted Masons purportedly traced its lineage back to the medieval stonecutters' guilds (and thence, in legend, to ancient Egypt, the land of the pyramids), but became a widespread international association in the eighteenth century and an important vehicle for the spread of Enlightened doctrines such as political liberalism and religious tolerance. Persecuted by organs of traditional authority, including the Catholic Church and the autocratic monarchies of Europe, the Masons had elaborate rites of initiation and secret signals (the famous handshake, for instance) by which members could recognize one another.

The plot of *The Magic Flute* concerns the efforts of Tamino, a Javanese prince, and Pamina, his beloved, to gain admission to the temple of Isis (the Earth- or Mother-goddess of ancient Egypt), presided over by Sarastro, the Priest of Light. Tamino is accompanied by a sidekick, the birdcatcher Papageno (played by Schikaneder himself in the original production; see Fig. 28-10), who in his cowardice and ignorance cannot gain admittance to the mysteries of the temple but is rewarded for his simple-hearted goodness with an equally appealing wife. The chief opposition comes from Pamina's mother, the Queen of the Night, and from Monostatos, the blackamoor who guards the temple (a clear throwback to Osmin in *Die Entführung*). The allegory

FIG. 28-8   Sarastro arrives on his chariot in act I of Mozart's *Die Zauberflöte*. Engraving published in an illustrated monthly to herald the first performance of the opera in Brünn (now Brno, Czech Republic) in 1793.

Papageno.

FIG. 28-9   Emanuel Schikaneder in the role of Papageno in the first production of *Die Zauberflöte* (Theater auf der Wieden, Vienna, 1791).

proclaims Enlightened belief in equality of class (as represented by Tamino and Papageno) and sex (as represented by Tamino and Pamina) within reason's domain. Even Monostatos's humanity is recognized, betokening a belief in the equality of races. On seeing him, Papageno (who first sounds the opera's essential theme when he responds to Prince Tamino's question as to his identity by saying "A man, like you") reflects, after an initial fright, that if there can be black birds, why not black men?

The range of styles encompassed by the music in *The Magic Flute* is enormous — wider than Mozart had ever before attempted. At one extreme is the folk-song idiom of Papageno, "Mr. Natural." At the other are the musical manifestations of the two opposing supernatural beings — the forces, respectively, of darkness (The Queen of the Night) and light (Sarastro) — both represented by *opera seria* idioms, altogether outlandish in a singspiel. In act II, the Queen, seeing her efforts to thwart the noble pair coming to nought, gets to sing the rage aria to end all rage arias (Ex. 28-7a). Its repeated ascents to high F *in altissimo* are a legendary test for coloratura sopranos to this day. (That pitch had actually been exceeded, incidentally, in a coloratura aria — or rather, a spoof of coloratura arias — that Mozart tossed off early in 1786 as the centerpiece of a little farce called *Der Schauspieldirektor* or "The Impresario," sung at its first performance by his sister-in-law Aloysia).

Sarastro, in the scene that immediately follows, expresses the opera's humanistic creed in the purest, most exalted sacerdotal manner (Ex 28-7b). George Bernard Shaw, the famous British playwright, worked in his youth as a professional music critic. Perhaps his most famous observation in that capacity pertained to this very aria of Sarastro's, which he called the only music ever composed by mortal man that would not sound out of place in the mouth of God.[24] That is as good a testimony as any to the hold Mozart has had over posterity, but it is also worth quoting to reemphasize the point that such sublime music was composed for use in a singspiel, then thought (because it was sung in the German vernacular) to be the lowliest of all operatic genres. That was in itself a token of Enlightened attitudes. In such company, the lyrical idiom of the lovers Tamino and Pamina occupies the middle ground, the roles (so to speak) of *mezzo carattere*.

Mozart's last stage work, an *opera seria* called *La clemenza di Tito* ("The clemency of Titus"), was composed to one of Metastasio's most frequently set librettos, one that had been first set to music almost sixty years before by Antonio Caldara, then Vice-Kapellmeister to the Austrian court. Its revival was commissioned, symbolically as it might seem, to celebrate the accession to the Austrian throne of Joseph II's younger

FIG. 28-10   Pamina, Tamino, and Papageno in a scene from act II of *Die Zauberföte* (Brünn, 1793).

brother, the Emperor Leopold II, who would rule for only two years—just enough time to undo all of his Enlightened predecessor's reforms. Just so, it could seem as though Mozart's reversion to a stiffly conventional aristocratic drama of sacrifice "undid" the modern realistic comedies that had preceded them—though of course no one had any premonition that this was to be his last opera.

EX. 28-7A   W. A. Mozart, *Magic Flute*, "Der Hölle Rache" (The Queen of the Night), mm. 21–47

EX. 28-7A (continued)

EX. 28-7B W. A. Mozart, *Magic Flute*, "In diesen heil'gen Hallen" (Sarastro), mm. 16–26

EX. 28-7B   (continued)

It has been claimed that Mozart accepted the commission with reluctance; but while his letters complain of some fatigue (and although he had to work in haste, farming out the recitatives to a pupil, Franz Xaver Süssmayr), there is no evidence that he felt the century-old genre of *opera seria* to be an unwelcome constraint. In any case, his setting of *La Clemenza* was fated to be the last masterpiece of that venerable genre, which barely survived the eighteenth century.

DON GIOVANNI CLOSE UP

For a closer look at the team of Mozart and Da Ponte in action, we can focus in on what the librettist proudly called "the best opera in the world." Many have endorsed Da Ponte's seemingly bumptious claim on behalf of *Don Giovanni*. For two centuries this opera has exerted a virtually matchless fascination on generations of listeners and commentators — the latter including distinguished authors, philosophers, and even later musicians, who "commented" in music.

For E. T. A. Hoffmann (1776–1822), a German writer (and dilettante composer) famous for his romantic tales, it was the "opera of operas," altogether transcending its paltry ribald plot — about "a debauchee," as Hoffmann put it, "who likes wine and women to excess and who cheerfully invites to his rowdy table the stone statue representing the old man whom he struck down in self-defense" — and becoming, through its music, the very embodiment of every noble heart's "insatiable, burning desire" to exceed "the common features of life" and "attain on earth that which dwells in our breast as a heavenly promise only, that very longing for the infinite which links us directly to the world above."[25] There could be no better evidence of the way in which Mozart's

FIG. 28-11   Poster announcing the first performance of Mozart's *Don Giovanni* (Prague, 1787).

music reflected to a sensitive listener an image of his own idealized humanity, however at variance with the composer's.

For Søren Kierkegaard (1813–55), the great Danish religious philosopher, *Don Giovanni* was Mozart's greatest work (hence the greatest of all art works) because in it the greatest of all composers tackled the subject matter that music was uniquely equipped to represent. "There is only one work," he wrote (and that work is *Don Giovanni*), "of which it can be said that its idea is altogether musical in such a way that the music does not merely serve as accompaniment but discloses its own innermost nature as it discloses the idea."[26] Once again, that essence or innermost idea is desire, the sensation that lies at the universal core of consciousness. It is by representing desire that music can represent to us an image of our own subjectivity. That representation undoubtedly became the virtually universal aim of musicians during the age of so-called Romanticism, an age that saw its own beginnings in the music of Mozart's time, and in *Don Giovanni* preeminently. The title character's insatiable erotic appetite, and the voracious amatory quests on which it led him, became a symbol — or more precisely, a *metonymy*, an attribute standing in for the whole — of human aspiration, and music became the primary vehicle for its artistic modeling.

That is because polyphonic music in common European practice had, in its basic harmonic and formal processes, long provided superlative models of tension and release, of loss and recovery, of transport and return, of complication and consummation. These processes could be represented in dramatic action as well as musical composition, and the task of dramatic musician and musical poet alike became that of fashioning explicit analogies between the two signifying media. The shape of the comic opera libretto, with its two acts, perfectly analogized these patterns of musical modeling. The two acts observed opposite trajectories, the first culminating in the *imbroglio* or tangle, the second in the crisis and the swift sorting out of threads. The first could be likened to dissonance, to remote tonality, to the "far out point"; the second — to resolution, restoration of the home key, harmonic and formal closure. The comic libretto, in short, was a "binary" form, and could be ideally elaborated by using all of the musical means associated with that most basic of "closed" musical formats.

And just as the musical process works itself out through points of harmonic repose (cadences) and passages of harmonic motion or "modulation," so the libretto structure made provision for points of stasis and passages of kinetic energy. The former were of course the arias, like the ones we have been sampling from Mozart's earlier output. In this the *buffa* did not differ greatly from the *seria*. The kinetic passages were the novelty, and for the composer the greatest opportunity. These were long passages of continuous music, already sampled in Piccinni's second-act finale from *La buona figliuola*, in which swift dramatic action, leading either toward imbroglio or toward closure, was to be embodied in music that was (unlike recitative) fully composed, with full use of the orchestra and sung throughout to lyrically conceived, well-shaped melodies. But at the same time it was (unlike an aria) forwardly progressing rather than rounded or symmetrical in harmony and phraseology.

Usually there were three main kinetic sections in a late eighteenth-century *opera buffa*: the *introduzione* to the first act, in which the plot was set in motion and given a maximum "spin"; the first-act finale, in which the imbroglio reached its peak; and the second-act finale, in which the action was driven home to closure. (The second act generally began at a low point of dramatic pressure, so that there could be a new buildup to the culmination; in most comic operas, the second-act curtain rose on simple recitative.) As Da Ponte himself remarked in his memoirs, the finale was the key to the libretto, and mastering its conventions was the test of a true musical dramatist, whether poet or composer. "This *finale*," he wrote in mock complaint:

> which must remain intimately connected with the opera as a whole, is nevertheless a sort of little comedy or operette all by itself, and requires a new plot and an unusually high pitch of interest. The *finale*, chiefly, must glow with the genius of the composer, the power of the voices, the grandest dramatic effects. Recitative is banned from the *finale*: everybody sings; and every form of singing must be available—the adagio, the allegro, the andante, the intimate, the harmonious and then—noise, noise, noise; for the *finale* [to the first act] almost always closes in an uproar: which, in musical jargon, is called the *chiusa*, or rather the *stretta* [literally, "squeeze" or "pinch"], I know not whether because in it, the whole power of the drama is drawn or "pinched" together, or because it gives generally not one pinch but a hundred to the poor brain of the poet who must supply the words. The *finale* must, through a dogma of the theatre, produce on the stage every singer of the cast, be there three hundred of them, and whether by ones, by twos, by threes or by sixes, tens or sixties; and they must have solos, duets, terzets, tenets, sixtyets; and if the plot of the drama does not permit, the poet must find a way to make it permit, in the face of reason, good sense, Aristotle, and all the powers of heaven or earth; and if then the *finale* happens to go badly, so much the worse for him![27]

We can observe concretely everything that has been described up to now in the abstract, and at the same time justify the eloquent but somewhat mysterious pronouncements of Hoffmann and Kierkegaard, by examining in some detail the *introduzione* and the two finales from *Don Giovanni*, noting at all times how the libretto mediates between plot (action) and music, cementing their affinities. The following sections of close descriptive commentary should be read with vocal score in hand.

MUSIC AS A SOCIAL MIRROR

Since it is attached directly to the *introduzione*, of which it is actually a part—and since, therefore it ends not with a cadence (except in its specially adapted "concert version") but with a modulation—the overture (or, as Mozart called it, the sinfonia) to *Don Giovanni* must also figure in our discussion. Like the drama to which it is appended, the sinfonia by Mozart's day was no longer a little three-movement suite but more often a single quick (Allegro) movement in binary (there-and-back) form. At the beginning, Mozart appended a startling andante that gives a forecast of the plot's grisly resolution, also forecast in the opera's subtitle, *Il dissoluto punito* (The immoralist punished).

The forecast is one not only of musical theme and mood but also of key. It was a convention of the *opera buffa* that the second-act finale end in the key in which the sinfonia begins, thus matching musically the resolution of the plot. As Daniel Heartz has pointed out, there were in practice only three tonics that could be used in this way: namely C, D, and E-flat, the keys of the natural trumpets and horns that would normally figure at the opera's loudest moments, including its launching and its culmination.

The dire prognosis having been given, the key shifts over to the parallel major for a typically effervescent *buffo* Allegro. Except for the horrific *introduzione*, in which a murder will take place before the eyes of the audience, and its harsh consequences in the last finale, the opera will adhere to the tradition of the Don Juan plays of the past, which was a tradition of farce. The form of the fast main body of the overture is essentially that of the J. C. Bach sonata allegro studied in the previous chapter (Ex. 27-6), also in D major. This coincidence is no surprise; we have already identified J. C. Bach as an important formative model for Mozart. In both Allegros, a theme in the tonic with fanfare characteristics (note the sudden loud entry of winds, brass and timpani in m. 38, between the phrases of Mozart's first Allegro theme) is contrasted with a pair of themes in the dominant, in which a decisive form-defining cadence is marked (at the double bar in J. C. Bach, followed by a repeat; in m. 120 of Mozart's overture, from which a repeat might just as easily have been made were it conventional to do so in an overture).

The cadence on the dominant is then followed in both pieces by a section that moves out to the FOP. In J. C. Bach, this is B minor (vi with respect to the tonic); in Mozart's case it is B-flat major, which has the same degree function with respect to the *original* tonic, namely the D minor of the andante—thus, it could be argued, again foreshadowing the drama's dénouement. As is typical of orchestral pieces (as opposed to keyboard sonatas), the thematic content of the freely modulating section containing the FOP is largely based on motives taken from the opening section of the piece, in new juxtapositions and new tonalities. The return to the tonic is signaled in both JC's piece and Mozart's by the all-important "double return," in which the first theme comes back in its original key, which is then maintained to the end. In Mozart's case this simply means transposing the big chunk of music first heard between m. 56 and m. 115 down a fifth, so that what had been originally cast in the dominant is now securely in the tonic. But then the coda (mm. 277 to the end) unexpectedly dissolves into a modulation, preparing the key of the first vocal number in the *introduzione* (F major) by coming to rest on its dominant, just as the awesome andante had come to rest on the dominant of D major, the key of the Allegro. Cadences on the dominant (also known as half-cadences), which need to be resolved, are the most efficient means of maintaining the all-important forward momentum that the large kinetic sections of an *opera buffa* required.

That first vocal number belongs to the noble title character's grumpy manservant (here named Leporello), a stock *opera buffa* type always sung by a bass. Its opening march-like ritornello sketches his impatient pacing and stamping as he awaits the return of his master. Its diminutive "rondo" form (ABCB) with refrain, permits the repetition of Leporello's envious line, "I'd like to be the master for a change," with its reminder of all the licenses and privileges that Don Giovanni enjoys—and abuses. Just as in the overture, the last cadence of the vocal melody is trumped by a modulation. That modulation, from F major to B-flat major, casts Leporello's whole song in retrospect as a sort of upbeat in the dominant to the first bit of kinetic action, corresponding to Don Giovanni's entrance, pursued by the enraged Donna Anna, the lady with whom he has been keeping company while his servant had been outside, stewing.

The three characters now on stage sing a tense trio in B-flat major, Donna Anna accusing the Don of attempted rape and calling for help, the Don attempting to flee, and Leporello cowering off to one side. This little number, too, fails to make complete closure: tremolando violins intrude upon its final cadence, and a bass figure introduces an incongruous F-sharp to coincide with the entrance of the Commander, Donna Anna's father, in response to her screams. That F-sharp, a leading tone, wrenches the tonality into an unstable G minor, the relative minor of the previous key, for another trio, much shorter than the one preceding, in which the two noblemen exchange threats and Leporello continues his horrified commentary from his hiding place.

The final cadence of the male trio is on D minor, a significant key that had already served for the menacing slow introduction to the overture. The men draw swords and fight to the strains of an orchestral passage making frantic modulations around the circle of fifths, but ending on a diminished-seventh chord that coincides with Don Giovanni's fatal thrust. The tempo now changes radically as the Commander, mortally wounded, falters and dies, while Don Giovanni gloats and Leporello panics, all in the remote key of F minor — remote, that is, in terms of the immediately preceding music, but coming full circle with respect to the opening of the *introduzione*, which had begun with Leporello's pouting song in F major.

Not even this ending section of the *introduzione*, though, makes a full cadence. The last dominant chord peters out into *its* dominant, the harpsichord takes over, and only now do we hear the first recitatives, inaugurating the "normal" succession of recitative and fully elaborated aria. In the space of less than two hundred measures, lasting only a few minutes, we have met four characters, witnessed an attempted arrest and a murder, and been through a veritable tonal whirlwind. This kind of uninterrupted action music seemed to eighteenth-century listeners to reproduce the rhythms and the passions of life itself. Its sustained dramatic pressure was unprecedented.

But now things settle down into a more orderly (that is, a more obviously contrived) rhythm, as the traditional farcical plot takes over. A series of closed numbers, linked by recitatives, ensues. Don Giovanni and Leporello scurry off and Donna Anna returns, accompanied by her fiancé, Don Ottavio. They vow revenge in passionate duet. Don Giovanni and Leporello regroup in another part of town, where they come upon and observe Donna Elvira, an old flame of the Don's traveling incognito. She is the opera's *mezzo carattere* role. Her raillery at her betrayer is cast in a coloratura aria reminiscent of the *opera seria*, while their mock-sympathetic asides are of the purest *buffo* manner. When Don Giovanni approaches her with an eye toward conquest, she hurls abuse at him. He withdraws, leaving her alone with Leporello, who "consoles" her with a leering "catalogue aria" listing all the Don's conquests (640 in Italy, 230 in Germany, 100 in France, 91 in Turkey, but in Spain 1003).

The scene changes to a peasant wedding. Don Giovanni is attracted to the bride, Zerlina, and invites everyone to his house, thinking thereby to seduce her. The groom, Masetto, flies into an aria of impotent rage; he is dragged off while the Don, preposterously proposing marriage in a duet with Zerlina, manages to gain her assent to a tryst. Donna Elvira arrives in pursuit. She warns Zerlina off in a brief coloratura explosion. Donna Anna and Don Ottavio appear. With Donna Elvira and Don Giovanni, whom at first they do not recognize in the daylight, they sing a brief quartet. With the help of Donna Elvira's insinuations, Donna Anna understands that Don Giovanni is none other than her villain seducer from the night before. Anna, Elvira, and Ottavio join forces to bring him to justice. Donna Anna sings another noble aria of vengeance. Don Ottavio, left briefly alone, sings of his devotion to her.

The remaining arias before the first finale are two: Don Giovanni's madcap "Champagne aria," in which he lustily looks forward to the orgy where he thinks a combination of wine and increasingly vigorous dancing (minuet, then "follia," then "allemande") will result in the addition of a dozen or so new names, including Zerlina's, to his catalogue; and a dulcet aria in which Zerlina manages to appease Masetto with the help of an unctuous obbligato cello.

This brings us to the act I finale, the first "little comedy in itself" as Da Ponte described it. Its self-contained quality is emphasized by its own tonal closure. It begins and ends in C major — another good trumpet key, and one that stands in relation to the original (and ultimate) tonic like a "far out point," reflecting its dramatic function as the peak of imbroglio, a "dissonance" in the plot that stands in urgent need of resolution.

It begins with a little "quarrel duet" between Masetto and Zerlina, he expressing suspicion, she exasperation; he hides as Don Giovanni appears, shouting instructions to his servants. The wedding party is invited inside, but Don Giovanni spies Zerlina and detains her outside the house as the music modulates to F major. He woos; she resists. All at once he spies Masetto, as the music makes a feint toward the relative minor. Thinking quickly, the Don reassures Masetto that Zerlina has been looking for him, invites them both in, and the music returns to the security of the major key.

From within, the sound of the Don Giovanni's hired (onstage) orchestra is heard, playing a contredanse. The counterpoint of stage music (that is to say, music "heard" by the characters on stage as actual performed music) and the "metaphorical" music of the singers and the pit orchestra (representing the characters' speech, thoughts, feelings, and actions, "heard" as music only by the audience), will henceforth be virtuosically exploited as a dramaturgical gimmick throughout the finale. It is a distinction all operagoers learn to make "instinctively." Only rarely is it thematized — made overt and explicit by the composer as a dramatic effect — the way it is here.

The stage music is silenced (for the audience) by the sudden appearance of Don Giovanni's pursuers — Don Ottavio, Donna Anna, and Donna Elvira, wearing masks — as the music takes a decisive turn to the minor, symbolizing their caustic frame of mind. Leporello throws open a window from within, and once again the Don's orchestra is heard, this time playing a stately minuet. Leporello, spying the maskers (whom he fails to recognize), tells his master of their presence. They, too, are of course invited to the ball.

Once again the stage music falls silent from the audience's perspective, as the pit orchestra focuses in like a zoom lens on the maskers. The change of tempo — to adagio — and of key — to B-flat, again casting the preceding music retrospectively as a dominant — announces a moment of solemn "inwardness," as they utter a prayer for heavenly assistance in revenge (a "silent" prayer, we understand, since they sing not in dialogue but as an ensemble).

The prayer being done, the music again lurches forward along the circle of fifths, to E-flat (another "horn key"), as the stage set opens in on the Don's glittering ballroom. All but the sulking Masetto enter into the festive spirit, egged on by the orchestra's jig rhythms. As the maskers enter they are greeted by an abrupt change to C major; trumpets now pompously replace the horns, and the trio of "strangers" exchange formal greetings with their quarry, joining in (but of course ironically) when the Don sings the praises of the "freedom" his generous hospitality betokens.

At Don Giovanni's signal, the stage orchestra strikes up the minuet again to inaugurate the main dance episode, one of Mozart's most famous tours de force. Taking his cue, evidently, from the dances named in the "Champagne aria" (minuet, follia, allemande), Mozart superimposes three dances, played by three sub-orchestras in various corners of the room, in a kind of collage. They represent the various social classes who are mixed harum-scarum in this weird ball that Don Giovanni's irrepressible libido has engineered.

Thus atop the noble minuet, in a stately triple meter, the rustic contredanse (or "country dance") heard earlier in the scene is superimposed, presumably for the benefit of the peasants from the wedding party. (It is introduced, wittily, by some suitable tuning-up noises from the second orchestra.) Its duple meter contradicts that of the dance already in progress, three measures of contredanse equaling two of minuet. The two dances are cleverly harmonized by the composer, however, so as to create no dissonances with one another.

Everyone but Masetto now dancing to one orchestra or another, Don Giovanni starts to lead Zerlina offstage. He tells Leporello to keep Masetto at bay, and Leporello signals to the third group of musicians, who strike up the "allemande," or rather the "Teitsch," as Mozart now designates it. Like allemande, the word *Teitsch* means "German"; the more usual term for this dance of Mozart's time was the *Deutscher Tanz*. A far cry from the dignified allemande of the old French dance suite, the Deutscher was a boisterous, whirling affair, the progenitor of the waltz. One of its fast triple measures equals a single beat of the concurrent minuet and contredanse. As soon as it starts, Leporello seizes Masetto and twirls him around while the Don slips away with Zerlina. Leporello, noticing her resistance and fearful at the possible outcome, abandons the whirling, confused Masetto and follows them.

Once off stage Zerlina lets out a bloodcurdling scream for help. Its outlandish harmonization, a sudden dominant-seventh chord on B-flat, utterly disrupts the complicated proceedings on stage and ushers in the "noise, noise, noise" with which a first-act finale must conclude. The tempo is now marked allegro assai, the fastest designation then in common use — and it will get faster. Everyone begins chasing after Don Giovanni, who comes out dragging Leporello and accusing him of having been Zerlina's abductor. The maskers are not taken in; they reveal themselves to Don Giovanni, who makes a desperate exit, leaving all the rest in confusion.

With each turn of events, the harmony is wrenched accordingly. There are many feints. E-flat seems to give way to the dominant of D, but instead F arrives with Don Giovanni's impetuous accusation. The maskers threaten in a C major liberally mixed with jarring notes borrowed from the parallel minor. At the last moment, as the Don makes his frantic escape, the tempo is "pinched" up even beyond allegro assai by means of the marking *più stretto*, as if quoted from Da Ponte's description. The imbroglio has indeed reached an unsurpassable peak.

MUSIC AND (OR AS) MORALITY

In the second act the trajectory is reversed, leading to the Don's inevitable downfall. The first scene finds him farcically brazen as ever, rejecting Leporello's advice to mend his ways and wooing Elvira's maidservant with a serenade. In the second scene, both noble ladies are cynically shown wavering in their hatred of the irresistible Don. The third scene is the turning point. Don Giovanni, having escaped another scrape by leaping a wall into a graveyard, and having revealed the true depths to which he can descend (now he's been dallying with Leporello's girl!), is brought up short by the voice of the Commander from beyond the grave (accompanied by sepuchrally solemn trombones). He sends Leporello to see where the voice is coming from, and they discover the Commander's monument. With his usual bravado, Don Giovanni bids Leporello invite the statue to dinner. To Leporello's great fright and Don Giovanni's bewilderment, the statue nods assent.

As a foil to the horrific finale, a tender scene for Don Ottavio and Donna Anna now ensues, in which she promises to marry him, but only after she's settled her score and rid herself of her obsession.

FIG. 28-12 Don Giovanni meets his doom. Engraving by P. Bolt after a drawing by Vincenz Georg Kinninger, used as the frontispiece to the first edition of the vocal score (Leipzig: Breitkopf und Härtel, 1801).

And now the second-act finale. Like the previous finale, it is a party scene: Don Giovanni, with renewed bravado, is getting ready for the repast to which he had mockingly invited the Commander.

And so, again like the previous finale, it features stage music: a wind octet such as actually did furnish dinner music at aristocratic salons (and for which many composers, including Mozart, made arrangements of popular numbers from operas). They play three actual excerpts from the current *opera buffa* repertory as of 1787 (for all that the ostensible setting of the opera is "the sixteenth century"). First comes an excerpt from *Una cosa rara* (full title, "A rare thing: beauty and honesty together"), by one of Mozart's rivals, Martìn y Soler, to a libretto by Da Ponte, premiered in Vienna only the year before (Don Giovanni's comment: "a tasty dish!"). Next, a tune from *Fra i due litiganti il terzo gode* ("While two dispute, a third rejoices") by Giuseppe Sarti (libretto by Carlo Goldoni), just then the most popular of all operas on the Vienna stage (Leporello greets it with delight). Finally, the musicians strike up one of the hit tunes from Mozart and Da Ponte's own *Le nozze di Figaro* (Leporello, in mock disgust: "Now that one I know all too well!").

These gay snatches have not only been entertaining the pair on stage and the audience in the opera house; they have also been establishing the finale's fluid tonal scheme and staking its limits: the first in D major, the key both of the overture at the front of the opera and of the looming final cadence; the second in F major, the flat mediant, which shares its signature of one flat with the parallel minor key, in which the statue music will be played; and the third in B-flat major, the flat submediant (linked through its relative minor with G major, which will also figure prominently in the design). These keys also — and probably deliberately — recapitulate the opening tonalities of the *introduzione* (overture, Leporello's pacing, the Don's entrance).

The final cadence of the *Figaro* snatch is bizarrely elided into loud chords signaling the sudden arrival of Donna Elvira, in a state of feverish anxiety. Somehow she has had a premonition of the Don's impending doom and has come to warn him. In an agitated trio, he meets her concern with derision, finally addressing to her the same insultingly insouciant invitation to sit herself down and dine with him that he had previously addressed to the statue of the Commander. At this even Leporello has to reprove his master's hard-heartedness.

Elvira rushes off in despair but rushes right back on again in horror, her scream matched in the orchestra by a bellowing diminished-seventh chord, horror-harmony par excellence. She flies out at the opposite end of the stage and Don Giovanni sends Leporello to investigate. Leporello, too, recoils to the same horror-harmony, transposed up a step and sounding even ghastlier because the chord of its implied resolution is now the chord of D minor that will spell death to Don Giovanni. In a breathless duet, the voice parts interrupted by panting rests, Leporello explains that he has seen him, "the man of stone, the white man" and imitates his crushing gait, "ta! ta! ta! ta!"

With undiminished bravado, Don Giovanni flings open the door. His gesture is greeted by what was surely the most awful noise that ever sounded in an opera house: yet another diminished-seventh chord, this one blasted in his face by the full orchestra, augmented by the three trombones from the graveyard scene, to announce the Commander's arrival. The harmony is the very one that accompanied Don Giovanni's fatal thrust in the introduzione; its recurrence seems to bracket the whole intervening action and cast the whole opera in terms of a single horrible deed and its expiation.

The stone guest now enters, accompanied by the grim music that had so unexpectedly launched the overture, thus providing a musical recapitulation to correspond with the fulfillment of the subtitle's prophecy. The Don continues to resist against the evidence of his own eyes. A hideous trio of three basses develops as the statue advances, the Don scoffs, and Leporello trembles. Here Mozart came as close as he would ever come to violating his own conceit — the bedrock precept of all "Enlightened" aesthetics — that *music, even in the most terrible situations, must never offend the ear, but must please the hearer.* Here his music gives intimations not of beauty but of what must at the very least be called sublime: matters vast and grave, awesome to contemplate.

Things get worse. The statue's command that Don Giovanni repent is sung to another gruesomely portentous recapitulation: the duel music from the *introduzione* that had accompanied Don Giovanni's most horrible crime. The Don remains proudly unrepentant: that is his idea of courage. But at the icy touch of the statue's hand, his demeanor crumbles into one of rack and ruin; the statue is replaced by a unison chorus of hellish spirits; the harmony is riddled with searing dissonance as the orchestra's noisiest resources are summoned up: trombone sforzandi, timpani rolls, string tremolos. Music like this, to say the least, had never figured before in any *opera buffa.* As the Don disappears, screaming in agony, the orchestra settles in on a chord of D major. The change of mode offers no consolation, though: it is more like the *tierce de picardie,* the "Picardy third" (a famous misnomer derived from *tierce picarte,* "sharp third"), the major chord that was used to end solemn organ preludes and toccatas in the minor in days of old.

And now the resolution: D major resolves to G major as dominant to tonic, the stage brightens, and (according to the old prescription), the librettist assembles all the remaining characters on stage on a flimsy pretext: Donna Anna, Donna Elvira (who has presumably summoned the rest), Don Ottavio, Zerlina, and Masetto (the last pair unseen since the first act) all rush on stage, together with some policemen who never get to sing, to join the dazed Leporello. The five pursuers, singing in a sort of chorus, interrogate Leporello about Don Giovanni's fate.

When all are satisfied that the Don has truly perished ("Ah, it must have been that ghost I saw!" says Elvira knowingly to the others), they react by turning their attention to the future, symbolizing the end of Don Giovanni's reign, and (like the harmony) providing the action with its long-awaited closure — a closure that could not take place so long as the Don's disruptive force was abroad in the opera's world. In a tender larghetto, Don Ottavio and Donna Anna make their plans to marry (in a year, at her insistence, so that she may fully mourn her father). Elvira announces that she is bound for a convent. Zerlina and Masetto agree to patch things up and resume their domesticity. Leporello vows to find himself a better master.

Meanwhile, the harmony has been quietly veering back to D major through its dominant on which the larghetto makes its (half) cadence. It is time to wrap things up in D major with a moral, launched presto by the women's voices in what sounds for all the world like the beginning of a fugue, Donna Anna and Elvira with the subject, Zerlina with the answer. (It was for touches like this that Mozart had the reputation of being a "difficult" composer.) But no, all six characters continue in chorus to the final cadence, to the accompaniment of ripping scales and fanfares in the orchestra, in a fully restored *buffa* style.

Together, Mozart and Da Ponte brought to a new height the faculty of imagining (or, in this case, re-imagining) a dramatic action in terms suitable for musical elaboration. In Mozart's case, the achievement had mainly to do with the unique skill with which he interwove the voices of his characters in ensembles — a variegated play of vocal color that made his finales flash and glitter, moving with unprecedented speed and flexibility. His finales were a powerful influence on later composers: indeed, as we shall see, the history of opera during the nineteenth century could be described as the genre's gradual transformation into one great big continuous "finale," lasting from curtain to curtain.

But it also had to do with fine calibrations of rhythm and harmony to underscore shifting sentiments and passions, finally homing in as if inevitably on the indispensable closure, lending a sense of surefooted progression — that is, of real dynamism — to that newly speedy yet flexible pace. These were the devices by which, more compellingly than ever, Mozart could "move an audience through representations of its own humanity," lending his music the aspect that the Enlightenment prized above all — the achievement of a "universal portrait" of mankind.

Nowadays, of course, it is easy to see how far such a representation fell short of true universality. In the case of *Don Giovanni*, as in that of *Così fan tutte*, the viewpoint that claims universality is clearly the viewpoint of a male ego. The "insatiable, burning desire" to exceed "the common features of life" and "attain on earth that which dwells in our breast as a heavenly promise" that so affected Hoffmann is all too clearly the barely sublimated male sexual drive. The "altogether musical idea" that Don Giovanni "disclosed" to Kierkegaard was likewise a reflection of the philosopher's maleness and its attendant desires.

It follows from this that all the women in the opera, even the noblest, are mocked and negated in varying degrees, regarded finally as catalogue entries — sexual "objects," rather than what a philosopher like Kierkegaard would have called a true "subject," which is to say an independent agent. Donna Elvira is willing up to the bitter end to suffer humiliation for the Don's sake; Donna Anna is more than faintly ridiculous in her constant deferral of her marriage plans, and painful to observe in her progressively deteriorating moral condition over the course of the opera; Zerlina is a virtual mirror reflection of the Don himself — a cruelly manipulative creature ruled by her animal appetites. Don Giovanni's, in short, is the viewpoint that ultimately prevails in the opera, his bad end and all attendant moralizing notwithstanding. Not for nothing has the critic Joseph Kerman dared suggest that the "closure ensemble" that follow the Don's demise is a dramatic failure, a "dead spot" that only "goes to show how drab life is without the Don."[28] It would be hard to argue that sneaking admiration for the villain has not been widely shared ever since the opera's première. Those, after all, were the cynical "gender politics" of Mozart's time, and it would not be reasonable to expect to find them transcended in a work that aspired to popular success. Much more recently, in the early part of the twentieth century, Feruccio Busoni, a great late-Romantic pianist and composer, professed his admiration for Don Giovanni as "the man who gave every woman the supreme experience of happiness." One might want to ask Donna Elvira or Donna Anna about that. Or so we are quick nowadays to object. In Mozart's day, or even in Busoni's, no one would have posed the question. It would not have been thought reasonable. Now it gives discomfort.

But that is the paradox of all "Enlightened" thinking. Reason's promise can be kept only provisionally. Its answers are inevitably superseded by others that will be superseded in their turn. To insist on their universal applicability—on a final, single truth—can only end in dogmatism or hypocrisy. And only dogmatism or hypocrisy will condemn the attempt to place the morality of great works of art, even works as great as *Don Giovanni*, in historical perspective.

Instrumental Music Lifts Off

THE EIGHTEENTH-CENTURY SYMPHONY; HAYDN

PARTY MUSIC GOES PUBLIC

In one or another linguistic variant, the term "symphony" (*symphonia, sinfonia*) has been in the European musical vocabulary since the ninth century. At first it meant what we now call "consonance," a term that merely substitutes Latin roots for Greek ones meaning "together-sounding" (*con = sym; sonus = phonos*). By the turn of the seventeenth century, the term had resurfaced as a prestigious "humanistic" (pseudo-Greeky) cognate to the homelier *concerto* in the original meaning of the word, designating a composition that mixed vocal and instrumental forces over a basso continuo, as in Gabrieli's (and later Schütz's) *Symphoniae sacrae*.

By the beginning of the eighteenth century, the term had become attached to the Italian opera, where it designated what the French called the *ouverture*, or opener, the orchestral curtain-raiser. As we may recall from chapter 23, the Italian *sinfonia avanti l'opera* as employed by the theater composers of Alessandro Scarlatti's generation was a short three- or (very occasionally) four-movement suite akin to what the string-players of Corelli's generation might have called a *concerto da camera* (see Ex. 23-4). Being meant for the larger space of a theater rather than an aristocratic salon, it was usually scored for oboes and horns or trumpets in addition to strings. The brass instruments set limits on harmonic complexity.

But still the term, and the associated genre, would not stay put. By the end of the eighteenth century, 16,558 symphonies had been written (probably many more: the number is merely the sum total of items listed in the *Union Thematic Catalogue of Eighteenth-Century Symphonies, c1720–c1810*, compiled in the 1960s and 1970s under the direction of the American musicologist Jan LaRue). That is many times more than the number of operas. Symphonies were living a life of their own, as free-standing three- or four-movement orchestral compositions, and were being produced in unprecedented quantities.

Immense production, of course, implies immense consumption. A new pattern of consumption implies a new demand; and a new demand implies a change of taste (or "esthetic"). Such changes have social as well as esthetic causes. And that will be the key to understanding what the term-and-genre "symphony" came to mean over the course of the eighteenth century. For as Jan LaRue has pointed out, the term "symphony" was not uniformly associated with the genre that now bears the name. It only gradually won out over a welter of synonyms that included, in a fashion that can seem bewildering to today's musicians who are used to hard-and-fast dictionary definitions, "overture" and "concerto," as well as many terms no longer associated with orchestral music, such as "sonata," "partita," "trio," "quartetto," "quintetto," and so on practically ad infinitum. Neither was the genre of free- standing symphony strictly distinguished from that of *sinfonia avanti l'opera*. Sometimes opera overtures were detached from their operas and performed as symphonies. Sometimes symphonies got attached to operas and were performed as overtures. Sometimes symphonies that never had any operas attached were called overtures out of habit, or because they opened concert programs.

But if we tend to rely on textbook or dictionary definitions for our idea of genres, eighteenth-century musicians and listeners identified them by their contexts and uses. For them, and so for us, a symphony will be any multimovement orchestral piece performed at certain kinds of social occasions. A crucial hint to the nature of the social occasions at which those thousands of free-standing symphonies were performed comes by way of some other early synonyms for the term in its new usage, including "divertimento," "scherzando," "serenata," "notturno," and "cassatione." "Divertimento" comes from the Italian verb *divertire*, and means "entertainment music." "Scherzando" comes from *scherzare*, to have fun. "Serenata" comes from *sera*, evening; "notturno" from *notte*, night. "Cassatione," though disguised as an Italian word (suggesting an improbable derivation from *cassare*, to dismiss or rescind, or an even more improbable one from the French *casser*, to break) actually comes from the Austrian German noun *Gasse*, meaning street: hence, "street (or outdoor) music."

To sum up, then, the free-standing orchestral symphony, produced in great numbers all over Europe beginning in the 1720s and 1730s, was originally a genre of entertainment music, usually performed in the evenings, sometimes out of doors. In short, the term meant aristocratic party music, which over the course of the century, responding to forces of urbanization and the economic empowerment of the bourgeoisie, became more and more available to public access. In the course of its becoming public it became more and more the pretext for the occasions at which it was performed, rather than their mere accompaniment. Thus, finally, the growth of the symphony paralleled the growth of the concert as we know it today — a growth that in turn paralleled a vastly increasing taste for esthetically beguiling or emotionally stirring instrumental music, sought out for the sake of its sheer sensuous and imaginative appeal, and listened to, increasingly, in silent absorption. This was indeed a momentous esthetic change, indeed a revolution. Its beginnings, however, were modest and artistically unpretentious in the extreme.

CONCERT LIFE IS BORN

The word "concert," originally, was merely the French form of the word "concerto." And it was in France — in 1725, to be exact — that the word was first used in its modern sense. It was in France, then, the cradle of Enlightenment and "civilized" taste, that the modern vogue for public instrumental music — "concert music" — was born. That first French usage was associated with the earliest significant and lasting European concert series, the Concert Spirituel (literally, "sacred concert"), organized in Paris by the minor court composer Anne Danican Philidor (1681–1728), son and brother to several other Parisian musicians, including François-André Philidor, who although a successful composer of operas was (and remains) much better known as one of the greatest chess players of all time.

The Concert Spirituel was intended as an excuse for musical entertainments on religious holidays, and especially during the Lenten season, when opera houses were closed. It had a remote ancestor in London, that great mercantile city, where an enterprising musician named John Banister rented a public building and put on what seem to have been rather shoddy musical programs almost fifty years earlier; it did not catch on (see Weiss and Taruskin, *Music in the Western World*, No. 57). At the much more lavishly endowed Concert Spirituel the staple fare was pious cantatas and concerted (vocal-instrumental) *grands motets* in keeping with its "spiritual" nature; but since it was a substitute for opera, it began with an overture—that is, a *sinfonia* or "symphonie"—which thus at the outset retained its traditional position as festive curtain-raiser.

At the very first concert spirituel, 18 March 1725, Corelli's famous "Christmas Concerto" (Ex. 24-8) served this purpose, which certainly illustrates the fluidity of genres and terms at this early period of concert life. But specially composed symphonies after the Italian operatic model quickly became the order of the day; indeed, it was the existence of the concert series that stimulated their production. The sacred vocal works were likewise interspersed with virtuoso instrumental solos, often composed and performed by the great Italian-trained violinist Jean-Marie Leclair, the "French Vivaldi."

The Concert Spirituel, which lasted until 1790, thus set the tone for concert programs throughout the eighteenth century. Almost always, and almost everywhere, concerts were variety shows mixing vocal music with instrumental and sacred with secular. A typical concert program from Vienna, dated 16 April 1791, printed in both German and Italian (Fig. 29-1), begins with a "grande Sinfonia della composizione del Sig. *Mozart*" as curtain raiser, followed by some opera arias by Mozart and Paisiello; a cello concerto by Ignatz Pleyel, a former apprentice of Haydn then working in Strasbourg; a choral *Alleluja* by the Vienna court composer Johann Georg Albrechtsberger, the most famous music pedagogue of the day; and *per finale*, a "harmonie," or wind-band partita "first performed in honor of the coronation of his Imperial Majesty" Leopold II, by Georg Druschetzky, a famous regimental musician of the day.

Except for outdoor band concerts consisting entirely of partitas like Druschetzky's (alias serenatas, cassations, notturnos, and the like), there were no all-instrumental concerts until the first decade of the nineteenth century. The idea of what we now call a "symphony concert," with the audience paying rapt attention to one orchestral work after another, was unheard of; the symphony was just one of the ingredients and almost always the opener. (In the opera house, free-standing symphonies were eventually performed from the pit as entertainment or sonic wallpaper between the acts; according to contemporary witnesses, they were usually ignored by the audience.)

The Viennese concert listed above was actually not called a concert but an *Akademie* or *academia*—a term that goes back, as we know, to sixteenth-century Italy, where it

FIG. 29-1   Bilingual handbill for a Tonkunstler-Sozietät concert in Vienna, 1791.

already designated aristocratic house concerts. And northern Italy was, after France, the next great venue for public concerts in the eighteenth century. A particular center was Milan, where Lenten "academie di sinfonia e di canto" were a fixture beginning in the 1730s. Their director, Giovanni Battista Sammartini (or San Martini, 1700–75), was both the *maestro di cappella* at the Milan cathedral and a leading composer of operas for the city's ducal theater. At first he adapted his operatic *sinfonie* for use at concerts, later he wrote them especially for concert use, in great quantities. Sixty-eight such works by Sammartini survive, making his the first big name in the history of the genre.

A "Sinfonia del Signor St Martini" (Ex. 29-1), now found in a Paris manuscript collection assembled in the 1740s, probably dates from the previous decade, making it one of the earliest free-standing concert symphonies now extant, and one that very likely served its festive purpose both in its city of origin and in the French capital. It is in four movements, of which all but the tiny second one (little more than a snatch of chordal connective tissue) are cast in binary form. The third and fourth movements, respectively a gigue and a minuet, are traditional dance-suite (or *concerto da camera*) items. Their harmonically defined form—the usual pendular swing from tonic to dominant and back (the return trip by way of a FOP)—plays itself out through a parallel thematic structure, as one would find in a suite by Bach, at this time (lest we forget) still very much alive and working in Leipzig.

Their style, however, has been modified by their Italian operatic background in ways that Bach would have despised ("the little Dresden tunes!"), but that his sons were much drawn to, as we have known since chapter 27. These telltale traits include their relatively homophonic texture and their relatively slow and regular "harmonic rhythm" (rate of chord change) — which, however, by no means precluded an interesting phrase structure. The concluding minuet, with its varied reprise standing as a middle section, is reminiscent of the keyboard sonatas examined in chapter 27.

EX. 29-1A Giovanni Battista Sammartini, Sinfonia in G, from Fonds Blancheton, mm. 1–17

EX. 29-1A (continued)

EX. 29-1B Giovanni Battista Sammartini, Sinfonia in G, from Fonds Blancheton, mm. 23–34

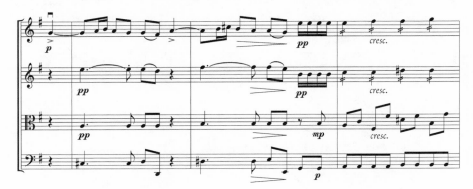

EX. 29-1B (*continued*)

It is the first movement that differs most strikingly from anything J. S. Bach could ever have written and reminds us most of his sons' work—or rather, the work his sons would later produce under the influence of music like Sammartini's. Although in dance-form, it is not a dance. In rhythm it resembles a march, and the brassy fanfarelike chords at the outset, so appropriate to a concert symphony's festive function, strengthen the military association (or "topic," to use a properly eighteenth-century term) even though only strings are used.

Like the work of Bach's sons, the opening section (Ex. 29-1a) moves not through a continuously developing or "spun out" melodic line (such as Bach the Father might have provided), but through a series of well-articulated, contrasting ideas (mm. 1–2,

3–5, 6–7, 9–11, 12–14). The last two measures close the section off with a reference to the opening music, but with its scoring as if "reversed." There is a noticeable inclination to "dramatize" the harmony: for example, the short sequence leading to the dominant (mm. 9–11) culminates in a complete diminished-seventh chord, rather a spicy harmony to use without any textual motivation.

The second half begins as if it were going to parallel the thematic structure of the first, but after four measures a long bout of modulating sequences sets in (Ex. 29-1b), putting continuity in place of contrast and dramatizing the onset of the journey to the Far Out Point. The journey is vividly contrasted in direction, with a passage of sharpward-leaning chromaticism (introducing D♯ as leading tone to vi, the FOP) not only followed but strongly contradicted by a flatward-leaning cascade that gets as far as the previous limit's enharmonic equivalent, E♭ (functioning here as the third of a minor subdominant triad), before veering in toward home.

As in the work of Bach's sons (and also Domenico Scarlatti), "home" means not only a returning key, but a returning theme as well: the "double return" has now already become fully established in Sammartini's style as the normal procedure for rounding off the opening movement of an orchestral *sinfonia*, whether intended for theater or "academy." From now on we will call the expanded binary form with dramatized key contrasts and double returns the "symphonic binary" form in recognition of its origin in the operatic sinfonia and its concert offshoot.

And now recall the overture (or sinfonia) to Mozart's *Don Giovanni*, discussed in the previous chapter, and notice that in form it is in all essentials identical to Sammartini's first movement, albeit far more elaborately worked out. The process of that elaboration—the evolution of the symphonic binary form (more commonly known today as "sonata form") over the course of the later eighteenth century—is one of the things this chapter will trace with particular zeal, for it gave rise to what would be the dominating genre of instrumental music for more than a century, a genre that would reach levels of development, both as to dimensions and as to elaborated content, that could never have been predicted before the advent of the concert symphony.

The spread of that magnificently fertile genre was facilitated by a number of political and social factors. During the eighteenth century Milan, Sammartini's city (along with all the rest of northern Italy, then called "Lombardy and Venetia"), was under Austrian rule. Musical developments there spread rapidly to Vienna, the Hapsburg capital, thence outward to all the other cities and courts within the Hapsburg ("Holy Roman") realm. Musical academies with their brilliant orchestral adornments became a site of conspicuous aristocratic, then (beginning in the 1770s) public, musical consumption throughout the Empire. Though practiced and supported elsewhere, and although it had other centers (notably Paris), the concert symphony became the Austrian genre *par excellence*, and the virtuoso orchestra (also emulated in Paris) became an Austrian specialty.

AN ARMY OF GENERALS

As Lombardy-Venetia marked the Austrian Empire's southern frontier, so the so-called Rhine Palatinate (now part of Bavaria in southern Germany) was its most westerly extension, bordering France. The name goes back to late Roman times, when the title Count Palatine was bestowed on the Emperor's chief vassal in the region, and so it remained under the "Holy Roman" Empire, when the ruler of the region became known as the Elector Palatine, one of the foremost nobles in the whole Hapsburg hierarchy. In the early eighteenth century, the seat of this substantial court was unexpectedly moved from Heidelberg, a large city whose castle had been ravaged during the War of the Spanish Succession, to Mannheim, a small town on the right bank of the Rhine.

A new capital had to be established, which meant building a large palace and equipping it with all the attributes of majesty. The town had no opera house, and so court instrumental music — semiweekly "académies de musique" — suddenly became one of the Elector Palatine's chief vehicles for displays of what sociologists call "quantitative luxury." The court musical establishment grew accordingly by leaps and bounds, especially during the reign of the Elector Carl Theodor (1743–78), himself a musical amateur.

In the seventh year of his reign, there were sixty-one musicians on his payroll. By the last year, when Mozart visited Mannheim and described the place in an enthusiastic letter to his father, there were ninety, of whom no fewer than sixty (many of them famous virtuosos) were members of what was by then the largest, most famous, and by all accounts most accomplished orchestra in Europe. Dr. Burney, another visitor, wrote in 1772 that "there are more solo players and good composers in this than perhaps in any other orchestra; it is an army of generals, equally fit to plan a battle as to fight it."[1] Many of these musical generals — particularly the wind players (including virtuosos of the clarinet, the latest instrument to join the standard orches-

tral complement) — had been brought in from the easterly portion of the Elector's realm, known as the Upper Palatinate, which bordered on or overlapped with Bohemia, the part of central Europe now known as the Czech Lands. The leader of the band under Carl Theodor, and its very exacting trainer, was a Bohemian violinist and composer named Jan Václav Stamic (1717–57, known in German as Johann Wenzel Stamitz or Steinmetz), whose son Carl (1745–1801) became even more famous than his father. (Carl toured the continent as a violin virtuoso and finally settled in Paris, where he became a favorite at the Concert Spirituel both as performer and as a composer specializing in *symphonies concertantes*, symphonies full of virtuoso solo passages for outstanding members of the orchestra.)

FIG. 29-2 Carl Theodor, Elector Palatine, who maintained the Mannheim orchestra at his court.

Under Stamitz senior and his successor Christian Cannabich (1731–98), a native Mannheimer whose conducting Mozart observed and admired, the Palatine orchestra became famous for its quasi-military discipline and the exquisite effects that such discipline enabled. "Its *forte* is a thunderclap," wrote another visitor, the poet and musical journalist Christian Friedrich Schubart, "its crescendo a cataract, its diminuendo a crystal stream babbling away into the distance, its *piano* a breath of spring."[2] The composing members of this band became the virtuoso orchestrators of their day, exploiting all kinds of special effects that acquired nicknames: "rockets" (quick rising passages, often arpeggiated), "steamrollers" (crescendos over ostinatos), and of course the explosive beginning, known as the *premier coup d'archet* ("first stroke of the bow"). Needless to say, Mannheim became a major spawning ground for concert symphonies.

In his short career Stamitz produced about seventy symphonies, of which ten were written in three-part score and are sometimes called "orchestral trios." The title page of Stamitz's op. 1, a collection of six such works published in Paris in 1755, reads *Six Sonates à Trois parties concertantes qui sont faites pour Exécuter ou à trois, ou avec toutes l'Orchestre*: "Six sonatas in three solo parts that are made to be performed either as a trio or with the whole orchestra." In their scoring alternatives these pieces occupied a middle position between chamber music (played, according to the modern definition, by one player on each part) and orchestra music (played with "doubling" of parts, especially string parts, by as many musicians as desired, and with the bass line doubled at the octave and joined by a continuo keyboard). They could be performed, in other words, either privately or publicly. That was true of many early symphonies, including the one by Sammartini with which we are already familiar, and it was almost always true, too, of works designated "divertimento" or "serenade." Stamitz's symphony or orchestra-trio in C minor, the third item in his posthumously published op. 4 (Paris, 1758), is a particularly distinguished yet fully representative example of his practice. All four of its movements are in binary form, and the sequence is similar to that in Sammartini's symphony: a marchlike first movement, a slower lyrical second, and two suite dances. Stamitz has reversed the order of the concluding pair, so that a stately minuet precedes a rollicking gigue marked *prestissimo*, evidently meant (like many Mannheim finales) as a showpiece of precision execution.

Like many orchestral minuets going all the way back to the time of Lully, the one in Stamitz's symphony is actually a pair of minuets, played *da capo*. This was a custom that originated in the aristocratic ballroom, where the full set of required dance steps or "figures" came to exceed the number of measures a single dance could reasonably provide. The second of the pair, in a related key and traditionally played by a smaller complement of instruments, was for that reason called the "trio." The term is redundant in the context of Stamitz's symphony, which is scored in trio texture throughout. But that just goes to show that it was truly a custom, like the pairing of dances itself. Like many customs, they persisted long after their practical necessity had been obviated and the reason for their existence forgotten.

The gigue finale is an impressively extended composition. Its tonal trajectory embodies a number of interestingly adventurous key relations, including a vagary into

E-flat minor, in modern parlance the "parallel minor of the relative major." Among its admirers, evidently, was Beethoven, who probably encountered Stamitz's works during his formative years in Bonn, his native town, then another Electoral seat on the Rhine at the western extremity of the Austrian empire, where his father and grandfather before him had served as Electoral court musicians. As we will see in chapter 32, the third movement of Beethoven's famous Fifth Symphony contains the same unusual modulation to E-flat minor and even contains a perhaps unwitting quotation from Stamitz's work, the sincerest form of tribute (see Ex. 32-12a–b on p. 719). Stamitz's work had thus achieved "classic" status; it was a work suitable for study and quotation.

THE BACH SONS AS "SYMPHONISTS"

Among the other composers of concert symphonies whose works became early classics of the genre were two of J. S. Bach's sons. Johann Christian Bach, a prolific composer of *opera seria* and, later in life, a concert impresario in his own right, naturally gravitated toward the genre as a spinoff from his primary activities. The interchangeability of opera overture and early symphony, both as genres and as terms, is well illustrated by J. C. Bach's popular Symphony in B♭, op. 18 no. 2. It was originally composed in 1774 as the *sinfonia avanti l'opera* preceding Bach's *Lucio Silla*. Publication followed seven years later in London, in a set entitled "Six Grand Overtures," of which two others were actual operatic sinfonias and the remaining three were symphonies composed for concert use. The use of the word "overture" to refer to what we now call symphonies persisted in London to the end of the century.

Bach's *Lucio Silla* was first performed in November 1775, at the court of Mannheim, which by then boasted a major opera house. (The libretto had already been set three years earlier by Mozart for performance in Milan.) The orchestra for which it was written, then, was the very same Mannheim orchestra whose feats of virtuoso concert execution had become legend. Bach's symphony (or "overture") can thus serve as an illustration of the fabled Mannheim style. The tempo marking, allegro assai, is already a mark of confidence in the band's virtuosity. The scoring is rich, with ten wind parts including clarinets, a Mannheim specialty. The first sound heard, a loud tutti on the tonic triad rhythmically repeated four times, is the redoubtable *premier coup d'archet*. It is immediately (and typically) contrasted with a quiet or "charming" passage for the three upper string parts, after which the two violins reapproach the fanfare through a quick rising passage marked with a crescendo—in other words, a "rocket." All of this is shown in Ex. 29-2a.

The festive fanfare mood is maintained throughout. (The ending—the "dernier coup d'archet," so to speak—is an even more emphatic paraphrase of the beginning.) While clearly organized around the binary (tonic/dominant) axis, the form of the piece is somewhat nonchalant, with the "double return" preceding rather than following the main modulatory section. The latter rather unusually includes a cadence on IV (E♭), possibly chosen for the same reason it was often avoided by other composers: like the tonic and the dominant, the subdominant is another major triad, no farther away from the tonic than the dominant along the circle of fifths (but in the opposite direction). Thus it offers little in the way of variety or adventure, but in compensation it continually reinforces the festive fanfare affect (Ex. 29-2b). The piece is an unmitigated celebration (of the Electoral presence in the opera house, of the London customers in the stalls) and an unclouded entertainment. As well as any compositions of their kind, J. C. Bach's symphonies (like those of Carl Friedrich Abel, his London business partner) uphold the ideal of high-class party music, transferred to a public occasion.

It is therefore especially interesting to compare them with the symphonies of his older half-brother Carl Philipp Emanuel Bach. Like his father, C. P. E. Bach never wrote an opera (hence never wrote a *sinfonia avanti l'opera*), yet he nevertheless contributed some twenty symphonies to the burgeoning orchestral repertoire, mostly rather late in his career. Many of them exhibit the stern and stormy, harmonically restless and unpredictable idiom identified in chapter 27 as the *empfindsamer Stil*, the "sentimental" or "pathetic" style—a style reserved, as CPE put it himself, *für Kenner und Liebhaber* ("for connoisseurs and amateurs" of the art), not for the average partygoer.

EX. 29-2A   J. C. Bach, Sinfonia, Op. 18, no. 2, mm. 1–7

EX. 29-2A (*continued*)

Six of Emanuel's symphonies, scored for strings alone, were composed in 1773 on commission from Baron van Swieten, the Vienna antiquarian, who absolutely personified the connoisseur-amateur type. Another set of four, composed in 1776 when the composer was sixty-two, was dedicated to Prince Frederick William of Prussia, the nephew and eventual successor of Emanuel's old patron, King Frederick the Great. The younger Frederick was an enthusiastic and skilled cellist who if it were possible would have outdone his flute-playing uncle in arts patronage.

The 1776 symphonies were published in Leipzig in 1780 with a curious title page that somewhat oversold them as *Orchester-Sinfonien* ("Orchestral symphonies," as if there were another kind) and advertised the fact that they were scored *mit 12 obligaten Stimmen*, that is, in twelve instrumental parts, all of which take solo passages and hence cannot be omitted. In many early symphonies, including some by CPE, the wind parts were an optional harmonic reinforcement and filler that merely took over the function of the continuo keyboard, which it tended to replace until the orchestra, by the end of the eighteenth century, was generally continuo-free. That is why in the eighteenth century wind ensembles were often called "Harmonie," as in the partita by Albrechtsberger encountered earlier on a Viennese concert program. In C. P. E. Bach's

"Orchester-Sinfonien," the wind scoring is elaborately detailed and virtuosic, and there are many passages where the continuo "flügel" (keyboard) is explicitly suppressed. This was an extremely, indeed self-consciously modern style of orchestration, all the more remarkable in view of the composer's age and his relative aloofness from the theater.

The first movement from the first of these symphonies shows off Emanuel's singular symphonic style at full potency. The orchestra is handled brilliantly, and in a way that especially dramatizes the "symphonic binary" form. The solo wind writing is contrasted strategically with the continuoless strings. It is the latter group—two violins, viola, and cello without double bass support or keyboard—that get to play the rhythmically agitated and tonally inconclusive opening theme (Ex. 29-3a). (Note particularly the use of the C-natural, which turns the tonic into the "V of IV" before it has even had a chance to establish itself through a cadence.) A stressful tutti, erupting in diminished-seventh chords, makes a headlong dash to the contrasting (dominant) key; and when that key arrives, the solo winds enter with a placid, harmonically stable theme of their own, creating a maximum of contrast with the earlier music (Ex. 29-3b).

EX. 29-2B   J. C. Bach, Sinfonia, Op. 18, no. 2, mm. 81–87

EX. 29-2B (*continued*)

EX. 29-3A   C. P. E. Bach, first Orchestral Symphony (Wotquenne. 183; 1776), mm. 1–19

EX. 29-3A   *(continued)*

EX. 29-3B C. P. E. Bach, first Orchestral Symphony (Wotquenne. 183; 1776), mm. 35–48

This strongly established contrast serves as a compass for the listener as the movement proceeds, since the composer's efforts seem mainly bent on maintaining an impetuous momentum, and incorporating a maximum of surface diversity, deployed with fantasialike (that is, unpredictable) caprice. Although the form is recognizably binary, there is no double bar dividing the two sections, and no repeats. Instead, the opening theme (associated with the continuoless strings) serves as a formal marker, somewhat in the manner of a ritornello. It resurfaces in the dominant at the halfway point, to set the tonal trajectory on its complicated homeward path, and again when the home key is reached (m. 136), providing the crucial "double return."

Although the recurrences of the opening theme thus provide an orientation point, its harmonic instability lends the whole movement a tonally precarious (hence emotionally fraught) aspect. The only points of harmonic repose are the contrasting wind solos, the first confirming arrival in the dominant and the second reconfirming the tonic. The obbligato wind theme is thus given a unique function in the movement's unfolding. The rigorous contrast in timbres—solo strings versus solo winds—reinforces a thematic dualism that reflects and dramatizes the tonal dualism on which this movement, like any binary movement, is constructed.

Thematic dualism of this kind would eventually become such an important ingredient of standard symphonic procedure as virtually to define it. Textbook descriptions of "sonata form" would eventually identify thematic dualism as its procedural basis. As we can see from this example, however, thematic dualism arose as an epiphenomenon—a surface event—to mirror, and thus to dramatize (as well as clarify), the underlying harmonic basis of the form.

The most spectacular display of harmonic instability comes at the very end of the movement (Ex. 29-3c), when the D major tonic suddenly dissolves without warning into the dominant of E-flat, the key of the next movement. It seems a radical, tonality-defying effect—so radical, in fact, that we might easily forget its many precedents. Those precedents are found in the opera, particularly the comic opera with its *introduzioni* and *finali*, long sections that depend for their continuity on the ability to make many

EX. 29-3C   C. P. E. Bach, first Orchestral Symphony (Wotquenne. 183; 1776), mm. 206–17

kinds of transition—abrupt or graded, as the situation demands—between keys. In connection with C. P. E. Bach's symphony we might recall the end of the *Don Giovanni* overture, which dissolves in an almost identical way into the dominant of Leporello's first aria.

Thus the opera continues, even in the hands of a non-operatic composer like C. P. E. Bach, to provide the concert symphony with its most important precedents. In its most elaborated form, the new genre was a veritable—or better, a virtual—instrumental drama.

HAYDN

By far the most influential—and in that sense the most important—composer of symphonies in the mid-to-late eighteenth century was (Franz) Joseph Haydn (1732–1809), who in two momentous ways established the genre for posterity. First, by creating an unusually large and impressive body of works in the genre that became

EX. 29-3C   (*continued*)

EX. 29-3C *(continued)*

the object of widespread emulation, Haydn did more by his example than any other composer to standardize the "classical" symphony, as it has come to be called. And second, by once and for all taking the genre out of the aristocratic salon and into the public sphere, Haydn considerably enlarged both its dimensions and its cultural significance, and laid the foundation for the modern concert repertory, in which several of his symphonies are still staples.

He did not do these things singlehandedly, or by sheer force of will, or even intentionally, as the word is usually understood, but in miraculous symbiosis with his times — that is, by adapting with phenomenal success to the changing social conditions of his time, and the concomitantly changing social role of musicians. The word "miraculous" seems appropriate because Haydn's great success seems to have been owed in equal measure to talent — for music, to be sure, but also for seizing opportunities — and to luck. The luck would not have done a less gifted and avid man any comparable good, but without it talent and productivity alone would never have sufficed. Haydn's great good fortune has become ours, for we have inherited its results.

THE PERFECT CAREER

Perhaps the most vivid measure of that synergy of capacity and contingency is the fact that Haydn was (like Handel) what we would now call a self-made man—a very modern sort of hero, the story of whose career reads a bit like an inspirational novel by Horatio Alger. Unlike the Bachs, unlike Mozart, and unlike Beethoven, Haydn was not born into an established musical family. His father was a village wheelwright in southeastern Austria near the border of what was then considered Hungary but is now Croatia. Though a master craftsman, the elder Haydn (unlike Handel's father, a prosperous surgeon) was neither a highly educated nor a particularly well-to-do man, and there was no way in the world that his son's future career could have

FIG. 29-3   Franz Joseph Haydn at the height of his fame, engraved by Thomas Bush Hardy "from an Original Picture in the Possession of J. Bland" (i.e., John Bland, the London publisher).

been predicted. Haydn was acutely aware of the distance his talent and good fortune had taken him. To one of his several contemporary biographers, Albert Christoph Dies, the venerable composer offered himself as an inspiration to the young, "who may see from my example that something may indeed come from nothing."[3] And his modern biographer, H. C. Robbins Landon, cast his whole enterprise as an enlargement of that remark, tracing "the life of a boy who began in abject poverty, half-trained and largely self-educated, who rose to be the leading musical figure of Europe by the 1790s and achieved greater popularity in his own lifetime than any composer before him," becoming in the process the wealthiest of all pre-twentieth-century professional musicians (Handel alone excepted), and an expert courtier, at home in high society and even "gently manipulating Princes of the Holy Roman Empire."[4]

The immediate result of Haydn's first sign of talent was his removal from his family. At the age of six he was sent to live with a cousin, Franck by name, who worked as a schoolmaster and church choirmaster in a neighboring town. There he had his only formal schooling—reading, writing, and catechism, besides the rudiments of music. By the age of eight he was earning his own keep as a musician, at first as a choirboy at St. Stephen's Cathedral, the main Viennese church, where he had been brought by a passing nobleman who had happened to hear him sing: his first stroke of luck. His solo singing brought Haydn while still a child to the attention of the Empress Maria Theresa, but his success as a church singer was short-lived. When his voice broke (not until the age of seventeen, as was usual in those days owing to a diet that would now be thought of as malnourishing), Haydn lost his place as soloist in the choir to his own younger brother Johann Michael (1737–1806), who also made a distinguished career as a composer, though nothing like Joseph's.

FIG. 29-4   St. Stephen's cathedral, Vienna, in 1792.

A rather terrible time followed—years of near-starvation in Vienna, where Haydn studied voraciously, gave lessons to children, and took any musical odd job that came his way, like playing violin for a pittance in street-music entertainments—serenades, cassations, and the like. Among the books he studied were Fux's *Gradus ad Parnassum*, the bible of the *stile antico* (that is, strict counterpoint), and C. P. E. Bach's "Prussian" sonatas, which we sampled two chapters back (Ex. 27-3), and which had a decided influence on Haydn's style. He also apprenticed himself for a while to Nicola Porpora (1686–1768), a famous Italian opera composer and singing teacher, who lived in Vienna between 1753 and 1760. In return for instruction Haydn accompanied Porpora's pupils at their lessons and (as he told his biographers) shined his master's boots.

Haydn's earliest compositions date from this wretched period, and all of them, a few church pieces excepted, were merry entertainments composed for ready market consumption. They included singspiels of the most plebeian sort, roughly on the order of Punch-and-Judy skits (or Hanswurst—"Johnny Sausage"—shows, as they were known in Vienna). The music for these carnival frolics is lost, or perhaps preserved anonymously, but the titles of two of them are known: *Der krumme Teufel* ("The foxy devil") and *Der neue krumme Teufel* (roughly, "A new foxy-devil show"). First performed in 1753 and 1757 respectively in the Kärntnerthor Theater, the official German-language (i.e., lower-class) house, they became very popular and gave Haydn his first local celebrity.

Another early success came in the form of instrumental works that straddled the nebulous line between orchestral and chamber music, presaging that vast portion of Haydn's output on which his historical reputation now rests. At various times Haydn called them cassations, at other times notturni, at still others divertimenti. Six were published with a title page that called them "Sinfonies ou Quatuors" (Symphonies or Quartets). The product of the years 1757–58, they are now classified in most lists of Haydn's works as his earliest string quartets (opus 1 and opus 2), because their four parts are earmarked for two violins, viola, and "basso," which could mean cello.

There is no reason why they could not be performed, like Stamitz's "orchestra-trios," with doubled parts, however; and the designation "basso" could certainly be read as implying the participation of a continuo. Nor is the addition of supplementary wind parts out of the question: manuscript sources of uncertain origin so equip some of them. The only thing one can say with certainty is that these works, along with a few others that are scored in three and five parts, stand at the beginning of Haydn's production of instrumental concert music, the field that he would decisively transform and standardize, in the process finally distinguishing between chamber and orchestral genres as we know them today.

Haydn's op. 1 and op. 2 must have been highly adaptable to varying combinations of instruments, because they were best sellers, circulating as far south as Naples and as far north (and east) as Königsberg (now the Russian city of Kaliningrad). They even found their way to North America when the Moravian composer Johann Friedrich Peter (1746–1813), who had copied them out, settled in Pennsylvania in 1770. (Peter himself would make a contribution to the chamber divertimento genre with a set of string quintets, composed in Salem, North Carolina in 1789: the first chamber music composed on American soil.)

Their symmetrical or palindromic sequence of five movements—fast "sonata form"/minuet-&-trio/slow/minuet-&-trio/fast finale—was typical of Viennese street music, but when performed by four solo strings the works were ideally suitable for home recreation as well. Haydn was again showing an understanding of the emergent music market, a business sense that would have marked him out for a successful freelance career if need be.

But he did not need it. On the strength of these early successes, Haydn found a permanent position as music director (Kapellmeister) in (or "to") a noble household. Such a position—essentially that of a highly regarded and somewhat privileged domestic servant—may appear demeaning to us, with our romantic notion of what an "artist" is. It was, however, the very best fate to which a professional musician in mid-eighteenth-century Vienna could aspire, unless, like Mozart, he was a performing virtuoso (as Haydn was not). In addition to a relatively high salary, a musician who landed such a post was given free lodging and board at the equivalent of an officers' mess. It was, especially by contrast with Haydn's former plight, a bountiful, carefree existence.

This stroke of good fortune befell Haydn in 1759, when he was hired by Count Karl Joseph Franz von Morzin (1717–83), a Bohemian aristocrat who maintained a huge residence in Vienna during the winters, as well as a family summer estate called Lukavec, near the Czech town of Plzen (Pilsen in German), famous for its breweries. The title of Kapellmeister originally meant "chapel master" (that is, choirmaster), but in secular courts and homes it meant director of musical entertainments. The post put Haydn in charge of an orchestra, and it was for this band that he wrote (or adapted) his first real symphonies.

There are seven such pieces dating from the Morzin period. They include the first five in the standard list of Haydn's symphonies, totaling 104, first drawn up early in the twentieth century, since which time two more have been unearthed. With two exceptions these early symphonies are three-movement works on the old *sinfonia avanti l'opera* model: a fast "symphonic binary" movement, a slow movement, and a dancelike finale, usually a gigue (less often a minuet). Of the two four-movement symphonies, one (no. 3 in G major) is cast in the format that Haydn would later establish as the norm: (1) symphonic binary, (2) slow, (3) minuet & trio, (4) fast finale. The other (no. 5 in A major) seems to be descended from the old church sonata. Its first movement is an Adagio, followed by an Allegro, both in binary form; then comes a minuet and trio; last a Presto finale in duple meter and binary form. Movement sequence was as yet a fluid affair.

What is already remarkably consistent, though, is Haydn's personal manner of inflecting the "symphonic binary" or "sonata" form: like the four-movement sequence of Symphony no. 3, it would eventually become standard practice thanks to his example. Let the first movement of Symphony "A" (Ex. 29-4), one of the recently discovered pieces and possibly the earliest of the lot, serve as prototype.

The special Haydnesque features are two. First, the movement's closing section, beginning with the "double return," closely parallels or recapitulates the whole opening section to the first double bar theme by theme, with only such truncations and adjustments as are necessary to keep the whole closing section in the tonic key rather than modulating again to the dominant. Second, the lengthy passage (Ex. 29-4a) extending from the first double bar to the double return, embodying the most radical tonal trajectory in the movement (from dominant to FOP to retransition), is quite rigorously, and very ingeniously, based melodically on motives drawn from the themes heard in the opening section. They are recombined, sequentially extended or otherwise paraphrased, using techniques collectively described in German by the term *thematische Arbeit* ("thematic work"), for which "development" is the word commonly employed in English.

EX. 29-4A   Franz Joseph Haydn, Symphony "A," I, mm. 43–79

EX. 29-4A (*continued*)

EX. 29-4A   (*continued*)

EX. 29-4A (*continued*)

EX. 29-4B   Franz Joseph Haydn, Symphony "A," I, mm. 1–4

EX. 29-4C   Franz Joseph Haydn, Symphony "A," I, mm. 31–37

EX. 29-4D   Franz Joseph Haydn, Symphony "A," I, mm. 23–27

Thus, to pick some examples, the figure tossed back and forth by the two violin parts in mm. 43–49 turns out to be a conflation of the first measure of the opening arpeggio or "rocket" (Ex. 29-4b) and a sixteenth-note turn from the quiet "second theme" in the dominant (Ex. 29-4c). The figure that elaborates the FOP (G minor or *vi*) in mm. 62–64 is drawn from the earlier transition to the dominant (Ex. 29-4d). The passage leading to the retransition (mm. 68–79) is a paraphrase of Ex. 29-4c.

In terms of its thematic or melodic content, then, Haydn's version of the "symphonic binary" form is articulated in three distinct parts, the first coinciding with the first harmonic "paragraph" of the binary form (I→V), and the second and third Haydnesque parts together comprising the second binary paragraph (V→I). The first and the last parts being similar in thematic content and sequence, they are often termed the exposition and the recapitulation. The middle part, containing the redeployment of motives originally "exposed" (or is it expounded?) in the first part, is often termed the development section in English. (The corresponding term in German, *Mittelsatz*, although it simply means the "middle section," carries the equivalent meaning when used in this context.)

This thematic structure — exposition, development, recapitulation — is obviously related to the old *da capo* aria form, from which it derives its very satisfying stability. What it amounts to is a sort of flexible "ternary" overlay coexisting with and reinforcing the binary harmonic structure. The relationship between the two elements — the three-part thematic structure and the two-part harmonic structure — could be endlessly varied. Its combination of flexibility and solidity, or (to put it another way) of complexity and clarity, made the resulting "sonata form" or "sonata-allegro form" or "first-movement form" (to give three terms now in common use to denote it) one of the most adaptable, durable, and potentially eloquent formal procedures ever devised for instrumental music in all media, from solo sonata to orchestral symphony or overture. It was largely thanks to this happy synthesis — and to Haydn, the synthesizer in chief — that instrumental music would enjoy a triumphant (and unforeseen) career over the next two centuries that in a curiously fitting way paralleled the course of Haydn's own life: from poor relation to dominant force. It too was a sort of Horatio Alger tale.

THE ESTERHÁZY YEARS

It might never have happened if Haydn had not had his next and biggest break, through which he was able to develop his gifts, and the media through which he exercised them, to the fullest. On 1 May 1761, still in his twenties, Haydn signed a contract as "Vice-Capellmeister in the service of his Serene Highness Paul Anton, Prince of the Holy Roman Empire, of Esterháza and Galantha, etc. etc." The benevolent patronage Haydn thus secured would last nearly five decades, to the end of his life. Three of the five decades were spent in active, and well-nigh incredibly fertile, Kapellmeisterly duty, the remaining two as a pensioned, still tirelessly creative, world celebrity.

The Esterházy family was the foremost princely house of Hungary. Their pre-eminence went back about a century before Haydn went to work for them, to the grandfather of the Prince who signed Haydn on, also named Paul, who was elected to the office of Hungarian Palatine in 1681, distinguished himself in the defense of Vienna against the forces of Suleiman the Magnificent two years later, and led the ensuing reconquest of Hungary from the Ottoman Turks, for which he was created a hereditary Prince of the Holy Roman Empire in 1687. This was the highest rank to which a nonmember of the house of Hapsburg could be admitted. It thus placed the Esterházy Princes on a level exceeded within the Empire only by the Imperial family itself. Not even the Elector Palatine at Mannheim could compete with them in noble standing.

With that standing went a commensurately heroic standard of living, entailing a household and a court second only to the Emperor's—or Empress's, for throughout most of the years of Haydn's active service the effective Austrian ruler was the dowager Empress Maria Theresa, who occasionally visited her near peer Prince Esterházy and thus got a Haydn symphony (no. 48 in C, with trumpets and drums) named after her. At the time of Haydn's employment the Prince had two main residences, the Palais Esterházy in Vienna, and the ancestral estate at Eisenstadt (Kismarton in Hungarian), on the western shore of Lake Neusiedl in Burgenland, the easternmost province of present-day Austria.

The Esterházy musical establishment was huge, and almost immediately after Haydn's employment was secured it grew beyond all imagining—not simply because of Haydn's presence on the payroll but because Prince Paul Anton was succeeded in 1762 by his brother Nikolaus Joseph, known as *der Prachtliebende* ("The magnificent," or more literally, "The ostentatious"), a fanatical music lover who built the gorgeous Eszterháza summer palace at the southern end of the lake, just where present-day Austria abuts present-day Hungary. Construction of this mini-Versailles was begun in 1766, just as Haydn acceded to the post of chief Kapellmeister for the Esterházy court on the death of his predecessor Gregor Joseph Werner. The whole estate, replete with parks, fountains, pleasure pavilions, and servant houses, was not completed until 1784, six years before Nikolaus's death. Bombed out and rebuilt after the Second World War, it is now maintained as a museum by the Hungarian government (see Fig. 29-5).

The Eszterháza palace compound contained two theaters, one for opera and the other for marionette plays. In addition there were two concert rooms in the palace itself, a large hall that could accommodate an orchestra and an audience to match, and a smaller chamber for what is (yes, for that reason) known as chamber music. Haydn's duties, reminiscent of Bach's in Leipzig, included the supervision of a regular round of performances—one opera and two concerts a week, as specified by the contract, with additional major performances for important guests like the Empress, and daily chamber music at the Prince's pleasure—as well as composition. It is no wonder that his output, like Bach's, has proved to be literally innumerable.

For the princely theaters Haydn composed some twenty Italian operas, mostly comic, and half a dozen singspiels for the puppet house. For the weekly musicales he composed at least seventy-five of his extant symphonies (a few of them reusing material from the operas) and dozens of divertimenti (mostly published as quartets). But

FIG. 29-5   Main gate of the summer palace at Eszterháza (now Fertöd, Hungary).

the fairest measure of the pace Haydn had to keep as music-purveyor to his voracious patron would be the music that was ordered à la carte, so to speak, "at the Prince's pleasure," much of it for the Prince himself to play.

Prince Nikolaus was an enthusiast of the baryton (or *viola paradon*), an unusual and unwieldy stringed instrument consisting of a bass viola da gamba with a widened neck that contained a set of wire "sympathetic strings" that mostly resonated with the bowed ones, creating a sort of shimmering harmonic aura surrounding the played melody, but that could also be plucked by the left thumb through a hole in the back of the neck, so that the instrument could provide its own rudimentary bass to accompany the bowed melody (Fig. 29-6). This contraption was used almost exclusively in Austria, where a few virtuosos lived, but it had

FIG. 29-6   Prince Nikolaus Esterhazy's baryton.

no literature to speak of. So Haydn had to create one from scratch. Over a rough decade from 1765 to 1776, Haydn furnished Prince Nikolaus with upwards of 175 three-movement divertimenti scored for baryton solo, discreetly accompanied by viola and "basso" (cello). He also composed a quantity of duets for two barytons, which he himself played with the Prince, having learned the instrument on demand, and larger chamber works, many of them birthday serenades for eight instruments, with easy baryton parts for the honoree to play.

But the Prince was not only a ravenous consumer of music, and Haydn was not merely prolific. His employer was also a true *Kenner und Liebhaber*, in C. P. E. Bach's phrase, who appreciated, as few of his contemporaries could, the specialness of Haydn's gifts. In what has become one of the most famous of the many reminiscences his biographers have recorded, Haydn reflected on the uniquely auspicious combination of circumstances that enabled his gifts — particularly his gifts as a "symphonist" — to flourish in the relative isolation of Eisenstadt and Eszterháza. "My prince was content with all my works," Haydn told Georg August Griesinger, a publisher's representative, "I received approval for anything I did. As head of an orchestra, I could make experiments, observe what enhanced an effect, and what weakened it, thus improving, adding to it, taking away from it, and running risks. I was cut off from the world, there was nobody in my vicinity to make me unsure of myself or interfere with me in my course, and so I was forced to become original."[5]

This testimony is an important document of the era of aristocratic patronage, because it attests to the symbiosis between talent and calling, between demand and supply, that could take effect when patronage operated to best advantage. The employer's needs — whether measured in idealized terms of artistic satisfaction or in crasser terms of blue-blood exhibitionism (*Prachtlieb* or "quantitative luxury") — were met. And the employee was liberated by his very exploitation, as it were, to develop his skills freely, knowing that the products of their free exercise would translate, from the employer's standpoint, into uniquely distinguished and valuable possessions.

Haydn's delight with his new working conditions is apparent in the very first symphonies he wrote for the Esterházys: a trilogy (nos. 6–8) bearing the subtitles "Morning, Noon, and Night" (*Le Matin, Le Midi, Le Soir*), and overflowing with special instrumental effects that exploited the virtuoso soloists in the orchestra, including *concertante* solo strings. In other pieces, he was very likely stimulated by the actual physical conditions of the halls in which he was privileged to work. The larger concert room was of really exceptional size, with a lengthy reverberation time like that of a church. That may be one reason why early on Haydn began experimenting with augmented orchestras, particularly with a complement of four horns that shows up in several Esterházy symphonies (and is given virtuoso treatment in no. 31, subtitled "Hornsignal"), but did not become standard in orchestras until well into the nineteenth century.

NORMS AND DEVIATIONS: CREATING MUSICAL MEANING

For an idea of Haydn at his most "original," and for a glimpse of that symbiosis between courtier-Kapellmeister and patron (leading to what Landon called the former's "gentle manipulation" of the latter), we can turn to Symphony no. 45, first performed, under very unusual circumstances, at the summer palace in November 1772. November is obviously not a summer month. That is what was so unusual about the circumstances — and, as a result, about the symphony.

Its key alone — F♯ minor — makes it unique among Haydn's symphonies and practically unique in the music of its time. (There is no other symphony in F♯ minor among the 12,000-odd entries in LaRue's *Union Thematic Catalogue*.) The character of its first movement is worlds away from the "festive fanfare mood" that typified the early concert symphony in keeping with its usual function. In form, too, the movement is famously enigmatic. And the concluding movement is so outlandish that without knowledge of the circumstances of its composition it would be altogether baffling.

The strange and squally first movement, with its uniquely "remote" key and its consequently anomalous timbre (at least when played on the winds and horns of Haydn's time), is the most extreme representative of a special group of symphonic compositions Haydn produced in the early 1770s, often associated with a similarly frenzied tendency in German drama and literature. The literary movement was known as *Sturm und Drang* ("Storm and stress") after the subtitle of a sensational play — *Die Wirrwarr* ("Turmoil" or "Confusion," 1776) — by F. M. von Klinger, a close friend of Goethe, whom he influenced with this work. With its glorification of the "state of nature," its emphasis on subjective, often violent moods, and its portrayals of social alienation, *Sturm und Drang* (as observed in chapter 27) had obvious affinities with the

Empfindsamkeit ("Sentimentality") of earlier German poetry that was directly reflected in the music of C. P. E. Bach, who as we know had a formative influence on Haydn's style. The *Sturm und Drang* movement also led, or fed, into the main stream of Romanticism that would soon engulf European art, and for the first time put German artists at the forefront of European culture.

EX. 29-5A Franz Joseph Haydn, Symphony no. 45 in F-sharp minor ("Farewell"), I, mm. 1–16

EX. 29-5A (*continued*)

Its actual connection with Haydn may be disputed; no direct evidence associates the composer with the actual products of the *Sturm und Drang* movement or its leaders. But the character of the opening movement of Symphony no. 45 is undeniably one of turmoil, and Haydn was clearly aiming to give something of the impression through it of a *Wirrwarr*, an emotional confusion. The unremitting syncopations in the accompaniment to the opening theme (Ex. 29-5a) are one symptom of this. A far more significant symptom, however, is the eccentric treatment given the sonata form. The contrasting second theme comes not before but after the double bar and is cast in neither the dominant nor the relative major, the "normal," therefore expectable (hence expressively neutral), alternate keys in a minor-mode movement.

(Those keys had already had their own little drama in the movement. As a look at the score will confirm, the relative major was deliberately prepared and avoided in mm. 37–38 by a sudden feint: the substitution of C-natural for C-sharp, changing A major to A minor. The actual sectional cadence takes place in C-sharp minor, the "minor dominant," but is contradicted on the other side of the double bar by another sudden feint: a switch to A major, the key originally expected and deferred.) The key of the lyrical "second theme" in this movement (Ex. 29-5b) is actually that of the FOP (D major, the submediant). This is perhaps the most serious departure from the conventions of sonata form as practiced (and established) by Haydn himself, according to which the FOP is to be reached through *thematische Arbeit*, not suddenly introduced by way of arbitrarily invented material. (It is true, by the way, that the theme in question bears some small if demonstrable resemblance to a motive in the exposition, and the resemblance has been cited by those who prefer to explain away its strangeness. But one has to hunt for it; the motivic relationship is only putative. By contrast, there is no need to hunt for the strangeness; it stares you challengingly in the face.)

As if that were not enough, this placidly beautiful D-major theme is approached and left not by transitions but by pauses on either side. It has the air of an intrusion, not a development, further set off from its surroundings by its "bassless" initial scoring. And it comes to no cadence: rather, it seems (by the use of an arpeggiated diminished-seventh

EX. 29-5B   Franz Joseph Haydn, Symphony no. 45 in F-sharp minor ("Farewell"), I, mm. 108–15

chord) to dissolve into thin air (like a mirage, as the Haydn specialist James Webster has suggested). There can be no question that this music is deliberately enigmatic. It is so because it departs for no apparent reason from what had become accepted norms of composition (that is, of behavior) by the time it was written — especially at the Esterházy court, where Haydn's music was especially familiar. As the saying goes, Haydn was honoring the norms he had created "in the breach," and could only have been expecting his audience to notice the fact and be bewildered.

From this example one might generalize further about the use and purposes of compositional "norms," so many of which can be credited to Haydn. One of their

EX. 29-5C   Franz Joseph Haydn, Symphony no. 45 in F-sharp minor ("Farewell"), III, mm. 1–12

EX. 29-5C (*continued*)

main uses—and purposes—is revealed precisely in departures from them like this one. In other words, norms are not laws that must be adhered to simply for the sake of coherence or intelligibility, although that is their primary purpose. Absolutely unchallenged "normality" is perhaps the most boring mode of discourse. One rarely finds it in Haydn, or in any imaginative or interesting composer. Rather it is the existence of norms that allows departures to become meaningful—and thereby expressive. In that sense, rules are indeed made to be broken.

But expressive of what? That is often a teasing question in instrumental music, as we know. An answer must await knowledge of what follows. The idea of leaving a movement "hanging" expressively, to become meaningful only in retrospect, or in conjunction with the other movements, is to create the aspect of a narrative connecting all the movements in the symphony. It both introduces an "extramusical" presence into the content of the work and at the same time binds its constituent parts that much more compellingly into a coordinated, coherent whole. In both of these aspects, Haydn's symphony was very much a harbinger of a new expressive range, and a new importance, that instrumental music would claim, especially in the German-speaking lands. This, too, was an aspect of German music that tied it to nascent Romanticism, and to Germany's new position of leadership in European art.

The overall shape of Symphony no. 45 is as strange—and therefore as telling—as that of its first movement. For most of its duration it seems to follow what had for a dozen years been the standard procedure: a fast symphonic binary movement or "sonata allegro," however eccentric; a slow movement, a minuet and trio, and a finale in Haydn's favorite meter-tempo combination (Presto in $\frac{2}{2}$ or "cut time"). The keys are closely related to those of the first movement: slow movement in A (relative major); minuet in F♯ (parallel major), finale in the original key.

One noteworthy harmonic touch, in view of what has gone before, occurs at the beginning of the minuet (Ex. 29-5c), where the first tutti blusters in on a boisterous chord of the flat submediant (D major), palpably intruding on the soft beginning of the tune. This, of course, is the key of the enigmatically intrusive "second theme" in the first movement. But where the D-major tonality had dissolved mysteriously in the

EX. 29-5D   Franz Joseph Haydn, Symphony no. 45 in F-sharp minor ("Farewell"), end of the symphony

EX. 29-5D (continued)

EX. 29-5D (continued)

EX. 29-5D   *(continued)*

first movement, here it is allowed to resolve in normal fashion to the dominant, as if to
suggest that the wildness of the opening is in the process of being tamed.

The biggest surprise, however, comes midway through the finale, when the
movement suddenly fizzles out on the dominant and is replaced, seemingly for no good
reason, by what sounds like another minuet, as graceful as its predecessor had been blunt
and very richly scored (four desks of violins, each with its own part), that enters in the
key of the relative major, thus replaying the sudden harmonic succession — dominant
to relative major — that had enigmatically surrounded the double bar in the first
movement. It then proceeds, through a resumption of the dominant, to the parallel
major (the rare and extravagant tonality of six sharps, at the farthest, i. e., diametrical,
reach of the circle of fifths from C, the conventional starting point), where the symphony
is finally allowed to end, in a quietly joyous mood uncannily similar to that of the first
movement's mysterious second theme.

Most enigmatic of all is the way in which this concluding dance proceeds through an
inexorable composed diminuendo, the instruments of the orchestra dropping out one

by one (including a bassoon, relegated in the three preceding movements to doubling the bass line, which enters briefly as a soloist, it seems, just so as to be able to make an exit). Ex. 29-5d shows the end of the movement. Only the strings remain at this point, and then they too bow out: first the double bass (after an extravagant and virtually unprecedented solo turn) and the two "extra" violins, then the cello, eventually everybody. As an extra surprise, the "extra" violins return to finish the movement, having donned their mutes. Their softly beatific murmurings finally fade out into silence.

What can this strange "story" mean? It was a response to circumstances that have been recounted (after Haydn's own recollections) by all of his biographers. This is Griesinger's version, first published in 1810:

> Among Prince Esterházy's *Kapelle* [orchestra] there were several vigorous young married men who in summer, when the Prince stayed at Eszterháza, were obliged to leave their wives behind in Eisenstadt. Contrary to his custom, the Prince once extended his sojourn in Eszterháza by several weeks: the loving husbands, thoroughly dismayed over this news, went to Haydn and asked for his advice.
>
> Haydn had the inspiration of writing a symphony (which is now known under the title of "Farewell" Symphony), in which one instrument after another is silent. This Symphony was performed as soon as possible in front of the Prince, and each of the musicians was instructed, as soon as his part was finished, to blow out his candle and to leave with his instrument under his arm.
>
> The Prince now rose and said, "If they all leave, we must leave, too." The musicians had meanwhile collected in the *antechamber*, where the Prince found them, and smiling said: "I understand, Haydn; tomorrow the men may all leave," whereupon he gave the necessary order to have the princely horses and carriages made ready for the trip.[6]

This story has lent the name "Farewell" to Symphony no. 45 irrevocably, and probably accounts for its survival in active repertory long after most of Haydn's Esterházy symphonies had been eclipsed by his later ones. Its fame is well deserved. It casts an appealing light on Haydn's relationship with his patron, being the prime instance of the "gentle manipulation" to which Landon called admiring attention. Casting Haydn as one of those "self-made men" who could command the personal respect of the nobility by dint of their achievements, it is a model embodiment of the bourgeois work ethic. But there is nothing subversive about such a message: it is just as much a flattering reflection on the liberality of the Prince, who becomes through it a model of "enlightened despotism."

Such stories about artists have a long history. They were not an eighteenth-century invention, whether enlightened or bourgeois. The one about the "Farewell" Symphony has a direct sixteenth-century precedent within this very book, in fact: the reader may already have recalled Glareanus's story, recounted in chapter 14, about Josquin des Prez and King Louis XII of France, in which the composer gently manipulated his master, reminding him of a forgotten promise by setting some verses from Psalm 119 ("Remember Thy word unto Thy servant") as a motet. There is an important difference between the stories, however, and one that does indeed set the time of Haydn decisively apart from the time of Josquin.

SIGN SYSTEMS

That difference lies in the respective media employed. For Josquin, the primary means at his disposal was a vocal composition, in which it was actually the words that conveyed the message he wished to impart. For Haydn, a wordless instrumental composition was the preferred medium for a no less pointed message. Instrumental music was effectively displacing vocal music as the medium of greatest cultural prestige. That was already something unthinkable in Josquin's time. But even more important, instrumental music gained that prestige by developing what was previously an unthinkably precise and powerful expressive potential.

That potential was realized through a newly complex and versatile process of signification, made possible by the rise of harmonically governed forms articulated through *thematische Arbeit*. The conventions through which motives derived from themes now functioned dynamically in conjunction with the tonal trajectory opened up a whole new level of musical signification, giving instrumental music in effect a double sign system.

On the one hand there were the old conventions, inherited from earlier styles and repertoires, whereby music could represent the sights and sounds of the natural world and the moods and feelings of the human world: onomatopoeia, iconicity, metaphor, metonymy—all that can be subsumed under the general heading of *extroversive semiotics* (literally, "pointing outward"). For music this included the sounds of other music—hunting horns, courtly dances, quotations of famous pieces, whatever—and their built-in associations.

On the other hand there was the newly important domain of *introversive semiotics* ("pointing inward")—a sign system made up of sounds that pointed to other sounds or musical events within the work itself. The most basic of these, perhaps, was the relationship of dominant and tonic—a normative relationship of two triads that marked them as signs of tension and repose, respectively. In a major key, the dominant triad is structurally and sonically indistinguishable from the tonic. It is only a convention set up by the context that marks the one as a pointer to the other. Similar conventions cause us to expect a modulation away from the tonic in the first half of a piece and a modulation back through a Far Out Point in the second half. Each event in the unfolding of the piece, then, carries implications for future unfolding, even as it seems to be a consequence of past unfolding. Thus everything that happens within the piece can be construed as a pointer toward some other thing—or better, toward all the other things—taking place within the piece.

The "Farewell" Symphony conveyed its meaning to the Prince through a unique interaction of introversive and extroversive signs. When its meaning is explained nowadays, it is apt to be the simplest extroversive signals that receive the emphasis: the musicians dropping out one by one from the last movement (and, as we know from the story, blowing out their reading candles and physically leaving the performing space as they did so). In the absence of all other factors, these gestures seem to be gestures of farewell to the Prince himself and to Eszterháza. But that does not tell the whole story; nor could it alone have conveyed the whole message of the symphony as the

Prince successfully received it. As James Webster has pointed out, the whole symphony participates in the unfolding of the message, beginning with the very strangely shaped first movement.[7] Its introversive semiotic requires a well-attuned perceiver; that is why it is not usually included in the story as adapted for "music appreciation" purposes. But that is precisely why it will repay our close attention here; it offers a matchless opportunity for attuning our ears to the introversive sign system on which Haydn relied.

As Landon reminds us in his account of the work, "Prince Esterházy was a trained and performing musician: he will have heard the very odd sound of this movement; and he will have noted that the subsidiary subject [or "second theme"] appears only once, in D major, in the development section," and so on.[8] In other words, he will have noticed the many departures or deviations from established norms — that is, failures of conventional implication and consequence — that Haydn deliberately planted in the work to raise questions in a sophisticated listener's mind.

But introversive and extroversive semiotics, while distinguishable, do not operate in mutual isolation. Just as potent a poser of questions is the radical contrast in "affect" (always an extroversive factor) between the movement's two themes: the one of a theatrically exaggerated stressfulness and tonal "remoteness" (matching the physical remoteness of the summer palace from "civilization"), the other, coming out of nowhere and prematurely disappearing, of an equally exaggerated blissfulness and tonal repose. Its disruption of introversive norms marks its blissfulness as unreal, an uncanny dream.

And it remains an obsessive presence, an object of longing, as the dissonant recurrence of its keynote (D) in the minuet bears out. When the long minuetlike Adagio coda intrudes on the last movement, there is the same sense of tonal disruption, the same sense of an alternative reality, into which the members of the orchestra now disappear one by one. As they blow out their candles as if retiring for the night amid this ambience of unreal, longed-for bliss, the suggestion that the bliss in question is conjugal bliss becomes so palpable as to be, in the context of an eighteenth-century court soirée, practically lewd. (Another reason, perhaps, why the story, as adapted nowadays for students and kiddies, is apt to leave out the connections between the various movements.)

We are dealing, then, with a mode of instrumental discourse capable of very subtle shades of allusion and irony. Haydn does not normally draw as extensively on all of its representational resources as he does in the "Farewell" Symphony, nor does he often write a multimovement work in which the different movements are, semiotically or narratively speaking, so firmly and obviously linked. The work is a unique tour de force within his output. But the resources on which he drew so extravagantly in this one case were permanent and ubiquitous resources for his music — and, by dint of their widespread emulation, for all European instrumental music. Introversive semiotics, in particular, had been brought permanently to a new level of refinement and consequence.

More commonly, introversive semiotics became for Haydn a site for the virtuoso exercise of wit. His mature instrumental music is forever commenting ironically and amusingly on its own unfolding, making his art an unprecedentedly self-conscious one, and one that seems uncommonly given to complimenting the discernment of its listeners. These are all aspects of *politesse*, refined "company" behavior. The music of this lower-Austrian wheelwright's son thus represents an epitome of aristocratic art.

Haydn's maturest instrumental style is often said to date from the 1780s, when after a long interval Haydn resumed composing string quartets and thereafter concentrated on them to a remarkable degree, creating in the process what he himself saw fit to describe (in a couple of business letters written in December 1781) as "a new and special manner." The phrase has been much debated. It has been suggested that Haydn was just trying to drum up commercial interest in his latest work at a time when his patron, in view of Haydn's great and unanticipated celebrity, had at last granted him dispensation from the exclusivity clause in his contract, freeing him to conclude subsidiary deals with publishers and individual noble purchasers. And yet a new motivic tightness and intricacy in Haydn's writing does emerge at this point, betokening a new fascination — first his, now ours — with introversive semiotics.

Unlike his symphonies, Haydn's quartets carry opus numbers. This directly reflects his new circumstances; they were written for publication (i.e., for profit), and they bore dedications to other important aristocrats besides Prince Esterházy, for which an additional honorarium could be expected. The set of six issued as op. 33 in 1782 was the first set to be published by the Vienna house of Artaria, from then on Haydn's main publisher. They bore dedication to the Grand Duke (later Tsar) Paul of Russia, for which reason they are sometimes called the "Russian" Quartets.

Perhaps most significant of all, they were the first quartets by Haydn that were not alternatively billed as divertimentos. Like the concert symphony, the quartet genre had solidified by then, in large part thanks to Haydn. The symphony and the quartet could be regarded by the 1780s, then, as two solid precipitates (one "public," the other "private") from the earlier all-purpose instrumental blend. The great distinguishing feature of op. 33, and possibly one of the elements that Haydn thought of as a "new and special" manner, was a newly versatile texture, no longer nearly so dominated by the first violin.

It had been anticipated in the last set of "Divertimentos," published as op. 20 in 1774; but there the liberation of the subordinate voices had come about largely as the by-product of an experimental, somewhat show-offy revival of archaic contrapuntal genres like double and triple fugues. In op. 33, the heightened contrapuntal interest was fully integrated into

FIG. 29-7   Tsar Paul I of Russia, to whom Haydn dedicated his "Russian" quartets.

the taut motivic elaboration. In effect, there were henceforth two dimensions of introversive pointing: horizontal ("structural") and vertical ("textural"). This supple warp and woof was indeed a new and special manner, and it was taken up with a will by all the other practitioners of what would be retrospectively and admiringly (if also misleadingly) dubbed *Wiener Klassik*—"Viennese classicism"—by the historians and pedagogues of the nineteenth and early twentieth centuries.

Haydn followed up on op. 33 with no fewer than five more quartet sets, each containing six: op. 50 (1787), opp. 54/55 (composed in 1788, split up into threes for publication in 1789 and 1790), op. 64 (1790, published 1791), opp. 71/74 (composed in 1793, published by threes in 1795 and 1796), and op. 76 (composed in 1797, published in 1799). There were also four odd items, one published as op. 42 in 1786, two as op. 77 in 1802, and one last unfinished quartet (two movements, evidently the middle ones) published as op. 103, Haydn's swansong, in 1806. Haydn's lifetime total of 68 quartets is exceeded only by his symphonies; and during his last decade of active creative life, from 1793, they were his primary interest.

ANATOMY OF A JOKE

No single item from such a list could possibly be wholly representative, but for a look at the "new and special manner" and its implications, the Quartet in E-flat major, op. 33, no. 2 is a reasonable choice. It sports a rather coarse nickname, "The Joke," in English; but since the joke in question is the quartet's ending gesture, a particularly well-aimed stroke of wit based entirely on the sending of a false "introversive" signal, the nickname arises directly out of the compositional strategies that are of interest to us now. Observing them minutely for a while will amply repay the effort it will cost by heightening sensitivity to the kind of significant detail that *Kenner und Liebhaber* prize. The discussion that follows must be read with the score close at hand. The first movement's exposition, which will be given an especially close analysis, is shown in Ex. 29-6a.

EX. 29-6A   Franz Joseph Haydn, Quartet in E-flat, Op. 33, no. 2 ("The Joke"), I, mm. 1–32

EX. 29-6A   (*continued*)

EX. 29-6A (continued)

EX. 29-6A   *(continued)*

Leaving the big titular joke for the end does not mean we will be deprived of humor till then. The first movement is inexhaustibly rife with little jokes of the same kind — or rather, little jolts of wit, which the dictionary defines as "the keen perception and cleverly apt expression of those connections between ideas which awaken pleasure and especially amusement." Unexpected introversive connections are the key — and such connections, in Haydn's music, consist preeminently of motivic relationships. The exploration of motivic relationships, and their shrewd recombination, has always been a feature of *thematische Arbeit*. Only now we will find such things happening not just in the designated development but from the word go, and pervading the whole texture besides.

The opening theme's initial four-bar phrase, in which the first violin is straightforwardly accompanied by the rest of the band, already harbors a clever motivic transformation. The fourth eighth note of the second measure, the melodic high point, is unexpectedly, arbitrarily broken (or so it seems) into a pair of sixteenths, with the second of the pair descending a fourth to anticipate the note on the next strong beat. Compare the very beginning of the melody (the first violin's anticipatory pickup to the first strong beat), and observe a neat motivic inversion (or — take your pick — a "crab" or mirror reversal).

Such a thing, done just for its own sake, would be as dull, ultimately, as a gratuitous pun: too much of that, and a conversationalist seems no longer witty but annoying. Haydn does not do it just for its own sake, though. First he redeems it by incorporating its rhythm into the fourth measure (the opening four-bar phrase now falling in retrospect into two rhythmically identical, balanced pairs). But then he derives the entire four-bar continuation (mm. 5–8) from varied recombinations of the three-note motive (two sixteenths anticipating an eighth) thus isolated. Its opening skip is progressively widened in the first violin from a fourth to a full octave. This is done in two stages, separated by pauses during which the second violin and viola add their two cents' worth of motivic echo, substituting chromatic leading tones for the initial skip of a fourth. Then the first violin, having reached the octave by way of a sixth and a seventh, turns that progression around, still maintaining the rhythm of the opening motive and compressing it into a measure of continuous sixteenth notes to match a melodic climax with a rhythmic one.

The second phrase is followed by a repetition of the first (the only change being the addition of a grace note to the half note in m. 11, so that there will be a greater resemblance to the by now strongly "motivated" two-note pickup). The opening period having thus been closed off in a minuscule *da capo*, the transition to the dominant is due. Now for the first time we get a contrapuntal montage of motivically related phrases. The first violin begins at m. 13 with the same pickup as before, extended to a sixth. Meanwhile, the remaining three instruments, up to now discreet accompanists, have struck up a conversation among themselves, initiated by the cello's immediate repetition of the first violin's motivically saturated ending phrase in m. 12. The six-note fragment is tossed from cello to viola to second violin (supported by the cello again) until the first violin receives it like a pass in m. 14 and tosses it back and forth with the second violin. The first violin's four-bar transitional passage from m. 15 to m. 18 is wholly derived from the same fragment, first repeated four-fold in the form received from the other instruments, and then in a rhythmic compression based entirely on the off-beat component, [8/16/16], first heard as such in m. 2.

Measures 19–22 are saturated in all four parts with further reminiscences of the opening three-note pickup idea, sometimes in its leading-tone variant, sometimes in its reversed ("off-beat") variant, and once, climactically, in its original form (pickup to m. 21) to zero in emphatically on the new tonic. The material from m. 23 to m. 28, which elaborates a cadence to establish the goal of the tonal trajectory from tonic to dominant (B-flat major), is not obviously related to the fund of motives we have been tracing. Neither is it particularly distinctive as thematic material. Its function is to provide some neutral space to support a harmonic close.

Harmonic closure having been achieved (on the third beat of m. 28), the old fund of motives is reasserted to provide a suitable melodic close. First the second violin enters with the original three-note group—on its original pitches, too (allowing for an octave transposition), only now functioning not as tonic but as subdominant. This is a typically ironic "introversive" reference: recalling the opening melodic phrase just to point up the changed harmonic context. Having been recalled, the three-note motive generates a four-beat phrase, answered by the first violin in m. 30 with a phrase reminiscent of its passage in mm. 17–18, itself derived originally from the phrase-closing motive in m. 4, which referred yet further back to the melodic peak in m. 2.

The exchange is repeated and "doubled": viola and cello in m. 31 (the cello recalling the first violin's octaves in mm. 6–7) and the two violins in m. 32. The last three notes of the first violin part before the double bar are nothing but a transposition to the dominant of its first three notes, the original "three-note anticipatory motive," rounding off the whole exposition with an elegant show of symmetry — and some more "introversive irony," the opening gesture now transformed into a closing gesture to give a foretaste of (or a precedent to) the ending "joke" after which the quartet as a whole was nicknamed.

That show of symmetry has a more immediate payoff when the exposition is repeated. After its second playing, the tonal trajectory goes into reverse, and the movement reaches that phase (the so-called development) most firmly associated with motivic derivations and recombinations, on the way to the FOP. It is precisely here that, in an ironic gesture of our own, we will stop tracing Haydn's *thematische Arbeit*. It is not just that blow-by-blow verbal descriptions of musical processes are ultimately supererogatory (not to mention tedious). It is also apparent, or should be, that the "development section" has no special lock on motivic development. Motivic elaboration — a newly enriched elaborative process in which the whole texture participates — is a constant characteristic of Haydn's "new and special manner." What is distinctive about the section between the double bar and the double return is its harmonic instability, not its thematic or motivic content.

The second movement of the quartet is the minuet, placed ahead of the slow movement rather than afterwards. This is not all that unusual. The all-purpose divertimentos out of which the mature quartet genre "precipitated" often had two minuets, one before the slow movement, the other after; for Haydn it was just a choice, so to speak, of which minuet to drop. More unusual as of 1781 was the use of the word "scherzo" (or *scherzando*) to designate this one movement rather than the divertimento as a whole, for which the word was an occasional synonym.

EX. 29-6B   Franz Joseph Haydn, Quartet in E-flat, Op. 33, no. 2 ("The Joke"), II, mm. 1–10, 21–26

EX. 29-6B   *(continued)*

As we may recall from Monteverdi's prior employment of the word (see chapter 20), its literal meaning is "joke" or "jest," which might possibly seem to be the source of the quartet's familiar nickname. But no, all the minuets in op. 33 sport the designation (and four out of six are placed like this one, as the second movement). The meaning might seem more a performance direction than a category: do the minuet a little faster than usual (hence the explicit instruction "allegro"), and do it playfully. Playfulness is built in, though: the eight-bar opening phrase is extended to an asymmetrical ten because of the stalling (or echo) tactics of the two violins in mm. 5–6. And then the silly wobble on the "dominant ninth" (C-flat) gets "developed" sequentially in mm. 21–24, dignifying it ironically by introversive recall (see Ex. 29-6b). A mock-silly piece, then?

Perhaps so, but with an important qualification. If we look at the scherzo with minuettish expectations, we immediately notice something "wrong." The tonal trajectory is askew. The first strain never leaves the tonic. The modulation to the dominant takes place at the beginning of the second strain, and serves in lieu of a FOP. (To the extent that there is a FOP, it is just the little chromatic extension provided by the development of the "wobble," as noted.) And the traditional final gesture, the double return, here amounts to a full, literal restatement of the first strain, pointless wobble and all. This impoverished sequence of events — failure to modulate before the double bar; the use of the dominant as FOP; full literal restatement of the first strain at the double return — is scrupulously reproduced in the Trio, marking it not as a casual departure from normal procedure, but as a sort of alternative normal procedure in its own right. The texture, too, now seems impoverished: it is just the sort of rigidly layered texture — first violin melody over second violin figuration over downbeat punctuations in the bass, the viola rendered altogether superfluous and dispensable — that one might have found in a "divertimento" before Haydn ever started fashioning his new and special manner of quartet writing (Ex. 29-6c).

EX. 29-6C   Franz Joseph Haydn, Quartet in E-flat, Op. 33, no. 2 ("The Joke"), II, mm. 35–42 (first strain of the Trio)

What we are dealing with then, is not so much a mock-silly piece as a mock-primitive one — a highly sophisticated composer imitating (thus mocking) the efforts of uncouth village musicians. (For the ultimate in this sort of slumming spoof see Mozart's hilarious if far from subtle Divertimento in F, K. 522, subtitled *Ein musikalischer Spass*, "A Musical Joke" [= scherzo].) In Haydn's late symphonies, too, one often finds the evocation of folk or peasant styles in the minuets (there more as a matter of harmonic or "modal" color, often involving the raised or "Lydian" fourth degree over a bagpipelike drone bass). There is also a whole group of late symphonic minuets in which the first strain is recapitulated in the second; but in these the first strain had made its customary modulation, and so its "recapitulation" is adjusted to reaffirm the tonic, just as in the "sonata form." The late symphonic minuet is thus a sonata hybrid, and extra sophisticated.

That cannot be said of the scherzi in op. 33. They are "extroversively ironic," evoking a folkish or "country" style just to point up the distance from there to courtly perfection. Thus while Haydn is often applauded for his peasant origins (even by himself in retrospect when talking to fawning biographers), it is evident that his artistic loyalties and sympathies were entirely aristocratic, and that his frequent evocations of peasant music were no manifestation of class solidarity, as they might have been in a nineteenth-century composer, but a bit of humorous rustic exoticism.

A folkish style, in any case, had only a "class" or "regional" connotation for a composer in eighteenth-century Austria, never a "national" one. Folkishness was marked as bumpkinry and regarded with condescension vis-à-vis the unmarked (cosmopolitan, aristocratic) default style of "quality." That was only inevitable in Haydn's time and place, especially in the multinational Hapsburg ("Holy Roman") Empire, whose identity was associated not with any ethnicity, nor even with any place, but with an ancient dynasty. Haydn's politics, like that of his patrons, was a dynastic politics, and nowhere is this more apparent than when he trades in "rustic" or "ethnic" stereotypes.

The quartet's slow movement, as usual, is cast in the most "original," least classifiable form; but (again as usual) that form is based on very familiar and intelligible procedures. The opening eight-bar duet (Ex. 29-6d), in which the viola, very strikingly, gets to enunciate the movement's lyrical main theme (thus reasserting its courtly "emancipated" role after its rustic subordination), is repeated three more times in different instrumental pairings, with textural elaborations in the form of countermelodies, and with intervening episodes to provide tonal contrasts. That's all there is to it; the charm of this movement lies in the detail work.

EX. 29-6D Franz Joseph Haydn, Quartet in E-flat, Op. 33, no. 2 ("The Joke"), III, mm. 1–8

The four varied repetitions of the melody exhaust the "rational" pairs into which the four instruments in a string quartet can be grouped. After the unaccompanied duet for the two lower instruments, the first repetition, which takes place immediately, is scored for the "upper pair," that is, the two violins, minimally accompanied by a murmur in the cello that bridges the caesura between the phrases in a manner that might recall (and thus restore to courtly grace) the rustic "wobble" from the preceding movement. After an episode in echo style that pulls the music out of its tonic and returns it (like a good "development section") to its dominant, the theme returns in the "inner" pair (second violin and viola), while the first violin keeps up the cello's "murmur" as a steady accompaniment of sixteenth notes.

Another echo episode, melodically similar to the first but harmonically different, leads the music on another wayward path to the dominant to prepare the final statement of the main theme, by the "outer pair" (first violin and cello, with the second violin occasionally taking the notes of the lower voice so as to free the cello to provide a better bass). Now the viola provides the running murmur and the second violin, when not spelling the cello, contributes a harmonic filler. The coda unites reminiscences of the theme with reminiscences of the episodes.

And now at last to the movement that gave the "Joke" Quartet its nickname. The theme of the finale is shaped exactly like those of the Scherzo and Trio: a repeated eight-bar strain that cadences in the tonic key (Ex. 29-6e), followed by a second strain that moves out to the dominant and ends there with a literal repeat of the first strain. Minus the repeats, this theme comes back literally halfway through the movement, marking the movement as a rondo and the material between the two statements of the theme as a motivically "developmental" episode. These are the internal relationships on which the movement's "introversive" signaling will depend.

EX. 29-6E   Franz Joseph Haydn, Quartet in E-flat, Op. 33, no. 2 ("The Joke"), IV, mm. 1–8

Several features of the theme are tailor-made for such treatment. For one thing, its first note, repeated over the bar for emphasis, is the third degree of the scale, expressed as the middle member of the tonic triad. That is no accident. It enables Haydn to precede each repetition (both of the whole theme and of its final "recapitulatory" strain) with a jolly maximum of pseudo-suspense, produced each time by a dominant-seventh chord with the dissonant tone exposed on top and followed by a rest to boost the sense of urgency toward predictable resolution on the first note of the theme. These chords all but palpably point at their successors: that is introversive semiotics at its rawest and bluntest — so much so that Haydn is moved to spoof the effect in mm. 137 – 40 with superfluous repetitions and fermatas (Ex. 29-6f).

EX. 29-6F   Franz Joseph Haydn, Quartet in E-flat, Op. 33, no. 2 ("The Joke"), IV, mm. 133 – 140

Also deliberately blunt and stolid is the way the opening strain of the theme (Ex. 29-6e) ends in m. 8: right on the beat without the characteristic ♩♩♩ ♪ fall-off rhythm found at all analogous points in the tune (compare mm. 2 and 4). This too gets joshed with a fermata on its last repetition. But although brought about by the same stop-time effect, this spoof is the virtual opposite of the one that came before. What made the fermatas in Ex. 29-6f funny was absolute certainty as to what would have to follow. In m. 148, the premature closure of the phrase creates real doubt as to what will follow. Haydn has engineered a deliberate breakdown of the introversive signaling system.

He capitalizes on the breakdown by producing something utterly unexpected: a repetition of mm. 145 – 48 (the final phrase of the theme) in a ludicrous mock-tragic tone, produced by a switch to adagio tempo, heavy chords (one of them an extra-dissonant "dominant ninth") marked *forte*, and a panting "speech rhythm" in the first violin (Ex. 29-6g). One last, hesitant, repetition of the rondo theme, all the phrases spaced out with "general pauses," brings the movement to an embarrassed end (Ex. 29-6h). Or tries to. The stubbornly incomplete final phrase again proves inadequate. And so, after four measures of mock indecision, the first phrase gets pressed into duty as an emergency last phrase. It has the correct harmonic content and it has the correct rhythmic weight (with a proper ♩ ♩ ♩ ♪ at the end). Its fatal drawback, of course, is that it has been marked by many repetitions, each one setting an "introversive" precedent, as an opener, not a closer.

And so whenever this ending is performed, it takes the audience an extra second or so to recover its wits and realize that the piece is indeed over. The result is an inevitable giggle — the same giggle that overtakes a prestidigitator's audience when it realizes that it has been "had." Haydn's titular joke is thus not an "anecdote" but a "practical joke," the product of misdirection.

Of course nothing so thoroughly spoils a good joke as an endeavor like the one now underway to explain it verbally. Like any attempt to manipulate an audience's expectations, this one succeeds unawares or not at all. But what Haydn did here for once broadly and obviously, he does subtly and artfully on every page of his mature instrumental music, as inspecting the first movement of this very quartet has already established for us. Like the "Farewell" Symphony, it illustrates the symbiosis that subsisted between a composer of superb self-consciousness and a correspondingly

EX. 29-6G Franz Joseph Haydn, Quartet in E-flat, Op. 33, no. 2 ("The Joke"), IV, mm. 145–152

EX. 29-6H Franz Joseph Haydn, Quartet in E-flat, Op. 33, no. 2 ("The Joke"), IV, end

discerning patron. The prince's demands gave Haydn many specific projects into which he could channel the spontaneous promptings of his creative urge. As Jean-Jacques Rousseau might have said, the conditions of his existence, a bondage to many, paradoxically forced Haydn to be free.

THE LONDON TOURS

Haydn remained in active service to the Esterházys, and in full-time residence on their estates, until Prince Nikolaus's sudden death on 28 September 1790. The latter's son and successor, Prince Anton, uninterested in music, disbanded his father's orchestra and opera establishment. This was no disaster for Haydn but yet another stroke of good fortune. He remained, according to the terms of Prince Nikolaus's will, on full salary as titular Kapellmeister, and drew a pension on top of it, but was no longer under any actual obligation to his patron. He was able to settle in Vienna and pursue a fully subsidized life as a freelance artist. As things turned out, his new status made it possible for him to accept a fantastic offer that unexpectedly came his way and embark on a what amounted to a new career as international celebrity under newly viable economic and social conditions.

At the time of Prince Nikolaus's death, a German-born violinist and minor composer named Johann Peter Salomon, who had moved to England and set himself up as a concert entrepreneur, happened to be in Cologne to recruit talent for his upcoming London season. Immediately on reading in the newspapers of the Prince's demise, he swooped down on Haydn in Vienna, barging in on the composer

one evening with the announcement (as Haydn later punningly paraphrased it to his biographers), "I am Salomon of London and have come to fetch you. Tomorrow we will arrange an *accord*" (that is, sign a contract — or tune up a fiddle, play in tune, etc.).[9]

The contract was signed by 8 December. According to its terms, Salomon undertook to pay Haydn a huge fee in return for an opera, six symphonies, and some other miscellaneous pieces, all to be performed under Haydn's personal direction at a series of twelve London subscription concerts to be given at Salomon's risk at a public concert hall on Hanover Square that had formerly been used for the Bach-Abel concerts. It had a seating capacity of around eight hundred. When standees were present, the room could accommodate well over a thousand.

FIG. 29-8 Johann Peter Salomon, Haydn's promoter, in a portrait by Thomas Hardy. This painting was then engraved by Hardy and hawked by the London publisher John Bland.

Salomon and Haydn crossed the English Channel together on New Year's Day, 1791, for what would prove to be for Haydn the first of two extended, acclaimed, and highly lucrative stays in the British capital. The first concert took place on Friday, 11 March, and the series continued on Fridays thereafter until 3 June. The first-night program was typical of the lot. As always, it was a miscellany. Although Haydn "presided at the harpsichord" as his contract stipulated, most of the music performed — various vocal and instrumental solos, including a "Concertante" for harp and piano by the Czech composer Jan Ladislav Dussek — was actually by other composers. The *pièce de resistance*, which occupied the place of honor at the opening of the concert's second half, was Haydn's "New Grand Overture," as the program put it. At all subsequent Salomon concerts the new Haydn piece would occupy this position in the program. It was the favored place because it was only then that the whole audience could be reliably assumed to have assembled. As one member of the first-night public put it, "by the beginning of the second act we concluded that all had arrived who intended to come."[10] The "New Grand Overture" given its first performance at the first Haydn-Salomon concert was actually his Symphony no. 92 in G major, composed in 1789, not yet one of the new symphonies Salomon had commissioned, but new to London. (It is now nicknamed the "Oxford" Symphony because it was given again at a concert in July at the University of Oxford, where Haydn had been invited to receive an honorary Doctor of Music degree.) It was repeated a week later, at the second Salomon concert, before a much larger crowd, along with one of the quartets from Haydn's op. 64. The first of Haydn's actual "Salomon" Symphonies to be performed — that is, the first symphony actually composed in London for the Salomon series — was the one now known as No. 96 in D major. It was given for the first time at the fourth concert on Friday, 1 April. (It now has the nickname "Miracle" because according to Haydn's biographer Dies, at a subsequent performance the audience is said to have arisen spontaneously at its conclusion and come forward toward the stage, thus evading a large chandelier that happened to fall at that moment.)

The next year, 1792, a new Haydn-Salomon Friday subscription series began on 17 February and lasted until 18 May. By now Haydn had had a chance to compose several major works on English soil, and his concerts contained many world premières of now-classic compositions. To choose one for a close look is as arbitrary and invidious an exercise as ever; but a special combination of typical and unique features recommends the symphony first performed on the evening of 23 March, shortly before Haydn's sixtieth birthday.

Its typical features are those of what amounted to a new genre: what the English were calling the "Grand Overture," and what we might half-facetiously call the Subscription Symphony — concert symphonies written not for aristocratic salons where the audience might number perhaps a hundred, but for big public halls where the audience might number a thousand. At the time of his London visit, Haydn already had some experience composing on this new "heroic" scale. He had been writing subscription symphonies since about 1785, when he received a commission from Paris for a set of six symphonies to be performed at a new concert series set up in competition with the venerable Concert Spirituel, where Haydn's works had become popular.

The new sponsoring organization, called Le Concert de la Loge Olympique, was run by a Masonic lodge that included among its members many aristocratic amateurs. Its orchestra was huge; when playing at full strength it could draw on forty violins and ten double basses. Its chief patron, Claude-François-Marie Rigoley, the Count d'Ogny, offered Haydn a fee larger by orders of magnitude than any he had ever received, and which he at first did not believe. Under the circumstances, it is hardly surprising that Haydn's "Paris" Symphonies—nos. 82–87 in the standard numbering—have a notably expanded format. His new, much grander style would henceforth be Haydn's normal symphonic practice, since a composer of Haydn's celebrity could now count on "subscription" performances for all his orchestral works.

Opening movements were now apt to be preceded by somewhat portentous slow introductions, sometimes soft and mysterious, more often in the manner of a fanfare. This was a practical move as much as an esthetic one: the dimming of lights in concert halls was something that electricity would not make possible for another hundred years or so; the audience needed a signal to pay attention. The inner movements grew significantly in dimensions. The minuets in particular took on girth, and this affected not only their duration but also their shape. As a way of controlling the longer duration, the use of a "double return" (or quasi-recapitulation) of the first strain at the end of the second became standard practice. (This is now often called the "rounded binary" form.) In addition, the trio was now apt to contrast decisively—in tempo, in scoring, often in mode or harmonic idiom—with the minuet that enclosed it. Finally, the concluding movements were apt to be cast in a fast $\frac{2}{4}$ meter derived from the contredanse (thus creating a dance pair with the minuet that actually reflected the contemporary ballroom repertoire); and their form was greatly expanded by putting "development sections," full of harmonic adventure and motivic ingenuity, in place of the neutral "episodes" of the simpler rondo form.

ADDRESSING THRONGS

Every point made in the foregoing paragraph applies fully to the Symphony in G major (no. 94 in the standard numbering), the one first given in London on 23 March 1792. Everything about it exemplifies the trend toward big public utterance. Most conspicuously, the London symphonies augment the sheer performing forces so that the normal Haydn orchestra now includes, as standard operating equipment, pairs of flutes, oboes, bassoons, trumpets, and horns, as well as

FIG. 29-9 Anonymous portrait of Haydn painted in 1795, showing the score of the "Surprise" Symphony open on the piano.

kettledrums. A close look at the first movement of No. 94, moreover, will reveal another aspect of "Grand Overture" style—the rhetorical techniques by which Haydn now addressed large crowds. Again, having the score at hand is highly recommended.

The slow introduction (Ex. 29-7a) begins on a pastoral note, unmistakably sounded by the horn with its bagpiper drones on the tonic pitch. "Characteristic" or "topical" gestures like this were practically *de rigueur* in big public symphonies. The biggest success Haydn ever enjoyed with a London audience came with another G-major symphony (no. 100 in the standard numbering), first performed on 31 March 1794, during Haydn's second London visit. Its slow movement featured unexpected solos for bass drum, triangle, and cymbal—marching-band percussion—for which reason the work became immediately famous as the "Military" Symphony. Like all symphonic slow introductions, the one in Symphony no. 94 proceeds through a FOP to a "half cadence" on the dominant: its essential function is to enable a running harmonic jump on the fast music to enhance the all-important rhythmic/tonal momentum that is the virtual *raison d'être* of a "subscription symphony's" first movement.

EX. 29-7A   Franz Joseph Haydn, Symphony no. 94 in G ("Surprise"), I, slow introduction

Notice a trick already familiar from the "Joke" Quartet: Haydn leaves the slow introduction hanging on the seventh of the dominant-seventh chord, so as to "point" all the more urgently at the main body of the movement and produce a moment of "electric" silence, the silence of intense expectation. There will be a lot of electric silence in this movement, as in all of the "London" symphonies. Another thing that breaking off on the seventh of the chord mandates, of course, is that the first note of the main theme is going to have to be the third degree of the scale, the note to which the seventh has to resolve. This happens so often with Haydn that a theme beginning on the third degree is virtually his stylistic fingerprint.

The amazingly pliant theme that now begins in this way is novel in our experience: everything about it is geared toward momentum, with the result that it almost doesn't register as a melody the way previous Haydn themes have done. It never has a chance. It is only four bars long—or not even that long, really, since (and this is the real point) it does not come to a proper end. Its interrupted cadence is the most significant and calculated thing about it (Ex. 29-7b).

Taking an even closer look, we see that the whole structure of this tiny theme is pointed ineluctably toward the cadence that never happens. The tune begins on

EX. 29-7A   (continued)

EX. 29-7A   (continued)

the second half of the bar and unfolds sequentially, which means that every measure points rhythmically to the next — and harmonically, too, since the initial pickup is unexpectedly harmonized with a chromatic tone — G♯, the leading tone of the "V of ii" — initiating a miniature tonal trajectory that proceeds by half measures through the circle of fifths, putting off the tonic demanded by the slow introduction for another couple of measures. And when it comes, on the downbeat of the second full measure, that long-awaited tonic is immediately weakened by the use of contrapuntal sleight-of-hand: an accented passing tone in the first violin, followed by an inversion of the whole texture, the second violin entering in the second half of the bar with a rhythmically compressed imitation at the lower octave of the first violin's opening phrase, while the first violin immediately cancels the G with the second violin's old G♯, thus initiating a replay of the whole circle-of-fifths trajectory.

Thus the downbeat of the fourth full measure has taken on a huge significance in advance: it has been multiply marked (by rhythm and harmony) as the defining cadence of the opening theme. What every musically sensitive ear now expects is a cadence note,

EX. 29-7A *(continued)*

a caesura (little rest to denote a phrase end), and then probably a repetition of the four bars (as in Ex. 29-7c), to form a "parallel period," presumably to be followed by some contrasting material and possibly a return to the opening to round things off.

And that is precisely what does not happen. Instead, the whole orchestra suddenly pounces on the moment that had been, so to speak, reserved for the thematic cadence, preempting it and (what is most startling) eliding the caesura, the expected moment of demarcative silence. This "elided cadence," as we may call it, introduced by an unanticipated loud tutti, is one of Haydn's trustiest devices to get the rhythmic and harmonic ball rolling at the beginning of a "subscription symphony." By the time one has heard a number of them, one anticipates the "unanticipated" tutti. But even if one has learned to expect it, its function as a disruptive event remains clear and potent.

The present case is an extreme one. Usually Haydn allows the equivalent of what is shown in Ex. 29-7c to take place before lopping off the ending with an elision and a tutti. Compare, for example, the analogous spot in Symphony no. 96, premiered during the

EX. 29-7B   Franz Joseph Haydn, Symphony no. 94 in G ("Surprise"), I, Vivace assai, mm. 1–5

1791 season, where two phrases sound as antecedent and consequence before the Big Bang (Ex. 29-7d). The quicker progress toward the interrupted cadence in Symphony No. 94 only intensifies momentum, because the function of the passage the Big Bang introduces is to modulate to the secondary key. Thus the tonic is being abandoned here almost before it has had a chance to assert itself. The ratio between theme and transition in this movement is skewed heavily in favor of the latter. The emphasis, even more than usually, will be on process, not presentation. Tonally speaking, we are in for a roller-coaster ride.

And in this particular movement, as befits the truncated thematic presentation, the ride is going to be an exceptionally twisty and angular one, fuller than ever of characteristically Haydnesque feints. The telltale moment in any tonal transition is

EX. 29-7C Franz Joseph Haydn, Symphony no. 94 in G ("Surprise"), hypothetical "symmetrical" version of Ex. 29–7b

EX. 29-7D Franz Joseph Haydn, Symphony no. 96, I, mm. 18–26

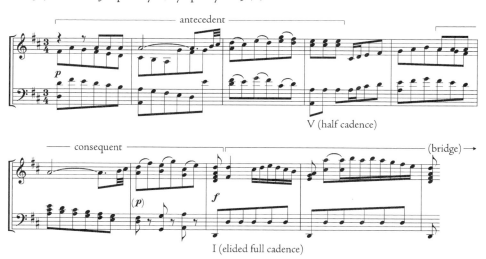

the moment when the leading tone to the new tonic appears. This happens in m. 30, with the introduction (typically, smuggled in on the weaker beat of the bar) of the C♯, prefiguring a cadence on D, the dominant. But a scant three bars later the C♯ is neutralized by a C-natural, and the harmony veers back unexpectedly to the starting point, the C-natural (the "seventh" of the dominant) getting its usual heavy emphasis (mm. 35–38) to heighten the expectation of the tonic's return (Ex. 29-7e).

We seem to be back at the starting point; but this time the elided cadence (m. 43) does produce the inevitable modulation to the dominant. (And that is the purpose of the initial avoidance: to stave off the inevitable is the essence of suspense, as any dramatist knows.) Even this time, though, there is a feint: in m. 54 the opening themelet comes back in D minor, from which D major, the dominant, must be reapproached. Both the return of the theme and the key in which it is couched come off like impromptu diversionary tactics, an essential part of the movement's highly calculated strategy.

The arrival of the dominant (m. 66) is marked by a slyly flatfooted vamp—an accompaniment in search of a tune. (The term "vamp," while often used in connection with twentieth-century popular music, is not in fact an anachronism; its use can been traced as far back as the early eighteenth century, and it is found in Dr. Burney's *History*.) What seems to be the awaited tune (m. 70) only prolongs the vamp with an aimless scale. But all at once the scale veers into a cadence (m. 77–79) that at last introduces what might be called a "second theme" (mm. 80–94) in the dominant, hardly less laconic than its predecessor in the tonic. It is quickly superseded by closing fanfares.

The exposition's final eccentricity is the way it ends (Ex. 29-7f), not on the expected D but on another suspenseful "vamp," a repeated B in the first violins. This is the note

EX. 29-7E Franz Joseph Haydn, Symphony no. 94 in G ("Surprise"), I, mm. 30–38

EX. 29-7E (*continued*)

with which the first theme began, of course, and it makes possible, first, a delightfully unpredictable lurch into the repeat and, second, an immediate point of departure into the tonal vagaries of the development.

As in the case of the "Joke" Quartet, it would be best to leave off the detailed descriptive commentary at this point, before the inevitable tedium of blow-by-blow description sets in. By now, in any case, the point has been made: the important matter in this symphonic "argument" is not the thematic content but the tonal trajectory, to which the themes are accessories. And yet Haydn remains sensitive enough to the need for thematic integrity that he builds the movement's coda — unexpectedly, but very satisfyingly — into the originally expected "full statement" of the first theme as a balanced pair of cadenced phrases (compare Ex. 29-7g with Ex. 29-7c).

There is a hint of a moral here, a gratifying sense that unfinished business has at last been attended to, giving the whole movement a sense of achieved and unified

EX. 29-7F   Franz Joseph Haydn, Symphony no. 94 in G ("Surprise"), I, mm. 101–107

design in which the thematic content and the tonal trajectory have cooperated. And yet in a "subscription symphony," there can be no doubt about priorities. The tonal trajectory is what finally counts. It has been turned into a very dramatic—that is, a highly "dramatized"—affair, in which harmonic and (especially) dynamic feints are the active ingredients, and in which the dual rhetorical strategy is that of building suspense, only to take the listener by surprise.

And that is why Symphony no. 94 is in its way the quintessential Haydn "subscription symphony": it is the one that is actually called the "Surprise" Symphony, a nickname that might have been applied to any or all of its counterparts. The reason why this particular symphony was so singled out has to do with the second movement, the Andante, which is cast as a set of variations on a theme in C major.

VARIATION AND DEVELOPMENT

The theme is cast in as regular and symmetrical a binary structure as Haydn ever employed: thirty-two bars in all, cast in repeated parallel periods (the first eight bars reaching a half cadence and then repeated; the second eight, beginning similarly, achieving full closure and then repeated). Haydn actually sketched the theme out as a pair of eight-bar phrases with repeats (see Fig. 29-11). But then he got another idea (Ex. 29-8a), one of his most famous inspirations.

What throws all symmetry out of whack (and the word is chosen advisedly) is the big thump at the end of m. 16. It comes at the least expectable place, the off beat of the last bar of an eight-bar phrase. That beat is unaccented at no fewer than five metrical levels: the measure of which it is an unaccented part is the unaccented member of a pair with its predecessor; that pair of measures is the unaccented member of a pair with its two-bar predecessor; that group of four measures is the unaccented member of a pair with its four-bar predecessor; and the whole resultant eight-bar phrase is the unaccented repetition of the movement's opening eight-bar phrase. Haydn has bent even further over backward to lull the listener into a state of complacency by marking the repetition of the opening phrase at a softer dynamic level (*pianissimo*, a direction he used only for special effects), by removing the second violins from the melody line, and by having the three lower parts plucked rather than bowed, all of which made it necessary to write all sixteen bars out in full rather than relying on a repeat sign as in the first draft.

EX. 29-7G Franz Joseph Haydn, Symphony no. 94 in G ("Surprise"), I, mm. 218–228

EX. 29-7G *(continued)*

The sudden blast is marked *forte* in the winds, *fortissimo* in the strings, and beefed up into "triple stops" (three-note chords) in the two violin parts. Most unusually, even recklessly, the timpani part is marked *fortissimo*, practically insuring that the drumbeat will drown all the other instruments out. And such seems to have been the calculation: the symphony is actually called *Symphonie mit dem Paukenschlag* ("Symphony with that kettledrum stroke") in German. The English sobriquet was given it almost immediately after the first performance. The *Oracle*, a London newspaper, reported the next morning that

> Act 2nd opened with a first performance of the GRAND OVERTURE composed by HAYDN for that evening. The Second Movement was equal to the happiest of this great Master's conceptions. The surprise might not be unaptly likened to the situation of a beautiful Shepherdess who, lulled to slumber by the murmur of a distant Waterfall, starts alarmed by the unexpected firing of a fowling- piece.[11]

It was Andrew Ashe, the first flutist in Salomon's orchestra, who claimed responsibility for the actual nickname. In a memoir set down in 1803, he wrote of the symphony that "I christened it the *Surprise* when I announced it for my Benefit Concert & my valued friend Haydn thank'd me for giving it such an appropriate Name."[12]

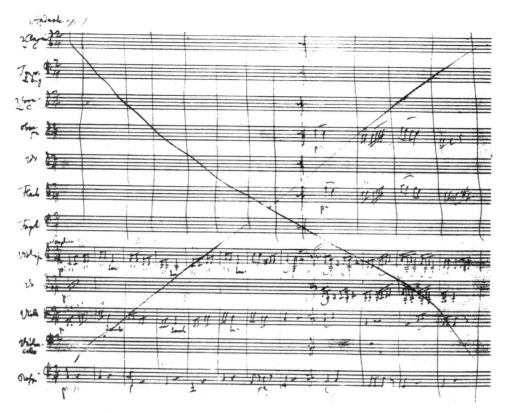

FIG. 29-10 Haydn's surpriseless original sketch for the Andante of Symphony no. 94.

People speculated wildly as to the reason for the strange event. There was certainly call for such speculation, since the big noise was (to put it mildly) "introversively underdetermined." There was nothing to motivate it from within; it pointed to nothing else in the score (except, perhaps, ironically). And so an extroversive explanation was sought. The reviewer for the *Oracle* accounted for it, as we have seen, by inventing a story for it to "imitate." A more general opinion was that it was meant to awaken sleepers in the hall. Dies, one of Haydn's biographers, is probably responsible for its spread in

EX. 29-8A Franz Joseph Haydn, Symphony no. 94 in G ("Surprise"), II, mm. 1–16

EX. 29-8A *(continued)*

subsequent accounts (including some versions in which it is old Prince Esterházy, two years dead by then, whom Haydn is supposedly nudging out of slumber). Griesinger, the competing biographer, put the matter to Haydn in an interview:

> I asked him once in jest if it were true that he wrote the Andante with the kettledrum beat in order to waken the English public that had gone to sleep at his concert. "No," he answered me. "Rather it was my wish to surprise the public with something new, and to make a début in a brilliant manner so as not to be outdone by my pupil [Ignaz] Pleyel, who at that time was engaged by an orchestra in London which had begun its concert series eight days before mine."[13]

In this very plausible anecdote, the big surprise was motivated as a sort of practical joke, or what we would now call a publicity stunt, to get people talking or (more likely) writing in the papers, and to outshine an upstart competitor. What makes the story plausible is the way it embodies a response to circumstances — for Haydn, new circumstances that would increasingly come to characterize the social and economic aspects of European music making in the new nineteenth century. Concert life — first of all in England, where in 1792 it was not at all a new thing, but everywhere soon enough — would henceforth function as something of a free market, in which composers had not only to address large crowds but to lure them, and in which professional reviewers acted as middlemen, mediating on behalf of artists (or against them!) and influencing public taste. The role and the function of arts criticism as we know it today were the creations of the English public and of the professional concert life that first got under way in England, and Haydn was one of the early objects of its ministrations. He was first of all its beneficiary, but he was not unaffected by its influence, since we are perhaps most easily influenced by those who praise us (and pay us).

Thus Haydn's "surprise" was an amiable early symptom of change to a new rhetorical manner that arose from a new musical ecosystem, conditioning a radical augmentation in the sheer dimensions of symphonic music and also a revolution in its content, which was increasingly likely to embody extroversive (or, in contemporary language, "characteristic") references.

As to the further progress of Haydn's slow movement, one particular variation should be singled out for the neat way it delineates the difference between "variation" and "development" as ways of elaborating on themes. That variation is second, cast in the parallel minor. Despite the changed mode, the first half of it hardly differs from the preceding variation, wherein the theme, given to the second violin, had acted as a cantus firmus against which the first violin (doubled once at the octave by the flute) contributed a "division" or filigree counterpoint. That is an unusually simple and old-fashioned sort of variation, but in its simplicity it illustrates the essential characteristic of the variation genre, namely adherence to the basic shape — the phrase structure and the harmonic trajectory — of the theme.

Just so, the first half of the minor-mode variation hews closely to the rhythmic and tonal shape of the theme. It is the same eight bars in length; the caesuras come at the same place, and its cadential destination is the same, making allowance for the changed mode (III rather than V being the usual half-cadence point in the minor). The second half of the variation might have been written to the same prescription: it might have started on E♭ or its dominant, had a caesura after four measures on the dominant of C minor, and made full closure on the tonic in the eighth measure. That would have been the normal, predictable procedure.

Instead, Haydn begins the second half on E♭, all right, but he aims it at the original dominant (G) rather than the tonic; and once having reached it, draws it out for its suspense value, as one might do in a "retransition" before a double return. Thus the whole variation is cast retrospectively as tonally "open" and unstable: it begins in one place and ends in another, on a note of unresolved tension that must await resolution in the next variation. The second half is unrepeated and asymmetrical in phrase structure. With a length of eighteen measures, it can only be parsed into pairs once before hitting an unreducible (odd) number. It contains no regular caesuras; rather, its one caesura, separating the main body of the section from the single-line "drawing-out" of the dominant, divides its 18 bars into 13 + 5, two prime numbers. Above all, it does not reproduce the melody of the theme as such but rather plays upon a motive extracted from it, tossed sequentially between the bass and viola parts (see Ex. 29-8b) to sustain the harmonic momentum.

EX. 29-8B   Comparison of the opening of Ex. 29-8a with its "development" in the minor variation

All of these traits — harmonic instability, asymmetry of phrase structure, *thematische Arbeit* (extraction and recombination of motives) — are traits that collectively describe the "development," as opposed to the mere "variation," of themes. Haydn certainly recognized this distinction and traded on it. The sudden introduction of restless and exciting developmental writing into the placid confines of a variations movement was another glorious surprise, no less worthy of immortality than the redoubtable kettledrum stroke. It serves further to "symphonicize" — to make impressively public and rhetorical — the music of a "subscription symphony," which was becoming an increasingly monumental genre.

Once the tonic is regained at m. 75 it is never again challenged; in compensation, however, the variations become ever quirkier and more "surprising." The nattering oboe solo at m. 75, for example, holds good only for half of a binary half, so to speak: just the first "A" out of AABB. Instead of being repeated, it is replaced at m. 83 by another "cantus firmus" variation, in which the original theme is played by the violins to support a woodwind obbligato. That texture then holds good for both B phrases, getting us as far as m. 107, where a pair of "sandwich" variations begins. The big and brassy tutti, led by the violins in sextolets, is dropped after eight measures in favor of an utterly contrasting idea marked *pianissimo e dolce* (very soft and sweet). The soft and sweet idea continues into the B phrase, but the big and brassy tutti is resumed for conclusion, thus: *AabB*, where capital letters stand for big-and-brassy and small letters for soft-and-sweet. The coda, derived (that is, "developed") from the "A" material, harbors one last surprise: the use of soft but very dissonant harmony (dominant-ninth chords on tonic and dominant over a tonic pedal) to lend an air of uncanny poignancy.

MORE SURPRISES

No less surprising is this symphony's minuet, marked at an outlandish tempo (allegro molto) that turns it into another dance altogether: a *Deutscher* (or "Teitsch"), the "German dance" familiar to us from the ballroom scene in *Don Giovanni*, where it served to accompany the lubberly steps of that unlikeliest of couples, Leporello and Masetto. It comes (or at least begins) in Haydn replete with its traditional oom-pah-pah accompaniment. As danced in the Austrian countryside the *Deutscher* was known as the *Walzer* (from *wälzen*, "to roll") after its characteristic whirling step. Within a generation this adapted peasant dance, known variously as *valse* or *waltz*, would be the main high-society ballroom dance throughout Europe and in all its cultural colonies.

Haydn played an important role in this dissemination. His use of this exotic dance type in his Salomon symphonies was a novelty to the London audience and caused a sensation. Haydn responded to the demand thus created with a set of a dozen *Deutsche Tänze* set for a typical Viennese dance band (clarinets among the winds, no violas). What is of particular historical significance is the fact that the famous composer of concert music also considered it a part of his job description to furnish ballroom dances for the use of the same social set who attended his concerts. Thus, although the symphony and its performance occasions were becoming increasingly specialized, they were not as yet altogether cut off from more utilitarian genres, and neither was the composer. Haydn's concert audiences, both at home and abroad, thus heard actual ballroom dances in contemporary use (minuets, contredanses, waltzes) as part of the typical symphony. And thus, ineluctably, they had a different relationship to the genre, and a different attitude toward it, from any that we (for whom all its dances are obsolete "museum pieces") can have today. Concert music, however monumentalized or rarefied, still enjoyed some semblance of symbiosis with eighteenth-century daily life. The concert hall was not yet a museum.

This holds especially for the finale of the "Surprise" Symphony, which is cast in the meter and tempo of a perfectly recognizable (and danceable) contredanse — or "country dance," as the Londoners still knew it and danced it.

This finale is a remarkable tour de force, one of Haydn's most accomplished hybrids or syntheses of rondo and "sonata" forms. Its main theme, whose first pair of balanced phrases is given in Ex. 29-9a, is thirty-eight bars long and has a fully articulated and "closed" shape. In its self-sufficiency it contrasts starkly with the terse little phrase that

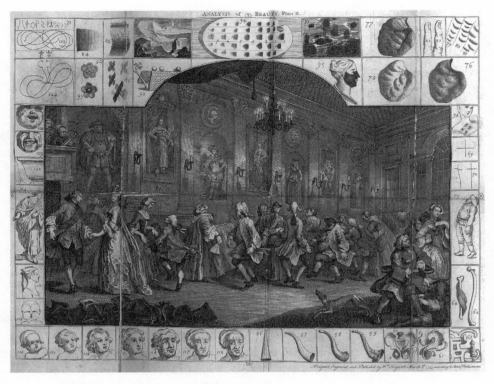

FIG. 29-11 *Country Dance*, by Hogarth (*The Analysis of Beauty*, 1753).

EX. 29-9A Franz Joseph Haydn, Symphony no. 94 in G ("Surprise"), IV, mm. 1–8

EX. 29-9B   Franz Joseph Haydn, Symphony no. 94 in G ("Surprise"), IV, mm. 138–48

gets the first movement going. Such structural self-sufficiency stamps it immediately as the theme of a rondo, not a "sonata-allegro." But at its very conclusion the theme is cut off before its time by an elided cadence, dramatized by a sudden tutti attack — the "Big Bang" familiar to us from the first movement, and to Haydn's London subscribers from just about every first and last movement they heard from his pen. This was the essential "subscription symphony" idea, and immediately stamps the movement as one that will emphasize the tonal trajectory. Unlike a simple rondo, it is to be a thing not of well-shaped themes but of departures, transitions, and arrivals in the manner of the "sonata" form.

That sudden tutti initiates the expected swing to the dominant, where a second theme awaits. In what by now seems a typical gesture, Haydn prolongs the wait with a bar of silence (m. 74) just to get the audience to sit up and beg. And if we may press the canine analogy just a bit farther, Haydn throws a bone to the *Kenner und Liebhaber* in the house by fashioning the accompaniment to the second theme out of the opening motive from the first theme. At m. 87 another tutti attack on an elided cadence reasserts the momentum of the tonal trajectory. The characteristically heavy insistence on the seventh of the dominant seventh (first presented as a brute unison in m. 100) unmistakably signals a return of the rondo theme in the tonic — something that would be unthinkable in "pure" sonata form. The heaviness of the insistence is a typically surprising yet communicative introversive sign, meant to give the audience a pleasurable jolt.

Note, by the way, that once again a main theme has been constructed with an emphasis on the third degree of the scale (in this case preceded by a two-note pickup, ubiquitous in Haydn finale themes). In fact, the whole formal strategy of the movement is implicit in the way that opening motive highlights the third degree, and might have been predicted. Its reprise halfway through the movement exhibits another typically Haydnesque touch: the doubling of the violins by the bassoon at the lower octave (for precedents within this very symphony, see the coda to the Andante and the trio section of the minuet). Here it is virtually mandated by the unison "middle Cs" in mm. 100–102: only a B in the bassoon register will give the C its proper resolution.

The tutti that next interrupts the rondo theme (m. 112) stands in for the sonata-form "development" — that is, the section that will arrive by dint of sustained *thematische Arbeit* at the FOP. And here Haydn pulls off a marvelous harmonic pun. The FOP is iii (B minor), the virtually inevitable choice given the way the note B has been spotlit in so much of the symphony's thematic content. The decisive cadence to B minor is initiated in m. 138 with the cadential $^6_4$ harmony that promises a dominant/tonic follow-through. The importance and the finality of the cadential gesture are signaled by the motivic work: an arpeggio in the first violin that rides the opening motive of the main theme through almost two octaves.

And then the engine stalls. After a bit of coughing and knocking, the first violins are left alone with the opening motive, still implicitly harmonized by the cadential $^6_4$ of B minor. And then, at the pickup to m. 146, the change of a single note (F♯ to G) allows the transformation of the stalled passage into the main rondo theme, and we're off and running again (see Ex. 29-9b).

Virtually every late Haydn finale has a passage in which something far out hooks up "unexpectedly" with the pickup to the rondo theme — here too we learn to expect the "unexpected" and wait gleefully for it. But Haydn, knowing this, lets it happen again (at the upbeat to m. 182, made less predictable by modifying the pickup figure) so that he can truly take us by surprise. The version of the rondo theme thus initiated acts like the sonata-form "recapitulation," bringing the second theme and a "developing" coda in tow, the harmonic surprise of the latter (m. 234) anticipated by another timpani shock to match (and recall) the one in the Andante.

THE CULMINATING WORK

As Landon has noted, the "Surprise" Symphony "has justly become a symbol for all Haydn's music."[14] That is not only because the symphony became the emblematic Haydn genre but also because of the way Haydn transformed the symphony, not only in style but above all in status. When Haydn found it the symphony was just a distinguished sort of party music. He left it a monumental genre that formed the cornerstone of a *canon*, a publically recognized body of works deemed by lovers of art to have universal or defining value within their culture — a value, be it noted, no longer associated exclusively with a single social class. In their public eloquence, Haydn's late "subscription symphonies" thus symbolized the nascent democratization of high art. In this way this former retainer to a princely house became one of the emblematic figures of the Enlightenment.

Which is not to say that Haydn consciously thought of himself as a *philosophe*, an Enlightened thinker, still less that he harbored (any more than Mozart did) the sort of subversive or anti-aristocratic sentiments we now tend, rather romantically, to associate with the era in which he lived. Nowhere in Haydn's works, his correspondence, or the vast posthumous biographical literature about him, for example, does he make any reference at all to the French Revolution, the most cataclysmic political event of the century. Indeed, his very late works give us reason to believe that he deplored the Revolution's consequences. In a pair of monumental Masses — "In Time of War" (*In tempore belli*, 1796) and "In Distress" (*In angustiis*, 1798, dedicated to Lord Nelson, the British naval hero) — Haydn appeared as a kind of Official Austrian or composer laureate, giving voice to his Empire's determined opposition to Napoleon. The same military "topic" that produced giggles in Symphony No. 100 produces shudders when it accompanies the prayer for peace at the end of the Mass in Time of War.

Even the London "public" to which Haydn's subscription symphonies made their appeal, while broader than any cohort he had previously addressed with his music, remained a largely aristocratic (or at least propertied) "high society"; the advertisements for Salomon's concerts were always pitched to "the Nobility and Gentry" (the latter term referring to property owners, noble or not). Haydn was privileged to move at the very highest levels of the notoriously class-conscious British society. He found his access to the high aristocracy highly agreeable and took very seriously King George III's invitation to settle permanently as a free artist in England under crown patronage.

This invitation was issued during Haydn's second stay in the English capital (1794–95), which was even more successful than the first. Haydn was received by the royal family on 1 February 1795, after which he wrote in his diary that "the King, who hitherto could or would only hear Handel's music, was attentive to mine."[15] Indeed, the king's evident intention in trying to secure Haydn's permanent attachment to his court was to make another Handel of him, and to establish Haydn's concerts as a national institution in perpetuity, like the Handel oratorio festivals given at Westminster Abbey every year, which Haydn found dazzlingly impressive and inspiring.

In addition to royal blandishments and bedazzlement with the magnificence of English performance traditions, Haydn faced other enticements as well. His diary following the concert of 4 May 1795 contains this entry:

> A new Symphony in D, the twelfth and last of the English;. . . The whole company was thoroughly pleased and so was I. I made four thousand Gulden on this evening. Such a thing is only possible in England.[16]

The newspaper reviews were fulsome in their praise of the work, showing Haydn to be already a sort of national monument. "He rewarded the good intentions of his friends," wrote one reviewer,

> by writing a new Overture for the occasion, which for fullness, richness, and majesty, in all its parts, is thought by some of the best judges to surpass all his other compositions. A Gentleman, eminent for his musical knowledge, taste, and sound criticism, declared this to be his opinion, That, for fifty years to come Musical Composers would be little better than imitators of Haydn; and would do little more than pour water on his leaves. We hope the prophecy may prove false; but probability seems to confirm the prediction.[17]

In some ways the prediction was indeed borne out, because Haydn's London symphonies have never left the repertory, and all subsequent composers in the genre, up to our own time, have perforce had to compete with them. Haydn's quartets and symphonies, like Mozart's operas, became the first canonical works of their kind. The culminating symphony (no. 104 in the standard numbering), which bears the same nickname ("London") as the whole series of twelve, set a benchmark for structural efficiency toward which composers have ever afterward aspired. Its historical fame and its enormous authority demand that we inspect its first movement (preferably, as always, with score at the ready).

But before we do, it is important to understand why Haydn's structural efficiency came to command such authority. Haydn himself gave the reason for valuing it when he wrote of another composer's work in his diary that he flitted from idea to idea, made nothing of his themes, and so one was left "with nothing in one's heart."[18] The economy and logic of thematic development for which Haydn became famous (and which is often — erroneously — looked upon as the "main point" or motivating idea of the sonata form) was valued not as a demonstration of technical virtuosity but as an intensifier, and a deepener, of sentiment. With this caveat in mind, we may indeed find

Haydn's technical virtuosity as astounding as did his contemporaries, to say nothing of the generations of composers who have avidly studied and emulated his work.

The slow introduction (Ex. 29-10a) is proclamatory—the audience-summoning fanfare most typical of subscription symphonies. One lady in the first-night audience thought the rising fifth, dramatized by fermatas, was a recollection of a vendor's cry ("Fresh cod!") that Haydn heard in the market. (There was an old tradition of "Cryes" in English music, as we may recall from chapter 22.) Whatever its source, Haydn makes of the rising fifth and its immediate "tonal" inversion (falling fourth) the theme for one of the most compressed and concentrated symphonic structures ever composed.

EX. 29-10A   Franz Joseph Haydn, Symphony no. 104 ("London"), I, slow introduction

EX. 29-10A *(continued)*

EX. 29-10A (*continued*)

EX. 29-10B Franz Joseph Haydn, Symphony no. 104 ("London"), I, beginning of the Allegro

EX. 29-10B *(continued)*

EX. 29-10C Franz Joseph Haydn, Symphony no. 104 ("London"), I, mm. 32–7

EX. 29-10C *(continued)*

In its scant sixteen-measure span the slow introduction encompasses a complete tonal trajectory, enunciated through a rigorous process of *thematische Arbeit*. It is, in short, a minuscule but a fully elaborated sonata form in its own right. Compare mm. 1–2 with mm. 7–8 and mm. 14–15, and you will see a progression from tonic (D minor) to relative major (F major) and back. The progression out is very direct, taking no more than four measures. The progression back (mm. 9–13) is, as always, more tortuous; it uses its extra measure to reach a FOP (actually a series of unstable diminished harmonies) and gains extra "psychological" length by doubling the harmonic rhythm and then doubling it again. Both the progression out and the progression back are carried by a clear motivic derivation from the theme: its rhythm is abstracted and applied to stepwise melodic motion, while the inversion contour is maintained by the use of a rhythmically compressed answer in the first violins that falls (usually a semitone, inflected in m. 5 to a whole tone to produce the marvelously pithy modulation to III) to counterbalance the rising bass. On regaining the tonic in m. 14–15, Haydn with equal economy of means inflects the inversion to a falling fifth in place of the original fourth, reaching IV (harmonized as a "Neapolitan sixth") and thus preparing a half cadence on V, so that the slow introduction might properly provide the running leap into the tonic and the new tempo.

What is noteworthy about the diminutive "sonata form" thus constructed is that it has only one theme. That may not seem remarkable in a 16-measure composition, but it is certainly remarkable in the 277-measure Allegro that follows. This nearly monothematic symphonic movement, by so advertising its economy, looks like a deviation from a norm if a bithematic exposition is taken as "normal" symphonic procedure. It is so taken in most descriptions — the same descriptions that usually describe the overall shape of the movement, with its exposition, development, and recapitulation, as "ternary" on the *da capo* model, rather than an expanded ("symphonic") binary form.

This bithematic ternary model, still taught in most textbooks, originated not in compositional practice but in earlier textbooks written in the 1830s for use in conservatory and university courses at Paris and Berlin. And that is why the first movement of Haydn's "London" Symphony is indispensable to any properly historical treatment of the composer and his musical accomplishments. The discrepancy between Haydn's own culminating and epitomizing symphonic movement and the later academic description of "sonata form" is an integral part of the history of nineteenth-century music and music education, but it ought not color our understanding of eighteenth-century musical style. For Haydn and his audience, the sonata form was made intelligible through a tonal, not a thematic, contrast. The thematic requirement was not contrast but *Arbeit*. These were the musical events and processes that left one with "something in one's heart."

And that is what Haydn provided in this movement with such remarkable concentration. In contrast to the opening theme of the "Surprise" Symphony, the opening theme here consists of a full sixteen-bar parallel period, eight bars to a half cadence (as shown in Ex. 29-10b), and then a repetition to a full cadence. The elision of the full cadence by a dramatic tutti signals the first major step along the tonal trajectory: thirty-four measures without a caesura (as it were, without a gulp of air), ending on the "V of V" to prepare the arrival of the "tonicized" dominant.

A closer look at the transitional or modulatory passage shows its close rhythmic relationship to the theme, further evidence of deliberate frugality of means. The rhythm of the main melody in mm. 32–35 (Ex. 29-10c) reproduces and repeats the rhythm heard at the beginning of Ex. 29-10b. The rhythm of the first violins, flutes, and (especially) first oboe at mm. 50–51 (Ex. 29-10d) is distinctly related to both the rhythm and the pitch repetitions in mm. 3–4 of Ex. 29-10b. Once this point is noticed, one notices further that the four-note pitch repetition first heard in Ex. 29-10b is often reproduced and extended in the bass (cf. Ex. 29-10e).

And so it may occasion in us a bit less anachronistic surprise when the first theme returns wholesale to express the secondary key. This time the transitional passage that interrupts it with an elided cadence makes reference to the theme's syncopated inner voice (compare the bass in Ex. 29-10f with mm. 4–6 of Ex. 29-10b), as well as to both of

EX. 29-10D   Franz Joseph Haydn, Symphony no. 104 ("London"), I, mm. 50–53

the motivic relationships already pointed out — more insistence on extreme thematic parsimony. Indeed, the only "new" thematic material in the exposition comes in the coda, though even here there are definite (if subtle) motivic correspondences with the main theme: those with score in hand will notice that the melodic figure in the first violins in mm. 104, 106, and (in other instruments) mm. 108 and 110 is the inversion of the opening figure in the theme (and we have encountered far too many important inversion relationships in the structure of this movement to regard this one as a happenstance).

After so much demonstrative economizing on thematic content in the exposition, one is ready for anything in the development, where motivic economy is always prized. But even so, one cannot fail to be impressed by the yield Haydn manages to harvest from the two-measure repeated-note idea first heard in the third and fourth measures of Ex. 29-10b. The first restatements of it after the double bar (mm. 124–127) are nearly literal ones, merely substituting a minor-inflected semitone for the original whole tone in the second measure. Thereafter, the idea is altered melodically in various ways over the invariant original rhythm: cf. the exchange for winds and bass in mm. 131–35 (Ex. 29-10f).

EX. 29-10E Franz Joseph Haydn, Symphony no. 104 ("London"), I, mm. 58–60

EX. 29-10F Franz Joseph Haydn, Symphony no. 104 ("London"), I, mm. 124–35

EX. 29-10F   (*continued*)

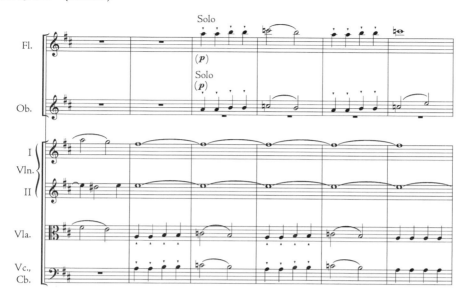

It would be an instructive exercise to analyze this development section to see where (if anywhere) the motive extracted from Ex. 29-10b, or at least one of its constituent measures, does *not* figure in the melodic elaboration. Even where the principal melodic line seems to have another source (e.g., Ex. 29-10g, expressing the FOP through a recall of the coda or "closing theme" at mm. 104 ff), the chugging repeated quarters in the bass are still derived from the main motive (and the way they are spotlit by the bassoon in mm. 150–55 leaves no doubt as to the purposefulness of the reference). But one could go much farther than that if one is willing to allow that the falling seconds in Ex. 29-10g and its counterparts in the coda is motivically related to the falling second in Ex. 29-10b and its many echoes in the development section. (Alternatively, one could describe the first-violin figure in the first, third, seventh, and ninth measures of Ex. 29-10g as the inversion of the first measure in Ex. 29-10b.) In that case one could describe Ex. 29-10g as a contrapuntal montage of the movement's two main motivic ideas.

EX. 29-10G   Franz Joseph Haydn, Symphony no. 104 ("London"), I, mm. 146–55

EX. 29-10G (*continued*)

Recalling that the main theme begins (as so often with Haydn) on the third degree of the scale, one might well predict the way in which the double return is prepared. The reassertion of the original key carries a heavier emotional payload than usual in this movement, since the development section had been confined so perspicuously (and so unexpectedly) to minor tonalities. Indeed, thanks to some particularly ingenious deceptive cadences, it is a wider range of minor tonalities than we have ever encountered before in direct succession, including two (C♯ and G♯ minor) that lack even a secondary function in the home key, making the passage in Ex. 29-11g a farther-out FOP than any previous Haydn symphony.

To the very end, then, Haydn was expanding the horizons of his signature genre and enhancing its import in response to the new importance of the subscription public to his art. The radical economy of thematic content together with the generous expansion of the tonal trajectory combine vastly to enlarge the music's "meaningfulness." The apparent thematic miserliness makes introversive reference pervasive: that is its true purpose and achievement. In such a situation practically every phrase relates motivically to music previously heard and putatively forecasts the music to come. And projecting this network of introversive signaling over an enriched tonal compass has the effect of increasing the scope—one might almost say the spatial reach—of introversive resonance and allowing it to combine more freely with the traditional vocabulary of pathos. The more consistent and rigorous the thematic process, and the more adventurous the tonal range, the more one is left with in one's heart.

The Composer's Voice

Mozart's Piano Concertos; His Last Symphonies; The Fantasia as Style and as Metaphor

ART FOR ART'S SAKE?

To cap the point on which the previous chapter came to rest, and appreciate the range and depth to which subjective emotional declaration could now be brought within the reach of late eighteenth-century instrumental style, consider a symphonic movement by Mozart, Haydn's great contemporary, whose short life came to an end during Haydn's first London tour. Owing to the vastly different conditions of his career, symphonies and quartets were never as central to Mozart's output as they were to Haydn's—or rather, they attracted his intense interest only rather late in the game, not long before its premature termination. Until the mid-1780s, they remained for him light entertainment genres. For Mozart, the symphony, especially, remained close to its sources in the opera pit and its frequent garden-party function. One of his best-known symphonies, no. 35 in D, subtitled "Haffner," was actually composed (as late as July 1782) as a serenade to entertain a party celebrating the ennoblement of a Mozart family friend, and became a concert symphony by losing its introductory march and its second minuet.

Mozart's instrumental style underwent an appreciable deepening after his move to Vienna in his late twenties and the start of a risky new life as a "free artist." Meeting Haydn and playing quartets with him—Haydn on violin, Mozart on viola—was one of the catalysts. Mozart wrote a set of six quartets—"the fruits of long and laborious endeavor," he called them—as if in direct response to Haydn's op. 33 (then Haydn's latest works) and published them in 1785 with a title page announcing that they were *Dedicati al Signor Giuseppe Haydn, Maestro di Cappella di S. A. il Principe d'Esterhazy &c &c, Dal Suo Amico W. A. Mozart, Opera X* ("Dedicated to Mr. Joseph Haydn, Music Director to His Highness the Prince of Esterhazy, etc. etc., by his friend W. A. Mozart, op. 10").[1] The features of texture and motivic saturation that so distinguished Haydn's quartets were a powerful stimulus to Mozart's imagination, with results that caused an astonished Haydn to exclaim to Leopold Mozart (at another Vienna quartet party), "Before God, and as an honest man, I tell you that your son is the greatest composer known to me in person or by name. He has taste, and, what is more, the greatest knowledge of composition."[2]

What he did not have was a steady job. In the years following his boot from Salzburg, Mozart lived what was by comparison with Haydn, or even with his

FIG. 30-1 Five-octave piano customary in Mozart's time (Ferdinand Hoffman, Vienna).

own father, the life of a veritable vagabond, enjoying a precarious love-hate relationship with a fickle public and its novel institutions of collective patronage. The very fact that Mozart dedicated his quartet volume to Haydn rather than to a prospective noble patron is an indication of his unusually autonomous, hazardous, and self-centered existence. For his livelihood he relied most on something Haydn did not have: surpassing performance skills. Mozart's most characteristic and important instrumental music, for that reason, usually involved the piano. Because they did not, symphonies and quartets had perforce to take a back seat.

But in the summer of 1788, in the happy aftermath of the Vienna première of *Don Giovanni*, Mozart composed the three symphonies that turned out to be his last: no. 39 in E♭, K. 543 (finished 26 June); no. 40 in G minor, K. 550 (finished 25 July); no. 41 in C, K. 551 (known as "Jupiter," finished 10 August). They are not known to have been commissioned for any occasion; and while Mozart surely hoped to make money from them, either by putting on subscription concerts or selling them to a publisher, they seem (like the "Haydn" quartets) to have been written "on spec," as the saying now goes among professionals — without immediate prospects, on the composer's own impulse, at his own risk.

This was not then a "normal" modus operandi for musicians; in somewhat hyperbolical historical hindsight these works loom as the earliest symphonies to be composed as "art for art's sake" — or, at the very least, for the sake of the composer's own creative satisfaction. (This of course is not in the least to imply that other composers did not derive satisfaction from their achievements; only that under conditions of "daily business" such as eighteenth-century musicians thought normal, creative satisfaction was the result of their effort, not its driving force.) Is there anything about their style, craft, or content that reflects this unusual status?

An argument could certainly be made that they are more reflective than most "public" music of the kind of subjectivity associated — like the very act of composing "for no reason" — with romanticism. It is a point similar to one made in a previous chapter about Mozart's operatic music and its emotional iconicity, its way of appearing, through the exact representation of "body language," to offer an internal portrait of a character to which listeners could compare their own inner life. The difference, of course, is that in the case of a symphony there is no mediating, "objectively" rendered stage character; there is only the "subject persona" evoked by the sounds of the music, easily (and under romanticism, conventionally) associated with the composer's own person. There is no hard evidence to support the view that Mozart's music contains a Romantic emotional self-portrait; there is just the widespread opinion of his contemporaries, and the supposition that the composer, late in life, may have subscribed to what was fast becoming a conventional code.

The supposition is often supported by citing the virtually operatic first movement of the G-minor Symphony, with its atmosphere of pathos, so unlike the traditional affect of what was still regarded in Vienna as party (or at least as festive) music. That atmosphere is conjured up by two highly contrasted, lyrical themes, a wealth of melting chromaticism, and a high level of rhythmic agitation. As with Haydn's extraordinary concision, Mozart's lyrical profusion is perhaps his most conspicuous feature. And yet it would be a pity to overlook, in our fascination with Mozart's prodigal outpouring of seemingly spontaneous emotion, the high technical craft with which a motive derived from the first three notes of the first theme — exactly as in Haydn's "Joke" Quartet (Ex. 29-6) — is made to pervade the whole musical fabric, turning up in all kinds of shrewd variations and contrapuntal combinations. It is the balance between ingenious calculation and (seemingly) ingenuous spontaneity, and the way in which the former serves to engineer the latter, that can so astonish listeners in Mozart's instrumental music.

Mozart was keenly aware of the relationship in his work between ingenuity of calculation and spontaneity of effect, and the special knack he had for pleasing the connoisseurs without diminishing the emotional impact of his music on the crowd. His letters are full of somewhat bumptious comments to the effect that (to quote one, to his father, from 1782): "there are passages here and there from which only *Kenner* can derive satisfaction; but these passages are written in such a way that the less learned (*nicht-kenner*) cannot fail to be pleased, though without knowing why."[3]

PSYCHOANALYZING MUSIC

So it is no exaggeration to claim that when Mozart is functioning at the top of his form, it is precisely the hidden craft that creates the impression of intense subjective emotion, and that without the concealed devices that only technical analysis can uncover, the emotion could never reach such intensity. A matchless case in point is the slow second movement of the Symphony no. 39 in E♭, K. 543, the first of the "self-motivated" and possibly self-centered 1788 trilogy. What follows will be the closest technical analysis yet attempted in this book, focusing in as it will on the career of a single pitch over the course of the movement (so keep the score at hand). Ultimately, however, the object of analysis will be not so much the recondite technical means as the palpable expressive achievement.

The unfolding of this *Andante con moto* in A♭ major conforms to no established format. Attempts to pigeonhole the movement according to the forms that were later codified in textbooks result in clumsy circumlocutions that betray their anachronism. The Scottish composer Donald Francis Tovey, one of the great music analysts of the early twentieth century, once found himself in precisely this quandary, reduced to describing the movement chiefly in terms of what it did *not* contain:

> The form of the whole is roughly that of a first movement [i.e., a "sonata form"] with no repeats (I am not considering the small repeats of the two portions of the "binary" first theme), and with no development section, but with a full recapitulation and a final return to the first theme by way of coda.[4]

But no one ever listens to music like that. Any meaningful description of the movement will have to account for what it does contain, not what it doesn't, beginning with a main theme (Ex. 30-1a) that, as Tovey observed, is presented as a fully elaborated, closed binary structure. This, of course, is something that never happens in a "first-movement" form, where the whole chain of events is inevitably set in motion by the

EX. 30-1A   W. A. Mozart, Symphony no. 39 in E-flat, II, opening

EX. 30-1A (*continued*)

interruption or elision of the theme's final close. If we must pigeonhole, the category that is most likely to occur to us as a working hypothesis while listening is that of rondo. And there would be some corroboration for this conjecture later on, as we shall see, in the form of contrasting "episodes" (again reminiscent of those encountered in the slow movement of Haydn's "Joke" Quartet, to which the present Andante is formally related). But it would still be better to take things as they come and regard the form of the piece as a result or outcome of a sequence of meaningful acts or "gestures," some of them now and then recalling this or that familiar formal strategy.

The two halves of the opening theme are related in a way that recalls "sonata form," with the second half encompassing some motivic development, especially of the unaccompanied violin phrase first heard in mm. 2–3, and then a double return. That double return is tinged with irony, though, in the form of a modal mixture—the substitution of the parallel minor for the original tonic in mm. 22–25. The return is no return. You can't go back again. Experience has cast a pall. The inflection of C to C♭, the tiniest inflection possible, makes a huge difference. Mozart was very fond of half-step adjustments that have outsized repercussions. Looking back at the first half of the theme, for example, we notice how he has managed to reroute the second cadence to the dominant just by inflecting the signature D♭, as heard in m. 3, to D natural in m. 7.

The inflection to C♭ means a lot more. It bodes ill. As the music historian Leo Treitler memorably put it, the seemingly unmotivated modal mixture is "a signal of a coming complication, or perhaps it is better understood as a provocation—the injection without warning of an element, however small, that is uncongenial to the prevailing atmosphere and inevitably provokes trouble."⁵ Indeed it will. And yet the theme's final cadence puts the intruder out of mind as though nothing had happened. In psychological terms, the C♭ and its troubling implications have been "repressed," as one might repress a disagreeable passing thought. But as a result that cheery final cadence has an ironic tinge; it is covering something up. One has the uneasy feeling that "something" will be back.

And sure enough, a new intruder now bursts upon the scene: the wind instruments, silent up to now, enter on the dominant of F minor, the relative minor of the main key, and force the music into a new harmonic domain. The element of force is palpable, not only because of the peremptoriness of the winds' maneuver, but because of the completely unexpected nature of the strings' response: stormy, anguished, protesting (or, in "objective" musical terms, abruptly loud, syncopated, dissonant). Most significant of all, what finally forces the bass instruments off their *tremolando* F is the reappearance in m. 33, in a much more dissonant (diminished-seventh) context, of the repressed C♭, now a far more active ingredient, harmonically speaking, than it had been before (Ex. 30-1b). The repressed has returned; and, as always, it has returned in a more threatening guise. In m. 35 it actually takes over briefly as harmonic root (of a "German sixth" chord) before resolving, its force spent, to the dominant of V.

Again it has been repressed, but with much greater effort than before, and incompletely. In mm. 39–45 the winds and basses try to recover the poise of the motivic dialogue first heard in mm. 9–14, but the unremitting tremolo in the violins acts as a continuing irritant, and another anguished response bursts out at m. 46, leading to a recurrence of the repressed note in the bass (in its enharmonic variant, B natural) with gathering force (in m. 48 as a nonharmonic escape note, in m. 49 as the functional harmonic bass; see Ex. 30-1c). The first violins try to change the subject at m. 50, but they cannot shake the B natural; it keeps intruding in place of B♭ (its trespass or forced

EX. 30-1B   W. A. Mozart, Symphony no. 39 in E-flat, II, mm. 33–38

EX. 30-1C   W. A. Mozart, Symphony no. 39 in E-flat, II, mm. 48–53

entry underscored by its being sustained), and in m. 51 it is approached by a direct and highly disruptive leap of a tritone.

Now, ironically, it is the winds, the original disturbers of the peace, who intervene to calm things down. The long passage from m. 53 to m. 68, leading to a serenely harmonious reprise of the original theme in the original key, is dominated by two points of imitation in the winds, of which the subject is drawn from the first wind entrance at m. 28; an effort to "undo the damage" is perhaps connoted by the inversion of the sixteenth-note turn figure (compare m. 54 *et seq.* with the flute in m. 29). The whole passage that follows (through m. 90) sounds like a "recapitulation" of the original theme, with the strings and winds now cooperating amicably in bright and brainy counterpoints (some of them, particularly the winds' staccato scales in mm. 77–82, in a distinctly *opera buffa* spirit).

But in m. 91 (Ex. 30-1d) the repressed again returns with a vengeance, abetted by a portentous four-note chromatic segment in the winds that ushers in a passage of bizarre, almost bewildering commotion. It is the old storm-and-stress material first brought on by the winds in m. 28, only now transposed to B minor, a key so "far out" with respect to the original tonic as to have no normal functional relationship with it at all. Its relationship to the original "storm-and-stress" key, however, has been prefigured by that violin leap, already characterized as "disruptive," from F to B in m. 51. And of course its tonic pitch is none other than the foreign body the movement has been trying to eject since its first appearance in m. 24. The repressed thought has not only returned, it has become an anguished, controlling obsession.

EX. 30-1D   W. A. Mozart, Symphony no. 39 in E-flat, II, mm. 91–97

Now it can be ejected only by really drastic measures. To recount them briefly: after a first fitful attempt to dislodge the B-natural by chromatic steps, it returns (spelled C♭) and is resolved in mm. 103–4 by treating it as a dominant to F♭ (how many times could that note have functioned as a tonic in the eighteenth century?). In m. 105, the F♭, by picking up an augmented sixth (D natural in the winds), is identified as the flat submediant of A♭, the home key, and is finally resolved to E♭, the dominant, in m. 106 (see Ex. 30-1e).

EX. 30-1E   W. A. Mozart, Symphony no. 39 in E-flat, II, mm. 103–108

Still the repressed note does not give up without a fight. After one last resurgence of conflict (mm. 116–19), the first violins try to bridge the last gap to the tonic, but are stalled briefly (mm. 121–24) by a couple of "difficult" intervals — a diminished fifth, and finally a diminished seventh that softly insinuates the C♭ for the last time before the final subsidence into the tonic (Ex. 30-1f). When the main theme comes back for the last time (m. 144), its cadence is at last purged of modal mixture, as if to say "I'm cured." Even so, at m. 151 and again at m. 155 there are a couple of lingering, curiously nostalgic twinges (Ex. 30-1g). The C♭ comes back as a decorative bass note, always in conjunction (at first direct, then oblique) with D natural, with which it forms a "pre-dominant" diminished seventh, directing the harmony securely back to a tonic cadence that is repeated four times, the last time suddenly loud. This overly insistent close seems to protest a bit too much, as if to say "I'm OK! Really!"

The use of words like "repression" and "obsession" might seem carelessly anachronistic. They are (or, at least, can often be used as) psychoanalytical terms — terms that

EX. 30-1F   W. A. Mozart, Symphony no. 39 in E-flat, II, mm. 121–125

EX. 30-1G   W. A. Mozart, Symphony no. 39 in E-flat, II, end

had their main currency in the twentieth century. Obviously, Mozart could not have known them, just as he could not have known the work of Sigmund Freud (1856–1939), the main theorist of psychoanalysis, who was chiefly responsible for their vogue in twentieth-century parlance. But of course Freud knew Mozart, just as he knew the literary legacy of Romanticism, and repeatedly commented that his own contribution oftentimes amounted to no more than giving names and clinical interpretations to age-old psychological phenomena that poets (and, let us add, tone-poets) had long since portrayed artistically in their every detail.

Not only twentieth-century listeners, but Mozart's own contemporaries recognized that his instrumental music was unusually rich—unprecedentedly rich, they thought—in "inner portraiture." It was Mozart above all who prompted Wilhelm Wackenroder (1773–98), an early theorist of Romanticism whose life was even shorter then Mozart's, to formulate the very influential idea that "music reveals all the thousandfold transitional motions of our soul," and that symphonies, in particular, "present dramas such as no playwright can make," because they deal with the inner impulses that we can subjectively experience but that we cannot paraphrase in words.[6]

It was because of this perceived "new art" of subjective expression, as E. T. A. Hoffmann dubbed it, that symphonies, like all instrumental music, achieved an esthetic status far beyond anything they had formerly known, to the point where the instrumental medium could rival and even outstrip the vocal as an embodiment of human feeling. Hoffmann made the point quite explicitly and related it to the historical development traced in chapter 29. "In earlier days," Hoffmann wrote,

> one regarded symphonies merely as introductory pieces to any larger production whatsoever; the opera overtures themselves mostly consisted of several movements and were entitled "sinfonia." Since then our great masters of instrumental music have bestowed upon the symphony a tendency such that nowadays it has become an autonomous whole and, at the same time, the highest type of instrumental music.

And specifically about Mozart's Eb-major Symphony, K. 543, which contains the movement we have just examined in detail, Hoffmann wrote:

> Mozart leads us into the heart of the spirit realm. Fear takes us in its grasp, but without torturing us, so that it is more an intimation of the infinite. Love and melancholy call to us with lovely spirit voices; night comes on with a bright purple luster, and with inexpressible longing we follow those figures which, waving us familiarly into their train, soar through the clouds in eternal dances of the spheres.[7]

It is tempting to speculate that the novel impression of enhanced subjectivity in Mozart's instrumental music, and its vaunted autonomy (leading eventually to the idea, prized by the nineteenth century, of "absolute music" as the highest-aspiring of all the arts), had something to do with Mozart's own novel, relatively uncertain and stressful social situation, and the heightened sense that it might have entailed of himself as an autonomous individual subjectively registering an emotional (or "spiritual") reaction to the vicissitudes of his existence.

A number of critics have pointed to Mozart as the earliest composer in whose music one can recognize what one of them, Rose Rosengard Subotnik, has called the "critical world view" associated with modernity.[8] Such a view entails a sense of reality that is no longer fully supported by social norms accepted as universal, but that must be personally constructed and defended. Its ultimate reference point is subjective: not the Enlightenment's universal (and therefore impersonal) standard of reason, but the individual sentient self.

It is a less happy, less confident sense of reality than the one vouchsafed by unquestioned social convention, and it points the way to the "existential loneliness" or alienation associated with romanticism. Hoffmann himself, perhaps somewhat irreverently paraphrasing the words of Jesus, averred that the "kingdom" of art was "not of this world."[9] Artists who see themselves in this way are the ones most inclined to create "art for art's sake," as Mozart may have done in the case of his last three symphonies.

And yet, of course, it was a change in the social and economic structures mediating the production and dissemination of art—the conditions, in short, "of this world"—that gave artists such an idea of themselves. Mozart was the first great musician to have tried to make a career within these new market structures. We shall see their effects most clearly by turning now to the works he composed for himself to perform, particularly his concertos.

THE "SYMPHONIC" CONCERTO IS BORN

Despite Haydn's unprecedented achievements in the realm of instrumental music, his catalogue contains a notable gap. His output of concertos is relatively insignificant. Only two or three dozen works of that kind are securely attributed to him, which may sound prolific enough until his hundred-plus symphonies and eighty-plus quartets are set beside them. Nor are they of a quality to stand comparison with those better-known works. Among them are a couple of perky little items that still figure occasionally on concert programs: a harpsichord concerto in D major and an unusual one in E♭ for "clarino" (that is, trumpet played high), composed in London in 1796.

His two cello concertos, especially the rather lengthy one in D major composed in 1783 for Anton Kraft, the solo cellist in Prince Esterházy's orchestra (and once attributed to him), are played, some would suggest, more often than they deserve since today's virtuoso cellists have hardly any "classical" concertos in their repertory. The D-major concerto originally won its place in the modern concert hall thanks to a modernized arrangement by the Belgian music scholar François-Auguste Gevaert; its only "classical" counterpart in the cello repertory, a concerto in B♭ by Luigi Boccherini (1743–1805), was likewise popularized in an arrangement by the cellist Friedrich Grützmacher. It says a lot about Haydn's concertos that they have needed editorial modernization in order to reenter the modern repertory, while his late symphonies, never modernized, have never gone out of style.

Few but students play Haydn's four violin concertos any more, and a fair number of Haydn concertos are for instruments that nobody (well, hardly anybody) plays at all any more. Besides two concertos for Prince Nikolaus Esterházy's beloved baryton, there are five for a pair of *lire organizzate*, weird hybrid instruments resembling hurdy-gurdies, activated by turning a crank but equipped on the inside with organ pipes and miniature bellows along with (or instead of) the usual violin strings. Haydn's output for *lira organizzata* (including several "notturni" or serenades in addition to the concertos) were written quite late in his

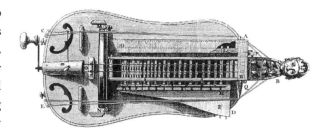

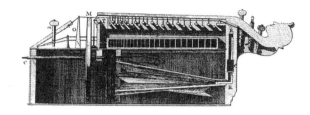

FIG. 30-2   Lira organizzata, for which Haydn wrote a set of concertos (Bèdos de Celles, *L'art du facteur d'orgues*, 1778).

career, between 1786 and 1794, on commission from Ferdinand IV, King of Naples, an enthusiast of the improbable contraption.

From this inventory of miscellaneous and rather perfunctory minor works a couple of important facts emerge. As the baryton and lira items suggest, Haydn's concertos were written to order, as the sometimes unpredictable occasion arose, and had little or nothing to do with the composer's personal predilections. Never once, moreover, did Haydn envision himself as the soloist in any of his concertos. He was not a virtuoso on any instrument, although he could function creditably as an ensemble violinist or a keyboard accompanist.

The situation with Mozart could not have been more different. His concertos were arguably the most vital and important portion of his instrumental output. Not only do they bulk larger in his catalogue, their total roughly equaling that of the symphonies, they also include some of his most original and influential work. As a result, Mozart's standing as a concerto composer is comparable to Haydn's in the realm of the symphony: he completely transformed the genre and provided the model on which all future concerto-writing depended. And that is largely because Mozart, as celebrated a performing virtuoso as he was a creative artist, was his own intended soloist—not only in his twenty-seven piano concertos but in his half-dozen violin concertos as well.

Mozart's earliest concertos were written at the age of eleven (at Salzburg in the spring and summer of 1767), for use as display pieces in his early tours as a child prodigy. They are not entirely original works but arrangements for harpsichord and small orchestra (oboes, horns, and strings) of sonata movements by several established composers including C. P. E. Bach and Hermann Friedrich Raupach, whom the seven-year-old Mozart had met in Paris during a five-month stay in 1763–64, his first tour abroad. A few years later, when he was sixteen, Mozart made similar touring arrangements of three sonatas by J. C. Bach, whom he had got to know well in London in 1765. These were scored for a really minimal band (two violins and bass) for which Mozart composed ritornellos to alternate phrase-by-phrase with the originals. These pieces may not amount to much, but they did set the tone for Mozart's lifetime output of concertos written for his own concert use.

Mozart's first entirely original piano concerto (now known as "No. 5" and listed in the Köchel catalogue as K. 175) was written back home in Salzburg in December 1773, shortly before the composer's eighteenth birthday. (He was still playing it in 1782, when he furnished it with a new finale for a concert in Vienna.) For the next two years, however, Mozart concentrated on the violin. His father, himself a famous violinist, encouraged him with the promise that if he applied himself, he could become the greatest violinist in Europe. As if to give himself an incentive to practice, Mozart composed five violin concertos between April and December 1775, as well as a curious piece he called "Concertone" (an invented word meaning "great big concerto") for two violins and orchestra, which he composed, perhaps to perform with his father, in May 1774.

Mozart never did become the greatest violinist in Europe, but his brash and entertaining violin concertos of 1775, composed at the age of nineteen, were nevertheless a watershed in his career. In them he began to combine the older ritornello form inherited from the concerto grosso with the idiosyncratic, highly contrasted thematic "dramaturgy" of the contemporary symphony, itself heavily indebted for its verve and variety to the comic opera. Out of this eclectic mixture came the concerto style that Mozart made his trademark.

The Salzburg violin concertos are light and witty works in the serenade or divertimento mold. The third (in G, K. 216) and fourth (in D, K. 218) are virtually identical in form. They begin with bright allegros in an expanded ritornello form; their middle movements are lyrical "arias" (actually marked *cantabile* — "songfully" — in no. 4) in which the soloist takes the lead throughout; and their finales, titled "rondeau" in the French manner, are dancelike compositions in which the most variegated episodes alternate playfully with a refrain. In no. 3 the refrain is in a lilting $\frac{3}{8}$ characteristic of the genre, but one of its episodes is a little march (preceded by an Andante in the minor). In no. 4 the recurrent tune itself alternates phrases in $\frac{2}{4}$ with phrases in $\frac{6}{8}$. This prankishly exaggerated heterogeneity — a Mozartean trademark! — lends these concluding movements something resembling the character of an *opera buffa* finale.

The fifth violin concerto (in A, K. 219) carries this comic opera effect to an extreme. Its finale, though not explicitly labeled "rondeau" since it has only one episode (resulting in the equally operatic *da capo* form), is an even wilder motley than its predecessors. The outer sections embody a gracious dancelike refrain in $\frac{3}{4}$ time marked "Tempo di Menuetto," while the middle of the piece consists of a riotous march or "quick-step" in the parallel minor, cast unexpectedly in the "alla turca" or "janissary" mode we have already encountered in *The Abduction from the Seraglio*, Mozart's boisterous singspiel of 1782. (Osmin's rage aria from that opera, we may recall, is also in A minor, as is the famous "Rondo alla turca" finale from the piano sonata, K. 331; it was Mozart's "Turkish" key, and the fifth violin concerto is sometimes called the "Turkish" concerto.)

The concerto's first movement opens with a droll sendup of the Mannheim orchestra's flashy routines, which Mozart had not yet actually heard on location, but which were avidly imitated, as we have seen, at the Parisian Concert Spirituel, which he did most enthusiastically attend as a boy. After a cheeky *premier coup d'archet* ("first stroke of the bow") comes a pair of "Mannheim rockets"—lithe arpeggios in the violins that rise to little sonic outbursts in mm. 5 and 9 (Ex. 30-2a). Thereafter the mood of this opening tutti seems to change like the weather, in a manner again recalling descriptions of the Mannheim orchestra and the showpieces composed for it: *pianissimos* alternating

EX. 30-2A   W. A. Mozart, Violin Concerto no. 5, K. 219, I, mm. 1–9

with *fortissimos*, chromatic harmonies with primary chords, marchlike rhythms with syncopations, all leading to a concluding "tag" or fanfare on the tonic triad, arpeggiated *all'unisono* (Ex. 30-2b).

And now the soloist enters—with an altogether unexpected lyrical *adagio* that proceeds through a really purple harmonic patch (a deceptive cadence to an augmented-sixth chord) and reaches yet another full stop on the tonic. Only now does the movement really seem to get under way, and very wittily, with the violin playing the main theme over a repetition by the orchestra of its opening Mannheim flourishes, now revealed as a mere accompaniment to the real substance of the movement (hence the implied satire on what for the Mannheimers was the main event).

Thereafter the whole opening tutti passes in review—with the very telling exception that it is now expanded by means of solo interpolations, and with the quietest passage from the opening tutti now transposed to the dominant, thus taking on the characteristics of a "second theme" in a "sonata-form" or symphonic exposition. More solo passagework intervenes between this transposed passage and the next theme recalled from the opening tutti, thus giving the latter the character of a codetta closing off the exposition and leading—through an unexpectedly "far-out" V of iii—into what is obviously going to be a "development" section.

Of course there has already been a fair amount of thematic development in the exposition, chiefly involving the "tag," which now comes twice—once in the tonic, to close off the "first theme," and once in the dominant, to close off the "second." The

EX. 30-2B   W. A. Mozart, Violin Concerto no. 5, K. 219, I, mm. 37–41

EX. 30-2C   W. A. Mozart, Violin Concerto no. 5, K. 219, I, mm. 61–73

first time around (Ex. 30-2c), its final rising arpeggio is immediately appropriated by the soloist, who trades it off with the orchestral basses three times, after which it goes into the orchestral first and second violins to accompany the modulation to the dominant. This merry interplay actually performs a subtle structural role: by initiating the exchange, the first rising bass arpeggio is simultaneously an ending (of the "tag") and a beginning (of the modulation). Its ambiguous status, in other words, provides the phrase elision or "elided cadence" traditionally invoked to cover the structural joint where theme gives way to "bridge" or transition.

Here, in embryo, we have the so-called "double exposition" technique through which the concerto form was modernized in the age of the symphony. The first compositions in which the technique can be identified are found in a set of six keyboard concertos by J. C. Bach, published in London as his opus 1 in 1763. These, possibly along with the unpublished but widely circulated concertos of C. P. E. Bach, may be regarded as Mozart's models. But although pioneered by the Bach brothers, the technique was used so consistently (and more to the point, varied so imaginatively) by Mozart, and became through him so influential, that since the end of the eighteenth century it has been thought of as the foundation of the "Mozartean" concerto style.

According to Heinrich Christoph Koch, the most encyclopedic music theorist and critic of the late eighteenth century, if one considers "Mozart's masterpieces in this category of art works, one has an exact description of the characteristics of a good concerto."[10] And according to Carl Czerny, a pupil of Beethoven, who wrote the most influential music textbooks of the early nineteenth century, the form of the solo concerto had been expressly established by Mozart as a vehicle for representing the same kind of intense subjective feeling we have already observed in his symphonies.[11] This simplified account of the concerto's genealogy is obviously colored by the mythology that grows up around any great creative figure, but (as in any myth) its departures from the literal truth give insight into cultural values. Like all the other genres of the late eighteenth century, the concerto was formally transformed in order to serve new social purposes and meet new expressive demands.

In the first movement of a modernized (or "symphonicized," or "Mozartean") concerto, the opening orchestral ritornello and the first solo episode contain the same thematic material, but with three significant differences the second time around. First, and most obviously, the themes are redistributed between the soloist and the band. Second, they are often augmented by passages and, occasionally, by whole themes newly contributed by the soloist, and thereafter reserved for the solo part. Third, and most important by far, the second statement (and only the second one) will make the intensifying modulation to the dominant without which there can be no properly symphonic form.

These modifications amount, in effect, to a way of "dynamizing" the statically sectional ritornello form in which concertos were formerly cast by adding to it the closed ("there and back") tonal trajectory of the symphonic binary form. It is true that even in a Vivaldi concerto the first ritornello stays in the tonic and the first solo moves out to the dominant (in the major). But the two sections in the earlier concerto did not share thematic material. It is the deployment of a similar melodic content toward crucially divergent ends that so dramatizes the symphonic concerto. By adding an element of overarching tonal drama to the form, Mozart's concertos serve further to dramatize the relationship between the soloist and the accompanying (or, as the case may be, dominating) group.

The technique was not christened "double-exposition" until the end of the nineteenth century. (The actual term was coined by Ebenezer Prout, a prolific British writer of conservatory textbooks, in 1895.)[12] But as early as 1793, only two years after Mozart's death, Koch described the contemporary concerto in terms of its relationship to the symphony, and so it is by no means anachronistic to view it so today. Indeed, there is no other way to account for the dynamic, dramatic, and expressive resources now employed by the composers (who were often also the performers) of concertos. They all had their origin in the symphony; but it could be argued that they reached their peak of development somewhat earlier, in Mozart's concertos.

MOZART IN THE MARKETPLACE

The works in which that peak was scaled were the piano concertos Mozart wrote for himself to perform during his last decade, when he was living in Vienna and trying to support himself—like increasing numbers of musicians at a time of radical transition in the economy of European music-making—as a freelance artist. The conditions that had so favored Haydn's development and nurtured his gifts were drying up. Julia Moore, the outstanding economic historian of musical Vienna, has summarized the catastrophic institutional and commercial changes that were taking place, to which Mozart, like countless lesser contemporaries, had to adapt as best he could. Until the middle of the 1770s, she records, court musical establishments or *Kapellen* were maintained not only by emperors and kings but also by princes, counts, and men without important titles. But between 1780 and 1795, most of the *Kapellen* in the Habsburg Empire were disbanded, except those at a few important courts, causing widespread unemployment among musicians and a huge surge in freelance activities.

Haydn himself experienced this change in 1790, when his chief patron died and he was put out to pasture. But he had already made his fortune, enjoyed a pension, and was soon visited in any case by a crowning stroke of good fortune when Salomon brought him to London as a celebrity freelancer and guaranteed his earnings. After his return to Vienna, he was a world luminary and was showered with "windfall patronage," aristocrats and wealthy merchants vying with one another to secure his prestigious and lavishly remunerated presence in their homes for an evening. At his death, Haydn left a net estate of over ten thousand florins, literally hundreds of times the median estate of a composer in late eighteenth-century Vienna, placing him solidly in the ranks of the upper middle class, otherwise populated by industrialists.

Mozart had traveled the length and breadth of Europe during the late 1770s in fruitless search of a *Kapelle* to direct. Once in Vienna, far from a world celebrity (except insofar as he was remembered from his childhood as a sort of freak), he had to rely on windfall patronage alone for his livelihood, which put him at the mercy of a notoriously fickle public.[13] His appearances as virtuoso at "academies" (concerts he put on himself, for which he sold subscriptions) and aristocratic soirées were his primary source of income, and his vehicles at these occasions were his piano concertos. And so during his Vienna years he composed on average about two a year, from the Concerto in F major (K. 413), now known as no. 11, composed in the winter of 1782–83, to the Concerto in

B♭ major (K. 595), now known as no. 27, completed on 5 January 1791, shortly before his last birthday. These seventeen concertos, created over a period of less than nine years, were arguably Mozart's most important and characteristic instrumental compositions.

Yet they were not evenly spread out over the time in question. In fact, a chronology of Mozart's concertos turns into an index of his fortunes in the musical marketplace. At first, as a novel presence in Vienna, he was very fashionable and sought-after. Between 1782 and 1786 he was allowed to rent the court theater every year for a gala concert; he gave frequent well-attended subscription academies; and he received frequent invitations to perform at aristocratic salons. He lived high during this period, in a luxury apartment, and had many "status" possessions including a horse and carriage.

At the pinnacle of his early success he proudly sent his father a list of his concert engagements during the Lenten season of 1784. Lent, when theaters were closed by law, was always the busiest time of year for concerts, and Mozart had twenty-one engagements over the five weeks between late February and early April. Most were aristocratic soirées, including five appearances at the residence of Prince Dmitriy Mikhailovich Galitzin (or Golitsyn), the Russian ambassador, and no fewer then nine (twice a week, on Mondays and Fridays) at the home of Count Johann (or János Nepomuk) Esterházy, a member of a lesser branch of the family that so famously patronized Haydn. Three were subscription concerts at the Trattnerhof Theater, and one, on the first of April, was an especially lucrative engagement at the court theater, where ticket prices could be set very high, and where Mozart could expect to net upwards of fifteen hundred florins.

All of these occasions undoubtedly included concerto performances, and so it is no wonder that Mozart completed no fewer than six concertos during the golden year of 1784, with three following in 1785 and another three in 1786. As Moore notes, however, the fact that Mozart never again secured the use of a court theater "indicates that he had become overexposed to the Viennese musical public by 1787."[14] His fortunes declined precipitously. By 1789 he could no longer subscribe academies to the point where they were profitable. "I circulated a subscription list for fourteen days," he complained in a letter to a friend, "and the only name on it is Swieten!"[15] He had to move to a smaller apartment, lost his status possessions, and, as all the world knows, went heavily into debt, so that at the time of his death his widow inherited liabilities totaling over a thousand florins (offset somewhat by the value of his clothing, a remnant from the fat years). The same ruinous decline is also reflected in his concerto output, with only two completed between the end of the year 1786 and his death five years later.

While it is no more realistic an endeavor to select a single "representative" Mozart concerto than it would be to select a single representative Haydn symphony, a combination of factors suggests the Concerto in G, K. 453, now known as no. 17, as a plausible candidate for the role. It was completed on 12 April 1784, immediately after the fabulous Lenten season described above, during Mozart's most productive concerto year. It was ostensibly written not for Mozart himself to perform but for Barbara Ployer, a Salzburg pianist who had been his pupil, and who was the daughter of a wealthy Salzburg official, who commissioned it; and so it has an unusually complete and painstaking score. Probably for the same reason it is not one of Mozart's most difficult concertos to perform; but as we shall see, the notated score of a Mozart concerto is by no means a reliable guide to its realization in performance. When Mozart himself played it, which he did often beginning in 1785, he surely embellished the rather modest solo part.

Like practically all solo concertos, still reflecting the century-old Vivaldian legacy, the work is cast in three movements, of which the first is in the "symphonicized" or "sonatafied" ritornello form described above. The two "expositions" are related according to a plan that was by 1784 habitual with Mozart. Comparing them from the moment of the piano's first solo entry, which takes the form of a little *Eingang* or "intro" preceding the first theme, it appears that the soloist takes over all the early thematic material the second time around—or rather, the piano replaces the strings in dialogue with the wind instruments. When the crucial modulation to the dominant finally takes place, the piano gets to announce the new key with an unaccompanied solo that contains a theme that was not part of the opening ritornello. It will remain the pianist's property to the end. The second theme from the opening orchestral ritornello, characteristically Mozartean in its operatic lyricism, eventually arrives in the dominant, with the pianist again replacing the strings in dialogue with the winds. The orchestral tutti that follows (and confirms) the piano's cadential trill at the end of the second exposition corresponds in function to the second ritornello in older concertos.

The moment corresponding to the final cadence of the ritornello is replaced by a "deceptive" move to a B♭ major harmony that in the local context sounds like the flat submediant. (In terms of the once and future tonic, it is of course the mediant of the parallel minor.) This chromatic intrusion launches a long modulatory section that reaches a surprising FOP on the diatonic mediant (B natural) with a borrowed major third, turning it into the "V of vi." A passage like this fulfills the structural function of a development section, finally enabling a satisfying resolution of tension in a "double return," with the tension stretched out just a mite by a typical feint in the solo part: an *Eingang* (m. 224) that leads not to the by now urgently expected first theme in the tonic, but to a teasingly reiterated dominant seventh.

A sneaky little extra *Eingang* for the violins finally reintroduces the first theme, and we get a slightly truncated "compromise" or integrated version of the exposition, which might be likened to a sonata recapitulation in that it stays in the tonic, but which actually owes a greater historical debt to the older precedent of the *da capo* aria. This final major section of the movement has all the thematic material from the modulating exposition, including the pianist's unaccompanied theme, and culminates in the solo cadenza. All of these details are summarized in Table 30-1.

The *cadenza*, another direct inheritance from the *da capo* aria, was literally an embellishment of the soloist's final *cadence*, or trill, preceding the last ritornello. At the hands of successive generations of virtuosi it kept on growing until Koch (writing in 1793) had forgotten the etymological link that defined the cadenza's initially rather modest cadential function. Calling the traditional term a misnomer, he defined the cadenza instead as being in reality "either a free fantasy or a capriccio"—that is, a fairly lengthy piece-within-a-piece to be improvised by the soloist on the spot.[16] According

TABLE 30-1 Mozart, Concerto no. 17 in G, K. 453, Movement I (Allegro)

1. *TUTTI ("1st exposition")*			2. *SOLO ("2nd exposition")*		
mm.	1–15	1st theme (I)	m.	74	*Eingang* for piano
	16–34	bridge (I)		75–93	1st theme (I)
	35–48	2nd theme (I)		94–109	bridge (I–V)
	49–56	chromatic excursion		110–25	"piano theme" (V)
	57–69	closing th. (I)		126–38	bridge
	69–74	cadential flourish		139–53	2nd theme (V)
				154–70	passagework
				171–78	closing theme (V)
				178–83	cadential flourish, interrupted by:
3. *CENTRAL PASSAGEWORK*			4. *INTEGRATED SOLO*		
(cf. development)			(cf. recapitulation)		
mm.	184–207	modulation to FOP	m.	226	*Eingang* for vlns.
	208–26	retransition (to V), using a motive derived from the "piano theme" (compare mm. 112, 120), leading to:		227–41	1st theme (I)
				242–56	bridge (I)
				257–76	"piano theme" (I)
				277–89	bridge
				290–304	2nd theme (I)
				304–27	passagework, leading to $I^6/_4$ to introduce
				327	CADENZA
				328–40	closing theme (I)
				340–49	cadential flourish (!!)

to the terms by which Koch designated it, the cadenza in his day was a piece in which the usual forms and rules of composition were in abeyance (as suggested by *capriccio*, "caprice") and in which the soloist could concentrate entirely on pursuing an untrammeled train of idiosyncratic musical thought (*fantasia*, "vagary"), as we may remember from the *empfindsamer Stil* compositions of C. P. E. Bach, the genre's pioneer (see Ex. 27-4).

COMPOSING AND PERFORMING

It is hard to tell just what these descriptions had to do with what Mozart himself might have played at the point marked "cadenza" in his concerto scores, since like all true virtuosos in his day he was an expert improviser, and played impromptu with the same mastery as when playing prepared compositions. Nor were the two styles completely separate. When playing a previously composed piece from memory, Mozart (as many earwitnesses report) felt completely free to reembroider or even recompose it on the spot. Only when he composed his concertos for others to perform (as in Concerto no. 17) did he even write out the solo part in full. Most of the existing manuscripts contain sections of sketchy writing that served as a blueprint for impromptu realization. (Nowadays such passages are all too often rendered literally by pianists who have been trained to play only what is written.) When playing a newly finished concerto for the first time, Mozart usually "improvised" the whole piano part from blank staves or a bass line (playing it, that is, half spontaneously, half from memory). For an idea of what he could do, compare the autograph of the opening of the second movement from his "Coronation" Concerto, K. 537, with the first published edition, issued three years after Mozart's death with a piano part supplied by an unidentified arranger (Fig. 30-3a,b).

FIG. 30-3A   Autograph page from Mozart, Concerto no. 26 in D, K. 537.

Nor was any public concert or salon complete without an "ex tempore" performance, often on themes submitted by the audience to make sure that what was billed as improvisation was truly that. Mozart was famous for his ability to improvise not only free fantasias or capriccios on such submitted themes but even sonatas and fugues. "Indeed," wrote an awestruck member of one of the largest audiences Mozart ever played to (in Prague, on 19 January 1787),

> we did not know what to admire the more—the extraordinary composition, or the extraordinary playing; both together made a total impression on our souls that could only be compared to sweet enchantment! But at the end of the concert, when Mozart extemporized alone for more than half an hour at the fortepiano, raising our delight to the highest degree, our enchantment dissolved into loud, overwhelming applause. And indeed, this extemporization exceeded anything normally understood by fortepiano playing, as the highest excellence in the art of composition was combined with the most perfect accomplishment in execution.[17]

From accounts like this, we may conclude that for Mozart, at any rate, the acts or professions of composing and performing were not nearly as separate as they have since become in the sphere of "classical" music. They are more reminiscent of the relationship that the two phases of musical creation have in the realms of jazz and pop music today. And so is the brisk interaction Mozart enjoyed with his audiences. The spontaneity of the Prague audience's reaction, as described in the extract above, applied not only to solo recitals, or concerto performances, but even to the performances of symphonies.

FIG. 30-3B The same passage from Mozart, Concerto no. 26 in D, K. 5, that was shown in Fig. 30-3A, as posthumously edited and printed

After the first performance of his Symphony in D Major, K. 297 (now known as Symphony no. 31), one of his most orchestrally brilliant scores, which took place in Paris before the most sophisticated paying public in Europe in June of 1778, Mozart wrote home exultantly:

> Just in the middle of the first Allegro there was a Passage I was sure would please. All the listeners went into raptures over it — applauded heartily. But as, when I

wrote it, I was quite aware of its Effect, I introduced it once more towards the end — and it was applauded all over again. . ... I had heard that final Allegros, here, must begin in the same way as the first ones, all the instruments playing together, mostly in unison. I began mine with nothing but the 1st and 2nd violins playing softly for 8 bars — then there is a sudden *forte*. Consequently, the listeners (just as I had anticipated) all went "Sh!" in the soft passage — then came the sudden *forte* — and no sooner did they hear the *forte* than they all clapped their hands.[18]

Such behavior would be inconceivable today at any concert where Mozart's music is played. And yet in Mozart's day it was considered normal, as this very letter reveals. Mozart expected the audience's spontaneous response and predicted it — or rather, knowing that it would be the sign of his success, he angled for it. Now only pop performers do that. Such reactions and such angling are now *déclassé* (debased, regarded as uncouth) in the "classical" concert hall. The story of how that change came about is one of the most important stories in the history of nineteenth-century music, and that is where it will be told.

PERFORMANCE AS SELF-DRAMATIZATION

When writing music out for others to perform, Mozart did occasionally provide cadenzas in advance to make the recipients look good, especially his sister Maria Anna ("Nannerl"), known in Salzburg as an excellent pianist in her own right, but not a composer. For the Concerto in G major, K. 453, composed for Barbara Ployer but also sent to Nannerl, he wrote out two different cadenzas for the first movement, and, rather unusually, for the second one as well — but that second movement is a rather unusual movement, as we shall see. The beginnings of the two first-movement cadenzas are set out for inspection in Ex. 30-3.

Like these, Mozart's written-out cadenzas usually took the form of short fantasias based more or less consistently on themes from the exposition. In the present case the first cadenza to the opening movement exemplifies the "thematic" style ("more consistently based"), the second the "passagework" style ("less consistently based"). In the latest and biggest concertos the thematic style predominates, often broken down into motivic work that begins to resemble "development." But whether these written cadenzas truly resemble anything Mozart would himself have played is difficult to guess. It seems unlikely that the pianist known among his fellow pianists as the greatest improviser of his time would have hewn so closely to the thematic content of the composed sections of the piece, or stayed so closely within the orbit of the original tonic. All the less likely does it seem if one considers Mozart's predilection for infusing his instrumental works with "personality" — creating, as we have already seen, the impression of spontaneous subjective expression. This histrionic posture could only have been heightened when he was taking an active part in the performance.

So let us imagine Mozart, not Barbara Ployer, as the soloist in the slow middle movement of the Concerto in G major, K. 453. The form of the piece is unusual on two counts. First, because it has a true symphonic binary shape, rarely found in a slow movement; and second, because that shape is complemented by a striking "motto" or ritornello idea.

The piece may be broken down into four large sections, each of them introduced by a strangely off-center phrase consisting of a single five-bar idea — or half idea, since it ends inconclusively, with a half cadence. The odd phrase length is achieved by drawing out a conventional four-bar phrase with a cadential embellishment that dramatizes its nonfinality, and then really insisting on its suspenseful nature with a rest that is further enhanced by a fermata. The phrase is almost literally a question — to which the ensuing music provides a provisional answer. In contour it strikingly resembles the beginning of the lyrical second theme from the first movement (see Ex. 30-4), and can probably be regarded as a conscious derivation from it (since anything that is likely to occur to us so readily is likely to have occurred just as readily to the composer).

EX. 30-3   W. A. Mozart, Concerto in G major, K. 453, I: beginnings of two different cadenzas

EX. 30-3   Beginning of second candenza

EX. 30-4A   W. A. Mozart, Concerto in G major, K. 453, II, mm. 1–5

EX. 30-4B   W. A. Mozart, Concerto in G major, K. 453, I, mm. 35 – 38

The four sections this motto phrase so suspensefully introduces could be described as corresponding, respectively, to an opening ritornello (or nonmodulating exposition), an opening solo (or modulating exposition), a development section, and a recapitulation. The coda, or closing segment following the cadenza, begins with what sounds like another repetition of the motto; but it differs very tellingly from the others, as we shall see.

Precisely because it does not come to a full stop but demands continuation, the prefatory motto lends the material that follows it a heightened air of expressive moment. That sense of poetic gravity is more than corroborated by the emotionally demonstrative behavior of the solo part. Once past the preliminaries, the first solo starts right off with an impetuous turn to the parallel minor (Ex. 30-5a) — always a sign of emotional combustion — reinforced by a sudden loudening of the volume and a thickening of the piano texture beyond anything heard in the first movement. The modulation to the dominant is accompanied by some very purple harmonies — Neapolitan sixth, diminished seventh — of a kind also largely avoided (or rather, unwanted) in the sunny first movement.

EX. 30-5A   W. A. Mozart, Concerto no. 17 in G major, K. 453, II, mm. 35 – 41

The temperature has cooled and the skies have lightened by the time the final cadence on the dominant is made and the next incantation of the motto begins. But as soon as the soloist returns (Ex. 30-5b), the mood becomes restless again. Another sudden shift to the parallel minor (this time on D, the root of the half cadence in the

EX. 30-5B   W. A. Mozart, Concerto no. 17 in G major, K. 453, II, mm. 69–86

EX. 30-5B *(continued)*

dominant) is followed by a fairly gruesome passage in which the harmony is violently forced backward along the circle of fifths through successive cadences on A minor, E minor, B minor, and even F♯ minor — all the way to C♯ minor, the tritone antipode of G, the concerto's nominal tonic. These cadence points are all introduced by disruptive applied dominants, and the last of them is followed by an augmented sixth (A-natural *vs.* F-double-sharp) that sets up a half cadence on its dominant, the almost unheard-of FOP of G♯ major.

What follows now is a tour de force of harmonic legerdemain. In a mere four bars, as if solving a chess problem in four moves, the orchestra moves in (mm. 86–89) and leads the G♯ major harmony through its parallel minor (altering one note), to a dominant seventh on E (achieved by splitting the D♯, so speak, into E and D, again altering a single note), thence to a dominant seventh on G (inflecting the G♯ to G and the E to F), the whole thus functioning as an incredibly rapid yet smooth retransition to the original tonic, C major (Ex. 30-5c). Its arrival, signaled by the motto phrase, provides an appropriately dramatic "double return." From this point to the end the accent is on progressive reconciliation and accommodation. The pianist gets one more outburst to parallel the one in m. 35; but although it still invokes a darkling minor coloration, it is the tonic minor that is invoked, and the cloud is that much more easily dispelled. Although, presumably, Mozart at the keyboard might have let loose a few more harmonic vagaries during the cadenza, the cadence thus embellished prepares the ultimate reconciliation of harmonic conflicts. Mutual adjustment and cooperation is beautifully symbolized by the final orchestral statement of the motto phrase (mm. 123 ff), which this time lacks its embellished half cadence and suspenseful fermata, but rather hooks up with a balancing phrase in the solo part to bring things back, peacefully and on harmonic schedule, to the tonic. Just as in the slow movement from Symphony no. 39 (Ex. 30-1), there are a few chromatic twinges in the closing bars to recall old aches, but the end comes quietly, with gracious resignation.

EX. 30-5C   W. A. Mozart, Concerto no. 17 in G major, K. 453, II, mm. 86–94

Again, as in the symphony, we have a kind of emotional diary in sound, but this time there is the complicating factor of the dual medium: piano plus (or, possibly, versus) orchestra. The heightened caprice and dynamism that Mozart (and before him, C. P. E. Bach) brought to the concerto genre caused a heightened awareness of its potentially symbolic or metaphorical aspect, its possible reading as a social paradigm or a venue for social commentary. Artists imbued with the individualistic spirit of Romanticism interpreted the paradigm as one of social opposition, of the One against the Many, with an outcome that could be either triumphant (if the One emerged victorious) or tragic (if the decision went the other way).

The interaction of the soloist and the orchestra in the slow movement of Concerto No. 17 has been splendid grist for such readings, including a vivid one by the feminist musicologist Susan McClary (whose social interpretation of Bach's Fifth Brandenburg Concerto was discussed in chapter 25). She reads the piece as a narrative of increasingly fraught contention between the orchestra and the defiant soloist, with that egregious FOP on a G♯ major triad signaling an impasse. "From the point of view of tonal norms," she writes (having already characterized tonal norms as a metaphor for social norms), "the piano has retreated to a position of the most extreme irrationality, and normal tonal logic cannot really be marshaled to salvage it."[19] And yet the orchestra, as we have already seen, succeeds in salvaging the tonic in a mere four bars. Such a quick victory, McClary argues, is itself "irrational," defiant of "the pure pristine logic of conventional tonality." Both the soloist and the orchestra have exhibited startling, not to say deviant, behavior — and deviance requires explanation. The explanation one chooses will reveal one's social attitudes. Does it seem that "the collective suddenly enters and saves the day"? If so, then one has confessed one's allegiance to the communal order. (McClary identifies this as the "Enlightened" position.) Or, conversely, does it seem that the "necessities of the individual are blatantly sacrificed to the overpowering requirements of social convention"?[20] This would betray one's identification with "the social protagonist," and cast the orchestra's behavior as exemplifying "the authoritarian force that social convention will draw upon if confronted by recalcitrant nonconformity."

In such a reading, a painful irony colors the final repetition of the opening motto, in which, we recall, the piano and the orchestra finally cooperate in a way that "delivers the long-awaited consequent phrase" that answers the motto's persistent question. The appearance of concord, McClary suggests, masks oppression and social alienation.

It is not difficult to raise objections to this reading, if one insists that a reading of a work of art directly represent or realize the author's intentions, and that those intentions are "immanent" — that is, inherent — in the work itself. One can cite biographical counterevidence: in 1784, the year in which Mozart composed this concerto, he was at the very peak of his early Viennese prosperity and showed few signs of alienation from the public whose favor he was then so successfully courting. (A possible rejoinder: we know, nevertheless, that the success was short-lived; and while Mozart could not know that, he did know very well that his freelance activity was risky and that his affluent lifestyle was precarious. This consciousness might well indeed have colored his attitude toward the society in which he was functioning, and made him anxious or mistrustful.) One may also doubt whether either the piano's tonal behavior or the orchestra's can really be classified as "irrational" within the listening conventions Mozart shared with his audience. Every symphonic composition reached a FOP, sometimes a very distant one (though, admittedly, rarely so distant as here). Mozart's techniques for achieving it in the present instance, while extreme in their result, were fully intelligible in their method. Quick chromatic or enharmonic returns to the tonic from distant points are something we have observed long ago in Scarlatti, after all, for whom it was sooner an amusing gesture than a troubling one.

Then too, the quick resolution of a seemingly hopeless imbroglio was the hallmark of the comic opera in which Mozart so excelled, and which (as we have seen) so informed the style of his concerto writing. Another music historian, Wye J. Allanbrook, calls the device the "comic closure," and maintains that the quicker and smoother the unexpected reconciliation, and the greater the harmonic distance covered by it,

FIG. 30-4 A Mozart family portrait, ca. 1780, by Johann Nepomuk della Croce. W. A. Mozart and his sister Maria Anna ("Nannerl") are at the keyboard; their father Leopold holds a violin; the portrait on the wall shows the composer's mother, who had died in 1778 in Paris while accompanying him on tour (Mozart House, Salzburg).

the more it reflected Mozart's essentially optimistic outlook on the workings of his society.[21] In this, Allanbrook concludes, Mozart was acting in a manner typical of eighteenth-century dramatists and, like them, expressing an ingenuous commitment to the social ideals of the Enlightenment.

Indeed, the interpretive descriptions of the concerto that have come down to us from the eighteenth century tend to place emphasis on a kind of co-participation in an expressive enterprise, rather than on social conflict. "I imagine the concerto," wrote Koch, "to be somewhat like the tragedy of the ancients, where the actor expressed his feelings not to the audience but to the chorus, which was involved most sparingly in the action, and at the same time was entitled to participate in the expression of the feelings."[22] Thus, in Koch's view, there is indeed an "emotive relationship" between the soloist and the orchestra. "To it," Koch writes (meaning the orchestra), "he displays his feelings, while it now beckons approval to him with short interspersed phrases, now affirms, as it were, his expression; now it tries in the Allegro to stir up his exalted feelings still more; now it pities him in the Adagio, now it consoles him." As Jane R. Stevens, the translator of this passage from Koch, comments, "instead of antagonists or simply cooperating partners, the solo and tutti are semi-independent, interacting elements in a sort of dramatic intercourse" — one designed not merely to represent a mode of interaction but to achieve a heightened expressive intensity for the audience to contemplate.[23]

And yet, even if it can be demonstrated conclusively that the idea of concerto as social paradigm was not the dominant view of Mozart's time, that does not by any means preclude or invalidate social or biographical readings of his contributions to the genre. The view of the concerto as a critical social microcosm seems to have come later than Mozart's time, but not much later. And when it came, it had surely been influenced by Mozart's example. Koch himself is a case in point. His remarks on the expressive meaning of the concerto are from his textbook, *An Essay in Composition Instruction* (*Versuch einer Anleitung zur Composition*), published in 1793. In this book, C. P. E. Bach is named as the exemplary concerto composer; Mozart's name is absent. Nine years later, in 1802, Koch published a *Musical Dictionary*, in which many of the same points are made, but now with Mozart as the prime example.

It was, in other words, only after Mozart's death that his concertos began to circulate outside of the narrow Vienna-Salzburg corridor and have a wider resonance. By then, Romanticism was burgeoning. The meanings and feelings that were drawn out of Mozart's music by his later interpreters probably no longer corresponded exactly with those that Mozart was aware of depositing there, so to speak. But a message received is just as much a message as a message sent. In this as in so many ways, Mozart — perhaps unwittingly, but no less powerfully — fostered the growth of musical Romanticism, and became its posthumous standard-bearer.

Whatever we may make of the closing bars of the middle movement, the finale of the Concerto in G, K. 453, like practically all of Mozart's concerto finales, is cast in the cheerful, conciliatory spirit of an *opera buffa* finale. While the rondo form remained the most popular framework for such pieces, a significant minority of concertos, including this one, used the theme and variation technique. In either case, the object was the same: to put a fetchingly contrasted cast of characters on stage and finally submerge their differences in conviviality. Mozart's stock of variational characters is replete, on the happy end, with jig rhythms for the piano and gossipy contrapuntal conversation for the winds; and, on the gloomy end, with mysterious syncopations in the parallel minor, all awaiting reconciliation in the coda.

That coda, when it comes, is even more *buffa*-like than most, thanks to its length and extraordinary precipitateness. With its bristling new tempo ("*Presto. Finale.*"), it takes the place of the *strepitoso* or *molto stretto* at the end of an operatic act, which (recalling Lorenzo Da Ponte's words) "always closes in an uproar" with every character cavorting on stage. Here all is given up to fanfares and madcap arpeggios (as Da Ponte would put it, to "noise, noise, noise!"), the texture teeming with rapid antiphonal exchanges and with muttered Leporelloish asides like the strange minor-mode string ostinato in whole notes that frames the frenetic last statement of the theme by the piano in characteristic dialogue with the winds (Ex. 30-6). The result, in the enthusiastic words of Donald Francis Tovey, the greatest of all program annotators, is "a comic wind-up big enough for *Figaro*."

THE TIP OF THE ICEBERG

Mozart's concertos, for all their superb originality, show him most clearly in a line of succession from the Bach sons — and, in particular, show him as the heir to C. P. E.

EX. 30-6   W. A. Mozart, Concerto no. 17 in G major, K. 453, III, mm. 218–29

EX. 30-7A   W. A. Mozart, Fantasia in D minor, K. 397, mm. 1–22

EX. 30-7A *(continued)*

Bach's proto-Romantic *empfindsamer Stil.* Mozart's keyboard fantasias are even better evidence of this important line of descent. There are only four of them, representing the tip of a huge iceberg of improvised music-making for which they are, along with the concerto cadenzas, our sole precious written remains. The one in D minor, K. 397, composed early in Mozart's Vienna period, might almost have been conceived in emulation of C. P. E. Bach's C-minor fantasia (Ex. 27-4). Like it, the work begins with inchoate exploratory strummings (Ex. 30-7a) reminiscent of the old lute "ricercars" described in a much earlier chapter of this book (see Fig. 15-2), alternatively known, even then, as "fantasias"—the remote but nevertheless direct ancestors of Mozart's keyboard improvisations.

Where the marking "Adagio" replaces the opening Andante, the music settles down into a recognizable thematic shape: four bars that break down two by two with complementary harmonies. A contrasting four bars lengthens the emergent theme to a full eight-bar period, ending on a half cadence. The expectation thus raised, of course, is that a parallel eight-bar period will follow, bringing things home with a full cadence on the tonic. Instead, this being a fantasia (rather than, say, a sonata), three chromatic bars ensue that take the harmony from the dominant to *its* dominant—i.e., farther away from closure: a deliberately puzzling effect. And puzzlement is compounded when that secondary dominant is resolved, through some suddenly agitated passagework, to the minor V, only to break off on a diminished harmony, followed by a rest-cum-fermata, the very emblem of suspense.

In other words, Mozart is doing everything he can to avoid the "logic" of functional harmony (everything, that is, short of denying the functions altogether and producing an uninteresting chaos) the more convincingly to suggest a spontaneous train of musical thought, triggered on the spur of the moment by the player's actual feelings in all their changeability.

From there on, interruption is the order of the day, with each thematic return — the main theme in A minor and then in D minor, the "agitated passagework" in G minor, producing an unusual FOP—halted in mid-career by some sort of rhythmically unmeasured "outside event," be it a *presto* flourish or a diminished-seventh arpeggio to a fermata. The two *presto* passages, interestingly, have opposite structural (or "syntactic") functions. The second of them, which precedes a "recapitulatory" idea (the main theme in the original key), is an *Eingang* or "lead-in," similar to what one finds in the concertos, if more intense. The first one, however, which breaks off on a diminished-seventh arpeggio to a time-out, could be called an *Abgang*. It "leads away" from the thematic material to points unknown (Ex. 30-7b).

EX. 30-7B   W. A. Mozart, Fantasia in D minor, K. 397, m. 34

And then, just when interruption is becoming "normal" for this piece, and therefore the expected thing, Mozart switches modes, ups the tempo to *allegretto*, and throws in a fully shaped and rounded theme of a sort that could easily serve for variation or rondo treatment. In the present context, where nothing can be taken for granted, the very regularity of the theme is a source of suspense (will it last? will the cadence come?). The continuation again seems regularity itself, until Mozart breaks it off on a diminished-seventh chord and follows through with a veritable spoof of a cadenza, replete with an inordinately prolonged cadential trill that never gets to make the cadence, followed by two attempts (the second of them successful) to bring the *allegretto* melody, and with it the entire piece, to a close.

The D-minor Fantasia, while typical of the genre, is mild. It was probably meant as practice material for one of Mozart's aristocratic pupils. For an idea of what a real Mozartean improvisation might have been like, we must turn to another piece, and a justly famous one: the C-minor Fantasia, K. 475. According to Mozart's own handwritten catalogue of his works, it was completed in Vienna on 20 May 1785 and was published later that year (as "opus 11") together with a piano sonata in the same key (K. 457), completed the year before.

The fantasia is designated as being in C minor, and it does begin on C, but to find an actual cadence in the titular key one must go to m. 173, only eight bars before the end of the piece, for only there is the tonality fully confirmed. Ex. 30-8 shows part of the opening section of the fantasia, and the parallel passage that closes the work. The opening section is harmonically one of the most uncanny compositions of its time — and it is in this, particularly, that it may be presumed to transmit the true style of a Mozartean improvisation, if earwitnesses are to be believed.

EX. 30-8A   W. A. Mozart, Fantasia in C minor, K. 475, mm. 1–22

EX. 30-8A   *(continued)*

The opening octave C in Ex. 30-8a is followed by an E♭ that seems to promise a (typical) tonic arpeggio; but the very next note (F♯), coming as it does in a rhythmically strong position, is profoundly disconfirming and destabilizing. (The off-beat G that follows it can only be heard now as a passing tone, not as the completion of the promised tonic arpeggio.) When compounded with the submediant A♭ at the peak of the phrase, the strong F♯ produces a disturbing diminished third — or rather, an inverted augmented sixth, an interval that ineluctably calls for a resolution to the dominant. The call is duly met in m. 2, the dominant thus being firmly established dozens of measures before the tonic.

Now of course it may be argued that to establish the dominant is to establish the tonic as well, since both terms describe not things in themselves but participants in a reciprocal relationship. And that is true — but only momentarily. The fleeting reference to the dominant is disconfirmed and destabilized in the very next measure, by the downbeat B♭, which is voiced exactly like the downbeat C and B-natural in the preceding measures, and seems all at once to be continuing a chromatic descent that they had (as if) surreptitiously begun.

Once we have noted the descending chromatic bass, we may be reminded (especially if we are eighteenth-century listeners by birth or education) of the old *passus duriusculus*, the "hard way down" from tonic to dominant, so familiar from the vocal and keyboard compositions of the seventeenth century and their myriad eighteenth-century progeny. Having recognized it, we are led to expect the dominant once more — to expect it, indeed, in the bass and in root position. And of course (this being a fantasia) we are in for a shocking surprise; for the bass gets stalled in the process of its descent, never making G (the dominant) at all, but coming prematurely to a most uneasy rest on A♭. From there it proceeds *up* by half steps, thus canceling the *passus duriusculus* and with it, all expectation of a dominant destination.

Will it perhaps, then, lead back to the tonic, establishing it at last? Not a chance. Again the bass stalls one degree short of the goal, on B-natural, and turns downward once more, this time with a greatly lessened sense of an implied goal, if indeed any is left at all. Since one of the notes the bass will now pass through is the G so spectacularly avoided the first time around, Mozart goes to amazing lengths not only to frustrate but actually to cancel the note's resolution tendency, finally dissolving the listener's tonal orientation once and (it could seem) for all. A new way of harmonizing the chromatic bass descent is introduced, now based on an older — indeed, "pre-tonal" — concept of harmony: the suspension chain, whereby sevenths resolve not as dominants, along the circle of fifths, but purely "intervallically," to sixths (see Ex. 30-8b).

EX. 30-8B   W. A. Mozart, Fantasia in C minor, K. 475, mm. 10–6 in harmonic reduction

By the time the G is reached, there has been a precedent for the 7–6 suspension resolution, and so the dominant seventh on G resolves not to the root-position triad on C that we have been waiting for, but resolves instead, hair-raisingly (if only apparently), to an inverted chord of E♭ minor. And now the best, most sophisticated feint of all: that chord, with G♭ in the bass, proceeds enharmonically to the dominant of B major. There has been a *passus duriusculus* after all, but it has gone from B down to F♯, not C to G. Mozart has misled our ears into accepting the wrong dominant. You might even say that he has transposed our hearing down a half step.

By now it may be needless to add that this ersatz dominant will no more likely achieve a normal resolution than any of the others. In mm. 16–17 resolution comes only on the weak beats, which makes the tonic so easy to trump by the deceptive cadence in m. 18. That deceptive cadence is to G major, of course, which is the original (long-expected) dominant. It comes in "tonicized" form, however, alternating with its own dominant, and devoid of any tendency to move on to C. On the contrary, in m. 21 the chord picks up an augmented sixth (E♯) that forces it back whence it sprang, to the dominant of B, thus turning the whole passage into a tease.

The tease continues past the end of Ex. 30-8a. The F♯ major triad alternates with the awaited B for awhile, but its persisting rhythmic advantage continues to hold off any real sense of closure. Then, almost sadistically, Mozart reiterates the ostensible dominant in the soprano no fewer than six times before failing yet again to resolve it. This particular failure is especially noteworthy: a rare form of deceptive cadence in which the dominant root is held but re-identified as a third, producing an unusual "flat mediant" progression with respect to the anticipated tonic.

This unexpected and remote key, D major, is — perversely! — then given the full functional treatment so conspicuously withheld from the tonic. It is made the bearer of a full-fledged theme (the first in the piece), replete with parallel-period structure and contrasting consequent. It almost comes to a full stop, but in m. 42 its subdominant is suddenly replaced by a replay of the progression that gave access to the key of D in the first place. A dominant "$^6_5$" on B picks up the circle of fifths left hanging in m. 25, a circle that in the ensuing *allegro* will go through six more progressions in rapid succession, until the key of F major is reached, and another seemingly random pause is made amid the harmonic flux to accommodate a new theme, unexpected and unrelated to what has gone before.

To describe these events, as always, takes much longer than it does to experience them. Suffice it then to announce that there will be another pause along the way for a new theme in B♭ major (Andantino) and a stormy quasi-development beginning in G minor that will eventually refocus on the original dominant to make a retransition to the opening material at m. 167, as shown in Ex. 30-8c. This is in fact the first thematic reprise in the composition, and it cleverly redirects the opening sequential ideas so as to lead back to, and finally confirm, the tonic. An especially effective touch, both witty and poignant, is the abandonment of melody altogether in m. 173, leaving only

EX. 30-8C   W. A. Mozart, Fantasia in C minor, K. 475, mm. 167–182

EX. 30-8C *(continued)*

a bare accompaniment figure to make the long-awaited cadential connection between dominant and tonic in a manner suggesting exhaustion.

To sum up this remarkable composition-in-the-form-of-an-improvisation, or improvisation-in-the-form-of-a-composition: its technique, basically, is that of withholding precisely what a sonata or symphonic exposition establishes, proceeding from key to key and theme to theme not by any predefined process of "logic," but in a "locally associative" process that at every turn (or, at any rate, until the retransition and recapitulation signal the approaching end) defies prediction. In place of a reassuring sense of order, the composer establishes a thrilling sense of danger—of imminent disintegration or collapse, to be averted only by an unending supply of delightfully surprising ideas such as only a Mozartean imagination can sustain. That sense of risks successfully negotiated is the same awareness that makes a virtuoso performance thrilling. In the fantasia, as in the improvisations it apes, composing and performing were one.

FANTASIA AS METAPHOR

Sometimes Mozart allowed the exploratory, improvisatory spirit of his keyboard fantasias to invade other genres. One of the most celebrated instances is the slow introduction to the first movement of Mozart's String Quartet in C major, K. 465, composed in Vienna just a few months before the keyboard fantasia in C minor. It was finished on 14 January 1785, and published later that year as the sixth and last in the set of quartets dedicated to Haydn.

One youthful experiment apart (K. 171, composed at the age of seventeen), this is the only one of Mozart's twenty-three quartets to begin with a slow introduction. It is clear that this little essay in uncanny chromaticism (thanks to which the whole work is now known as the "Dissonance" Quartet) was an import from another genre, a virtual keyboard improvisation set for four stringed instruments (Fig. 30-5).

The dissonance to which the quartet owes its nickname is the glaringly exposed cross relation, A♭ vs. A, that occurs between viola and first violin at their respective entrances. (The effect is repeated four bars later a whole step lower; there are also many more-or-less concealed cross relations in the introduction, for example between cello and viola in mm. 2–3 and 6–7). The harmony implied by this chromatic inflection suggests a move to the dominant (the A♭ being part of a Neapolitan sixth in the key of G, the A-natural the fifth of a "V$_2^4$" in the same key), and that is indeed the overall trajectory, as it is in all slow introductions. But, just as in the C-minor Fantasia, a *passus duriusculus* intervenes, falling by semitones in the bass and giving rise to a whole series of fugitive shadow-"keys" (B♭ minor, F major, C minor) along the way.

So eerie and bizarre is the effect of this seemingly wayward (but actually so unerringly calculated) little passage, that it became a *cause célèbre*. The first to attack it was Giuseppe Sarti, Mozart's older contemporary, whose opera *Fra i due litiganti* Mozart quoted in the banquet scene from *Don Giovanni* as a token of friendship. Sarti's essay, "Osservazioni critiche sopra un quartetto di Mozart" ("Carping comments about a Mozart quartet"), shows a far less friendly attitude toward Mozart, whom he dismisses as an upstart piano player with "spoiled ears."[24] As for cross relations, Sarti declared gruffly that there were only two kinds: those that should be avoided and those that were intolerable.

Probably written in St. Petersburg, Russia, where Sarti served the court of the Empress Catherine the Great, the essay did not see print in full until 1832, more

FIG. 30-5   Mozart, autograph score of String Quartet in C major, K. 465 ("Dissonance"), showing the celebrated slow introduction to the first movement and the beginning of the Allegro.

than four decades after Mozart's death (and three after Sarti's own). When it did, it prompted several attempts to "correct" Mozart's writing. The most interesting of these was by the Belgian scholar-critic François-Joseph Fétis, who changed no notes, only rhythms, but managed to avoid all the direct cross relations — an achievement as clever and skillful from the technical point of view as it was esthetically obtuse (Ex. 30-9).

In a way both Sarti and Fétis were correct: the former in recognizing that the style of the introduction was that of a "piano player," the latter in normalizing it according to the rules of formal composition customarily employed when writing "in parts,"

EX. 30-9   François-Joseph Fétis, rewrite of slow introduction to K. 465, I, mm. 1–5

as one does in a proper string quartet. But that only serves to confirm the surmise that the origins of Mozart's harmonic boldness lay in the unwritten traditions of free improvisation. His boldness consisted not so much in the harmonic transgressions his critics sought to eliminate, but, more basically by far, in the substitution of one set of generic norms for another.

One who mistook neither Mozart's purpose nor the effect of his achievement was the man to whom the quartet was dedicated. Haydn heard the piece the very day after it was completed, at a quartet evening in Vienna on 15 January 1785; it was then and there that he exclaimed to Leopold Mozart that the latter's son was the greatest musician of the age. He confessed his astonishment and admiration not only in words but also, later, in exquisite musical deed. More than a decade later, undoubtedly prompted and emboldened by the teasing memory of Mozart's little fantasia for quartet, Haydn wrote a magnificent full-length fantasia for orchestra, perhaps his most amazing composition and certainly his most unexpected one.

While in England with Salomon in 1791, Haydn had attended the great Handel Festival in Westminster Abbey. He immediately perceived something we have long since observed — that Handel's sacred oratorios, rendered in monumental performances, were for the British a symbol of nationhood, the first truly *nationalistic* musical genre in our modern sense of the word. Haydn wanted to offer something similar to the Austrian nation: a sacred oratorio with text not in Latin but in the language of the people, for performance not in a Catholic worship service but under secular auspices, as a unifier not of a religious body but of a body politic, to reinforce the Austrian nation in its loyalty not only to a dynastic crown but to a common soil.

When Thomas Linley, the director of the Drury Lane Oratorio Concerts, offered Haydn *The Creation*, a libretto based on Milton's *Paradise Lost* that had been prepared for Handel but never set, Haydn leapt at the chance. He took the text home with him to Vienna, had it translated (as *Die Schöpfung*) by Baron van Swieten, and began setting it to music in 1796. The resulting oratorio was very much in the Handelian tradition, including *da capo* arias and old-fashioned contrapuntal choruses. Its popularity in Austria following its 1798 première fulfilled Haydn's ambition for the work and sparked the composition of a sequel, an oratorio called *The Seasons* (*Die Jahreszeiten*), to a libretto by James Thomson, also revised and translated by van Swieten. First performed in Vienna in April 1801, it was Haydn's last major work (followed only by two Masses, one of them drawing on the music for *The Creation*).

One part of *The Creation*, however, had no Handelian counterpart and was anything but old-fashioned in conception. That was the very opening of the oratorio, the Introduction (*Einleitung*). Subtitled *Vorstellung des Chaos* — "The Representation of Chaos" — it was an unprecedented attempt to depict in music the disorder that preceded the biblical Beginning. Yet while the illustrative endeavor as such may have been unprecedented, the musical means by which it was accomplished had a precedent, and that precedent was the keyboard fantasia.

It has been suggested, by Donald Francis Tovey and others, that Haydn's pious depiction of Chaos and the formation of the Cosmos was influenced by what was then in fact the most advanced scientific theory of the origin of the universe: the so-called nebular hypothesis, first proposed by Immanuel Kant in 1755 and popularized by the French astronomer Pierre Simon, Marquis de Laplace, in his *Exposition du système du monde*, published in 1796, the very year in which Haydn began work on *The Creation*. According to the nebular hypothesis, the solar system originated as a nebula, an immense body of rarefied gas and dust swirling in space, that gradually cooled, contracted, and condensed to form the sun and the planets. Or, as the Bible put it, in the beginning "the earth was without form and void" until God gave the Word; whereupon the processes described in the nebular hypothesis commenced. Haydn's Representation of Chaos, then, was a representation of a process of Becoming, through which what was without form took shape.

"Here is your infinite empty space!" Tovey declared, referring to the sublimely hollow opening sonority (Ex. 30-10a), a gaping orchestral unison on the note C that discloses neither mode nor key.[25] It was an inspired interpretation, for it identified the crucial representational device: the functional degree relationships of tonality, or rather their anomalous withholding and gradual reassertion. A cadence identifying the tonic and dominant, normally given at the outset of a composition to set up the structural norms that will govern it, is deliberately suppressed. The expected thing is normally so routinely supplied by the opening thematic material as to be taken for granted, hardly noticed as such. Its suppression, repeatedly and teasingly replayed, is bizarre, making Haydn's Representation unique among his orchestral compositions and singularly memorable.

What Haydn did, in effect, was to turn the techniques of fantasia writing as we have observed them in Mozart into a metaphor. "Tonality," as Tovey brilliantly observed, "is Haydn's musical Cosmos." As inchoate matter strives, according to the nebular hypothesis, toward shape and differentiation, so the music strives toward the emergence of its tonic triad and all of the attendant degree functions. The means by which Haydn realized this metaphor, expertly prolonging and delaying the process of tonal clarification, strikingly parallels the harmonic vagaries we have observed both in Mozart's C-minor Fantasy and in the Adagio from the "Dissonance" Quartet.

As in both Mozartean precedents, so here, a bare C, tentatively identifiable as the tonic (and eventually established as such), is initially disconfirmed by an A-flat that turns it perceptually into the third of VI (or of a Neapolitan to V) rather than the root of I (compare Ex. 30-10a with Exx. 30-8 and 30-9).

Haydn dramatizes the frustration of his music's "will to form" with special rigor and emphasis. He follows the unison C in Ex. 30-10a, like Mozart in Ex. 30-8a, with an E♭ that at first appears to signal a gradual building-up of the full C-minor triad. That process is then explicitly contradicted by the A♭ contributed by the second violins. Once sounded, that disruptive note is held while the C and E♭ both slip down a half step and are joined by the first violins' F to form a classically ambiguous diminished-seventh chord. Only then does the A♭ move down to G; but the delayed resolution produces not a tonic triad but a dominant seventh, the opposite member of the awaited cadential pair. The resolution to the by now even more urgently expected tonic is deferred while the violins

EX. 30-10A Franz Joseph Haydn, *Creation*, *Vorstellung des Chaos* in piano reduction, mm. 1–10

decorate the dominant function with a chromatic ascent — F♯, G, A♭ — that might well have been copied right out of the opening phrase of Mozart's Fantasia. But when the resolution comes, on the downbeat of m. 4, it is once again sullied by the A♭ in place of G — once again a dull deceptive cadence has left the Cosmos "without form and void."

Now the whole opening gesture is replayed and intensified by compression. The first violins' F is pinched up to an F♯ in m. 6, producing a chromatically altered chord devoid of clear harmonic purpose. (Its reappearance decades later in the prelude to Richard Wagner's *Tristan und Isolde* will only confirm its tonally suspensive bent.) The chord gives way to the same diminished seventh as before, only now accompanied by a G in the bass that turns the harmony into an especially tense version of the dominant (the "dominant ninth"); but when the bass arpeggiation moves to a member of the tonic triad (E♭) in m. 7, the rest of the chord stays put, producing a wildly dissonant suspension. An unconventional resolution gets us closer to the tonic, increasing our agitated suspense. But the inverted tonic triad, rhythmically unstable, gives way in m. 8 to the submediant, which, having gained an augmented sixth (F♯), is now redirected, more powerfully than ever, to the dominant.

Yet that dominant never materializes, and of course neither does the tonic. At the downbeat of m. 9 the expected G in the bass is altogether confoundingly re-identified (or misidentified) as the third of the mediant triad, and all sense of propulsion toward C minor is lost. Not until m. 21 will any decisive cadence produce a strongly voiced triad in root position, and that triad will be rooted on D♭, a note not even found in the scale of C minor, the long-foreshadowed but now seemingly lost-forever tonic. Before the tonic has even been fairly established, in other words, Haydn (like Mozart in his Fantasia) has arrived at a FOP.

A fairly extended passage (mm. 26–30) that seems to stalk a cadence on E♭ major, the normal subsidiary region of a C-minor binary structure, suggests that Haydn's overall plan follows the broad outlines of "sonata form." That impression is strengthened by the passage beginning in m. 37 (Ex. 30-10b), which has all the earmarks of a retransition.

EX. 30-10B   Franz Joseph Haydn, *Creation, Vorstellung des Chaos* in piano reduction, mm. 37–44

EX. 30-10C   Franz Joseph Haydn, *Creation, Vorstellung des Chaos* in piano reduction, mm. 48–59

But when the moment of truth arrives (m. 40), in place of the full tonic triad the hollow unison C returns, now hammered out seven times for emphasis. We are still lost in "infinite empty space."

Only on the last forlorn try, beginning at m. 48 (Ex. 30-10c), does Haydn allow a full cadence on C minor to occur, *pianissimo*. What normally happens at the beginning — again compare Mozart's C-minor Fantasia — only gets to happen at the end. And here, too, there is an added metaphorical dimension, quickly made explicit by the entry of a bass singer impersonating the angel Raphael, who intones the opening words of the Book of Genesis: "In the Beginning God created the heavens and the earth." The imminence of Creation has been announced. But its first forecast was not the Angel's speech; it came wordlessly, in the soft C-minor triad played by the strings in mm. 58 – 59, finally fulfilling, in a whisper, the promise of form.

The familiar biblical account now continues in a remarkable recitative in which the chorus, which alone may impersonally represent the voice of God, takes part. Of the suddenly radiant passage (Ex. 30-11) that follows the first act of Creation (". . . and there was LIGHT"), Haydn once exclaimed, "It was not I who wrote that, but some higher power that guided my hand." All it is, though, is an ordinary (if unusually assertive) authentic cadence on C, of a kind that not only Haydn but every composer alive at the time, whether great or mediocre, wrote every single day. It is the very special context that creates its overwhelmingly fraught significance, reminding us that what freights any utterance with meaning is never confined to its bare immanent "content," but is the product of an interaction between sender, context, and receiver(s).

Of course the role of orchestration (that is, tone color) in producing the stunning effect of the passage should not be underestimated. Indeed, orchestration has been playing an almost unprecedented role throughout the Representation of Chaos as a "nebular" metaphor. Swirling figures in the woodwinds, including a couple of spectacular runs for the flute and for the still-novel clarinet, contribute tellingly to the uncanny effect of the whole, and it is the woodwinds and brass, entering suddenly *en masse* after a long silence, that produce the sublime and somewhat terrifying radiance at the appearance of God's light. The poetic art of orchestration, seemingly "created" here before our ears (but in fact prefigured in the opera house, as we know full well from Mozart's *Don Giovanni*), would reach an unimagined peak at the hands of the increasingly metaphor-minded composers of the incipient nineteenth century.

Nor is that all that Haydn bequeathed to them in the astounding Introduction to *The Creation*. Its tonal trajectory, too, from a dark and murky "unformed" C minor to a radiantly triumphant C major, became a *topos* — a narrative archetype — that would be replayed again and again in many expressive and dramatic contexts.

THE COMING OF MUSEUM CULTURE

And that is because Mozart and Haydn's progeny, far more than any previous generation of musicians, thought of themselves as just that — progeny. A sense of heirship, of tradition, of obligation to illustrious forebears and their great works becomes in the nineteenth century a stronger force in the history of musical composition than ever before. The reasons, as always, are many, but one of the most important is the growing sense of *canon*, of an accumulating body of permanent masterworks that never go out of style but form the bedrock of an everlasting and immutable repertory that alone can validate contemporary composers with its authority.

EX. 30-11 Franz Joseph Haydn, *Creation*, recitative with chorus in full score

The reasons for the emergence of this canon had to do with the same new economic conditions in which Mozart and Haydn worked at the ends of their lives. The prime venue of musical performance became the public subscription concert rather than the aristocratic salon. Not the needs of a patron but the communal judgment of a public (as arbitrated by a new class of public critics) now defined values.

And those values were defined in accordance with a new concept of the artistic masterwork—a consummate, inviolable, even sacred musical text that contained and transmitted the permanently valuable achievements of a master creator. Thanks to this new concept, the art of music now possessed artifacts of permanent value like the painter's colored canvas or the architect's solid edifice. And like paintings, stored increasingly in public museums, musical masterworks were now worshiped in public temples of art—that is, in modern concert halls, which took on more and more the aspect of museums.

Mozart and Haydn (with Handel a singular local prototype) were the first inhabitants of that museum, of which the first examples were figuratively "erected" in Handel's adopted city, London, with the institution of public concert series, like the so-called Academy of Antient [Ancient] Musick, devoted predominantly to the work of dead composers. That was the birth of "classical music," essentially a nineteenth-century invention. And that was what killed off the busy music marketplace, with its premium on spontaneous public invention, replacing it with our familiar "classical" curatorial function—faultless reproduction, heavy sense of obligation to texts, radical differentiation of creative and performing roles, the elevation of the literate tradition and the denigration of the oral one.

Although the process of its formation was well underway by the turn of the nineteenth century, the new museum-culture of "classical music" was much abetted by the advent of a powerful catalyst. His name was Beethoven. It is clear that the museum-culture would have prevailed in the long run even without Beethoven, since it was impelled by social and economic forces much more powerful than any individual artist's efforts could be. And it is equally clear that Beethoven would have become a greatly influential figure in nineteenth-century culture even without the force of the emergent museum-culture behind him. And yet neither the authority of the one nor the greatness of the other would have attained such a speedy elevation without their symbiosis. The museum culture helped create Beethoven, and he helped create it. That momentous story now lies directly in our path.

The First Romantics

Late Eighteenth-century Music Esthetics; Beethoven's Career and His Posthumous Legend

THE BEAUTIFUL AND THE SUBLIME

The earliest public critics were motivated by a concept or ideal called romanticism — an easy thing to spot in a writer or an artist, but notoriously difficult to define. And that is because romanticism was (and is) no single idea but a whole heap of ideas, some of them quite irreconcilable. Yet if it has a kernel, that kernel can be found in the opening paragraphs of a remarkable book that appeared in Paris in 1782 under the title *Confessions* — the last and (he thought) crowning work of Jean-Jacques Rousseau. "I am commencing an undertaking," he wrote,

> hitherto without precedent, and which will never find an imitator. I desire to set before my fellows the likeness of a man in all the truth of nature, and that man myself.
>
> Myself alone! I know the feelings of my heart, and I know men. I am not made like any of those I have seen; I venture to believe that I am not made like any of those who are in existence. If I am not better, at least I am different. Whether Nature has acted rightly or wrongly in destroying the mould in which she cast me, can only be decided after I have been read.[1]

To be romantic meant valuing difference and seeking one's uniqueness. It meant a life devoted to self-realization. It meant believing that the purpose of art was the expression of one's unique self, one's "original genius," a reality that only existed within. The purpose of such self-expression was the calling forth of a sympathetic response; but it had to be done "disinterestedly," for its own sake, out of an inner urge to communicate devoid of ulterior motive. It was that, and that alone, that could provide a truly "esthetic" experience (as defined by the philosopher Alexander Gottlieb Baumgarten, who coined the term in his treatise *Aesthetica* of 1750), as distinct from an intellectual or an ethical one. The only musical works we have encountered so far that could conceivably satisfy these requirements were the late symphonies of Mozart, described in the previous chapter. Not coincidentally, then, Mozart became for the critics of his own time and shortly thereafter the first and quintessential romantic artist, the more so since music was widely regarded as the most essentially romantic of all the arts.

What made it so, according to E. T. A. Hoffmann (1776–1822), the most influential music critic of the early nineteenth century, was not merely the power of music to engage the emotions, but rather the "fact" (as Hoffmann felt it to be) that "its sole subject is the infinite."[2] Precisely because music, unlike painting or poetry, has no necessary

FIG. 31-1   E. T. A. Hoffmann, self-portrait (ca. 1822).

model in nature, it "discloses to man an unknown realm, a world that has nothing in common with the external sensual world that surrounds him, a world in which he leaves behind him all definite feelings to surrender himself to an inexpressible longing." In opposition to "the external sensual world," then, music provides access to the inner spiritual world—but only if it resists all temptation to represent the outer world.

Thus, for romantics, instrumental music was an altogether more exalted art than vocal. This, too, was a novel idea, perhaps only even thinkable since Haydn's time. Rousseau himself, as we know, was of the opposite view, quoting Fontanelle's exasperated cry—"Sonate, que me veux-tu?" ("Sonata, what do you want from me?")—with approval, and adding that a taste for "purely harmonic" (i.e., instrumental) music was an "unnatural" taste. Even Kant, the greatest early theorizer of esthetics, thought instrumental music at once the pleasantest art and the least "cultured," since "it merely plays with sensations."[3] For Hoffmann, though, writing in 1813, the shoe was on the other foot. Words, for him, were the inferior element—by nature representational, hence merely "external." They pointed outside themselves, while music pointed within. Music, he allowed, definitely improved a text—"clothing it with the purple luster of romanticism"—but that was only because its inherently spiritual quality rendered our souls more susceptible to the externally motivated (hence, more ordinary, less artistic) emotions named by the poem.[4] The poem was transformed by union with music, but the music was inhibited by the poem. Eventually, wrote Hoffmann, music "had to break each chain that bound it to another art," leaving the other arts bereft and aspiring, in the words of Walter Pater, a latter-day romantic critic, "towards the condition of music."[5]

That condition is the condition of autonomous, "absolute" spirituality and expressivity. The whole history of music, as Hoffmann viewed it, was one of progressive emancipation of music from all bonds that compromised the autonomy and absoluteness of expression that Hoffmann took to be its essence. "That gifted composers have raised instrumental music to its present high estate," he wrote, is due not to the superior quality of modern instruments or the superior virtuosity of modern performers.[6] It is due solely to modern composers' "more profound, more intimate recognition of music's specific nature." The composer and the performing virtuoso were henceforth cast in opposition; virtuosity was just one more bond, one more tie to the external world, from which true music had to be emancipated.

All of this was utterly contrary to earlier notions of musical expression, which were founded staunchly on the ancient doctrine (stated most comprehensively by Aristotle) that art imitates nature. That doctrine had itself brought about a revolution in musical expression in its time, the sixteenth century, when musicians discovered the writings of ancient Greece and began, in madrigals and (later) in opera, to devise the "representational style" (*stile rappresentativo*) so as directly to imitate speech and, through it, the emotions expressed by speech. Like the later doctrine of affections, the *stile rappresentativo* was at the opposite pole from romantic notions of untrammeled musical expressivity.

For one thing, it depended on alliance with words — another art. For another, it expressed not the unique feelings of the composer but the archetypical feelings of characters, and hence emphasized general "human nature" as an object of *representation*, not the uniqueness of an individual self as an object of *expression*. For a third, it dealt with particular objectified categories of feeling that had names, that could be (and were) classified and catalogued, that were the common property of humanity. It was powerless to summon up the verbally inexpressible, the ineffable, the metaphysical or "infinite." Hence, it could communicate only through a repeatable process of objective intellectual cognition (or recognition), not transcendent subjective inspiration. It was not an absolute art, let alone an autonomous or emancipated one. It dealt in the common coin of shared humanity, not the elite currency of genius.

The "gifted composers" or geniuses to whom music owed its emancipation, Hoffmann declared, were Mozart and Haydn, the first true romantics. As "the creators of our present instrumental music," they were "the first to show us the art in its full glory."[7] But whereas Haydn "grasps romantically what is human in human life," Mozart reveals "the wondrous element that abides in inner being." Haydn, albeit with unique aptitude and empathy, manifests a general humanity, what Kant called the *sensus communis* — thoughts and feelings common to all ("all men," as people put it then), thus capable of fostering social union. Haydn is therefore "more commensurable" with ordinary folk, "more comprehensible for the majority." His art is democratic, in the spirit of Enlightenment.

Mozart, by contrast, expresses for Hoffmann something essential, ineffable, unique. His music "leads us into the heart of the spirit realm" — or those of "us," anyway, who are equipped (like Tamino, the hero of *The Magic Flute*) to make a spiritual journey. It springs, like all true romantic art, from an "attempt to transcend the sphere of cognition, to experience higher, more spiritual things, and to sense the presence of the ineffable."[8] That is the definition of romanticism given around 1835 by Gustav Schilling (1803–81), a German lexicographer.

For all these reasons Mozart's music, unlike Haydn's, gives rise not only to bliss but to fear and trembling, and to melancholy as well. To sum it all up in a single pair of opposing words, it was Mozart, according to Hoffmann and his contemporaries, who made the crucial romantic breakthrough — from the (merely) *beautiful* to the *sublime*.

We are perhaps no longer as sensitive to this distinction as were the theorists of romanticism. We may tend nowadays to interchange the words "beautiful" and "sublime" in our everyday language, perhaps even in our critical vocabulary. To say "Haydn's music is beautiful" may not seem to us to be very different in meaning or intent from saying "Mozart's music is sublime." It may even seem to us like a way of

FIG. 31-2   Caspar David Friedrich, *Moonrise on an Empty Shore* (1839). Friedrich's eerily lit landscapes often summon up moods of sublime immensity comparable to the "infinite longing" Hoffmann named as the latent subject matter of romantic art.

pairing or equating the two. But to a romantic, it meant radically distinguishing them. And that is because, from about the middle of the eighteenth century to about the middle of the nineteenth, the words were held to be virtual opposites.

For the English philosopher and statesman Edmund Burke (1729–97), writing in 1757 under the influence of Kant (whom he influenced in turn), they presented "a remarkable contrast," which he detailed as follows:

> Sublime objects are vast in their dimensions, beautiful ones comparatively small: beauty should be smooth and polished; the great is rugged and negligent; . . . beauty should not be obscure; the great ought to be dark and even gloomy: beauty should be light and delicate; the great ought to be solid and even massive. They are indeed ideas of a very different nature, one being founded on pain, the other on pleasure.[9]

This was, indeed, if not something new then at least something so old and forgotten as to seem new again: art founded on pain. Not since J. S. Bach have we encountered any notion that music should be anything but beautiful, and never have we encountered such a notion with reference to secular music. It implies an enormous change in the artist's attitude toward his audience; and this, too, is a crucial component in any adequate definition of romanticism. The history of music in the nineteenth century — at any rate, of a very significant portion of it — could be written (and, in this book, will be written) in terms of the encroachment of the sublime upon the domain of the beautiful, of the "great" upon the pleasant. And the process of encroachment applies to retrospective evaluation as well, as we are in the process of discovering where Mozart is concerned.

By characterizing Mozart's art as being "more an intimation of the infinite" than Haydn's, moreover, Hoffmann was implying (and claiming as one of its values) that it was inaccessible to the many. Romanticism, at least Hoffmann's brand of it, was profoundly elitist and anti-egalitarian. It was an agonized reaction to the "universalist" ideals of the Enlightenment, a recoil by thinkers (especially in England and Germany) who viewed the French Revolution and the disasters that ensued — regicide, mob rule, terror, mass executions, wars of Napoleonic conquest — as the bitter harvest of an arrogant Utopian dream. Indeed, the man who gave this opinion its most memorably eloquent expression was none other than Edmund Burke, our erstwhile theorist of the sublime, in his *Reflections on the Revolution in France*, published in 1790, and the even more embittered *Letters on a Regicide Peace* of 1795–97.

Examples of "painful" music are common enough in opera. The second-act finale of Mozart's *Don Giovanni* will surely come to mind in this connection, with its "devastating opening chords" that (in the words of Elaine Sisman, a perceptive writer on the musical sublime) "intensify almost unbearably the music of the overture by substituting the chord on which the Commendatore had been mortally wounded in the [Act I] duel."[10] The graveyard scene from the same opera had inspired actual "horror" in a contemporary reviewer, who commented that "Mozart seems to have learned the language of ghosts from Shakespeare."[11] Interestingly enough, Mozart, while working on *Idomeneo*, his most unremittingly serious opera, found fault with that very aspect of Shakespeare, commenting that "if the speech of the ghost in Hamlet were not so long it would be more effective."[12] He twice revised the trombone-laden music representing the terrifying subterranean voice of Neptune in *Idomeneo* — from seventy measures, to thirty-one, all the way down to nine — so as to achieve a proper sense of awe-inspiring shock, or (in a single word) sublimity.

But these were not the passages in Mozart that inspired Hoffmann to call him romantic, nor did even Haydn's overwhelming Representation of Chaos in *The Creation*, culminating in the famous burst of divine illumination, qualify for that honor. The latter was undeniably a sublime achievement. Schilling, the lexicographer, actually referred to it in his definition of *das Erhabene* (the sublime) in music, although that may have been because the opening words of the Book of Genesis were themselves often cited as the greatest of all models for sublime rhetoric.[13]

But there was a crucial difference between the sublime as represented in *The Creation* and the sublime as prized by romantics. Haydn's representation, like any representation, had a cognizable object, a fixed content that emanated from words, not music. Hence it was an example of "imitation" rather than expression, and therefore, to romantics, not romantic. For a mere imitation to venture intimations of the sublime could strike a romantic critic as a ridiculous misuse of music. "At Vienna, I heard Haydn's *Creation* performed by four hundred musicians," wrote Mme. de Staël, an exile from revolutionary France, in her travel memoir *De l'Allemagne* (From Germany; 1810):

> It was an entertainment worthy to be given in honor of the great work which it celebrated; but the skill of Haydn was sometimes even injurious to his talent: with these words of the Bible, "God said let there be light, and there was light," the accompaniment of the instruments was at first very soft so as scarcely to be heard, then all at once they broke out together with a terrible noise as if to express the sudden burst of light, which occasioned a witty remark "that at the appearance of

light it was necessary to stop one's ears." In several other passages of the *Creation*, the same labor of mind may often be censured.[14]

In this censure one can hear the authentic voice of early romanticism. It was not for *The Creation*, after all, that Hoffmann valued Haydn, but for his untitled instrumental works—works of ineffable content but powerful expressivity. That uncanny combination was the result of inspiration, and called forth inspiration from the listener.

The reason why Mozart was thought of—first in his day and then, more emphatically, in Hoffmann's—as the most romantically sublime of composers had to do, in the first place, with the discomfort of sensory overload. "Too many notes, my dear Mozart" complained the emperor in the famous story, and in so doing reacted to what Immanuel Kant called the "mathematical sublime," the awe that comes from contemplating what is countless, like the stars above.[15] The "difficulty" of Mozart's instrumental style was most spectacularly displayed, perhaps, in the densely grandiose fugal finale to his last symphony (in C major, K. 551), a movement that created, *without recourse to representation*, the same sort of awe that godly or ghostly apparitions created in opera. And that is why the symphony was nicknamed *Jupiter* (by J. P. Salomon, Haydn's promoter, as it happens). That awe was the painful gateway to the beatific contemplation of the infinite, the romantics' chosen work.

CLASSIC OR ROMANTIC?

Nowadays it is conventional, of course, to call Mozart and Haydn "classic" composers rather than "romantic" ones, and even to locate the essence of their "classicism" in the "absoluteness" of their music (construing "absoluteness" here to imply the absence of representation). This is due, in part, to a changed perspective, alluded to at the end of the previous chapter, from which we now tend to look back on Mozart-and-Haydn as the cornerstone of the permanent performing repertory or "canon," and "classic" is another way of saying "permanent." As early as 1829, the author of a history of romanticism recognized that in music more than in any other art, everything takes on a "classic" aspect as it ages: "As far as we are concerned," wrote F. R. de Toreinx (real name Eugène Ronteix), "Paisiello, Cimarosa and Mozart are classics, though their contemporaries regarded them as romantics."[16]

But there was more to it than that. Historical hindsight eventually led to a new periodization of music history that came into common parlance around 1840, parsing the most recent phase of that history into a "Classical" period and a "Romantic" one, with the break occurring around 1800. One of the earliest enunciations of this dichotomy, for a long time almost universally accepted by historians, was an essay, "Classisch und Romantisch" (1841), by Ferdinand Gelbcke (1812–92). The music of the late eighteenth century was a "Classical art" for Gelbcke because like all classical art it was "object-centered, contemplative rather than expressive," and—cliché of clichés!—because it struck a balance between form and content (or as Gelbcke put it, "between the art which shapes it and the material that is to be shaped").[17] Mozart, for Hoffmann a dangerous and "superhuman" (i.e., sublime) artist, was by Gelbcke's time the very epitome of orderly values:

That composure, that peace of mind, that serene and generous approach to life, that balance between ideas and the means of expression which is fundamental to the superb masterpieces of that unique man, these were the most blessed and fruitful characteristics of the age in which Mozart lived, characteristics that we have imperceptibly yet gradually lost.[18]

The view may be anachronistic, and it is surely forgetful of romanticism's original import (to say nothing of the actual conditions of Mozart's life). But like "Gregorian chant" or "English horn," the misnomer "Classical period" — corresponding exactly to what the earliest romantic critics called the earliest romantic phase of music — may be too firmly ensconced in the vocabulary of musicians to be dislodged by mere factual refutation. Nor is it without its own historical truth, so long as we remember that what we now call "classical" virtues, especially the virtues of artistic purity and self-sufficiency, are really romantic values in disguise.

Calling them "classical" expresses the nostalgia — an altogether "romanticized" nostalgia — that the artists and thinkers of post-Napoleonic Europe felt for the imagined stability and simplicity of the *ancien régime*. Gelbcke, unlike many later writers, makes no attempt to conceal his idyllic hankering for a bygone time he never knew. "When the Austrian Empire enjoyed a golden era of security, power, prosperity and peace under the reign of the Emperor Joseph II," he mused rhetorically,

> was this not the age of Haydn and Mozart? Although the storms were brewing elsewhere, within the Austrian Empire, nothing transpired to disturb the calm. So it was that both great composers were free to develop those qualities that have already been mentioned in connection with Mozart, qualities that they derived above all from the spirit of the age in which they lived.[19]

Like so many distinctions that try to pass themselves off as "purely" artistic, the Classic/Romantic dichotomy thus has a crucial political subtext. "Classic" was the age of settled aristocratic authority; "romantic" was the age of the restless burgeoning bourgeoisie. Yet even without looking beyond the boundaries of music, no one in the nineteenth century could evade the sense that a torrential watershed had intervened between the age of Mozart and Haydn and the present. Even Hoffmann, writing a generation before Gelbcke, acknowledged that a momentous metamorphosis had taken place, although he saw it as a culmination of a prior "romantic" tendency rather than a break with a "classic" one. A difference of degree can be so great, nevertheless, as to be tantamount to a difference in kind, and so it was for Hoffmann

FIG. 31-3 Sketches of Beethoven by L. P. A. Burmeister (Lyser), published with his signature by the printmaker E. H. Schroeder.

when he compared the work of Mozart and Haydn, "the creators of our present instrumental music," with that of "the man who then looked on it with all his love and penetrated its innermost being—Beethoven!"[20]

BEETHOVEN AND "BEETHOVEN"

The enthusiastic quote comes from Hoffmann's essay, "Beethoven's Instrumental Music," published in 1814 but based on articles and reviews written as early as 1810—and so do most of the other quotations from Hoffmann given above. Even as he waxed ardent about Mozart's romanticism and Haydn's, Hoffmann did so in the knowledge that they had been surpassed in all that made them great. Hoffmann's characterization of Beethoven, taken in conjunction with his analytical writings about several of Beethoven's works, does far more than reflect the romantic viewpoint of 1814. Hoffmann's view of Beethoven reflects assumptions about art and artists that have persisted ever since—ideas to which practically all readers of this book will have been exposed, and to many of which they will have subscribed, even readers who have never read a single word about Beethoven, or (for that matter) about music.

Ideas received in this way—informally, unconsciously, from "the air," without knowledge of their history (or even that they *have* a history)—are likely to be accepted as "truths held to be self-evident." In this way, Hoffmann's "Beethoven" stands for a great deal more than just Beethoven. It stands for the watershed that produced the modern musical world in which we all now live. To learn about it will be in large part to learn about ourselves. Before we can adequately understand Beethoven, then, or indeed anything that has happened since, we will need to know more about "Beethoven."

To begin with, Hoffmann's "Beethoven" was the idea of the romantic (or Kantian) sublime multiplied to the *n*th power. "Beethoven's music," Hoffmann raved,

> opens up to us the realm of the monstrous and the immeasurable. Burning flashes of light shoot through the deep night of this realm, and we become aware of giant shadows that surge back and forth, driving us into narrower and narrower confines until they destroy *us*—but not the pain of that endless longing in which each joy that has climbed aloft in jubilant song sinks back and is swallowed up, and it is only in this pain, which consumes love, hope, and happiness but does not destroy them, which seeks to burst our breasts with a many-voiced consonance of all the passions, that we live on, enchanted beholders of the supernatural![21]

The purpose of art, then, is to grant us an intensity of experience unavailable to our senses, and even (unless we too are geniuses) to our imaginations. But that intensity, to be felt at maximum strength, must be unattached to objects. It must be realer than what is merely present to the senses and nameable. Thus,

> Beethoven's music sets in motion the lever of fear, of awe, of horror, of suffering, and wakens just that infinite longing which is the essence of romanticism. He is accordingly a completely romantic composer, and is not this perhaps the reason why he has less success with vocal music, which excludes the character of indefinite longing, merely representing emotions defined by words as emotions experienced in the realm of the infinite?

The process whereby the great displaces the pleasant as the subject and purpose of art is well under way. And therefore, Hoffmann notes with perhaps a trace of an aristocratic smirk, "the musical rabble is oppressed by Beethoven's powerful genius; it seeks in vain to oppose it." But mere musicians, be they ever so learned in the craft of their profession, fare no better:

> Knowing critics, looking about them with a superior air, assure us that we may take their word for it as men of great intellect and deep insight that, while the excellent Beethoven can scarcely be denied a very fertile and lively imagination, he does not know how to bridle it! Thus, they say, he no longer bothers at all to select or to shape his ideas, but, following the so-called daemonic method, he dashes everything off exactly as his ardently active imagination dictates it to him.

While a romantic artist inevitably makes a demoniac impression, Hoffmann goes on to assert, a true genius can be "unbridled" in effect yet at the same time fully in control of his method. Discerning that control where others miss it is the function of the critic. A critic, he implies, can be inspired, too. He, too, can be a genius.

> The truth is that, as regards self-possession, Beethoven stands quite on a par with Haydn and Mozart and that, separating his ego from the inner realm of harmony, he rules over it as an absolute monarch. In Shakespeare, our knights of the aesthetic measuring-rod have often bewailed the utter lack of inner unity and inner continuity, although for those who look more deeply there springs forth, issuing from a single bud, a beautiful tree, with leaves, flowers, and fruit; thus, with Beethoven, it is only after a searching investigation of his instrumental music that the high self-possession inseparable from true genius and nourished by the study of the art stands revealed.[22]

What all of this amounts to is the idea, fundamental to the modern concept and practice of "classical music," of the lonely artist-hero whose suffering produces works of awe- inspiring greatness that give listeners otherwise unavailable access to an experience that transcends all worldly concerns. "His kingdom is not of this world," declared Hoffmann in another essay on Beethoven, making explicit reference to the figure regarded by Christians as the world-redeeming Messiah. And indeed, the romantic view was in essence a religious, "sacralizing" view. It was literally an article of faith to romantics that theirs was a specifically Christian idea of art — intent, like the Christian religion, on eternal values and on an intensity of experience that (as Schilling put it) might "transcend cognition" so that its communicants would "experience something higher, more spiritual." Therein lay the difference between romantic art and all previous art, even (or especially) that of classical antiquity. The beauty of all pre-Christian art was a materialistic beauty, as pagan religion was a materialistic religion. Its "classic" proportions and pleasing grace, inspiring though they had been to artists ever since the humanist revival, were hedonistic virtues, expressive of nothing (to quote Schilling once more) beyond a mere "refined and ennobled sensuality." Beauty, in the name of the new art-religion, had to give way before greatness. From now on music expressive of the new world-transcending values would be called not beautiful music but "great music." It is a term that is still preeminently used to describe—or at least to market—"classical music," and Beethoven is still its standard-bearer.

The newly sacralized view of art had immense and immediate repercussions on all aspects of daily musical life. Great works of music, like great paintings, were displayed in specially designed public spaces. The concert hall, like the museum, became a "temple of art" where people went not to be entertained but to be uplifted. The masterworks displayed there were treated with a reverence previously reserved for sacred texts. Indeed, the scores produced by Beethoven *were* sacred texts, and the function of displaying them took on, at the very least, the aspect of curatorship—and at the highest level, that of a ministry.

Where previously, as Carl Dahlhaus (1928-88) once memorably put it, the written text of a musical composition was "a mere recipe for a performance," it now became an inviolable authority object "whose meaning is to be deciphered with exegetical interpretations."[23] By invoking the concept of exegesis—scriptural commentary—Dahlhaus once again draws attention to the parallel between the new (or "strong") concept of art and that of religion. Music, because of its abstract or "absolute" character, required the most exegesis. It therefore became the art-religion par excellence, and provided the most work for an art-ministry—that is, criticism. Where previously the work served the performer, now the performer, and the critic too, were there to serve the work.

The scores of earlier "canonical" composers came to be treated with a similar reverence. But here the new treatment contrasted, and in some ways even conflicted, with the way such older works had been treated when they were new. Mozart did not scruple to alter his works in performance in order to please his audience with spontaneous shows of virtuosity, and neither did his contemporaries. Not only Mozart, but all performers of concertos and arias in his time improvised their passagework, "lead-ins," and cadenzas, and were considered remiss or incompetent if they did not. For them scores, even (or especially) their own scores, were "mere recipes," blueprints for flights of fancy, pretexts for display. Beginning in the early nineteenth century, however, spontaneous performance skills began to lose their prestige in favor of reverent curatorship.

Musicians were now trained (at conservatories, "keeping" institutions) to reproduce the letter of the text with a perfection no one had ever previously aspired to, and improvisation was neglected if not scorned outright. By the late nineteenth century, most instrumentalists played written-out cadenzas to all canonical concertos from memory; the cadenzas were now just as "canonical" as the rest of the piece. Beginning with Beethoven, composers actually set them down in their scores, expecting performers to reproduce them scrupulously. Nowadays, it is only the most exceptional pianist who has the wherewithal to improvise a cadenza, and those who do have it are as likely to be censured for their impertinence as praised for their know-how.

Improvisation skills have not died out by any means, but they have been excluded from the practice of "classical music." They continue to thrive only in nonliterate or semiliterate repertories such as jazz and what is now called "pop" or popular music, a concept that did not exist until "classical music" was sacralized in the nineteenth century.

If sacralization implied inhibition of spontaneous performer behavior, that is nothing compared with the constraints that were imposed on audiences, who were now expected (and are still expected) to behave in concert halls the way they behaved in church. Recalling Mozart's own description of the audience that greeted his *Paris* symphony with spontaneous applause wherever the music pleased them (as audiences still do when listening to pop performers), it is hard to avoid a sense of irony when contemplating the reverent passivity with which any audience today will receive the same symphony. Concert programs now even contain guides to "concert etiquette" in which new communicants at the shrine can receive instruction in the faith. One that appeared in New York "stagebills" during the 1980s even affected a parody of biblical language. When attending a concert, it reads:

> Thou Shalt Not:
> Talk . . .
> Hum, Sing, or Tap Fingers or Feet . . .
> Rustle Thy Program . . .
> Crack Thy Gum in Thy Neighbors' Ears . . .
> Wear Loud-Ticking Watches or Jangle
> Thy Jewelry . . .
> Open Cellophane-Wrapped Candies . . .
> Snap Open and Close Thy Purse . . .
> Sigh With Boredom . . .
> Read . . .
> Arrive Late or Leave Early . . .

This is only the latest version of a mode of discourse that began with critics like E. T. A. Hoffmann around 1810. As musicians and music lovers, we still live under the iron rule of romanticism.

KAMPF UND SIEG

Was Beethoven really responsible for all of this? Only in the sense that things were said and done in his name that, were it not for him, would have been said and done in the name of others, and perhaps differently. He became the protagonist and the beneficiary of an attitude that had been growing for almost half a century by the time he began making a name for himself, and that ultimately reflected changing social and economic conditions over which he had no more control than any other musician. His music was clearly affected by it; if it had not existed he would have composed very differently (in all likelihood more like Mozart). But by the force of his career and his accomplishments, and by the commanding mythology that grew up around his name, he mightily affected it in turn; without him it might not have achieved the authority his powerful example conferred upon it. In the "Beethoven watershed" we have one of the clearest examples of symbiosis between a powerful agent and the intellectual milieu in which he thrived.

FIG. 31-4 The house in Bonn where Beethoven was born.

In some important respects Beethoven shaped his time (and ours) in ways he could never have intended. He was born, on 16 December 1770, into a transplanted Flemish family of court musicians, like the Bachs but far less prestigious. His grandfather and namesake, Louis van Beethoven (1712–73), after occupying positions in several Belgian cities, accepted a singer's post at the minor Electoral court of Bonn, a smallish city on the Rhine (later the capital of the Federal Republic of Germany or "West Germany"), where he changed his name to Ludwig and in 1761 acceded to the Kapellmeistership, a position to which his son Johann, the composer's father, did not measure up.

The younger Ludwig was originally groomed for a career in the family mold. By the age of twelve, after establishing a local reputation as a piano prodigy, he was appointed assistant to the Electoral court organist. At eighteen, he took over some of his father's duties as singer and instrumentalist. His first important compositions date from 1790, when he was nineteen: a cantata on the death of his employer's elder brother, the emperor Joseph II, followed by another (this one actually commissioned) celebrating the coronation of Leopold II, Joseph's successor. This sort of piece was standard Kapellmeisterly fare.

Although neither cantata seems to have been performed at the time, they were shown to Haydn, who passed through Bonn en route to England in December of that year, and received his approval. After Haydn's return from his first London visit, late in 1792, the Elector arranged for Beethoven to study with the great man in Vienna. A line of succession was thus established. The lessons, confined in the main to basic training in counterpoint, did not last long. Haydn was summoned back to England early in 1794. In his absence Beethoven took instruction from some other local maestros — from Johann Georg Albrechtsberger (1736–1809), the Kapellmeister of St. Stephen's Cathedral; and possibly from Antonio Salieri (1750–1825), the imperial court Kapellmeister — and began making a name for himself as a pianist. He became the darling of the aristocratic salon set, and seemed to be duplicating, or even surpassing, Mozart's early Viennese success as virtuoso performer and improviser.

By the time Haydn returned in August 1795, Beethoven had become a household name among the noble music lovers of the capital. He had had his first big concert success, performing his Concerto in B♭ major (later published as his Second Concerto, op. 19), and had also published his opus 1. This was a set of three trios for piano, violin, and cello, dedicated to one of his patrons, Prince Karl von Lichnowsky (1761–1814). Haydn expressed regrets that Beethoven had published the third of these trios, a brusque work in the dark key of C minor. In retaliation, Beethoven refused to identify himself on the title page of his op. 2 (three piano sonatas) as Haydn's pupil, even though the sonatas were dedicated to his former master. (He claimed, when pressed, that although he had taken a few lessons from Haydn, he hadn't learned anything from him.) These acts of self-assertion, like the startling assertiveness of some of the early compositions, were probably the product of both sincere self-regard and self-promoting calculation. They later became key elements in the Beethoven myth.

Beginning in 1796 Beethoven made concert tours throughout the German-speaking lands. They were immensely successful, both in pecuniary terms and in terms of his spreading fame. The Czech composer Václav Tomášek (1774–1850) heard him in Prague in 1798; in memoirs he published near the end of his long life he averred that Beethoven was the greatest pianist he had ever heard. Beethoven's supremacy among composers of his generation was established by the turn of the century, especially after a concert he organized for his own benefit on 2 April 1800. The program contained works by Haydn and Mozart, another Beethoven concerto performed by the author, and, as always, an improvisation.

But it also contained two new Beethoven compositions without keyboard: the Septet for Winds and Strings, op. 20, which would remain one of his most popular works, and most important by far, the First Symphony, op. 21. This last was the crucial step, because with his symphonic debut Beethoven was now competing not only with other virtuoso composers of his own generation, but directly with Haydn on the master's own turf. The next year he published a set of six string quartets (op. 18) that challenged Haydn in his other genre of recognized preeminence. This secured Beethoven's claim, so to speak, as heir apparent to the throne Haydn's death would shortly vacate.

And now disaster. In a letter to a friend dated 29 June 1801, Beethoven confessed for the first time that, after several years of fearful uncertainty, he was now sure that he was losing his hearing. The immediate result of this devastating discovery was withdrawal from his glittering social life: "I find it impossible to say to people, I am deaf," he wrote. "If I had any other profession it would be easier, but in my profession it is a terrible handicap."[24] What an

FIG. 31-5 Piano by Sebastian Erard, presented to Beethoven by the maker in 1803.

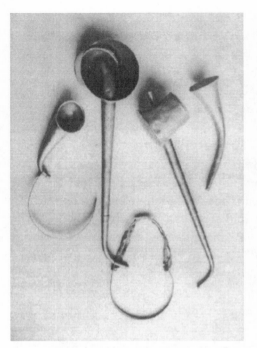

FIG. 31-6 Ear trumpets, made for Beethoven between 1812 and 1814 by Johann Nepomuk Maelzel, who was best known for his metronome.

understatement! And yet, while eventually he had to cease his concertizing, he did not give up his composing.

Indeed, as he told his brothers in a letter he addressed to them in October of the next year from a suburb of Vienna called Heiligenstadt, composing remained his chief consolation. The realization that he still had music in him, and that he had an obligation to share it with the world, had cured his obsessive thoughts of suicide. This letter, which he apparently never sent, was discovered among Beethoven's papers after his death. Its poignant mixture of despondency and resolution, and its depiction of a man facing unimaginable obstacles over which he was by then known to have triumphed, have made the Heiligenstadt Testament, as it has come to be known, perhaps the most famous personal utterance of any composer.[25] It has done more than any other single document to make Beethoven an object of inexhaustible human interest, the subject of biographical novels, whole galleries of idealized portraiture, and most recently, of biopics.

None of these books, pictures, or films would have been made, it could go without saying, were it not for the extraordinary musical output that followed the Heiligenstadt Testament. And yet perhaps it needs saying after all, for Beethoven's deafness not only became the chief basis of the Beethoven mystique, and the chief source of his unprecedented authority as a cultural figure; it also served as one of the chief avenues by which Beethoven's personal fate, as mediated through the critical literature we have been sampling, became the most commanding and regulating single influence on the whole field of musical activity from his time to ours.

The idea of a successful deaf composer is a virtually superhuman idea. It connotes superhuman suffering and superhuman victory, playing directly into the emerging quasi-religious romantic notion of the great artist as humanity's redeemer. That scenario — of suffering and victory, both experienced at the limits of intensity — became the ineluctable context in which Beethoven's music was received. And, as we shall shortly see, that very scenario was consciously encoded by the composer in some of his most celebrated works.

Yet there was also another factor at work, profoundly affecting Beethoven's output and his significance, and enabling him to facilitate by his example the inexorable romantic transformation of musical art and life. His deafness caused him to disappear physically from the musical scene. It removed him, so far as the musical world was concerned, from "real time," the time frame in which musical daily business was conducted. His creative activities now took place in an unimaginable transcendent space to which no one but he had access. The copious sketches he made for his compositions beginning in the late 1790s (and, somewhat bizarrely, kept in his possession throughout his life) have precisely for this reason exercised an enormous fascination — and not only on musicians or musicologists — as a lofty record of esthetic achievement, but also as an ethically and morally charged human document of *Kampf und Sieg* (struggle and victory).

The creative and performing functions were in Beethoven gradually but irrevocably severed, leaving only the first. And that sole survivor, the creative function, was now invested with a heroic import that cast the split — again, just as romantic theory would have it — in ethical, quasi-religious terms. Never again would the performing virtuoso composer, on the Mozartean model, be considered the ideal. The composer — the creator — became a truly Olympian being, far removed from the ephemeral transactions of everyday musical life — improvisations, cadenzas, performances in general — and yet a public figure withal, whose pronouncements were regarded as public events of the first magnitude. That was the difference between Beethoven and such earlier nonperforming composers as Haydn. Haydn passed most of his creative life in the closed-off, private world of aristocratic patronage, while Beethoven, even after his social alienation, spoke to the mass public that emerged only after the patronage system had begun to wither.

Beethoven's last appearance as concerto soloist took place at a concert on 22 December 1808 at which the Fifth and Sixth Symphonies both received their first performances, and Beethoven, in addition to improvising, performed his Fourth Piano Concerto and his so-called Choral Fantasy, a short but grandiose work that begins with a piano solo (extemporized at the first performance) and ends with a choral hymn that foreshadowed the gigantic "Ode to Joy" at the end of the Ninth Symphony. His last public appearance as pianist took place in the spring of 1814 (in the so-called "Archduke" Trio, op. 97), from which time onward, even down to the present, a "classical" composer's involvement in performance (except as conductor, another sort of silent dictator) would carry something of a stigma, a taint of compromise, as "art" (the province of creators) became ever more radically distinguished from "entertainment" (the province of performers). The distinction between art and entertainment is wholly the product of romantic esthetics. Mozart would not have understood it. Beethoven certainly did. The social and economic conditions that followed the demise of the private patronage system were its enablers. Critics like Hoffmann were its inventors.

THE *EROICA*

Whether it is fair to infer a causal nexus will forever be a matter for debate, but almost immediately after Beethoven's confession of his progressive deafness and his social alienation, his music underwent a momentous transformation in style. As early as 1798, the ambassador to Vienna from revolutionary France, General Bernadotte, suggested to Beethoven that he write a "heroic symphony" on the subject of the charismatic young general Napoleon Bonaparte, then riding the crest of adulation for his brilliant campaigns in Italy and Egypt. In the summer of 1803, with Napoleon now (as First

Consul) the effective dictator of France and idolized throughout Europe as the great exporter of political Enlightenment, Beethoven was moved to realize this plan.

The work he produced, a *sinfonia eroica* originally entitled "Bonaparte," was conceived on a hitherto unprecedented scale in every dimension: size of orchestra, sheer duration, "tonal drama," rhetorical vehemence, and (hardest to describe) a sense of overriding dynamic purpose uniting the four movements. The monumentally sublime or "heroic" style thus achieved became the mark of Beethoven's unique greatness and, for his romantic exegetes, a benchmark of musical attainment to which all had now, hopelessly, to try and measure up. The fact that Beethoven, enraged over Napoleon's crowning himself Emperor of the French in 1804, rescinded the dedication before the first performance of the work, substituting the possibly ironic title "Heroic Symphony Composed to Celebrate the Memory of a Great Man," only enhanced its sublimity. It took the work beyond the level of representation into the realm of transcendental ideas.

A quick survey of the first movement of the *Eroica*, as it is now familiarly called, will at once reveal the astonishing earmarks of the new heroic style that seemed so suddenly to spring from Beethoven fully armed, like Athena from the head of Zeus. Analysts and critics never tire of pointing out the insignificance of the theme from which the whole huge edifice derives (a veritable bugle call), or its fortuitous resemblance to the first four bars of a theme by the twelve-year-old Mozart. The latter comes at the beginning of the Intrada (overture) to a trivial little singspiel, *Bastien und Bastienne*, that the boy wonder tossed off to entertain the guests at a garden party hosted by Dr. Franz Mesmer, the quack healer (Ex. 31-1).

EX. 31-1A   W. A. Mozart, *Bastien und Bastienne*, first theme of intrada, mm. 1–8

EX. 31-1B   W. A. Mozart, *Bastien und Bastienne*, intrada, whole first period

EX. 31-1B (*continued*)

EX. 31-1C Ludwig van Beethoven, Symphony no. 3, Op. 55 (*Eroica*), I, mm. 1–44 in thematic outline

There is some point to this comparison. What it shows is not that Beethoven's theme is inane or insignificant, but more nearly the opposite: that his new style is founded on a new and explosively powerful concept of what produces a significant musical utterance. Mozart's theme, up to the point quoted in Ex. 31-1a, is entirely conventional in its symmetry. In fairness to the young composer, Ex. 31-1b shows how the continuation of the theme is cleverly "unbalanced." The second phrase is repeated, and its first two bars are extended in sequence, so that the total length of the theme up to the elided cadence is an interesting fourteen bars in length $(4 + 4 + 2 + 2 + 2)$. But even these departures honor symmetry in the breach. They are by no means unusual or atypical in the music of Haydn and Mozart's time.

Beethoven's treatment of the same four-bar fanfare idea is altogether unprecedented in manner (Ex. 31-1c). The C♯ that immediately follows the E♭-major arpeggio on the downbeat of m. 7 is possibly the most famous single note in the entire symphonic literature, for the way it flatly contradicts all the fanfare's implications. Rather than initiating a balancing phrase, like the fifth bar of Mozart's theme, it can only be heard (thanks to the slur) as a violently unbalancing extension—so violently unbalancing, in fact, that the first violins, entering immediately after the C♯, are made palpably to totter for two bars. Relative harmonic stability is restored in m. 9 by the resolution of the uncanny chromatic note back to a normal scale degree (the leading tone), marked with the first of countless *sforzandi* to give it the force necessary to prop the tottering violins. But the two-bar "time out" in mm. 7–8 has scotched all possibility of phrase symmetry—all possibility, that is, of "themehood," at least for the moment.

All one can do is try again. A cadence, reinforced by the wind instruments, clears the slate in mm. 14–15. (The first stab at the first theme, not counting the two-bar chordal preparation at the outset, has lasted not Mozart's interestingly subdivided fourteen bars, but an entirely undivided and indivisible fourteen—probably the most hopelessly and designedly off-balance opening in the symphonic literature.) Balance having been provisionally restored, the winds restate the opening four-bar fanfare. In dialogue with the strings the ascending arpeggio at the end is detached and developed sequentially until the dominant is reached; whereupon harmonic motion is stalled (m. 22), preventing closure.

The long series of syncopated *sforzandi* that now follows (mm. 24–33) seems to push hard against a implied harmonic barrier, until an exhilarating breakthrough to the tonic (m. 36) initiates what is obviously a climactic statement of the original fanfare motif, coinciding with the first orchestral *tutti*, replete with martial trumpets and drums. Even this statement, however, dissipates in a sequence without achieving closure. Instead, after eight bars (m. 42), a decisive pull away from the tonic (by means of an augmented sixth resolving to F, the dominant's dominant) launches the modulation to the secondary key.

What we have been given, in short, is a thematic exposition that furnishes no stable point of departure, but that instead involves us from the beginning in a sense of turbulent dynamic growth: not state, so to speak, but process; not being, to put it philosophically (and romantically), but Becoming. The theme is not so much presented as it is achieved—achieved through struggle. The clarity of metaphor here, instantly apprehended by contemporary listeners, lent this music from the beginning an unprecedented ethical potency.

Not that the metaphor was in any way categorical or determinate in meaning. As the music theorist Scott Burnham has put it, the struggle-and-achievement paradigm could be attached to Napoleon (as "Beethoven's hero") or to the composer himself (as "Beethoven Hero," Burnham's name for the "author-persona" of the *Eroica*).[26] It could as easily be felt as a metaphor for the listener's own inner life, thus potentially symbolizing bourgeois self-realization, or liberation, or religious transcendence. In any event, as Burnham points out, Beethoven's achievement provided the supreme symbolic expression of the chief philosophical and political ideals of its time and place. He calls it, in the tradition of German cultural history, the "Goethezeit," the time of the great polymath Johann Wolfgang von Goethe (1749–1832)—poet, playwright, philosopher, and natural scientist in one. He makes it clear, though, that the time might better have been called the "Beethovenzeit," for precisely with Beethoven, and by force of his example, music achieved its century-long preeminence in the eyes of all romantic artists.

But of course the *Eroica* movement is only just getting underway. Closure is deliberately, indeed demonstratively, withheld even from the climactic statement of the theme. Dynamic process continues through the modulatory section that now ensues, carrying the listener along through a great wealth of new melodic ideas before the

F I G. 31-7   *Goethe in the Roman Campagna* (1787) by Johann Heinrich Tischbein.

second theme is even reached — and when it finally arrives, at m. 83, it provides no more than a brief touching-down on the way to the main cadence of the exposition.

The formal development section having been reached, the same structural/ethical process that shaped the opening theme will be seen to operate at the global level as well, giving shape to the entire 691-measure movement, which thus emerges not as a gigantic sprawl but as a single directed span — or, to recall Goethe the naturalist, a single organic growth. The same rhetorical gesture that governed the very first statement of the fanfare — that of a disruptive detour enabling a triumphant return — will shape the movement as a whole, lending the opening statement a quality of prophesy and the whole a quality of fated consequence.

Of course the "there-and-back" or pendular harmonic plan had been a fundamental shaper of musical form for a hundred years or more when Beethoven composed the *Eroica*; of course his music was rooted in that tradition and depended on it both for its coherence and for its intelligibility. Moreover, his accomplishment could be looked upon as a continuation of Mozart's and (particularly) Haydn's earlier project of dramatizing the binary plan: that, we may recall, is what "symphonic" style was all about from the beginning. And yet the difference in degree of drama — or more to the point, of disruption and concomitant expansion — in Beethoven's treatment of the plan seemed to his contemporaries, and can easily still seem, to be tantamount to a difference in kind.

Consider the move to the "far-out point" (FOP) in the development section, starting (for those with access to the score) at m. 220. That measure recommends itself as an access point because tonal progress up to it has been slow. In fact, the harmony is the same E♭ triad that elsewhere in the piece functions as the tonic. Here, however, owing to its preparation (an augmented sixth on F♭, precisely analogous to the one on G♭ with which Ex. 31-1c ended) it is clearly identified as the local dominant of A♭, the global subdominant. The harmony rocks gently back and forth for a while between the local dominant and the local tonic before a move to F minor (m. 236) incites a fugato, a common tactic for speeding up harmonic rhythm toward an implied goal.

And then it happens. Just as in the exposition at m. 25 ff, the harmony stalls and strains against an invisible barrier suggested by the same syncopated *sforzandi* as before (Ex. 31-2). Only this time (m. 248) it stalls not on a primary harmonic function of whose eventual resolution there is no doubt, but on a diminished-seventh chord built on G♯ — enharmonically equivalent to A♭, the local tonic, but now implying resolution to A, a note altogether outside the tonic scale. The stall therefore arrests the harmonic motion at a far more threatening point; for even when resolution takes place (m. 254), there is no sense of achievement — just another stall. Six measures later the A minor harmony is resolved "Phrygianly" to an even more remote sonority, a dominant-seventh on B-natural, presaging even less satisfying prospects for resolution than before (see Ex. 31-2).

And it is indeed to that unlikely goal — E-natural, seemingly a further-out FOP than ever approached before — that resolution is eventually made, but not before one last detour through another set of wrenching harmonic stalls that finally reapproaches

EX. 31-2 Ludwig van Beethoven, Symphony no. 3, Op. 55 (*Eroica*), I, mm. 248–65

EX. 31-2   (*continued*)

the dominant-seventh-of-E through the Neapolitan of that unclassifiable key, expressed in a fiercely dissonant form that retains as a suspension the high flute E from the preceding C-major chord (the flat submediant of the looming key, suggesting that it will materialize in the minor). The suspended E rubs painfully against F, the chord root, in the other flute part. For fully four excruciating measures (mm. 276–279) this ear-splitting harmony is hammered out — and then simply dropped (Ex. 31-3).

The grating semitone between the flutes is never resolved; resolution takes place only by implication, in another register, played on other instruments (the E resolving to the first violins' D♯ in m. 280, the F, most unconventionally, to the viola F♯). The resolution chord, delayed by a disruptive rest on the downbeat of measure 280, still throbs tensely owing to the second violins' C-natural, suspended from the preceding chord, which adds a minor ninth to the dominant seventh on B. Tension is reduced by degrees: the C moves to B in measure 282, the remaining dissonance (A, the chord seventh) to G in measure 284. The smoke has metaphorically cleared, and we are left in E minor, the "unclassified" tonality adumbrated twenty-four measures before, with no immediate prospect of return to harmonic terra firma.

EX. 31-3   Ludwig van Beethoven, Symphony no. 3, Op. 55 (*Eroica*), I, mm. 276–288.

So far from home no symphonic development had ever seemed to stray before. Having dramatized the disruption, Beethoven now dramatizes the sense of distance by unexpectedly introducing a new theme in the unearthly new key (mm. 284ff). It has been argued that this theme is a counterpoint to an embellished variant of the main theme of the movement (see Ex. 31-4), hence not really a new theme at all. But even if one accepts the demonstration shown in Ex. 31-4, the novelty of the music at m. 284 is striking — as indeed it must be, because it performs an unprecedented function within the movement's dramatic unfolding. By far the most placid, most symmetrically presented melody in the movement, it expresses not "process" but "state" for a change — the state of being tonally adrift.

EX. 31-4   Ludwig van Beethoven, Symphony no. 3, Op. 55 (*Eroica*), I, the relationship between the E minor theme at mm. 284ff and the main theme of the first movement

And yet, there being only twelve possible tone centers, and only six degrees of remoteness (since once past the midpoint, whether reckoning by the circle of fifths or by the chromatic scale, one is circling not out but back), one is never quite as far away from home as one is made at such moments to feel. Beethoven engineers a "retransitional" coup similar to the one we have already encountered in the slow movement from Mozart's G-major piano concerto, K. 453 (Ex. 30-5), whereby the seeming outermost reaches of tonal space are traversed in a relative twinkling. But where Mozart did it with maximum smoothness, to amaze (and perhaps amuse), Beethoven does it with maximum drama, to inspire and thrill.

Understood enharmonically, as F♭, E-natural is equivalent to ♭II, the flatted or "Neapolitan" second degree of the scale, just a stone's throw from the tonic on the circle of fifths. Beethoven does not take quite such a direct route home; but he might as well have done, since by mm. 315–316 he has achieved the essential linkage, hooking up the flat supertonic broached in m. 284 with V and I of the original key, its implied successors along the circle of fifths. All harmonies on either side of this essential link amount to rhetorical feinting, staving off the inevitable moment of "double return," when the tonic key and the first theme will at last make explosive contact.

The purpose of strategic delay, or "deferred gratification," is, as always, the enhancement of the emotional payoff when the long-awaited event is finally allowed to occur. It does not happen until m. 398, by which time suspense has been deliberately jacked up to an unbearable degree (see Ex. 31-5, which begins twenty measures earlier) — so literally unbearable, in fact, that at m. 394 the first horn goes figuratively berserk, personifying and "acting out" the listener's agony of expectation by breaking in on the violins — still dissonantly and exasperatingly protracting the dominant function in a seemingly endless tremolo — with a premature entry on the first theme in the tonic.

EX. 31-5 Ludwig van Beethoven, Symphony no. 3, Op. 55 (*Eroica*), I, mm. 378 – 405

EX. 31-5 (continued)

So unprecedented was this bold psychological stroke that it was at first mistaken, even by the composer's close associates, for a sort of prank. His pupil and assistant Ferdinand Ries (1784–1838) described it in his memoirs as a "mischievous whim" (*böse Laune*), and recalled that

> At the first rehearsal of the symphony, which was horrible, but at which the horn player made his entry correctly, I stood beside Beethoven, and, thinking that a blunder had been made, I said: "Can't the damned hornist count?—it's so obviously wrong!" I think I came pretty close to receiving a box on the ear. Beethoven did not forgive the slip for a long time.[27]

Far from a blunder or a miscount, the horn entrance dramatizes once again in retrospect the unprecedented scope of the tonal journey the movement has traversed and the pent-up emotional stimulation such a journey generates as it nears its desired fulfillment.

Nor is this the only way in which Beethoven will exploit the sense of disruption caused within the movement by the digression in mid-development to a new theme in a remote key. As in the exposition of the first theme, what is done first at a local level is later recast on the global plane. Full redemption of the movement's disruptive forces, and full discharge of its tonal tensions will come only after the apparent end of the recapitulation, in a mammoth coda that begins at m. 557 with a shockingly sudden irruption of D♭, the enharmonic equivalent of the pitch that sounded the first disruptive note of all, way back in m. 7. This probably comes as a bigger surprise than anything else in the movement, but like most of Beethoven's "disruptions" it is a strategic maneuver, enabling the control of longer and longer time spans by a single functional impulse.

The coda thus convulsively introduced takes up and resolves two pieces of unfinished business. First it effectively recapitulates the E-minor theme within the normal purview of the tonic by having it appear in F minor, the ordinary diatonic ("unflatted") supertonic. But that is only by the way. The coda's main business is at last to provide the fully articulated, cadentially closed version of the opening theme that has been promised from the very start of the movement, but that has never materialized. It arrives at m. 631 in the form of a quietly confident horn solo that makes up, as it were, for the horn's harried "false entrance" 237 bars earlier. Its swingingly symmetrical eight-bar phrase finally juxtaposes tonic and dominant versions of the opening arpeggio, thus for the first time closing the harmonic circle at close range (Ex. 31-6).

Four times the phrase is repeated, together with its rushing countersubject, in a massive crescendo that ultimately engulfs the whole orchestra, the trumpets and drums entering on the third go-round with a military tattoo (pickup to m. 647) and, on the fourth, finally breaking the melodic surface in a final thematic peroration. Yet even this crest is immediately trumped by one final disruption, the diminished-seventh chord in mm. 663–664, with D♭/C♯ (what else?) as the climactic note in the bass. From here there is nothing left to do but retake the goal in one last eight-bar phrase, after which only a clinching I–V–I remains—with the V extended through one more characteristic "stall" (mm. 681 ff) to bring home the final pair of tonic chords (mirroring the pair at the other end of the movement and retrospectively justifying it) as one last victory through struggle.

One listens to a movement like this with a degree of mental and emotional engagement no previous music had demanded, and one is left after listening with a sense of satisfaction only strenuous exertions, successfully consummated, can vouchsafe. Beethoven's singular ability to summon that engagement and grant that satisfaction is what invested his "heroic" music with its irresistible sense of high ethical purpose and

EX. 31-6 Ludwig van Beethoven, Symphony no. 3, Op. 55 (*Eroica*), I, mm. 631–639

EX. 31-6 (continued)

power. It is not the devices themselves — anyone's devices, after all — that so enthrall the listener, but the singleness of design that they conspire to create, the scale on which they enable the composer to work, and the metaphors to which these stimuli give rise in the mind of the listener.

The exalted climactic statement of the opening theme in particular makes use of a cluster of devices — accumulating sonority over an ostinato swinging regularly between the harmonic poles — that as the "Rossini crescendo" would soon cap the overtures to the zaniest comic operas ever written, operas that ever after would scandalize Beethoven's high-minded German devotees with their Italianate frivolity. Anyone's devices indeed: their effect is entirely a matter of context.

In the Beethovenian context, far from a light amusement, the big regular crescendo brings long-awaited closure to a tonal drama of unprecedented scope. That long-deferred resolution is what creates in the listener what Hoffmann called the "unutterable portentous longing" that is the hallmark of romantic art. That "purely musical" tension and release, powerfully enacted in a wordless context, is what produces in the listener such a total immersion in what Hoffmann called "the spirit world of the infinite."

CRISIS AND REACTION

The great majority of Beethoven's works, to the end of the first decade of the new century (that is, up to the time of Hoffmann's decisively influential critiques), were marked by the new heroic style, whether opera (*Leonore*, later revised as *Fidelio*, on a subject supposedly borrowed from an actual incident from French revolutionary history), or symphony, whether chamber music (the three quartets published as op. 59 with a dedication to Count Razumovsky, the Russian ambassador) or piano sonata (the "Waldstein," op. 53, or especially the "Appassionata," op. 57).

Their prodigious dynamism not only transformed all the genres to which Beethoven applied himself, but also met with wild approval from an ever-widening bourgeois public who read in that dynamism a portent and a portrayal of their own social and spiritual triumph. For such listeners (as Hoffmann, their unwitting spokesman, put it explicitly), Beethoven finally realized the universal mission of music, just as they felt that in their own lives they were realizing the universal aspiration of mankind to political and economic autonomy — an aspiration defined as the superhuman realization of the "World Spirit" by Georg Wilhelm Friedrich Hegel (1770–1831), the great romantic philosopher of history and Beethoven's exact contemporary. To read Beethoven's music as a metaphor of the universal world spirit was as seductive a notion as it was perilous.

What made it perilous was the tendency it encouraged to cast one's own cherished values as "universal" values, good (and therefore binding) for all. To see all music that did not conform to the heroic Beethovenian model as deficient to the extent of the difference was to discriminate invidiously against other possible musical aims, uses, and styles. To the extent, for example, that the Beethovenian ideal was identified with virility, or with at times violently expressed "manly" ideals of strength and greatness, it invited or reinforced prejudice against women as composers, even as social agents. To the extent that it sanctioned neglect of the audience's pleasure, it could serve to underwrite gratuitous obscurity or difficulty. To the extent that it exalted the representation of violence, whether of *Kampf* (struggle) or *Sieg* (victory), it could serve as justification for aggressive or even militaristic action. To the extent that it was identified with German national aspirations or (as we will very shortly see) with a concept of German "national character," it encouraged chauvinism. To the extent that it was identified with middle-class norms of behavior, it paradoxically thwarted the expression of other, equally "romantic" forms of creative individualism.

That these unwarranted and undesirable side effects have at various times emerged from the Beethoven myth is a matter of historical fact. Whether they are implicit (or, to speak medically, "latent") in it is a matter for continued, and possibly unsettleable, debate.

That such attributes were not inherent in Beethoven but constructed by listeners and interpreters is certainly suggested by the facts of his actual career. The remarkable thing is the way in which he was accepted both by the new mass public and by the old aristocratic one, which continued as before to support him financially, albeit collectively rather than by direct employment. (It should be added that Beethoven's own social attitudes, as conveyed in documents and anecdotes, were ambiguous at best, and inconstant.) Thanks to that support, Beethoven was able to evade the prospect of steady work as Kapellmeister at the court of Westphalia in Kassel, where Napoleon had installed his youngest brother Jerome as king. A consortium of Viennese noblemen undertook in 1809 to guarantee Beethoven a lifetime annuity that more than matched the salary he was offered at Kassel, and that allowed him to devote his full time to composing as he wished, provided only that he remain in Vienna.

This consortium included the Archduke Rudolph, the emperor's younger brother and Beethoven's only composition (as opposed to piano) pupil, to whom the composer dedicated no fewer than ten works, including the "Archduke" Trio (op. 97, composed 1810–11), the "Emperor" Concerto (Piano Concerto no. 5, op. 73, composed 1809), and the Mass in D (*Missa solemnis*), op. 123 (1819–23), composed in celebration of Rudolph's investment as a cardinal of the Roman Catholic Church. The consortium also included Prince Joseph Franz Maximilian von Lobkowitz, scion of an ancient Bohemian family long famous for its arts patronage, who had underwritten the first performance of the *Eroica* Symphony at his own private residence in 1804, and to whom Beethoven dedicated not only the *Eroica* but six other works as well, including the op. 18 quartets and both the Fifth and the Sixth Symphonies.

From this evidence of mutual devotion between Beethoven and the Viennese aristocracy, it is clear that the idea of the composer as a musical revolutionist or Jacobin, widespread in the romanticizing literature that cast him as "The Man Who Freed Music" (the title of Robert Schauffler's 1929 biography), is as one-sided and misleading as the opposing image—that of the isolated, world-renouncing hermit on a lonely quest of saintly personal fulfillment, just as widespread in an opposing romanticizing literature that culminated in another influential book (J. W. N. Sullivan's *Beethoven: His Spiritual Development*, published in 1927, the centennial of the composer's death). These images, and many others, were partial readings of the life of Beethoven in support of one or another variant of the myth of Beethoven, for almost two centuries one of the most potent stimuli to musical thought and action in the West, but a fantastically various one.

The "heroic" phase of Beethoven's career lasted until around 1812, with the completion of his Eighth Symphony. He then lapsed, probably as a result of deepening deafness and personal frustrations, into a period of depression and evident decline. Goethe, who finally met his great contemporary at a Bohemian spa in the summer of 1811, remarked that Beethoven "was not altogether wrong in holding the world to be detestable, but surely does not make it any the more enjoyable either for himself or for others by his attitude," adding that his deafness "perhaps mars the musical part of his nature less than the social."[28] Between 1810 and 1812 the composer suffered repeated setbacks in his personal life. Increasingly desperate overtures to unwilling or unavailable prospective brides culminated in an enigmatic love letter to an unnamed "Immortal Beloved," written in the summer of 1812 and discovered unsent, like the Heiligenstadt Testament, among his posthumous effects. Beethoven being almost as much the object of "human interest" attention as he has been of musical, scholars and biographers and movie producers have devoted enormous energy to the problem of identifying Beethoven's mysterious love interest.

If Maynard Solomon, one of Beethoven's biographers, was right in advancing the name of Antonie Brentano, now regarded as the most plausible candidate, then Beethoven's fate as hopeless suitor has been intriguingly illuminated.[29] Frau Brentano, the sister-in-law of Bettina Brentano, a young piano pupil and friend of Beethoven's, was for two reasons out of reach: she was of aristocratic birth, and she was already married. Beethoven's lifetime status as a forlorn bachelor, another reason for his posthumous casting as a spiritual hermit, may well have been as much the result of psychological obstacles as actual social impediments. Brought to a state of turbulence by his multiple rejections and thwartings around 1812, they may have contributed to his creative silence in the years that followed.

Another painful emotional drain was Beethoven's involvement with his nephew and ward Karl van Beethoven, following the death of his brother Kaspar in 1815. The composer's possessive and destructive behavior, culminating in a successful but morally wounding four-year legal battle to wrest custody of the eight-year-old boy from his mother, testified to his deep longings and discontents but augured bleakly as to the welfare of any of the parties concerned. Eventually, in the summer of 1826, Karl attempted suicide, an emotionally shattering experience for his jealous uncle, who was described shortly afterward by a close associate as looking like a man of seventy. (He was in fact only fifty-five, but less than a year away from death.) The creative trough set off by the events of 1812 lasted about five years, during which time Beethoven wrote little of lasting significance. Of the little that he did write, some (inconveniently enough for his mythmakers) was of a calculated popular appeal, including a noisy "Battle Symphony" known as *Wellington's Victory*, celebrating Napoleon's defeat by combined British, Spanish, and Portuguese forces under Arthur Wellesley, the first Duke of Wellington, at the Battle of Vittoria in 1813. It was performed at huge (and hugely successful) charity concerts in December of that year (at which the Seventh Symphony was also unveiled), and again, "by popular demand," in February 1814 (at which time the Eighth Symphony was along for the ride).

This piece of orchestral claptrap, replete with fanfares, cannonades performed by an augmented percussion section, and a fugue on "God Save the King," was an early fruit of musical capitalism. It was the brainchild of an entrepreneur inventor named Johann Nepomuk Maelzel (1772–1838), who sought Beethoven's name appeal so as to attract crowds to view demonstrations of his panharmonicon, a "mechanical orchestra" (actually a mechanical organ with a variety of noisemaker attachments). Later, Maelzel invented a metronome for which Beethoven again provided testimonials and, more important for posterity, exact tempo settings for his symphonies and other important works. His collaborations with Maelzel cast Beethoven in a rather unheroic light, as a sort of musical market speculator. That was, however, no less typical or "progressive" a role for a musician in economically unsettled times.

Otherwise, Beethoven's output dwindled drastically. The only important compositions written between 1813 and 1818 are three piano sonatas culminating in the huge sonata in B♭, op. 106, with its famous post-Napoleonic subtitle (the apparently nationalistic *für das Hammerklavier* in place of the conventionally Italianate *per il pianoforte*); two cello sonatas, op. 102; and a group of songs united in a "cycle" by a recurring theme, with the poignant title *An die ferne Geliebte* ("To the far-off beloved") that must have had manifold personal resonances for the unhappy composer. The year 1817 went by without a single work of any consequence completed. Perhaps even more indicative of the composer's state of mind, during this period he worked on a number of sizeable projects — a piano concerto, a trio, a string quintet — that he finally abandoned, and that are known only from entries in his sketchbooks.

His largest and most ambitious compositional effort of the period was *Der glorreiche Augenblick*, a bombastic political potboiler of a cantata, unpublished during Beethoven's lifetime, intended for performance before the assembled crowned heads of Europe gathered for the Congress of Vienna in 1815 to celebrate "the glorious moment" of imperial restoration following on the final defeat and exile of Napoleon.

So utterly does this reactionary political harangue fail to accord with the Beethoven myth that when it was finally published, in 1837, its text was replaced by a more "esthetic" sort of celebration, *Preis der Tonkunst* ("In praise of music"), by Friedrich Rochlitz (1769–1842), who as editor of the *Allgemeine musikalische Zeitung*, the first important modern music magazine, was the most influential critic of his time. As such, he played almost as great a role as Hoffmann had played before him in the early propagation of the Beethoven myth.

Beethoven began to shake off his creative torpor toward the end of 1817, possibly spurred by a flattering invitation from the Philharmonic Society of London to compose two "grand symphonies" for the coming concert season and present them in person. He

FIG. 31-8A   A historical painting by Jean Baptiste Isabey: Napeoléon Bonaparte as First Consul (1804). Napoléon was the intended dedicatee of Beethoven's Third Symphony.

FIG. 31-8B Jean Baptiste Isabey, The Congress of Vienna (1814).

never composed either symphony, and never duplicated Haydn's triumphant success with a trip to London, but he was sufficiently energized to embark on the "Hammerklavier" sonata, even though it took him almost a whole year to complete it. Successful completion of this first large project in two or three years brought back his old creative euphoria.

When Anton Diabelli (1781–1858), a minor composer but a major music publisher, asked Beethoven to contribute a variation on a trivial little waltz tune Diabelli had written, for publication in a "patriotic anthology" featuring the work of some fifty Austrian and German composers (including the young Franz Schubert, the eleven-year-old boy wonder Franz Liszt, and Beethoven's own pupil Archduke Rudolph), Beethoven responded not with one variation but with twenty. Realizing that he had burst the bounds of the commission he had received, he held them back until he had time to complete what had turned into a monumental project. The full set of thirty-three *Diabelli Variations*, one of Beethoven's crowning works, was completed in 1822 and published as his op. 120, long before the omnibus album finally appeared. Concurrently with the second phase of work on the Variations, Beethoven composed three short but very intense piano sonatas, the last of which (no. 32 in C minor, op. 111) was finished almost simultaneously with the Variations.

A similar indication of Beethoven's regained ebullience, and the creative overfulfillment to which it could lead, was the Mass he undertook to compose on hearing that Archduke Rudolph was to be elevated to the rank of cardinal and installed as Archbishop of Olomouc, an important ecclesiastical seat in what is now the Czech

Republic. He had meant to have it ready for the installation ceremony in March 1820, but the music expanded irrepressibly under his hand, and the whole vast design, now called the *Missa solemnis* (Solemn Mass), op. 123, was only completed in the early months of 1823. Beethoven had not only missed the deadline by three years; he had also ended up with a work whose stupendous length precluded its forming part of an actual church service. The first performance took place under secular auspices in St. Petersburg on 7 April 1824, on the initiative of Prince Nikolai Borisovich Golitsyn (1794–1866), a Russian nobleman and chamber music enthusiast who became one of the outstanding patrons of Beethoven's last years.

THE "NINTH"

Beethoven now undertook to compose a symphony, his first in more than a decade. Like the Variations and the Mass, it broke all generic precedents, encompassing in its last movement what was for all the world a virtual oratorio, for soloists, chorus, and an orchestra augmented by a whole battery of "Turkish" instruments, on the text of Friedrich Schiller's famous poem, *An die Freude* (known in English as the "Ode to Joy"). Feeling that his music was no longer fashionable in Vienna (then in the throes of infatuation with the operas of Rossini and with a new breed of concerto virtuosi), Beethoven made inquiries with an eye toward having the new symphony, the Ninth (op. 125), introduced in Berlin.

On hearing of this, a group of his admirers — among them his old patron Prince Lichnowsky, his new publisher Diabelli, and his last important pupil Karl Czerny (1791–1857) — tendered him a "memo" or open letter imploring that he not forsake his "second native city." It is one of the most affecting documents of the incipient romantic art-religion (now significantly tinged with post-Napoleonic nationalism), and impressive testimony to Beethoven's central place in its ideology.

> Although Beethoven's name and creations belong to all contemporaneous humanity and every country which opens a susceptible bosom to art, it is Austria which is best entitled to claim him as her own. Among her inhabitants appreciation for the great and immortal works which Mozart and Haydn created for all time within the lap of their homes still lives, and they are conscious with joyous pride that the sacred triad in which these names and yours glow as the symbol of the highest within the spiritual realm of tones, sprang from the soil of their fatherland. All the more painful must it have been for you to feel that a foreign power has invaded this royal citadel of the noblest, that above the mounds of the dead and around the dwelling-place of the only survivor of the band, phantoms are leading the dance who can boast of no kinship with the princely spirits of those royal houses; that shallowness is abusing the name and insignia of art, and unworthy dalliance with sacred things is beclouding and dissipating appreciation for the pure and eternally beautiful.
>
> For this reason they feel a greater and livelier sense than ever before that the great need of the present moment is a new impulse directed by a powerful hand, a new advent of the ruler in his domain . . . . For years, ever since the thunders of the Victory at Vittoria ceased to reverberate, we have waited and hoped to see you distribute new gifts from the fulness of your riches to the circle of your friends. Do not longer disappoint the general expectations![30]

FIG. 31-9 Kärntnertortheater, Vienna, site of the first performance of Beethoven's Ninth Symphony.

Moved by the tribute, Beethoven decided to come out of retirement for what would be the last time. He agreed to a public concert, his first in a decade, to be held at the same theater in which, some thirty years before, Mozart's *Magic Flute* had first been given, and where, ten years before, his own much-revised opera *Leonore* (now called *Fidelio*) had finally met with favor from the public that had formerly spurned it.

The official announcement read:

GRAND
　　MUSICAL CONCERT
by
　　HERR L. v. BEETHOVEN which will take place Tomorrow, May 7, 1824 in the Royal Imperial Theater beside the Kärntnerthor.
　　The musical pieces to be performed are the latest works of Herr Ludwig van Beethoven.
　　First: A Grand Overture ["The Consecration of the House," op. 124]
　　Second: Three Grand Hymns with Solo and Choral Voices [i.e., the Kyrie, Credo, and Agnus Dei from the *Missa solemnis*]
　　Third: A Grand Symphony with Solo and Chorus Voices entering in the finale on Schiller's Ode to Joy. The solos will be performed by the Demoiselles Sontag and Unger and the Herren Haizinger and Seipelt. Herr Schuppanzigh has undertaken the direction of the orchestra, Herr Kapellmeister Umlauf the direction of the whole, and the Music Society the augmentation of the chorus and orchestra as a favor.
　　Herr Ludwig van Beethoven will himself participate in the general direction.
　　Prices of admission as usual.
　　Beginning at seven o'clock in the evening.[31]

As promised, the composer, by then stone deaf for almost a decade, did stand before the assembled orchestra and chorus and wave his arms, but according to the later recollection of the pianist Sigismund Thalberg, who as a twelve-year-old prodigy attended the concert, the court conductor Michael Umlauf, listed as general overseer in the advertisement above, "had told the choir and orchestra to pay no attention whatever to Beethoven's beating of the time but all to watch him."[32] The most famous story of this great event, for which we have not only Thalberg's memory to rely on but also corroborating testimony from other witnesses and participants, relates how "after the Scherzo of the Ninth Symphony Beethoven stood turning over the leaves of his score utterly deaf to the immense applause, and [the contralto soloist Karoline] Unger pulled him by the sleeve, and then pointed to the audience, whereupon he turned and bowed." Of all Beethoven's works, the Ninth Symphony cast the longest shadow over the rest of the nineteenth century, and has continued to lower over the music of the twentieth century as well. In its awe-inspiring vastness it has been so long and so often compared to a mountain that as recently as 1967, the critic and musicologist Joseph Kerman could write, simply, that "we live in the valley of the Ninth Symphony." Immediately notorious, it has been as strenuously resisted as it has been enthusiastically submitted to. Both submission and resistance have been eloquent testimonials not only to the work itself, but to the cultural attitudes that it quickened and polarized.

One of the most telling contemporary comments was that of Louis Spohr (1784–1859), a violinist and, later in life, the first virtuoso baton conductor in the modern sense of the word. It was the reaction of one who had known and played under Beethoven in his youth, but who could not accept the new turn the master's art was taking. For Spohr the Ninth was a monstrosity that could only be explained in terms of its creator's deafness.

> His constant endeavor to be original and to open new paths, could no longer as formerly, be preserved from error by the guidance of the ear. Was it then to be wondered at that his works became more and more eccentric, unconnected, and incomprehensible? Yes! I must even reckon the much admired Ninth Symphony among them, the three first movements of which, in spite of some solitary flashes of genius, are to me worse than all of the eight previous Symphonies, the fourth movement of which is in my opinion so monstrous and tasteless, and in its grasp of Schiller's Ode so trivial, that I cannot even now understand how a genius like Beethoven's could have written it. I find in it another proof of what I already remarked in Vienna, that Beethoven was wanting in aesthetical feeling and in a sense of the beautiful.[33]

Recalling Edmund Burke's elaborate set of contrasts between the sublime and the beautiful, one can only agree with Spohr's comment, though not necessarily with its intent. If to be beautiful meant to be pleasing, then Beethoven did indeed lack a sense of beauty. Or rather, he rejected the assumption on which Spohr based his judgment, that to be beautiful (that is, to please) was the only proper aim of art. Like Bach before him (though he could scarcely have known it), Beethoven in the Ninth did at times deliberately assault the ear, most famously and extravagantly with the fanfares — Richard Wagner called them *Schreckensfanfaren*, "horror fanfares" — that introduce the finale containing the "Ode to Joy" (Ex. 31-7). In the second of them, the D minor triad and the diminished-seventh chord on its leading tone are sounded together as a seven-tone harmony with a level of dissonance that would not be reached again until the very end of the century.

EX. 31-7   Ludwig van Beethoven, Symphony no. 9, Op. 125, IV, *"Schreckensfanfare"*(arr. Franz Liszt)

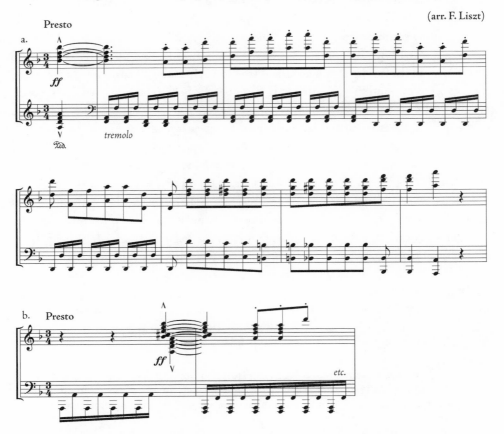

(arr. F. Liszt)

However much music like this may move or thrill, it cannot be said to please the listener. By Mozartean standards (recalling his letter about Osmin's rage aria in *The Abduction from the Seraglio*, quoted in chapter 28), it isn't music. By composing it, Beethoven tells us that he doesn't care what we think of it (or of him); that it is bigger than we are. It was, to many, an insulting message, a sort of declaration of composerly independence, an arrogant emancipation proclamation.

Spohr's seemingly contradictory charge of triviality was aimed at the famous melody to which Beethoven set Schiller's Ode. In its folklike simplicity it seemed a sort of urban popular tune, out of place in the lofty precincts of the rest of the symphony; and Beethoven did his best to accentuate its low-class associations by giving it a "Turkish" parade variation that turned it, for all the world, into Viennese street music (Ex. 31-8).

The most radical move, however, was to load the symphony down with a great freight of imagery and symbolism, but an imagery and a symbolism that is not fully explained either within the work itself or by reference to any public code. Maynard Solomon has identified in the symphony a great deal of conventional musical

EX. 31-8A Ludwig van Beethoven, Symphony no. 9, IV, "Ode to Joy" theme

EX. 31-8B Ludwig van Beethoven, beginning of "Turkish" variation on the "Ode to Joy" (arr. Liszt)

imagery — martial, pastoral, ecclesiastical — that any audience familiar with the works of Mozart and Haydn would have instantly recognized. He has also pointed to an elaborate network within the work of thematic reminiscences and forecasts that unite all of the movements into a single expressive whole. Most particularly, these thematic forecasts prefigure the "Ode to Joy" melody in the finale, and turn the whole symphony (it is possible to argue) into a single quest for "Elysium," the mythical abode where heroes and other fortunate shades are rewarded by the Gods with the Joy whose praises Schiller sings (Ex. 31-9).

These are the "introversive" and "extroversive" sign systems we first encountered and discussed as expressive media in connection with Haydn's instrumental music. As always, the two are fully separable only in theory. The Joy Theme that is prefigured in the early movements by a process of introversive signification is itself an extroversive sign, pointing outside of the work to words like "Joy" and "Elysium" and the concepts for which they stand.

But as in every other way, Beethoven maximized and transformed his heritage to the point where, as Hoffmann was first to suggest, it crossed the threshold into a difference not only in degree but in kind. Specifically, by withholding an explicit key to the sign systems on whose importance he nevertheless insists, by offering no explanation of the meanings to which those systems may give rise, Beethoven enlists all listeners in another "quest" — a never-ending process of interpretation. "The precise nature of Beethoven's programmatic intentions," Maynard Solomon cautions, "will always remain open," turning the Ninth Symphony into a vast symbol, "the totality of whose referents cannot be known and whose full effects will never be experienced."[34] And this ultimate uncertainty, Solomon avers somewhat more controversially (but very much in the romantic spirit), is "true to the nature of music, whose meanings are beyond translation — and beyond intentionality." The message — Solomon's, to be sure, but perhaps Beethoven's as well — is clear. We may interpret Beethoven's meanings in endless ways, depending on our perspicacity and our interests. What we may not do, on the one hand, is to claim to have arrived at a definitive interpretation, or, on the other, to deny the reality of the semiotic dimension or its relevance to the meanings of the work.

This is romanticism of the purest strain. What must forever remain controversial about it is the implication (which Solomon, if not Beethoven, makes explicit) that such is "the nature of music." Meanings like those Solomon describes had not figured in previous musical discourse, at least not instrumental discourse. The eighteenth century had its semiotic codes, of course: there was the *Affektenlehre* or system of symbolic figures on which Bach and Handel and their contemporaries had drawn to depict their character's emotions. And there was the so-called *sinfonia caratteristica*, the "characteristic" (that is, pictorial) symphony, to which works like Beethoven's Sixth ("Pastoral") Symphony belonged, with its "Scene by the Brook" and its vividly graphic "Storm." (The *Eroica*, too, might be called a *sinfonia caratteristica* in view of all of its military imagery, beginning with that bugle call of a first theme.) The difference was that conventionally embodied meanings like these, whether emotive or descriptive, were always *public* meanings. No one needs to interpret the "Pastoral"

EX. 31-9A   Ludwig van Beethoven, Symphony no. 9, foreshadowing the "Ode to Joy" in earlier movements

EX. 31-9B   Ludwig van Beethoven, Symphony no. 9, foreshadowing the "Ode to Joy" in earlier movements

EX. 31-9C   Ludwig van Beethoven, Symphony no. 9, foreshadowing the "Ode to Joy" in earlier movements

Symphony, just as no one needed to explain to Prince Esterházy what Haydn was getting at with his "Farewell" Symphony. If certain eighteenth-century genres do need to be interpreted now by historians—the expressive conventions of the *opera seria*, for example—that is only because we have lost the code through disuse, not because it was esoteric. Some eighteenth-century sacred genres such as the Bach cantatas did occasionally embody esoteric meanings, it is true, to which hermeneutic techniques have to be applied. But such theological, often numerological symbolism was a survival of a pre-Enlightenment esthetic and was rejected between Bach's time and Beethoven's.

The meanings embodied in Beethoven's Ninth Symphony are no longer public in this way. Though they are clearly crucial components of the work, they cannot be fully comprehended according to some socially sanctioned code. They have become subjective, hermetic, gnomic, "not of this world." They are not so private as to render the musical discourse unintelligible, but they do render its message ineffable and inexhaustible and, to that extent, oracular. Intuitive grasp, aided of course by whatever can be gleaned by code or study or experience, is the only mode of understanding available. Just as often we may be deeply moved without quite knowing why or how. And that must be what Beethoven meant by insisting, in his late years, that he was not merely a composer (*Tonsetzer*) but a "tone-poet" (*Tondichter*).

INWARDNESS

Beethoven lived less than three years after the premiere of the Ninth Symphony, finally succumbing to the effects of liver disease (itself the result, it is speculated, of heavy drinking) on 26 March 1827. During this final phase he returned to the string quartet, another genre he had not touched in more than a decade, and devoted himself to it almost exclusively. The immediate stimulus came from Prince Golitsyn, the Russian nobleman who arranged the first performance of the *Missa solemnis*. In the fall of 1822 he had invited Beethoven to compose anywhere from one to three quartets for him, and to name his price. In the end Beethoven completed six works for string quartet, including the three commissioned by Golitsyn and dedicated to him (opp. 127, 130, 132), and two more full-scale works in the genre (in C-sharp minor, op. 131, gratefully dedicated to a certain Baron von Stutterheim who had accepted the Beethoven's nephew Karl into his guards regiment after the boy's attempted suicide; and in F major, op. 135).

The remaining work was a "Great Fugue" (*Grosse Fuge*) that was originally planned as the finale of the Quartet in B-flat major, op. 130. When Diabelli, his publisher, pointed out that at six movements the quartet was long even without the mammoth finale, and that the fugue was not only huge but inordinately difficult to play, Beethoven agreed to detach the fugue for separate publication (as op. 133, dedicated to Archduke, now Archbishop, Rudolph) and to compose a dancelike rondo to provide a more conventional, less taxing conclusion to what was already a somewhat suitelike composition resembling a divertimento of old. The substitute finale of op. 130, delivered to the publisher in November 1826, was Beethoven's last completed work.

The steadfastness of Beethoven's late interest in the quartet medium can be partially accounted for by the devotion of Ignaz Schuppanzigh (1776–1830), the violinist who served as orchestra leader (or "concertmaster" as we now say) at the momentous concert in which the Ninth Symphony was unveiled. He had been the leader of Prince Lichnowsky's private string quartet since the 1790s, and Beethoven had relied upon his counsel from the very beginning of his career as a quartet composer. Following the general trend of the time, Schuppanzigh reconstituted his quartet as a freelance ensemble during the winter of 1804–5 and began giving subscription con-

FIG. 31-10   Beethoven's study in the Schwarspanierhaus, his last residence.

certs in Vienna. These were among the first regular public chamber music concerts anywhere. It was at these concerts that Beethoven's "middle" quartets were first performed, notably the "Razumovsky" series, op. 59, commissioned by the Russian ambassador in Vienna. Razumovsky later employed Schuppanzigh's quartet and lavishly subsidized its activities until 1814, when his palace burned down.

From 1816 until 1823, probably owing to his connection with Razumovsky, Schuppanzigh relocated in St. Petersburg, the Russian capital, where he was very active in promoting Beethoven's works, and not only quartets. It was he who put Prince Golitsyn in touch with Beethoven, thus serving as the late quartets' catalyst. His own professional ensemble, again reconstituted in Vienna in 1823 and again offering regular subscription concerts, gave the first performances of the three Golitsyn quartets, as well as the posthumous premiere of Opus 135, Beethoven's swan song. Schuppanzigh's readiness for creative collaboration with Beethoven was surely among the most potent stimuli on the composer's "quartet imagination."

And yet there came a point where Beethoven's burgeoning romantic idealism doomed any true symbiosis with performers. A much-repeated story that may be true recounts Beethoven's contemptuous retort when Schuppanzigh complained that a certain passage in one of the late quartets was too difficult to play effectively: "Do you fancy I am thinking of your puking little fiddle when the muse confides in me?" he is supposed to have said. In fact, in Beethoven's choice of the verb "confide" we may encounter another reason for Beethoven's late preoccupation with the quartet medium:

its privateness, or, as the German romantics characteristically put it, its "inwardness" (*Innigkeit* or *Innerlichkeit*).

The intimacy of chamber music offered the composer the possibility of a heightened subjectivity, a medium where he could speak his inmost, private thoughts and confide his deepest private moods as if to a musical diary. There are pages in the late quartets that can seem almost embarrassing to hear in public, as if hearing were overhearing—eavesdropping on the composer's afflicted personal existence, invading his privacy. One of these is the fifth movement of the Quartet in B♭ major, op. 130. Its tempo is Adagio molto espressivo; the parts are marked *sotto voce* (in an undertone); and it is subtitled "Cavatina," which to Beethoven meant a short, slow operatic aria of particular poignancy. (The Countess's "Porgi amor" in Mozart's *Marriage of Figaro*, in which a betrayed wife gives vent to her misery, is a classic of the genre.)

The impression is unmistakable that Beethoven is confiding his private grief; and in case anyone should mistake it, the composer makes it even more explicit near the end (Ex. 31-10), where the dynamic level becomes even more hushed ("sempre pp"), the harmony slips unexpectedly and mysteriously into the flat submediant region, and the first violin, in a passage marked *Beklemmt* (constricted or stifled, "all choked up"), effectively loses its voice, its line being continually interrupted by rests as if racked by sobs.

EX. 31-10   Ludwig van Beethoven, Quartet no. 13 in B-flat, Op. 130, V ("Cavatina")

EX. 31-10 (continued)

This was not in fact the first time Beethoven had used this device. A comparable, though much shorter, passage had occurred at the end of the second movement ("Marcia funebre," "funeral march") in the *Eroica* Symphony more than twenty years earlier (Ex. 31-11). But what had the appearance of a public orator's rhetorical ploy in the symphony now has the aspect of a private disclosure. The voice appears to belong this time not to a public "persona" but to an actual person, recalling the inscription

EX. 31-11A Ludwig van Beethoven, Symphony no. 3, II ("Marcia funebre"), first violin, mm. 1–8

EX. 31-11B Ludwig van Beethoven, Symphony no. 3, II ("Marcia funebre"), first violin, mm. 238–47

Beethoven placed on the first page of the *Missa solemnis* autograph, "From the heart: May it also go to the heart" (*Von Herzen — Möge es wieder — zu Herzen gehn!*).

In the wake of this movement and others like it, the key of the flat submediant became a virtual symbol of *Innigkeit* — "inwardness of expression" — for Beethoven's successors, particularly Franz Schubert, his fellow Viennese. Here Beethoven bequeathed to future composers of the romantic persuasion not only an esthetic purpose, and not only a general approach to instrumental music that invested it with "voice," but an actual *topos* — an expressive "topic" or sign referent. For a musical work may indeed point outside itself to another musical work, and after Beethoven, the work that failed to point to his colossal example was a rarity. One can fairly say that virtually the whole corpus of German instrumental (and not only instrumental) music composed in the nineteenth century was a commentary on Beethoven.

In the appropriation of a vocal genre lay a further clue as to why Beethoven spent his last, semiretired years with the string quartet rather than what would seem for him an equally private medium, namely the piano. In fact he did continue to write for the piano, and with emphatic "privacy," after completing the *Diabelli Variations*, concentrating on short, strongly characterized pieces he called *Bagatelles* (French for "trifles"). He had been writing them for decades; one, a little rondo composed in 1808 and published with the subtitle "Für Elise" (For Eliza), has become a ubiquitous children's practice piece. The late ones, composed between 1820 and 1824 and published in two sets (op. 119 and op. 126), are definitely not for the young. They are gnomic, often enigmatic pieces that find their echo in some of the more grotesque little movements in the late quartets (for instance, the tiny *presto* that forms the second movement of the same B♭ major quartet that also contains the heartrending Cavatina).

But the piano could not give the illusion of "vocality" on which Beethoven now relied for intimately "innig" utterance. His preoccupation with the vocal, moreover, was also strangely bound up with archaism — an archaism already evident in his predilection for fugues in many of his late works, including three of the late piano sonatas (opp. 101, 106, and 110). Taken in conjunction with the political sentiments expressed in *Der glorreiche Augenblick*, this archaism has been interpreted as a religious gesture, and a sign of Beethoven's disillusioned acquiescence in the spirit of post-Napoleonic reaction. That reading gains some support from the late quartets, for now Beethoven pushed back beyond fugues to imitations or evocations of earlier modes of religious vocal polyphony — his own version of a *stile antico*.

This new-old inclination, and its highly personal meaning for Beethoven, is vividly embodied in the slow movement of the Quartet in A minor, op. 132, composed in 1825. Beethoven had spent the month of April and part of May that year gravely sick in bed, and the movement, composed later that spring, bears the heading *Heiliger Dankgesang eines Genesenen an die Gottheit, in der lydischen Tonart* ("Sacred Hymn of Thanksgiving from a Convalescent to the Deity, in the Lydian Mode"). It is in effect a sort of motet with variations, on a theme reminiscent of an old chorale (Ex. 31-12), summoning up (in Joseph Kerman's words) "some infinitely remote liturgy, a ritual music of romance," interspersed with a contrasting exultant dance in D major, marked "Neue Kraft fühlend"

(Feeling new strength), that also returns in varied form.[35] The variation technique is itself an archaic one: "divisions," as they were called in the seventeenth century, whereby the rhythmic activity is continually heightened by breaking the long notes values down into shorter and shorter ones.

EX. 31-12   Ludwig van Beethoven, Quartet no. 15 in A minor ("chorale" tune), Op. 132, III ("Heiliger Dankgesang"), reconstructed from mm. 3–7, 9–13, 15–19, 21–25

The "Lydian mode" is of course another archaism, the most obvious one of all, and the most romantic. For as we have known since chapter 3, the actual Lydian mode of medieval music theory had been regularly adjusted into what we call the major mode from the beginning. Beethoven's version of the mode is thus no medieval restoration but a romantically exotic invention: a strange F major notated without a B♭ in the key signature, with all the B-naturals (and they are quite rare) applied as leading tones to C, the dominant, or used within a transposed statement of the choralelike subject that is harmonized in C.

What makes the imaginary archaism of the music evident to all listeners is the contrapuntal nature of the writing, the use of "freely canonic" imitation at the octave and unison, the cantus firmus textures, particularly the liberal use of dotted note values on the weak beats, typical of school counterpoint even today but unusual in any other context. In reality, the seemingly archaic contrapuntal style gives Beethoven access to a level of pure diatonic "linear" dissonance that must have struck his earliest listeners as nothing short of modernistic. It is used to project an overwhelming intensity of subjective feeling at which Beethoven hints verbally in the last and rhythmically most complex variation, where he writes that the instruments are to be played *Mit innigster Empfindung* ("With the most inward expression"), actually using the word that would become for all German composers the very motto of romanticism (Ex. 31-13).

And yet despite all privacy and inwardness in thought and apparent purpose, Beethoven at the time of his death was far more a public figure than any composer had ever been before; and that, too, was part of the legacy of romanticism. The streets of Vienna were thronged on the morning of his funeral, 29 March 1827. Police estimates put the crowd at ten thousand.

EX. 31-13   Ludwig van Beethoven, Quartet no. 15 in A minor, Op. 132, III, Last variation on the "Heiliger Dankgesang"

FIG. 31-11   Beethoven's funeral procession, by Franz Stoeber (Beethoven House, Bonn).

At the graveside, an oration by the dramatist Franz Grillparzer (1791–1872) was declaimed in high tragic tones by a famous actor, Heinrich Anschütz. Like the letter of 1824 imploring for Vienna the rights to first hearing of the Ninth Symphony, Grillparzer's eulogy placed the emphasis on nationality, comparing Beethoven with Goethe (the "hero of verse in German speech and tongue") and tracing for him a historically spurious but heavily symbolic musical genealogy from Handel and Bach. "Standing by the grave of him who has passed away," Grillparzer's homily began,

> we are in a manner the representatives of an entire nation, of the whole German people, mourning the loss of the one highly acclaimed half of that which was left us of the departed splendor of our native art, of the fatherland's full spiritual bloom. There yet lives — and may his life be long! — the hero of verse in German speech and tongue; but the last master of tuneful song, the organ of soulful concord, the heir and amplifier of Handel and Bach's, of Haydn and Mozart's immortal fame is now no more, and we stand weeping over the riven strings of the harp that is hushed.[36]

Forever afterward it would be an article of faith for German artists that Beethoven's stature was unequalable ("He who comes after him will not continue him," Grillparzer declared), that with Beethoven the age of heroes had ended. The Napoleonic myth and the Beethoven myth — as can only seem inevitable in retrospect — had fused. And yet all who came after would nevertheless be under an onus to strive toward the unreachable mark Beethoven's legacy had set. The concept of music and the role of the composer had both been irrevocably transformed by romanticism, and enormously enlarged. Beethoven had been at once the protagonist of these transformations, and their vessel.

C-Minor Moods

THE "STRUGGLE AND VICTORY" NARRATIVE AND ITS RELATIONSHIP TO FOUR C-MINOR WORKS OF BEETHOVEN

DEVOTION AND DERISION

The *New Grove Dictionary of Music and Musicians* calls Beethoven "the most admired composer in the history of Western music," and we have seen some of the reasons for that. Not only has Beethoven been admired by other musicians and by his composing progeny; he has also been consistently the most popular composer with concert audiences over a period now approaching two centuries, during which the makeup of the concert audience has undergone repeated profound change. But it is also true that for just as long a period, and in the same tradition, Beethoven has been among the most feared, resisted, and even hated of composers, and we shall see the reasons for that, too, as our investigation of nineteenth- and twentieth-century music proceeds.

Both admiration and resistance have a single source; in fact they are the two sides of a single coin. They have arisen in reaction to Beethoven's looming, unshakeable presence as the most authoritative and influential figure in the tradition of which this book is the history — a tradition that has yet fully to outgrow its romantic phase, the phase that was formed, so to speak, in the image of Beethoven. For a century and a half and more, in short, Beethoven has been the one to beat.

So a book like this needs more than an account of Beethoven's life in relation to his art, or an appreciation of his cultural and esthetic significance. We need a survey of his actual musical achievement as well — one that is at once comprehensive, representative, reflective of his influence, and still relatively brief. That is a tall order, especially the last requirement. Perhaps the best way to fill it would be to concentrate on the music that has most exercised posterity, fastening in particular on two categories: the music that has been the most popular, and the music that has been the most notorious or controversial.

Indeed, it turns out that both categories are the same; or rather, that a small number of famous works inhabit both categories. And it further turns out that many of these works share the same key: the quintessentially "Beethovenian" key of C minor. What Joseph Kerman calls Beethoven's "C-minor mood," the one most firmly associated with the composer by posterity, has been an object of devotion and derision in equal measure.[1] In its dynamic, even terrifying agitation and disquiet it concentrates our image of Beethoven as an unruly "unlicked bear" (as his high-society patrons called him in his youth), as the tormented soul he became in mature isolation, and as the enigmatic visionary of his last decade.

From the beginning, the prevalence of C minor sharply delineated Beethoven's distance from the spiritual world of Haydn and Mozart, who used the key quite sparingly. The fact that a C-minor work has nevertheless figured prominently in our discussions of both men — the Fantasia, K. 475, in the case of Mozart; the *Creation* Prologue in that of Haydn — betrays the bias that those discussions necessarily share with all descriptions that serve the purposes of historical narrative. Our discussions of Mozart and Haydn, in other words, were written in the knowledge — knowledge unavailable to Mozart and Haydn — that Beethoven was coming, and that we would have to take account of his relationship to them. For however rare their use of the key, it was Mozart and Haydn who — inevitably — provided Beethoven with the precedent on which he based his conception of it.

For devotion to the C-minor Beethoven, we may turn to any of the critics (beginning once again with E. T. A. Hoffmann) or composers (beginning with Robert Schumann, who was also a critic), not to mention the countless audiences, who have viewed the Fifth Symphony, this chapter's centerpiece, as the Beethovenian epitome, hence the epitome of "classical music" outright. Schumann linked it up in especially direct fashion with the "romantic sublime" by refusing to write at length about it. "Let us be silent about this work!" he bade his readers.[2] "No matter how frequently heard, whether at home [played on the piano] or in the concert hall, this symphony invariably wields its power over men of every age like those great phenomena of nature that fill us with fear and admiration at all times, no matter how frequently we may experience them."

Derision began early, too, and found a willing spokesman, once again, in Louis Spohr, for whom the work "did not add up to a classical [that is, a beautiful] whole," since the first movement "lacked the dignity essential to the opening of a symphony," and the last movement was merely "empty noise." Prime time for Beethoven-scorn, however, was the disillusioned aftermath of the First World War. To the great British music scholar Edward J. Dent (1876–1957), writing in that fallen moment, the Beethoven of the C-minor mood symbolized everything that was outmoded in European culture. Having been promoted by the musicians and critics of the Victorian age as "the great musician of moral uplift," Beethoven was now suspect in the eyes of youth.[3]

Though he remained unwilling or unable to level the charge of charlatanry at Beethoven himself, Dent saw in Beethoven-worship the origin of a sanctimonious and baleful tendency — the tendency for

> every little scribbler to regard himself as a prophet, and the tendency of music-lovers in general to exhibit a ludicrously exaggerated reverence for the artist — a reverence, it need hardly be said, which the artist, and especially the charlatan, has lost no time in exploiting to the full.[4]

As a result, Beethoven's work, however genuine its inspiration or its musical distinction, has been resisted by many modern thinkers as being, like other varieties of moral conviction, a kind of "false consciousness" masking hypocritical complacency. "The lofty idealism of Beethoven," Dent wrote, "is a thing which we cannot possibly deny or ignore; but we may justly question whether the artistic expression of it is still convincing to modern ears."[5] These were the words of one resigned to reluctant disbelief—a voice raised in protest against Beethoven's continuing, unassailable, but (for Dent) no longer fitting ascendancy. Were Beethoven not still a dominating presence in the minds of all musicians a full century after his death, there would have been no reason at so late a date to renounce him. Beethoven, and Beethovenian values, have become so synonymous with the culture of "classical music" that one can chart the checkered course of musical esthetics since his time simply by examining reactions to him.

Dent was not only a professor; in 1926, when he wrote the words just quoted, he was also a founding member and first president of the International Society of Contemporary Music, a concert-sponsoring organization that was then the leading forum for the performance and dissemination of the works of all the most advanced composers of the day. Dent was speaking, then, not only on behalf of contemporary scholars and listeners, but on behalf of contemporary artists as well, and his words found many echoes, at least for a while, among creative musicians.

One of the most colorful was an exchange between Marcel Proust, the French novelist, and Igor Stravinsky, then a youngish Russian composer at the pinnacle of Parisian prestige, at a reception held for Stravinsky at a swanky Paris hotel in the late spring of 1922. As recalled by Clive Bell, an English biographer of Proust, who overheard it, the conversation went like this:

> "Doubtless you admire Beethoven," Proust began. "I detest Beethoven," was all he got for answer. "But *mon cher maître* [my dear master], surely those late sonatas and quartets . . . ?" "*Pire que les autres* [the worst of all]," growled Stravinsky.[6]

Stravinsky, who later professed as profound an admiration[7] for Beethoven as one could expect from another composer (and for the late quartets in particular), admitted in his autobiography that his earlier antipathy was a pose brought on by a surfeit of oppressively enforced reverence, and by disgust at the mythology that had grown up around Beethoven, surrounding him with a fog of pious words about "his famous *Weltschmerz* [world-weariness], together with his 'tragedy' and all the commonplace utterances voiced for more than a century about this composer."[8] As Stravinsky put it in retrospect, unthinking deification "alienated me from Beethoven for many years," until, at last, he was "cured and matured by age."

The experience was typical. With the passing of that aggressively "modern" moment after World War I, doubts about Beethoven were for a time put to rest; but they dependably resurface whenever a new artistic tendency needs to clear a musical space for itself. John Cage, for instance, an avant-garde musician of the post–World War II period, went on renewed offensive against Beethoven in 1948, claiming that the whole concept of "composition defined by harmony" was "in error," and that "Beethoven's influence, which has been as extensive as it is lamentable, has been deadening to the art of music."[9]

As the persistent need to attack him attests better than anyone's praise, the Beethoven of the C-minor mood remains a touchstone of music's full potential within the European fine-art tradition, and will undoubtedly retain that position as long as the tradition persists. For he (or rather "it" — the touchstone, not the man) has become the tradition's virtual definer for the listeners on whom it depends for its subsistence.

Yet to describe the distinctive Beethovenian tone simply as the "C-minor mood" is woefully inadequate. It is not just incomplete: such a description leaves out the chief thing that has given Beethoven his hold on the minds and hearts of so many generations of listeners. For the "C-minor mood" is really not a mood at all. A mood is static. What Beethoven offers, as always, is a trajectory. Most of the works we shall examine begin in C minor and end in C major; and the ones that do not make a point of the fact.

Thus, time and again over the whole course of his career, Beethoven seemed to replay, as if under a compulsion, that sublime moment in Haydn's *Creation* when the dark of chaos yielded to the light of primeval day. The many inflections he gave the basic opposition, from consoling to triumphal to quiescent, have given rise to as many metaphorical interpretations, and to as many moral or ethical readings. Adolf Bernhard Marx (1795–1866) caught the Haydn resonance and drew out its implications with great acumen when he wrote of the Fifth Symphony that its overall theme was "Durch Nacht zum Licht! Durch Kampf zum Sieg!" ("Through night to light! Through struggle to victory!"), sounding a keynote for Beethoven interpretation that has resonated over the centuries on many levels from the biographical or psychological to the nationalistic, and from the benignly auspicious to the potentially sinister.[10]

TRANSGRESSION

As we may remember from the previous chapter, it was the key (or mood) of C minor that got Beethoven into trouble for the first time. We can get the whole story now from Beethoven's pupil Ferdinand Ries, who claimed to have had it from Beethoven himself. It took place around the end of 1793 or the beginning of 1794, when Beethoven, sent to Vienna by his earliest patron Count Waldstein "to receive the deceased Mozart's spirit from Haydn's hands," had been living in the capital for about a year.[11] Now it was time to make good on the count's happy (but for Beethoven, perhaps, somewhat unnerving) prediction. "It was planned," Ries wrote in a memoir published in 1838,

> to introduce the first three Trios of Beethoven, which were about to be published as Opus 1, to the artistic world at a soirée at Prince Lichnowsky's, to whom they were dedicated. Most of the artists and music-lovers were invited, especially Haydn, for whose opinion all were eager. The Trios were played and at once commanded extraordinary attention. Haydn also said many pretty things about them, but advised Beethoven not to publish the third, in C minor. This astonished Beethoven, inasmuch as he considered the third the best of the Trios, as it is still the one which gives the greatest pleasure and makes the greatest effect. Consequently, Haydn's remark left a bad impression on Beethoven and led him to think that Haydn was envious, jealous and ill-disposed toward him. I confess that when Beethoven told me of this I gave it little credence. I therefore took occasion to ask Haydn himself about it. His answer, however, confirmed Beethoven's statement; he said he had not believed that this Trio would be so quickly and easily understood and so favorably received by the public.[12]

Note that, contrary to a frequent but unjustified interpretation of this incident, Haydn is not portrayed as disliking or misunderstanding the Trio himself, only as anticipating a poor reception from the paying public. Haydn himself had recently had a sour experience with a piece in C minor. His Symphony no. 95, for the first London series, was the only one without a slow introduction and the only one in a minor key. The public didn't like it; and as Elaine Sisman puts it, "he didn't make the mistake again."[13] So, far from wishing to suppress a young rival, he was in all likelihood motivated by concern for his former pupil's reputation and commercial prospects. Additional reasons for that concern are not difficult to surmise. They had to do with the genre in which Beethoven was making his debut.

Today's standard nomenclature for late-eighteenth- and nineteenth-century chamber ensembles of three or more, or pieces written for them, is based simply on the number of instruments participating: for example, string or piano "trio," string or piano "quartet," "quintet," and so on. In the eighteenth century, however, as we have already observed in chapter 27, ensembles with fully notated piano parts were generally deemed to be amplified or "accompanied" piano sonatas. What we call a violin sonata (say, by Mozart) would have been called a piano sonata with violin; and what we call a piano trio by Mozart or Haydn would have been called a "sonata con violino e basso," or a "sonata pour le piano-forte avec accompagnement de violon et violoncello," to quote from the title page of a set of three such pieces by Haydn that was published in London in 1794, the same year as the tryout of Beethoven's op. 1.

(French was often the language of such title pages, no matter where published, because the piano trio genre was traditionally deemed a French one, going back to the *Pièces de clavecin en concerts* — "Harpsichord pieces arranged in sets with accompanying parts" — by Jean-Philippe Rameau, published in 1741.)

In such pieces the violin occasionally got to sing its own tunes, but the cello part was largely confined to doubling the piano left hand. That is because the accompanied piano sonata was, in its origins and usual aim, an unambitious and undemanding household genre. Further evidence of its modesty was its traditional brevity. Except for two early specimens (one of them never published during his lifetime), Haydn's typically huge output of forty-one trios never exceeded three movements, and nine of them, including a pair composed in the 1790s, have only two. Mozart's eight trios (one of them with clarinet in place of violin) all have three movements.

Not only that, but the use of minor keys was extremely rare in such pieces, as it was in all domestic entertainment genres. Mozart never wrote a trio in the minor mode, and Haydn wrote only six. The one that shared Beethoven's key of C minor, composed in the late 1780s, compensated for its seriousness by being cast in only two movements, of which the second (and longer) one was demonstratively marked "gay and witty" (*Allegro spirituoso*) and cast in C major to dispel the gloom. Weightiness, agitation, dark moods — such characteristics were simply not associated with the genre. They were implicitly undesirable. That is what Haydn was getting at.

Now compare Beethoven's op. 1, no. 3. All three trios in op. 1 have four movements — that is, they all have both a slow movement and a minuet between ample allegros, as in a symphony. That amplitude of form was already unprecedented, and so was the willingness it implied to transgress the obligations of genre in the interests of expression — or of making an impression. (Not for nothing did Haydn once refer to Beethoven, behind his back, as the "Grand Mogul from Bonn.")[14] To compound the infraction by the use of C minor, a key associated not with home amusements but with theatrical pathos, was to put op. 1, no. 3, for Haydn, altogether beyond the pale of decorum. From the older composer's point of view, the younger one was committing an act of gratuitous, arrogant aggression against his potential audience. Haydn, who spent his life as a sort of courtier, failed to foresee that Beethoven's public would respond to his aggression with delight. He can be forgiven.

For it was indeed that grand theatrical pathos, vulgar in courtly eyes, to which Beethoven was aspiring. This is evident from the very beginning of the Trio, in a theme that plays a very conspicuous but ambiguous role in the work (Ex. 32-1). It is not hard to see that it is modeled directly on the ominous opening theme of Mozart's Piano Concerto no. 24, K. 491, composed in 1786, one of only two minor-mode Mozartean concertos out of a total of over fifty. (The fact that both are among Mozart's most famous works — the other is the Piano Concerto no. 20 in D minor, K. 466 — could be read either as a simple mark of their quality, or, more complexly, as a sign that Mozart's works have been selectively valued by a posterity that knew Beethoven.)

Note particularly the way the dominant degree (G) is circled in both themes by half steps on either side (Ab, F#), so that a dissonant augmented sixth — or its inversion, an even more dissonant diminished third — is built right into the theme. It is almost as if Beethoven were announcing that what had been a mood of extreme rarity — or of rare extremity — in Mozart or Haydn would be "normal" for him.

EX. 32-1A   Ludwig van Beethoven, Piano Trio in C minor, Op. 1, no. 3, I, mm. 1–10

EX. 32-1B   W. A. Mozart, Piano Concerto in C minor, K. 491, opening theme

Beethoven's theme, with its portentously theatrical fermata, plays a somewhat ambiguous role in the first movement of the Trio. It is not exactly the "first theme" in sonata form. That role is taken by the theme that immediately follows the phrase quoted in Ex. 32-1, a melody built up out of repetitions of a restless motive beginning with a long upbeat of three eighth notes. (We shall see later what a characteristic

"Beethoven rhythm" this motive is!) That is the theme from which Beethoven derives most of the movement's continuity. The opening idea, rather, seems reserved for almost the opposite purpose, that of interrupting—or actually disrupting—the course of the music for important announcements, many of them ending with fermatas, and most of them involving chromatic turns—or wrenches—in harmony. Its role is an essentially dramatic or rhetorical one, as befits the theatrical pathos of its style.

In m. 31, for example, the "announcement" theme returns in the form of a deceptive cadence that leads almost immediately to a weird F♭-major arpeggio that can only in retrospect be interpreted as the Neapolitan sixth of the relative major, the key of the second theme (Ex. 32-2a). At the beginning of the development section (m. 138), the theme comes back again (Ex. 32-2b) to nudge the harmony from its comfortable cadence on E♭ toward the Far Out Point, by substituting the parallel minor and leading from there, very briefly, into the mysterious territory of the flat submediant (here spelled enharmonically, as B major). And in the recapitulation (mm. 214 ff), after announcing

EX. 32-2A   Ludwig van Beethoven, Piano Trio in C minor (Op. 1, no. 3), I, mm. 29–36

EX. 32-2B   Ludwig van Beethoven, Piano Trio in C minor (Op. 1, no. 3), I, mm. 138–49

EX. 32-2C   Ludwig van Beethoven, Piano Trio in C minor (Op. 1, no. 3), I, mm. 224–35

the double return, the theme makes another abrupt harmonic turn (Ex. 32-2c; just where, as Haydn probably pointed out, the listener least expects it) into the actual key, not just the chord, of the "Neapolitan" degree, ♭II (D♭ major). Thanks to these surprising modulations, the tonic key has been shadowed on both sides by chromatic half steps, just the way the dominant is shadowed by the notes of the theme itself. More harmonically abandoned than this, music rarely got before the nineteenth century, and never in a trio.

Of course the "announcement theme" gets to announce important events of a more structural kind as well. As we have seen, it introduces the recapitulation. Broken down into motives, it sustains the first part of the development section, as earlier it had provided the exposition with its climax. In all its functions it serves as the vehicle, or channeler, of high rhetoric. Despite its ambiguous structural role, it provides the music that makes the most lasting impression on the listener.

And Beethoven needs to make sure that the impression lasts, for with the arrival of the impetuous *prestissimo* finale, we are confronted with another bold "announcement theme" (this time replete with "Mannheim rocket") that ends, like the one in the first movement, on a dominant half cadence that is underscored by a fermata (Ex. 32-3a). With something of a start, we realize that this theme is not merely similar in function to the theme heard at the Trio's outset. It is an actual variant of the earlier theme, in much the same way that the earlier theme had been a variant of a theme from Mozart's concerto.

EX. 32-3A   Ludwig van Beethoven, Piano Trio in C minor (Op. 1, no. 3), Finale, mm. 1–8

EX. 32-3B   Ludwig van Beethoven, Piano Trio in C minor (Op. 1, no. 3), Finale, end

EX. 32-3B (continued)

Thus Beethoven uses a single "basic melodic shape" or *Grundgestalt* (to use an apt term invented a century later by the Austrian composer Arnold Schoenberg) to secure the entire four-movement structure, at once more sprawling and more tautly unified than had previously been the norm. That tandem of unprecedented rhetorical amplitude and tight structural control would remain the Beethovenian standard. Following romantic theories of esthetics that likened works of art to living organisms in their properties of growth, it quickly became known as Beethovenian "organic" form — the norm against which the work of all composers would soon be measured, up to Schoenberg's time and even beyond.

After all the stormy impetuosity of the outer movements, the end of the Trio comes as another calculated surprise. After hitting a peak of energy with a passage based on a sequential extension of the opening "rocket" motive to a point of great harmonic tension on a diminished-seventh chord, the movement subsides by degrees. *Sforzando* accents apart, there is no dynamic marking above *piano* in the last 86 measures of the Finale. The music seems palpably to deflate in a marvelously calculated unison descent that implies a sophisticated harmonic pun: treating the dominant as if it were an augmented sixth chord (a technique that would become much more common in the early nineteenth century), allowing the tonal structure almost visibly to "sag" a semitone.

The end of the movement (and the trio) is given in Ex. 32-3b. The task this coda must perform is that of gradually building back up from B to C, but the effort seems costly. Emotional fatigue seems implicit in the obsessively repeated half-step descents to the tonic C, until the string instruments, seemingly drained of the energy it takes to play a theme, can only vamp the notes of the tonic triad, while the piano deploys its last remaining strength in a series of tonic scales, *pianissimo*.

The tonic, it will certainly not be missed, has relaxed into the major, invoked here, it would seem, as a symbol or metaphor of final repose, or possibly of resignation. Beethoven duplicated this final mode switch, from C minor to C major, many times over the course of his career, in many emotional contexts. Its persistence shows that this heavily fraught progression, according as it did with Haydn's monumental example in the *Creation*, was as much a part of Beethoven's "C-minor mood" as the choice of tonic key itself. The move from minor to major, often played out over a large multimovement span, was not only a spiritually symbolic device but also Beethoven's ultimate unifying stratagem, encompassing complex works within a single narrative or dramatic unfolding.

What is most remarkable is the variety of emotionally resonant stories Beethoven was able, in this way, to tell. By projecting emotionally engaging tonal narratives or dramas over ever longer musical spans, Beethoven forever changed the nature of instrumental music, and the expectations it aroused in audiences. If at the beginning of his career Beethoven seemed careless of those expectations, it was because he sought in the end to transform them. That goal is evident even in his op. 1.

MORTI DI EROI

The choice of C minor as a key that would play a central role in enunciating Beethoven's heroic stance was no surprise. It was virtually mandated by its traditional theatrical associations and reputation. These were well summed up by Francesco Galeazzi (1758–1819), an Italian violinist and composer who between 1791 and 1796 published an encyclopedic music treatise called *Elementi teorico-pratici di musica* (The Theoretical and Practical Elements of Music).

The key of C minor, Galeazzi wrote, was "the tragic key, suitable for expressing great misfortunes like the deaths of Heroes (*morti di Eroi*)."[15] Though Galeazzi was writing out of the tradition of Italian opera, his description of the key accords so tellingly with Beethoven's use of the key in his instrumental music that it almost seems to sum up Beethoven's achievement in transforming the instrumental genres of his day into virtual dramas.

Twice, in fact, Beethoven used the key to portray exactly the occasion for which Galeazzi proclaimed it best suited. One is already familiar: the end of the second movement of the *Eroica* Symphony, which is cast as a *Marcia funebre*, a Funeral March in C minor, literally marking the death of a Hero. An even more pointed and "literary" use of the key to symbolize heroic tragedy comes in the Overture Beethoven wrote in 1807 to *Coriolan*, a *Trauerspiel* or "mourning play" by the Austrian poet Heinrich Josef von Collin (1771–1811).

Though sometimes translated simply as "tragedy," the word *Trauerspiel* connotes (in the words of John Daverio, a cultural historian of German music) an unmitigated "display of human misery, wretchedness, and suffering."[16] It arose in the mid-seventeenth century as a typically fulsome manifestation of "baroque" theater, dealing, in the words of a contemporary observer, with "nothing but killings, despair, infanticide and patricide, conflagration, incest, war and commotion, lamentation, weeping, sighing, and suchlike."[17] Now there is a list of C-minor moods!

Collin's *Trauerspiel* concerned the fate of the Roman general Gnaeus Marcius Coriolanus as related by Plutarch. (Shakespeare's tragedy *Coriolanus* is a treatment of the same story.) He made his fame (and earned his name) by capturing the Volscian city of Corioli, but was then expelled from Rome for tyrannical acts. Joining with the Volscians, his former enemy, he avenged himself by attacking Rome, which he would have destroyed, but was dissuaded by the tears of his wife and his mother. For his fatal vacillation the Volscians condemned him to death by torture.

Beethoven's overture to this dismal play encapsulates its desperate emotional content, beginning with ponderous unison Cs and slashing chords that wed the blunt opening of Haydn's *Creation* Prologue to the restless harmony of Mozart's C-minor Concerto, K. 491 (Ex. 32-4a). A second theme offers major-mode relief, but comfort is short-lived; C minor, and with it the "C-minor mood," quickly reasserts itself (Ex. 32-4b). That second theme, however, offers a possible way to achieve C major in the recapitulation, and the promise seems briefly to be kept. The even quicker quashing of the major, however, where its retention and eventual exaltation might have been expected, epitomizes, more eloquently perhaps than any words could do, the hopelessness of the drama. The return of the violent opening gesture, the hollow unisons now reinforced with additional winds, seems virtually to portray the Hero's murder, and in the final coda, with its composed deceleration of the "first theme" music

EX. 32-4A   Ludwig van Beethoven, *Coriolan* Overture, mm. 1–21

EX. 32-4B   Ludwig van Beethoven, *Coriolan* Overture, mm. 52–75

EX. 32-4B (*continued*)

EX. 32-4C Ludwig van Beethoven, *Coriolan* Overture, end

from the exposition, we seem to witness the wasting of his energies and his anguished demise (Ex. 32-4c).

This is horror music. And the horror is conveyed as much by what does not happen, by what is deliberately withheld, as by anything that actually occurs. The trajectory from C minor to C major is cut off as palpably as the Hero's life. All the more powerfully, then, does the completed narrative sound forth in what has to be regarded as the *Coriolan* Overture's counterpart: Beethoven's Fifth Symphony, op. 67, the most famous symphony in the world.

Its status was confirmed, almost from the beginning, by E. T. A. Hoffmann, who cast his most extensive blast of romanticist propaganda in the form of an extended description of the Fifth. This famous essay of 1810 stands today as an early landmark of music analysis, a then wholly new form of writing about music, in which technical observations were linked up directly with expressive interpretations, in a manner that emphatically paralleled and positively reinforced the equally novel (and equally zealous) intentions of contemporary composers. Where composers proceeded from causes to effects, exegetical critics like Hoffmann endeavored to work back from the effect to uncover the cause.

In the case of Hoffmann himself, who was not only a musician but an outstanding literary figure as well, analysis (to paraphrase a famous remark by the musicologist

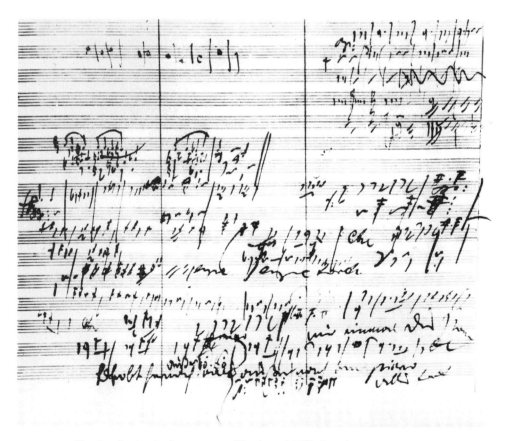

FIG. 32-1   Sketches for the third movement of Beethoven's Fifth Symphony.

Manfred Bukofzer) could fairly be described as "composition in reverse." It became the distinguishing feature of German instrumental music that it attracted this sort of exegetical interpretation. Alongside verbal interpretations like Hoffmann's (and later Robert Schumann's), there also arose the "interpretations" of master performers, including the first baton ("maestro") conductors. In this as in so many other ways, Beethoven's music was the preeminent catalyst, remaking the world of music in what we still recognize today as its modern image.

Hoffmann used the Fifth to demonstrate, on the "micro" level, the organic unity of the composition; and on the "macro" level, the expressive power to which that unity gave rise. Very significantly, if a little predictably, he finds Beethoven's truest forebear in Shakespeare, worshipped by German romantics as the greatest of all dramatists. It was a romantic mission to rescue Shakespeare from the low status to which he had been consigned by the dogmatic "neoclassical" critics of the French Enlightenment, who (basing themselves on Aristotle's authority) charged him with formlessness. Hoffmann's task, then, was to demonstrate the organic growth of tree from seed in order to certify Beethoven's supreme mastery, not only of compositional technique, but of transcendent expression as well. The two, Hoffmann strongly argued, were the two sides of a single coin, and the Fifth offered the ultimate proof:

> Can there be any work of Beethoven's that confirms all this to a higher degree than his indescribably profound, magnificent symphony in C minor? . . . No doubt the whole rushes like an ingenious rhapsody past many a man, but the soul of each thoughtful listener is assuredly stirred . . . . The internal structure of the movements, their execution, their instrumentation, the way in which they follow one another — everything contributes to a single end; above all, it is the intimate interrelationship among the themes that engenders that unity which alone has the power to hold the listener firmly in a single mood. This relationship is sometimes clear to the listener when he overhears it in the connecting of two movements or discovers it in the fundamental bass they have in common; a deeper relationship which does not reveal itself in this way speaks at other times only from mind to mind, and it is precisely this relationship that prevails between sections of the two Allegros and the Minuet and which imperiously proclaims the controlling force of the master's genius.[18]

In this remarkable paragraph Hoffmann has alluded both to the "micro" and the "macro" structures of the symphony and suggested both the ways in which the levels are mutually reinforcing or "synergistic," and the ways in which structural unity and powerful expression exhibit in Beethoven a comparable synergy. Indeed, there is synergy between composition and critique as well, for surely there is no work by Beethoven (or by any other composer) that so flaunts the derivation of the whole from a single "germinal seed," the four notes proclaimed at the very outset in the gruff unison so endemic to the C-minor mood.

GERMINATION AND GROWTH

This famous opening (Ex. 32-5a) has many points of congruence with the opening of the Trio, op. 1, no. 3 — the unison, the fermata, and the use of a brusque "announcement theme" to arrest the attention before the actual, structurally functioning "first theme" gets underway (m. 6). What is new and noteworthy in the Fifth is the way the first theme is related to the announcement theme. It is built up out of a multitude — a veritable mosaic — of motivic repetitions, all derived from the opening four-note group as if to demonstrate the process of germination. It is a theme that no one instrumental part ever gets to play in its entirety, as if to demonstrate the way in which the whole, as in any organism, transcends the mere sum of its parts.

And now notice that the four notes of the symphony's "germinal seed" are grouped in exactly the same rhythm — an upbeat of three short notes to a long downbeat note — as the much-repeated idea from which the first theme in the first movement

EX. 32-5A   Ludwig van Beethoven, Symphony no. 5 in C minor, Op. 67, mm. 1–24

EX. 32-5A   *(continued)*

EX. 32-5B   Ludwig van Beethoven, Symphony no. 5 in C minor, Op. 67, mm. 62–65 (strings only)

of the Trio, op. 1, no. 3, is built up (beginning in the piano part at m. 10), already referred to in the discussion of that piece as a distinctive "Beethoven rhythm" because of its pronounced forward thrust (see the end of Ex. 32-1a). That propulsive force, as Hoffmann noted, is virtually unremitting in the first movement of the Fifth, accounting for the "interrelationship among the themes that engenders that unity which alone has the power to hold the listener firmly in a single mood." It continues to sound, for example, in the cellos and basses while the other instruments turn their attention to the ostensibly contrasting "second theme" (Ex. 32-5b), and returns in full force to inform the codetta or closing theme at the end of the exposition, as Beethoven insists on our noticing with his unusual beaming of the eighth notes (Ex. 32-5c).

E X. 32-5C   Ludwig van Beethoven, Symphony no. 5 in C minor, Op. 67, mm. 109–21

EX. 32-5C   (continued)

Nor is that the only way in which the "germinal seed" makes its presence known. It recurs significantly in the other movements as well, extending "organic" unity over the entire four-movement span. One can hear it ticking like a time bomb in the second violins and violas at mm. 76–77 in the second (slow) movement (Ex. 32-6a), and

EX. 32-6A   Ludwig van Beethoven, Symphony no. 5 in C minor, Op. 67, II, mm. 76–77

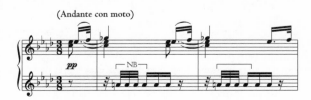

EX. 32-6B   Ludwig van Beethoven, Symphony no. 5 in C minor, Op. 67, II, mm. 88–96

EX. 32-6C   Ludwig van Beethoven, Symphony no. 5 in C minor, Op. 67, III, mm. 19–26

again in the cellos at mm. 88–96 (Ex. 32-6b). Transformed into a two-measure idea, it informs the main theme of the third movement (informally known as the scherzo although Beethoven did not so designate it) beginning at m. 19 (Ex. 32-6c), and comes back along with the theme itself during the famously enigmatic reprise of the scherzo theme in the finale.

But that is far from its only role in the finale. As shown in Ex. 32-7a, the germinal seed-rhythm is firmly embedded in the finale's jubilant main theme, and actually leads the theme to its highest point. More obviously, the germinal rhythm, now expressed in triplets, informs the finale's second theme as well (Ex. 32-7b). Even the codetta is implicitly informed by it, as evidenced by the threefold pitch repetitions on the upbeats (Ex. 32-7c).

Finally, expressed as a sort of hocket, the germinal seed-rhythm launches the headlong coda of the finale on its way (Ex. 32-8a) and then, at the Presto (m. 414, Ex. 32-8b) makes explicit (in the cellos and basses) what had formerly been the "implicit" derivation of the finale's codetta theme from the germinal seed (Ex. 32-8b).

It was the Austrian music theorist Heinrich Schenker (1868–1935) who first proposed that the original "germinal seed" be regarded as consisting not in the first four-note unison alone, but in both unison phrases, as shown in Ex. 32-9a. Only in this way, he argued, can the organic unity of the first movement be understood to the full. Indeed, when this conceptual adjustment is made, the horn call that serves as brisk transition to the second theme (Ex. 32-9b) stands revealed as the germinal theme's direct offspring (derived by expanding the thirds to fifths).

Even more significantly, the relationship (or, at least, a relationship) becomes clear between the mysteriously becalmed, harmonically outlandish retransition (Ex. 32-9c) and the music that it interrupts. The antiphonal pairs of half notes are a sequential extension of the "horn call" idea, and the further reduction to single chords hocketing between strings and winds can now be related, through the mediating horn call, to the germinal motif.

EX. 32-7A   Ludwig van Beethoven, Symphony no. 5 in C minor, Op. 67, IV, mm. 1–12, piccolo

EX. 32-7B   Ludwig van Beethoven, Symphony no. 5 in C minor, Op. 67, IV, mm. 45–48, first violins

EX. 32-7C   Ludwig van Beethoven, Symphony no. 5 in C minor, Op. 67, IV, mm. 64–70, violas

EX. 32-8A   Ludwig van Beethoven, Symphony no. 5 in C minor, Op. 67, IV, mm. 402–404

EX. 32-8B   Ludwig van Beethoven, Symphony no. 5, in C minor, Op. 67, IV, Presto, outer string parts

The so-called "new theme" in the coda (Ex. 32-10) has been another site of contention among critics. Some have touted it as a bold deviation from the overall "organic" plan, while others have argued that it is more readily understood as a rhythmic regrouping or reaccenting of the original four-note germinal motive: ˘˘˘ˉ instead of ˉ˘˘˘. On this point there has grown up a large literature of sharp, occasionally acrid, debate.

The point, from a historical vantage point, is not to adjudicate the dispute but to characterize it. It is a new sort of musical argument, in which the *meaning* of instrumental

EX. 32-9A Ludwig van Beethoven, Symphony no. 5, in C minor, Op. 67, I, opening unisons (mm. 1–5)

EX. 32-9B Ludwig van Beethoven, Symphony no. 5, in C minor, Op. 67, I, horn call (mm. 59–63)

EX. 32-9C Ludwig van Beethoven, Symphony no. 5, in C minor, Op. 67, I, mm. 195–231

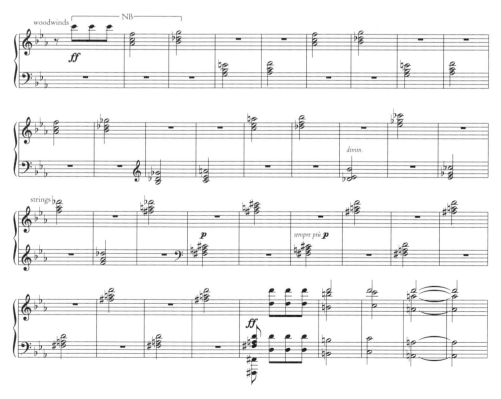

EX. 32-10   Ludwig van Beethoven, Symphony no. 5 in C minor, Op. 67, first movement coda

music is discussed in terms of its *structure*. The meaning has been internalized, and the job of the critic is not so much to judge the music as to understand it, or (more practically) to help listeners understand it by explicating it. That is what was meant, later, when German critics began talking about and touting the value of "absolute" music. It meant exactly what Hoffmann meant when he called Beethoven's instrumental music "romantic" — that is, capable of expressing what is otherwise inexpressible (and in particular, inexpressible in words). A later German composer, Richard Wagner (1813–83), defined absolute music as music that can convey "an unsayable content."[19] So it should never be imagined that "absolute" instrumental music contained or expressed nothing beyond its "organic" sound structure. The organic sound structure was the vehicle or gateway to a hitherto inaccessible realm of transcendent or ineffable meaning. The best possible illustration, as it happens, comes in the second movement of the Fifth, where as we have already observed, the germinal motive can be discerned at certain points, ticking away ("like a time bomb"). What sort of detonation does that ticking presage, and what does it mean?

The second movement of the Fifth, marked *Andante con moto*, is a broadly conceived, rather unusual set of variations on a theme — or to be more exact, a broadly conceived theme and two *doubles*, or embellished repetitions, with an extended coda — in the fairly unusual key of A♭ major, the submediant degree with respect to the original tonic scale. The reason for its selection will become apparent when we consider the structure of the theme and the thrice-repeated tonal trajectory that it embodies.

The opening eight-bar phrase (Ex. 32-11a), while it cadences quite normally, has a somewhat bizarre middle. The fourth bar, which might be expected to contain a caesura (a brief point of rest or articulation), instead sounds a note of unexpected tension — an

EX. 32-11A   Ludwig van Beethoven, Symphony no. 5 in C minor, Op. 67, II, mm. 1–8

E-natural, identified by the succeeding notes as the leading tone in an applied dominant (V of vi). The tension is quickly (and "normally") resolved in a circle of fifths, but the brief shock fixes the fourth measure's errant harmony in the mind: a C major triad. Beethoven acknowledges the force of the shock by compensating for it with a fivefold embellished and then foreshortened repetition of the perfect cadence in mm. 6–8, reverberations that do not die down completely until m. 22.

The two-bar phrase that begins with the upbeat to m. 23 (Ex. 32-11b) can be identified as an expansion of the three-note incipit, or opening motive, of the original theme. It is followed by a phrase (mm. 25–26 with pickup) that continues the same trajectory to the next tonic chord tone. But then once again the unexpected intervenes: yet another sequential continuation (mm. 26–27) moves not to another stable tone, but to a wildly unstable G♭, a chromatic tone that fundamentally threatens the identity of the tonic by turning it into the V of IV. Its instability is immediately reinforced

EX. 32-11B   Ludwig van Beethoven, Symphony no. 5 in C minor, Op. 67, II, mm. 23–31

EX. 32-11B (*continued*)

by another chromatic tone, the A-natural in the second violin and viola that forms a diminished seventh against the intruder. The diminished seventh harmony is then repeated in the kind of suspenseful stall familiar from the ones encountered in the *Eroica* Symphony in the previous chapter.

And now the denouement. In m. 30 the A-natural falls back to A♭, the G♭ is respelled F♯, and the resulting augmented sixth, reinforced by a sudden orchestral tutti, *fortissimo*, resolves the only way it can—to the same C major triad that had briefly intruded in the first phrase of the theme; but this time it is immediately confirmed by a brilliantly fulfilling—that is, tonicizing—cadence. The sense of breakthrough, achieved by a great effort, is shattering. *Durch Kampf nach Sieg!*

The reason for the unconventional choice of A♭ as the tonic for the second movement is now clear. It was chosen strategically, to enable this sudden, surprising (and elating) breakthrough to the key that will eventually discharge the violent C-minor mood of the first movement. It offers a foretaste of the outcome we have by now learned to associate with Beethoven's heroic narratives, the narratives that so decisively transformed the meaning of music for nineteenth-century audiences.

The horns, trumpets, and drums now exult in the brightness of the new key, blaring out in C major the same music that had been played *piano* and *dolce* (softly and sweetly) in mm. 22–26 by the clarinets and bassoons, and reminding us that—according to the same Galeazzi whose characterization of C minor so agreed with Beethoven's practice—the key of C major is *grandioso, militare*. The foretaste of victory lasts for six blazing bars (mm. 32–38). Achieved by rupture, however, and prematurely, it is impermanent. The strings insinuate a soft but decisive destabilizing harmony in m. 39—another diminished seventh chord that resolves through another drawn-out suspense passage, a tortuously chromatic vagary that lasts fully nine bars (mm. 39–48) until it arrives at the dominant of the A♭ and the first *double* can begin.

It is in the course of that *double* that the mysterious references to the germinal motive ("ticking like a time bomb") appear; and their appearances coincide exactly with the "suspense passages" that surround the second explosion of C major. Beethoven has contrived, in other words, to bring a reminder of the "C-minor mood" of the opening movement into direct conjunction with the foretaste of C-major victory. It is a moment fraught with multiple "introversive" resonances, as defined in chapter 29, resonances that connect both with what is past and with what still (potentially, or hopefully) lies ahead.

These are dramatists' devices. Beethoven was not the first composer to apply them to instrumental music. We have observed similar gestures in the symphonies of Mozart and (particularly) Haydn. But by using them so much more pervasively than his predecessors, and so intensifying their effect, Beethoven seemed, to Hoffmann and his contemporaries, to have ushered in a new musical era—the era that Hoffmann so influentially dubbed romantic. Of paramount significance is the fact, emphasized by the prophetically discerning Hoffmann, that the technical achievement (organically unified form) and the expressive or dramaturgical achievement (creating a meaningfully related sequence of musically represented moods that plays overwhelmingly upon the listener's nerves) are one and the same achievement, variously described.

To return to the narrative: the premature thrusts toward the light in the second movement are effectively (though not hopelessly) canceled by the coda, in which the augmented sixth chord that had so stunningly rerouted the harmony toward C major in the variations is neutralized by the soothing bassoon solo. The F♯ is respelled (or re-respelled) G♭, the chord is re-resolved as a V of IV, and the local tonic A♭, a weak secondary function with respect to the symphony's once and future tonics, is temporarily reconfirmed. The trajectory of struggle and victory has its vacillations, its setbacks.

The scherzo, consequently, is dark — another C-minor mood, replete with a unison "announcing theme" and fermatas. The darkness is expressed both in the tone color (muttering cellos and basses, *pianissimo*) and in the harmony: the jarring cross-relation between the outer voices as the second fermata is approached. Amazingly enough in view of its seeming originality, this very spot (mm. 16–20) in Beethoven's scherzo virtually reproduces a five-bar sequence from the last movement of Stamitz's Orchestra Trio in C minor (op. 4, no. 3), one of the early symphonies investigated in chapter 29. The two little passages, which encompass not only the unusual cadence with a false relation but also the beginning of a contrasting idea, are laid out for comparison in Ex. 32-12.

Was it an old memory from Beethoven's Bonn years, treacherously disguised as imagination, that resurfaced here in the form of an unwitting quotation from Stamitz, his grandfather's counterpart at Mannheim? Or was it a deliberate "extroversive" allusion, the point of which we no longer get? Beethoven's music, as we have already learned in our brief consideration of the Ninth Symphony (in the previous chapter), teems with riddles like these, as does most romantic symphonic music composed in its wake. The Fifth Symphony, perhaps even more than the Ninth, was a landmark of "coded utterance" — the use of obvious but tantalizingly unexplained signaling, both introversive and extroversive — in instrumental music. And the enigmatic complex comprising the symphony's scherzo and finale is what chiefly made it so.

As Hoffmann has already alerted us, and as the most cursory glance at the score reveals, the two movements are joined like Siamese twins, their joining furnishing the means for not merely the juxtaposition of C minor and C major, but the direct transformation of the one into the other, through which the symphony's "overarching single gesture" is consummated at last. The point is made with suitable drama — a lengthy dominant pedal to gather and focus tension, by way of *molto crescendo* and tremolos, not to mention the contrast between the nattering, muttering dissolve with which the scherzo comes to its inconclusive end, *pianissimo*, and the dazzling brassy blast that launches the finale on its triumphant course.

For early audiences, that blast was magnified far beyond its present power to shock by the unexpected sound of trombones in their symphonic debut. (Up to now we have encountered them only in church and in the opera pit, where they were employed for their religious — or, in Gluck's *Orfeo* and Mozart's *Don Giovanni*, their infernal — associations.) In the finale of the Fifth, they are accompanied by the contrabassoon and piccolo, both used until that very moment solely in military bands. Thus the "grand military" affect associated with C major by Galeazzi is once again invoked and quite literally reinforced. Unlike the *Eroica*, however, the Fifth is not generally thought to carry explicitly military associations. It is generally agreed that its military affect is metaphorical, symbolizing a triumph that is experienced (whether externally, with respect to the composer, or internally, by a sympathetically identifying listener) as personal.

But that is not the full extent of the interrelationship of scherzo and finale. It is no such simple contrast. There is also the reprise of the scherzo within the finale, at

EX. 32-12A   Carl Stamitz, Trio, Op. 4, no. 3, IV, mm. 141–164

EX. 32-12B   Ludwig van Beethoven, Symphony no. 5, in C minor, Op. 67, III, mm. 1–20

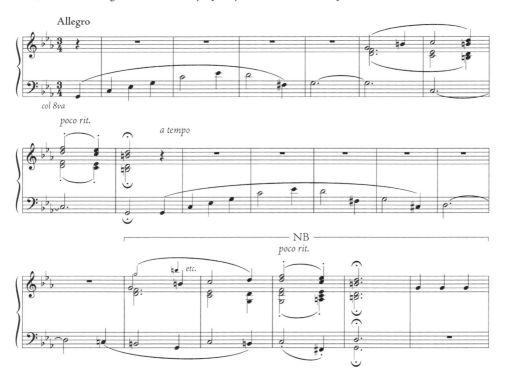

a point that could not be more disruptive: during the retransition, right before the recapitulation, where it seems to reintroduce C minor, most unwelcomely, right as the dominant is about to resolve for the last time to the tonic major. In a larger sense, of course, the scherzo reprise serves a strategic purpose, prolonging as it does the suspense of "dominant tension," and enabling a replay of the transitional passage so as to launch the recapitulation with a blast comparable to the one that had launched the exposition. Triumph, it could be argued, is not compromised but actually enhanced by the overcoming of one last setback.

But that is only one possible argument, one possible rough verbal paraphrase of a specifically musical reality. We have here one of the very earliest instances of the sort of situation, at once fascinating and frustrating, that became increasingly the norm in the symphonic music of the nineteenth century — music that at once demands and thwarts paraphrase. As the pianist and critic Charles Rosen has characterized it, the dilemma is that for music in the post-Beethoven tradition, "metaphorical description is called for, and even necessary," but "none will be satisfactory or definitive."[20]

The dilemma, of course, is ours, not music's. From the quintessentially romantic situation Rosen describes, music comes out the winner — as a medium transcending paraphrase and metaphor, and hence privy to a mode of expression that transcends what is fully expressible with blunt, all-too-human instruments like language and logic. Music all at once became a matter of intense interest (and envy) not only for artists in all media, but for philosophers as well. Different romantic philosophers have had different ways of getting at musical transcendence, though all agreed that it left phenomenal reality (that is, what can be apprehended through the senses alone) far behind and seemed to approach what Kant (following Plato) called the noumenal: the irreducible, ineffable essence of things, the reality that lay behind all appearance. Where other arts could only describe or reproduce appearances, music had access to the thing itself.

Beethoven, possibly reacting to Hoffmann's critiques, had put it this way to a friend (who immediately quoted it in a letter to Goethe) as early as 1810: "I despise the world which does not intuitively feel that music is a higher revelation than all wisdom and philosophy."[21] "Intuitively feel" rather than "understand," because such knowledge can come only as revelation. Like religious faith, it is inaccessible and impervious to sense or reason. As the philosopher Arthur Schopenhauer (1788–1860) would later put it, where the other arts were confined to *representing* the world, music could actually *present* the underlying reality, or what Schopenhauer called the Will.

And, as Schopenhauer insisted, it did so in ways that even a composer could not fully explain. "The composer," Schopenhauer wrote, "reveals the inner nature of the world and expresses the deepest wisdom in a language which his reason does not understand."[22] Beethoven was the first composer to be self-consciously aware of this great romantic truth and to act on that awareness.

LETTING GO

Schopenhauer was the most radically romantic thinker in Germany during the last decade of Beethoven's life. Like Beethoven a lonely man, he evolved an influential philosophy of pessimism. As manifested in the strivings of individuals, he taught, the Will produces inevitable strife and frustration, dooming all inhabitants of the world to a life of unsatisfied cravings and spiritual pain. Ultimately the only way out was renunciation of desire, implying transcendence of the individual will — an idea for which Schopenhauer was indebted to Buddhist teachings, making him one of the earliest European bridge-builders to Asian culture. Short of full renunciation, some temporary assuagement of worldly pain can be found in philosophy and art — particularly in music, whose inherent faculty of transcendence could model, and perhaps even induce, the spiritual quiescence at which Schopenhauer's philosophy aimed.

These ideas, which found their first expression in *The World as Will and Representation*, a treatise that Schopenhauer published in 1818 at the age of thirty, would seem likely to appeal powerfully to a spirit as thwarted and tortured as Beethoven. We have no direct evidence of Beethoven's contact with Schopenhauer's philosophy or its "Eastern" antecedents, only the tenuous circumstance that intellectual Vienna was talking about it. But there is at least one late work of Beethoven's that seems to prefigure a Schopenhauerian *Weltanschauung*, or outlook on life, and that is the last of his piano sonatas, No. 32 in C minor, op. 111, composed in 1821–22 and consisting of two large movements: one in the titular key of C minor, and the other in C major.

We have seen Haydn's primal dark/light opposition of C minor and C major played out by now in several very different Beethovenian narratives. In op. 1, no. 3, the major came gently, as relaxation or solace. In the Fifth Symphony it came spectacularly, as victory, symbolized by the finale's fifty-four-bar coda, consisting of nothing but manically reiterated tonic cadences and triads (one of the most fanatically adored and, in consequence, fiercely lampooned pages in all of symphonic music). In the *Coriolan* Overture it never came at all, betokening in its withholding the tragic outcome of the drama.

Now, in op. 111, C major assumes a luminous (or, in the quasi-sacred terms Beethoven probably intended, a numinous) aura. It serves as the medium for metaphysical disclosure, conjuring an oceanic vista in which the desiring subject can finally lose itself. The late-Beethovenian religious impulse, already observed in the previous chapter, that found expression not only in sacred compositions like the *Missa solemnis* but in secular ones as well (the Ninth Symphony; the Quartet in A minor, op. 132, with its "Heiliger Dankgesang"), here reaches an early pinnacle.

That religiosity, betokening a turning-away from the world and its vicissitudes, found its most conspicuous (or most conspicuously *musical*) outlet in Beethoven's sudden infatuation with the fugue. By the end of the eighteenth century, fugal writing was a decidedly archaic device that had only one surviving application in a living genre: the Mass or oratorio chorus. Before 1815, that was where Beethoven had used it, with a single well-known exception: the finale of his Quartet in C major, op. 59, no. 3 (the last of the "Razumovsky" set, composed in 1806), in which the fugal technique, applied to a rollicking subject, set up a tour de force of performance virtuosity. Thanks to the fugal organization, listeners knew in advance that the cello was going to have to play at a tempo that was already taxing enough for the violins. This kind of whimsical fugalism was of a piece with the kind found occasionally in the quartets of Haydn (op. 20) and Mozart (K. 387).

From 1814–15, however, there was a big change; and it is impossible not to suspect a connection between the change in Beethoven and the political changes that took place over that momentous year of post-Napoleonic Restoration. As noted in the previous chapter, Beethoven contributed an oratorio, *Der glorreiche Augenblick* ("The glorious moment"), to the festivities that greeted the reactionary Congress of Vienna.

The offering ended with a grandiose and sentimental finale in which the chorus, divided into separate groups of *Frauen* (sopranos and altos) and *Männer* (tenors and basses), is joined by a choir of *Kinder* (child sopranos and altos of both genders). The three groups first step forward one by one to pay a quasi-religious tribute to the assembled crowned heads of Europe:

Frauen:	Es treten hervor	Now we step forward,
	die Schaaren der Frauen,	the host of women,
	den glänzenden Chor	to behold the shining
	der Fürsten zu schauen,	throng of princes,
	auf alle die Kronen	and to lay a holy
	den heiligen Segen	mothers' benediction
	der Mütter zu legen.	on all the crowned heads.
Kinder:	Die Unschuld als Chor,	Innocence itself
	sie wagt es zu kommen,	now ventures to come forth
	es treten hervor	in a choir of children, all
	die Kinder, die frommen,	righteous and meek, to bind
	Herz, Himmel und Scepter	heart, heaven, and scepter
	mit Blumengewinden	together with
	zusammen zu binden.	garlands of flowers.

FIG. 32-2 Masked ball in the Redoutensaal (Vienna) celebrating the Congress of Vienna, following performances of Beethoven's Seventh Symphony and *Wellington's Victory*, or "Battle" Symphony.

Männer: Auch wir treten vor,   We, too, come forth,
                 die Mannen der Heere,   we men of battle,
                 ein Kriegrischer Chor   in martial chorus
                 mit Fahnen und Wehre,   with arms and colors flying
                 und fühlen die höchste   and feeling the highest
                 der Vaterland's-wonnen   delight in our Fatherland,
                 sich also zu sonnen.   thus we bask in its glory.

All then come together in a rousing choral fugue (Ex. 32-13) that invokes Vienna by its ancient Latin name: "Vindobona, may you prosper! World, your great moment is at hand!"

The poetry is doggerel. The music, hurriedly composed, is undistinguished. Overall, *Der glorreiche Augenblick* (no doubt owing in part to its political message, so offensive to

EX. 32-13   Ludwig van Beethoven, *Der glorreiche Augenblick*, final Presto, beginning of fugal exposition

modern liberalism) is commonly regarded as Beethoven's closest approach to drivel. And yet despite its occasional nature, its repugnant sentiments, and its artistic insignificance, the work may hold a key to some of Beethoven's most sublime utterances — provided we remember what the adjective "sublime" properly connotes.

The Latin epithet ("Vindobona!") and the choral fugue had a similar import. Both were archaic references that invoked antiquity — that is, long-lastingness, which is ultimately to imply the timeless or eternally valid. That, of course, was precisely the political import of the Congress of Vienna: the purported reinstatement of ancient, divinely ordained, and timeless principles of social order in place of novel principles arrogantly conceived by the rational mind of man and still more impudently instituted on earth by the likes of Napoleon. It was a fierce reactionary rebuke to the Enlightenment, and so was much of romanticism.

In place of the optimistic, melioristic Enlightened vision, lately come to grief, political and philosophical romanticism offered a sentence of stasis, terrible or comforting depending on one's point of view. The world has been created for all time by God. It cannot be improved (said political romanticists), only at best secured. It cannot be improved (said philosophical romanticists), only at best escaped. Both safeguard and escape signal acceptance of the status quo, or at the very least, resignation to it.

Perhaps the best way of viewing Beethoven's post-1815 fugal frenzy, then, would be to regard it as having been induced or inspired by political romanticism, to which Beethoven is known to have responded with pessimistic gusto. In conversation with Ferdinand Hiller shortly before his death, he mocked the great watchword of political reform: *Vox populi, vox Dei*, "The voice of the people is the voice of God." (It is attributed to Charlemagne's adviser Alcuin, long familiar to readers of this book.) "I never believed it," Beethoven scoffed.[23] It was a disclaimer many disillusioned or nervous former champions of democracy were making. At the same time Beethoven declared Handel, the supreme master of the political fugue, to have been the greatest of all composers.

The resigned, disappointed public temper of post-Napoleonic Europe, with its hankering after the security of a timeless social order, found a private echo in the context of Beethoven's instrumental music. Fugues began turning up in bizarre profusion — and in the strangest places. What, for instance, could be an unlikelier place for a fugue than the finale of a cello sonata? And yet that is how Beethoven's fifth cello sonata (in D major, op. 102, no. 2) ends. It was composed in 1815, almost immediately after *Der glorreiche Augenblick* was first performed (Ex. 32-14a).

It was the first of many. The next year, 1816, Beethoven wrote a fugal finale for the Piano Sonata in A major, op. 101 (Ex. 32-14b). In 1818 there followed a truly colossal fugue, the one that caps the "Hammerklavier" Sonata, op. 106 (Ex. 32-14c). In between, perhaps most tellingly of all, came 1817, Beethoven's most barren year, in which he managed to complete only one work, and an insignificant one at that. And yet that one completed composition was still and all a small fugue (for string quintet, published posthumously as opus 137). All through this period Beethoven sketched as well at other, uncompleted, fugues. Example 32-14 gives the subject and answer from the expositions of the three main "finale fugues" of the period.

EX. 32-14A   Ludwig van Beethoven, late fugue subjects, Cello Sonata in D, Op. 102, no. 2 (Finale)

EX. 32-14B   Ludwig van Beethoven, late fugue subjects, Piano Sonata in A, Op. 101 (Finale)

EX. 32-14C   Ludwig van Beethoven, late fugue subjects, "Hammerklavier" Sonata in B-flat, Op. 106 (Finale)

Later there would be fugues in the Piano Sonata in A♭ (op. 110, 1822), the *Diabelli Variations* (op. 120, 1819–23), and the very Handelian *Consecration of the House* Overture (op. 124, 1822), as well as in two quartets: the C# minor, op. 131 (first movement), and the B♭ major, op. 130 (finale, later published separately as the *Grosse Fuge*, op. 133). Nor do even these exhaust the list.

The idea of incorporating fugues into sonatas is in some ways an incongruous one. To put it very bluntly, a fugue is a one-idea piece while a sonata is a two-idea piece. Consisting as it does of a single subject viewed as it were from all sides, a fugue is contemplative and, when sufficiently big, monumental. Consisting as it does of a tonal and (usually) thematic polarity worked through to a reconciliation, a sonata is dialectical and, when sufficiently big, dramatic. So different do the genres appear in their implications that in 1913 an influential German scholar named August Halm published a book, *Von zwei Kulturen der Musik* ("On the two cultures of music"), that tried to cast the entire history of music in terms of their opposition.

Before Beethoven's late period, no one had really tried to reconcile the two genres, or use them in genuine tandem. When Haydn or Mozart wrote "fugal" sonata movements (or when Beethoven himself did it up to the quartets of op. 59), all that it usually meant was casting the first theme in the form of a fugal exposition, and then recapitulating it with a new countersubject, often ingeniously derived from another theme. Alternatively, it could mean casting the development section, or part of it, in the form of a *fugato*. "Real" thoroughgoing fugues were simply (and rightly) thought impossible to reconcile with the dynamics of sonata form.

Partly it is a matter of the structure of the theme itself. As we have long known, but as the subjects in Ex. 32-14 (especially the immense one from the "Hammerklavier" sonata) will remind us, a typical fugue theme has a well-etched beginning but a very hazy ending. Fuguelike themes typically recede into an evenly flowing "time-river." Resisting dynamism, they cannot be brought to climax except by patently artificial means — mounting sequences, inflated dynamics, tacked-on codas, or the like.

It is not surprising, then, that Beethoven's late fugal preoccupation focused at first on finales, where the fugue could stand in for the traditional rondo — a form that was, like the fugue itself, monothematic in content and episodic in form. The periodic fugal expositions provided an easily comprehended analogy for the recurring rondo theme. No conceptual damage was done. But when the fugue form takes over the first-movement function, as it does in the Quartet in C♯ minor, op. 131, we can really sense an invasion of rhythmic and tonal quiescence, pessimistically usurping the place of a dynamic process that had formerly homed strategically (and optimistically) in on a dramatically satisfying closure.

The greatest "conceptual damage" done by fugue to sonata in late Beethoven occurs in the first movement of the Piano Sonata in C minor, op. 111, which is unequivocally in sonata form and not overly burdened, except in the development section, with imitative counterpoint. It is therefore, strictly speaking, not a fugue at all. But in some very telling ways it behaves like one, and by doing so signals the fundamental changes that have taken place in Beethoven's whole musical (and cultural, and political, and social) outlook.

The sonata begins with a slow introduction (*maestoso*) that almost seems an intensified replay of the famous slow introduction to another C minor sonata (op. 13, subtitled "Pathétique") composed almost a quarter of a century earlier (see Ex. 32-15). Both introductions feature dramatic diminished-seventh harmonies directed at the dominant and tonic in turn. The later sonata — by dispensing with the preliminary tonic, by resolving the second diminished seventh not to the tonic but to a strained "V of iv," by spacing the harmonies so that they seem to cover the length and breadth of the keyboard, and by piling on additional diminished-seventh chords in bewildering profusion — boosts the pathos level beyond anything Beethoven (or any composer) would have imagined or dared in 1797.

The exaggerated pathos, as we will discover, is a dramatic foil. Meanwhile, the main body of the movement, the *Allegro con brio ed appassionato*, establishes itself (Ex. 32-16a) with a cluster of signs we have long associated with "C-minor moods": unison writing, fermata (m. 20), a melodic diminished seventh (m. 21, preceded by an even more dissonantly "C-minorish" diminished fourth in m. 20). But the theme behaves like no sonata theme we have yet encountered. The unison writing goes on at extravagant length (more than ten measures, from m. 18 to m. 28), and the phrase that descends a diminished fifth (first heard in mm. 21–22) is on two further appearances (mm. 22–23, 30–31) marked *portato* (separated by dots within a slur, normally a bowing indication for strings) and *poco ritenente*, "holding back slightly," to emphasize its doleful, "cast down" effect.

The headlong dash so typical of Beethoven's sonata expositions is being deliberately frustrated, not only by the *poco ritenente*, but also by the theme itself, which is so obviously structured like a fugue subject. Instead of driving forward, it peters out into a time-river of steady sixteenth notes. And yet the expected fugal answer, normally

EX. 32-15A   Ludwig van Beethoven, Piano Sonata no. 8, Op. 13 ("Pathétique"), beginning of the slow introduction

EX. 32-15B   Ludwig van Beethoven, Piano Sonata no. 32, Op. 111, beginning of slow introduction

prepared by the rhythmic dissolution of the subject, never materializes. The whole movement is one unconsummated gesture after another. It never manages to define itself either as a fugue or as a sonata. Forever frustrated in its immediate purposes, it is forever in search of a way out, symbolized here (as in the Ninth Symphony) by a brief second theme (m. 50 ff) in the "Elysian" key of the submediant. Here, as everywhere, cadences are highly attenuated: the only complete A♭-major triads in the section of the piece nominally in that key are placed in weak metrical positions, and in unstable inversions to boot. The cadence in the secondary key (m. 69) is made only at the end of another fuguelike time-river passage *all'unisono*.

The development, exceedingly brief or even stunted, begins with a number of gambits that go nowhere: first, a sort of *passus duriusculus* formed by repeating the diminished fourth from the first theme in a chromatic descending sequence; next, a passage that before petering out in yet another time-river negotiates the circle of fifths with a series of imitative, quasi-fugal entries on a countersubject to the same theme, now stretched to encompass a diminished seventh instead of a diminished fourth; finally, another go around a circle of fifths by way of retransition, each stage of its progress stabbed out with a diminished-seventh chord, *sforzando*. Of all Beethoven compositions, this one must be the most saturated with diminished-seventh harmonies, making it the most pungently and pervasively dissonant movement Beethoven (or anyone since Bach, who had very different reasons) had ever composed.

And suddenly (m. 92) the struggle leaves off. The recapitulation repeats all the same futile gestures previously assayed in the exposition. As in the *Coriolan* Overture, the parallel major takes the place of the secondary key (mm. 116 ff), providing a brief ray of light or hope, but one that is dispelled even more quickly than in the Overture,

EX. 32-16A   Ludwig van Beethoven, Piano Sonata no. 32 in C minor, Op. 111, I, mm. 17 – 31

EX. 32-16A   (*continued*)

EX. 32-16B   Ludwig van Beethoven, Piano Sonata no. 32 in C minor, Op. 111, I, mm. 146–end

and with the same dispiritingly "tragic" effect. Finally, as in the Trio, op. 1, no. 3, C major returns (Ex. 32-16b) in conjunction with a concluding diminuendo to end the movement, somewhat unexpectedly, on a note of alleviation or relief.

Or escape. In the Sonata, unlike the Trio, the strangely abrupt mood of serenity into which the music is suddenly allowed to relax does not end the composition. It is, rather, picked up and sustained throughout the movement that follows. More than twice the length of the first, the second movement of op. 111 is a set of variations on a pristine binary theme (Ex. 32-17a); but it carries a significant subtitle, *Arietta*, a simple song or hymn. Like the Cavatina in the Quartet in B♭, op. 130 (Ex. 31-10), or the Song of Thanksgiving in the Quartet in A minor, op. 132 (see Ex. 31-12), the movement conveys the impression of an especially immediate and personal utterance, even if the nonsustaining piano tone cannot impersonate a human voice as naturally as strings.

EX. 32-17A   Ludwig van Beethoven, Piano Sonata no. 32 in C minor, Op. 111, II, *Arietta* (mm. 1–18)

It is also one of the slowest and "raptest" pieces Beethoven ever wrote, despite the seemingly paradoxical use of tiny note values. At times the music practically reaches a point of stasis or suspended motion, as if Beethoven were putting into practice the advice he gave an aspiring composer, one Xaver Schneider, in a letter of 1812: "Continue to raise yourself higher and higher into the divine realm of art; for there is no more undisturbed, more unalloyed or purer pleasure than that which comes from such an experience."[24]

Just so, we can almost hear Beethoven taking imaginative leave of the world, retreating—or, as he would no doubt have preferred to put it, ascending—into the higher realm of art, where quiet ecstasy abides. (And now recall all the depressingly reiterated melodic descents in the first movement to which the lofty ascent of the Arietta is an answer.) To paraphrase a famous remark of Friedrich Schiller, the poet of the Ninth Symphony's "Ode to Joy," the movement stands as an "effigy of the ideal," perhaps the most literal embodiment Beethoven ever gave to the "longing for the infinite" that E. T. A. Hoffmann identified as the romantic essence of his art.

The attempt to adumbrate the infinite can be viewed in many dimensions. The most puzzling aspect of the movement, its notation, seems to be an effort to overwhelm the player or reader of the score with what Kant called the "mathematical sublime"—awesome, ungraspable profusion, as preeminently represented for Kant (in a passage Beethoven copied out and underscored) by "the starry sky above." Notating the op. III variations in miniaturized $\frac{9}{16}$ time, with the beat falling on the dotted eighth, gives the page a similarly uncanny, immeasurably proliferous look. By the time the third or fourth variation is reached, the beat has been progressively divided into sixteenths, thirty-seconds, and sixty-fourths. Finally, triplets of thirty-seconds turn every beat into a miniaturized ($\frac{9}{32}$) version of the full measure (Ex. 32-17b). Single measures stretch across whole systems in the score and one is faced, so to speak, with as many notes as there are stars in the sky.

Nor is this the only way in which Beethoven tries to represent what is normally measured in music as immeasurable. The next stage of rhythmic diminution, finally reached after a little cadenza into which the fourth variation dissolves, is the unmeasured trill—a kind of aural vanishing point, in which all sense of countable time is lost (Ex. 32-17c). The most arresting effect comes in mm. 112–114, a triple trill (almost impossible—that is, *infinitely* hard—to perform) that lasts for seven beats, during which time seems to come literally to a halt despite the repeated notes in the bass.

This symbol of infinite duration or boundless time returns in m. 160 to accompany the last, exalted statement of the theme in its original note values, bringing things full circle—or rather, full spiral, since the trills unmistakably signal a higher, transfigured mode of existence (Ex. 32-17d). As the latest, greatest philosophical romanticist, Friedrich Nietzsche (1844–1900), later put it of the similarly indefinite *tremolando* rhythms at the beginning of the Ninth Symphony, to listen is to feel oneself "floating above the earth in an astral dome, with the dream of immortality in one's heart."[25] The trills serve another purpose as well, and one that is equally sublime. The ones in Ex. 32-17c introduce the only modulation ever to intrude, in this movement, upon the limpid C-major tonality of the whole. The triple trill takes place on a harmony that can only be interpreted as the dominant of E♭ major; and, after a virtual eternity of trilling, chromatically (and timelessly) ascending into the musical ether, the tonic of that key finally materializes in m. 118, somewhat weakly but nevertheless definitely expressed (in first inversion), and confirmed by an allusion to the second phrase of the original melody.

By analyzing a number of late works (along, in some cases, with their sketches), the pianist and Beethoven scholar William Kinderman identified the combination of high pitch and a modulation to E♭ as Beethoven's "symbol for the Deity," directly related to (or inspired by) Kant's invocation of the starry sky.[26] That is a private meaning and an arcane one, deducible not from listening but only by dint of scholarly inquiry. What is available to every listener, though, and overwhelming in its effect, is the virtually fathomless distance that separates the pianist's hands at this point: almost five octaves where E♭ is first invoked, and almost five and one-half octaves on the next downbeat, where the right hand's melodic arc reaches its zenith. That is yet another

EX. 32-17B   Ludwig van Beethoven, Piano Sonata no. 32 in C minor, Op. 111, II, mm. 72–80

EX. 32-17C   Ludwig van Beethoven, Piano Sonata no. 32 in C minor, Op. 111, II, mm. 106–20

kind of musical infinity. It conjures up another sort of boundlessness — not of time but of space.

It is also a recollection of the first movement — or rather, a reference to what in retrospect now stands revealed as a forecast in the first movement of the second movement's oceanic vista. In mm. 48–49 of the first movement, and again in mm. 114–115 (see Ex. 32-18), the pianist's right hand is required to traverse the whole breadth of the keyboard in great arcs, approaching and then exceeding five octaves in expanse. These sublime moments introduce the second theme in the exposition and the recapitulation respectively. The latter, actually the biggest registral leap in the entire sonata, takes place immediately before the one brief foretaste in the first movement of C major — the tonality that, in the second movement, will finally supplant its agonized C-minor contortions with a transcendent, rapturous stillness.

EX. 32-17D   Ludwig van Beethoven, Piano Sonata no. 32 in C minor, Op. 111, II, mm. 160–69

EX. 32-18   Ludwig van Beethoven, Piano Sonata no. 32 in C minor, Op. 111, I, mm. 48–49, 114–116

With its extremes of rapidity and stillness, its ability to make rapidity seem to merge with stillness, and its uncanny quality of hovering (most spectacularly in Ex. 32-19, mm. 89–92), the second movement of op. 111 was one of many romantic attempts — and perhaps the first fully conscious and considered one — to render the infinite palpable through music. If Hoffmann was right to insist that romanticism was music's natural birthright, it would have happened anyway without Beethoven; we will never know.

EX. 32-19   Ludwig van Beethoven, Piano Sonata no. 32 in C minor, Op. 111, II, mm. 89–92

THE MUSIC CENTURY

But of course there was a Beethoven. And, owing in some large measure to that fact and to the enormous force of his example, the nineteenth century, especially in the

FIG. 32-3 House of the music publishing firm of Nikolaus Simrock (Bonn), which issued the first editions of many of Beethoven's compositions.

German-speaking lands but not only there, was preeminently the music century. It was the century in which music embodied visionary philosophy, provided its audience with a medium in which they could live vicarious emotional lives, and became the object of emulation for all the other arts. It was the century in which composers could become culture heroes and political activists, could become champions of whole nations, could even define nationhood in new and powerful ways.

And that is because it was the century in which the audience for art music increased a hundredfold. As Arnold Hauser, the great social historian of art, would emphasize, from now on the middle class, not the aristocracy, would become the chief consumer of music, and music would become the favorite art of the middle class, "the form in which it could express its emotional life more directly and with less hindrance than in any other."[27] The vastly increasing size and importance of the middle-class public gave rise to a whole new class of public spokesmen and public educators for music. Thus the nineteenth century was also the century in which modern music journalism, music criticism, music scholarship, and music historiography were born. It was the century in which instrumental design and concert-hall construction rose to the challenge of the new mass audience with an unprecedented burst of technological advancement, when parlor pianos became standard middle-class furniture and had to be mass-produced to meet the demand, and when music publishing, benefiting from the industrial revolution, ballooned into a big business. The nineteenth century was the first great century of musical commerce and publicity.

It was also the century in which institutions of standardized professional instruction in music flourished, thanks to the public conservatory system that had originated in revolutionary France and had been exported as a by-product of Napoleon's conquests. It found its most fertile soil in Germany, whence it spread to outlying regions like Russia and the United States, colonizing them in the name of the newly emancipated art of music. The nineteenth century was the great century of music education. Many of the important composers of the century — Felix Mendelssohn in Germany, Anton Rubinstein in Russia, Luigi Cherubini in France — became conservatory professors, training their pupils in an increasingly rigorous and standard academic discipline of composition. (What we now call "sonata form," for example, was first described as such by Anton Reicha, a transplanted Bohemian composer, in a classroom textbook devised for the Paris Conservatory and published in 1824.) Yet just as many important composers — Robert Schumann in Germany, Hector Berlioz in France, the lesser known Alexander Serov and César Cui in Russia (just coming into its own as a music-consuming power) — went into public journalism rather than professional instruction. Criticism was an activity made both possible and necessary by the commercial and industrial explosion and its attendant publicity machine, but its practitioners, romantics all, adopted a distinctly "contrarian" position with respect to the institutions that sustained them, leading to a widening rift between the mass audience and the composers it idolized and supported.

Schumann's activity expressed the contradiction best. For his journalistic purposes, undertaken in response to the growth of public appetite for art, he invented a fictional mouthpiece called the "League of David" (*Davidsbund*), a band of idealistic musicians (all based on aspects of Schumann's own personality) that did battle on the one hand with that very public, now branded the "Philistines," and on the other hand against the "industrialized" routines of academic training, which fostered stylistic uniformity and conservatism.

In seeming paradox, the nineteenth century, the century of burgeoning commerce, technology, industry, and mass education, was also the century in which composers cultivated introspection to the point of near incomprehensibility, defied and rejected their preceptors and predecessors, asserted the claim that they were more important than their patrons and audiences, and (in a pair of closely related, quintessentially romantic terms) purported to *emancipate* themselves and their art, and to render both their art and themselves *autonomous*. It was thus the great century of artistic individualism.

The paradox, however, was only on the surface, for individualism and self-expression was also a prime middle-class virtue or ideal. In seeming to oppose their public, musicians were actually imitating it, for emancipation — political, social, economic — was their common goal. Both the composers and their listeners idealized the "self-made man." Thus the "autonomous" musical work, the work of an "emancipated" creator, although touted as the work of world-transcending, "disinterested" (and therefore apolitical) genius, was equally a potent political symbol.

As Hauser pointed out, as composers were emancipated from the service class (or, as one could also put it, as composers were cut adrift from the secure social structures that had formerly supported them), and their music was no longer written to specific order but created "on spec" (that is, in the expectation of a demand that had to be created), they came to despise the idea of composing as an "official" activity of any kind — which of course does not at all mean that they stopped doing such work, only that (to adopt Hauser's Marxist vocabulary for a moment) they became "alienated" from the utilitarian aspects of their work. Hauser diagnoses this as a "conflict of conscience and a crisis where in earlier times no antithesis of any kind had been suspected to exist."[28] We have already seen how Beethoven's forced social alienation (by reason of his deafness) contributed to his prestige. His handicap was read in retrospect as emancipation — as was Mozart's falling out with his employer, the Archbishop of Salzburg. At the time both were experienced as catastrophes; in legend both were transformed into salvation.

These legends were the product and the vehicle of canonization — turning Mozart and Beethoven, with Haydn, into timeless preceptors of art as the standard concert repertory took shape around their works (first, as we have seen, in England, the great commercial empire, but soon thereafter in Germany). All of these nineteenth-century expansions and developments, all these claims and counterclaims, however difficult to reconcile, could find precedent and validation in Mozart and (especially) Beethoven, and therefore no longer needed reconciling.

Thus Beethoven became the authoritative — at times, even, the authoritarian — symbol of the age, the one who in the words of one self-appointed disciple, Richard Wagner, had shown "the only possible way" for music to develop further.[29] And in becoming that, Beethoven (as we have seen at the beginning of this chapter) also became the chief butt and target of all who resisted that way and that development. Today more than ever, in fact, artists have felt the need to resist the universalizing or (in a term much favored by resisters) the "hegemonic" claims of romanticism, of aggressive heroism, of philosophical grandiosity — in a word, of Germany.

And here we come to the untold story of musical classicism and musical emancipation. It represented the victory of German art, and so its history was written from the standpoint of the victors. The particular origins of the style and attitude represented by Beethoven were suppressed — even their origin in Beethoven. The origins were displaced to a more mythological time — that of Bach, Haydn, and Mozart, the earliest "canonized" composers — and the style was represented as an "unmarked" or transparent one that was said (in language drawn from the discourse of the Enlightenment) to represent "universal" and therefore timeless human values.

This was the discourse of "classical music," which, when purveyed by concert-giving and educational institutions in the guise of "music appreciation," became (for one last paradox) the vehicle for the commercial (and, even more covertly, the political) exploitation of a product that was touted precisely as something above commerce and politics. For an example, here is a description of "Classicism" by Paul Henry Lang, the author of *Music in Western Civilization* (1941), the most successful music appreciation textbook of the mid-twentieth century:

> By the end of the eighteenth century we no longer speak of German music, for this music became the musical language of the world, as in the two previous supreme syntheses the musical language of the Franco-Flemish composers and later of the Neapolitans became the language of the world [in sixteenth-century church music and eighteenth-century opera, respectively]. For in the symphonies of Haydn, as in the works of Mozart and of the other masters of the era, there speaks a musicianship that is universal, timeless, and valid under all circumstances. This music is not one solution or one aspect, nor is it a personal matter; it speaks to all peoples.[30]

By now it is easy to see that this is not a statement of fact but rather a polemic. (It is quite contradictory, in fact — if the Franco-Flemish and the Neapolitan "syntheses" did not ultimately prove to be "universal, timeless, and valid under all circumstances," why should we expect the German one to do so?) "There are universal values," the historian

Stanley Hoffman has written, "and they happen to be mine."[31] That is Hoffman's sardonic definition not of genuine universality, of course, but of ethnocentrism—a single (and therefore partial) viewpoint, asserted on behalf of a powerful nation, that seeks dominance by representing itself as universal and impartial.

The same debasement of Enlightened "universalism" has been used on behalf of many "centrisms." In American politics, for example, it has found echo whenever defenders of the status quo have tried to discredit legislation on behalf of the civil or economic rights of minorities, of women, of labor, or of the indigent as "special interest" legislation, implying that what favored the interests of rich white men served the interests of all. Ruling out personal decision in favor of an obligatory consensus (as Lang explicitly does on behalf of German "classicism") is another move that nowadays advertises its political character more obviously than it did before World War II, explicitly a war fought against totalitarianism.

Even Lang, after the war, muted his universal claims for Germany: his last book was a 1966 biography of Handel that zealously represented the composer as an Englishman by choice, against those who emphasized his German birth. There was still, of course, a universalist component in the argument, but now it was advanced on behalf of "cold war" values: the free enterprise, laissez-faire politics, and individual self-definition available on the Western side of the wall that by then divided Germany. It is more obvious than ever that the concept of "classicism," for music, initially the creation of romanticism, was perennially available for tweaking on behalf of whatever values or interests might be contending at a given time for "universal" dominance.

If historically factual proof of its origins, or of its political nature, is needed, moreover, it can be furnished. The first writer to speak of a "classical period" in music history, comprising the work of Haydn, Mozart, Beethoven, and their lesser contemporaries, was the Leipzig music critic Johann Gottlieb Wendt, who wrote under the Mozartean pen name Amadeus Wendt, Amadeus being a translation of his second given name. He coined the term in a book with the unwieldy but revealing title *Über den gegenwärtigen Zustand der Musik besonders in Deutschland und wie er geworden: Eine beurtheilende Schilderung* ("On the present state of music, especially in Germany, and how it got that way: A critical sketch"), published in 1836, almost a decade after Beethoven's death, and more than a quarter century after writers like E. T. A. Hoffmann began describing the three Viennese composers, but particularly Beethoven, as the founders of musical romanticism. Wendt's title betrays the link between the discourse of classicism as a timeless or universal standard, and the discourse of nationalism: Germany as exemplary music-nation, whose values are (or should be) those of all peoples.

It is easy to see now why Beethoven has always been "the one to beat." One can sympathize with those who have opposed his authority, and one can do so without any loss of belief in his greatness. The very fact that after two centuries Beethoven is still the standard-bearer of the universalizing claims of classical music, and still receives the brickbats of resisters, is all the evidence we need of his centrality to the musical culture that we have inherited, and that is now ours to modify as we see fit.

Notes

CHAPTER 20: OPERA FROM MONTEVERDI TO MONTEVERDI

1 Pirrotta, "Monteverdi and the Problems of Opera," in *Music and Culture in Italy from the Middle Ages to the Baroque* (Cambridge: Harvard University Press, 1984), p. 248.

2 The letter may be found complete, in English translation, in *The Monteverdi Companion*, ed. Denis Arnold and Nigel Fortune (New York: Norton, 1968, pp. 52–56,) or in P. Weiss and R. Taruskin, *Music in the Western World: A History in Documents* (New York: Schirmer, 1984), pp. 181–84.

3 Trans. R. Taruskin in Weiss and Taruskin, *Music in the Western World*, pp. 173–74.

4 See Ellen Rosand, "The Descending Tetrachord: An Emblem of Lament," *Musical Quarterly* LXV (1979): 346–59.

5 Ellen Rosand, *Opera in Seventeenth-Century Venice: The Creation of a Genre* (Berkeley and Los Angeles: University of California Press, 1991), p. 1.

6 Leo Schrade, *Monteverdi, Creator of Modern Music* (New York: Norton, 1950).

7 Manfred Bukofzer, *Music in the Baroque Era* (New York: Norton, 1947), pp. 394–95.

8 Bukofzer, *Music in the Baroque Era*, p. 398.

9 Rosand, *Opera in Seventeenth-Century Venice*, p. 7.

10 John Roselli, *New Grove Dictionary of Opera* (London: Macmillan, 1992), s.v. "castrato."

11 Percy A. Scholes, ed., *Dr. Burney's Musical Tours in Europe*, Vol. I (London: Oxford University Press, 1959), pp. 247–48.

12 Quoted in Rosand, *Opera in Seventeenth-Century Venice*, p. 11.

13 See Susan McClary, "Constructions of Gender in Monteverdi's Dramatic Music," *Cambridge Opera Journal* I (1989): 203–23.

14 Trans. Arthur Jacobs, in Monteverde, *L'Incoronazione di Poppea*, Libretto by G. F. Busenello, English version by Arthur Jacobs (London: Novello, 1989).

CHAPTER 21: FAT TIMES AND LEAN

1 Maugars's whole letter, translated by Walter H. Bishop, may be found in Weiss and Taruskin, *Music in the Western World: A History in Documents* (New York: Schirmer, 1984), pp. 194–97.

2 Lorenzo Bianconi, *Music in the Seventeenth Century*, trans. David Bryant (Cambridge: Cambridge University Press, 1987), p. 101.

3 Bianconi, *Music in the Seventeenth Century*, p. 103.

4 Trans. by R. Taruskin from the Italian given in Bianconi, p. 102.

5 Quoted in Richard Hudson, *Passacaglio and Ciaconna from Guitar Music to Italian Keyboard Variations in the Seventeenth Century* (Ann Arbor: UMI Research Press, 1981), p. 237.

6 Hudson, *Passacaglio and Ciaconna*, p. 237.

7 Quoted in Bianconi, *Music in the Seventeenth Century*, p. 95.

8 Johann Mattheson, *Grundlage einer Ehren-Pforte* (Hamburg, 1740), quoted in R. Tollefsen and P. Dirksen, "Sweelinck," in *New Grove Dictionary of Music and Musicians*, Vol. XXIV (2nd ed., New York: Grove, 2000), p. 771.

9 Heinrich Schütz, letter to the Elector of Saxony (1651), trans. Piero Weiss, in P. Weiss, *Letters of Composers Through Six Centuries* (Philadelphia: Chilton Books, 1967), pp. 46–51; abridged in P. Weiss and R. Taruskin, *Music in the Western World*, pp. 184–86.

10 See *The Treatises of Christoph Bernhard*, trans. Walter Hilse, *The Music Forum*, Vol. III (New York: Columbia University Press, 1973); excerpts printed in P. Weiss and R. Taruskin, *Music in the Western World*, pp. 187–89.

11 Aaron Copland, "The Teacher: Nadia Boulanger," in *Copland on Music* (New York: Norton, 1963), p. 85.

12 Anthony Newcomb, "Courtesans, Muses, or Musicians? Professional Women Musicians in Sixteenth-Century Italy," in *Women Making Music: The Western Art Tradition, 1150–1950*, eds. J. Bowers and J. Tick (Urbana: University of Illinois Press, 1986), p. 103.

13 Ellen Rosand, "Barbara Strozzi, *Virtuosissima cantatrice*: The Composer's Voice," *JAMS* XXXI (1978): 252.

14 See Suzanne G. Cusick, "Thinking from Women's Lives: Francesca Caccini after 1627," *Musical Quarterly* LXXVII (1993): 484–507.

CHAPTER 22: COURTS RESPLENDENT, OVERTHROWN, RESTORED

1 Jacques Bonnet, *Histoire de la musique*, Vol. III (Amsterdam, 1725), p. 322.

2 Quoted in Oliver Strunk, *Source Readings in Music History* (New York: Norton, 1950), p. 483 (translation slightly adapted).

3 Strunk, *Source Readings in Music History*, pp. 485–86.

4 Quoted in P. Weiss and R. Taruskin, *Music in the Western World: A History in Documents* (New York: Schirmer, 1984), p. 202.

5 Pierre Corneille, *Oeuvres complètes*, Vol. I (Paris, 1834), p. 570.

6 Jean de la Bruyère, *Les Caractères* (Paris, 1874), p. 21.

7 Madelleine Laurain-Portemer, *Études Mazarines* (Paris, 1981), quoted in Neal Zaslaw, "The First Operas in Paris: A Study in the Politics of Art," in *Jean-Baptiste Lully and the Music of the French Baroque: Essays in Honor of James R. Anthony*, ed. J. Heyer (Cambridge: Cambridge University Press, 1989), p. 8.

8 Zaslaw, "*Scylla et Glaucis*: A Case Study," *Cambridge Opera Journal* IV (1992): 199.

9 Voltaire, *Le siècle de Louis XIV* (1751), cited in Lois Rosow, "Atys," *New Grove Dictionary of Opera*, Vol. I (London: Macmillan, 1992), p. 242.

10 Letter of August 1675, ed. Jean Duron in booklet accompanying *Atys, de M. de Lully*, recording by William Christie and Les Arts Florissants, Harmonia Mundi France HMC 1257.59 (1987), p. 21.

11 Letter of August 1675, *Atys* booklet, p. 21.

12 See Denis Diderot, *Les bijoux indiscrets, Au Monomotapa* (Paris: Durand, 1748).

13 J. J. Rousseau, *Confessions* (New York: Modern Library [Random House], n.d.), p. 395; see also Rousseau's *Lettre sur la musique française* (1753), in Strunk, *Source Readings*, pp. 636–54.

14 John Wilson, ed., *Roger North on Music* (London: Novello, 1959), pp. 10–11.

15 See, for example, Ernst H. Meyer, *English Chamber Music* (London: Lawrence & Wishart, 1946).

16 Thomas Mace, *Musick's Monument* (London: T. Ratcliffe and N. Thompson, 1676; facsimile ed. New York: Broude Bros., 1966), p. 245.

17 Thomas Babington Macaulay, *History of England from the Accession of James II*, Vol. I (1849), Chap. 1, part v.

18 Quoted in Murray Lefkowitz, *William Lawes* (London: Routledge and Kegan Paul, 1960), p. 37.

19 Keith Walker, "In the Merry Monarchy," *Times Literary Supplement*, 1 September 1995, p. 26.

20 Curtis Price, *Henry Purcell and the London Stage* (Cambridge: Cambridge University Press, 1984), p. 320.

21 See John Buttrey, "Dating Purcell's Dido and Aeneas," *Proceedings of the Royal Musical Association* XCVI (1967–68): 52–60; also Purcell, *Dido and Aeneas*, ed. Curtis Price (Norton Critical Scores; New York: Norton, 1986), pp. 6–12.

22 Dan H. Lawrence, ed., *Shaw's Music: The Complete Musical Criticism in Three Volumes*, Vol. I (London: Bodley Head, 1981), p. 559.

CHAPTER 23: CLASS AND CLASSICISM

1 Donald Jay Grout, *Alessandro Scarlatti: An Introduction to His Operas* (Berkeley and Los Angeles: University of California Press, 1979), p. 15.

2 Marita McClymonds, "Opera seria," in *New Grove Dictionary of Opera*, Vol. III (London: Macmillan, 1992), p. 698.

3 Grout, *Alessandro Scarlatti*, p. 9.

4 Pietro Metastasio to Johann Adolf Hasse, 20 October 1749, trans. John Hoole, in Patrick J. Smith, *The Tenth Muse: A Historical Study of the Opera Libretto* (New York: Knopf, 1970), p. 403.

5 *Ibid.*, p. 405.

6 Smith, *The Tenth Muse*, p. 96.

7 Metastasio to Hasse, in Smith, *The Tenth Muse*, pp. 407–8.

8 *The Works of Metastasio*, trans. John Hoole, Vol. I (London: T. Davis, 1767), p. 3.

9 Martha Feldman, "Magic Mirrors and the *Seria* Stage: Thoughts toward a Ritual View," *JAMS* XLVIII (1995): 454–55.

10 Dale E. Monson, "Carestini, Giovanni," in *New Grove Dictionary of Opera*, Vol. I (London: Macmillan, 1992), p. 731.

11 Charles Burney, *A General History of Music*, Vol. II, ed. Frank Mercer (New York: Dover, 1957), p. 917.

12 Pier Francesco Tosi, *Observations on the Florid Song; or, Sentiments on the Ancient and Modern Singers*, trans. J. E. Galliard (London, 1742), p. 126.

13 It is published in facsimile in Hans-Peter Schmitz, *Die Kunst der Verzierung im 18. Jahrhundert* (Kassel: Bärenreiter, 1955), pp. 76–93.

14 Tosi, *Observations on the Florid Song*, pp. 128–29.

15 Donald Jay Grout, "On Historical Authenticity in the Performance of Old Music," in *Essays on Music in Honor of Archibald Thompson Davison* (Cambridge: Harvard University Press, 1957), p. 343.

16 Angus Heriot, *The Castrati in Opera* (London: Secker and Warburg, 1956), pp. 144–45.

17 Feldman, "Magic Mirrors and the *Seria* Stage," p. 480.

18 *New Grove Dictionary of Opera*, Vol. III, p. 700.

19 Feldman, "Magic Mirrors and the *Seria* Stage," p. 444.

CHAPTER 24: THE ITALIAN CONCERTO STYLE AND THE RISE OF TONALITY-DRIVEN FORM

1 John Wilson, ed., *Roger North on Music* (London: Novello, 1959), p. 11.

2 Jonathan Freeman-Attwood, review of Purcell, *12 Sonatas in Three Parts* (L'Oiseau-Lyre CD 444 499-2OH), *Gramophone*, April 1996, p. 67.

3 Henry Purcell, preface to *Sonnatas of Three Parts: Two Violins and Bass, to the Organ or Harpsecord* (London, 1683); reprinted in facsimile in Purcell, *Works*, Vol. V (London, 1983).

4 The term is Leonard B. Meyer's; for the most extensive treatment see Eugene Narmour, *The Analysis and Cognition of Basic Melodic Complexity: The Implication-Realization Model* (Chicago: University of Chicago Press, 1992).

5 Quoted in Jean-Jacques Rousseau, *Dictionnaire de musique* (Paris, 1768), p. 452.

6 Charles de Brosses, *Lettres familières sur Italie*, quoted in Marc Pincherle, *Vivaldi*, trans. Christopher Hatch (New York: Norton, 1962), p. 19.

7 Eberhard Preussner, *Die musikalischen Reisen des Herrn von Uffenbach* (Kassel: Bärenreiter, 1949), p. 67; trans. Piero Weiss, in P. Weiss and R. Taruskin, *Music in the Western World: A History in Documents* (New York: Schirmer, 1984), p. 236.

8 Johann Joachim Quantz, *On Playing the Flute*, trans. Edward R. Reilly (New York: Schirmer, 1975), p. 311.

9 Francesco Geminiani, *The Art of Playing on the Violin* (London, 1751), p. 1.

CHAPTER 25: CLASS OF 1685 (I)

1 Manfred F. Bukofzer, *Music in the Baroque Era* (New York: Norton, 1947), p. 303.

2 Johann Joachim Quantz, *On Playing the Flute*, trans. Edward R. Reilly (New York: Schirmer, 1975), p. 341.

3 Susan McClary, "The Blasphemy of Talking Politics during Bach Year," in *Music and Society: The Politics of Composition, Performance and Reception*, eds. S. McClary and R. Leppert (Cambridge: Cambridge University Press, 1987), p. 26.

4 *Ibid.*, p. 41.

5 *Ibid.*, p. 40.

6 Michael Marissen, *The Social and Religious Designs of J. S. Bach's Brandenburg Concertos* (Princeton: Princeton University Press, 1995), pp. 114–15.

CHAPTER 26: CLASS OF 1685 (II)

1 Robert D. Hume, "The Beggar's Opera," in *New Grove Dictionary of Opera*, Vol. I (London: Macmillan, 1992), p. 377.

2 John Dennis, "An Essay on the Opera's [sic] after the Italian Manner, Which are about to be Establish'd on the English Stage: With Some Reflections on the Damage Which They May Bring to the Publick" (1706), quoted in Richard Leppert, "Imagery, Musical Confrontation and Cultural Difference in Early 18th-Century London," *Early Music* XIV (1986): 337.

3 *The Spectator*, no. 205 (25 October 1711); quoted in Leppert, "Imagery, Musical Confrontation and Cultural Difference," p. 331.

4 Christopher Hogwood, *Handel* (London: Thames and Hudson, 1984), p. 142.

5 "R. W.," letter to the *London Daily Post*, 18 April 1739; Otto Eric Deutsch, *Handel: A Documentary Biography* (London: A. & C. Black, 1955), pp. 544–45.

6 Ruth Smith, *Handel's Oratorios and Eighteenth-Century Thought* (Cambridge: Cambridge University Press, 1995), pp. 288–89.

7 John Brown, *A Dissertation on the Rise, Union, and Power, the Progressions, Separations, and Corruptions, of Poetry and Music* (London: L. Davis and C. Reymers, 1763), p. 218; quoted in Howard E. Smither, *A History of the Oratorio*, Vol. II (Chapel Hill: University of North Carolina Press, 1977), p. 255.

8 John Roberts, "Handel and Vinci's 'Didone Abbandonata': Revisions and Borrowings," *Music & Letters* LXVIII (1987): 149.

9 Donald Jay Grout, *A History of Western Music* (New York: Norton, 1960), p. 410.

10 Peter Kivy, *Sound and Semblance: Reflections on Musical Representation* (Princeton: Princeton University Press, 1984), pp. 210–11.

11 Roberts, "Handel and Vinci's 'Didone Abbandonata,'" p. 149.

12 Quoted in John Roberts, "Handel and Charles Jennens's Italian Opera Manuscripts," in *Music and Theatre: Essays in Honour of Winton Dean*, ed. Nigel Fortune (Cambridge: Cambridge University Press, 1987), p. 192.

13 Jens Peter Larsen, *Handel's Messiah* (2nd ed., New York: Norton, 1972), p. 83.

14 Leppert, "Imagery, Musical Confrontation and Cultural Difference," p. 331.

15 S. L. Gulich, ed., *Some Unpublished Letters of Lord Chesterfield* (Berkeley and Los Angeles: University of California Press, 1937), p. 78.

16 "Short But Most Necessary Draft for a Well-Appointed Church Music," in *The Bach Reader*, eds. Hans T. David and Arthur Mendel (rev. ed., New York: Norton, 1966), pp. 120–24.

17 Joshua Rifkin, "Bach's Chorus," *Musical Times* CXXIII (1982): 747–54; the controversy over this article has lasted more than twenty years and generated a sizeable literature of books, articles and manifestoes.

18 Burney, *A General History of Music*, ed. F. Mercer, Vol. I (New York: Dover, 1957), p. 21.

19 Carl Friedrich Zelter to Johann Wolfgang von Goethe (1827), quoted in R. Taruskin, *Text and Act* (New York: Oxford University Press, 1995), p. 310.

20 See Eric Chafe, *Tonal Allegory in the Vocal Music of J. S. Bach* (Berkeley and Los Angeles: University of California Press, 1991), p. 15.

21 Johann Adolph Scheibe, "Letter from an Able Musikant Abroad" (1737), in David and Mendel, *The Bach Reader*, p. 238.

22 See Cecelia Hopkins Porter, "The New Public and the Reordering of the Musical Establishment: The Lower Rhine Music festivals, 1818–67," 19th *Century Music* III (1979–80): 211–24.

23 "Musikalische," *Neue Zeitschrift für Musik* (19 February 1841), quoted in Cecelia Hopkins Porter, *The Rhine as Musical Metaphor: Cultural Identity in German Romantic Music* (Boston: Northeastern University Press, 1996), p. 66.

24 Johann Nikolaus Forkel, *Johann Sebastian Bach: His Life, Art, and Work* (London: Constable and Co., 1920), p. xxv.

25 *Ibid.*, p. 152

26 Domenico Scarlatti, Preface to *Essercizi per gravicembalo* (London, 1738); quoted in Ralph Kirkpatrick, *Domenico Scarlatti* (Princeton: Princeton University Press, 1953), p. 102.

27 Thomas Twining, *Aristotle's Treatise on Poetry, Translated: With Notes on the Translation, and on the Original; And Two Dissertations, on Poetical, and Musical, Imitation* (2nd ed., London, 1812), p. 66.

28 Title page of *XLII Suites de Pieces Pour le Clavecin. En deux Volumes. Composées par Domenico Scarlatti. . .Carefully Revised & Corrected from the Errors of the Press [by] Thos. Roseingrave* (London: B. Cooke, [1739]).

29 Francesco Geminiani, *Treatise of Good Taste in the Art of Musick* (London, 1749), p. 4.

30 Burney, *A General History of Music*, ed., F. Mercer, Vol. II, p. 706.

31 Ralph Kirkpatrick, *Domenico Scarlatti*, p. 266.32.

32 Fernando Valenti, liner note to Domenico Scarlatti, *Sonatas for Harpsichord* (Westminster Records, 1952).

33 Edward E. Lowinsky, *Tonality and Atonality in Sixteenth-Century Music* (Berkeley and Los Angeles: University of California Press, 1962), p. 74.

34 Igor Stravinsky, Foreword to Lowinsky, *Tonality and Atonality*, p. viii.

CHAPTER 27: THE COMIC STYLE

1 First reported (or invented) in Friedrich Rochlitz, "Karl Philipp Emmanuel Bach," *Für Freunde der Tonkus*, Vol. IV (1832), p. 308.

2 See H. Riemann, Introduction to *Sinfonien der pfalzbayerischen Schule*, Denkmäler der Tonkunst in Bayern, Vol. IV, Jahrgang iii/1 (1902).

3 See F. Torrefranca, *Le origini italiane del romanticismo musicale: I primitivi della sonata moderna* (Turin, 1930).

4 See W. Fischer, *Wiener Instrumentalmusik vor und um 1750*, Vol. II, Denkmäler der Tonkunst in Österreich, Vol. XXXIX, Jahrgang xix/2 (1912).

5 Daniel Heartz, *Haydn, Mozart and the Viennese School: 1740–1780* (New York: W. W. Norton, 1995); eight years later Heartz published a thousand-page sequel, *Music in European Capitals: The Galant Style, 1720–1780* (New York: Norton, 2003).

6 Daniel Heartz, "Approaching a History of Eighteenth-Century Music," *Current Musicology* 9 (1969): 92–93.

7 F. W. Marpurg, *Der critische Musicus an der Spree*, no. 27 (Berlin, 2 September 1749), p. 215.

8 C. P. E. Bach, *Versuch über die wahre Art das Clavier zu spielen* (Berlin, 1753), p. 119.

9 C. P. E. Bach, *Versuch*, pp. 122–23, trans. Piero Weiss in P. Weiss and R. Taruskin, *Music in the Western World: A History in Documents* (New York: Schirmer, 1984), p. 272.

10 C. P. E. Bach, *Essay on the True Art of Playing Keyboard Instruments*, trans. William J. Mitchell (New York: Norton, 1949), p. 430.

11 Heinrich Wilhelm von Gerstenberg, letter to Friedrich Nicolai (1767), quoted in Eugene Helm, "The 'Hamlet' Fantasy and the Literary Element in C. P. E. Bach's Music," *Musical Quarterly* LVIII (1972): 279.

12 Carl Friedrich Cramer, *Flora* (Hamburg, 1787), p. xiii; quoted in Helm, "The 'Hamlet' Fantasy," p. 287.

13 C. P. E. Bach to H. W. von Gerstenberg (1773); quoted in Helm, "The 'Hamlet' Fantasy," p. 291.

14 C. P. E. Bach, *Versuch*, p. 121, trans. Piero Weiss in P. Weiss and R. Taruskin, *Music in the Western World*, p. 272.

15 Burney, *A General History of Music*, Vol. II, ed. F. Mercer (New York: Dover, 1957), p. 866.

16 Burney, *A General History of Music*, Vol. II, ed. F. Mercer, p. 866.

17 William S. Newman, *The Sonata in the Classic Era* (2nd ed., New York: Norton, 1972), p. 621.

18 Quoted in Stephen Roe, "Johann Christian Bach," in *New Grove Dictionary of Music and Musicians*, Vol. II (2nd ed., New York: Grove, 2000), p. 417.

19 See Piero Weiss, "Baroque Opera and the Two Verisimilitudes," in *Music and Civilization: Essays in Honor of Paul Henry Lang*, eds. E. Strainchamps and M. R. Maniates (New York: Norton, 1984), pp. 117–26; *idem*, "La diffusione del repertorio operistico nell'Italia del Settecento: Il caso dell'opera buffa," in S. Davoli, ed., *Civiltà*

teatrale e Settecento emiliano (Bologna, 1986), pp. 241–56; idem, "Ancora sulle origini dell'opera comica: Il linguaggio," *Studi pergolesiani/Pergolesi Studies* I (1986): 124–48; and especially Wye J. Allanbrook, "Comic Flux and Comic Precision," and "A Voiceless Mimesis," lectures delivered at the University of California at Berkeley, in the fall of 1994 while this book was being drafted, forthcoming as *The Secular Commedia: Comic Mimesis in Late Eighteenth-Century Music* (Ernest Bloch Lectures, Berkeley and Los Angeles: University of California Press).

20 Aristotle, *Poetics*, trans. Kenneth A. Telford (Chicago: Regnery, 1961), pp. 10–29.

21 Denis Diderot, *Le Neveu de Rameau*, trans. Wye J. Allanbrook in "Comic Flux and Comic Precision."

CHAPTER 28: ENLIGHTENMENT AND REFORM

1 Johann Adam Hiller, *Wöchentliche Nachrichten und Anmerkungen, die Musik betreffend*, Vol. III, p. 8 (22 August 1768), trans. Piero Weiss in P. Weiss and R. Taruskin, *Music in the Western World: A History in Documents* (New York: Schirmer, 1984), pp. 282–83.

2 Carlo Goldoni, Preface to *La buona figliuola*, trans. Catherine Silberblatt Woflthal in the notes to Fonit Cetra LMA 3012 (Niccolò Piccinni, *La buuona figliola* [sic]), ca. 1981.

3 William C. Holmes, "Pamela Transformed," *Musical Quarterly* XXXVIII (1952): 589.

4 Christoph Willibald Gluck, Preface to *Alceste*, trans. Piero Weiss in P. Weiss and R. Taruskin, *Music in the Western World*, p. 301.

5 I. F. Edlen von Mosel, *Ueber das Leben und die Werke des Anton Salieri, K. k. Hofkepellmeister* (Vienna, 1827), p. 93; trans. Daniel Heartz in "Coming of Age in Bohemia: The Musical Apprenticeships of Benda and Gluck," *Journal of Musicology* VI (1988): 524.

6 Ranieri de Calzabigi, "Lettre au rédacteur du Mercure de France" (signed 25 June 1784), *Mercure de France*, 21 August 1784.

7 Alfred Einstein, *Gluck*, trans. Eric Blom (London: Dent, 1936), p. 82.

8 M. Boyé, *L'Expression musicale, mise au rang des Chimères* (Amsterdam, 1779), p. 14.

9 Eduard Hanslick, *On the Musically Beautiful* (*Vom Musikalisch-Schönen*, 1854), trans. Geoffrey Payzant (Indianapolis: Hackett, 1986), pp. 16–17.

10 J. J. Rousseau, *Extrait d'une réponse du petit faiseur à son prête-nom, sur un morceau de l'Orphée de M. le chevalier Gluck* (Geneva, 1781).

11 Letter from Gluck to François Louis Du Roullet, in *L'Année litteraire*, 1777; quoted in Einstein, *Gluck*, pp. 146–47.

12 Wye J. Allanbrook, *Rhythmic Gesture in Mozart* (Chicago: University of Chicago Press, 1983), p. 16.

13 Immanuel Kant, "An Answer to the Question: What is Enlightenment?" (*Beantwortung der Frage: Was ist Aufklärung?*, 1784), trans. James Schmidt, in *What is Enlightenment? Eighteenth-Century Answers and Twentieth-Century Questions*, ed. J. Schmidt (Berkeley and Los Angeles: University of California Press, 1996), p. 58.

14 Kant, "An Answer," trans. Schmidt, p. 59.

15 See Maynard Solomon, "Mozart: The Myth of the Eternal Child," 19th *Century Music* XV (1991–2): 95–106; incorporated in Solomon, *Mozart: A Life* (New York: HarperCollins, 1995).

16 Daniel Heartz, *Mozart's Operas* (Berkeley and Los Angeles: University of California Press, 1990), p. 9.

17 Melchior von Grimm, *Correspondance littéraire*, Vol. V, p. 461(1 March 1764); quoted in Heartz, *Mozart's Operas*, p. 9.

18 Eric Blom, ed., *Mozart's Letters*, trans. Emily Anderson (Harmondsworth: Penguin Books, 1956), pp. 181–82.

19 Blom, ed., *Mozart's Letters*, p. 182.

20 Blom, ed., *Mozart's Letters*, Ibid., p. 208.

21 Blom, ed., *Mozart's Letters*, Ibid., p. 208.

22 Heartz, *Mozart's Operas*, p. 108.

23 *The Memoirs of Lorenzo Da Ponte*, trans. Elisabeth Abbott (New York: Orion Press, 1959), p. 232.

24 George Bernard Shaw, quoted in *The Encyclopedia Brittanica*, s.v. "Opera" (www.britannica.com/eb/print?eu=118789).

25 E. T. A. Hoffmann, "A Tale of Don Juan" (1813), in *Pleasures of Music*, trans. Jacques Barzun (New York: Viking, 1960), p. 28.

26 S. Kierkegaard, *Eithor/Or*, Part I, trans. H. V. Hong and E. H. Hong (Princeton: Princeton University Press, 1987), p. 57.

27 *The Memoirs of Lorenzo Da Ponte*, pp. 59–60.

28 Joseph Kerman, *Opera as Drama* (New York: Knopf, 1956), p. 122.

CHAPTER 29: INSTRUMENTAL MUSIC LIFTS OFF

1 Charles Burney, *The Present State of Music in Germany, the Netherlands, and United Provinces* (2nd ed., London, 1775), p. 95.

2 C. F. D. Schubart, *Ideen zu einer Ästhetik der Tonkunst* (Vienna, 1806), p. 130 (describing a performance heard in 1784).

3 A. C. Dies, interview with Haydn, 15 April 1805; in Dies, A. C. Dies: *Biographische Nachrichten von Joseph Haydn* (Vienna, 1810), p. 17.

4 H. C. Robbins Landon, *Haydn: Chronicle and Works*, Vol. I (Bloomington: Indiana University Press, 1980), p. 11.

5 Georg August Griesinger, *Biographische Notizen über Joseph Haydn* (Leipzig: Breitkopf und Härtel, 1810), p. 17.

6 Griesinger, *Biographische Notizen*, p. 19; third paragraph follows Dies, *Biographische Nachrichten*, p. 48.

7 J. Webster, *Haydn's "Farewell" Symphony and the Idea of Classical Style* (Cambridge: Cambridge University Press, 1991), p. 45: "Since the [D-major] interlude remains unexplained, never returning, it too forms part of the 'problem' of the work. Its resolution can only come *elsewhere* — on a level which involves the entire symphony."

8   H. C. Robbins Landon, *Haydn: Chronicle and Works*, Vol. II (Bloomington: Indiana University Press, 1978), p. 302.

9   Dies, *Biographische Nachrichten*, p. 80.

10 Diary of Charlotte Papendiek, quoted in H. C. Robbins Landon, *Haydn: Chronicle and Works*, Vol. III (Bloomington: Indiana University Press, 1976), p. 52.

11 Quoted in Landon, *Haydn: Chronicle and Works*, Vol. III, p. 150.

12 Quoted in Landon, *Haydn: Chronicle and Works*, Vol. III, p. 149.

13 Griesinger, *Biographische Notizen*, p. 32.

14 Landon, *Haydn: Chronicle and Works*, Vol. III, p. 531.

15 Quoted in Landon, *Haydn: Chronicle and Works*, Vol. III, p. 283.

16 Quoted in Landon, *Haydn: Chronicle and Works*, Vol. III, p. 309.

17 Quoted in Landon, *Haydn: Chronicle and Works*, Vol. III, p. 308.

18 Griesinger, *Biographische Notizen*, p. 60.

CHAPTER 30: THE COMPOSER'S VOICE

1   Mozart, Dedication of "Six Quartets, op. 10" (Vienna: Artaria, 1785).

2   Leopold Mozart to Maria Anna Mozart, February 1782; quoted in H. C. Robbins Landon, *Haydn: Chronicle and Works*, Vol. II (Bloomington: Indiana University Press, 1976), pp. 508–9.

3   Mozart to his father, 28 December 1782; Eric Blom, ed., *Mozart's Letters*, trans. Emily Anderson (Harmondsworth: Penguin Books, 1956), p. 204.

4   Donald Francis Tovey, *Essays in Musical Analysis*, Vol. I (London: Oxford University Press, 1935), p. 189.

5   Leo Treitler, "Mozart and the Idea of Absolute Music," in *Music and the Historical Imagination* (Cambridge: Harvard University Press, 1989), p. 206.

6   Wilhelm Wackenroder, *Phantasien über die Kunst, für Freunde der Kunst* (Hamburg, 1799); in Wackenroder, *Werke und Briefe* (Heidelberg, 1967), p. 254.

7   E. T. A. Hoffmann, "Beethoven's Instrumental Music" (1813), in Oliver Strunk, *Source Readings in Music History* (New York: Norton, 1950), p. 777.

8   See R. R. Subotnik, "Evidence of a Critical World View in Mozart's Last Three Symphonies," in *Music and Civilisation: Essays in Honor of Paul Henry Lang*, ed. E. Strainchamps, M. R. Maniates, and C. Hatch (New York: Norton, 1984), pp. 29–43.

9   E. T. A. Hoffmann, *Kreisleriana* (1813), trans. Stephen Rumph in "A Kingdom Not of This World: The Political Context of E. T. A. Hoffmann's Beethoven Criticism," 19th *Century Music* XIX (1995–96): 50.

10 Heinrich Christoph Koch, *Musikalisches Lexicon* (Frankfurt am Main: A. Hermann der junger, 1802), col. 354.

11 C. Czerny, *Vollständiges Lehrbuch der musikalischen Composition*, Vol. I (Vienna, 1834), p. 159; see Jane R. Stevens, "Theme, Harmony, and Texture in Classic-Romantic Descriptions of Concerto First-Movement Form," *JAMS* XXVII (1974): 47.

12 Ebenezer Prout, *Applied Forms* (London, 1895), pp. 203–4; quoted in Jane R. Stevens, "An Eighteenth-Century Description of Concerto First-Movement Form," *JAMS* XXIV (1971): 85.

13 Julia Moore, "Mozart in the Market-Place," *Journal of the Royal Musical Association* CXIV (1989): 22.

14 Moore, "Mozart in the Market-Place," p. 23.

15 Mozart to Michael Puchberg, 12–14 July 1789; *Mozart's Letters*, p. 242.

16 H. C. Koch, *Versuch einer Anleitung zur Composition*, Vol. III (Leipzig, 1793), p. 339; quoted in Stevens, "An Eighteenth-Century Description," p. 91.

17 Quoted by Neal Zaslaw in "Mozart: Piano Concertos K. 456 and 459," booklet notes accompanying Archiv Produktion CD 415 111–2 (Hamburg: Polydor International, 1986).

18 Mozart to his father, 3 July 1778; *Mozart's Letters*, pp. 107–8.

19 Susan McClary, "A Musical Dialectic from the Enlightenment: Mozart's *Piano Concerto in G Major, K. 453, Movement 2,*" *Cultural Critique* 4 (Fall 1986): 149.

20 McClary, "A Musical Dialectic," p. 151.

21 Wye J. Allanbrook, *The Secular Commedia* (forthcoming, Berkeley and Los Angeles: University of California Press).

22 Koch, *Versuch einer Anleitung*, Vol. III, p. 332; quoted in Stevens, "An Eighteenth-Century Description," p. 94.

23 Stevens, "An Eighteenth-Century Description," p. 94.

24 Quoted in Julie Anne Vertrees, "Mozart's String Quartet K. 465: The History of a Controversy," *Current Musicology* 17 (1974): 97.

25 Donald Francis Tovey, *Essays in Musical Analysis*, Vol. V (London: Oxford University Press, 1937), p. 115.

Chapter 31: The First Romantics

1 *The Confessions of Jean-Jacques Rousseau* (New York: Random House [Modern Library], n.d.), p. 1.

2 E. T. A. Hoffmann, "Beethoven's Instrumental Music" (1813), in Oliver Strunk, *Source Readings in Music History* (New York: Norton, 1950), p. 775.

3 Immanuel Kant, *Critique of Judgment* (1790), trans. J. H. Bernard (New York: Hafner, 1951), p. 174.

4 Quoted in Strunk, *Source Readings*, p. 776.

5 Walter Pater, "The School of Giorgione" (1873), in *The Aesthetes: A Sourcebook*, ed. Ian Small (London: Routledge and Kegan Paul, 1979), p. 15.

6 Quoted in Strunk, *Source Readings*, p. 776.

7 Hoffmann, quoted in Strunk, *Source Readings*, p. 776.

8 Gustav Schilling, *Encyklopädie der gesammte musikalischen Wissenschaften, oder Universal-Lexicon der Tonkunst*, Vol. VI (Stuttgart 1837), in *Music and Aesthetics in the Eighteenth and Early-Nineteenth Centuries*, eds., P. le Huray and J. Day (Cambridge: Cambridge University Press, 1981), p. 470.

9 Edmund Burke, *A Philosophical Enquiry into the Origin of Our Ideas of the Sublime and the Beautiful* (1757), in *Music and Aesthetics in the Eighteenth and Early-Nineteenth Centuries*, eds. P. le Huray and J. Day, pp. 70–71.

10 Elaine R. Sisman, *Mozart: The 'Jupiter' Symphony* (Cambridge Music Handbooks; Cambridge: Cambridge University Press, 1993), p. 18.

11 *Dramaturgische Blätter* (Frankfurt, 1789); quoted in Sisman, *'Jupiter' Symphony*, p. 18.

12 Mozart to his father, 29 November 1780; quoted in Sisman, *'Jupiter' Symphony*, p. 17.

13 Quoted in le Huray and Day, *Music and Aesthetics in the Eighteenth and Early-Nineteenth Centuries*, p. 474.

14 Quoted in le Huray and Day, *Music and Aesthetics in the Eighteenth and Early-Nineteenth Centuries*, p. 302.

15 Or, as first reported, "Too beautiful for our ears, my dear Mozart, and monstrous many notes!" (Franz Niemtschek, *Leben des K. K. Kapellmeisters Wolfgang Gottlieb Mozart, nach Originalquellen beschrieben* [Prague, 1798]; quoted in Thomas Bauman, *W. A. Mozart: Die Entführung aus dem Serail* [Cambridge Opera Handbooks; Cambridge: Cambridge University Press, 1987], p. 89).

16 F. R. Toreinz, *L'Histoire du romantisme* (1829); quoted in le Huray and Day, *Music and Aesthetics in the Eighteenth and Early-Nineteenth Centuries*, p. 415.

17 Ferdinand Adolf Gelbcke, "Classisch und Romantisch: Ein Beitrag zur Geschichtsschreibung der Musik unserer Zeit," in *Neue Zeitschrift für Musik* (1841); quoted in le Huray and Day, *Music and Aesthetics in the Eighteenth and Early-Nineteenth Centuries*, p. 525.

18 *Ibid.*, p. 527.

19 *Ibid.*, p. 528.

20 Hoffmann, quoted in Strunk, *Source Readings*, p. 776.

21 *Ibid.*, p. 777.

22 *Ibid.*, p. 778.

23 Carl Dahlhaus, *Nineteenth-Century Music*, trans. J. B. Robinson (Berkeley and Los Angeles: University of California Press, 1989), p. 9.

24 Beethoven to Franz Wegeler, 29 June 1801; in *Beethoven: Letters, Journals and Conversations* trans. Michael Hamburger (Garden City, N.Y.: Doubleday and Co., 1960), p. 24.

25 For the full text, trans. Piero Weiss, see P. Weiss and R. Taruskin, *Music in the Western World: A History in Documents* (New York: Schirmer Books, 1984), pp. 326–28.

26 See Scott Burnham, *Beethoven Hero* (Princeton: Princeton University Press, 1995), p. xviii.

27 Ferdinand Ries, *Biographische Notizen über Ludwig van Beethoven* (1838), in *Beethoven: Impressions By His Contemporaries*, ed. O. G. Sonneck, (New York: Schirmer, 1926), p. 54.

28 Goethe to Carl Friedrich Zelter, 2 September 1812; in *Beethoven: Impressions by His Contemporaries*, ed. O. G. Sonneck (New York: Schirmer, 1926), p. 88.

29 See M. Solomon, "New Light on Beethoven's Letter to an Unknown Woman," *Musical Quarterly* LVIII (1972): 572–87; also M. Solomon, *Beethoven* (New York: Schirmer, 1977), Chap. 15.

30 Elliot Forbes, ed., *Thayer's Life of Beethoven* (Princeton: Princeton University Press, 1967), pp. 897–98.

31 Forbes, ed., *Thayer's Life of Beethoven*, pp. 907–8.

32 Quoted in Forbes, ed., *Thayer's Life of Beethoven*, p. 909.

33 *Louis Spohr's Autobiography* (London: Longman, Green, 1865), pp. 188–89.

34 M. Solomon, "Beethoven's Ninth Symphony: A Quest for Order," *19th-Century Music* X (1986–87): 8, 10–11.

35 Joseph Kerman, *The Beethoven Quartets* (New York: Norton, 1979), p. 254.

36 Forbes, ed., *Thayer's Life of Beethoven*, p. 1057.

Chapter 32: C-Minor Moods

1 For devotion see Joseph Kerman, "Beethoven's Minority," in *Write All These Down: Essays on Music* (Berkeley and Los Angeles: University of California Press, 1994), pp. 217–37; for derision see Kerman, *The Beethoven Quartets*, pp. 70–71.

2 Robert Schumann, *On Music and Musicians*, ed. Konrad Wolff, trans. Paul Rosenfeld (New York: Norton, 1969), p. 95.

3 Edward J. Dent, *Terpander; or, Music and the Future* (New York: E. P. Dutton, 1927), p. 64.

4 Edward J. Dent, "The Problems of Modern Music" (1925), in *Selected Essays*, ed. Hugh Taylor (Cambridge: Cambridge University Press, 1979), p. 98.

5 Dent, *Terpander*, p. 91.

6 Clive Bell, *Old Friends* (London, 1956); quoted in Eric Walter White, *Stravinsky: The Composer and His Works* (Berkeley and Los Angeles: University of California Press, 1966), p. 60.

7 See Stravinsky's review (ghostwritten by his assistant Robert Craft) of Kerman's *The Beethoven Quartets* in *The New York Review of Books*, 26 September 1968; reprinted in Igor Stravinsky and Robert Craft, *Retrospectives and Conclusion* (New York: Knopf, 1969), pp. 130–42.

8 *Stravinsky: An Autobiography* (New York: Simon and Schuster, 1936), p. 181.

9 Quoted in David Revill, *The Roaring Silence: John Cage, A Life* (New York: Arcade, 1992), pp. 95–96.

10 Adolf Bernhard Marx, *Ludwig van Beethoven: Leben und Schaffen*, 6th ed., ed. and rev. Gustav Behncke, Vol. II (Berlin: Otto Janke, 1908), p. 62.

11 Album inscription, quoted in *Thayer's Life of Beethoven*, ed. Elliot Forbes (Princeton: Princeton University Press, 1967), p. 115.

12 Ferdinand Ries, *Biographische Notizen über Ludwig van Beethoven* (1838), in *Beethoven: Impressions By His Contemporaries*, ed. O. G. Sonneck (New York: Schirmer, 1926), p. 74.

13 Personal communication to author.

14 A. C. Kalischer, *Beetnoven und Wien* (Berlin, 1910), p. 8.

15 Quoted in Rita Steblin, *A History of Key Characteristics in the Eighteenth and Early Nineteenth Centuries* (Ann Arbor: UMI Research Press, 1983), p. 109.

16 John Daverio, *Robert Schumann: Herald of a "New Poetic Age"* (New York: Oxford University Press, 1997), p. 345.

17 Martin Opitz, *Prosodia Germanica* (ca. 1650); quoted in Daverio, *Schumann*, p. 345.

18 E. T. A. Hoffmann, "Beethoven's Instrumental Music" (1813), in Oliver Strunk, *Source Readings in Music History* (New York: Norton, 1950), p. 778.

19 Richard Wagner, *Das Judenthum in der Musik* (1850), in *Judaism in Music and Other Essays*, trans. W. Ashton Ellis (Lincoln: University of Nebraska Press, 1995), p. 96.

20 Charles Rosen, *Critical Entertainments: Music Old and New* (Cambridge: Harvard University Press, 2000), p. 267.

21 Bettina von Arnim to Goethe, 28 May 1810; in *Beethoven: Impressions by His Contemporaries*, ed. O. G. Sonneck (New York: Schirmer, 1926), p. 80.

22 Artur Schopenhauer, *The World as Will and Representation*, trans. E. F. J. Payne, Vol. I (New York: Dover, 1966), p. 260.

23 Quoted in Forbes, ed. *Thayer's Life of Beethoven*, p. 1046.

24 Quoted in *Beethoven: Letters, Journals and Conversations*, trans. and ed. Michael Hamburger (Garden City, N.Y.: Doubleday, 1960), p. 151.

25 Friedrich Nietzsche, *Menschliches Allzumenschliches* (1878); quoted in Leo Treitler, *Music and the Historical Imagination* (Cambridge: Harvard University Press, 1989), p. 61.

26 See William Kinderman, "Beethoven's Symbol for the Deity in the *Missa solemnis* and the Ninth Symphony," *19th-Century Music* XI (1985): 102–18.

27 Arnold Hauser, *The Social History of Art*, trans. Stanley Godman (New York: Vintage, n.d.), Vol. III, p. 82.

28 Hauser, *Social History of Art*, Vol. III, p. 82.

29 Richard Wagner, *The Art-Work of the Future*, in *Richard Wagner's Prose Works*, trans. W. Ashton Ellis, Vol. I (London, 1895), p. 123.

30 Paul Henry Lang, "Music and History" (1952), in *Musicology and Performance*, ed. P. H. Lang (New Haven: Yale University Press, 1997), p. 38.

31 Stanley Hoffman, "Us and Them," *The New Republic*, 12 July 1993, p. 32.

Art Credits

23-6 Pier Leone Ghezzi, Biblioteca Apostolica Vaticana, Rome, © Biblioteca Apostolica Vaticana.

23-7 Jacopo Amigoni 1682–1752 Italian. Portrait group: The singer Farinelli and friends ca. 1750–52. Oil on canvas 172.8 x 245.1 cm Felton Bequest, 1949 National Gallery of Victoria, Melbourne, Australia.

24-1 Estienne Roger and Michel Charles Le Cène, ca. 1715, Bibliothèque Nationale, Paris, © Giraudon / Art Resource, NY.

24-2 Adapted from G. Faber, *Musicae practicae erotematum*, Basel 1553.

24-3 Russian State Library.

24-4 Pier Leone Ghezzi, Biblioteca Apostolica Vacticana, Rome, akg-images.

25-1 Cartography by Bill Nelson.

25-2 Johann Ernst Rentsch, ca. 1715, Erfurt Stadtmuseum, © Bildarchiv Preussischer Kulturbesitz, Berlin, 2003.

25-3 Matthaeus Seutter III, early 18th century, © Foto Marburg / Art Resource, NY.

25-4 Johann-Gottfried Krugner, Musée des Arts Decoratifs, Paris, © Bridgeman-Giraudon / Art Resource, NY.

25-5 Thomaskirche, Leipzig, © Foto Marburg / Art Resource, NY.

25-6 © Bildarchiv Preussischer Kulturbesitz, Berlin, 2003.

25-7 Staatsbibliothek zu Berlin, Berlin, © Bildarchiv Preussischer Kulturbesitz / Art Resource, NY.

25-8 Anonymous, 17th century, Chateaux de Versailles et de Trianon, Versailles, © Erich Lessing / Art Resource, NY.

25-9 Paris: Ballard, 1793.

25-10 E. G. Houssmann, 1727, Stadtgeschichtliches Museum, Leipzig.

25-11 © Bildarchiv Preussischer Kulturbesitz, Berlin, 2003.

26-1a Miniature stolen from museum in 1948. Copy by Luzie Schneider. Händel-Haus, Halle.

26-1b Louis François Roubiliac, Victoria and Albert Museum, London, © Victoria & Albert Museum / Art Resource, NY.

26-2 William Hogarth, Victoria and Albert Museum, London, © Victoria & Albert Museum / Art Resource, NY.

26-3 William Hogarth, 1731, Tate Gallery, © Tate Gallery, London / Art Resource, NY.

26-4 Fotomas Index UK.

26-5 John Sanders, ca. 1774, Coram Foundation, Foundling Museum, London / Bridgeman Art Library.

26-6 Copperplate engraving by Christian Fritzsch © Bildarchiv Preussischer Kulturbesitz, Berlin, 2003.

26-7 © Bildarchiv Preussischer Kulturbesitz, Berlin, 2003.

26-8 © Giraudon / Art Resource, NY.

27-1 Anonymous contemporary etching, © Bildarchiv Preussischer Kulturbesitz, Berlin, 2003.

27-2 Anonymous pencil sketch, © Bildarchiv Preussischer Kulturbesitz, Berlin, 2003.

27-3	Adolf von Menzel, Nationalgalerie, Staatliche Museen zu Berlin, Berlin, © Bildarchiv Preussischer Kulturbesitz, Berlin, 2003.
27-4	Thomas Gainsborough, Civico Museo Bibliografico Musicale, Bologna, © Scala / Art Resource, NY.
27-5	Thomas Gainsborough, before 1774. Courtesy of the Huntington Library, Art Collections, and Botanical Gardens, San Marino, California.
27-6	17th century engraving by Duclos, after design by Saint Aubin. The Metropolitan Museum of Art, Harris Brisbane Dick Fund, 1933 (33.56.34).
27-7	Maurice-Quentin de La Tour, Musée Antoine Lecuyer, Saint-Quentin, © Réunion des Musées Nationaux / Art Resource, NY.
27-8	General Research Division, New York Public Library, Astor, Lenox, and Tilden Foundations.
27-9a	Pier Leone Ghezzi. © Biblioteca Apostolica Vaticana.
27-9b	© Giraudon / Art Resource, NY.
27-10	Maurice-Quentin de La Tour, Musée Antoine Lecuyer, Saint-Quentin, © Réunion des Musées Nationaux / Art Resource, NY.
28-1	Joseph Siffred Duplessis, Private Collection, Paris, © Scala / Art Resource, NY.
28-2	Painting by Johann F. Grieppel, Kunsthistorisches Museum, Vienna, Austria, © Erich Lessing / Art Resource, NY.
28-3	Anonymous, 18th century, Civico Museo Bibliografico Musicale, Bologna, © Art Resource, NY.
28-4	Anonymous, 18th century, Mozart House, Salzburg, © Scala / Art Resource, NY.
28-5	Courtesy of the Metropolitan Opera.
28-6	Carl Schuetz, Historisches Museum der Stadt Wien, Vienna, © by Direktion der Museen der Stadt Wien.
28-7	engraving by Michele Pekenino after a painting by Nathaniel Rogers, akg-images.
28-8	Joseph and Peter Schaffer, ca. 1793, Mozarteum, Salzburg, © Erich Lessing / Art Resource, NY.
28-9	Stadtarchiv Augsburg.
28-10	Joseph and Peter Schaffer, ca. 1793, Mozarteum, Salzburg, © Erich Lessing / Art Resource, NY.
28-11	OPERA NEWS / The Metropolitan Opera Guild, Inc.
28-12	Bildarchiv d. ÖNB, Wien.
29-1	Österreichisches Theatermuseum.
29-2	Bayerisches Nationalmuseum, Munich, © Foto Marburg / Art Resource, NY.
29-3	cliché Bibliothèque nationale de France.
29-4	Carl Schuetz, 1792, Historisches Museum der Stadt Wien, Vienna, © By Direktion der Museen der Stadt Wien.
29-5	© Erich Lessing / Art Resource, NY.

29-6   Hungarian National Museum.

29-7   Johann Baptist Lampi, © Foto Marburg / Art Resource, NY.

29-8   Thomas Hardy, second half of 18th century, Royal Academy of Arts, London, © Erich Lessing / Art Resource, NY.

29-9   Anonymous, 1795, Oesterreichische Galerie, Vienna, © Erich Lessing / Art Resource, NY.

29-10   Library of Congress.

29-11   William Hogarth, 1753. General Research Division, The New York Public Library, Astor, Lenox and Tilden Foundations.

30-1   The Metropolitan Museum of Art, Gift of Geraldine C. Herzfeld in memory of her husband, Monroe Eliot Hemmerdinger, 1984 (1984.34).

30-2   Bédos de Celles, *L'art du facteur d'orgues', iv*, 1778.

30-3a   The Pierpont Morgan Library, New York, Dannie and Hettie Heineman Collection.

30-3b   K00980 Mozart Piano Concertos, by permission, Warner Brothers Publications.

30-4   Johann Nepomuk della Croce, Mozarteum, Salzburg, © Erich Lessing / Art Resource, NY.

30-5   British Museum, Add.ms. 37763 fol. 57, akg-images.

31-1   © Foto Marburg / Art Resource, NY.

31-2   Caspar David Friedrich, *Moonrise on an Empty Shore*, Patron's Permanent Fund, Image © 2004 Board of Trustees, National Gallery of Art, Washington.

31-3   The Metropolitan Museum of Art, The Crosby Brown Collection, 1901 (01.2.38).

31-4   cliché Bibliothèque nationale de France.

31-5   akg-images.

31-6   cliché Bibliothèque nationale de France.

31-7   Johann Heinrich Tischbein, 1787, Staedelsches Kunstinstitut, Frankfurt am Main, © Art Resource, NY.

31-8a   Jean Baptiste Isabeym, 1804, Chateaux de Malmaison et Bois-Preau, Rueil-Malmaison, © Giraudon / Art Resource, NY.

31-8b   Jean Baptiste Isabey, 1814, Museo del Risorgimento, Milan, © Scala / Art Resource, NY.

31-9   © by Direktion der Museen der Stadt Wien.

31-10   Johann Baptist Hoechle, Historisches Museum der Stadt Wien, © by Direktion der Museen der Stadt Wien.

31-11   Franz Stoeber, Beethoven House, Bonn, © Erich Lessing / Art Resource, NY.

32-1   Vienna Gesellschaft der Musikfreunde, akg-images.

32-2   Carl Schuetz, ca. 1815, Historisches Museum der Stadt Wien, © by Direktion der Museen der Stadt Wien.

32-3   E. Meurer, Stadtarchiv und Stadthistorische Bibliothek, Bonn.